KT-521-349

ITALIAN
DICTIONARY

ITALIAN-ENGLISH
ENGLISH-ITALIAN

HUGO'S LANGUAGE BOOKS LTD
LONDON

This impression 1987

© 1971 Hugo's Language Books Ltd
ISBN 0 85285 078 6

Printed in Great Britain

DIZIONARIO
INGLESE

ITALIANO-INGLESE
INGLESE-ITALIANO

PREFAZIONE.

————

Coll'uso si troverà che il dizionario da tasca "Hugo" è un libro di referenza molto utile. Contiene in spazio ristretto le parole che sono necessarie nella vita ordinaria. Si è impiegato il rinomato sistema di pronuncia figurata "Hugo." Questo metodo d'indicare la pronuncia è così semplice che chiunque può usarlo immediatamente senza la minima difficoltà (vedansi le pagine x, xii e xiii). *Non vi sono chiavi complicate da studiare.*

Le parole che hanno la stessa radice e che non appaiono nella sezione Italiana-Inglese si troveranno generalmente nella sezione Inglese-Italiana. Abbiamo adottato questo piano affine di lasciar spazio per il maggior numero possibile di parole.

PREFACE.

Hugo's Italian Dictionary will be found a most serviceable pocket reference-book. It contains in a small space the words that are needed in everyday life. Hugo's well-known system of Imitated Pronunciation has been employed. This method of imparting the pronunciation is so simple that anyone can use it at once without the slightest trouble (see page xi). *There is no complicated key to be mastered.*

Words belonging to the same root not given in the Italian-English section will generally be found in the English-Italian section. This plan has been followed to provide space for the greatest possible number of words.

TAVOLA COMPARATIVA
di misure e pesi inglesi ed italiani.

MISURE LINEARI

1 inch (pollice)=m. 0,025	1 foot (piede)=m. 0,300
1 yard (iarda) = „ 0,914	1 fathom = „ 1,828
1 furlong = „ 201,16	1 mile (miglio)
1 knot (nodo) = „ 1852	= m. 1609,31

MISURE DI SUPERFICIE

1 square inch=6 cm²	1 square yard=8361 cm²
1 square foot = 929 cm²	1 acre = 40 are

MISURE DI CAPACITÀ

1 pint = litri 0,567	1 gallon (gallone)
1 quart = „ 1,135	= litri 4,54

PESI (avoirdupois)

1 grain (grano)=gr. 0,065
1 ounce (oncia)=gr. 28,35
1 pound (1 lb., una libbra)=gr. 453,59
1 hundredweight (1 cwt. 1 quintale)=51 chilogrammi
1 ton (una tonnellata inglese)=1016 chilogrammi

(troy)

1 grain = gr. 0,065	1 pennyweight=gr. 1,555
1 ounce = gr. 31,15	1 pound=gr. 373,25

TERMOMETRO

32° Fahrenheit=0° centigradi
212° Fahrenheit=100° centigradi
quindi 9° Fahrenheit=5° centigradi

Per convertire gradi centigradi in gradi
Fahrenheit si moltiplica per 9, divide per 5
e aggiunge 32.

COMPARATIVE TABLE
of the
Italian-English measures, and weights.

LINEAL MEASURES

The metro is the basis of the Italian system of measures, and weights. It is equal to 39·37 inches.

1 centimetro = ·39 inch   1 millimetro = ·039 inch
1 ettometro = 109 yards
1 chilometro (1000 metri) = 1094 yards

SQUARE MEASURES

1 aro (100 square metri) = 0·988 rod
1 centiara (1 square metro) = 1·196 yard
1 ettaro (10,000 metri) = 2·471 acres

CUBIC MEASURES

Solids.—1 stero = 1·31 cubic yard
Liquids.—1 litro = 1·760 pint
1 ettolitro = 22·009 gallons

WEIGHTS

1 grammo = 15·43 grains
1 centigrammo = ·154 grain
1 milligrammo = ·0154 grain
1 ettogrammo (100 grammi) = 3·527 oz.
1 chilogrammo (1000 grammi) = 2·204 lbs.
1 tonnellata (1000 chilogrammi) = 2205 lbs.

THERMOMETER

0° centigradi = 32° Fahrenheit
100° centigradi = 212° Fahrenheit
Therefore 5° centigradi = 9° Fahrenheit.
To convert Fahrenheit into centigradi, subtract 32, multiply by 5, and divide by 9.

SPIEGAZIONE DELLE ABBREVIATURE.

a.	aggettivo	n.	nome
adv.	avverbio	naut.	nautico
art.	articolo	p.p.	participio passato
conj.	congiunzione	parl.	parlamento
eccl.	ecclesiastico	pl.	plurale
f.	femminile	poet.	poesia
fam.	familiare	pop.	popolare
fig.	figuratamente	prep.	preposizione
gram.	grammatica	pron.	pronome
interj.	interiezione	refl.	riflessivo
m.	maschile	sing.	singolare
mech.	meccanica	tech.	tecnico
med.	medico	v.	verbo
mil.	militare	vulg.	volgare
mus.	musicale		

GENERE DEI SOSTANTIVI.

Tutti i sostantivi inglesi sono di genere neutro, eccettuati quelli che si riferiscono alle persone.

PRONUNCIA FIGURATA.

Avvertenza.—Siccome la pronuncia figurata nella parte Inglese-Italiana è esclusivamente ad uso degli Italiani, i suoni inglesi sono rappresentati da lettere e gruppi di lettere di origine italiana. Non si deve, perciò, tener conto di qualunque critica fatta da stranieri giacchè questi si dimenticano che la pronuncia figurata non si basa sulla fonetica del loro idioma. Reciprocamente, la pronuncia figurata nella parte Italiana-Inglese solo interessa le persone che parlano inglese.

ABBREVIATIONS.

a.	adjective	n.	noun
adv.	adverb	naut.	nautical
art.	article	p.p.	past participle
conj.	conjunction	parl.	parliament
eccl.	ecclesiastical	pl.	plural
f.	feminine	poet.	poetry
fam.	familiar	pop.	popular
fig.	figuratively	prep.	preposition
gram.	grammar	pron.	pronoun
interj.	interjection	refl.	reflexive
m.	masculine	sing.	singular
mech.	mechanics	tech.	technical
med.	medical	v.	verb
mil.	military	vulg.	vulgar
mus.	musical		

IMITATED PRONUNCIATION.—CAUTION.

The imitated pronunciation in the Italian-English section, being for English people only, is framed in accordance with English "sound-spelling" principles. Users of this Dictionary should beware of criticisms from foreigners who forget that this imitated pronunciation is not based upon their own phonetics.

Vice versa, the imitated pronunciation in the English-Italian section is for Italian people only.

ALFABETO INGLESE.

a, b, c, d, e, f, g, h, **i,** j, **k,** l, m, n, o, **p,**
q, r, s, t, u, v, w, x, y, z.

PRONUNCIA IMITATA.

Ci sono nella lingua inglese suoni, che assolutamente non hanno corrispondenti nella lingua italiana e che non possono pertanto essere accuratamente imitati col mezzo di sillabe italiane. Coloro, che usano questo dizionario, tuttavia, si faranno capire dagli Inglesi, se si atterranno scrupolosamente alle seguenti istruzioni.

VOCALI.

aa a lunga, come **â** nelle parole francesi 'fâché, tâche.'

ei e chiuso, come in 'godere,' seguito da una debole i pronunciata rapidamente.

ĕ come **eu** nelle parole francesi 'peur, fleur.'

ii i lungo.

ŏ rappresenta un suono breve tra **eu** e **a** delle parole francesi 'fleur, lac.'

oo o lungo.

ou o lungo seguito da **u** pronunciato rapidamente e leggermente.

uu u lungo.

Le vocali lunghe **aa, ii, oo, uu** rappresentano un suono unico.

La vocale in grassetto deve essere pronunciata più forte delle altre lettere nella stessa sillaba.

(vedi pagina xii.)

THE ITALIAN ALPHABET.—a, b, c, d, e, f, g, h, i, j, l, m, n, o, p, q, r, s, t, u, v, z.

The IMITATED PRONUNCIATION

will always be understood by natives provided each syllable is pronounced as if it were part of an English word, and due attention is paid to the stress; but the exact sound will be still more nearly obtained if the following instructions are borne in mind:—

1.—**VOWELS.**—Practically each Vowel has only one sound in Italian, usually pronounced long, but naturally shortened when the stress is on another syllable, or when two or more consonants follow.

a is pronounced like **ah**		**i** is pronounced like **ee**	
e " " **ay**		**o** " " **oh**	
	u is pronounced like **oo**		

2.—**CONSONANTS.**—When a Consonant is doubled, it is almost pronounced twice. That is to say, it must be lingered on, and pronounced more slowly. Examples: classe, **klahss-**say; città, chit-**tah.**

3.—In the Imitated Pronunciation, "**r**" is printed in thicker type after a Vowel as a reminder that this letter is to be pronounced more strongly than in English. This must not be taken to mean that the syllable in which the "**r**" occurs is stressed.

4.—The stressed syllable, (usually the last but one), is indicated throughout the Italian-English part of this Dictionary in larger type, thus: ah-ne-**mah**-lay, ven-**too**-ro (animale, venturo).

ADVERBS.

Many Adverbs are formed in Italian by adding "mente" (corresponding to the English "ly") to the Adjective in the feminine singular. Example: raro (masc.), rara (fem.), raramente, rarely conveniente (m. & f.) convenientemente, conveniently

A final **e** preceded by **l** or **r** is omitted before adding "mente," as: eguale, egualmente, equally particolare, particolarmente, particularly

Adjectives from which Adverbs can thus be formed are marked with an asterisk (*).

a, e, i, o, u (corsivo). In molte parole inglesi, le vocali delle sillabe disaccentate hanno un suono non definito alquanto simile a quello dell' e francese in de, que, me, le. Questo suono è imitato qui a mezzo di *a, e, i, o, u,* in corsivo, cosicchè l'apparenza della parola venga mutata il meno possibile; ma il suono reale della vocale non deve essere sentito. L'e nelle summenzionate parole francesi (de, que, me, le) è l'imitazione più prossima ed è il suono, che si deve udire sia per *a, e, i, o* sia per *u*. In qualche finale, lo stesso suono cupo ed indistinto è indicato dall' omissione della vocale : maiden, meid'-n.

CONSONANTI.

c   mai come c in 'cena.' Davanti a, o, u, e davanti una consonante, come k in 'kino '(cinema); davanti a, i, y, come s in 'solo.'

r   (corsivo) è pronunciato molto debolmente ed appena udibile.

ɳ   (corsivo) indicante un suono nasale, non è pronunciato separatamente.

sh   come sc in 'scena.'

sh (grassetto) come j nelle parole francesi 'jour, jamais.'

ch   come c in 'cena.'

ch (grassetto) come g in 'già.'

s   indica un suono dolce come quello della s in 'chiesa.'

s   come la s in 'senso, solo.'

h   deve essere aspirata distintamente.

g   come g in 'gallo,' prima di a, o, u (con poche eccezioni).

g   come g in 'già,' prima di e (con poche eccezioni).

xii.

I DUE SUONI DI 'TH.'

z th (forte). Questo suono si ottiene mettendo la lingua fra i denti e pronunciando una **s**.

D th (debole). Il suono è lo stesso ma più dolce e preceduto da una **d** molto leggermente pronunciata.

LETTERA 'R.'

Quando questa lettera non è immediatamente seguita da una vocale, è quasi muta o pronunciata molto debolmente a Londra ed in tutto il **sud** d'Inghilterra.

ACCENTO TONICO.

Il segno ′ mostra che la sillaba precedente **deve** essere pronunciata con maggior forza che le **altre**.

AVVERBI.

Il segno * indica quegli aggettivi ai quali è sufficiente aggiungere **ly**, che corrisponde alla **finale** **mente** in italiano, per trasformarli in avverbi.

Es.: **wise**, savio; **wisely**, saviamente.

GEOGRAPHICAL NAMES
NOMI GEOGRAFICI

Pronuncia figurata.	Imitated pronunciation.
Abyssinia, *a*-bis-sii′-ni-*a*	Abissinia, f., ah-biss-**see**-ne′ah
Africa, *a*′-fri-ka	Africa, f., ah-**fre**-kah
Algeria, al-chi′-ri-*a*	Algeria, f., ahl-jay-ree-ah
America, *a*-mei′-ri-ka	America, f., ah-**may**-re-kah
Asia, ei′-sha	Asia, f., ah-ze′ah
Australia, oos-trei′-li-*a*	Australia, f., ah′oo-**strah**-le′ah
(cont. pag. seguente)	**(continued overleaf)**

GEOGRAPHICAL NAMES (continuation)
NOMI GEOGRAFICI (continuazione)

Austria, oos'-tri-*a* — Austria, f., ah'oo-stre'ah

Belgium, bel'-chi-*o*m — Belgio, m., bell-je'o

Brazil, bra-*s*iil' — Brasile, m., brah-zee-lay

Great Britain, greit brit'-n — Gran Bretagna, f., grahn bray-tah-n'yah

Bulgaria, bŏl-gheir'-i-*a* — Bulgaria, f., bool-gah-ree-ah

Canada, ka'-na-d*a* — Canadà, m., kah-nah-dah

China, chaai'-n*a* — Cina, f., chee-nah

Denmark, den'-maar*k* — Danimarca, f., dah-ne-mar-kah

Egypt, ii'-chipt — Egitto, m., ay-jeet-to

England, ing'-ghland — Inghilterra, f., in-gheel-tair-rah

Europe, iuu'-röp — Europa, f., ay'oo-ro-pah

France, fraans — Francia, f., frahn-che'ah

Germany, chĕr'-ma-ni — Germania, f., jayr-mah-ne'ah

Greece, griis — Grecia, f., gray-che'ah

Holland, hol'-land — Olanda, f., o-lahn-dah

Hungary, hŏng'-ga-ri — Ungheria, f., oonn-gay-ree-ah

India, in'-di-*a* — India, f., in-de'ah

Ireland, air'-land — Irlanda, f., eer-lahn-dah

Italy, i'-tal-i — Italia, f., e-tah-le'ah

Japan, cha-pan' — Giappone, m., je'ahp-po-nay

Mexico, meks'-i-ko — Messico, m., mess-se-ko

Morocco, m*o*-ro'-kou — Marocco, m., mah-rock-ko

Netherlands, neds'-*r*-land*s* — Paesi Bassi, m. pl., pah'ay-ze bahss-se

New Zealand, niuu *s*ii'-land — Nuova Zelanda, f., noo'o-vah zay-lahn-dah

Norway, noor'-uei — Norvegia f., nor-vay-je'ah

Portugal, por'-tu-gal — Portogallo, m., por-to-gahl-lo

Russia, rösh'-*a* — Russia, f., rooss-se'ah

Scotland, skot'-land — Scozia, f., sko-tse'ah

Spain, spein — Spagna, f., spah-ne'ah

Sweden, suid'-n — Svezia, f., zvay-tse'ah

Switzerland, suitz'-er-land — Svizzera, f., sveet-tsay-rah

Turkey, těr'-ki	Turchia, f., toohr-**ke**-ah
(the) United States,	(Gli) Stati Uniti, m. pl.,
(Di) iu-nai'-ted steits	(l'yee)**stah**-te oo-**nee**-te
Wales, uels	Galles, m., **gahl**-layss

American,	Americano, a.,
a-mei'-ri-k*a*n	ah-may-re-**kah**-no
Australian,	Australiano, a.,
oos-trei'-li-*a*n	ah'oo-strah-le-**ah**-no
Belgian, bel'-**ch**i-*a*n	Belga, a., **bell**-gah
British,	Britannico, a.,
brit'-ish	bre-**tahn**-ne-ko
Canadian,	Canadese, a.,
k*a*-nei'-di-*a*n	kah-nah-**day**-zay
Danish, dei'-nish	Danese, a., dah-**nay**-zay
Dutch, dŏch	Olandese, a.,
	o-lahn-**day**-zay
English, ing'-ghlish	Inglese, a., in-**glay**-zay
French,	Francese, a.,
french	frahn-**chay**-zay
German, ch**ě**r'-man	Tedesco, a., tay-**day**-sko
Irish,	Irlandese, a.,
air'-ish	eer-lahn-**day**-zay
Italian, i-tal'-i-*a*n	Italiano, a.,e-tah-le'**ah**-no
Norwegian,	Norvegese, a.,
noor-uii'-**ch**i-*a*n	nor-vay-**jay**-zay
Portuguese,	Portoghese, a.,
por'-tiu-ghiis	por-to-**gay**-zay
Russian, rŏsh'-i-*a*n	Russo, a., **rooss**-so
Scotch, skoch	Scozzese, a., skot-**tsay**-zay
Spanish,	Spagnuolo, a.,
span'-ish	spah-n'yoo-o-lo
Swedish, suid'-ish	Svedese, a., zvay-**day**-zay
Swiss, suis	Svizzero, a.,
	sveet-tsay-ro
Welsh, uelsh	Gallese, a., gahl-**lay**-zay

Antwerp, an'-tu**ě**rp	Anversa, f., ahn-**vair**-sah
Athens, aZ'-n**s**	Atene, f., ah-**tay**-nay
Berlin, b**ě**r'-lin	Berlino, f., bair-**lee**-no
Brussels, brŏs'-sl**s**	Bruxelles, f., broo-**sell**
Cairo, kai'-rou	Il Cairo, m., eel **kah**'e-ro

Cape Town, **keip taun**	Città del Capo, f., **chit-tah dell kah-po**
Geneva, chi-**nii'-va**	Ginevra, f., je-**nay-vrah**
Genoa, **chen'-ou-a**	Genova, f., **jay-no-vah**
Gibraltar, **chi-brool'-ta**	Gibilterra, f., je-beel-**tair-rah**
Hague, **heigh**	L'Aja, f., **lah-yah**
Lisbon, lis'-**bon**	Lisbona, f., le-**sbo**-nah
London, lŏn'-dn	Londra, f., **lon**-drah
Madrid, ma-**driid'**	Madrid, m., mah-**drid**
Marseilles, maar-**sels'**	Marsiglia, f., mar-see-l'yah
Milan, mi-lan'	Milano, f., me-**lah**-no
Naples, nei'-**pls**	Napoli, f., **nah**-po-le
New York, niuu **lork**	Nuova York, f., noo'o-vah **york**
Paris, pa'-ris	Parigi, f., pah-**ree**-dje
Rome, rŏum	Roma, f., **ro**-mah
Tangiers, tan'-**chiirs**	Tangeri, m., tahn-**jay**-re
Venice, ven'-is	Venezia, f., vay-**nay**-tse'ah
Vienna, vi-en'-a	Vienna, f., ve'en-nah
Warsaw, uoor'-so	Varsavia, f., var-**sah**-ve'ah

Alps, alps	Alpi, m. pl., **ahl**-pe
Black Sea, blak **sii**	Mar Nero, m., mar **nay**-ro
Caucasus, kau'-ka-**ses**	Caucaso, m., **kah**'oo-kah-zo
Danube, dan'-lub	Danubio, m., dah-noo-be'o
Dolomites, dol'-o-maits	Dolomiti, f.pl., do-lo-**mee**-te
Mediterranean, med-i-těr-ei'-ni-an	Mediterraneo, m., may-de-tair-**rah**-nay-o
Nile, nail	Nilo, m., **nee**-lo
North Sea, norZ **sii**	Mare del Nord, m., **mah**-ray del nord
Ocean, oo'-shn	Oceano, m., o-**chay**-ah-no
Pyrenees, pi-**ren**-iis'	Pirenei, m., pe-ray-**nay**-e
Seine, sein	Senna, f., **sen**-nah
Thames, tem**s**	Tamigi, m., tah-**mee**-je
Tiber, tai'-ba	Tevere, m., **tay**-vay-ray
Vosges, voosh	Vosgi, m. pl., **vo**-zje

xvi.

ITALIAN-ENGLISH DICTIONARY

a, ah, prep., to ; by ; at ; with

abaco, ah-bah-ko, m., plinth

abate, ah-bah-tay, m., abbot

abbacchiare, ahb-bahk-ke'ah-ray, v., to knock down

abbacinare, ahb-bah-che-nah-ray, v., to dazzle

abbadare, ahb-bah-dah-ray, v., to pay attention

abbadessa, ahb-bah-dess-sah, f., abbess

abbagliare, ahb-bah-l'yah-ray, v., to dazzle ; to mislead ; to astonish

abbaglio, ahb-bah-l'yo, m., dazzling ; mistake

abbaiamento, ahb-bah'e-yah-men-to, m., barking

abbaiare, ahb-bah'e-yah-ray, v., to bark ; to scream

abbaiata, ahb-bah'e-yah-tah, f., barking ; hooting

abbaino, ahb-bah'ee-no, m., skylight

abbandonare, ahb-bahn-do-nah-ray, v., to abandon, to give up

abbandono, ahb-bahn-do-no, m., abandonment

abbarcare, ahb-bar-kah-ray, v., to pile up

abbassamento, ahb-bahss-sah-men-to, m., lowering, abasement

abbassare, ahb-bahss-sah-ray, v., to lower

abbassarsi, ahb-bahss-sar-se, v., to stoop down

abbasso, ahb-bahss-so, adv., below, down

abbastanza, ahb-bah-stahn-tsah, adv., enough

abbattere, ahb-baht-tay-ray, v., to throw down ; to slaughter ; to demolish ; to fell

abbattimento, ahb-baht-te-men-to, m., discour- [agement

abbazia, ahb-bah-tsee-ah, f., abbey

abbellire, ahb-bell-lee-ray, v., to embellish ; to deck

abbeverare, ahb-bay-vay-rah-ray, v., to water

abbeveratoio, ahb-bay-vay-rah-to-e'o, m., horse-trough, cattle-trough, watering-place

abbici, ahb-be-chee, m., alphabet

abbietto*, ahb-be'ayt-to, a., abject [clothing

abbigliamento, ahb-be-l'yah-men-to, m., dress, clothing

abbigliarsi, ahb-be-l'yar-se, v., to dress oneself

abbindolamento, ahb-bin-do-lah-men-to, m., trick, cheat

ABB 2 ABI

abbindolare, ahb-bin-do-lah-ray, v., to cheat

abbisognare, ahb-be-zo-n'yah-ray, v., to need, to want ; to necessitate

abboccamento, ahb-bok-kah-men-to, m., interview

abboccare, ahb-bok-kah-ray, v., to bite ; to seize

abboccarsi, ahb-bok-kar-se, v., to have an interview

abbominabile, ahb-bo-me-nah-be-lay, a., abominable, odious

abbonamento, ahb-bo-nah-men-to, m., subscription

abbonare, ahb-bo-nah-ray, v., to subscribe ; to im-

abbonarsi, ahb-bo-nar-se, v., to subscribe [prove

abbondante, ahb-bon-dahn-tay, a., abundant

abbondare, ahb-bon-dah-ray, v., to abound

abbordare, ahb-bor-dah-ray, v., to accost ; (naut.) to draw alongside ; (naut.) to foul

abbordo, ahb-bor-do, m., access, approach

abbottonare, ahb-bot-to-nah-ray, v., to button

abbozzare, ahb-bot-tsah-ray, v., to sketch ; (sculpture) to rough out

abbozzo, ahb-bot-tso, m., sketch, outline

abbracciare, ahb-braht-chah-ray, v., to embrace

abbraccio, ahb-braht-cho, m., embrace

abbreviare, ahb-bray-ve'ah-ray, v., to abbreviate

abbreviatura, ahb-bray-ve'ah-too-rah, f., abbreviation

abbrividire, ahb-bre-ve-dee-ray, v., to shiver with cold, etc.

abbronzire, ahb-bron-tsee-ray, v., to sunburn

abbruciare, ahb-broo-chah-ray, v., to burn

abbrunamento, ahb-broo-nah-men-to, m., darkening ; blackening

abbrunare, ahb-broo-nah-ray, v., to get dark

abbrustolire, ahb-brooss-to-lee-ray, v., to toast, to grill

abbrutire, ahb-broo-tee-ray, v., to brutalize

abbuiare, ahb-boo-yah-ray, v., to get dark ; to obscure ; to darken ; to hide, to conceal

abdicare, ahb-de-kah-ray, v., to abdicate

aberrazione, ah-bair-rah-tse'o-nay, f., aberration

abete, ah-bay-tay, m., fir-tree

abile, ah-be-lay, a., skilful, able, clever

abilità, ah-be-le-tah, f., cleverness, skilfulness
abilitare, ah-be-le-tah-ray, v., to enable ; to qualify
abilmente, ah-bil-men-tay, adv., ably, cleverly
abisso, ah-biss-so, m., abyss
abitante, ah-be-tahn-tay, m., inhabitant
abitare, ah-be-tah-ray, v., to inhabit
abitazione, ah-be-tah-tse'o-nay, f., dwelling
abito, ah-be-to, m., garment ; custom
abituale, ah-be-too'ah-lay, a., usual, customary
abitualmente, ah-be-too'ahl-men-tay,adv.,usually
abituare, ah-be-too'ah-ray, v., to accustom
abituarsi, ah-be-too'ar-se, v., to get used to
abitudine, ah-be-too-de-nay, f., habit
abiurare, ah-be'oo-rah-ray, v., to abjure
abluzione, ah-bloo-tse'o-nay, f., ablution
abolire, ah-bo-lee-ray, v., to abolish ; to cancel
abominare, ah-bo-me-nah-ray, v., to abominate
abominevole,ah-bo-me-nay-vo-lay, a.,abominable
aborrire, ah-bor-ree-ray, v., to abhor
abortire, ah-bor-tee-ray, v., to miscarry
aborto, ah-bor-to, m., abortion
abrasione, ah-brah-ze'o-nay, f., abrasion
abusare, ah-boo-zah-ray, v., to abuse
abusivo⁶, ah-boo-zee-vo, a., abusive
abuso, ah-boo-zo, m., abuse
accademia, ahk-kah-day-me'ah, f., academy
accadere, ahk-kah-day-ray, v., to happen, to occur
accaduto, ahk-kah-doo-to, m., happening
accagliare, ahk-kah-l'yah-ray, v., to curdle
accalappiare, ahk-kah-lahp-pe'ah-ray, v., to ensnare ; to deceive
accalcare, ahk-kahl-kah-ray, v., to heap ; to crowd
accampare, ahk-kahm-pah-ray, v., to camp
accanire, ahk-kah-nee-ray, v., to embitter
accanto, ahk-kahn-to, adv., near, close
accaparrare, ahk-kah-par-rah-ray, v., to buy up
accappatoio, ahk-kahp-pah-to-e'o, m., dressing-
gown ; bathing-gown
accarezzamento, ahk-kah-ret-tsah-men-to, m.,
caress
accarezzare, ahk-kah-ret-tsah-ray, v., to caress
accasarsi, ahk-kah-zar-se, v., to marry

accasciarsi, ahk-kah-she'ar-se, v., to get discouraged ; to mope

accatastare, ahk-kah-tahss-tah-ray, v., to pile up

accattabrighe, ahk-kaht-tah-bree-gay,m.,caviller

accattare, ahk-kaht-tah-ray, v., to beg

accattone, ahk-kaht-to-nay, m., beggar

accecare, aht-chay-kah-ray, v., to blind ; to dazzle

accedere, aht-chay-day-ray, v., to approach

accelerare, aht-chay-lay-rah-ray, v., to accelerate

accendere, aht-chen-day-ray, v., to light

accenditore, aht-chen-de-tor-ay, m., lighter

accennare, aht-chen-nah-ray, v., to beckon ; to show ; to hint

accenno, aht-chen-no, m., nod ; hint

accensione, aht-chen-se'o-nay, f., lighting

accento, aht-chen-to, m., accent

accentuare, aht-chen-too'ah-ray, v., to accentuate

accerchiare, aht-chair-ke'ah-ray, v., to encircle

accertamento, aht-chair-tah-men-to, m., confirmation ; ascertainment

accertare, aht-chair-tah-ray, v., to assure ; to ascertain

accessibile, aht-chess-see-be-lay, a., accessible

accesso, aht-chess-so, m., access

accessorio, aht-chess-so're'o, m., accessory

accetta, aht-chet-tah, f., hatchet

accettabile, aht-chet-tah-be-lay, a., acceptable

accettare, aht-chet-tah-ray, v., to accept

accettazione,aht-chet-tah-tse'o-nay,f.,acceptation

acchetare, ahk-kay-tah-ray, v., to calm, to appease

acchiappare, ahk-ke'ahp-pah-ray, v., to catch

acciacco, aht-chahk-ko, m., infirmity

acciaio, aht-chah-e'o, m., steel

accidentale, aht-che-den-tah-lay, a., accidental

accidente, aht-che-den-tay, m., accident ; stroke

accidia, aht-che-de'ah, f., laziness, indolence

accidioso*, aht-che-de'o-zo, a., bad-tempered ; idle

accigliato*, aht-che-l'yah-to, a., sullen, haughty

acciò, acciocchè, aht-cho, aht-chok-kay, conj., in order that, so that

acciuga, aht-choo-gah, f., anchovy

acclamare, ahk-klah-mah-ray, v., to acclaim

acclamazione, ahk-klah-mah-tse'o-nay, f., acclamation

accludere, ahk-kloo-day-ray, v., to enclose

accoglienza, ahk-ko-l'yen-tsah, f., reception, welcome

accogliere, ahk-ko-l'yay-ray, v., to receive

accollatario, ahk-koll-lah-tah-re'o, m., contractor

accolta, ahk-koll-tah, f., assembly

accomandante, ahk-ko-mahn-dahn-tay, m., sleeping-partner

accomandatario, ahk-ko-mahn-dah-tah-re'o, m., working-partner [pany

accomandita, ahk-ko-mahn-de-tah, f., Ltd. Com-

accomodare, ahk-ko-mo-dah-ray, v., to repair; to accommodate

accomodarsi, ahk-ko-mo-dar-se, v., to take a seat

accompagnatore, ahk-kom-pah-n'yah-tor-ay, m., accompanist; companion

acconciare, ahk-kon-chah-ray, v., to attire; to arrange

acconciatura, ahk-kon-chah-too-rah, f., hair-dress; attire

acconcio*, ahk-kon-cho, a., suitable

acconsentire, ahk-kon-sen-tee-ray, v., to consent

accontentare, ahk-kon-ten-tah-ray, v., to satisfy

acconto, ahk-kon-to, m., account; instalment

accoppiare, ahk-kop-pe'ah-ray, v., to pair; to mate

accoramento, ahk-ko-rah-men-to, m., affliction, sorrow; pang

accorare, ahk-ko-rah-ray, v., to afflict; to grie

accorciare, ahk-kor-chah-ray, v., to shorten

accordare, ahk-kor-dah-ray, v., to grant; to t

accordo, ahk-kor-do, m., accord, harmony

accorgersi, ahk-kor-jair-se, v., to perceive

accorrere, ahk-kor-ray-ray, v., to run, to hur

accorto*, ahk-kor-to, a., shrewd, cunning;

accostamento, ahk-koss-tah-men-to, m., app

accostare, ahk-koss-tah-ray, v., to accost; to

accosto, ahk-koss-to, adv., near

accostumare, ahk-koss-too-mah-ray, v., custom

accozzaglia, ahk-kot-tsah-l'yah, f., rabbl

accozzamento, ahk-kot-tsah-**men**-to, m., collection ; heap

accozzare, ahk-kot-**tsah**-ray, v., to heap ; to collect

accreditare, ahk-kray-de-tah-ray, v., to accredit ; to credit

accrescere, ahk-**kray**-shay-ray, v., to increase

accudire, ahk-koo-**dee**-ray, v., to attend to

accumulare, ahk-koo-moo-**lah**-ray, v., to accumulate

accuratezza, ahk-koo-rah-**tayt**-tsah, f., accuracy

accurato*, ahk-koo-**rah**-to, a., accurate

accusa, ahk-**koo**-zah, f., accusation

accusare, ahk-koo-**zah**-ray, v., to accuse

accusatore, ahk-koo-zah-**tor**-ay, m., accuser

acerbo*, ah-**chair**-bo, a., bitter, sour, stern, pungent

acero, ah-**chay**-ro, m., maple

aceto, ah-**chay**-to, m., vinegar

acetosa, ah-chay-**to**-zah, f., sorrel

acetoso, ah-chay-**to**-zo, a., acid

acidezza, ah-che-**dayt**-tsah, f., acidity

acido, ah-**che**-do, m., acid. a.,* acid

aconito, ah-**ko**-ne-to, m., aconite

acqua, **ahk**-kwah, f., water

acquattarsi, ahk-kwaht-**tar**-se, v., to crouch

acquavite, ahk-kwah-**vee**-tay, f., crude brandy

acquazzone, ahk-kwaht-**tso**-nay, m., downpour

acquedotto, ahk-kway-**dot**-to, m., aqueduct

acquerello, ahk-kway-**rell**-lo, m., water-colour

acquietare, ahk-kwe'ay-**tah**-ray, v., to appease, to quiet

acquistare, ahk-kwiss-**tah**-ray, v., to acquire ; to buy

acquisto, ahk-**kwiss**-to, m., acquisition ; shopping ;

acquoso, ahk-koo'**o**-zo, a., watery [buying

acre, ah-kray, a., acrid ; harsh

acredine, ah-**kray**-de-nay, f.,pungency ; acrimony

acuire, ah-**kwee**-ray, v., to sharpen ; to embitter

acuità, ah-kwe-**tah**, f., acuteness

acume, ah-**koo**-may, m., acumen ; subtleness

acuminare, ah-koo-me-**nah**-ray, v., to point

acutezza, ah-koo-**tayt**-tsah, f., sharpness

acuto*, ah-**koo**-to, a., sharp, pointed ; keen

adagiare, ah-dah-**jah**-ray, v., to lay down

adagiarsi, ah-dah-jar-se, v., to lie down
adagio, ah-dah-jo, adv., slowly. m., adage
adattare, ah-daht-tah-ray, v., to adapt
adatto°, ah-daht-to, a., suitable ; capable
addebitare, ahd-day-be-tah-ray, v., to debit
addebito, ahd-day-be-to, m., imputation
addensare,ahd-den-sah-ray,v.,to thicken; to crowd
addentare, ah-den-tah-ray, v., to seize with the teeth ; to indent
addentrare, ahd-den-trah-ray, v., to penetrate
addentro, ahd-den-tro, adv., within, inside
addestrare, ahd-dess-trah-ray, v., to train
addetto, ah-det-to, a., addict ; attached
addi, a dì, ahd-dee, ah dee, adv., on the day of
addietro, ah-de'ay-tro, adv., behind
addio, ah-dee-o, interj., good-bye
addirittura, ahd-de-rit-too-rah, adv., absolutely ; straight away, interj., indeed !
addirizzare, ahd-de-rit-tsah-ray, v., to straighten
addirsi, ahd-deer-se, v., to devote oneself to
additare, ah-de-tah-ray, v., to indicate
addizione, ah-de-tse'o-nay, f., addition
addobbare, ah-dob-bah-ray, v., to decorate
addolcire, ahd-dol-chee-ray, v., to sweeten ; (fig.) to soothe
addolorare, ahd-do-lo-rah-ray,v.,to grieve ; to pain
addome, ah-do-may, m., abdomen
addomesticare, ahd-do-mess-te-kah-ray, v., to domesticate ; to tame ; to break in
addormentare, ahd-dor-men-tah-ray, v., to put asleep
addormentarsi, ahd-dor-men-tar-se, v., to go to sleep
addossare, ahd-doss-sah-ray, v., to load ; to lean against
addossarsi, ahd-doss-sar-se,v.,to take upon oneself
addosso, ahd-doss-so, prep. & adv., on, against
addurre, ahd-doohr-ray, v., to allege ; to lead
adeguare, ah-day-goo'ah-ray, v., to equalize
adeguato°, ah-day-goo'ah-to, a., adequate
adempiere, adempire, ah-dem-pe'ay-ray, ah-dem-pee-ray, v., to fulfil ; to perform

aderenza, ah-day-ren-tsah, f., adherence; (pl.) con-
aderire, ah-day-ree-ray, v., to adhere [nections
adescare, ah-dess-kah-ray, v., to bait, to lure
adesione, ah-day-ze'o-nay, f., adhesion
adesso, ah-dess-so, adv., now; presently
adiacente, ah-de'ah-chen-tay, a., adjacent
adipe, ah-de-pay, m., fat, grease
adiramento, ah-de-rah-men-to, m., wrath
adirare, ah-de-rah-ray, v., to anger
adirato*, ah-de-rah-to, a., angry
adire, ah-dee-ray, v., to acquire by inheritance, etc.
adito, ah-de-to, m., access, entrance, inlet
adocchiare, ah-dock-ke'ah-ray, v., to ogle; to
    wink; to observe for a moment
adombrare, ah-dom-brah-ray, v., to shade [front
adontare, ah-don-tah-ray, v., to reproach; to af-
adontarsi, ah-don-tar-se, v., to be offended
adoperare, ah-do-pay-rah-ray, v., to use
adorabile, ah-do-rah-be-lay, a., adorable
adornamento, ah-dor-nah-men-to, m., ornament
adornare, ah-dor-nah-ray, v., to adorn
adottare, ah-dot-tah-ray, v., to adopt
adozione, ah-do-tse'o-nay, f., adoption
adulare, ah-doo-lah-ray, v., to flatter
adulterare, ah-dool-tay-rah-ray, v., to adulterate
adunanza, ah-doo-nahn-tsah, f., meeting
adunare, ah-doo-nah-ray, v., to assemble; to gather
aduncare, ah-doonn-kah-ray, v., to shape hook-
    beaked
adunco, ah-doonn-ko, a., hooked
adunghiare, ah-doonn-ghe'ah-ray, v., to seize with
    the claws
adunque, ah-doonn-kway, adv., so, therefore, thus
aerare, ah-ay-rah-ray, v., to air
aere, ah-ay-ray, m., air, wind
aereo, ah-ay-ray-o, m., aeroplane. a., aerial
aeronauta, ah-ay-ro-nah'oo-tah, m., aeronaut
aeronave, ah-ay-ro-nah-vay, f., airship
aeroplano, ah-ay-ro-plah-no, m., aeroplane
aeroporto, ah-ay-ro-por-to, m., airport
aerostato, ah-ay-ross-tah-to, m., air-balloon
afa, ah-fah, f., sultriness

affabile, ahf-**fah**-be-lay, a., affable

affaccendarsi, ahf-faht-chen-**dar**-se, v., to get busy

affaccendato*, ahf-faht-chen-**dah**-to, a., busy

affacchinarsi, ahf-fahk-ke-**nar**-se, v., to toil

affacciarsi, ahf-faht-**char**-se, v., to look out of the window

affagottare, ahf-fah-got-**tah**-ray, v., to bundle up

affamare, ahf-fah-**mah**-ray, v., to starve out

affamato*, ahf-fah-**mah**-to, a., hungry, starved

affannare, ahf-fahn-**nah**-ray, v., to grieve, to worry

affannarsi, ahf-fahn-nar-se, v., to bustle ; to fret

affannato*, ahf-fahn-**nah**-to, a., out of breath

affanno, ahf-**fahn**-no, m., difficulty of breath, asthma ; sorrow

affardellare, ahf-far-dell-**lah**-ray, v., to bundle up ; to wrap up ; to pack

affare, ahf-**fah**-ray, m., business, affair ; enterprise

affarista, ahf-fah-**riss**-tah, m., promoter ; tricky business man ; busybody

affascinamento, ahf-fah-she-nah-**men**-to, m., fascination

affascinante, ahf-fah-she-**nahn**-tay, a., fascinating

affascinare, ahf-fah-she-**nah**-ray, v., to fascinate

affaticamento, ahf-fah-te-kah-**men**-to, m., fatigue

affaticare, ahf-fah-te-**kah**-ray, v., to tire, to fatigue

affatto, ahf-**faht**-to, adv., nothing at all ; entirely

affermare, ahf-fair-**mah**-ray, v., to affirm

afferrare, ahf-fair-**rah**-ray, v., to seize ; to cling

affettare, ahf-fet-**tah**-ray, v., to affect, to pretend

affettato, ahf-fet-**tah**-to, a., affected, conceited

affetto, ahf-**fet**-to, m., affection. a., affected

affettuoso*, ahf-fet-too'**o**-zo, a., affectionate

affezione, ahf-fay-tse'**o**-nay, f., affection

affiatare, ahf-fe'ah-**tah**-ray, v., to tune ; to get on well together

affibbiare, ahf-fib-be'**ah**-ray, v., to buckle

affibbiatura, ahf-fib-be'ah-**too**-rah, f., buckling ; hooks and eyes

affidare, ahf-fe-**dah**-ray, v., to entrust, to rely on

affievolire, ahf-fe'ay-vo-lee-ray, v., to weaken

affiggere, ahf-**feed**-jay-ray, v., to placard ; to advertise ; to fasten

affilare, ahf-fe-lah-ray, v., to sharpen; to whet
affilato*, ahf-fe-lah-to, a., sharpened, stropped
affinare, ahf-fe-nah-ray, v., to refine
affinchè, ahf-fin-kay, conj., in order that
affine, ahf-fee-nay, a., akin
affissare, ahf-fiss-sah-ray, v., to stare at; **to concentrate;** to post up
affissione, ahf-fiss-se'O-nay, f., bill-posting
affisso, ahf-fiss-so, m., poster, placard
affittaiuolo, ahf-fit-tah'e-oo-O-lo, m., small farmer
affittare, ahf-fit-tah-ray, v., to rent; to lease
affitto, ahf-fit-to, m., rent; lease
affittuario, ahf-fit-too'ah-re'o, m., tenant; renter
affliggere, ahf-fleed-jay-ray, v., to afflict; **to** trouble; to pain
afflitto*, ahf-flit-to, a., afflicted
afflizione, ahf-fle-tse'O-nay, f., affliction
affloscire, ahf-flo-shee-ray, v., to get limp
affluente, ahf-floo'en-tay, m., tributary, a., abundant
affluenza, ahf-floo'en-tsah, f., abundance, plenty
affluire, ahf-floo'ee-ray, v., to flow into; to flock; to abound
afflusso, ahf-flooss-so, m., afflux, flow
affogamento, ahf-fo-gah-men-to, m., drowning
affogare, ahf-fo-gah-ray, v., to drown
affollamento, ahf-fol-lah-men-to, m., **gathering**
affollare, ahf-fol-lah-ray, v., to crowd
affondare, ahf-fon-dah-ray, v., to sink
affrancare, ahf-frahn-kah-ray, v., to stamp **letters;** to prepay; to release; to redeem
affranto*, ahf-frahn-to, a., worn out
affrettare, ahf-fret-tah-ray, v., to hasten
affrontare, ahf-fron-tah-ray, v., to affront; to face
affumicare, ahf-foo-me-kah-ray, v., to fumigate, to smoke
affusto, ahf-fooss-to, m., gun-carriage
afono*, ah-fo-no, a., voiceless, aphonous
agente, ah-jen-tay, m., agent
agenzia, ah-jen-tsee-ah, f., agency
agevolare, ah-jay-vo-lah-ray, v., to facilitate
agevole, ah-jay-vo-lay, a., easy, manageable
agevolezza, ah-jay-vo-let-tsah, f., facility, **ease**

agganciare, ahg-gahn-chah-ray, v., to hook, to hang up ; to clasp

aggettivo, ahd-jet-tee-vo, m., adjective

agghiacciare, ahg-ghe'aht-chah-ray, v., to freeze

agghindare, ahg-ghin-dah-ray, v., to dress in one's best

aggio, ahd-jo, m., interest ; usury ; premium

aggiogare, ahd-jo-gah-ray, v., to yoke

aggiornamento, ahd-jor-nah-men-to, m., adjournment, postponement

aggiornare, ahd-jor-nah-ray, v., to postpone ; to bring up to date

aggirare, ahd-je-rah-ray, v., to whirl ; to dupe

aggiudicare, ahd-joo-de-kah-ray, v., to adjudge

aggiungere, ahd-joonn-jay-ray, v., to add, to link

aggiunta, ahd-joonn-tah, f., addition ; joining

aggiuntare, ahd-joonn-tah-ray, v., to couple ; to add

aggiunto, ahd-joonn-to, m., assistant. a., added

aggiustare, ahd-jooss-tah-ray, v., to adjust ; to mend ; to settle

aggomitolare, ahg-go-me-to-lah-ray, v., to roll up ; to crouch

aggradare, ahg-grah-dah-ray, v., to please ; to oblige

aggradevole, ahg-grah-day-vo-lay, a., agreeable

aggradire, ahg-grah-dee-ray, v., to agree to ; to please

aggranchiare, ahg-grahn-ke'ah-ray, v., to get the cramp ; to benumb

aggrandire, ahg-grahn-dee-ray, v., to enlarge

aggranfiare, ahg-grahn-fe'ah-ray, v., to grasp, to clutch

aggrappare, ahg-grahp-pah-ray, v., to grapple

aggravare, ahg-grah-vah-ray, v., to aggravate

aggravio, ahg-grah-ve'o, m., burden ; (fig.)injury

aggraziato*, ahg-grah-tse'ah-to, a., pleasant, sweet ; affected

aggredire, ahg-gray-dee-ray, v., to assault

aggregare, ahg-gray-gah-ray, v., to aggregate

aggressore, ahg-gress-sor-ay, m., aggressor

aggrinzare, ahg-grin-tsah-ray, v., to wrinkle ; to wizen

aggrottare, ahg-grot-tah-ray, v., to frown

aggrumarsi, ahg-groo-mar-se, v., to clot

aggruppare, ahg-groop-pah-ray, v., to group

agguagliamento, ahg-goo'ah-l'yah-men-to, m., equalization

agguagliare, ahg-goo'ah-l'yah-ray, v., to equalize ; to compare

agguantare, ahg-goo'ahn-tah-ray, v., to seize, to catch

agguato, ahg-goo'ah-to, m., ambush

aghetto, ahg-ghet-to, m., aiglet ; tag

agiatamente, ah-jah-tah-men-tay, adv., easily

agiatezza, ah-jah-tet-tsah, f., comfort

agiato°, ah-jah-to, a., wealthy ; comfortable

agile, ah-je-lay, a., agile, alert

agio, ah-jo, m., comfort, repose ; convenience

agire, ah-jee-ray, v., to act

agitare, ah-je-tah-ray, v., to agitate

aglio, ah-l'yo, m., garlic

agnella, ah-n'yell-lah, f., ewe-lamb

agnello, ah-n'yell-lo, m., lamb

ago, ah-go, m., needle   [nately

agognare, ah-go-n'yah-ray, v., to desire inordi-

agonia, ah-go-nee-ah, f., agony

agosto, ah-goss-to, m., August

agreste, ah-gress-tay, a., wild ; rustic

agrezza, ah-gret-tsah, f., sourness, acidity

agricoltore, ah-gre-kol-tor-ay, m., agriculturist

agricoltura, ah-gre-kol-too-rah, f., agriculture

agrifoglio, ah-gre-fo-l'yo, m., holly

agrimensore, ah-gre-men-sor-ay, m., land surveyor

agrimensura, ah-gre-men-soo-rah, f., land sur-

agro, ah-gro, a., sharp, sour ; pungent   [veying

agrodolce, ah-gro-doll-chay, m., bitter-sweet

agronomo, ah-gro-no-mo, m., agronomist

agrumi, ah-groo-me, m. pl., citric fruits

aguzzare, ah-goot-tsah-ray, v., to sharpen

aguzzino, ah-goot-tsee-no, m., cruel overseer

aguzzo°, ah-goot-tso, a., sharp ; pointed

ah ! ah ! ! ah, ah'e, interj., oh ! ah ! alas !

ahimè, ah'e-may, interj., alas ! poor me !

aia, ah'e-ah, f., nurse ; threshing-floor

aio, ah'e-o, m., tutor
airone, ah'e-ro-nay, m., heron
aitante, ah'e-tahn-tay, a., strong, fine
aiuola, ah-yoo-o-lah, f., flower-bed
aiutante, ah-yoo-tahn-tay, m., adjutant ; **helper**
aiutare, ah-yoo-tah-ray, v., to assist, to help
aiuto, ah-yoo-to, m., help ; support
aizzare, ah'it-tsah-ray, v., to instigate, to goad
ala, ah-lah, f., wing ; aisle
alabarda, ah-lah-bar-dah, f., halberd
alacre, ah-lah-kray, a., active ; cheerful ; **brisk**
alamari, ah-lah-mah-re, m. pl., braiding
alano, ah-lah-no, m., great Dane
alare, ah-lah-ray, m., andiron
alato, ah-lah-to, a., winged
alba, ahl-bah, f., day-break
albagia, ahl-bah-jee-ah, f., pride ; haughtiness
albeggiare, ahl-bayd-jah-ray, v., to dawn [hoist
alberare, ahl-bay-rah-ray, v., to plant trees ; to
albereto, ahl-bay-ray-to, m., cluster of trees
albergare, ahl-bair-gah-ray, v., to lodge, to shelter
albergatore, ahl-bair-gah-tor-ay, m., inn-keeper
albergo, ahl-bair-go, m., hotel ; country hotel
albero, ahl-bay-ro, m., tree ; shaft ; mast
albicocca, ahl-be-kok-kah, f., apricot
albicocco, ahl-be-kok-ko, m., apricot-tree
albume, ahl-boo-may, m., albumen
alcione, ahl-cho-nay, m., halcyon ; king-fisher
alcool, ahl-ko-ol, m., alcohol
alcova, ahl-ko-vah, f., alcove, recess
alcunchè, ahl-koonn-kay, m., something, a little
alcuno, ahl-koo-no, a., some. m., someone
alea, ah-lay-ah, f., risk
alfabeto, ahl-fah-bay-to, m., alphabet
alfiere, ahl-fe'ay-ray, m., ensign ; midshipman
alfine, ahl-fee-nay, adv., at last
alga, ahl-gah, f., sea-weed
alice, ah-lee-chay, f., anchovy
alienare, ah-le'ay-nah-ray, v., to alienate
alieno, ah-le'ay-no, a., not inclined ; adverse [fish
aligusta [*or* **aragosta**], ah-le-gooss-tah, f., craw-
alimentare, ah-le-men-tah-ray, v., to feed

alimento, ah-le-men-to, m., food

alitare, ah-le-tah-ray, v., to pant; to blow gently

alito, ah-le-to, m., breath; breeze

allacciare, ahl-laht-chah-ray, v., to fasten; to lace up; to link; to entice

allargare, ahl-lar-gah-ray, v., to broaden; to outstretch; to relax

allarmare, ahl-lar-mah-ray, v., to alarm

allarme, ahl-lar-may, m., alarm

allato, ahl-lah-to, adv., beside, near

allattare, ahl-laht-tah-ray, v., to feed; to nurse

alleanza, ahl-lay-ahn-tsah, f., alliance

alleato, ahl-lay-ah-to, m., ally. a., allied

allegare, ahl-lay-gah-ray, v., to allege; to attach

allegato, ahl-lay-gah-to, m., enclosure

allegazione, ahl-lay-gah-tse'o-nay, f., allegation

alleggerire, ahl-led-jay-ree-ray, v., to lighten

allegrare, ahl-lay-grah-ray, v., to cheer up

allegrezza, ahl-lay-gret-tsah, f., cheerfulness

allegria, ahl-lay-gree-ah, f., merriment, joy

allegro*, ahl-lay-gro, a., gay, merry

allenamento, ahl-lay-nah-men-to, m., training

allenare, ahl-lay-nah-ray, v., to exercise, to train

allenire, ahl-lay-nee-ray, v., to allay

allentare, ahl-len-tah-ray, v., to slow down

allestimento, ahl-less-te-men-to, m., completion; fitting out

allestire, ahl-less-tee-ray, v., to prepare

allettamento, ahl-let-tah-men-to, m., allurement

allettare, ahl-let-tah-ray, v., to allure

allettato, ahl-let-tah-to, a., bed-ridden

allevamento, ahl-lay-vah-men-to, m., breeding

allevare, ahl-lay-vah-ray, v., to bring up, to breed

alleviamento, ahl-lay-ve'ah-men-to, m., relief

alleviare, ahl-lay-ve'ah-ray, v., to alleviate

allibire, ahl-le-bee-ray, v., to be bewildered

allietare, ahl-le'ay-tah-ray, v., to cheer up

allievo, ahl-le'ay-vo, m., pupil, scholar

allineamento, ahl-le-nay-ah-men-to, m., alignment

allineare, ahl-le-nay-ah-ray, v., to set in line

allividire, ahl-le-ve-dee-ray, v., to turn pale

allocco, ahl-lok-ko, m., owl; (fig.) dunce

allodola, ahl-lo-do-lah, f., lark

allogamento, ahl-lo-gah-men-to, m., placing ; investment ; letting ; billeting

allogare, ahl-lo-gah-ray, v., to place ; to let ; to invest

alloggiare, ahl-lod-jah-ray, v., to lodge, to dwell

alloggio, ahl-lod-jo, m., lodging, abode

allontanamento, ahl-lon-tah-nah-men-to, m., departure ; parting ; absence ; removal ; neglect

allontanare, ahl-lon-tah-nah-ray, v., to send away

allora, ahl-lo-rah, adv., then ; in such a case

allorchè, ahl-lor-kay, adv., when, while, at the time

alloro, ahl-lo-ro, m., laurel

allorquando, ahl-lor-kwahn-do, adv., when

allucinazione, ahl-loo-che-nah-tse'o-nay, f., hallucination

alludere, ahl-loo-day-ray, v., to allude   [cination

allume, ahl-loo-may, m., alum

alluminio, ahl-loo-mee-ne'o, m., aluminium

allungare, ahl-loonn-gah-ray, v., to prolong ; to lengthen

alma, ahl-mah, f., (poet.) soul

almanacco, ahl-mah-nak-ko, m.,almanac,calendar

almanco, ahl-mahn-ko, adv., at least

almeno, ahl-may-no, adv., at least

aloe, ah-lo-ay, m., aloes

alone, ah-lo-nay, m., halo

alpestre, ahl-pess-tray, a., alpine

alquanto, ahl-kwahn-to, adv., somewhat

altalena, ahl-tah-lay-nah, f., see-saw ; swing

altare, ahl-tah-ray, m., altar

alterare, ahl-tay-rah-ray, v., to alter

altercare, ahl-tair-kah-ray, v., to quarrel

alterezza, ahl-tay-ret-tsah, f., haughtiness, pride

alternare, ahl-tair-nah-ray, v., to alternate

alterno*, ahl-tair-no, a., alternate

altero*, ahl-tay-ro, a., haughty

altezza, ahl-tet-tsah, f., height ; Highness

altiero*, ahl-te'ay-ro, a., haughty

altipiano, ahl-te-pe'ah-no, m., plateau

alto³, ahl-to, a., high ; tall ; loud

altolocato, ahl-to-lo-kah-to, a., highly placed

altri, ahl-tre, pron., somebody else ; others

altrimenti, ahl-tre-**men**-te, adv., else ; on the contrary

altro, ahl-tro, a., other

altronde, ahl-**tron**-day, adv., elsewhere ; d'—, besides, on the other hand

altrove, ahl-tro-vay, adv., elsewhere

altrui, ahl-**troo**-e, pron., others ; somebody else's

altura, ahl-**too**-rah, f., altitude ; hillock

alunno, ah-**loonn**-no, m., pupil

alveare, ahl-vay-ah-ray, m., bee-hive

alveo, ahl-vay-o, m., river-bed

alzare, ahl-**tsah**-ray, v., to raise ; to hoist ; to weigh

alzarsi, ahl-**tsar**-se, v., to get up ; to sit up

alzata, ahl-**tsah**-tah, f., rise, rising ; shelf

amabile, ah-**mah**-be-lay, a., amiable, charming

amaca, ah-**mah**-kah, f., hammock

amante, ah-**mahn**-tay, m. & f., lover

amarasco, ah-mah-**rahss**-ko, m., morello-tree

amare, ah-**mah**-ray, v., to love, to cherish

amareggiare, ah-mah-red-jah-ray, v., to embitter

amarena, ah-mah-**ray**-nah, f., bitter cherry

amaretto, ah-mah-**ret**-to, m., macaroon

amarezza, ah-mah-**ret**-tsah, f., bitterness ; grief

amaro°, ah-**mah**-ro, a., bitter

amarrare, ah-mar-**rah**-ray, v., to moor

amarume, ah-mah-**roo**-may, m., bitterness

amatista, ah-mah-**tiss**-tah, f., amethyst

amato, ah-**mah**-to, m., beloved. a., loved

ambasceria, ahm-bah-shay-**ree**-ah, f., embassy

ambascia, ahm-bah-she'ah, f., sorrow, pain

ambasciata, ahm-bah-she'**ah**-tah, f., (see **ambasceria**)

ambasciatore, ahm-bah-she'ah-**tor**-ay, m., ambassador

ambedue, ahm-bay-**doo**-ay, pron., both   [sador

ambiente, ahm-be'**en**-tay, m., room ; environment ; circle ; midst

ambiguo°, ahm-bee-goo'o, a., ambiguous

ambire, ahm-bee-ray, v., to long or crave for

ambito, **ahm**-be-to, m., circle ; relationship

ambito, ahm-bee-to, a., coveted

ambizioso°, ahm-be-tse'**o**-so, a., ambitious

ambo, ahm-bo, m., couple. a., both

ambra, **ahm**-brah, f., amber

ambulante, ahm-boo-**lahn**-tay, a., itinerant

ambulanza, ahm-boo-**lahn**-tsah, f., ambulance

amenità, ah-may-ne-**tah**, f., amenity

ameno*, ah-**may**-no, a., pleasant ; mild ; entertain-ing [ing

ametista, ah-may-**tiss**-tah, f., amethyst

amianto, ah-me'**ahn**-to, m., asbestos

amica, ah-**mee**-kah, f., lady-friend

amichevole, ah-me-**kay**-vo-lay, a., amiable

amicizia, ah-me-**chee**-tse-ah, f., friendship

amico, ah-**mee**-ko, m., friend. a.,* friendly

amido, ah-**me**-do, m., starch [crush

ammaccare, ahm-mahk-**kah**-ray, v., to bruise ; to

ammaccatura, ahm-mahk-kah-**too**-rah, f., bruise

ammaestramento, ahm-mah-ess-trah-**men**-to, m., training, instruction

ammaestrare, ahm-mah-ess-**trah**-ray, v., to train

ammaestrato, ahm-mah-ess-**trah**-to, a., trained

ammainare, ahm-mah'e-**nah**-ray, v., to take in sails ; to hoist the boats *or* anchor ; to strike colours

ammalare, ahm-mah-**lah**-ray, v., to make un-well ; to become ill

ammalato, ahm-mah-**lah**-to, m., sick person ; invalid. a., diseased ; sick ; ailing

ammaliare, ahm-mah-le'**ah**-ray, v., to bewitch

ammanco, ah-**mahn**-ko, m., a falling short [cuff

ammanettare, ahm-mah-net-**tah**-ray, v., to hand-

ammansare, ahm-mahn-**sah**-ray, v., to tame

ammansare, ahm-mahn-**tah**-ray, v., to cloak

ammanto, ahm-**mahn**-to, m., mantle, cloak

ammassare, ahm-mahss-**sah**-ray, v., to amass

ammasso, ahm-**mahss**-so, m., heap

ammattire, ahm-maht-**tee**-ray, v., to go mad

ammazzare, ahm-maht-**tsah**-ray, v., to kill

ammazzasette, ahm-maht-tsah-**set**-tay, m., bully

ammazzatoio, ahm - maht - tsah - to - e'o, m., slaughter-house

ammenare, ahm-may-**nah**-ray, v., to strike

ammenda, ahm-**men**-dah, f., fine ; amends

ammendare, ahm-men-**dah**-ray, v., to amend

ammettere, ahm-**met**-tay-ray, v., to admit

ammezzare, ahm-met-**tsah**-ray, v., to halve

ammiccare, ahm-mick-**kah**-ray. v., to wink
amministratore, ahm-me-niss-trah-**tor**-ay, m., managing director ; trustee
ammirabile, ahm-me-**rah**-be-lay, a., admirable
ammiraglio, ahm-me-**rah**-l'yo, m., admiral
ammirare, ahm-me-**rah**-ray, v., to admire
ammirevole, ahm-me-ray-vo-lay, a., admirable
ammiserire, ahm-me-say-**ree**-ray, v., to impoverish
ammissibile, ahm-miss-**see**-be-lay, a., admissible
ammobiliamento, ahm-mo-be-l'yah-**men**-to, m., furniture
ammobiliare, ahm-mo-be-l'**yah**-ray, v., to furnish
ammodo, ahm-**mo**-do, a., well to do. adv., well
ammogliarsi, ahm-mo-l'**yar**-se, v., (man) to marry
ammollare, ahm-moll-**lah**-ray, v., to soak : to soften
ammollire, ahm-moll-**lee**-ray, v., to mollify
ammollirsi, ahm-moll-**leer**-se, v., to become effeminate
ammoniaca, ahm-mo-**nee**-ah-kah, f., ammonia
ammonimento, ahm-mo-ne-**men**-to, m., admonition ; warning
ammonire, ahm-mo-**nee**-ray, v., to admonish
ammontare, ahm-mon-**tah**-ray, m., sum. v., to heap
ammonticchiare, ahm-mon-tick-ke'**ah**-ray, v., to heap together ; to hoard
ammorbare, ahm-mor-**bah**-ray, v., to infect
ammorbidire, ahm-mor-be-**dee**-ray, v., to soften
ammortamento, ahm-mor-tah-**men**-to, m., settlement of debts by sinking fund
ammortire, ahm-mor-**tee**-ray, v., to deaden ; to redeem
ammortizzare, ahm-mor-tit-**tsah**-ray, v., to pay off a debt by instalments
ammorzare, ahm-mor-**tsah**-ray, v., to extinguish
ammoscire, ahm-mo-**shee**-ray, v., to become soft ; to fade ; to wither
ammucchiare, ahm-mook-ke'**ah**-ray, v., to pile up
ammuffire, ahm-**moof**-fee-ray, v., to get mouldy
ammutinamento, ahm-moo-te-nah-**men**-to, m., mutiny ; uprising
ammutinarsi, ahm-moo-te-**nar**-se, v., to mutiny
ammutire, ahm-moo-**tee**-ray, v., to become dumb

ammutolire, ahm-moo-to-lee-ray, v., to become mute

amnistia, ahm-niss-tee-ah, f., amnesty

amnistiare, ahm-niss-te'ah-ray, v.,to grant pardon

amo, ah-mo. m., fishing-hook

amore, ah-mo-ray, m., love

amoreggiare, ah-mo-red-jah-ray, v., to woo

amorevole, ah-mo-ray-vo-lay, a., endearing

amorevolezza,ah-mo-ray-vo-let-tsah,f.,lovingness

amorino, ah-mo-ree-no, m., mignonette

amoroso, ah-mo-ro-zo, m., lover. a.,* amorous

ampio*, ahm-pe'o, a., ample

amplesso, ahm-pless-so, m., embrace

ampliare, ahm-ple'ah-ray, v., to enlarge

ampolla, ahm-poll-lah, f., phial ; cruet-bottle

ampolliera, ahm-poll-le'ay-rah, f., cruet-stand

ampolloso*, ahm-poll-lo-zo, a., bombastic

amputare, ahm-poo-tah-ray, v., to amputate

anagrafe, ah-nah-grah-fay, f., census

analfabeta, ah-nahl-fah-bay-tah, a., illiterate

analisi, ah-nah-le-ze, f., analysis. **in ultima —**, in short, after all, in a word

analizzare, ah-nah-lit-tsah-ray, v., to analyse

analogo*, ah-nah-lo-go, a., analogous

ananasso, ah-nah-nahss-so, m., pine-apple

anarchico, ah-nar-ke-ko, m., anarchist

anatomia, ah-nah-to-mee-ah, f., anatomy

anatra, anitra, ah-nah-trah, **ah**-ne-trah, f., **duck**

anca, ahn-kah, f., hip ; haunch

ancella, ahn-chell-lah, f., maid

anche, ahn-kay, adv., still ; even ; too

ancora, ahn-ko-rah, adv., yet ; again ; more

áncora, ahn-ko-rah, f., anchor

ancorchè, ahn-kor-kay, adv., even ; although

andamento, ahn-dah-men-to, m., gait ; trend

andante, ahn-dahn-tay, a., current ; **fair.** m., (mus.) andante

andare, ahn-dah-ray, v., to go ; to walk

andarsene, ahn-dar-say-nay, v., to leave, to depart

andata, ahn-dah-tah, f., departure ; single journey

andato, ahn-dah-to, p.p., gone ; (fig.) ruined

andatura, ahn-dah-too-rah, f., gait, walking

andirivieni, ahn-de-re-ve'ay-ne, m., hurry-skurry
andito, ahn-de-to, m., corridor
androne, ahn-dro-nay, m., anteroom ; hall
aneddoto, ah-ned-do-to, m., anecdote
anelare, ah-nay-lah-ray, v., to pant ; to long for
anelito, ah-nay-le-to, m., breath ; gasp ; craving
anello, ah-nell-lo, m., ring, ringlet ; link ; curly-lock
anemia, ah-nay-mee-ah, f., anæmia
anestetico, ah-nay-stay-te-ko, m., anæsthetic
anfibio, ahn-fee-be'o, a., amphibious
angariare, ahn-gah-re'ah-ray, v., to torment
angelo, ahn-jay-lo, m., angel
angolare, ahn-go-lah-ray, a., angular
angolo, ahn-go-lo, m., corner, angle
angoscia, ahn-go-she'ah, f., anguish
anguilla, ahn-goo'eel-lah, f., eel
anguria, ahn-goo-re'ah, f., water-melon
angustia, ahn-gooss-te'ah, f., sorrow ; misery
angusto*, ahn-gooss-to, a., narrow ; poor, modest
anice, ah-ne-chay, m., aniseed
anima, ah-ne-mah, f., soul
animare, ah-ne-mah-ray, v., to animate   [to
animarsi, ah-ne-mar-se, v., to take heart ; to come
animella, ah-ne-mel-lah, f., sweet-bread
animo, ah-ne-mo, m., mind, thought, soul ; courage ;
     leaning ; presentiment
animoso*, ah-ne-mo-zo, a., intrepid, brave
anitra, ah-ne-trah, f., duck
anitrotto, ah-ne-trot-to, m., duckling
annacquare, ahn-nahk-kwah-ray, v., to dilute
annaffiare, ahn-nahf-fe'ah-ray, v., to water   [can
annaffiatoio, ahn-nahf-fe'ah-to-e'o, m., watering-
annali, ahn-nah-le, m. pl., annals
annaspare, ahn-nah-spah-ray, v., to reel ; to gasp
annata, ahn-nah-tah, f., year ; year's profits
annebbiare, ahn-neb-be'ah-ray, v., to dim, to mist
annegare, ahn-nay-gah-ray, v., to drown
annerire, ahn-nay-ree-ray, v., to blacken
annessi, ahn-ness-se, m. pl., out-buildings
annessione, ahn-ness-se'o-nay, f., annexion
annesso, ahn-ness-so, p.p. & a., annexed   [nate
annestare, ahn-nay-stah-ray, v., to graft ; to vacci-

annettere, ahn-**net**-tay-ray. v., to annex
annichilire, ahn-ne-ke-lee-ray. v., to annihilate
annidare, ahn-ne-**dah**-ray. v., to build a nest
annientare, ahn-ne'en-**tah**-ray. v., to annihilate
anniversario, ahn-ne-vair-sah-re'o. m., anniversary ; birthday
anno, **ahn**-no. m., year. **Capo d'anno**, New Year's Day
annodare, ahn-no-**dah**-ray. v., to tie ; to bind
annoiare, ahn-no-**yah**-ray. v., to annoy ; (fam.) to tease
annotare, ahn-no-**tah**-ray. v., to take a note of
annoverare, ahn-no-vay-**rah**-ray. v., to enumerate
annuale, ahn-noo'**ah**-lay. a., yearly
annualità, ahn-noo'ah-le-**tah**. f., annuity
annuire, ahn-noo'**ee**-ray. v., to assent ; to nod
annuità, ahn-noo'e-**tah**. f., annuity
annullare, ahn-nooll-**lah**-ray. v., to annul
annunziare, ahn-noonn-tse'**ah**-ray. v., to announce
annunzio, ahn-**noonn**-tse'o. m., advertisement ; notice, declaration ; poster
annuo, **ahn**-noo'o. a., annual
annusare, ahn-noo-**sah**-ray. v., to sniff ; to scent
annuvolarsi, ahn-noo-vo-lar-se. v., to become [cloudy
anomalo, ah-**no**-mah-lo. a., anomalous
anonima, ah-**no**-ne-mah. a., **Società anonima,** Ltd. Company
anormale, ah-nor-**mah**-lay. a., abnormal
ansa, **ahn**-sah. f., loop
ansamento, ahn-sah-**men**-to. m., short breathing
ansare, ahn-**sah**-ray. v., to pant, to be out of breath
ansia, ahn-se'ah. f., longing
ansietà, ahn-se'ay-**tah**. f., anxiety ; agitation
antecedente, ahn-tay-chay-**den**-tay. a., antecedent
antecedenza, ahn-tay-chay-den-tsah. f., antecedence
antecessore, ahn-tay-chess-**sor**-ay. m., predecessor
antenato, ahn-tay-**nah**-to. m., ancestor
antenna, ahn-**ten**-nah. f., antenna ; (wireless) aerial
anteporre, ahn-tay-**por**-ray. v., to prefer
anteriore, ahn-tay-re'**o**-ray. a., anterior, prior, first
anticaglia, ahn-te-**kah**-l'yah. f., old curiosities

anticaglie, ahn-te-kah-l'yay, f.pl., antiquities

anticamente, ahn-te-kah-men-tay, adv., in by-gone times, formerly, of yore

anticamera, ahn-te-**kah**-may-rah, f., ante-chamber. **fare —**, to wait

antichità, ahn-te-ke-tah, f., antiquity

anticipare, ahn-te-che-pah-ray, v., to anticipate

anticipato*, ahn-te-che-pah-to, a., in advance

antico*, ahn-tee-ko, a., antique

antidata, ahn-te-dah-tah, f., antedate

antilope, ahn-tee-lo-pay, f., antelope

antimeridiano, ahn-te-may-re-de'**ah**-no, a. morning, a.m.

antimonio, ahn-te-mo-ne'o, m., antimony

antipasto, ahn-te-**pahss**-to, m., hors-d'œuvre

antipodi, ahn-tee-po-de, m.pl., antipodes [date

antiquato*, ahn-te-kwah-to, a., obsolete ; out-of-

antivedere, ahn-te-vay-day-ray, v., to foresee

antiveleno, ahn-te-vay-lay-no, m., counter-poison

antracite, ahn-trah-chee-tay, f., anthracite

antro, ahn-tro, m., cave, den, lair

antropofago, ahn-tro-po-fah-go, m., cannibal

anulare, ah-noo-lah-ray, m., ring-finger

anzi, ahn-tse, adv., rather ; even ; just the opposite

anzianità, ahn-tse'ah-ne-tah, f., seniority

anziano, ahn-tse'ah-no, a., aged, elder, senior

anziché, ahn-tse-kay, conj., rather than

anzidetto, ahn-tse-det-to, a., aforesaid

apatia, ah-pah-tee-ah, f., apathy, insensibility

apatico*, ah-pah-te-ko, a., apathetic, indifferent

ape, ah-pay, f., bee

aperitivo, ah-pay-re-tee-vo, m., appetizer ; (med.) aperient

aperto*, ah-pair-to, a., open, candid

apertura, ah-pair-too-rah, f., aperture

apice, ah-pe-chay, m., apex, top ; (fig.) summit

apologia, ah-po-lo-jee-ah, f., apology

apoplessia, ah-po-pless-see-ah, f., apoplexy

apostolo, ah-poss-to-lo, m., apostle [tion

appagamento, ahp-pah-gah-men-to, m., satisfac-

appagare, ahp-pah-gah-ray, v., to satisfy, to content

appaiare, ahp-pah-yah-ray, v., to match

appalesare, ahp-pah-lay-sah-ray, v., to disclose, to divulge

appaltare, ahp-pahl-tah-ray, v., to lease out; to adjudge

appaltatore, ahp-pahl-tah-tor-ay, m., contractor

appalto, ahp-pahl-to, m., contract; monopoly

appannaggio, ahp-pahn-nahd-jo, m., allowance; alimony

appannare, ahp-pahn-nah-ray, v., to dull, to dim

apparato, ahp-pah-rah-to, m., apparatus; (fig.) pomp, show

apparecchiare, ahp-pah-reck-ke'ah-ray, v., to prepare; to lay the table

apparecchio, ahp-pah-reck-ke'o, m., apparatus; outfit; (med.) dressing

apparente, ahp-pah-ren-tay, a., apparent

apparenza, ahp-pah-ren-tsah, f., appearance

apparire, ahp-pah-ree-ray, v., to appear

appartamento, ahp-par-tah-men-to, m., flat

appartare, ahp-par-tah-ray, v., to set aside

appartarsi, ahp-par-tar-se, v., to withdraw oneself

appartenere, ahp-par-tay-nay-ray, v., to belong

appassimento, ahp-pahss-se-men-to, m., fading

appassionamento, ahp-pahss-se'o-nah-men-to, m., passion, ardour

appassionarsi, ahp-pahss-se'o-nar-se, v., to become impassioned; to love

appassionato*, ahp-pahss-se'o-nah-to, p. p. & a., passionate; affectionate

appassire, ahp-pahss-see-ray, v., to wizen, to fade

appellare, ahp-pell-lah-ray, v., to call; to name; to summon; (law) to appeal

appello, ahp-pell-lo, m., call; appeal; roll-call

appena, ahp-pay-nah, adv., barely, hardly. —**che**, as soon as

appendere, ahp-pen-day-ray, v., to hang up

appestare, ahp-pay-stah-ray, v., to infect, to taint

appetito, ahp-pay-tee-to, m., appetite

appetto, ahp-pet-to, prep., in comparison with

appezzare, ahp-pet-tsah-ray, v., to patch; to allot

appianare, ahp-pe'ah-nah-ray, v., to smooth; to level

appiattarsi, ahp-pe'aht-**tar**-se, v., to hide ; to lay in wait

appiattire, ahp-pe'aht-**tee**-ray, v., to flatten ; to beat

appiccicare, ahp-pit-che-**kah**-ray, v., to stick

appiccicaticcio, ahp-pit-che-kah-**tit**-cho, a., sticky

appiccinire, ahp-pit-che-**nee**-ray, v., to belittle

appicco, ahp-**pick**-ko, m., (fig.) pretext

appiè, ahp-pe'**ay**, adv., at the foot

appieno, ahp-pe'**ay**-no, adv., entirely, completely

appigionare, ahp-pe-jo-**nah**-ray, v., to let out

appigliarsi, ahp-pe-l'**yar**-se, v., to cling

appiglio, ahp-**pee**-l'yo, m., pretext ; grip

appiombo, ahp-pe'**om**-bo, adv., perpendicularly

appioppare, ahp-pe'op-**pah**-ray, v., (pop.) to hit

applaudire, ahp-plah'oo-**dee**-ray, v., to applaud

applicare, ahp-ple-**kah**-ray, v., to apply

appoggiare, ahp-pod-**jah**-ray, v., to lean ; to help

appoggiarsi, ahp-pod-**jar**-se, v., to lean against ; to rely upon

appoggio, ahp-**pod**-jo, m., support, protection

apporre, ahp-**por**-ray, v., to affix, to appose

apportare, ahp-por-**tah**-ray, v., to bring ; to carry

apporto, ahp-**por**-to, m., contribution

apposito*, ahp-**po**-ze-to, a., apposite ; made to order

apposizione, ahp-po-ze-tse'**o**-nay, f., affixing

apposta, ahp-**poss**-tah, adv., for the express purpose

appostamento, ahp-poss-tah-**men**-to, m., watching ; ambush

apprendere, ahp-**pren**-day-ray, v., to learn

apprendista, ahp-pren-**diss**-tah, m. & f., apprentice ; articled clerk

apprensione, ahp-pren-se'**o**-nay, f., apprehension

appressare, ahp-press-**sah**-ray, v., to approach

appresso, ahp-**press**-so, adv., near, close ; after

apprestamento, ahp-press-tah-**men**-to, m., preparation ; provision ; clearing for action

apprestare, ahp-press-**tah**-ray, v., to prepare

apprezzare, ahp-pret-**tsah**-ray, v., to appreciate

approdare, ahp-pro-**dah**-ray, v., to land ; to come alongside

approdo, ahp-**pro**-do, m., landing ; landing-place

approfittare, ahp-pro-fit-**tah**-ray, v., to profit

approfondare, ahp-pro-fon-**dah**-ray, v., to deepen ;
  to dredge ; to dig ; to fathom

approntare, ahp-pron-**tah**-ray, v., to get ready

approssimarsi, ahp-pross-se-**mar**-se, v., to approach, to approximate ; to accost

approvare, ahp-pro-**vah**-ray, v., to approve

approvazione, ahp-pro-vah-tse'**o**-nay, f., approval

approvvigionare, ahp-prov-ve-jo-**nah**-ray, v., to
  supply ; to victual ; to provide

appuntamento, ahp-poonn-tah-**men**-to, m., appointment ; meeting

appuntare, ahp-poonn-**tah**-ray, v., to pin ; to
  point ; to blame

appuntato, ahp-poonn-**tah**-to, a., pointed ; qualified

appuntellare, ahp-poonn-tell-**lah**-ray, v., to prop

appuntino, ahp-poonn-**tee**-no, adv., quite so ;
  very precisely ; as it should be

appunto, ahp-**poonn**-to, m., blame ; note.
  adv., precisely, quite so ; exactly

appurare, ahp-poo-**rah**-ray, v., to verify ; to
  clear up

appuzzare, ahp-poot-**tsah**-ray, v., to contaminate
  with a bad odour

aprile, ah-**pree**-lay, m., April

aprire, ah-**pree**-ray, v., to open

aquila, ah-**kwe**-lah, f., eagle

ara, ah-rah, f., (poet.) altar

arabile, ah-rah-**be**-lay, a., arable

aragosta [or **aligusta**], ah-rah-**goss**-tah, f., craw-
araldica, ah-**rahl**-de-kah, f., heraldry   [fish

araldo, ah-**rahl**-do, m., herald

arancia, ah-**rahn**-chah, f., orange

aranciata, ah-**rahn**-chah-tah, f., orangeade

arancio, ah-**rahn**-cho, m., orange-tree

arare, ah-**rah**-ray, v., to plough

aratore, ah-rah-**tor**-ay, m., ploughman

aratro, ah-**rah**-tro, m., plough

arazzo, ah-**raht**-tso, m., tapestry

arbitrare, ahr-be-**trah**-ray, v., to arbitrate

arbitrio, ahr-bee-**tre**'o, m., arbitrary act ; free
  agency

arbitro, ahr-**be**-tro, m., arbiter, umpire

arboscello, ahr-bo-shell-lo, m., shrub

arbusto, ahr-booss-to, m., shrub

arca, ahr-kah, f., ark, chest ; tomb

arcade, ahr-kah-day, m., Arcadian

arcata, ahr-kah-tah, f., arcade ; stroke of the bow

arcato°, ahr-kah-to, a., curved ; crescent shaped

archeggiare, ahr-ked-jah-ray, v., to arch ; to fiddle

archetto, ahr-ket-to, m., violin-bow ; bird-trap ; fret-saw

archivio, ahr-kee-ve'o, m., archives

arcidiacono, ahr-che-de'ah-ko-no, m., archdeacon

arciduca, ahr-che-doo-kah, m., archduke

arcigno°, ahr-chee-n'yo, a., surly

arcivescovo, ahr-che-vess-ko-vo, m., archbishop

arco, ahr-ko, m., arch ; bow

arcobaleno, ahr-ko-bah-lay-no, m., rainbow

arcuato°, ahr-koo'ah-to, a., arched, curved

ardente, ahr-den-tay, a., ardent

ardenza, ahr-den-tsah, f., ardour

ardere, ahr-day-ray, v., to burn

ardesia, ahr-day-se'ah, f., slate

ardire, ahr-dee-ray, v., to dare

arditezza, ahr-de-tet-tsah, f., boldness, audacity

ardito°, ahr-dee-to, a., daring ; (pop.) plucky

ardore, ahr-dor-ay, m., ardour

arduo°, ahr-doo'o, a., arduous

arena, ah-ray-nah, f., sand ; arena

arenoso, ah-ray-no-zo, a., sandy

areostato, ah-ray-o-stah-to, m., air-balloon

arganello, ahr-gah-nell-lo, m., turnstile

argano, ahr-gah-no, m., capstan

argentare, ahr-jen-tah-ray, v., to plate with silver

argenteria, ahr-jen-tay-re'ah, f., silver-plate

argentiere, ahr-jen-te'ay-ray, m., silversmith

argentino, ahr-jen-tee-no, a., silvery ; harmonious

argento, ahr-jen-to, m., silver

argilla, ahr-jill-lah, f., clay

arginare, ahr-je-nah-ray, v., to dam   [way

argine, ahr-je-nay, m., embankment, dyke, cause-

argomentare, ahr-go-men-tah-ray, v., to argue

argomento, ahr-go-men-to, m., argument ; reason ; summary

arguire, ahr-goo'ee-ray, v., to argue ; to infer

argutezza, ahr-goo-tet-tsah, f., acuteness, subtlety

arguto°, ahr-goo'to, a., sharp, witty, acute

aria, ah-re'ah, f., air, mien ; refrain

arido°, ah-re-do, a., dry, barren, sterile

arieggiare, ah-re-aid-jah-ray, v., to ventilate ; to resemble

ariete, ah-re'ay-tay, m., ram, goat ; (naut.) ram

arietta, ah-re'ayt-tah, f., light musical air ; breeze

aringa, ah-reen-gah, f., herring

arioso°, ah-re'o-zo, a., airy, well-aired [racy

aristocrazia, ah-re-sto-krah-tsee-ah, f., aristoc-

aritmetica, ah-rit-may-te-kah, f., arithmetic

arlecchino, ahr-lek-kee-no, m., harlequin

arma, ahr-mah, f., arm, weapon

armacollo(ad), ahr-mah-koll-lo, adv., slung across the shoulders

armadio, ahr-mah-de'o, m., wardrobe

armaiuolo, ahr-mah-e'oo-o-lo, m., gunsmith

armare, ahr-mah-ray, v., to arm ; (naut.) to com-mission ; (naut.) to charter

armata, ahr-mah-tah, f., army

armatore, ahr-mah-tor-ay, m., shipowner

armatura, ahr-mah-too-rah, f., armour ; structure

arme, ahr-may, f., arm, weapon

armellino, ahr-mell-lee-no, m., ermine ; ermine-fur

armento, ahr-men-to, m., herd of cattle

armeria, ahr-may-ree-ah, f., arsenal ; armoury

armi, ahr-me, f. pl., arms ; alle —, with the colours

armistizio, ahr-miss-tee-tse'o, m., armistice

armonia, ahr-mo-nee-ah, f., harmony

armonio, ahr-mo-ne'o, m., harmonium [nize

armonizzare, ahr-mo-nit-tsah-ray, v., to harmo-

arnese, ahr-nay-zay, m., tool ; harness

arnia, ahr-nee-ah, f., bee-hive

aro, ah-ro, m., are (100 square metres)

arpa, ahr-pah, f., harp

arpione, ahr-pe'o-nay, m., harpoon ; hook

arra, ahr-rah, f., token ; earnest money

arrabattarsi, ahr-rah-baht-tar-se, v., to take pains, to exert oneself

arrabbiarsi, ahr-rahb-be'ar-se. v., to get angry

arrabbiato, ahr-rahb-be'ah-to. a., (dog) mad

arraffare, ahr-rahf-fah-ray. v., to snatch; to seize

arrampicarsi, ahr-rahm-pe-kar-se, v., to climb up

arrancare, ahr-rahn-kah-ray, v., to limp; to row fast

arrangiare, ahr-rahn-jah-ray, v., to arrange

arrecare, ahr-ray-kah-ray, v., to bring about

arredare, ahr-ray-dah-ray, v., to furnish, to fit out

arredo, ahr-ray-do. m., furniture; outfit

arrenare, ahr-ray-nah-ray, v., to run aground

arrendersi, ahr-ren-dair-se, v., to surrender

arrendevole, ahr-ren-day-vo-lay, a., flexible

arrestare, ahr-ress-tah-ray, v., to arrest

arretrarsi, ahr-ray-trar-se, v., to recede; to draw [back

arretrati, ahr-ray-trah-te, m. pl., arrears

arricchirsi, ahr-rik-keer-se, v., to grow rich

arricciare, ahr-rit-chah-ray, v., to curl

arridere, ahr-ree-day-ray, v., to smile upon

arringa, ahr-rin-gah. f., harangue; pleading

arringare, ahr-rin-gah-ray, v., to harangue

arrischiare, ahr-riss-ke'ah-ray, v., to risk

arrivare, ahr-re-vah-ray, v., to arrive; to reach

arrivo, ahr-ree-vo, m., arrival

arroganza, ahr-ro-gahn-tsah, f., arrogance

arrogare, ahr-ro-gah-ray, v., to arrogate, to adopt

arrossire, ahr-ross-see-ray, v., to blush; to become red

arrostire, ahr-ross-tee-ray, v., to roast; to toast

arrosto, ahr-ross-to, m., roast

arrotare, ahr-ro-tah-ray, v., to sharpen

arrotino, ahr-ro-tee-no, m., knife-grinder

arrotolare, ahr-ro-to-lah-ray, v., to roll up

arrotondare, ahr-ro-ton-dah-ray, v., to make round

arrovellarsi, ahr-ro-vell-lar-se, v., to cudgel one's brain

arroventare, ahr-ro-ven-tah-ray, v., to make red or white hot

arrovesciare, ahr-ro-vay-she'ah-ray, v., to upset, to overturn, to overthrow

arrovescio, ahr-ro-vay-she'o, adv., on the contrary; inside out

arruffare, ahr-roof-fah-ray, v., to ruffle the hair, to dishevel; to entangle

arrugginire, ahr-rood-je-nee-ray, v., to get rusty

arruolare, ahr-roo'o-lah-ray, v., to enrol; to enlist

arruvidire, ahr-roo-ve-dee-ray, v., to roughen

arsella, ahr-sell-lah, f., mussel

arsenale, ahr-say-nah-lay, m., arsenal; dockyard

arsicciare, ahr-sit-chah-ray, v., to scorch; to singe

arso, ahr-so, a., burnt, scorched

arsura, ahr-soo-rah, f., drought; great thirst; stifling heat

arte, ahr-tay, f., art; skill

artefatto*, ahr-tay-faht-to, a., artificial; adulterated

artefice, ahr-tay-fe-chay, m., artisan

arteria, ahr-tay-re'ah, f., artery

articolare, ahr-te-ko-lah-ray, v., to articulate

articolo, ahr-tee-ko-lo, m., article; clause

artiere, ahr-te'ay-ray, m., artisan

artificiale, ahr-te-fe-chah-lay, a., artificial

artificio, ahr-te-fee-cho, m., artifice, trick

artigiano, ahr-te-jah-no, m., artisan

artigliere, ahr-te-l'yay-ray, m., gunner

artiglieria, ahr-te-l'yay-ree-ah, f., artillery

artiglio, ahr-tee-l'yo, m., claw, talon

artista, ahr-tiss-tah, m. & f., artist

arto, ahr-to, m., (anatomy) member, limb

artrite, ahr-tree-tay, f., arthritis

arzigogolo, ahr-dze-go-go-lo, m., whim; prank

arzillo*, ahr-dzeell-lo, a., vigorous, lively

asbesto, ahss-bess-to, m., asbestos

ascella, ah-shell-lah, f., arm-pit

ascendente, ah-shen-den-tay, m., ascendant

ascendenza, ah-shen-den-tsah, f., ascendency

ascendere, ah-shen-day-ray, v., to ascend, to climb

ascensione, ah-shen-se'o-nay, f., ascension

ascensore, ah-shen-sor-ay, m., lift

ascesso, ah-shess-so, m., abscess

asceta, ah-shay-tah, m., ascetic

ascia, ah-she'ah, f., axe

asciare, ah-she'ah-ray, v., to chop, to hew

asciugamano, ah-she'oo-gah-mah-no, m., towel

asciugare, ah-she'oo-gah-ray, v., to dry ; to wipe ; to blot

asciugatoio, ah-she'oo-gah-to-e'o, m., towel

asciutto*, ah-she'oot-to, a., dry ; lean

ascoltare, ahss-koll-tah-ray, v., to listen

ascoltatore, ahss-koll-tah-tor-ay, m., listener

ascrivere, ahss-kree-vay-ray, v., to ascribe

asfalto, ahss-fahl-to, m., asphalt

asfissia, ahss-**fiss**-se'ah, f., asphyxy

asilo, ah-zee-lo, m., asylum ; shelter

asinata, ah-ze-nah-tah, f., stupidity, **silliness**

asino, ah-ze-no, m., ass

asma, ahss-mah, f., asthma

asola, ah-zo-lah, f., button-hole

asparago, ahss-pah-rah-go, m., asparagus

aspergere, ahss-pair-jay-ray, v., to sprinkle

aspettare, ahss-pet-tah-ray, v., to wait ; to expect

aspettativa, ahss-pet-tah-tee-vah, f., expectation

aspetto, ahss-pet-to, m., aspect ; appearance. **sala d'—**, f., waiting-room

aspide, **ahss**-pe-day, f., asp

aspirante, ahss-pe-rahn-tay, m. & f., candidate

aspirare, ahss-pe-rah-ray, v., to inhale ; to aspirate ; to aim at

aspo, ahss-po, m., reel ; skein-winder

asportare, ahss-por-tah-ray, v., to remove, to extirpate

asprezza, ahss-**pret**-tsah, f., harshness ; rudeness

aspro*, ahss-pro, a., sour ; bitter ; rough

assaggiare, ahss-sahd-jah-ray,v.,to test ; to sample

assai, ahss-sah'e, adv., much, plenty, very much

assalire, ahss-sah-lee-ray, v., to assault, to attack

assaltatore, ahss-sahl-tah-tor-ay, m., aggressor

assalto, ahss-sahl-to, m., attack ; fit

assaporare, ahss-sah-po-rah-ray, v., to taste

assaporire, ahss-sah-po-ree-ray, v., to flavour

assassinare, ahss-sahss-se-nah-ray, v., to assassinate ; to murder

assassinio, ahss-sahss-see-ne'o, m., murder

assassino, ahss-sahss-see-no, m., murderer

asse, ahss-say, f., plank ; axle ; shaft ; axis

assecondare, ahss-say-kon-dah-ray, v., to second

assediare, ahss-say-de'ah-ray, v., to besiege

assedio, ahss-say-de'o, m., siege; importunity

assegnamento, ahss-say-n'yah-men-to, m., allowance; assignment; alimony; appointment

assegnare, ahss-say-n'yah-ray, v., to assign, to appoint, to attribute, to make a settlement on

assegno, ahss-say-n'yo, m., allowance; cheque; pension

assembramento, ahss-sem-brah-men-to, m., assembly, crowd, throng

assembrare, ahss-sem-brah-ray, v., to assemble

assennato*, ahss-sen-nah-to, a., prudent, wise

assentarsi, ahss-sen-tar-se, v., to absent oneself

assente, ahss-sen-tay, a., absent

assentire, ahss-sen-tee-ray, v., to assent, to agree

assenza, ahss-sen-tsah, f., absence

assenzio, ahss-sen-tse'o, m., absinthe, wormwood

asserire, ahss-say-ree-ray, v., to assert

asserzione, ahss-sair-tse'o-nay, f., assertion

assestare, ahss-sess-tah-ray, v., to adjust; to put in order

assesto, ahss-sess-to, m., settlement, regulation

assetato, ahss-say-tah-to, a., thirsty

assettamento, ahss-set-tah-men-to, m., tidying

assettare, ahss-set-tah-ray, v., to put in order

assetto, ahss-set-to, m., order; adjustment

asseverare, ahss-say-vay-rah-ray, v., to affirm

assicurare, ahss-se-koo-rah-ray, v., to affirm; to assure, to insure

assicuratore, ahss-se-koo-rah-tor-ay, m., insurer; assurer; underwriter

assicurazione, ahss-se-koo-rah-tse'o-nay, f., insurance; assurance

assiderato, ahss-se-day-rah-to, a., frozen

assidersi, ahss-see-dair-se, v., to sit down

assiduità, ahss-se-doo'e-tah, f., assiduity, diligence

assiduo*, ahss-see-doo'o, a., assiduous

assieme, ahss-se'ay-may, adv., together

assiepare, ahss-se'ay-pah-ray, v., to hedge; to crowd

assillato*, ahss-sill-lah-to, a., busy; worried; annoyed

assillo, ahss-sill-lo, m., worry, anguish

assimilare, ahss-se-me-lah-ray, v., to assimilate

assioma, ahss-se'o-mah, m., axiom

assisa, ahss-see-zah, f., uniform, livery

assise, ahss-see-zay, f. pl., court of assizes

assistente, ahss-siss-ten-tay, m. & f., assistant

assistenza, ahss-siss-ten-tsah, f., assistance

assistere, ahss-siss-tay-ray, v., to assist ; to attend

asso, ahss-so, m., ace

associare, ahss-so-chah-ray, v., to associate

associato, ahss-so-chah-to, m., partner, associate

associazione, ahss-so-chah-tse'o-nay, f., association ; company

assodare, ahss-so-dah-ray, v., to investigate

assoggettare, ahss-sod-jet-tah-ray, v., to subdue

assoldare, ahss-soll-dah-ray, v., to enrol ; to engage

assoluto°, ahss-so-loo to, a., absolute ; precise

assoluzione, ahss-so-loo-tse'o-nay, f., absolution

assolvere, ahss-soll-vay-ray, v., to absolve

assomigliare, ahss-so-me-le'ah-ray, v., to resemble ; to compare

assonnato°, ahss-son-nah to, a., sleepy

assopimento, ahss-so-pe-men-to, m., drowsiness

assopirsi, ahss-so-peer-se, v., to get sleepy, to become drowsy

assorbente, ahss-sor-ben-tay, f., absorbent, a., absorbing

assorbimento, ahss-sor-be-men-to, m., absorption

assorbipolvere, ahss-sor-be-poll-vay-ray, m., vacuum cleaner

assorbire, ahss-sor-bee-ray, v., to absorb ; to swallow up

assordare [*or* **assordire**], ahss-sor-dah-ray, v., to deafen ; to become deaf

assortire, ahss-sor-tee-ray, v., to match ; to assort

assorto°, ahss-sor-to, a., absorbed ; immersed

assottigliare, ahss-sot-te-l'yah-ray, v., to make thin ; to sharpen

assuefare, ahss-soo'ay-fah-ray, v., to accustom

assuefazione, ahss-soo'ay-fah-tse'o-nay, f., addiction, habit

assumere, ahss-soo-may-ray, v., to assume

assunto, ahss-soonn-to, m., task ; assertion

assunzione, ahss-soonn-tse'o-nay, f., assumption

assurdità, ahss-soohr-de-tah. f., absurdity

assurdo°, ahss-soohr-do. a., absurd

asta, ahss-tah, f., staff ; pole ; auction

astemio, ahss-tay-me'o.m.,teetotaler. a.,abstemious

astenersi, ahss-tay-nair-se. v., to abstain

astensione, ahss-ten-se'o-nay, f., abstention

astergere, ahss-tair-jay-ray, v., to wipe, to clean

asteria, ahss-tay-re'ah, f., star-fish

astice, ahss-te-chay, m., lobster

astinenza, ahss-te-nen-tsah, f.,abstinence, sobriety

astio, ahss-te'o, m., spite, hatred

astioso°, ahss-te'o-zo, a., malicious

astrarre, ahss-trar-ray, v., to abstract

astratto°, ahss-traht-to, a., absent-minded

astrazione, ahss-trah-tse'o-nay, f., abstraction

astringente, ahss-trin-jen-tay, m., astringent.
   a., astringent

astringere, ahss-trin-jay-ray, v., to restrain ;
   to astringe

astro, ahss-tro, m., star

astronomia, ahss-tro-no-mee-ah. f., astronomy

astruso°, ahss-troo-zo, a., abstruse. enigmatic

astuccio, ahss-toot-cho, m., case, box ; sheath

astuto°, ahss-too-to. a., cunning, artful, astute

astuzia, ahss-too-tse'ah, f., astuteness

ateo, ah-tay'o, m., atheist

atleta, aht-lay-tah, m., athlete

atmosfera, aht-moss-fay-rah, f., atmosphere

atomo, ah-to-mo, m., atom

atrio, ah-tre'o, m., entrance-hall, vestibule

atro°, ah-tro, a., dark, gloomy ; dreadful

atroce, ah-tro-chay, a., atrocious

attaccabrighe, aht-tahk-kah-bree-gay, m. & f.,
   provoking individual

attaccamento, aht-tahk-kah-men-to, m., attach-
   ment ; linking

attaccare, aht-tahk-kah-ray, v., to attach, to tie
   to ; to attack

attacco, aht-tahk-ko, m., attack ; connection

attecchire, aht-teck-kee-ray, v., to take well ;
   to thrive

atteggiamento, aht-ted-jah-**men**-to, m., attitude ; mood

attempato, aht-tem-**pah**-to, a., elderly

attendente, aht-ten-**den**-tay, m., (mil.) orderly

attendere, aht-**ten**-day-ray, v., to attend to ; **to mind** ; to expect

attenente, aht-tay-**nen**-tay, a., adjoining

attenersi, aht-tay-**nair**-se, v., to abide by

attentare, aht-ten-**tah**-ray, v., to attempt

attentato, aht-ten-**tah**-to, m., attempt

attento*, aht-**ten**-to, a., attentive

attenuare, aht-tay-noo'**ah**-ray, v., to attenuate

attenuazione, aht-tay-noo'ah-tse'**o**-nay, f., attenuation

attenzione, aht-ten-tse'**o**-nay, f., attention

atterraggio, aht-tair-**rahd**-jo, m., alighting of aircraft

atterrare, aht-tair-**rah**-ray, v., to throw to the ground ; (aircraft) to land

atterrire, aht-tair-**ree**-ray, v., to terrify

attesa, aht-**tay**-zah, f., awaiting

atteso, aht-**tay**-zo, p.p.,expected. prep., considering

attestare, aht-tess-**tah**-ray, v., to attest

attestato, aht-tess-**tah**-to, m., certificate ; testimonial

atti, aht-te, m. pl., behaviour ; (law) deeds   [nial

attico, **aht**-te-ko, m., attic

attiguo*, aht-**tee**-goo'o, a., adjoining, contiguous

attillarsi, aht-till-**lar**-se, v., to dress oneself with exaggerated care ; to deck oneself

attillatezza, aht-till-lah-**tet**-tsah, f., dandyism

attillato*, aht-till-**lah**-to, a., dandified

attimo, **aht**-te-mo, m., instant

attinente, aht-te-**nen**-tay, a., referring to

attingere, aht-**teen**-jay-ray, v., to draw up water or wine

attirare, aht-te-**rah**-ray, v., to attract

attitudine, aht-te-**too**-de-nay, f., attitude ; inclination, bent ; mood

attivare, aht-te-**vah**-ray, v., to urge ; to hasten

attività, aht-te-ve-**tah**, f., activity

attivo, aht-**tee**-vo, a.,* active. m., assets

attizzare, aht-tit-**tsah**-ray, v., to poke ; to rouse up

attizzatoio, aht-tit-tsah-to-e'o, m., poker

atto, aht-to, m., act; document. a.,* qualified, capable, adapted to

attonare, aht-to-nah-ray, v., to strengthen; to corroborate

attonito*, aht-to-ne-to, a., astonished

attorcigliarsi, aht-tor-che-l'yar-se, v., to creep around; to wind around

attore, aht-tor-ay, m., actor; plaintiff

attorniare, aht-tor-ne'ah-ray, v., to encircle

attorno, aht-tor-no, adv., round about

attortigliare, aht-tor-te-l'yah-ray, v., to twist

attraente, aht-trah-enn-tay, a., attractive

attrarre, aht-**trar**-ray, v., to attract

attraversare, aht-trah-vair-sah-ray, v., to traverse, to cross over, to frustrate

attraverso, aht-trah-**vair**-so, adv.,across; through

attrezzare, aht-tret-tsah-ray, v., to fit up; to rig

attrezzo, aht-**tret**-tso, m., tool, implement; utensil

attribuire, aht-tre-boo'ee-ray, v., to attribute

attrice, aht-**tree**-chay, f., actress; plaintiff

attristare, aht-triss-**tah**-ray, v.,to sadden, to grieve

attrito, aht-**tree**-to, m., friction; abrasion

attruppamento, aht-troop-pah-**men**-to, m., crowding

attrupparsi, aht-troop-**par**-se, v., to assemble

attuabile, aht-too'ah-be-lay, a., feasible

attuale, aht-too'ah-lay, a., actual; present

attuffare, aht-toof-fah-ray, v., to plunge, to dive

attutire, aht-too-tee-ray, v., to allay, to calm

audacemente, ah'oo-dah-chay-**men**-tay, adv., audaciously, daringly

audacia, ah'oo-**dah**-chah, f., audacity, impudence

auditore, ah'oo-de-tor-ay, m., judge; auditor

audizioni radiofoniche, ah'oo-de-tse'o-ne rah-de'o-fo-ne-kay, f. pl., broadcasting

augurare, ah'oo-goo-rah-ray,v.,to wish; to betoken

augurio, ah'oo-goo-re'o, m., wish, vow; omen

augusto*, ah'oo-**gooss**-to, a., august, lordly

aula, ah'oo-lah, f., hall; court; class-room

aumentare, ah'oo-men-**tah**-ray, v., to increase

aumento, ah'oo-**men**-to, m., increase; rise

aura, ah'oo-rah, f., breeze ; air ; (med.) **aura**

aureo, ah'oo-ray'o, a., golden, gilt

aureola, ah'oo-ray-o-lah, f., halo

aurora, ah'oo-RO-rah, f., dawn

ausiliare, ah'oo-ze-le'ah-ray, m. & f., auxillary. a., auxiliary

auspice, ah'oo-spe-chay, m., patron ; protector

austero, ah'oo-stay-ro, a., austere, stern

australe, ah'oo-strah-lay, a., southern

austro, ah'oo-stro, m., southern wind ; south

autenticare, ah'oo-ten-te-kah-ray, v., to authenticate ; to legalize

autenticità, ah'oo-ten-te-che-tah, f., authenticity

autista, ah'oo-tiss-tah, m., driver

autoblindata, ab'oo-to-blin-dah-tah, f., armoured

autobus, ah'oo-to-booss, m., motorbus [car

autocarro, ah'oo-to-kar-ro, m., motor-lorry

autocrate, ah'oo-to-krah-tay, m. & f., autocrat

autodromo, ah'oo-to-dro-mo, m., motor-track

autografo, ah'oo-to-grah-fo, m., autograph

automa, ah'oo-to-mah, m., automaton

automezzo, ah'oo-to-med-dzo, m., motor-vehicle

autopubblica, ah'oo-to-poob-ble-kah, f., taxi

autore, ah'oo-tor-ay, m., author

autorevole, ah'oo-to-ray-vo-lay, a., authoritative

autorimessa, ah'oo-to-re-mess-sah, f., garage

autorizzare, ah'oo-to-rid-dzah-ray, v., to authorize

autostrada, ah'oo-to-strah-dah, f., motor-road

autoveicolo, ah'oo-to-vay-ee-ko-lo, m., motor-car

autunnale, ah'oo-toonn-nah-lay, a., autumnal

autunno, ah'oo-toonn-no, m., autumn

avallo, ah-vahl-lo, m., security ; indorsement ; undertaking ; guarantee

avambraccio, ah-vahm-braht-cho, m., forearm

avanguardia, ah-vahm-goo-ar-de'ah, f., vanguard

avanguardista, ah-vahn-goo'ar-diss-tah, m., fascist boy scout

avanti, ah-vahn-te, adv.,forward. prep., in front of

avantieri, ah-vahn-te'ay-re, adv., the day before yesterday

avanzamento, ah-vahn-tsah-men-to, m., advancement, progress

avanzare, ah-vahn-tsah-ray, v., to advance; to improve

avanzato, ah-vahn-tsah-to, a., advanced; developed

avanzo, ah-vahn-tso, m., rest, residue; profit

avaria, ah-vah-ree-ah, f., damage; average

avariare, ah-vah-re'ah-ray, v., to damage

avaro, ah-vah-ro, m., miser. a.,* avaricious

ave! ah-vay, interj., hail! greetings!

avellana, ah-vell-lah-nah, f., filbert

avellano, ah-vell-lah-no, m., filbert-tree

avello, ah-vell-lo, m., grave, tomb

avena, ah-vay-nah, f., oats

avere, ah-vay-ray, m., property; credit. v., to have, to get, to possess

avi, ah-ve, m. pl., ancestors

aviatore, ah-ve'ah-tor-ay, m., aviator

avidità, ah-ve-de-tah, f., avidity

avido*, ah-ve-do, a., greedy; eager

aviere, ah-ve'ay-ray, m., airman

aviolinea, ah-ve'o-lee-nay-ah, f., air-service, air-way, air-line

avo, ah-vo, m., grandfather

avocare, ah-vo-kah-ray, v., to claim right to

avola, ah-vo-lah, f., grandmother

avoltoio, ah-voll-to-e'o, m., vulture

avorio, ah-vo-re'o, m., ivory

avvallamento, ahv-vahl-lah-men-to, m., land-slide; depression

avvalorare, ahv-vah-lo-rah-ray, v., to strengthen; to appraise, to value

avvampare, ahv-vahm-pah-ray, v., to blaze; to set fire to; to flare up

avvantaggio, ahv-vahn-tahd-jo, m., advantage

avvedersi, ahv-vay-dair-se, v., to perceive; to become aware of

avvedutezza, ahv-vay-doo-tet-tsah, f., insight, foresight

avveduto*, ahv-vay-doo-to, a., wary; keen

avvelenare, ahv-vay-lay-nah-ray, v., to poison

avvenente, ahv-vay-nen-tay, a., attractive, pretty, charming, prepossessing

avvenenza, ahv-vay-nen-tsah, f., charm, prettiness

avvenimento, ahv-vay-ne-men-to, m., event; happening

avvenire, ahv-vay-nee-ray, m., future. v., to happen, to take place

avventarsi, ahv-ven-tar-se, v., to hurl oneself, to rush against

avventato*, ahv-ven-tah-to, a., rash; risky

avventizio, ahv-ven-tee-tse'o, m., temporary clerk or workman. a.,* casual

avvento, ahv-ven-to, m., advent

avventore, ahv-ven-tor-ay, m., customer

avventurare, ahv-ven-too-rah-ray, v., to risk

avventuriere, ahv-ven-too-re'ay-ray, m., adventurer

avverare, ahv-vay-rah-ray, v., to verify [turer

avverbio, ahv-vair-be'o, m., adverb

avversare, ahv-vair-sah-ray, v., to oppose

avversario, ahv-vair-sah-re'o, a.,* unfriendly. m., opponent

avversità, ahv-vair-se-tah, f., adversity

avverso*, ahv-vair-so, a., adverse, opposed [tion

avvertenza, ahv-vair-ten-tsah, f., warning, atten-

avvertimento, ahv-vair-te-men-to, m., warning, notice; admonition

avvertire, ahv-vair-tee-ray, v., to warn, to give notice; to perceive

avvertitore, ahv-vair-te-tor-ay, m., indicator; warner

avvezzare, ahv-vet-tsah-ray, v., to train; to get used to

avviamento, ahv-ve'ah-men-to, m., starting

avviare, ahv-ve'ah-ray, v., to set up in, to start

avviatura, ahv-ve'ah-too-rah, f., beginning

avvicendare, ahv-ve-chen-dah-ray, v., to alternate

avvicinare, ahv-ve-che-nah-ray, v., to approach

avvilimento, ahv-ve-le-men-to, m., discouragement; degradation; humiliation

avvilire, ahv-ve-lee-ray, v., to degrade, to lower

avvilirsi, ahv-ve-leer-se, v., to get discouraged

avviluppare, ahv-ve-loop-pah-ray, v., to envelop, to wrap up; to entangle

avvincere, ahv-veen-chay-ray, v., to hug; to tie up; to convince

avvinghiare, ahv-veen-ghe'ah-ray, v., to grip; to claw

avvisare, ahv-ve-zah-ray, v., to advise

avvisatore, ahv-ve-zah-tor-ay, m., advertiser; informer; adviser

avviso, ahv-vee-zo, m., notice; warning; counsel; advertisement; opinion

avvistare, ahv-ve-stah-ray, v., to see, to sight

avvitare, ahv-ve-tah-ray, v., to screw

avviticchiare, ahv-ve-tick-ke'ah-ray, v., to curl round, to twine round; to hug tightly

avvivare, ahv-ve-vah-ray, v., to revive; to come to

avvizzire, ahv-vit-tsee-ray, v., to fade, to wizen

avvocato, ahv-vo-kah-to, m., lawyer, barrister

avvolgere, ahv-voll-jay-ray, v., to wrap up

avvolgimento, ahv-voll-je-men-to, m., wrapping

avvoltoio, ahv-voll-to-e'o, m., vulture

azalea, ah-dzah-lay-ah, f., azalea

azienda, ah-dze'en-dah, f., business; management

azionare, ah-tse'o-nah-ray, v., to start up

azione, ah-tse'o-nay, f., action; share

azionista, ah-tse'o-niss-tah, m. & f., shareholder

azzannare, ahd-dzahn-nah-ray, v., to snap

azzardare, ahd-dzar-dah-ray, v., to hazard

azzardo, ahd-dzar-do, m., hazard, risk

azzeccare, ahd-dzeck-kah-ray, v., to catch; to guess

azzimarsi, ahd-dze-mar-se, v., to dress extravagantly

azzimo, ahd-dze-mo, a., unleavened

azzuffarsi, ahd-dzoof-far-se, v., to scuffle

azzurro, ahd-dzoor-ro, m., azure. a., sky-blue

babbeo, bahb-bay-o, m., fool

babbo, bahb-bo, m., father, dad

babbuino, bahb-boo'ee-no, m., baboon

babordo, bah-bor-do, m., starboard

bacato, bah-kah-to, a., worm-eaten; degenerate

bacca, bahk-kah, f., berry

baccalà, bahk-kah-lah, m., dried codfish

baccano, bahk-kah-no, m., row, din

baccello, baht-chell-lo, m., pod, husk

bacchetta, bahk-ket-tah, f., wand; baton; rod

bachicultore, bah-ke-kooll-tor-ay, m., silk-worm breeder

baciare, bah-chah-ray, v., to kiss

bacile, bah-chee-lay, m., basin

bacillo, bah-chill-lo, m., bacillus

bacinella, bah-che-nell-lah, f., bowl, basin; pan

bacino, bah-chee-no, m., basin

bacio, bah-cho, m., kiss

baco, bah-ko, m., caterpillar; worm

bacologia, bak-o-lo-jee-ah, f., silk-worm culture

bada, bah-dah, **tenere a —**, to keep at bay or arm's length

badare, bah-dah-ray, v., to mind; to look after

badessa, bah-dess-sah, f., abbess

badia, bah-dee-ah, f., abbey

badile, bah-dee-lay, m., shovel

baffi, bahf-fe, m. pl., moustache

bagagliaio, bah-gah-l'yah-e'o, m., luggage-van

bagaglio, bah-gah-l'yo, m., luggage

bagatella, bah-gah-tell-lah, f., trifle

bagliore, bah-l'yo-ray, m., sudden flash of light

bagnare, bah-n'yah-ray, v., to wet, to bathe

bagno, bah-n'yo, m., bath; penal settlement

baia, bah'e-ah, f., bay; joke; hoot

baiata, bah'e-ah-tah, f., hooting

baio, bah'e-o, a., chestnut colour

baionetta, bah'e-o-net-tah, f., bayonet

balaustrata, bah-lah'ooss-trah-tah, f., balustrade

balbettare, bahl-bet-tah-ray, v., to stutter

balbo, bahl-bo, a., stammering

balbuzie, bahl-boo-tse'ay, f., stuttering, stammering

balcone, bahl-ko-nay, m., balcony

baldacchino, bahl-dahk-kee-no, m., canopy

baldanza, bahl-dahn-tsah, f., boldness

baldo*, bahl-do, a., bold, fearless

baldoria, bahl-do-re'ah, f., clamorous jollity

balena, bah-lay-nah, f., whale

balenare, bah-lay-nah-ray, v., to lighten

baleno, bah-lay-no, m., flash of lightning

balia, bah-le'ah, f., wet-nurse   [mercy

balia, bah-lee-ah, f., power, authority. **in —**, at the

balilla, bah-leell-lah, m., boy fascist

balla, bahl-lah, f., bale
ballabile, bahl-lah-be-lay, m., dance movement
ballare, bahl-lah-ray, v., to dance
ballata, bahl-lah-tah, f., dance ; ballad
ballerina, bahl-lay-ree-nah, f., dancer
balletto, bahl-let-to, m., ballet
ballo, bahl-lo, m., ball, dance
ballottaggio, bahl-lot-tahd-jo, m., second ballet
ballottare, bahl-lot-tah-ray, v., to ballot
baloccare, bah-lock-kah-ray, v., to play
balordo*, bah-lor-do, a., silly, stupid, foolish
baluardo, bah-loo'ar-do, m., bulwark
balza, bahl-tsah, f., rock
balzano*, bahl-tsah-no, a., funny, strange, crazy
balzare, bahl-tsah-ray, v., to bound ; to jump
balzo, bahl-tso, m., rebound ; jump
bambagia, bahm-bah-jah, f., cotton-wool
bambina, bahm-bee-nah, f., baby girl
bambinaia, bahm-be-nah-yah, f., nurse
bambinesco*, bahm-be-ness-ko, a., childish
bambino, bahm-bee-no, m., small boy ; baby
bambola, bahm-bo-lah, f., doll
banca, bahn-kah, f., bank
bancario, bahn-kah-re'o, a., banking
bancarotta, bahn-kah-rot-tah, f., bankruptcy
banchettare, bahn-ket-tah-ray, v., to banquet
banchetto, bahn-ket-to, m., banquet
banchiere, bahn-ke'ay-ray, m., banker
banchina, bahn-kee-nah, f., quay ; park-seat
banco, bahn-ko, m., bank ; pew ; bench ; counter ; bureau
banconota, bahn-ko-no-tah, f., bank-note
banda, bahn-dah, f., band ; troop ; side
banderuola, bahn-day-roo'o-lah, f., weathercock
bandiera, bahn-de'ay-rah, f., flag, banner, colours
bandire, bahn-dee-ray, v., to proclaim ; to banish
bandita, bahn-dee-tah, f., place protected by rights for shooting, fishing, etc.
bandito, bahn-dee-to, m., exile ; bandit
banditore, bahn-de-tor-ay, m., town-crier ; auctioneer
bando, bahn-do, m., proclamation ; banishment

bara, bah-rah, f., coffin

baracca, bah-rahk-kah, f., barrack ; wooden shed

baraonda, bah-rah-onn-dah, f., chaos, confusion

barare, bah-rah-ray, v., to cheat at cards, etc.

baratro, bah-rah-tro, m., abyss

barattare, bah-raht-tah-ray, v., to barter

baratteria, bah-raht-tay-ree-ah, f., swindling

barattiere, bah-raht-te'ay-ray, m., swindler

baratto, bah-raht-to, m., exchange

barba, bar-bah, f., beard ; long thin roots

barbabietola, bar-bah-be'ay-to-lah, f., beet-root

barbagianni, bar-bah-jahn-ne, m., owl

barbaro, bar-bah-ro, m., barbarian. a.,* barbarous

barbicare, bar-be-kah-ray, v., to take root

barbiere, bar-be'ay-ray, m., barber ; coiffeur

barbogio, bar-bo-jo, m., dotard

barbone, bar-bo-nay, m., large beard ; poodle

barbottare, bar-bot-tah-ray, v., to grumble

barbugliare, bar-boo-l'yah-ray, v., to stammer

barbuto, bar-boo-to, a., bearded

barca, bar-kah, f., boat

barcaccia, bar-kaht-chah, f., stage-box

barcaiuolo, bar-kah-e'oo-o-lo, m., boatman, waterman

barcamenare, bar-kah-may-nah-ray, v., to behave cleverly ; to manage well

barchetta, bar-ket-tah, f., small boat ; wherry

barcollare, bar-koll-lah-ray, v., to totter ; to falter

barcone, bar-ko-nay, m., barge

bardare, bar-dah-ray, v., to harness

barella, bah-rell-lah, f., stretcher ; hand-barrow

bargello, bar-jell-lo, m., sheriff

barile, bah-ree-lay, m., cask

barilotto, bah-re-lot-to, m., keg ; bull's eye

barlume, bar-loo-may, m., gleam, ray

baro, bah-ro, m., cheat

baroccio, bar-rot-cho, m., cart, waggon

barocco*, bah-rock-ko, a., grotesque, odd

baronata, bah-ro-nah-tah, f., swindling cheat

barone, bah-ro-nay, m., baron ; rascal

baronessa, bah-ro-ness-sah, f., baroness

barra, bar-rah, f., bar

barriera, bar-re'ay-rah, f., barrier ; gate

baruffa, bah-roof-fah, f., squabble

basamento, bah-zah-men-to, m., pedestal, socle

basare, bah-zah-ray, v., to base

base, bah-zay, f., base, foundation

basette, bah-zet-tay, f. pl., whiskers

bassezza, bahss-set-tsah, f., baseness, meanness

basso, bahss-so, m., bottom ; (mus.) bass. a.,* base, vulgar, common

bassofondo, bahss-so-fon-do, m., shallow

bassotto, bahss-sot-to, m., dachshund. a., squatty

bassura, bahss-soo-rah, f., lowness ; low ground

basta, bahss-tah, adv., enough

bastante, bahss-tahn-tay, a., sufficient

bastardo, bahss-tar-do, m., bastard ; mongrel

bastare, bahss-tah-ray, v., to suffice

bastimento, bahss-te-men-to, m., ship

basto, bahss-to, m., pack-saddle

bastonare, bahss-to-nah-ray, v., to chastise ; to cane

bastonata, bahss-to-nah-tah, f., caning, thrashing

bastone, bahss-to-nay, m., cudgel ; walking stick

batacchio, bah-tahk-ke'o, m., tongue of a bell ; knocker ; beater

batista, bah-tiss-tah, f., cambric

batosta, bah-toss-tah, f., reverse ; quarrel

battaglia, baht-tah-l'yah, f., battle

battagliare, baht-tah-l'yah-ray, v., to fight

battello, baht-tell-lo, m., boat ; skiff

battente, baht-ten-tay, m., knocker

battere, baht-tay-ray, v., to knock ; to forge

battesimo, baht-tay-ze-mo, m., christening

battezzare, baht-ted-dzah-ray, v., to baptize

battibecco, baht-te-beck-ko, m., altercation

batticuore, baht-te-koo'o-ray, m., palpitation

battimano, baht-te-mah-no, m., applause

battito, baht-te-to, m., beating ; clapping

battitoio, baht-te-to-e'o, m., beater ; threshing-machine

battitura, baht-te-too-rah, f., beating ; threshing

battuta, baht-too-tah, f., beat ; blow ; thrashing

baule, bah'oo-lay, m., trunk

bava, bah-vah, f., foam ; spittle

bavaglio, bah-vah-l'yo, m., bib ; gag
bavero, bah-vay-ro, m., collar ; bib
bavoso, bah-vo-zo, a., drivelling ; foaming
bazzicare, bahd-dze-kah-ray, v., to frequent
bazzotto, bahd-dzot-to, a., (egg) lightly boiled
bearsi, bay-ar-se, v., to rejoice
beato°, bay-ah-to, a., happy ; blessed
beccaccia, beck-kaht-chah, f., woodcock
beccaccino, beck-kaht-chee-no, m., snipe
beccafico, beck-kah-fee-ko, m., fig-eater
beccaio, beck-kah-e'o, m., butcher
beccare, beck-kah-ray, v., to peck
beccata, beck-kah-tah, f., a blow with the beak
beccheggio, beck-ked-jo, m., (naut.) pitching
beccheria, beck-kay-ree-ah, f., butcher's shop
becchino, beck-kee-no, m., grave-digger
becco, beck-ko, m., beak — di gas, gas-burner
befana, bay-fah-nah, f., Epiphany ; fairy visitor
beffa, bef-fah, f., mockery, derision
beffardo°, bef-far-do, a., mocking, scoffing
beffare, bef-fah-ray, v., to laugh at, to sneer at
beffeggiamento, bef-fed-jah-men-to, m., mockery
beffeggiare, bef-fed-jah-ray, v., to ridicule
bega, bay-gah, f., dispute
beghina, bay-ghee-nah, f., bigot ; affected devotee
belare, bay-lah-ray, v., to bleat
belletto, bell-let-to, m., rouge
bellezza, bell-let-tsah, f., beauty
bellico°, bell-le-ko, a., warlike
bellimbusto, bell-lim-booss-to, m., a beau
bello°, bell-lo, a., beautiful ; good looking
beltà, bell-tah, f., beauty
belva, bell-vah, f., wild beast
benchè, ben-kay, conj., though, although
bencreato, ben-kray-ah-to, a., well-bred
benda, ben-dah, f., bandage ; headband
bendare, ben-dah-ray, v., to bind up ; to blindfold
bene, bay-nay, m., property, goods. adv., well
benedetto°, bay-nay-det-to, a., blessed, holy
benedire, bay-nay-dee-ray, v., to bless
beneficio, bay-nay-fee-cho, m., benefit ; favour
benefico, bay-nay-fe-ko, a., beneficent, generous

benemerenza, bay-nay-may-ren-tsah, f., merit
benemerito, bay-nay-may-re-to, a., meritorious
beneplacito, bay-nay-plah-che-to, m., consent; will; pleasure
benessere, bay-ness-say-ray, m., comfort
benestante, bay-nay-stahn-tay, m., a person of independent means
benevolo, bay-nay-vo-lo, a., benevolent
benigno*, bay-nee-n'yo, a., affable; good
benino, bay-nee-no, adv., pretty well
beninteso, bay-nin-tay-zo, adv., of course
benissimo, bay-niss-se-mo, adv., very well
benone, bay-no-nay, adv., very well
benservito, ben-sair-vee-to, m., reference
bensi, ben-see, adv., on the contrary; but
benzina, ben-dzee-nah, f., benzine; petrol
beone, bay-o-nay, m., drunkard
bere, bay-ray, v., to drink
bernoccolo, bair-nock-ko-lo, m., bump
berretta, bair-ret-tah, f., cap; cardinal's hat
berretto, bair-ret-to, m., cap
bersagliare, bair-sah-l'yah-ray, v., to hit a target or a person; (fig.) to torment
bersaglio, bair-sah-l'yo. m., target
bertuccia, bair-toot-chah, f., little monkey
bestemmia, bess-tem-me'ah, f., blasphemy
bestemmiare, bess-tem-me'ah-ray, v., to blaspheme
bestia, bess-te'ah, f., beast; brute; fool
bestiale, bess-te'ah-lay, a., brutal
bestiame, bess-te'ah-may, m., cattle
bettola, bet-to-lah, f., tavern, pub
betulla, bay-tooll-lah, f., birch-tree
bevanda, bay-vahn-dah, f., beverage
beveraggio, bay-vay-rahd-jo,m.,beverage; potion
bevere, bay-vay-ray, v., to drink
bevibile, bay-vee-be-lay, a., drinkable
bevuta, bay-voo-tah, f., draught
biacca, be'ahk-kah, f., ceruse; white paint
biade, be'ah-day, f. pl., standing crops of cereals
biancastro, be'ahn-kahss-tro, a., whitish [white
biancheggiare, be'ahn-ked-jah-ray, v., to turn
biancheria, be'ahn-kay-ree-ah, f., linen

bianchezza, be'ahn-**ket**-tsah, f., whiteness

bianco, be'**ahn**-ko, m., white, blank. a., white, blank

biancospino, be'ahn-ko-**spee**-no, m., hawthorn

biascicare, be'ah-she-**kah**-ray, v., to mumble. to murmur

biasimare, be'ah-ze-**mah**-ray, v., to blame

biasimevole, be'ah-ze-**may**-vo-lay, a., blamable

biasimo, be'**ah**-ze-mo, m., blame, fault

bibbia, **bib**-be'ah, f., Bible

bibita, bee-be-tah, f., beverage

bibliotecario, be-ble'o-tay-**kah**-re'o, m., librarian

bicchiere, bik-ke-**ay**-ray, m.,tumbler; goblet; glass

bicicletta, be-che-**klet**-tah, f., bicycle

bicocca, be-**kock**-kah, f., hut, poor cottage

bidello, be-**dell**-lo, m., beadle

bieco*, be'**ay**-ko, a., askew, cross; squinting

biella, be'**ell**-lah, f., connecting-rod

bietola, be'**ay**-to-lah, f., beet

bifolco, be-**fol**-ko, m., rustic   [off

biforcarsi, be-for-**kar**-se, v.,to bifurcate, to branch

bigamo, bee-**gah**-mo, m., bigamist

bigatto, be-**gaht**-to, m., silk-worm

bighellone, be-ghell-**lo**-nay, m., lounger

bigio, bee-jo, a., grey

bigliardo, be-l'yar-do, m., billiards

bigliettaio, be-l'yet-**tah**-e'o, m., booking-office clerk; conductor

biglietto, be-l'yet-to, m., note; ticket; card

bigotto, be-**got**-to, m., bigot, devotee

bilancia, be-lahn-chah, f., weighing-machine

bilanciare, be-lahn-**chah**-ray, v., to balance; to weigh

bilancio, be-**lahn**-cho, m., budget; balance-sheet

bile, bee-lay, f., bile; (fig.) anger

bilia, bee-le'ah, f., billiard-ball

biliardo, be-l'yar-do, m., billiards; billiard-room

bilico, bee-le-ko, m., equilibrium

bilione, be-le'o-nay, m., billion

bimbo, **beem**-bo, m., child; baby

bimensile, be-men-see-lay, a., bi-monthly

binario, be-nah-re'o, m., railway-track   [glass

binoccolo, be-**nock**-ko-lo, m., opera-glass; field-

biondo, be'onn-do, a., fair
birbante, beer-bahn-tay, m., rogue   [rogue
birbo [*or* birbone], beer-bo, m., rascal, scoundrel
biricchino, be-rick-kee-no, m., naughty boy
birra, beer-rah, f., beer
birraio, beer-rah-e'o, m., brewer
birreria, beer-ray-ree-ah, f., brewery
bis, biss, adv., twice. interj., encore !
bisava, be-zah-vah, f., great-grandmother
bisavo, be-zah-vo, m., great-grandfather
bisbetico*, biss-bay-te-ko, a., cross, irritable
bisbigliare, biss-be-l'yah-ray, v., to whisper
bisbiglio, biss-bee-l'yo, m., whisper
bisca, biss-kah, f., gambling-den
biscazziere, biss-kaht-tse'ay-ray, m., croupier ;
   owner of a gambling house
biscia, bee-she'ah, f., snake
biscotto, biss-kot-to, m., biscuit
bisestile, be-zess-tee-lay, a., **anno —**, leap-year
bislacco*, biss-lack-ko, a., queer
bislungo, biss-loonn-go, a., oblong
bisogna, be-zo-n'yah, f., business ; work ; task
bisognare, be-zo-n'yah-ray, v., to be necessary
bisogno, be-zo-n'yo, m., need, necessity
bissare, biss-sah-ray, v., to encore
bistecca, biss-teck-kah, f., (beef) steak
bisticcio, biss-teet-cho, m., dispute ; pun
bistorto*, biss-tor-to, a., twisted, crooked
bisunto, be-zoonn-to, a., very greasy
bitorzolo, be-tor-tso-lo, m., wart
bivio, bee-ve'o, m., cross-road
bizza, beed-dzah, f., anger ; fancy
bizzarro*, beed-dzar-ro, a., odd, queer
bizzeffe, bit-tsef-fay, adv., **a —**, in abundance
blandire, blahn-dee-ray, v., to allure, to cajole
blando*, blahn-do, a., soft ; mild
blocco, block-ko, m., blockade ; block
blu, bloo, m., blue. a., blue
bocca, bock-kah, f., mouth ; muzzle ; **gap**
boccale, bock-kah-lay, m., jar ; mug
boccetta, bot-chet-tah, f., phial   [mouth
bocchino, bock-kee-no, m., mouth-piece ; pretty

boccia, bot-chah, f., bottle : (game) bowls
bocciolo, bot-cho-lo, m., bud
boccone, bock-ko-nay, m., mouthful
bocconi, bock-ko-ne, adv., lying face downwards
boia, bo-e'ah, m., executioner
bolla, boll-lah, f., bubble ; blister
bollare, boll-lah-ray, v., to stamp, to brand
bollente, boll-len-tay, a., boiling ; hot ; (fig.) hasty
bolletta, boll-let-tah, f., receipt ; bill
bollettino, boll-let-tee-no, m., bulletin
bollire, boll-lee-ray, v., to boil
bollitore, boll-le-tor-ay, m., boiler
bollo, boll-lo, m., stamp
bolsaggine, boll-sahd-je-nay, f., (horse) asthma
bolscevico, boll-shay-vee-ko, a., bolshevik
bolso*, boll-so, a., asthmatic ; short of breath
bomba, bom-bah, f., bomb
bombardare, bom-bar-dah-ray, v., to bombard
bompresso, bom-press-so, m., bowsprit
bonaccia, bo-naht-chah, f., calm at sea : prosperity
bonaccione, bo-naht-cho-nay, m., good-natured person
bonanima, bo-nah-ne-mah, m. & f., (defunct) dear old soul
bonario*, bo-nah-re'o, a., simple, naïve : kindly
bonificare, bo-ne-fe-kah-ray, v., to deduct : to re-
bontà, bon-tah, f., goodness   [claim
borace, bo-rah-chay, m., borax
borbottare, bor-bot-tah-ray, v., to grumble ; to murmur
bordello, bor-dell-lo, m., brothel
bordo, bor-do, m., edge ; hem ; brim ; margin ; (naut.) board
bordone, bor-do-nay, m., tener —, to abet
borgata, bor-gah-tah, f., suburb, village
borghese, bor-gay-zay, m., citizen ; civilian. in —, in plain clothes
borghesia, bor-gay-zee-ah, f., middle-class
borgo, bor-go, m., suburb ; hamlet
boria, bo-re'ah, f., vanity, haughtiness
borioso*, bo-re'o-zo, a., boastful
borraccia, bor-raht-chah, f., flask

borsa, bor-sah, f., purse ; pouch ; stock-exchange
borsai[u]olo, bor-sah-yo-lo, m., pickpocket
bosco, boss-ko. m., wood
bosso, boss-so. m., box-tree ; box-wood
botanica, bo-tah-ne-kah, f., botany
botola, bo-to-lah, f., trap-door
botta, bot-tah. f., blow
bottaio, bot-tah-e'o, m., cooper
botte, bot-tay. f., cask, barrel
bottega, bot-tay-gah. f., shop
bottegaio, bot-tay-gah-e'o, m., shop-keeper
bottiglia, bot-tee-l'yah, f., bottle
bottino, bot-tee-no. m., booty
bottoncino, bot-ton-chee-no,m.,bud ; small button
bottone, bot-to-nay, m., button ; bud ; stud
bovaro, bo-vah-ro, m., drover
bove, bo-vay, m., ox
bozza, bot-tsah. f., sketch
bozzolo, bot-tso-lo, m., cocoon
braccialetto, braht-chah-let-to, m., bracelet
braccio, braht-cho, m., arm. —di mare, channel
bracciuolo, braht-choo'o-lo, m., arm of a seat
bracco, brahk-ko, m., hound
brache, brah-kay. f. pl., trousers
braciere, brah-chay-ray, m., brazier
braciola, brah-cho-lah, f., chop
brama, brah-mah, f., lust
bramare, brah-mah-ray, v., to covet
bramoso*, brah-mo-zo, a., eager
branca, brahn-kah, f., tentacle ; branch
branchie, brahn-ke'ay, f. pl., gills
branco, brahn-ko, m., flock, herd
brancolare, brahn-ko-lah-ray, v., to grope
branda, brahn-dah, f., hammock ; bunk
brandello, brahn-dell-lo, m., rag, tatter
brandire, brahn-dee-ray, v., to brandish
brando, brahn-do. m., sword
brano, brah-no. m., slip, piece
bravaccio, brah-vaht-cho, m., braggart
bravo, brah-vo. a.,* able ; brave ; good. m., hired
    ruffian. interj., bravo !
bravura, brah-voo-rah, f., bravery ; skill

1—3

breccia, bret-chah, f., breach
brefotrofio, bray-fo-tro-fe'o, m., foundling hospi-
bretelle, bray-tell-lay, f. pl., braces   [tal
breve, bray-vay, a., brief. m., papal brief
brevettare, bray-vet-tah-ray, v., to patent
brevetto, bray-vet-to, m., patent
brezza, bret-tsah, f., breeze
briaco, bre'ah-ko, a., tipsy
bricco, brik-ko, m., kettle
briccone, brik-ko-nay, m., rascal
briciola, bree-cho-lah, f., crumb
briga, bree-gah, f., trouble
brigare, bre-gah-ray, v., to intrigue
brigata, bre-gah-tah, f., gang ; party ; flock ; bevy ;
    (mil.) brigade
briglia, bree-l'yah, f., bridle
brillante, bril-lahn-tay, m., diamond. a., brilliant
brillare, bril-lah-ray, v., to glitter, to shine
brillo, bril-lo, a., muzzy
brina, bree-nah, f., hoar-frost
brindare, brin-dah-ray, v., (to drink) to toast
brindisi, breen-de-ze, m., (speech) toast
brio, bree-o, m., wit ; liveliness
brioso*, bre'o-zo, a., full of life and wit
brivido, bree-ve-do, m., shiver
brizzolato, brit-tso-lah-to, a., iron grey
brocca, brock-kah, f., pitcher, jug
brodo, bro-do, m., broth
brogliare, bro-l'yah-ray, v., to intrigue
broglio, bro-l'yo, m., intrigue
bromuro, bro-moo-ro, m., bromide
bronchi, bron-ke, m. pl., bronchial tubes
broncio, bron-cho, m., sulkiness. avere il —,
    to be angry
brontolare, bron-to-lah-ray, v., to grumble
brontolio, bron-to-lee-o, m., growl
brontolone, bron-to-lo-nay, m., grumbler
bronzare, bron-dzah-ray, v., to bronze
bruciare, broo-chah-ray, v., to burn
bruciatura, broo-chah-too-rah, f., burn
bruciore, broo-cho-ray, m., burning sensation
bruco, broo-ko, m., caterpillar

brughiera, broo-ghe-**ay**-rah, f., moorland
brulicare, broo-le-**kah**-ray, v., to swarm
brullo, brooll-lo, a., barren
bruma, broo-mah, f., misty weather
brunetto, broo-**net**-to, a., brownish
brunire, broo-**nee**-ray, v., to burnish
bruno, broo-no, a., brown; dusky; dark
bruto, broo-to, m., brute. a.,* brutal
bruttezza, broot-**tet**-tsah, f., ugliness; brutality
brutto*, broot-to, a., ugly; (weight) gross
buca, boo-kah, f., hole. — **da lettere**, letter-box
bucare, boo-**kah**-ray, v., to pierce, to bore
bucato, boo-**kah**-to, m., washing
bucatura, boo-kah-**too**-rah, f., puncture
buccia, boot-chah, f., peel; skin; rind
buco, boo-ko, m., hole
budello, boo-**dell**-lo, m., bowel; gut
budino, boo-**dee**-no, m., pudding
bue, boo-ay, m., ox
bufera, boo-**fay**-rah, f., gale
buffo, boof-fo, m., comedian; gust; whiff. a.,* comical
buggerare, bood-jay-**rah**-ray, v., (pop.) to deceive
bugia, boo-**jee**-ah, f., lie; flat candlestick
bugiardo, boo-**jar**-do, m., liar. a.,* lying
buio, boo-e'o, m., darkness. a.,* dark
bulbo, booll-bo, m., bulb
bulgaro, booll-**gah**-ro, m., Bulgarian; russian leather
bulinare, boo-le-**nah**-ray, v., to chisel
bulino, boo-lee-no, m., graving tool
bulletta, booll-**let**-tah, f., tack; luggage-receipt
buonamano, boo'o-nah-**mah**-no, f., tip
buondi [or **bondì**], boo'on-**dee**, interj., good day! greetings!
buono, boo'o-no, m., welfare; bill; coupon. a.,* good, kind; proper
buontempone, boo'on-tem-**po**-nay, m., one who enjoys life to the full
burattino, boo-raht-**tee**-no, m., puppet, marionette
burbanza, boor-**bahn**-tsah, f., arrogance
burbero*, boor-**bay**-ro, a., surly, sullen
burla, boor-lah, f., joke; jest

burlare, boor-lah-ray, v., to make a fool of

burlone, boor-lo-nay, m., joker; (pop.) humbug

burrasca, boor-rahss-kah, f., gale

burro, boor-ro. m., butter

burrone, boor-ro-nay, m., precipice

busca, booss-kah, f., in —, in quest of

buscherata, booss-kay-rah-tah, f., nonsense; hoax

bussa, booss-sah, f., blow, stroke

bussare, booss-sah-ray, v., to knock; to chastise

bussata, booss-sah-tah, f., knocking

busse, booss-say, f. pl., thrashing, slapping

bussola, booss-so-lah, f., compass

bussolotto, booss-so-lot-to, m., dice-box

busta, booss-tah, f., envelope

busto, booss-to, m., bust; corset

buttare, boot-tah-ray, v., to throw; to cast off; to shoot up

buttero, boot-tay-ro, m., herdsman

cabala, kah-bah-lah, f., cabal

cabottaggio, kah-bot-tahd-jo, m., (trade) coasting

cacao, kah-kah-o, m., cocoa

caccia, kaht-chah, f., (game) shooting

cacciare, kaht-chah-ray, v., to chase; to shoot; to send away

cacciatore, kaht-chah-tor-ay, m., hunter

cacciavite, kaht-chah-vee-tay, m., screw-driver

cacio, kah-cho. m., cheese

cadauno, kah-dah'oo-no, pron., each

cadavere, kah-dah-vay-ray, m., corpse

cadere, kah-day-ray, v., to fall; to happen

cadetto, kah-det-to, m., cadet; younger son

caducità, kah-doo-che-tah, f., decay; short life

caduco, kah-doo-ko, a., short lived

caduta, kah-doo-tah, f., fall; misfortune

caffè, kahf-fay, m., coffee; café

caffettiera, kahf-fet-te'ay-rah, f., coffee-pot

cagionare, kah-jo-nah-ray, v., to cause

cagione, kah-jo-nay, f., cause

cagionevole, kah-jo-nay-vo-lay, a., delicate

caglio, kah-l'yo, m., rennet

cagna, kah-n'yah, f., bitch

cagnara, kah-n'yah-rah, f., tumult
cagnolino, kah-n'vo-lee-no, m., puppy ; small dog
caimano, kah-e-mah-no, m., alligator
cala, kah-lah, f., cove ; (naut.) hold
calabrone, kah-lah-bro-nay, m., hornet
calamaio, kah-lah-mah-e'o, m., inkstand ; cuttle-fish
calamita, kah-lah-mee-tah, f., magnet
calamità, kah-lah-me-tah, f., calamity
calamitare, kah-lah-me-tah-ray, v., to magnetize
calamitoso*, kah-lah-me-to-zo, a., disastrous
calare, kah-lah-ray, v., to lower ; to sink ; to set
calata, kah-lah-tah, f., fall ; quay
calca, kahl-kah, f., crowd
calcagno, kahl-kah-n'yo, m., heel
calcare, kahl-kah-ray, v., to trample ; to press
calce, kahl-chay, f., lime ; mortar
calcestruzzo, kahl-chess-troot-tso, m., concrete
calciare, kahl-chah-ray, v., to kick
calcina, kahl-chee-nah, f., lime
calcio, kahl-cho, m., kick ; calcium ; butt
calcitrare, kahl-che-trah-ray, v., to resist ; to kick
calcolo, kahl-ko-lo, m., calculation ; (med.) gravel
calda, kahl-dah, f., heating
caldaia, kahl-dah-e'ah, f., boiler
calderino, kahl-day-ree-no, m., kettle ; small pan
calderone, kahl-day-ro-nay, f., cauldron
caldo, kahl-do, m., heat, warmth. a.,* warm, hot
calere, kah-lay-ray, v., to matter ; to care for
calice, kah-le-chay, m., chalice ; communion-cup
caligine, kah-lee-je-nay, f., fog ; obscurity
calle, kahl-lay, f., Venetian street
callista, kahl-liss-tah, m. & f., chiropodist
callo, kahl-lo, m., corn, hard skin
calloso*, kahl-lo-zo, a., callous
calmante, kahl-mahn-tay, m., soothing draught.
  a., soothing, calming
calo, kah-lo, m., drop in price ; descent ; waste
calore, kah-lor-ay, m., heat, warmth ; affection
calorifero, kah-lor-e-fay-ro, m., central heating ;
  radiator
calotta, kah-lot-tah, f., skull-cap ; dome

calpestare, kahl-pay-**stah**-ray, v., to trample upon

calunnia, kah-**loonn**-ne'ah, f., calumny

calunniare, kah-loonn-ne'ah-ray, v., to slander

calunniatore, kah-loonn-ne'ah-**tor**-ay, m., slanderer

calura, kah-loo-rah, f., heat-wave   [derer

calvizie, kahl-**vee**-tse-ay, f., baldness

calvo, **kahl**-vo, a., bald

calza, **kahl**-tsah, f., stocking, sock   [shoes

calzare, kahl-**tsah**-ray, v., to supply with *or* put on

calzature, kahl-tsah-**too**-ray, f. pl., shoes and boots

calzetto, kahl-**tset**-to, m., sock

calzolaio, kahl-tso-**lah**-e'o, m., shoemaker

calzoleria, kahl-tso-lay-**ree**-ah, f., shoemaker's shop

calzoni, kahl-**tso**-ne, m. pl., trousers

camaleonte, kah-mah-lay-**on**-tay, m., chameleon

camarilla, kah-mah-**rill**-lah, f., (coterie) set

cambiabile, kahm-be'**ah**-be-lay, a., changeable

cambiale, kahm-be'ah-lay, f., bill of exchange, draft

cambiamento, kahm-be'ah-**men**-to, m., change

cambiamonete [*or* **cambiavalute**], kahm-be'ah-mo-**nay**-tay, m., bureau de change

cambiare, kahm-be'**ah**-ray, v., to change

cambio, **kahm**-be'o, m., change ; rate of exchange

cambista, kahm-**biss**-tah, m., money-changer

camera, **kah**-may-rah, f., room ; chamber. — **d'aria**, inner tube. — **dei deputati**, House of Commons. — **dei senatori**, House of Lords

camerata, kah-may-**rah**-tah, m. & f., comrade, companion, f., dormitory

cameratismo, kah-may-rah-**tiss**-mo, m., comradeship

cameriera, kah-may-re'**ay**-rah, f., chambermaid ; waitress ; parlourmaid

cameriere, kah-may-re'**ay**-ray, m., waiter ; valet

camerino, kah-may-**ree**-no, m., closet ; cabin

camice, **kah**-me-chay, m., overall ; surplice

camicetta, kah-me-**chet**-tah, f., blouse

camicia, kah-**mee**-chah, f., shirt ; chemise

camiciola, kah-me-**cho**-lah, f., bodice, chemise

caminetto, kah-me-**net**-to, m., chimney-piece

camino, kah-**mee**-no, m., fire-place ; chimney

camionale, kah-me'o-**nah**-lay, f., motor-road

camione, kah-me'o-nay, m., lorry ; truck
cammello, kahm-mell-lo, m., camel
camminare, kahm-me-nah-ray, v., to walk
camminata, kahm-me-nah-tah, f., walk, stroll
cammino, kahm-mee-no, m., road, way
camorra, kah-mor-rah, f., gang ; criminal **society**
camoscio, kah-mo-she'o, m., chamois
campagna, kahm-pah-n'yah, f., country ; campaign
campagnuolo, kahm-pah-n'yoo-o-lo, m., peasant
campana, kahm-pah-nah, f., bell
campanello, kahm-pah-nell-lo, m., small bell
campanile, kahm-pah-nee-lay, m., steeple
campanula, kahm-pah-noo-lah, f., bell-flower
campare, kahm-pah-ray, v., to earn one's daily bread
campeggiare, kahm-ped-jah-ray, v., to encamp
campeggio, kahm-ped-jo, m., encampment
campestre, kahm-pess-tray, a., rural
campionario, kahm-pe'o-nah-re'o, m., samples
campionato, kahm-pe'o-nah-to, m., championship
campione, kahm-pe'o-nay, m., sample ; champion
campo, kahm-po, m., field ; camp ; time
camposanto, kahm-po-sahn-to, m., church**yard**
camuffare, kah-moof-fah-ray, v., to disguise
canaglia, kah-nah-l'yah, f., rabble
canale, kah-nah-lay, m., canal
canapa, kah-nah-pah, f., hemp
canapè, kah-nah-pay, m., settee
canapo, kah-nah-po, m., hawser
canarino, kah-nah-ree-no, m., canary
canavaccio, kah-nah-vaht-cho, m., canvas ; mop ; (play) outline
cancellare, kahn-chell-lah-ray, v., to cancel
cancellatura, kahn-chell-lah-too-rah, f., annulment ; erasure
cancelleria, kahn-chell-lay-ree-ah, f., chancery
cancelliere, kahn-chell-le'ay-ray, m., chancellor
cancello, kahn-chell-lo, m., gate ; stile
cancrena, kahn-kray-nah, f., gangrene
cancro, kahn-kro, m., cancer
candela, kahn-day-lah, f., candle
candelabro, kahn-day-lah-bro, m., chandelier
candeliere, kahn-day-le'ay-ray, m., candlestick

candidato, kahn-de-dah-to, m., candidate ; applicant

candidezza, kahn-de-det-tsah, f., whiteness ; innocence

candido*, **kahn**-de-do, a., white ; (fig.) candid

candore, kahn-dor-ay, m.,whiteness ; (fig.) candour

cane, kah-nay, m., dog ; (gun) cock

canestro, kah-ness-tro, m., basket

canfora, **kahn**-fo-rah, f., camphor

cangiare, kahn-jah-ray, v., to change

canguro, kahn-goo-ro, m., kangaroo

canile, kah-nee-lay, m., dog-kennel

canina, kah-nee-nah, a., **tosse** —, whooping-cough

canizie, kah-nee-tse'ay, f., white hair ; (fig.) old age

canna, **kahn**-nah, f., cane, reed ; (gun) barrel

cannella, kahn-nell-lah, f., cinnamon

cannello, kahn-nell-lo, m., thin pipe, stem, or hose

cannocchiale, kahn-nock-ke'ah-lay, m., operaglass ; telescope

cannone, kahn-no-nay, m., cannon, gun

cannoniera, kahn-no-ne'ay-rah, f., gun-boat

cannoniere, kahn-no-ne'ay-ray, m., gunner

canonico*, kah-no-ne-ko, m., canon. a., canonical

canoro*, kah-no-ro, a., (mus. & poet.) harmonious

canotto, kah-not-to, m., canoe ; rowing boat

canova, kah-no-vah, f., cave ; tavern ; cellar

canovaccio, kah-no-vaht-cho, m., canvas ; towel

cantante, kahn-tahn-tay, m.& f., singer. a.,singing

cantare, kahn-tah-ray, v., to sing. — **da gallo**, to

cantico, **kahn**-te-ko, m., canticle ; carol   [crow

cantiere, kahn-te'ay-ray, m., dockyard

cantina, kahn-tee-nah, f., cellar ; canteen

cantiniere, kahn-te-ne'ay-ray, m., wine-butler ; canteen-keeper

canto, **kahn**-to, m., song ; corner

cantone, kahn-to-nay, m., corner, angle ; canton

cantoniere, kahn-to-ne'ay-ray, m., signalman ; road-caretaker

cantuccio, kahn-toot-cho, m., nook

canuto, kah-noo-to, a., snow-white haired

canzonaccia, kahn-tso-naht-chah, f., ribald song

canzonare, kahn-tso-nah-ray, v., to make fun of

canzonatura, kahn-tso-nah-**too**-rah, f., hoax, rail-
canzone, kahn-tso-nay, f., song ; tune : carol [lery
caos, **kah**-oss, m., chaos
capace, kah-**pah**-chay, a., capable, able ; capacious
capacitare, kah-pah-che-**tah**-ray, v., to convince ;
 to enable
capanna, kah-**pahn**-nah, f., hut, shed
capannello, kah-pahn-**nell**-lo, m., group ; hut
capannone, kah-pahn-**no**-nay, m., hangar ; outhouse
caparbietà, kah-par-be'ay-**tah**, f., stubborness
caparbio*, kah-**par**-be'o, a., obstinate ; restive
caparra, kah-**par**-rah, f., earnest money ; token
capello, kah-**pell**-lo, m., hair
capelluto, kah-pell-**loo**-to, a., hairy [fern
capelvenere, kah-pell-**vay**-nay-ray, m., maiden-hair
capestro, kah-**pess**-tro, m., noose, halter
capezzale, kah-pet-**tsah**-lay, m., pillow ; bolster
capezzolo, kah-pet-**tso**-lo, m., nipple ; teat ; pap
capigliatura, kah-pe-l'yah-**too**-rah, f., hair ; plaits ;
capire, kah-**pee**-ray, v., to understand [locks
capitare, kah-pe-**tah**-ray, v., to arrive ; to occur
capitello, kah-pe-**tell**-lo, m., (architecture) capital
capitolo, kah-**pee**-to-lo, m., chapter
capo, **kah**-po, m., head ; principal ; end ; cape.
 — **d'anno**, New Year's Day
capofabbrica, kah-po-**fahb**-bre-kah, m., foreman
capogiro, kah-po-**jee**-ro, m., giddiness
capolavoro, kah-po-lah-**vo**-ro, m., masterpiece
capolinea, kah-po-lee-nay-ah, f., terminus
caporale, kah-po-**rah**-lay, m., corporal
caporione, kah-po-re'**o**-nay, m., ringleader
caposquadra, kah-po-**skwah**-drah, f., overseer ;
 team-captain
capovolgere, kah-po-**voll**-jay-ray, v., to upset ; to
cappa, **kahp**-pah, f., cape [turn turtle
cappella, kahp-**pell**-lah, f., chapel
cappellaio, kahp-pell-lah-e'o, m., hatter
cappellano, kahp-pell-**lah**-no, m., chaplain
cappelleria, kahp-pell-lay-ree-ah, f., hat-shop
cappelliera, kahp-pell-le'**ay**-rah, f., hat-box
cappellino, kahp-pell-lee-no, m., bonnet
cappello, kahp-**pell**-lo, m., hat

capperi, kahp-pay-re, m. pl., capers. interj., wonderful ! good gracious ! oh !
cappio, kahp-pe'o, m., loop
cappotto, kahp-pot-to, m., overcoat
cappuccio, kahp-**poot**-cho, m., hood
capra, kah-prah, f., she-goat
capraro, kah-prah-ro, m., goat-herd
capretto, kah-pret-to, m., kid [goat
capro, kah-pro, m.,he-goat. — **espiatorio,** scape-
capriccio, kah-preet-cho, m., caprice
caprifoglio, kah-pre-fo-l'yo, m., honeysuckle
capriola, kah-pre'o-lah, f., roe-deer ; somersault
captare, kahp-tah-ray, v., to catch ; to win
capzioso, kahp-tse'o-zo, a., fraudulent ; rebellious
caraffa, kah-rahf-fah, f., decanter
carambola, kah-**rahm**-bo-lah, f.,(billiards) cannon
caramella, kah-rah-mell-lah, f., sweet ; monocle
carato, kah-**rah**-to, m., carat
carattere, kah-**raht**-tay-ray, m., character ; handwriting
carbonaia, kar-bo-**nah**-e'ah, f.,coal-cellar ; bunker
carbonaio, kar-bo-**nah**-e'o, m., coalman ; trimmer
carbonchio, kar-bon-ke'o, m., anthrax
carbone, kar-bo-nay, m., coal ; charcoal
carbonio, kar-bo-ne'o, m., carbon
carburante, kar-boo-**rahn**-tay, m., fuel
carcame, kar-**kah**-may, m., carcass
carcerato, kar-chay-**rah**-to, m., prisoner
carcere, kar-chay-ray, m., prison
carceriere, kar-chay-re'ay-ray, m., gaoler
carciofo, kar-cho-fo, m., artichoke
cardare, kar-dah-ray, v., (wool) to card
cardellino, kar-dell-lee-no, m., goldfinch
cardine, kar-de-nay, m., hinge ; pivot
cardo, kar-do, m., cardoon
cardone, kar-**do**-nay, m., thistle
carena, kah-**ray**-nah, f., keel
carestia, kah-ress-**tee**-ah, f., dearth
carezza, kah-**ret**-tsah, f., caress ; costliness
carezzare, kah-ret-**tsah**-ray, v., to caress
carica, kah-re-kah, f., charge ; position, rank
caricare, kah-re-**kah**-ray, v., to load

carico, kah-re-ko, m., freight ; loading ; responsibility. **polizza di —,** bill of lading

cariglione, kah-re-l'yo-nay, m., chimes

carino, kah-ree-no, a., nice ; cosy ; charming ; dear

carità, kah-re-**tah,** f., charity

caritatevole, hah-re-tah-**tay**-vo-lay, a.,charitable ;
 merciful

carlinga, kar-lin-gah, f., aeroplane-body

carminio, kar-mee-n'yo, m., carmine red

carnagione, kar-nah-jo-nay, f., complexion

carne, kar-nay, f., flesh ; meat

carnefice, kar-nay-fe-chay, m., executioner

carneficina, kar-nay-fe-chee-nah, f., shambles

carniera, kar-ne'ay-rah, f., game-pouch

carnoso°, kar-no-zo, a., fleshy ; muscular

caro°, kah-ro, a., dear

carogna, kah-ro-n'yah, f., carrion

carota, kah-ro-tah, f., carrot ; (fig.) fairy tales

caroviveri, kah-ro-vee-vay-re, m., higher living
 [costs

carpire, kar-pee-ray, v., to seize

carponi, kar-po-ne, a —, on all fours

carrello, kar-rell-lo, m., trolley ; under-carriage

carretta, kar-ret-tah, f., cart

carrettiere, kar-ret-te'ay-ray, m., carman

carretto, kar-ret-to, m., wheel-barrow ; hand-cart

carriera, kar-re'ay-rah, f., career ; full gallop

carro, kar-ro, m., waggon ; truck

carrozza, kar-rot-tsah, f., carriage ; coach

carrozzabile, kar-rot-tsah-be-lay, a., for carriages

carrozzella, kar-rot-tsell-lah, f., pram ; pony cart

carrozziere, kar-rot-tse'ay-ray, m., coach-builder

carrucola, kar-roo-ko-lah, f., pulley

carta, kar-tah, f., paper ; bill ; map. **— asciugante,** blotting-paper. **—da visita,** visiting-
 card. **— straccia,** waste-paper

cartapecora, kar-tah-pay-ko-rah, f., parchment,
 vellum

carteggiare, kar-ted-jah-ray, v., to correspond

cartella, kar-tell-lah, f., wrapper ; satchel

cartellino, kar-tell-lee-no, m., label ; card ; ticket

cartello, kar-tell-lo, m., sign ; poster ; label ;
 (business) trust. **— di sfida,** challenge

cartellone, kar-tell-lo-nay, m., poster
cartiera, kar-te'ay-rah, f., paper-mill
cartilagine, kar-te-lah-je-nay, f., cartilage
cartoccio, kar-tot-cho, m., cone ; bundle ; cornet
cartolaio, kar-to-lah-e'o, m., stationer
cartoleria, kar-to-lay-ree-ah, f., stationer's shop
cartolina, kar-to-lee-nah, f., post-card
cartone, kar-to-nay, m., cardboard
cartuccia, kar-toot-chah, f., cartridge
carvi, kar-ve, m. pl., caraway seeds
casa, kah-zah, f., house ; home. **— di salute,** nursing-home
casale, kah-zah-lay, m., hamlet   [ticated
casalingo, kah-zah-leen-go, a., home-like ; domes-
casato, kah-zah-to, m., surname ; family
cascami, kahss-kah-me, m. pl., wool waste, etc.
cascare, kahss-kah-ray, v., to fall, to tumble
cascata, kahss-kah-tah, f., waterfall
casco, kahss-ko, m., helmet, head-piece
casella, kah-zell-lah, f., pigeon-hole. **— postale,** (address) P.O. box
casello, kah-zell-lo, m., road-minder's house ; signalman's box
caserma, kah-zair-mah, f., barracks   [house
casino, kah-zee-no, m., country-house ; club ; bawdy-
caso, kah-zo, m., case ; chance ; befalling
cassa, kahss-sah, f., case ; box. **— forte,** safe. **— da morto,** coffin. **— di risparmio,** savings-bank
cassare, kahss-sah-ray, v., to cancel
cassetta, kahss-set-tah, f., cash-box ; little box
cassetto, kahss-set-to, m., drawer
cassiere, kahss-se'ay-ray, m., cashier
cassone, kahss-so-nay, m., large case or box
casta, kahss-tah, f., caste, rank
castagna, kahss-tah-n'yah, f., chestnut
castagno, kahss-tah-n'yo, m., chestnut-tree
castello, kahss-tell-lo, m., castle
castigare, kahss-te-gah-ray, v., to chastise
castigo, kahss-tee-go, m., punishment
castità, kahss-te-tah, f., chastity
casto°, kahss-to, a., chaste
castoro, kahss-to-ro, m., beaver

castrare, kahss-**trah-ray**, v., to castrate. to doctor
castrato, kahss-**trah-to**, m., mutton ; eunuch
casualità, kah-zoo'ah-le-**tah**, f., casualty ; hazard
casupola, kah-**zoo**-po-lah, f., hovel
catalessi, kah-tah-**less-se**, f., catalepsy
catapecchia, kah-tah-**peck-ke'ah**, f., tumble-down
    house ; hovel ; dirty attic
cataplasma, kah-tah-**plahss-mah**, m., poultice
catarro, kah-**tar**-ro, m., catarrh
catasta, kah-**tahss**-tah, f., stack ; heap [property
catasto, kah-**tahss**-to, m., survey and valuation of
catena, kah-**tay**-nah, f., chain ; linking tie
catenaccio, kah-tay-**naht**-cho, m., bolt ; padlock
catera, kah-**tay**-rah, f., green almond
cateratta, kah-tay-**raht**-tah, f., cataract
caterva, kah-**tair**-vah, f., band, troop ; heap
catinella, kah-te-**nell**-lah, f., basin ; washhand
catino, kah-**tee**-no, m., basin   [basin
catramare, kah-trah-**mah-ray**, v., to tar
catrame, kah-**trah**-may, m., tar
cattedra, **kaht**-tay-drah, f., pulpit ; chair
cattedratico, kaht-tay-**drah**-te-ko, m., pedant.
    a. * pedant
cattivare, kaht-te-**vah-ray**, v., to captivate
cattiveria, kah-te-vay-re'ah, f., wickedness
cattivo*, kaht-**tee**-vo, a., naughty ; wicked
cattura, kaht-**too**-rah, f., capture ; seizure
catturare, kaht-too-**rah-ray**, v., to capture ; to
caucciù, kah'oot-**choo**, m., India-rubber   [seize
causa, kah'oo-zah, f., cause ; case ; trial
causare, kah'oo-**zah**-ray, v., to cause
cautela, kah'oo-**tay**-lah, f., caution
cauto*, **kah**'oo-to, a., cautious
cauzione, kah'oo-tse'o-nay, f., bail ; security
cava, **kah**-vah, f., cave ; cellar ; quarry
cavadenti, kah-vah-**den**-te, m., dentist
cavafango, kah-vah-**fahn**-go, m., dredger
cavalcare, kah-vahl-**kah**-ray, v., to ride
cavalcata, kah-vahl-**kah**-tah, f., ride ; cavalcade
cavalcatura, kah-vahl-kah-**too**-rah, f., mount
cavalcavia, kah-vahl-kah-**vee**-ah, m., viaduct
cavalcioni, kah-vahl-**cho**-ne. a —, astride

cavaliere, kah-vah-le'ay-ray, m., knight ; rider. a., courteous

cavalla, kah-vahl-lah, f., mare

cavalleresco°, kah-vahl-lay-ress-ko, a., chivalrous

cavalleria, kahl-vahl-lay-ree-ah, f., cavalry ; knighthood ; gallantry

cavalletta, kah-vahl-let-tah, f., grasshopper ; locust ; (game) leap-frog

cavalletto, kah-vahl-let-to, m., trestle ; easel

cavallino, kah-vahl-lee-no, m., pony

cavallo, kah-vahl-lo, m., horse ; (chess) knight

cavalloni, kah-vahl-lo-ne, m. pl., (sea) breakers

cavare, kah-vah-ray, v., to extract ; to subtract ; to mine

cavastivali, kah-vah-ste-vah-le, m., boot-jack

cavaturacciolo, kah-vah-too-raht cho-lo,m.,cork-

caverna, kah-vair-nah, f., cavern, cave [screw

cavezza, kah-vet-tsah, f., halter

caviale, kah-ve'ah-lay, m., caviar

cavicchio, kah-veek-ke'o, m., peg ; plug

caviglia, kah-vee-l'yah, f., ankle ; bolt

cavillare, kah-vil-lah-ray, v., to quibble

cavillo, kah-vil-lo, m., cavil, quibble

cavo, kah-vo, m., cable. a., hollow

cavolfiore, kah-vol-fe'O-ray, m., cauliflower

cavolo, kah-vo-lo, m., cabbage

cazza, kaht-tsah, f., crucible, melting-pot

cazzarola, kaht-tsah-ro-lah, f., casserole

cazzotto, kaht-tsot-to, m., blow

cazzuola, kaht-tsoo'o-lah, f., trowel

ce, chay, pron., us, to us. adv., there ; here

cece, chay-chay, m., chick-pea

cecità, chay-che-tah, f., blindness

ceco°, chay-ko, a., (see **cieco**)

cedere, chay-day-ray, v., to cede

cedibile, chay-dee-be-lay, a., transferable

cedola, chay-do-lah, f., coupon

cedro, chay-dro, m., cedar

cefalo, chay-fah-lo, m., mullet

ceffata, chayf-fah-tah, f., smack

ceffo, chayf-fo, m., snout

ceffone, chayf-fo-nay, m., slap

celare, chay-lah-ray, v., to conceal
celebramento, chay-lay-brah-men-to, m., celebration ; praise
celebrare, chay-lay-brah-ray, v., to celebrate
celebre, chay-lay-bray, a., renowned
celere, chay-lay-ray, a., rapid ; speedy
celeste, chay-less-tay, a., celestial
celia, chay-le'ah, f., joke, fun
celiare, chay-le'ah-ray, v., to joke ; to make fun
celibato, chay-le-bah-to, m., celibacy
celibe, chay-le-bay, m., bachelor
cella, chell-lah, f., cell ; chamber
celluloide, chell-loo-lo-e-day, m., celluloid
celo, chay-lo, m., (see cielo)
cemento, chay-men-to, m., cement
cena, chay-nah, f., supper
cenare, chay-nah-ray, v., to take supper
cenciaiuolo, chen-chah-e'oo-0-lo, m., rag-man
cencio, chen-cho, m., rag, tatter
cencioso*, chen-cho-zo, a., ragged, tattered
cenere, chay-nay-ray, f., ashes. a., ash-colour
cenerentola, chay-nay-ren-to-lah, f., cinderella
cenno, chen-no, m., nod ; signal, hint
cenobio, chay-no-be'o, m.,monastery ; brotherhood
censimento, chen-se-men-to, m., census
censire, chen-see-ray, v., to tax ; to take a census
censo, chen-so, m., census ; assessment ; income
censore, chen-sor-ay, m., censor
censurare, chen-soo-rah-ray, v., to censure
centellinare, chen-tell-le-nah-ray, v., to sip
centesimo, chen-tay-ze-mo, m., centime ; hundredth part. a., hundredth
centinaio, chen-te-nah-e'o, m., about a hundred
cento, chen-to, a., hundred
centralino, chen-trah-lee-no, m., telephone exchange
centuplo, chen-too-plo, m., hundredfold
centuria, chen-too-re'ah, f., one hundred men, etc.
centurino, chen-too-ree-no, m., waist-belt ; girdle
ceppo, chep-po, m., stump of a tree ; block
cera, chay-rah, f., wax ; complexion ; mien
ceralacca, chay-rah-lahk-kah, f., sealing-wax

cerata, chay-rah-tah, a., **tela —**, tarpaulin; American cloth

cerbottana, chair-bot-tah-nah, f., pea-shooter; arrow; blow-pipe

cerca, chair-kah, f., search; quest

cercare, chair-kah-ray, v., to seek; to fetch

cerchiare, chair-ke'ah-ray, v., to surround; to hoop

cerchio, chair-ke'o, m., circle; ring; hoop

cereale, chay-ray-ah-lay, m., cereal

cerebro, chay-ray-bro, m., brain

cereo, chay-ray-o, a., waxen

cerimonia, chay-re-mo-ne'ah, f., ceremony

cerino, chay-ree-no, m., wax-match

cerna, chair-nah, f., choice, selection

cernere, chair-nay-ray, v., to choose

cerniera, chair-ne'ay-rah, f., hinge

cero, chay-ro, m., large wax-candle

cerotto, chay-rot-to, m., plaster

certezza, chair-tet-tsah, f., certainty

certificato, chair-te-fe-kah-to, m., certificate

certuni, chair-too-ne, pron., several, some

ceruleo, chay-roo-lay-o, a., light blue, sky-blue

cerva, chair-vah, f., hind

cervella, chair-vell-lah, f.pl., brains

cervello, chair-vell-lo, m., brain

cervice, chair-vee-chay, f., nape

cervo, chair-vo, m., stag

cesello, chay-zell-lo, m., chisel

cesoie, chay-zo-e'ay, f.pl., scissors; shears

cespuglio, chess-poo-l'yo, m., thicket, bush

cessare, chess-sah-ray, v., to cease

cessione, chess-se'o-nay, f., cession; assignment

cesso, chess-so, m., water-closet

cesta, chess-tah, f., basket, hamper

cestinare, chess-te-nah-ray, v., to throw paper into the basket; to shelve

cestino, chess-tee-no, m., small basket

ceto, chay-to, m., social rank

cetra, chay-trah, f., lyre

cetriolo, chay-tre'o-lo, m., cucumber; gherkin

che, kay, pron., who, whom; which; **what**. conj., that; than. interj., what!

checchè, kayk-**kay**, pron., whatever
checchessia, kayk-kess-**see**-ah, pron., whatsoever
cherica, **kay**-re-kah, f., tonsure
cherico, **kay**-re-ko, m., choir-boy ; young priest
chermisi, kair-me-**zee**, m., crimson. a., crimson
cheto°, **kay**-to, a., quiet, silent
chi, kee, pron., who, whom ; which
chiacchiera, ke'ahk-ke'**ay**-rah, f., idle talk
chiacchierare, ke'ahk-ke'ay-**rah**-ray, v., to chatter
chiacchierone, ke'ahk-ke'ay-**ro**-nay, m., chatter-box ; gossiper
chiamare, ke'ah-**mah**-ray, v., to call
chiamata, ke'ah-**mah**-tah, f., appeal ; call
chiappa, ke'**ahp**-pah, f., hold ; buttock
chiappare, ke'ahp-**pah**-ray, v., to catch ; to entrap
chiarezza, ke'ah-**ret**-tsah, f., clearness
chiarificare, ke'ah-re-fe-**kah**-ray, v., to clarify
chiarire, ke'ah-**ree**-ray, v., to make clear
chiaro, ke'**ah**-ro, m., light. a.,° clear
chiaroscuro, ke'ah-ro-**skoo**-ro, m., light and shade
chiaroveggente, ke'ah-ro-ved-**jen**-tay, m. & f., clairvoyant
chia.sare, ke'ahss-**sah**-ray, v., to make a din
chiasso, ke'**ahss**-so, m., noise ; bustle
chiatta, ke'**aht**-tah, f., lighter, barge
chiavaio, ke'ah-**vah**-e'o, m., locksmith
chiavarda, ke'ah-**var**-dah, f., screw-bolt
chiavare, ke'ah-**vah**-ray, v., to lock up
chiave, ke'ah-**vay**, f., key. — inglese, spanner
chiavistello, ke'ah-ve-**stell**-lo, m., bolt
chiazza, ke'**aht**-tsah, f., spot, stain ; mottle
chiazzare, ke'aht-**tsah**-ray, v., to stain ; to mottle
chicca, keek-kah, f., sweet ; dainty bits
chicchessia, keek-kess-**see**-ah, pron., whosoever
chicco, keek-ko, m., pip ; seed ; bean ; stone ; grain
chiedere, ke'ay-**day**-ray, v., to ask, to demand
chiesa, ke'**ay**-zah, f., church
chiesta, ke'**ess**-tah, f., request, demand
chiglia, kee-**le'ah**, f., keel
chilo, kee-lo, m., kilogram
chimerico°, ke-**may**-re-ko, a., imaginar-
chimica, kee-me-kah, f., chemistry

chimico, kee-me-ko, m., chemist. a., chemical

china, kee-nah, f., slope, declivity

chinarsi, ke-nar-se, v., to bend oneself ; to stoop

chincaglieria, keen-kah-l'yay-ree-ah, f., earthenware, hardware

chinina, ke-nee-nah, f., quinine

chioccia, ke'ot-chah, f., brooding-hen

chiocciare, ke'ot-chah-ray, v.,to cackle ; to scream

chiocciola, ke'ot-cho-lah, f., snail. scala a —, winding staircase

chiodo, ke'o-do, m., nail

chioma, ke'o-mah, f., locks, flowing hair

chiosa, ke'o-zah, f., glossary, annotation

chiosare, ke'o-zah-ray, v., to comment, to explain

chiostro, ke'oss-tro, m., cloister

chiromante, ke-ro-mahn-tay, m., chiromancer

chirurgico, ke-roohr-je-ko, a., surgical

chirurgo, ke-roohr-go, m., surgeon

chissà, kiss-sah, adv., perhaps, maybe

chitarra, ke-tar-rah, f., guitar

chiudere, ke'oo-day-ray, v., to close

chiunque, ke'oonn-kway, pron., whoever

chiusa, ke'oo-zah, f., lock, barrier ; enclosure

chiuso, ke'oo-zo, m., (cattle, etc.) pen ; fold

chiusura, ke'oo-zoo-rah, f., lock ; enclosure. — lampo, zip-fastener

ci, chee, pron., us, to us. adv., there ; here

ciabatta, che'ah-baht-tah, f., slipper ; old shoe

ciabattino, che'ah-baht-tee-no, m., cobbler

cialda, che'ahl-dah, f., wafer

cialtrone, che'ahl-tro-nay, m., churl ; rogue

ciambella, che'ahm-bell-lah, f., cake

ciambellano,che'ahm-bell-lah-no,m.,chamberlain

ciao, chah'o, interj., greetings ! cheerio !

ciarla, che'ar-lah, f., false report ; tattle

ciarlare, che'ar-lah-ray, v., to chatter, to gossip

ciarlatano, che'ar-lah-tah-no, m., charlatan

ciarlone, che'ar-lo-nay, m., chatterbox

ciarpa, che'ar-pah, f., scarf

ciascuno, che'ahss-koo-no, pron., each one, every one. a., each

cibare, che-bah-ray, v., to feed

cibo, chee-bo, m., food
cicala, che-kah-lah, f., cricket
cicalare, che-kah-lah-ray, v., to chirp; to blab
cicatrice, che-kah-tree-chay, f., scar
cicca, chick-kah, f., cigar *or* cigarette end
ciccare, chick-kah-ray, v., to chew tobacco
ciclo, chee-klo, m., cycle
cicogna, che-ko-n'yah, f., stork
cicuta, che-koo-tah, f., hemlock
cieco*, che'ay-ko, a., blind
cielo, che'ay-lo, m., heaven; sky
ciera, che'ay-rah, f., looks, mien, appearance
cifra, chee-frah, f., cipher
ciglio, chee-l'yo, m., eyelash; edge. **sopracciglio,** eyebrow
cigno, chee-n'yo, m., swan
cigolare, che-go-lah-ray, v., to creak
cigolio, che-go-lee-o, m., creaking
ciliegia, che-le'ay-jah, f., cherry
ciliegio, che-le'ay-jo, m., cherry-tree
cilindrare, che-lin-drah-ray, v., to roll
cima, chee-mah, f., summit
cimelio, che-may-l'yo, m., relic; old curiosity
cimentare, che-men-tah-ray, v., to tease; to try
cimice, chee-me-chay, f., bug
ciminiera, che-me-ne'ay-rah, f., funnel; chimney-
cimitero, che-me-tay-ro, m., cemetery [stack
cimurro, che-moohr-ro, m., (disease) distemper
cingere, chin-jay-ray, v., to hug; to tie round;
   to surround
cinghia, chin-ghe'ah, f., strap; belt
cinghiale, chin-ghe'ah-lay, m., wild boar [chirp
cinguettare, chin-goo'et-tah-ray, v., to chatter; to
cinico, chee-ne-ko, m., cynic. a.,* cynical
cinquanta, chin-kwahn-tah, a., fifty
cinquantesimo, chin-kwahn-tay-se-mo, a., fiftieth
cinque, chin-kway, a., five
cinto, chin-to, m., truss
cintola, chin-to-lah, f., girdle
cintura, chin-too-rah, f., belt; waist
ciò, cho, pron., that; it
ciocca, chock-kah, f., (hair) lock

ciocchè, chock-**kay**, pron., that which ; what
cioccolata, chock-ko-lah-tah, f., chocolate
cioè, cho-ay, adv., namely, that is to say
ciondolare, chon-do-lah-ray, v., to dangle
ciondolo, chon-do-lo, m., trinket ; fob ; pendant
ciotola, cho-to-lah, f., bowl
ciottolo, chot-to-lo, m., pebble
cipiglio, che-pee-l'yo, m., frown
cipolla, che-pol-lah, f., onion ; (nozzle) rose
cipollina, che-pol-lee-nah, f., chive
cipolline, che-pol-lee-nay, f. pl., little onions
cipresso, che-press-so, m., cypress
cipria, chee-pre-ah, f., toilet-powder
circa, cheer-kah, prep., about, regarding, adv., about
circo, cheer-ko, m., circus ; amphitheatre [cular
circolare, cheer-ko-lah-ray, v., to circulate, f., cir-
circolo, cheer-ko-lo, m., circle ; club
circoncidere, cheer-kon-chee-day-ray, v., to
   circumcise
circondare, cheer-kon-dah-ray, v., to surround
circondario, cheer-kon-dah-re'o, m., district
circuire, cheer-koo'ee-ray, v., to surround
cisposo*, chiss-po-zo, a., blear-eyed
citare, che-tah-ray, v., to cite ; to summons
citrullo, che-trooll-lo, m., blockhead. a.,* stupid
città, chit-tah, f., city ; town
cittadino, chit-tah-dee-no, m., citizen ; inhabitant
ciuco, choo-ko, m., donkey
ciuffo, choof-fo, m., tuft of hair
ciurma, choor-mah, f., crew ; riffraff
civetta, che-vet-tah, f., owl ; coquette
civettare, che-vet-tah-ray, v., to flirt
civile, che-vee-lay, a., civil, courteous
civiltà, che-vil-tah, f., civility
clamore, klah-mor-ay, m., clamour
clamoroso*, klah-mo-ro-zo, a., clamorous
claretto, klah-ret-to, m., claret
classico, klahss-se-ko, m., classic. a., classical
classificare, klahss-se-fe-kah-ray, v., to classify
claudia, klah'oo-de'ah, f., greengage
clausola, klah'oo-zo-lah, f., clause, stipulation
clausura, klah'oo-zoo-rah, f., seclusion ; enclosure

clava, klah-vah. f., (bludgeon) club
clavicola, klah-vee-ko-lah, f., collar-bone, **clavicule**
clemenza, klay-men-tsah, f., clemency ; **mildness**
clericale, klay-re-kah-lay, a., clerical
clero, klay-ro, m., clergy
cliente, kle-en-tay, m. & f., client
clima, klee-mah, m., climate ; region
clistere, kliss-tay-ray, m., enema
cloaca, klo-ah-kah, f., sewer, drain
cloro, klo-ro, m., chlorine
cloruro, klo-roo-ro, m., chloride
coadesione, ko-ah-day-ze'o-nay, f., cohesion
coadiuvare, ko-ah-de'oo-vah-ray, v., to assist
coattivo*, ko-aht-tee-vo, a., coercive
coatto, ko-aht-to, m., prisoner. a., compelled
cocca, kock-kah, f., notch
coccarda, kock-kar-dah, f., cockade
cocchiere, kock-ke'ay-ray, m., coachman
cocchio, kock-ke'o, m., carriage, vehicle
cocciuto*, kot-choo-to, a., stubborn, obstinate
cocco, kock-ko, m., cocoa-nut
coccodrillo, kock-ko-dreel-lo, m., crocodile
cocente, ko-chen-tay, a., burning
cocere, ko-chay-ray, v., to cook
cocomero, ko-ko-may-ro, m., water-melon
cocuzzolo, ko-koot-tso-lo, m., summit, top
coda, ko-dah, f., tail ; queue ; (dress) train
codardia, ko-dar-dee-ah, f., cowardice
codardo, ko-dar-do, m., coward
codazzo, ko-daht-tso, m., suite, attendance
codesto, ko-dess-to, pron., that. a., that
codice, ko-de-chay. m., code ; codex
codicillo, ko-de-cheel-lo, m., codicil
codino, ko-dee-no, m., pig-tail
coerede, ko-ay-ray-day, m. & f., co-heir ; co-heiress
coerente, ko-ay-ren-tay, a., coherent ; united
coetaneo, ko-ay-tah-nay-o, a., contemporary
coevo, ko-ay-vo, m., of same period
cofano, ko-fah-no, m., trunk, box
coffa, kof-fah, f., (ship) crow's nest
cogliere, ko-l'yay-ray, v., to gather ; to catch
coglione, ko-l'yo-nay, m., testicle ; (fig.) dunce

coglitore, ko-l'ye-tor-ay, m., gatherer, harvester

cognata, ko-n'yah-tah, f., sister-in-law

cognato, ko-n'yah-to, m., brother-in-law. a., related

cognito, ko-n'ye-to, a., known

cognizione, ko-n'ye-tse'o-nay, f., knowledge

cognome, ko-n'yo-may, m., surname, family-name

coi, ko'e, (=con i), with the

coiame, ko-c-yah-may, m., leather, hides

coincidenza, ko-in-che-den-tsah, f., coincidence ; (train, etc.) connection

col, kol, (=con il), with the

colà, ko-lah, adv., there, yonder

colare, ko-lah-ray, v., to flow, to drip ; to strain

colatoio, ko-lah-to-e'o, m., sieve ; colander

colazione, ko-lah-tse'o-nay, f., lunch. **prima colazione**, breakfast

colla, koll-lah, f., glue ; paste

collana, koll-lah-nah, f., necklace

collare, koll-lah-ray, m., collar ; band

collasso, koll-lahss-so, m., collapse

colle, koll-lay, m., hill ; pass

collegio, koll-lay-jo, m., college ; community

collera, koll-lay-rah, f., anger

colletta, koll-let-tah, f., collection

colletto, koll-let-to, m., collar

collezione, koll-lay-tse'o-nay, f., collection ; choice

collina, koll-lee-nah, f., hillock

collo, koll-lo, m., neck ; parcel ; packet

collo, koll-lo, (=con lo), with the

collocamento, koll-lo-kah-men-to, m., employment ; appointment

collocare, koll-lo-kah-ray, v., to place

colloquio, koll-lo-kwe'o, m., interview ; conference

colluttazione, koll-loot-tah-tse'o-nay, f., struggle

colmare, koll-mah-ray, v., to fill up

colmo, koll-mo, m., top ; acme. a., full

colomba, ko-lomm-bah, m., dove

colombaia, ko-lomm-bah-e'ah, f., pigeon-house

colombario, ko-lomm-bah-re'o, m., burial niche

colonia, ko-lo-ne'ah, f., colony

coloniali, ko-lo-ne'ah-le, m. pl., groceries ; drugs

colonna, ko-lon-nah, f., column

colono, ko-lo-no, m., colonist, settler ; farmer

colorare, ko-lo-**rah**-ray, v., to colour

colore, ko-lo-ray, m., colour

coloro, ko-lo-ro, pron., those ; they

colpa, koll-pah, f., fault ; guilt ; offence

colpevole, koll-**pay**-vo-lay, a., guilty. m., culprit

colpire, koll-pee-ray, v., to hit

colpo, koll-po, m., blow ; shot   [ing-knife

coltellaccio, koll-tell-laht-cho, m., cutlass ; hunt-

coltellata, koll-tell-lah-tah, f., stab

coltellinaio, koll-tell-le-nah-e'o, m., cutler

coltello, koll-tell-lo, m., knife

colto*, koll-to, a., educated ; cultivated

coltre, koll-tray, f., quilt ; coverlet

colubro, ko-loo-bro, m., serpent

colui, ko-loo-e, pron., he, him ; that

comandare, ko-mahn-**dah**-ray, v., to command

comandita, ko-**mahn**-de-tah, f., joint-stock com-

comando, ko-**mahn**-do, m., command   [pany

comare, ko-mah-ray, f., midwife ; gossip

combaciare, kom-bah-**chah**-ray, v., to join

combattere, kom-**baht**-tay-ray, v., to fight

combattimento, kom-baht-te-**men**-to, m., fight

combinare, kom-be-nah-ray, v., to combine

combriccola, kom-**brick**-ko-lah, f., gang ; clique

combustibile, kom-booss-tee-be-lay, m., fuel

come, ko-may, adv., so ; as ; like ; while ; how

comecchessia, ko-meck-kess-see-ah, adv., be it
as it may

cometa, ko-**may**-tah, f., comet ; (fig.) bolt from
the blue

comico, ko-me-ko, m., comedian. a.,* comical

comignolo, ko-mee-n'yo-lo, m., chimney-stack

cominciamento, ko-min-chah-**men**-to, m., commencement

cominciante, ko-min-**chahn**-tay, m., beginner

cominciare, ko-min-**chah**-ray, v., to begin

comitato, ko-me-tah-to, m., committee

comitiva, ko-me-tee-vah, f., party

comizio, ko-mee-tse'o, m., meeting

commediante, kom-may-de-**ahn**-tay, m. & f., comedian, actor, actress

commendare, kom-men-dah-ray, v., to praise
commendevole, kom-men-day-vo-lay, a., praise-worthy
commensale, kom-men-sah-lay, m. & f., table-companion
commentare, kom-men-tah-ray, v., to comment
commerciale, kom-mair-chah-lay, a., commercial
commerciante, kom-mair-chahn-tay, m., trader
commerciare, kom-mair-chah-ray, v., to trade
commercio, kom-mair-cho, m., commerce
commesso, kom-mess-so, m., clerk ; shop-assistant
commestibile, kom-mess-tee-be-lay, m., victual. a., eatable
commettere, kom-met-tay-ray, v., to commit ; to commiato, kom-me'ah-to, m., leave [order
commilitone, kom-me-le-to-nay, m., comrade
comminare, kom-me-nah-ray, v., to threaten
commiserare, kom-me-zay-rah-ray, v., to pity
commissionario, kom-miss-se'o-nah-re'o, m., commission-agent
committente, kom-mit-ten-tay, m., customer
commovente, kom-mo-ven-tay, a., touching
commuovere, kom-moo'o-vay-ray, v., to affect
commuoversi, kom-moo'o-vair-se, v., to be moved
commutare, kom-moo-tah-ray, v., to change
commutatore, kom-moo-tah-tor-ay, m., (electric) switch
comodità, ko-mo-de-tah, f., commodity ; comfort ; opportunity
comodo*, ko-mo-do, a., commodious
compagnia, kom-pah-n'yee-ah, f., company; society
compagno, kom-pah-n'yo, m., companion ; partner
comparabile, kom-pah-rah-be-lay, a., comparable
comparare, kom-pah-rah-ray, v., to compare
compare, kom-pah-ray, m., godfather ; (pop.) pal
comparire, kom-pah-ree-ray, v., to appear
comparsa, kom-par-sah, f., appearance ; straw-man ; (stage) figurante
compartecipare, kom-par-tay-che-pah-ray, v., to participate
compartimento, kom-par-te-men-to, m., compartment ; division ; section

compartire, kom-par-tee-ray, v., to distribute

compassionevole, kom-pahss-se'o-**nay**-vo-lay, a., pitiable, moving, touching

compasso, kom-**pahss**-so, m.,compass ; compasses

compatimento, kom-pah-te-**men**-to, m., compassion ; indulgence

compatire, kom-pah-**tee**-ray, v.,to pity ; to absolve

compatto*, kom-**paht**-to, a., compact

compendio, kom-**pen**-de'o, m., abridgment

compenso, kom-**pen**-so, m., compensation ; reward ; balance

compera, kom-**pay**-rah, f., purchase

competente, kom-pay-**ten**-tay, a., competent. m. & f., expert

competere, kom-**pay**-tay-ray, v., to compete ; to be incumbent upon

compiacente, kom-pe'ah-**chen**-tay, a., obliging

compiacenza, kom-pe'ah-**chen**-tsah, f., kindness

compiacere, kom-pe'ah-**chay**-ray, v., to oblige ; to please

compiacimento, kom-pe'ah-che-**men**-to, m., pleasure ; consent

compiangere, kom-pe'**ahn**-jay-ray, v., to bewail

compianto, kom-pe'**ahn**-to, m., lamentation

compiere, compire, kom-pe'**ay**-ray, kom-**pee**-ray, v., to complete ; to fulfil

compilare, kom-pe-**lah**-ray, v., to compile

compimento, kom-pe-**men**-to, m., accomplishment ; fulfilment ; completion

compitare, kom-pe-**tah**-ray, v., to spell ; to reckon

compitezza, kom-pe-**tet**-tsah, f., politeness

compito*, kom-**pee**-to, a., accomplished, complete

compito, **kom**-pe-to, m., task ; duty ; homework

compiuto*, kom-pe'**oo**-to, a., ended, completed

compleanno, kom-play-**ahn**-no, m., birthday

complementare, kom-play-men-**tah**-ray, a., additional ; auxiliary

complessione, kom-pless-se'o-**nay**, f., constitution

complessivo, kom-pless-**see**-vo, a., comprehensive. m., sum total

complesso, kom-**pless**-so, a., complex ; whole

completare, kom-play-**tah**-ray, v., to complete

completo*, kom-play-to, a., complete ; full up

complicare, kom-ple-kah-ray, v., to complicate

complice, kom-ple-chay, m. & f., accomplice

complimento, kom-ple-men-to, m., compliment

componente, kom-po-nen-tay, m., component ; member

componimento, kom-po-ne-men-to, m., composition

comporre, kom-por-ray, v., to compose ; to adjust differences ; to compound

comportabile, kom-por-tah-be-lay, a., tolerable

comportare, kom-por-tah-ray, v., to tolerate

comportarsi, kom-por-tar-se, v., to behave

compositore, kom-po-ze-tor-ay, m., composer ; compositor

composizione, kom-po-ze-tse'o-nay, f., composition ; settlement ; arrangement

composta, kom-poss-tah, f., stewed fruit

composto, kom-poss-to, m., mixture, compound

compra, kom-prah, f., purchase

comprare, kom-prah-ray, v., to purchase

compratore, kom-prah-tor-ay, m., buyer

comprendere, kom-pren-day-ray, v., to understand ; to include

comprensibile, kom-pren-see-be-lay, a., comprehensible

comprensibilità, kom-pren-se-be-le-tah, f., comprehension

compressa, kom-press-sah, f., compress

comprimere, kom-pree-may-ray, v., to compress

compromettere, kom-pro-met-tay-ray, v., to compromise

comprovare, kom-pro-vah-ray, v., to prove

compunto*, kom-poonn-to, a., repentant   [tion

compunzione, kom-poonn-tse'o-nay, f., compunc-

computare, kom-poo-tah-ray, v., to compute

computista, kom-poo-tiss-tah, m., reckoner

computo, kom-poo-to, m., reckoning, account

comune, ko-moo-nay, m., commune. a., usual, trivial, vulgar

comunicarsi, ko-moo-ne-kar-se, v., to receive the Holy Communion

comunismo, ko-moo-niss'mo, m., communism
comunque, ko-moon'kway, adv., however
con, kon, prep., with ; by
conato, ko-nah'to, m., effort ; vain attempt
conca, kon'kah, f., basin ; shell ; broad valley
concatenare, kon-kah-tay-nah-ray, v., to link up
concausa, kon-kah'oo-zah, f., joint cause
concavo*, kon-kah'vo, a., concave
concedere, kon-chay-day-ray, v., to concede
concentrare, kon-chen-trah'ray, v., to concentrate
concepibile, kon-chay-pee-be-lay, a., conceivable
conceria, kon-chay-ree-ah, f., tannery
concernere, kon-chair-nay-ray, v., to concern
concertare, kon-chair-tah-ray, v., to concert
concerto, kon-chair-to, m., concert ; scheme
concessionario, kon-chess-se'o-nah-re'o, m., grantee
concessione, kon-chess-se'O-nay, f., concession
concetto, kon-chet-to, m., sense ; aim ; matter
concezione, kon-chay-tse'o-nay, f., conception
conchiglia, kon-kee-l'yah, f., shell ; shell-fish
conchiudere, kon-ke'oo-day-ray, v., to conclude
concia, kon-chah, f., tanning ; tan
conciare, kon-chah-ray, v., to tan ; to preserve
conciatore, kon-chah-tor-ay, m., tanner
conciliare, kon-che-le'ah-ray, v., to conciliate
conciliazione, kon-che-le'ah-tse'o-nay, f., reconciliation ; conciliation ; agreement
concilio, kon-chee-le'o, m., council ; assembly
concime, kon-chee-may, m., manure ; fertiliser
concisione, kon-che-ze'O-nay, f., conciseness
conciso*, kon-chee-zo, a., concise
concitare, kon-che-tah-ray, v., to stir up
concittadino, kon-chit-tah-dee-no, m., fellow-citizen
conclave, kon-klah-vay, m., conclave
concludere, kon-kloo-day-ray, v., to conclude
conclusivo*, kon-kloo-see-vo, a., conclusive
concordare, kon-kor-dah-ray, v., to reconcile ; to agree
concordato, kon-kor-dah-to, m., settlement ; composition ; convention
concorde, kon-kor-day, a., unanimous ; agreeable

concordia, kon-kor-de'ah, f., harmony, concord
concorrente, kon-kor-ren-tay, m. & f., competitor
concorrenza, kon-kor-ren-tsah, f., competition
concorrere, kon-kor-ray-ray, v., to compete
concorso, kon-kor-so, m., competition ; concourse
concubito, kon-koo-be-to, m., sleeping together
condanna, kon-dahn-nah, f., condemnation
condannare, kon-dahn-nah-ray, v., to condemn
condannato, kon-dahn-nah-to, m., convict
condensatore, kon-den-sah-tor-ay, m., condenser
condimento, kon-de-men-to, m., seasoning ; vim
condire, kon-dee-ray, v., to season
condiscendere, kon-de-shen-day-ray, v., to condescend
condiscepolo, kon-de-shay-po-lo, m., school-fellow
condividere, kon-de-vee-day-ray v., to share with
condizionare, kon-de-tse'o-nah-ray, v., to condition ; to subject to conditions
condizione, kon-de-tse'o-nay, f., condition ; rank ; calling
condoglianza, kon-do-l'yahn-tsah, f., condolence
condominio, kon-do-mee-ne'o, m., joint-rule ; joint-property
condonare, kon-do-nah-ray, v., to pardon
condotta, kon-dot-tah, f.,conduct ; administration
condottiere, kon-dot-te'ay-ray, m., leader
condotto, kon-dot-to, m., conduit. **medico —,** panel-doctor
conducente, kon-doo-chen-tay, m. & f., driver ; guide. **conducive** a., leading
condurre, kon-doohr-ray, v., to conduct ; to lead ; to drive
conduttore, kon-doot-tor-ay, m., guide ; driver
confederale, kon-fay-day-rah-lay, a., confederate
conferenza, kon-fay-ren-tsah, f., conference ; lecture ; interview
conferenziere, kon-fay-ren-tse'ay-ray, m.,lecturer
conferire, kon-fay-ree-ray, v., to confer, to bestow
conferma, kon-fair-mah, f., confirmation
confermare, kon-fair-mah-ray, v., to confirm ; to sanction
confessare, kon-fess-sah-ray, v., to confess

confessione, kon-fess-se'o-nay, f., confession

confetteria, kon-fet-tay-ree-ah, f., confectionery

confettiere, kon-fet-te'ay-ray, m., confectioner

confetto, kon-fet-to, m., sweet; candy

confettura, kon-fet-too-rah, f., preserve; sweetmeat; jam

confezionare, kon-fay-tse'o-nah-ray, v., to manufacture

confezioni, kon-fay-tse'o-ne, f. pl., ready-made clothes

conficcare, kon-fick-kah-ray, v., to nail in; to peg

confidare, kon-fe-dah-ray, v., to confide; to rely upon

confidenza, kon-fe-den-tsah, f., confidence, familiarity

configgere, kon-feed-jay-ray, v., to fix into

confinare, kon-fe-nah-ray, v., to banish; to limit; to border upon

confinato, kon-fe-nah-to, m., temporarily banished

confine, kon-fee-nay, m., boundary; exile

confino, kon-fee-no, m., temporary banishment

confisca, kon-fiss-kah, f., confiscation

conflitto, kon-flit-to, m., conflict; dispute

confondere, kon-fon-day-ray, v., to confound

conformare, kon-for-mah-ray, v., to conform

confortare, kon-for-tah-ray, v., to comfort

confortevole, kon-for-tay-vo-lay, a., comforting

conforto, kon-for-to, m., comfort

confrontare, kon-fron-tah-ray, v., to confront; to compare

confusamente, kon-foo-zah-men-tay, adv., in confusion; indistinctly

confuso*, kon-foo-zo, a., confused; obscure

confutare, kon-foo-tah-ray, v., to confute

congedare, kon-jay-dah-ray, v., to dismiss

congedo, kon-jay-do, m., leave, furlough; discharge

congegnare, kon-jay-n'yah-ray, v., to assemble; to plot; to devise

congegno, kon-jay-n'yo, m., mechanism; device

congelare, kon-jay-lah-ray, v., to congeal

congettura, kon-jet-too-rah, f., conjecture

congetturare, kon-jet-too-rah-ray, v., to surmise

congiungere, kon-joonn-jay-ray, v., to join [ed
congiunto, kon-joonn-to, m., relation. a., connect-
congiuntura, kon-joonn-too-rah, f., conjuncture
congiunzione, kon-joonn-tse'o-nay, f., conjunction ; connection
congiura, kon-joo-rah, f., conspiracy
congiuraro, kon-joo-rah-ray, v., to conjure ; to plot
congiurato, kon-joo-rah-to, m., conspirator
congratulare, kon-grah-too-lah-ray, v., to congratulate
congregare, kon-gray-gah-ray, v., to assemble
congresso, kon-gress-so, m., congress ; assembly
congrua, kon-groo-ah, f., clerical stipend
congruo, kon-groo'o, a., suitable. fit
coniare, ko-ne'ah-ray, v., to coin ; to invent
conico, ko-ne-ko, a., conical
coniglio, ko-nee-l'yo, m., rabbit ; (fig.) coward
conio, ko-ne'o, m., die ; coinage
coniugale, ko-ne'oo-gah-lay, a., conjugal
coniugare, ko-ne'oo-gah-ray, v., to conjugate
coniugato, ko-ne'oo-gah-to, a., married
coniuge, ko-ne'oo-jay, m. & f., husband ; wife
connazionale, kon-nah-tse'o-nah-lay, m., fellow-
   countryman
connessione, kon-ness-se'o-nay, f., connection
connettere, kon-net-tay-ray, v., to connect
connivenza, kon-ne-ven-tsah, f., connivance
connotati, kon-no-tah-te, m.pl., marks of identity
connubio, kon-noo-be'o, m., marriage ; union
cono, ko-no, m., cone
conocchia, ko-nock-ke'ah, f., distaff
conoscente, ko-no-shen-tay, m. & f., acquaintance
conoscenza, ko-no-shen-tsah, f., knowledge ; acquaintance
conoscere, ko-no-shay-ray, v., to know
conoscibile, ko-no-shee-be-lay, m., all-knowledge
conoscitore, ko-no-she-tor-ay, m., connoisseur
conosciuto, ko-no-she'oo-to, a., known, renowned
conquista, kon-kwiss-tah, f., conquest
conquistare, kon-kwiss-tah-ray, v., to conquer
conquistatore, kon-kwiss-tah-tor-ay, m., conqueror

consacrare, kon-sah-**krah**-ray, v., to consecrate
consanguineo*, kon-sahn-goo'ee-nay-o, a., kin
consapevole, kon-sah-**pay**-vo-lay, a., conscious of
conscio*, kon-**she**'o, a., conscious
consegna, kon-**say**-n'yah, f., consignment ; password
consegnare, kon-say-n'yah-ray, v., to consign ; to confine
consegnatario, kon-say-n'yah-tah-re'o, m., consignee
conseguente, kon-say-goo'en-tay, a., ensuing
conseguire, kon-say-goo'ee-ray, v., to obtain
consenso, kon-**sen**-so, m., consent
consentaneo*, kon-sen-**tah**-nay-o, a., suitable
consentire, kon-sen-**tee**-ray, v., to consent
consenziente, kon-sen-tse'en-tay, a.,consenting to
conserva, kon-**sair**-vah, f., preserve
conservatore, kon-sair-vah-**tor**-ay, m., preservative ; (archives) keeper
conservazione, kon-sair-vah-tse'**o**-nay, f., conservation, preservation
consesso, kon-**sess**-so, m., council ; assembly
considerare, kon-se-day-**rah**-ray, v., to consider
considerevole, kon-se-day-**ray**-vo-lay, a., considerable ; important
consigliare, kon-se-l'yah-ray, v., to advise
consigliere, kon-se-l'yay-ray, m., adviser ; councillor
consiglio, kon-**see**-l'yo,m.,advice ; counsel ; council
consimile, kon-see-me-lay, a., similar, alike, akin
consistente, kon-siss-ten-tay, a., firm ; tenacious
consistenza,kon-siss-ten-tsah,f.,firmness;tenacity
consistere, kon-**siss**-tay-ray, v., to consist
consociare, kon-so-**chah**-ray, v., to associate ; to take into partnership
consocio, kon-so-cho, m., co-partner
consolare, kon-so-lah-ray, v., to console
consolato, kon-so-**lah**-to, m., consulate
console, kon-so-lay, m., consul
consolidare, kon-so-le-**dah**-ray, v., to consolidate
consono, kon-so-no, a., consistent ; conforming
consorte, kon-**sor**-tay, m. & f., consort

consorzio, kon-**sor**-tse'o,m.,partnership ; syndicate

constare, kon-**stah**-ray, v., to be evident ; to consist of

constatare, kon-stah-**tah**-ray, v., to ascertain

consueto*, kon-soo'**ay**-to, a., usual, habitual

consuetudine, kon-soo'ay-**too**-de-nay, f., custom

consulente, kon-soo-**len**-tay, a., consulting. m., counsel

consultare, kon-sooll-**tah**-ray, v., to consult

consulto, kon-**sooll**-to, m., (med.) consultation

consumare, kon-soo-**mah**-ray, v., to consume

consumo, kon-**soo**-mo, m., consumption ; waste. dazio —, excise

consuntivo, kon-soonn-**tee**-vo, a., consumptive. conto —, (commercial) final balance

consunzione, kon-soonn-tse'o-nay, f.,consumption

contabile, kon-**tah**-be-lay, m., book-keeper ; bank-accountant

contabilità, kon-tah-be-le-**tah**, f., book-keeping

contachilometri, kon - tah - ke - **lo** - may - tre, m., speedometer

contadinesco*, kon-tah-de-**ness**-ko. a., rustic

contadino, kon-tah-**dee**-no, m., peasant

contado, kon-**tah**-do, m., country-side

contagiare,kon-tah-**jah**-ray,v.,to infect ; to corrupt

contagio, kon-**tah**-jo, m., contagion ; (fig.) plague

contaminare, kon-tah-me-**nah**-ray, v., to contaminate

contanti, kon-**tahn**-te, m. pl., cash

contare, kon-**tah**-ray, v., to count. — **su**, to rely upon

contatore, kon-tah-**tor**-ay, m., meter

contatto, kon-**taht**-to, m., contact ; touch

conte, **kon**-tay, m., count

contea, kon-**tay**-ah, f., county

conteggiare, kon-ted-**jah**-ray, v., to calculate

contegno, kon-**tay**-n'yo, m., behaviour ; aspect

contegnoso*,kon-tay-n'yo-zo.a.,reserved; haughty

contemplare, kon-tem-**plah**-ray, v., to contemplate ; to include

contemporaneo, kon-tem-po-**rah**-nay-o, m., contemporary. a.,* contemporary

contendere, kon-ten-day-ray, v., to contend; to forbid

contenente, kon-tay-nen-tay, a., containing

contenenza, kon-tay-nen-tsah, f., contents

contenere, kon-tay-nay-ray, v., to contain; to restrain; to hold back

contentare, kon-ten-tah-ray, v., to content

contentezza, kon-ten-tet-tsah, f., contentment; pleasure

contenuto, kon-tay-noo-to, m., contents

conteria, kon-tay-ree-ah, f., jet; beads

contesa, kon-tay-zah, f., dispute; contest

contessa, kon-tess-sah, f., countess

contessere, kon-tess-say-ray, v., to entwine

contestare, kon-tay-stah-ray, v., to contest

contestazione, kon-tay-stah-tse'o-nay, f., contest; debate; denial

contesto, kon-tess-to, m., context

contiguo*, kon-tee-goo'o, a., contiguous, near

continenza, kon-te-nen-tsah, f., continence, forbearance

contingentamento, kon-tin-jen-tah-men-to, m., apportionment per quota

contingente, kon-tin-jen-tay, m., contingent; quantity; share. a., contingent

continuare, kon-te-noo'ah-ray, v., to continue

continuità, kon-te-noo'e-tah, f., continuity; constancy

continuo*, kon-tee-noo'o, a., continuous

conto, kon-to, m., account, bill; story

contorcere, kon-tor-chay-ray, v., to contort; to writhe

contornare, kon-tor-nah-ray, v., to frame; to surround

contorno, kon-tor-no, m., circuit; edge; outline

contorto*, kon-tor-to, a., twisted; crooked

contra, kon-trah, prep., opposite to, against

contrabbandiere, kon-trahb-bahn-de'ay-ray, m., smuggler

contrabbando, kon-trahb-bahn-do, m., smuggling; contraband

contrabbasso, kon-trahb-bahss-so, m., double-bass

contraccambiare, kon-trahk-kahm-be'ah-ray, v., to reciprocate

contraccolpo, kon-trahk-**koll**-po, m., counter-blow; recoil; rebound; consequence

contrada, kon-trah-dah, f., road; country, region

contraddire, kon-trahd-**dee**-ray, v., to contradict; to deny

contradditorio, kon-trah-de-tor-e'o, a.,*contradictory; opposed. m., cross-examination

contradizione, kon-trah-de-tse'o-nay, f., contradiction

contraente, kon-trah-en-tay, m.,contracting party

contraffare, kon-trahf-**fah**-ray, v., to counterfeit, to adulterate

contraffattore, kon-trahf-faht-**tor**-ay, m., forger; imitator

contraffazione, kon-trahf-fah-tse'o-nay, f., forgery

contrafforte, kon-trahf-**for**-tay, m., buttress

contrammandare, kon-trahm-mahn-**dah**-ray, v., to countermand, to cancel

contrammarca, kon-trahm-**mar**-kah, f., counter-mark; check

contrammiraglio, kon-trahm-me-**rah**-l'yo, m., rear-admiral

contrappesare, kon-trahp-pay-**zah**-ray, v., to counterbalance; to estimate; to examine

contrappeso, kon-trahp-**pay**-zo, m., counter-weight; counterpoise

contrapporre, kon-trahp-**por**-ray, v., to oppose; to compare

contrariare, kon-trah-re'**ah**-ray, v., to gainsay

contrarietà, kon-trah-re'ay-**tah,** f., disappointment; hinderance

contrario, kon-**trah**-re'o, m., contrary; opponent. a.,* opposite; inimical; adverse

contrarre, kon-**trar**-ray, v., to contract; to shrink

contrarrestare, kon-trar-ray-**stah**-ray, v., to put a stop to

contrassegnare, kon-trahss-say-n'**yah**-ray, v., to countersign; to place a mark upon

contrassegno, kon-trahss-**say**-n'yo, m., counter-sign; mark; proof

contrastare, kon-trah-**stah**-ray, v., to contrast ; to oppose ; to compare ; to refute

contrattabile, kon-traht-tah-be-lay, a., negotiable

contrattare, kon-traht-tah-ray, v., to contract

contrattempo, kon-traht-**tem**-po, m., untoward event ; misfortune, mishap

contrattuale, kon-traht-too'**ah**-lay, a., in accordance with agreement

contravveleno, kon-trahv-vay-lay-no, m., antidote

contravvenire, kon-trahv-vay-ne-ray, v., to contravene

contravventore, kon-trahv-ven-**tor**-ay, m., infringer

contravviso, kon-trahv-**vee**-zo, m., countermand

contribuente, kon-tre-boo'**en**-tay, m., contributor ; tax-payer

contributo, kon-tre-**boo**-to, m., participation ; voluntary contribution

contristare, kon-tre-**stah**-ray, v., to sadden ; to afflict

contrito*, kon-**tree**-to, a., repentant

contrizione, kon-tre-tse'**o**-nay, f., contrition

contro, **kon**-tro, prep., against ; contrary to. di —, facing

controllo, kon-**troll**-lo, m., control, checking

contrordinare, kon-tror-de-nah-ray, v., to countermand

controverso*, kon-tro-**vair**-so, a., debated ; questionable

contumace, kon-too-**mah**-chay, a., contumacious ; defaulting. m. & f., defaulter

contumelia, kon-too-**may**-le'ah, f., abuse ; offence

contundente, kon-toonn-**den**-tay, a., blunt

conturbare, kon-toohr-**bah**-ray, v., to trouble

contuso, kon-**too**-zo, a., hurt, bruised

contuttochè, kon - toot - to - **kay**, conj., though, although

contuttociò, kon-toot-to-**cho**, adv., however, yet

convalescenza, kon-vah-lay-**shen**-tsah, f., recovery, convalescence

convalidare, kon-vah-le-**dah**-ray, v., to confirm ; to render valid ; to corroborate

convegno, kon-**vay**-n'yo,m.,appointment; congress

convenevoli, kon-vay-**nay**-vo-le, m. pl., compliments

conveniente, kon-vay-ne-**en**-tay, a., convenient, fitting ; decent

convenire, kon-vay-**nee**-ray, v., to agree ; **to fit** ; to suit

convento, kon-**ven**-to, m., convent

conventuale, kon-ven-too-**ah**-lay, a., conventual ; monastic

convenuto, kon-vay-**noo**-to, m., dependant ; agreement. a., agreed upon

convenzione, kon-ven-tse'o-nay, f., convention

convergere, kon-**vair**-jay-ray, v., to converge

conversare, kon-**vair**-sah-ray, v., to converse

conversazione, kon-vair-sah-tse'o-nay, f., conversation ; chat

convertire, kon-vair-**tee**-ray, v., to convert

convertito, kon-vair-**tee**-to, m., convert. a., converso°

convesso°, kon-**vess**-so, a., convex [verted

convincente, kon-veen-**chen**-tay, a., convincing

convincere, kon-**veen**-chay-ray, v., to convince

convinto°, kon-**veen**-to, a., convinced, persuaded

convitato, kon-ve-**tah**-to, m., guest. a., invited

convito, kon-**vee**-to, m., invitation ; party

convitto, kon-**veet**-to, m., boarding-school

convittore, kon-veet-**tor**-ay, m., boarder

convivere, kon-**vee**-vay-ray, v., to live with

convocare, kon-vo-**kah**-ray, v., to call together

convocazione, kon-vo-kah-tse'o-nay, f., meeting ; summon ; summons

convogliare, kon-vo-l'**yah**-ray, v., to convoy

convoglio, kon-vo-l'yo, m., train ; convoy

convulso°, kon-**vool**-so, a., convulsed

cooperare, ko-o-pay-**rah**-ray, v., to co-operate

coordinare, ko-or-de-**nah**-ray, v., to set in order

coperchio, ko-**pair**-ke'o, m., cover, lid

coperta, ko-**pair**-tah, f.,blanket ;cover ;upper-deck

copertina, ko-pair-**tee**-nah, f., wrapper

coperto, ko-**pair**-to, m., cover ; refuge. a.,° covered ; overcast ; (mil.) hidden

copertone, ko-pair-**to**-nay, m., tarpaulin ; tyre

copertura, ko-pair-too-rah, f., cover ; roof ; surety
copia, ko-pee-ah, f., copy ; plenty
copiare, ko-pe'ah-ray, v., to copy
copiativo, ko-pe'ah-tee-vo,a.,(ink or pencil)copying
copiatura, ko-pe'ah-too-rah, f., copy ; imitation
copiosità, ko-pe'o-ze-tah, f., abundance, plenty
copista, ko-piss-tah, m., copyist, transcriber
coppa, kop-pah, f., cup ; back of the head
coppia, kop-pe'ah, f., couple, brace
copripiedi, ko-pre-pe'ay-de, m., travelling-rug
coprire, ko-pree-ray, v., to cover ; to hide
copritavola, ko-pre-tah-vo-lah, f., table-cloth
coraggio, ko-rahd-jo, m., courage ; (fig.) cheek
corale, ko-rah-lay, m., chorus. a., choral
corallo, ko-rahl-lo, m., coral
corame, ko-rah-may, m., leather
coramella, ko-rah-mell-lah, f., razor-strop
corazza, ko-raht-tsah, f., cuirass, breastplate
corazzata, ko-raht-tsah-tah, f., battleship
corba, kor-bah, f., basket
corbellare, kor-bell-lah-ray, v.,to mock, to laugh at
corbelleria, kor-bell-lay-ree-ah, f., tomfoolery
corbello, kor-bell-lo, m., basket
corbezzoli, kor-bet-tso-le, interj., by Jove ! egad !
corda, kor-dah, f., string ; sinew ; gut
cordaio, kor-dah-e'o, m., rope-maker
cordame, kor-dah-may, m., rigging ; ropes
cordella, kor-dell-lah, f., tape
cordellare, kor-dell-lah-ray, v., to twist ; to braid
corderia, kor-day-ree-ah, f., rope-manufactory
cordialità, kor-de'ah-le-tah, f., cordiality
cordoglio, kor-do-l'yo, m., grief ; heart-break
cordone, kor-do-nay, m., braid
coreggia, ko-red-jah, f., leather-strop ; thong
coricarsi, ko-re-kar-se, v., to go to bed ; to lie flat
coricino, ko-re-chee-no, m., little darling
corista, ko-riss-tah, m. & f., chorister ; tuning-fork
cornacchia, kor-nahk-ke'ah, f., rook ; chatterer
cornamusa, kor-nah-moo-zah, f., bag-pipe
corneo, kor-nay-o, a., horny
cornetta, kor-net-tah, f., cornet ; horn
cornetto, kor-net-to, m., little horn ; lump

cornice, kor-nee-chay, f., cornice ; frame
corno, kor-no, m., horn
cornuto*, kor-noo-to, a., horned. m., cuckold
coro, ko-ro, m., chorus ; choir
corona, ko-ro-nah. f., crown ; wreath
coronare, ko-ro-nah-ray, v., to crown
corpacciuto, kor-paht-choo-to, a., corpulent
corpetto, kor-pet-to, m., jersey ; doublet
corpo, kor-po, m., body ; society ; mass
corpulenza, kor-poo-len-tsah, f., corpulence
corpuscolo, kor-pooss-ko-lo, m., corpuscle ; atom
corredare, kor-ray-dah-ray, v., to equip ; to adorn
corredo, kor-ray-do, m., outfit ; trousseau
correggere, kor-red-jay-ray, v., to correct
correggia, kor-red-jah, f., leather-strap
correlativo*, kor-ray-lah-tee-vo, a., correlative
corrente, kor-ren-tay, f., stream ; draught.
  a., flowing ; usual ; (month) instant
correntista, kor-ren-tiss-tah, m. & f., current
  account holder
correre, kor-ray-ray, v., to run ; to stream
correspettivo, kor-ress-pet-tee-vo, a.,* relative.
  m., equivalent
corretto*, kor-ret-to, a., correct ; exact
correttore, kor-ret-tor-ay, m., (press) reader
corridoio, kor-re-do-e'o, m., corridor
corridore, kor-re-dor-ay, m., runner
corriera, kor-re'ay-rah, f., mail-coach
corriere, kor-re'ay-ray, m., mail ; courier
corrispondere, kor-riss-pon-day-ray, v., to correspond
corroborare, kor-ro-bo-rah-ray, v., to corroborate
corrodere, kor-ro-day-ray, v., to corrode
corrompere, kor-rom-pay-ray, v., to corrupt
corrosione, kor-ro-ze'o-nay, f., corrosion
corrotto*, kor-rot-to, a., corrupted   [to vex
corrucciare, kor-root-chah-ray, v., to torment ;
corruccio, kor-root-cho, m., wrath ; vexation
corrugare, kor-roo-gah-ray, v., to corrugate ;
  to frown
corruscare, kor-roos-kah-ray, v., to glitter.
  to sparkle

corruttela, kor-root-tay-lah, f., corruption
corruttibile, kor-root-tee-be-lay, a., **corruptible**
corruzione, kor-roo-tse'o-nay, f., corruption
corsa, kor-sah, f., run ; race ; train
corsaletto, kor-sah-let-to, m., breastplate
corsaro, kor-sah-ro, m., corsair
corseggiare, kor-sed-jah-ray, v., to plunder
corsia, kor-see-ah, f., (in a ward) passage
corsiero, kor-se'ay-ro, m., steed
corsivo, kor-see-vo, m., italics
corso, kor-so, m., course ; main street ; **drive** ;
   exchange ; flow ; route
corte, kor-tay, f., court ; court-yard
corteccia, kor-tet-chah, f., bark ; skin
corteggiare, kor-ted-jah-ray, v., to court
corteggio, kor-ted-jo, m., retinue, attendance
corteo, kor-tay-o, m., procession
cortese, kor-tay-zay, a., courteous
cortezza, kor-tet-tsah, f., brevity, **shortness**
cortigiano, kor-te-jah-no, m., courtier
cortile, kor-tee-lay, m., court-yard
cortina, kor-tee-nah, f., curtain ; **screen**
corto*, kor-to, a., short
corvetta, kor-vet-tah, f., sloop
corvino, kor-vee-no, a., raven-black
corvo, kor-vo, m., crow
cosa, ko-zah, f., thing, matter
coscetto, ko-shet-to, m., leg of mutton
coscia, ko-she'ah, f., thigh
coscienza, ko-she'en-tsah, f., conscience
coscienzioso*, ko-she'en-tse'o-zo, a., conscientious
coscritto, ko-skrit-to, m., conscript
cosi, ko-zee, adv., so : thus : as. basta—! enough !
cosicchè, ko-zick-kay, conj., so that
cosino, ko-zee-no, m., little thing
coso, ko-zo, m., little thing ; (fig.) simpleton
cospargere, koss-par-jay-ray, v., to sprinkle, to
cospetto, koss-pet-to, m., presence   [strew
cospicuo*, koss-pee-koo'o, a., conspicuous
cospirare, koss-pe-rah-ray, v., to conspire
cospiratore, koss-pe-rah-tor-ay, m., **conspirator**
cospirazione, koss-pe-rah-tse'o-nay, f., **conspiracy**

costa, koss-tah, f., rib ; coast ; slope

costà, koss-tah, adv., there ; by there

costaggiù, koss-tahd-joo, adv., down there, yonder

costante, koss-tahn-tay, a., constant

costanza, koss-tahn-tsah, f., constancy

costare, koss-tah-ray, v., to cost

costassù, koss-tahss-soo, adv., up there ; there above

costatare, koss-tah-tah-ray, v., to prove ; to estab-

costato, koss-tah-to, m., breast, ribs [lish

costeggiare, koss-ted-jah-ray, v., to coast

costei, koss-tay-e, pron., she ; this woman

costellazione, koss-tell-lah-tse'o-nay, f., constel-
lation

costernarsi, koss-tair-nar-se, v., to be depressed

costernato, koss-tair-nah-to,a.,dismayed ; alarm-

costì, koss-tee, adv., there [ed

costiera, koss-te'ay-rah, f., coast ; cliffs

costipare, koss-te-pah-ray, v., to constipate

costipazione, koss-te-pah-tse'o-nay, f., constipation ; cold

costituire, koss-te-too'ee-ray, v., to constitute

costo, koss-to, m., cost

costola, koss-to-lah, f., rib

costoletta, koss-to-let-tah, f., cutlet

costoro, koss-to-ro, pron., these or those people

costoso, koss-to-zo, a., costly

costretto, koss-tret-to, a., compelled, forced

costringere, koss-treen-jay-ray, v., to compel

costruire, koss-troo'ee-ray, v., to construct

costrutto, koss-troot-to, m., construction ; advantage, profit

costruttore, koss-troot-tor-ay, m., constructor

costui, koss-too-e, pron., he ; this man

costumanza, koss-too-mahn-tsah, f., old custom

costumare, koss-too-mah-ray, v., to accustom,
to be in the habit of

costumato, koss-too-mah-to, a., well-bred ; well-
behaved

costume, koss-too-may, m., usage ; suit, dress

costura, koss-too-rah, f., seam

cotale, ko-tah-lay, pron., such a one

cotanto, ko-tahn-to, adv., so much ; so very

cotenna, ko-ten-nah, f., pig-skin : scalp

cotesto, ko-tess-to, a., this, that. pron., this one, that one

cotidiano*, ko-te-de'ah-no, a., daily

cotogna, ko-to-n'yah, f., quince

cotogno, ko-to-n'yo, m., quince-tree

cotone, ko-to-nay, m., cotton ; cotton-tree

cotonificio, ko-to-ne-fee-cho, m., cotton-mill

cotonina, ko-to-nee-nah, f., calico, cotton-cloth

cotta, kot-tah, f., surplice : cooking ; (fig.) drunken-ness ; (fig.) blind infatuation

cottimo, kot-te-mo, m., job ; by contract

cotto, kot-to, a., cooked, baked ; (fig.) drunken

cottura, kot-too-rah, f., cooking, baking

cova, ko-vah, f., nest ; den ; brooding

covare, ko-vah-ray, v., to sit brooding ; to hatch

covata, ko-vah-tah, f., brood ; eggs under brood-hen

covo, ko-vo, m., den, burrow, cave

covone, ko-vo-nay, m., sheaf

cozzare, kot-tsah-ray, v., to butt

cozzo, kot-tso, m., butting ; blow ; clash

crampo, krahm-po, m., cramp

cranio, krah-ne'o, m., skull

crapula, krah-poo-lah, f., debauch

crasso*, krahss-so, a., fat ; thick ; (fig.) dense

cratere, krah-tay-ray, m., crater

creanza, kray-ahn-tsah, f., good manners ; breeding

creanzato*, kray-ahn-tsah-to, a., well-bred ; polite

creare, kray-ah-ray, v., to create

creato, kray-ah-to, m., universe. p.p., created. mal —, ill-bred

creatore, kray-ah-tor-ay, m., creator

creatura, kray-ah-too-rah, f., creature : baby [tion

creazione, kray-ah-tse'o-nay, f., creation ; produc-

credente, kray-den-tay, m. & f., believer

credenza, kray-den-tsah, f., belief ; sideboard ; buffet. far —, to sell on credit

credenziale, kray-den-tse'ah-lay, f., letter of credit

credenziali, kray-den-tse'ah-le, pl., credentials

credere, kray-day-ray, v., to believe, to think

credito, kray-de-to, m., credit ; trust ; good name

creditore, kray-de-tor-ay, m., creditor

credo, kray-do, m., creed, belief

credulo*, kray-doo-lo, a., credulous

crema, kray-mah, f., cream

cremare, kray-mah-ray, v., to cremate

crematorio, kray-mah-tor-e'o, m., crematorium

cremisi, kray-me-ze, a., crimson

crepa, kray-pah, f., fissure

crepaccio, kray-paht-cho, m., cleft ; crack

crepacuore, kray-pah-koo'or-ay,m.,heart-breaking

crepare, kray-pah-ray, v., to crack ; to burst

crepatura, kray-pah-too-rah, f., crack

crepitare,kray-pe-tah-ray, v.,to crackle, to sparkle

crepitio, kray-pe-tee-o, m., cracking ; rattling

crepuscolo, kray-pooss-ko-lo, m., twilight

crescente, kray-shen-tay, a., increasing. m., (river) rise ; (moon) first quarter

crescenza, kray-shen-tsah, f., growth ; rise

crescere, kray-shay-ray, v., to increase ; to grow

crescione, kray-she'o-nay, m., water-cress

crescita, kray-she-tah, f., increase, growth

cresima, kray-se-mah, f., (eccl.) confirmation

cresimare, kray-se-mah-ray, v., (eccl.) to confirm

crespa, krayss-pah, f., wrinkle

crespare, krayss-pah-ray, v., to crisp, to plait

crespo, krayss-po, m., crape. a., curly

cresta, krayss-tah, f., crest ; (bird) comb

crestaia, krayss-tah-e'ah, f., milliner

creta, kray-tah, f., clay

cretino, kray-tee-no, m., cretin, idiot

cribro, kree-bro, m., sieve

cricca, krick-kah, f., clique ; crew

cricchiare, krick-ke'ah-ray, v., to creak

cricco, krick-ko, m., hand-jack

crimine, kree-me-nay, m., crime

crine, kree-nay, m., horse-hair ; mountain-ridge

criniera, kre-ne'ay-rah, f., mane

crisantemo, kre-zahn-tay-mo,m.,chrysanthemum

crisi, kree-ze, f., crisis

cristallo, kriss-tahl-lo, m., crystal

cristianità, kriss-te'ah-ne-tah, f., Christendom

criterio, kre-tay-re'o, m., criterion, judgment

critica, kree-te-kah, f., criticism ; censure

criticare, kre-te-kah-ray, v., to criticise ; to censure
critico, kree-te-ko, m., critic. a., critical
crivellare, kre-vell-lah-ray, v., to sift ; to riddle
crivello, kre-vell-lo, m., sieve
croccante, krock-kahn-tay, a., crunchy, crisp
crocchiare, krock-ke'ah-ray, v., to crunch ; to croak ; (joints) to crack
crocchio, krock-ke'o, m., gathering of persons
crocco, krock-ko, m., crook ; hook
croce, kro-chay, f., cross ; (fig.) torment
crocevia, kro-chay-vee-ah, f., cross-roads
crociata, kro-chah-tah, f., crusade ; cruise
crocicchio, kro-cheek-ke'o, m., cross-way
crociera, kro-chay-rah, f., cruise ; thoroughfare
crocifiggere, kro-che-fid-jay-ray, v., to crucify
crocifisso, kro-che-fiss-so, m., crucifix. a., crucified
croco, kro-ko, m., crocus
crogiuolo, kro-joo'o-lo, m., crucible   [fast
crollare, kroll-lah-ray, v., to tumble down ; to sink
crollo, kroll-lo, m., collapse ; ruin
croma, kro-mah, f., quaver
cromo, kro-mo, m., chromium ; chromo
cronaca, kro-nah-kah, f., chronicle : news ; review
cronico, kro-ne-ko, a., chronic ; of long standing
crosta, kross-tah, f., crust ; scab
crostaceo, kross-tah-chay-o, m., shell-fish
crostino, kross-tee-no, m., toasted bread
crucciarsi, kroot-char-se, v., to worry oneself
druccio, kroot-cho, m., anger ; spite
crudele, kroo-day-lay, a., cruel
crudeltà, kroo-dell-tah, f., cruelty
crudezza, kroo-det-tsah, f., crudity ; roughness
crudo, kroo-do, a., raw ; (fig.) uncouth
cruento, kroo-en-to, a., bloody ; dreadful
crumiro, kroo-mee-ro, m., black-leg
cruna, kroo-nah, f., eye of a needle
crusca, krooss-kah, f., bran ; chaff
cubo, koo-bo, m., cube. a., cubic
cuccagna, kook-kah-n'yah, f., greasy pole. **paese di —**, land of plenty
cucchiaio, kook-ke-ah-e'o, m., spoon
cuccia, koot-chah, f., kennel ; couch

cucciare, koot-**chah**-ray, v., to lie down
cucciolo, koot-cho-lo, m., puppy
cucco, kook-ko, m., fool, crank
cuccuma, kook-koo-mah, f., kettle ; coffee-pot
cucina, koo-**chee**-nah, f., kitchen ; cooking
cucinare, koo-che-**nah**-ray, v., to cook
cuciniera, koo-che-ne-**ay**-rah, f., woman-cook
cucire, koo-**chee**-ray, v., to sew
cucitrice, koo-che-**tree**-chay, f., seamstress
cucitura, koo-che-**too**-rah, f., seam
cuculo, koo-koo-lo, m., cuckoo
cuffia, koof-fe'ah, f., cap ; head-phone
cugina, koo-jee-nah, f., female cousin
cugino, koo-jee-no, m., male cousin
cui, koo'e, pron., of whom, to whom ; which
culatta, koo-laht-tah, f., buttock ; breech
culla, kooll-lah, f., cradle ; babyhood
cullare, kooll-**lah**-ray, v., to rock ; to lull
culminare, kooll-me-**nah**-ray, v., to culminate
culmine, kooll-me-nay, m., top ; height ; apex
culo, koo-lo, m., posterior ; rump ; bottom
culto, kooll-to, m., worship
cultore, kooll-**tor**-ay, m., farmer ; (fig.) patron
cultura, kooll-**too**-rah, f., culture
cumulare, koo-moo-**lah**-ray, v., to accumulate
cumulatore, koo-moo-lah-**tor**-ay, m., accumulator
cumulo, koo-moo-lo, m., heap, pile, hoard
cuneo, koo-nay-o, m., wedge
cuocere, koo'o-chay-ray, v., to cook
cuoco, koo'o-ko, m., man-cook
cuoio, koo'o-e'o, m., leather, hide
cuore, koo'o-ray, m., heart ; kernel
cupidigia, koo-pe-dee-jah, f., cupidity ; lust
cupido*, koo-pe-do, a.,* lusty ; covetous. m., cupid
cupo*, koo-po, a., gloomy ; sad ; musing
cura, koo-rah, f., care ; cure ; parish
curadenti, koo-rah-**den**-te, m., toothpick
curare, koo-**rah**-ray, v., to cure ; to care
curato, koo-**rah**-to, m., vicar
curatore, koo-rah-**tor**-ay, m., guardian ; trustee
curia, koo-re'ah, f., diocese ; court of justice
curioso*, koo-re'o-zo, a., curious, strange

cursore, koohr-sor-ay, m., courier; bailiff
curva, koohr-vah, f., curve, bend
curvare, koohr-vah-ray, v., to curve
curvatura, koohr-vah-too-rah, f., bend; warping
curvo°, koohr-vo, a., curved, warped; bent
cuscinetto, koo-she-net-to, m., small pad. **— a sfere,** ball-bearing
cuscino, koo-shee-no, m., cushion; pillow
cuspide, kooss-pe-day, f., spire; peak
custode, kooss-to-day, m., custodian
custodia, kooss-to-de'ah, f., custody [care of
custodire, kooss-to-dee-ray, v., to guard; to take
cutaneo, koo-tah-nay-o, a., cutaneous
cute, koo-tay, f., human skin
cutrettola, koo-tret-to-lah, f., wagtail

da, dah, prep., of, from; by; since; on; at; with
dabbene, dahb-bay-nay, a., good; honest
daccapo, dahk-kah-po, adv., again; once more
dacchè, dahk-kay, conj., since; as
dado, dah-do, m., die; **dadi,** dice
daga, dah-gah, f., dagger; bayonet
dagli, dah-l'ye, interj., stop him ! down with ... !
daino, dah'e-no, m., deer; buckskin
dalia, dah-le'ah, f., dahlia
d'altronde, dahl-tron-day, adv., besides; moreover; however
dama, dah-mah, f., lady; (game) draughts
damasco, dah-mahss-ko, m., damask
damerino, dah-may-ree-no, m., dandy, beau
damigella, dah-me-jell-lah, f., young lady; bridesmaid
damo, dah-mo, m., lover, gallant
danaro, dah-nah-ro, m., money; (cards) diamonds
danaroso, dah-nah-ro-zo, a., wealthy, well-off
dannabile, dahn-nah-be-lay, a., damnable
dannare, dahn-nah-ray, v., to damn
danneggiare, dahn-ned-jah-ray, v., to damage, to injure
danno, dahn-no, m., damage; loss
dannoso°, dahn-no-zo, a., detrimental; injurious
danza, dahn-tsah, f., dance

danzare, dahn-**tsah**-ray, v., to dance
dappertutto, dahp-pair-**toot**-to, adv., everywhere
dappoco*, dahp-**po**-ko, a., useless, worthless, idle
dappoi, dahp-**po**-e, adv., since; afterwards
dappoichè, dahp-po'e-**kay**, conj., since
dappresso, dahp-**press**-so, prep., close, **near by**
dapprima, dahp-**pree**-mah, adv., firstly; first
dardeggiare, dar-ded-**jah**-ray, v., to dart, to
  pierce, to shine fiercely
dardo, **dar**-do, m., dart; arrow
dare, **dah**-ray, v., to give; to grant
darsena, dar-**say**-nah, f., wet dock
darsi, **dar**-se, v., to addict oneself to [date
data, **dah**-tah, f., date. di fresca —, of recent
datare, dah-**tah**-ray, v., to date
dato, **dah**-to, m., fact; indication. p. p., given
datore, dah-**tor**-ay, m., — di lavoro, employer
dattero, **daht**-tay-ro, m., date; date-tree
dattilografa, daht-te-lo-grah-fah, f., (lady) typist
dattilografia, daht-te-lo-grah-**fee**-ah, f., typewriting
dattorno, daht-**tor**-no, adv., around
davanti, dah-**vahn**-te, m., front. adv., in front of
davanzale, dah-vahn-**tsah**-lay, m., window-sill
davvero, dahv-**vay**-ro, adv., indeed; truly
daziabile, dah-tse'**ah**-be-lay, a., subject to duty
dazio, **dah**-tse'o, m., excise
dea, **day**-ah, f., goddess [press
debellare, day-bell-**lah**-ray, v., to master; to sup-
debilitare, day-be-le-**tah**-ray, v., to debilitate;
  to enfeeble
debito, **day**-be-to, m., debt; obligation
debitore, day-be-**tor**-ay, m., debtor
debole, **day**-bo-lay, a., weak
debolezza, day-bo-**let**-tsah, f., weakness
debuttare, day-boot-**tah**-ray, v., to appear for
  the first time
decadenza, day-kah-**den**-tsah, f., decadence
decadere, day-**kah**-day-ray, v., to decline
decadimento, day-kah-de-**men**-to, m., decline
decampare, day-kahm-**pah**-ray, v., to withdraw;
decano, day-**kah**-no, m., dean [to cede
decantare, day-kahn-**tah**-ray, v., to praise

decapitare, day-kah-pe-tah-ray, v., to behead
decedere, day-chay-day-ray, v., to die
decennio, day-chen-ne'o, m., decade
decente, day-chen-tay, a., decent
decenza, day-chen-tsah, f., decency, decorum
decesso, day-chess-so, m., death, demise. a., dead
decidere, day-chee-day-ray, v., to decide
decifrare, day-che-frah-ray, v., to decipher
decima, day-che-mah, f., tenth part ; tithe
decimale, day-che-mah-lay, a., decimal
decimare, day-che-mah-ray, v., to decimate
decimo, day-che-mo, a., tenth
decisione, day-che-ze'o-nay, f., decision
decisivo*, day-che-zee-vo, a., decisive
declamare, day-klah-mah-ray, v., to declaim
declinare, day-kle-nah-ray, v., to decline
declivio, day-klee-ve'o, m., slope
decollare, day-koll-lah-ray, v., to decapitate ;
(aeroplane) to take off
decomporre, day-kom-por-ray, v., to decompose
decorare, day-ko-rah-ray, v., to decorate, to award
decorazione, day-ko-rah-tse'o-nay, f., decoration
decoroso*, day-ko-ro-zo, a., decorous
decorrenza, day-kor-ren-tsah, f., dating from :
lapse of time
decorrere, day-kor-ray-ray, v., to elapse, to run
decotto, day-kot-to, m., decoction
decrepito*, day-kray-pe-to, a., decrepit
decrescere, day-kray-shay-ray, v., to decrease
decretare, day-kray-tah-ray, v., to decree
decreto, day-kray-to, m., decree
decuplo, day-koo-plo, a., tenfold
decurtare, day-koohr-tah-ray, v., to shorten
dedalo, day-dah-lo, m., labyrinth, maze
dedica, day-de-kah, f., dedication
dedicare, day-de-kah-ray, v., to dedicate ; to vow
dedito, day-de-to, a., inclined to, addicted
dedizione, day-de-tse'o-nay, f., devotion ; yielding
dedurre, day-doohr-ray, v., to deduce ; to derive
deduzione, day-doo-tse'o-nay, f., deduction ;
abatement
defalcare, day-fahl-kah-ray, v., to deduct ; to abate

defalco, day-fahl-ko, m., defalcation; deduction
deferente, day-fay-ren-tay, a., deferent
deferenza, day-fay-ren-tsah, f., deference
deferire, day-fay-ree-ray, v., to defer; to condescend
defezione, day-fay-tse'o-nay, f., defection, abandoning
deficiente, day-fe-chen-tay, a., deficient, lacking
deficienza, day-fe-chen-tsah, f., deficiency
definire, day-fe-nee-ray, v., to decide; to define
definitivo*, day-fe-ne-tee-vo, a., definitive
definizione, day-fe-ne-tse'o-nay, f., definition
deflettere, day-flet-tay-ray, v., to deflect
deflorare, day-flo-rah-ray, v., to violate
deformare, day-for-mah-ray, v., to deform
deforme, day-for-may, a., deformed. m., cripple
deformità, day-for-me-tah, f., deformity
defraudare, day-frah'oo-dah-ray, v., to defraud
defunto, day-foonn-to, m., defunct. a., late, deceased
degenerare, day-jay-nay-rah-ray, v., to degenerate
degenere, day-jay-nay-ray, a., degenerate
degente, day-jen-tay, a., bedridden
degnare, day-n'yah-ray, v., to deign
degno*, day-n'yo, a., worthy, deserving
degradare, day-grah-dah-ray, v., to degrade
degradazione, day-grah-dah-tse'o-nay, f., degradation, abasement
degustare, day-gooss-tah-ray, v., to taste
deità, day-e-tah, f., divinity, deity
delatore, day-lah-tor-ay, m., informer, accuser
del credere, dell kray-day-ray, m., deduction against bad debts
delega, day-lay-gah, f., delegation
delegare, day-lay-gah-ray, v., to entrust, to delegate
delegato, day-lay-gah-to, m., delegate
deleterio*, day-lay-tay-re'o, a., injurious; harmful
delfino, del-fee-no, m., dolphin; dauphin
deliberare, day-le-bay-rah-ray, v., to deliberate
deliberatamente, day-le-bay-rah-tah-men-tay, adv., deliberately
deliberazione, day-le-bay-rah-tse'o-nay, f., deliberation
delicatezza, day-le-kah-tet-tsah, f., delicacy

delicato°, day-le-**kah**-to, a., delicate ; gentle

delineare, day-le-nay-**ah**-ray, v., to trace ; to delineate ; to describe ; to outline

delinquente, day-lin-**kwen**-tay, m. & f., offender

delinquenza, day-lin-**kwen**-tsah, f., delinquency

deliquio, day-lee-kwe'o, m., swoon

delirante, day-le-**rahn**-tay, a., delirious

delirare, day-le-**rah**-ray, v., to be delirious

delitto, day-**lit**-to, m., crime

delittuoso°, day-lit-too-**o**-zo, a., criminal

delizia, day-lee-**tse**'ah, f., delight

delizioso°, day-le-tse'**o**-zo, a., delicious

deludere, day-loo-day-ray, v., to delude ; to frustrate

deluso°, day-**loo**-zo, a., disappointed ; deluded

delusorio°, day-loo-zo-re'o, a., deceiving ; disappointing

demanio, day-**mah**-ne'o, m., public property

demarcare, day-mar-**kah**-ray, v., to indicate the limits

demente, day-**men**-tay, a., mad. m. & f., lunatic

demenza, day-**men**-tsah, f., madness

demerito, day-**may**-re-to, m., demerit

demolire, day-mo-lee-ray, v., to demolish

demolizione, day-mo-le-tse'**o**-nay, f., demolition

demonio, day-**mo**-ne'o, m., demon ; evil passion

demoralizzare, day-mo-rah-lid-**dzah**-ray, v., to demoralize

denaro, day-**nah**-ro, m., money ; ready cash

denaturato, day-nah-too-**rah**-to, a., adulterated

denegare, day-nay-**gah**-ray, v., to deny

denigrare, day-ne-**grah**-ray, v., to defame ; to disparage ; to tarnish

denominare, day-no-me-**nah**-ray, v., to denominate

denominazione, day-no-me-nah-tse'**o**-nay, f., denomination

denotare, day-no-**tah**-ray, v., to denote

densità, den-se-**tah**, f., density

denso°, **den**-so, a., dense

dentale, den-**tah**-lay, a., dental

dentatura, den-tah-**too**-rah, f., set of teeth

dente, **den**-tay, m., tooth ; cog

dentellare, den-tell-**lah**-ray, v., to indent ; to notch

dentiera, den-te'ay-rah, f., artificial set of teeth; dental plate

dentifricio, den-te-free-cho, m., tooth-paste; tooth-powder; mouth-wash

dentista, den-tiss-tah, m., dentist

dentizione, den-te-tse'o-nay, f., teething

dentro, den-tro, adv., in, inside, within

denudare, day-noo-dah-ray, v., to divest; to expose

denunciare, day-noonn-chah-ray, v., to denounce

denunzia, day-noonn-tse'ah, f., denunciation

depauperare, day-pah'oo-pay-rah-ray, v., to impoverish

deperire, day-pay-ree-ray, v., to waste away; to perish; to decay

depilare, day-pe-lah-ray, v., to remove hair

deplorabile, day-plo-rah-be-lay, a., deplorable

deplorare, day-plo-rah-ray, v., to deplore

deplorevole, day-plo-ray-vo-lay, a., deplorable

deporre, day-por-ray, v., to depose

deportare, day-por-tah-ray, v., to deport; to exile

deportazione, day-por-tah-tse'o-nay, f., deportation; banishment

depositare, day-po-ze-tah-ray, v., to deposit

deposito, day-po-ze-to, m., deposit; warehouse; depot; depository

deposizione, day-po-ze-tse'o-nay, f., deposition

depravare, day-prah-vah-ray, v., to deprave

deprecare, day-pray-kah-ray, v., to deprecate

depredare, day-pray-dah-ray, v., to rob, to plunder

depressione, day-press-se'o-nay, f., depression

depresso°, day-press-so, a., depressed

deprezzare, day-pret-tsah-ray, v., to depreciate

deprimere, day-pree-may-ray, v., to depress

depurare, day-poo-rah-ray, v., to purify, to cleanse

deputare, day-poo-tah-ray, v., to depute

deputato, day-poo-tah-to, m., deputy; M.P.

deputazione, day-poo-tah-tse'o-nay, f., deputation

deragliare, day-rah-l'yah-ray, v., to derail

derelitto, day-ray-lit-to, a., derelict; forsaken. m., wreck

deridere, day-ree-day-ray, v., to mock

derisione, day-re-ze'o-nay, f., derision

deriva, day-**ree**-vah, f., down stream ; **leeway**
derivare, day-re-**vah**-ray, v., to derive ; to drift
derivazione, day-re-vah-tse'**o**-nay, f., derivation ;
extension
derogatorio*, day-ro-gah-**tor**-e'o, a., derogatory
derrata, dair-**rah**-tah, f., merchandise ; foodstuffs
desco, **dess**-ko, m., desk ; long table : counter
descrittivo*, dess-krit-**tee**-vo, a., descriptive
descrivere, dess-**kree**-vay-ray, v., to describe
descrizione, dess-kre-tse'**o**-nay, f., description
deserto, day-**zair**-to, m., desert. a., deserted, bare
desiderabile, day-ze-day-rah-be-lay, a., desirable
desiderare, day-ze-day-**rah**-ray, v., to desire
desiderio, day-ze-**day**-re'o, m., desire, longing
desideroso*, day-ze-day-ro-zo, a., desirous
designare, day-ze-n'**yah**-ray, v., to designate
designazione, day-ze-n'yah-tse'**o**-nay, f., desig-
nation
desinare, day-ze-**nah**-ray, v., to dine. m., dinner
desistere, day-**ziss**-tay-ray, v., to desist, to leave off
desolato*, day-zo-**lah**-to, a., desolate ; sorrowful
despota, **dess**-po-tah, m., despot, tyrant ; ruler
despotico, dess-**po**-te-ko, a., despotic
destare, dess-**tah**-ray, v., to awaken
destinare, dess-te-**nah**-ray, v., to destine ; to assign
destinazione, dess-te-nah-tse'**o**-nay, f., destination
destino, dess-**tee**-no, m., destiny
destituire, dess-te-too-ee-ray, v., to deprive ; to
dismiss
destituito*, dess-te-too-e-to, a., destitute, poor
destituzione, dess-te-too-tse'**o**-nay, f., destitution ;
[dismissal]
desto, **dess**-to, a., wide-awake
destra, **dess**-trah, f., the right hand
destrezza, dess-**tret**-tsah, f., dexterity ; agility
destro*, **dess**-tro, a., dexterous ; right ; skilful
detenere, day-tay-**nay**-ray, v., to detain
detenuto, day-tay-**noo**-to, m., convict
detenzione, day-ten-tse'**o**-nay, f., detention
deteriorare, day-tay-re'o-**rah**-ray, v., to deteriorate
determinare, day-tair-me-**nah**-ray, v., to determine
determinazione, day-tair-me-nah-tse'**o**-nay, f.,
determination

detestare, day-tess-**tah**-ray, v., to detest
detonazione, day-to-nah-tse'o-nay, f., detonation
detrarre, day-**trar**-ray, v., to deduct
detrattore, day-traht-**tor**-ay, m., slanderer
detrazione, day-trah-tse'o-nay, f., detraction;
   defamation
detrimento, day-tre-**men**-to, m., detriment
detrito, day-**tree**-to, m., disintegrated material
detronizzare, day-tro-nid-**dzah**-ray,v.,to dethrone
dettagliante, det-tah-l'**yahn**-tay, m., retailer
dettagliare, det-tah-l'**yah**-ray, v., to detail
dettaglio, det-tah-l'**yo**, m., detail, particular
dettare, det-**tah**-ray, v., to dictate
dettato, det-**tah**-to, m., dictation; style
dettatura, det-tah-**too**-rah, f., dictation
detto, **det**-to, m., saying. a., called, named, said
deturpare, day-toohr-**pah**-ray, v., to disfigure
devastare, day-vahss-**tah**-ray, v., to devastate
devastazione, day-vahss-tah-tse'o-nay, f., devas-
   tation, ruin, destruction
deviare, day-ve'**ah**-ray, v., to deviate; to swerve
devolvere, day-**voll**-vay-ray, v., to devolve
devoto*, day-**vo**-to, a., devout; devoted
devozione, day-vo-tse'o-nay, f., devotion
di, dee, prep., of; with; from; by; on; in; to; after
di, dee. m., day
diabolico*, de'ah-bo-le-ko, a., diabolical
diacono, de'**ah**-ko-no, m., deacon
diadema, de'ah-**day**-mah, m., diadem
diafano, de'**ah**-fah-no, a., diaphanous, clear
diagonale, de'ah-go-**nah**-lay, a., diagonal
dialetto, de'ah-**let**-to, m., dialect
dialogo, de'**ah**-lo-go, m., dialogue
diamante, de'ah-**mahn**-tay, m., diamond
diametrale, de'ah-may-**trah**-lay, a., diametrical
diametro, de'**ah**-may-tro, m., diameter
diamine, de'**ah**-me-nay, interj., (pop.) the deuce!
dianzi, de'**ahn**-tse, adv., before; not long since
diapason, de'**ah**-pah-zon, m., tuning-fork
diaria, de'**ah**-re'ah, f., daily allowance
diario, de'**ah**-re'o, m., diary; day-book
diarrea, de'ahr-**ray**-ah, f., diarrhœa

diaspro, de-ahss-pro, m., jasper

diavolo, de'ah-vo-lo, m., devil; demon

dibattere, de-baht-tay-ray, v., to debate, to argue

dibattimento, de-baht-te-men-to, m., dispute; debate; legal argument

dibattito, de-baht-te-to, m., debate [ment

dicastero, de-kahss-tay-ro, m., government-depart-

dicembre, de-chem-bray, m., December

diceria, de-chay-ree-ah, f., tittle-tattle, rumours

dichiarare, de-ke'ah-rah-ray, v., to declare

dichiarazione, de-ke'ah-rah-tse'o-nay, f., declaration; explanation

diciannove, de-che'ahn-no-vay, a., nineteen

diciassette, de-che'ahss-set-tay, a., seventeen

diciotto, de-che'ot-to, a., eighteen

dicitura, de-che-too-rah, f., text; speech

dieci, de'ay-che, a., ten

dieta, de'ay-tah, f., diet; assembly

dietro, de'ay-tro, prep., behind; after

difalco, de-fahl-ko, m., defalcation; rebate

difendente, de-fen-den-tay, m. & f., defendant

difendere, de-fen-day-ray, v., to defend

difensore, de-fen-sor-ay, m., defender, protector

difesa, de-fay-zah, f., defence

difettivo°, de-fet-tee-vo, a., defective, faulty

difetto, de-fet-to, m., defect, fault, flaw

difettoso°, de-fet-to-zo, a., defective; faulty

diffamare, dif-fah-mah-ray, v., to defame

diffamatorio, dif-fah-mah-tor-e'o, a., slanderous

differenza, dif-fay-ren-tsah, f., difference

differibile, dif-fay-ree-be-lay, a., deferable

differimento, dif-fay-re-men-to, m., adjournment

differire, dif-fay-ree-ray, v., to differ; to postpone

difficile, dif-fee-chee-lay, a., difficult

diffida, dif-fee-dah, f., warning; intimation

diffidare, dif-fe-dah-ray, v., to mistrust; to intimate

diffidenza, dif-fe-den-tsah, f., diffidence

diffondere, dif-fon-day-ray, v., to diffuse; to broadcast

diffusione, dif-foo-ze'o-nay, f., broadcasting

diffusivo°, dif-foo-zee-vo, a., diffusive; prolix

diffuso°, dif-foo-zo, a., diffuse; widely spread; ample

diffusore, dif-foo-**zor**-ay, m., loud speaker
difterite, dif-tay-**ree**-tay, f., diphtheria
diga, dee-**gah**, f., dam ; dyke ; breakwater
digeribile, de-jay-**ree**-be-lay, a., digestible
digerire, de-jay-**ree**-ray, v., to digest
digestivo, de-jess-**tee**-vo, a., digestive
diggià, did-**jah**, adv., already
dighiacciare, de-ghe'aht-**chah**-ray, v., to thaw
digiunare, de-joo-**nah**-ray, v., to fast
digiuno, de-**joo**-no, m., fasting   [minish
digradare, de-grah-**dah**-ray, v., to degrade ; to di-
digredire, de-gray-**dee**-ray, v., to digress
digrignare, de-gre'n'**yah**-ray, v., to snarl ; to guash
dilagare, de-lah-**gah**-ray, v., to spill over ; to flood
dilapidare, de-lah-pe-**dah**-ray, v., to dilapidate
dilatare, de-lah-**tah**-ray, v., to dilate
dilazionare, de-lah-tse'o-**nah**-ray, v., to delay
dilazione, de-lah-tse'**o**-nay, f., delay ; respite
dileggiare, de-led-**jah**-ray, v., to scoff at
dilettabile, de-let-**tah**-be-lay, a., delectable
dilettare, de-let-**tah**-ray, v., to delight ; to charm
diletto, de-**let**-to, m., delight ; beloved
diligenza, de-le-**jen**-tsah, f., diligence ; care
dilucidare, de-loo-che-**dah**-ray, v., to elucidate
diluire, de-loo-**ee**-ray, v., to dilute
dilungare, de-loonn-**gah**-ray, v., to lengthen
dilungarsi, de-loonn-**gar**-se, v., to dwell upon
diluviare, de-loo-ve'**ah**-ray, v., to rain in torrents
diluvio, de-**loo**-ve'o, m., deluge, flood
dimagrare, de-mah-**grah**-ray, v., to become lean
dimagrire, de-mah-**gree**-ray, v., to grow thin
dimenare, de-may-**nah**-ray, v., to shake ; to wag
dimensione, de-men-se'**o**-nay, f., dimension
dimenticanza, de-men-te-**kahn**-tsah, f., over-
    sight ; oblivion
dimenticare, de-men-te-**kah**-ray, v., to forget
dimesso°, de-**mess**-so, a., shabby ; dismissed
dimettere, de-**met**-tay-ray, v., to dismiss
dimettersi, de-**met**-tair-se, v., to resign
dimezzare, de-med-**dzah**-ray, v., to halve
diminuire, de-me-noo'**ee**-ray, v., to diminish
diminutivo*, de-me-noo-**tee**-vo, a., diminutive

dimodochè, de-mo-do-**kay**, adv., in order that

dimora, de-**mo**-rah, f., abode; sojourn; delay; (botanical) permanent quarters

dimorare, de-mo-**rah**-ray, v., to dwell, to reside

dimostrare, de-moss-**trah**-ray, v., to demonstrate

dinamite, de-nah-**mee**-tay, f., dynamite

dinamo, dee-**nah**-mo, f., dynamo

dinanzi, de-**nahn**-tse, prep., before. m., front

dinastia, de-nahss-**tee**-ah, f., dynasty

dinegare, de-nay-**gah**-ray, v., to deny; to refuse

diniego, de-ne'**ay**-go, m., refusal; denial

dintorno, din-**tor**-no, m., neighbourhood.   adv., round about

Dio, dee-o, m., God

diocesano, de'o-chay-**sah**-no, a., diocesan

diocesi, de'o-chay-se, f., diocese

dipanare, de-pah-**nah**-ray, v., to unravel

dipartenza, de-par-**ten**-tsah, f., departure

dipartire, de-par-**tee**-ray, v., to depart; to separate

dipendente, de-pen-**den**-tay, a., dependent

dipendere, de-pen-**day**-ray, v., to depend [upon]

dipingere, de-pin-**jay**-ray, v., to paint; to describe

dipinto, de-**pin**-to, m., painting.   a., painted; made up

dipoi, de-po'e, adv., afterwards

dipopolare, de-po-po-**lah**-ray, v., to depopulate

diportamento, de-por-tah-**men**-to, m., deportment

diporto, de-**por**-to, m., recreation, amusement

dipresso, de-**press**-so, adv., approximately [out

diramazione, de-rah-mah-tse'o-nay, f., branching

dire, dee-ray, v., to say; to tell; to recite

diretto*, de-**ret**-to, a., straight; through; addressed to

direttore, de-ret-**tor**-ay, m., manager; director

direzione, de-ray-tse'o-nay, f., direction; management; board; steering; route

dirigere, de-**ree**-jay-ray, v., to direct; to steer

dirigibile, de-re-jee-be-lay, m., airship

dirimpetto, de-rim-**pet**-to, adv., facing; opposite to

diritta, de-**rit**-tah, f., right hand

diritto, de-**rit**-to, m., right; equity.   a.,* straight; upright.   adv., rightly; directly

dirittura, de-rit-**too**-rah, f., rectitude; integrity

dirizzare, de-rit-**tsah**-ray, v., to straighten; to lift

diroccare, de-rock-kah-ray, v., to dismantle; to pull down

dirompere, de-rom-pay-ray, v., to break; to disintegrate; to rot

dirotto, de-rot-to, a.,* excessive. **a —**, pouring

dirozzare, de-rod-dzah-ray, v., to educate; to rough-hew

dirupamento, de-roo-pah-men-to, m., subsidence; precipice

dirupo, de-roo-po, m., steep rocky ground

disabitato, de-zah-be-tah-to, a., uninhabited

disadatto, de-zah-daht-to, a., unfit; awkward

disadorno*, de-zah-dor-no, a., unadorned; bare

disagevole, de-zah-jay-vo-lay, a., difficult

disaggradevole, de-zahg-grah-day-vo-lay, a., displeasing, unpleasant, disagreeable

disaggradire, de-zahg-grah-dee-ray, v., to displease

disagiato*, de-zah-jah-to, a., inconvenient; needy

disagio, de-zah-jo, m., discomfort; trouble; want

disamina, de-zah-me-nah, f., careful consideration

disapprovare, de-zahp-pro-vah-ray, v., to disapprove; to reproach

disappunto, de-zahp-poonn-to, m., disappointment

disarmare, de-zar-mah-ray, v., to disarm

disarmo, de-zar-mo, m., disarmament

disarmonico*, de-zar-mo-ne-ko, a., discordant

disassuefare, de-zahss-soo'ay-fah-ray, v., to disaccustom

disastro, de-zahss-tro, m., disaster

disattento*, de-zaht-ten-to, a., inattentive, careless

disavanzo, de-zah-vahn-tso, m., deficit

disavventura, de-zahv-ven-too-rah, f., mishap

disborso, diz-bor-so, m., disbursement

disboscare, diz-boss-kah-ray, v., (woods) to clear

disbrigare, diz-bre-gah-ray, v., to extricate; to handle

disbrigo, diz-bree-go, m., tidying; handling

discapito, diss-kah-pe-to, m., loss; detriment

discaricare, diss-kah-re-kah-ray, v., to unload

discarico, diss-kah-re-ko, m., unloading; excuse

discendente, de-shen-den-tay, m. & f., descendant

discendenza, de-shen-den-tsah, f., descent; issue

discendere, de-shen-day-ray, **v.**, to descend; to derive; to come from

discepolo, de-shay-po-lo, **m.**, disciple; pupil

discernere, de-shair-nay-ray, **v.**, to discern

discesa, de-shay-sah, **f.**, descent

dischiudere, diss-ke'oo-day-ray, **v.**, to disclose

discinto°, de-sheen-to, **a.**, scantily dressed

disciogliere, de-she'o-l'yay-ray, **v.**, to dissolve

discioglimento, de-she'o-l'ye-men-to, **m.**, dissolution; dissolving; solution

disciplinare, de-she-ple-nah-ray, **v.**, to discipline

disco, diss-ko, **m.**, disc; dial; gramophone record

discobolo, diss-ko-bo-lo, **m.**, discus-thrower

discolo°, diss-ko-lo, **a.**, undisciplined

discolpare, diss-koll-pah-ray, **v.**, to excuse, to justify

disconoscere, diss-ko-no-shay-ray, **v.**, to ignore

discoprire, diss-ko-pree-ray, **v.**, to uncover

discoraggiare, diss-ko-rahd-djah-ray, **v.**, to discourage, to dishearten

discordare, diss-kor-dah-ray, **v.**, to disagree; to jar

discorrere, diss-kor-ray-ray, **v.**, to discourse

discorso, diss-kor-so, **m.**, speech; reasoning; lecture; sermon; scolding

discosto°, diss-koss-to, **a.**, at some distance

discretamente, diss-kray-tah-men-tay, **adv.**, discreetly; rather

discretezza, diss-kray-tet-tsah, **f.**, discretion

discreto°, diss-kray-to, **a.**, discreet

discucire, diss-koo-chee-ray, **v.**, to unsew

discutere, diss-koo-tay-ray, **v.**, to discuss; to dispute

disdegnare, diss-day-n'yah-ray, **v.**, to disdain

disdetta, diss-det-tah, **f.**, notice to quit; denial; ill-luck

disdire, diss-dee-ray, **v.**, to deny; to give notice

disegnare, de-zay-n'yah-ray, **v.**, to design, to draw; to describe

disegno, de-zay-n'yo, **m.**, design; drawing; project. — **di legge**, (parl.) bill

diseredare, de-zay-ray-dah-ray, **v.**, to disinherit

disertare, de-zair-tah-ray, **v.**, to desert

disertore, de-zair-tor-ay, **m.**, deserter

disfare, diss-fah-ray, **v.**, to undo; to defeat; to ruin

disfatta, diss-**faht**-tah, f., defeat, rout

disfida, diss-**fee**-dah, f., challenge; defiance

disgelo, diss-**jay**-lo, m., thaw

disgiungere, diss-**joonn**-jay-ray, v., to disjoin

disgombrare, diss-gom-**brah**-ray, v., to clear

disgradevole, diss-grah-**day**-vo-lay,a.,disagreeable

disgrazia, diss-grah-**tse**'ah, f., disgrace; bad luck; mishap

disgraziato°, diss-grah-**tse**'**ah**-to, a., unfortunate

disgregare, diss-gray-**gah**-ray, v., to separate

disguido, diss-goo'**ee**-do, m., misleading; going astray

disgustare,diss-gooss-**tah**-ray,v.,to disgust; to vex

disgusto, diss-**gooss**-to, m., disgust; vexation

disgustoso°, diss-gooss-**to**-zo, a., disgusting, unpalatable

disilludere, de-zill-**loo**-day-ray, v., to disillude

disimpegnare, de-zim-pay-n'**yah**-ray, v., to redeem; to free

disinfettare, de-zin-fet-**tah**-ray, v., to disinfect

disingannare, de-zin-gahn-**nah**-ray, v., to disillusion

disinvoltura, de-zin-voll-**too**-rah, f., grace of manner; coolness; dexterity; swagger

dislacciare, diss-laht-**chah**-ray, v., to unlace

dislocare, diss-lo-**kah**-ray, v., to displace

dislogare, diss-lo-**gah**-ray, v., to dislocate, to sprain

dislogazione, diss-lo-gah-**tse**'o-nay, f., dislocation

dismettere, diss-**met**-tay-ray, v., to dismiss; to leave off; to renounce; to give up

dismisura, diss-me-**zoo**-rah, f., excess

dismontare, diss-mon-**tah**-ray, v., to dismount

disobbligare, de-zob-ble-**gah**-ray, v., to disoblige

disoccupato, de-zock-koo-**pah**-to, a., disengaged; unemployed; leisured; idle

disonesto°, de-zo-**ness**-to, a., dishonest; fast

disonorare, de-zo-no-**rah**-ray, v., to dishonour

disonore, de-zo-**no**-ray, m., dishonour; discredit

disonorevole, de-zo-no-**ray**-vo-lay, a., dishonourable; disgraceful; blamable

disopra, de-**so**-prah, adv., on top, over, upstairs

disordinato°, de-zor-de-**nah**-to, a., disorderly

disordine, de-zor-de-nay, m., disorder; riot

disorganizzare, de-zor-gah-nit-tsah-ray, v., to disorganize, to muddle

disorientare, de-zor-e'en-tah-ray, v., to lose one's bearings; to mislead

disormeggiare, de-zor-med-jah-ray, v., (naut.) to unmoor

disotto, de-sot-to, adv., downstairs; underneath

dispacciare, diss-paht-chah-ray, v., to despatch

dispaccio, diss-paht-cho, m., despatch; telegram

disparato*, diss-pah-rah-to, a., diverse; odd

dispari, diss-pah-re, a., odd; unequal

disparte, diss-par-tay, adv., in —, aside, on one side

dispendio, diss-pen-de'o, m., expense, cost

dispendioso*, diss-pen-de'o-zo, a., expensive

dispensa, diss-pen-sah, f., distribution; exemption; larder; leave

dispensare, diss-pen-sah-ray, v., to dispense; to exempt

dispensario, diss-pen-sah-re'o, m., dispensary

disperare, diss-pay-rah-ray, v., to despair

disperato*, diss-pay-rah-to, a., desperate

disperdere, diss-pair-day-ray, v., to disperse

dispettoso⁵, diss-pet-to-zo, a., spiteful

dispiacente, diss-pe'ah-chen-tay, a., displeasing

dispiacere, diss-pe'ah-chay-ray, v., to displease. m., pain, sorrow

dispiacevole, diss-pe'ah-chay-vo-lay, a., disagreeable

dispiegare, diss-pe'ay-gah-ray, v., to unfold

dispogliare, diss-po-l'yah-ray, v., to fleece; to undress

disponibile, diss-po-nee-be-lay, a., available

disporre, diss-por-ray, v., to dispose; to arrange

disposto, diss-poss-to, a., disposed

dispotismo, diss-po-tiss-mo, m., despotism

disprezzante, diss-pret-tsahn-tay, a., disdainful

disprezzare, diss-pret-tsah-ray, v., to disparage; to contemn

disprezzo, diss-pret-tso, m., contempt

disputare, diss-poo-tah-ray, v., to dispute

disseccare, diss-seck-kah-ray, v., to dry up

disseminare, diss-say-me-nah-ray, v., to dissemi-

dissenso, diss-sen-so, m., dissension [nate

dissenteria, diss-sen-tay-ree-ah, f., dysentery

dissentire, diss-sen-tee-ray, v., to dissent, to differ

disserrare, diss-sair-rah-ray, v., to unfasten ; to disclose

dissetare, diss-sess-tah-ray, v., to involve in pecuniary difficulties

dissetare, diss-say-tah-ray, v., to quench thirst

dissettore, diss-set-tor-ay, m., dissector

dissidio, diss-see-de'o, m., dissention

dissimile, diss-see-me-lay, a., unlike

dissimulare, diss-se-moo-lah-ray, v., to hide ; to make pretence ; to camouflage

dissodare, diss-so-dah-ray, v., to break up ; to till

dissoluto*, diss-so-loo-to, a., dissolute

dissolvere, diss-soll-vay-ray, v., to dissolve

dissomigliare, diss-so-me-l'yah-ray, v., to be dissimilar

dissonante, diss-so-nahn-tay, a., discordant

dissuadere, diss-soo'ah-day-ray, v., to dissuade

distaccare, diss-tahk-kah-ray, v., to detach, to undo, to disjoin, to separate

distanza, diss-tahn-tsah, f., distance

distendere, diss-ten-day-ray, v., to distend, to enlarge, to spread ; to unfold

distesa, diss-tay-zah, f., expansion ; stretch

disteso*, diss-tay-zo, a.,wide ; extended, spread out

distillare, diss-till-lah-ray, v., to distil

distillatore, diss-till-lah-tor-ay, m., distiller ; still

distinguere, diss-tinn-goo'ay-ray,v.,to distinguish

distinta, diss-tinn-tah, f., list ; invoice ; inventory

distintivo, diss-tinn-tee-vo, m., sign, badge, a.,* distinctive

distinto*, diss-tinn-to, a., polished ; distinct

distogliere, diss-to-l'yay-ray, v., to dissuade ; to distract

distornare, diss-tor-nah-ray, v., to divert ; to embezzle ; to corrupt

distrarre, diss-trar-ray, v., to distract ; to amuse

distratto*, diss-traht-to, a., absent-minded

distretto, diss-tret-to, m., district ; territory

distribuire, diss-tre-boo'ee-ray, v., to distribute
distruggere, diss-trood-jay-ray, v., to destroy
distrutto, diss-troot-to, a., destroyed, wasted
disturbo, diss-toohr-bo, m., disturbance ; trouble
disubbidire, de-zoob-be-dee-ray, v., to disobey
disuguale, de-zoo-goo'ah-lay, a., uneven ; unequal
disunione, de-zoo-ne'o-nay, f., discord ; separation
disunire, de-zoo-nee-ray, v., to separate
disvio, diss-vee-o, m., misleading
ditale, de-tah-lay, m., thimble ; finger-stall
dito, dee-to, m., finger ; toe
ditta, dit-tah, f., firm, business concern
dittatore, dit-tah-tor-ay, m., dictator
dittatura, dit-tah-too-rah, f., dictatorship
dittongo, dit-tonn-go, m., diphthong
diurno*, de-oohr-no, a., daily
diva, dee-vah, f., goddess ; singer ; (stage) star
divagare, de-vah-gah-ray, v., to distract ; to wander
divario, de-vah-re'o, m., variation ; variance
divellere, de-vell-lay-ray, v., to pluck out, to uproot
divenire, de-vay-nee-ray, v., to become, to get
diverbio, de-vair-be'o, m., heated argument
divergere, de-vair-jay-ray, v., to diverge
diverso*, de-vair-so, a., diverse ; different
divertire, de-vair-tee-ray, v., to divert
divertirsi, de-vair-teer-se, v., to amuse oneself
divezzare, de-vet-tsah-ray, v., to wean
dividendo, de-ve-den-do, m., dividend
dividere, de-vee-day-ray, v., to divide ; to separate ;
    to cut ; to share, to apportion
divieto, de-ve-ay-to, m., prohibition
divinare, de-ve-nah-ray, v., to guess, to divine
divincolare, de-vin-ko-lah-ray, v., to wriggle ; to
divino*, de-vee-no, a., divine   [twist
divisa, de-vee-zah, f., uniform ; motto
divisare, de-ve-zah-ray, v., to devise, to scheme
divisione, de-ve-ze'o-nay, f., division ; hyphen
divorare, de-vo-rah-ray, v., to devour
divorziare, de-vor-tse'ah-ray, v., to divorce
divozione, de-vo-tse'o-nay, f., devotion
divulgare, de-vooll-gah-ray, v., to divulge
dizionario, de-tse'o-nah-re'o, m., dictionary

dizione, de-tse'o-nay, f., diction, locution

do, do, m., (mus.) Do, C

doccia, dot-chah, f., shower-bath

docente, do-chen-tay, m. & f., teacher

docile, do-che-lay, a., docile, pliable

docilità, do-che-le-tah, f., docility

dodicesimo, do-de-chay-ze-mo, a., twelfth

dodici, do-de-che, a., twelve

doga, do-gah, f., (cask) stave

dogana, do-gah-nah, f., custom-house

doganiere, do-gah-ne'ay-ray, m., customs officer

doglia, do-l'yah, f., pain, ache ; grief, affliction

doglianza, do-l'yahn-tsah, f., complaint

doglioso*, do-l'yo-zo, a., painful ; complaining

dolce, doll - chay, a., sweet ; soft ; gentle.
m., sweetmeat

dolcezza, doll-chet-tsah, f., sweetness ; grace

dolciumi, doll-choo-me, m.pl., sweets

dolente, do-len-tay, a., aching ; grieved

dolere, do-lay-ray, v., to ache ; to grieve

dolersi, do-layr-se, v., to complain ; to lament

dolore, do-lo-ray, m., pain, sorrow

doloroso*, do-lo-ro-zo, a., painful ; sore

doloso*, do-lo-zo, a., crafty ; fraudulent ; deceitful

domabile, do-mah-be-lay, a., tameable

domanda, do-mahn-dah, f., question ; demand

domandare, do-mahn-dah-ray, v., to demand ; to
ask ; to claim

domani, do-mah-ne, adv., to-morrow

domare, do-mah-ray, v., to tame

domatore, do-mah-tor-ay, m., tamer [morning

domattina, do-maht-tee-nah, adv., to-morrow

domenica, do-may-ne-kah, f., Sunday

domestico, do-mess-te-ko, m., man-servant.
a., domestic

domicilio, do-me-chee-le'o, m., domicile

dominare, do-me-nah-ray, v., to dominate

dominio, do-mee-ne'o, m.,dominion ; domain ; rule

domo, do-mo, m., cathedral ; dome. a., tamed

don [donno], don, m., padre ; Mr. [master]

donare, do-nah-ray, v., to give ; to present with

donde, don-day, adv., whence, why

dondolare, don-do-**lah**-ray, v., to swing ; to dangle
donna, don-nah,f., woman ; wife ; lady ; (fig.) queen
donnaccia, don-**naht**-chah, f., fast woman ; slut
donnaiuolo, don-nah-e'oo-**O**-lo, m., a fast man
donnesco*, don-**ness**-ko, a., womanly ; effeminate
donnola, don-no-lah, f., weasel, stoat
dono, do-no, m., gift ; knack
donzella, don-**dzell**-lah, f., girl ; maiden
dopo, do-po, prep., after ; behind ; since.   **—mez-**
    zogiorno or **—pranzo**, m., afternoon
doppiare, dop-pe'**ah**-ray, v., to double ; to fold
doppiere, dop-pe'**ay**-ray, m., candlestick
doppiezza, dop-pe'**et**-tsah, f., duplicity
doppio*, dop-pe'o, a., double ; twofold ; (fig.) false
dorare, do-**rah**-ray, v., to gild
dorato, do-**rah**-to, a., gilt
dormicchiare, dor-mick-ke'**ah**-ray, v., to slumber
dormiglione, dor-me-l'yo-nay, m., late riser
dormire, dor-**mee**-ray, v., to sleep
dormita, dor-**mee**-tah, f., nap ; long sleep
dorso, dor-so, m., back
dosare, do-**zah**-ray, v., to dose
dose, do-zay, f., dose
dosso, **doss**-so, m., back ; hillock
dotare, do-**tah**-ray, v., to endow
dote, do-tay, f., dowry ; settlement
dotto*, dot-to, a., learned
dottore, dot-tor-ay, m., doctor ; physician
dottrina, dot-**tree**-nah, f., doctrine ; culture
dove, do-vay, adv., where ; if
dovere, do-**vay**-ray, v., to owe ; to have to.
    m., duty ; homework
doveroso*, do-vay-**ro**-zo, a., due ; rightful
dovizia, do-vee-**tse**'ah, f., abundance
dovunque, do-**voonn**-kway, adv., anywhere,
    in any place
dozzina, dod-**dzee**-nah,f.,dozen ; board and lodging
dozzinante, dod-dze-**nahn**-tay, m.,boarder, lodger
draga, drah-gah, f., dredger
drago, drah-go, m., dragon
dragone, drah-**go**-nay, m., dragoon
dramma, **drahm**-mah, m., drama, tragedy

drammaturgo, drahm-mah-**toohr**-go, m., play-
drappello, drahp-**pell**-lo, m., squad ; flag　[wright
drapperia, drahp-pay-**ree**-ah, f., drapery
drappiere, drahp-pe'**ay**-ray, m., draper
drappo, drahp-po, m., cloth　　　　　[tion
drenaggio, dray-**nahd**-jo, m., drainage ; reclama-
drizzare, drit-**tsah**-ray, v., to right ; to raise ; to set
droga, dro-gah, f., drug
drogheria, dro-gay-**ree**-ah, f., druggist's shop
droghiere, dro-ghe'**ay**-ray, m., druggist ; grocer
drudo, droo-do, m., co-respondent
duale, doo-**ah**-lay, a., dual, twofold
dubbio, doob-be'o, m., doubt.　a.,* doubtful
dubbioso*, doob-be'**o**-zo, a., dubious
dubitare, doo-be-**tah**-ray, v., to doubt
duca, doo-kah, m., duke ; chief ; leader
ducato, doo-**kah**-to, m., duchy ; (coin) ducat
duce, doo-chay, m., leader ; guide
duchessa, doo-**kess**-sah, f., duchess
due, doo-ay, a., two
duello, doo-**el**-lo, m., duel
duennale, doo-en-**nah**-lay, a., biennial
duna, doo-nah, f., sand-dune
dunque, **doonn**-kway, conj., then, therefore
duomo, doo'o-mo, m., dome ; cathedral
duplicare, doo-ple-**kah**-ray, v., to duplicate
duplicità, doo-ple-che-**tah**, f., duplicity
durante, doo-**rahn**-tay, prep., during
durare, doo-**rah**-ray, v., to last
durevole, doo-**ray**-vo-lay, a., lasting
durezza, doo-**ret**-tsah, f., hardness ; harshness
duro*, doo-ro, a., hard ; firm ; stale
duttile, **doot**-te-lay, a., flexible ; ductile

e, ay, conj., and
ebanista, ay-bah-**niss**-tah, m., cabinet-maker
ebano, ay-bah-no, m., ebony ; ebony-tree
ebbene, ayb-bay-nay, interj., well then ! now then !
ebbrezza, ayb-**bret**-tsah, f., drunkenness
ebbro, ayb-bro, a., drunk
ebdomadario*, ayb-do-mah-**dah**-re'o, a., weekly
ebete, **ay**-bay-tay, a., feeble-minded

ebreo, ay-bray-o, m., Jew. Hebrew
eburneo, ay-boohr-nay-o, a., of ivory
eccedenza, ayt-chay-den-tsah, f., excess
eccedere, ayt-chay-day-ray, v., to exceed
eccellente, ayt-chell-len-tay, a., excellent
eccellere, ayt-chell-lay-ray, v., to excel
eccelso*, ayt-chell-so, a., eminent ; lofty
eccentrico*, ayt-chen-tre-ko, a., eccentric
eccepire, ayt-chay-pee-ray, v., to object to
eccessivo*, ayt-chayss-see-vo, a., excessive
eccesso, ayt-chayss-so, m., excess, superfluity
eccetto, ayt-chayt-to, prep., unless
eccettuare, ayt-chayt-too-ah-ray, v., to except
eccezione, ayt-chay-tse'o-nay, f., exception
eccidio, ayt-chee-de'o, m., slaughter
eccitabile, ayt-che-tah-be-lay, a., excitable
eccitare, ayt-che-tah-ray, v., to excite ; to incite
ecclissi, eck-kliss-se, f., eclipse
ecco, eck-ko, adv., here is, there is [or are]
echeggiare, ay-ked-jah-ray, v., to echo
eco, ay-ko, m. & f., echo
economia, ay-ko-no-mee-ah, f., economy
economo, ay-ko-no-mo, m., manager ; buyer ;
    purser. a., thrifty
ed, ayd, conj., and
edera, ay-day-rah, f., ivy
edicola, ay-dee-ko-lah, f., bookstall ; kiosk
edificare, ay-de-fe-kah-ray, v., to build ; to edify
edificio, ay-de-fee-cho, m., building
editore, ay-de-tor-ay, m., editor ; publisher
editto, ay-deet-to, m., edict, decree
edizione, ay-de-tse'o-nay, f., edition ; publication
efferatezza, ef-fay-rah-tet-tsah, f., cruelty ; ferocity
efferato*, ef-fay-rah-to, a., inhuman, cruel
effettivo, ef-fet-tee-vo, a., effective ; real. uffi-
    ciale —, m., regular officer
effetto, ef-fet-to, m., effect. — cambiario, m.,
    bill of exchange
efficace, ef-fe-kah-chay, a., efficacious
effimero*, ef-fee-may-ro, a., ephemeral
efflusso, ef-flooss-so, m., efflux
effluvio, ef-floo-ve'o, m., effluvium, exhalation

effondere, ef-fon-day-ray, v., to pour out ; to ema- [nate

egli, ay-l'ye, pron., he

eglino, ay-l'ye-no, pron., they

egoismo, ay-go'eess-mo, m., selfishness, egoism

egregio°, ay-gray-jo, a., egregious

egresso, ay-grayss-so, m., egress

eguaglianza, ay-goo'ah-l'yahn-tsah, f., equality

eguagliare, ay-goo'ah-l'yah-ray, v., to equalize

eguale, ay-goo'ah-lay, a., equal

elaborare, ay-lah-bo-rah-ray, v., to elaborate

elargire, ay-lar-jee-ray, v., to give generously

elasticità, ay-lahss-te-che-tah, f., elasticity

elefante, ay-lay-fahn-tay, m., elephant

eleganza, ay-lay-gahn-tsah, f.,elegance, smartness

eleggere, ay-led-jay-ray, v., to elect

elemento, ay-lay-men-to, m., element

elemosina, ay-lay-mo-ze-nah, f., alms

elencare, ay-len-kah-ray, v., to make a list of

elenco, ay-len-ko, m., list ; roll

eletta, ay-let-tah, f., election ; elite

elettivo, ay-let-tee-vo, a., elective

eletto, ay-let-to, a., elected ; chosen

elettore, ay-let-tor-ay, m., elector

elettricista, ay-let-tre-chiss-tah, m., electrician

elettrico°, ay-let-tre-ko, a., electric ; electrical

elettrizzare, ay-let-trid-dzah-ray, v., to electrify

elevare, ay-lay-vah-ray, v., to elevate, to lift up

elezione, ay-lay-tse'o-nay, f., election ; choice

elica, ay-le-kah, f., propeller, screw

eliminare, ay-le-me-nah-ray, v., to eliminate

elisir, ay-le-zeer, m., elixir

ella, el-lah, pron., she ; you

elle, el-lay, pron., they

elleno, el-lay-no, pron., they

elmo, el-mo, m., helmet

elogiare, ay-lo-jah-ray, v., to praise, to commend

elogio, ay-lo-jo, m., praise, eulogy

eloquio, ay-lo-kwe-o, m., speech, discourse

elsa, el-sah, f., hilt

eludere, ay-loo-day-ray, v., to elude

emaciare, ay-mah-chah-ray, v., to emaciate

emanare, ay-mah-nah-ray, v., to emanate

emancipare, ay-mahn-che-**pah**-ray, v., to emanci-
embrione, em-bre'**O**-nay, m., embryo   [pate
emendare, ay-men-**dah**-ray, v., to amend
emergere, ay-**mair**-jay-ray, v., to emerge
emerito°, ay-**may**-re-to, a., emeritus
emettere, ay-**met**-tay-ray, v., to emit ; to issue
emicrania, ay-me-**krah**-ne'ah, f., sick-headache
emigrare, ay-me-**grah**-ray, v., to emigrate
eminenza, ay-me-**nen**-tsah, f., eminence
emisfero, ay-miss-**fay**-ro, m., hemisphere
emissione, ay-miss-se'**O**-nay, f., emission ; issue
emorragia, ay-mor-rah-jee-ah, f., hemorrhage
emorroidi, ay-mor-**ro**'e-de, f.pl., hemorrhoids, piles
emozione, ay-mo-tse'**O**-nay, f., emotion
empiere, em-pe'ay-ray, v., to fill up
empietà, em-pe'ay-**tah**, f., impiety
empio, **em**-pe'o, a., impious
emporio, em-po-re'o, m., emporium
emulare, ay-moo-**lah**-ray, v., to emulate
emulo, **ay**-moo-lo, m., competitor
encomiare, en-ko-me'**ah**-ray, v., to praise, to extol
encomio, en-ko-me'o, m., praise, eulogy
endivia, en-dee-ve'ah, f., endive
energia, ay-nair-jee-ah, f., energy, strength
energumeno, ay-nair-goo-**may**-no, m., person
    beside himself with fury
enfasi, en-fah-ze, f., emphasis, stress
enfiagione, en-fe'ah-jo-nay, f., swelling
enfiare, en-fe'**ah**-ray, v., to swell
ennesimo, en-**nay**-ze-mo, a., limitless   [try
enologo, ay-**no**-lo-go, m., specialist in wine indus-
enorme, ay-**nor**-may, a., enormous
ente, **en**-tay, m., being. — **morale**, corporation
enterite, en-tay-ree-tay, f., enteritis
entrambi, en-**trahm**-be, m. pl., both
entrare, en-**trah**-ray, v., to enter
entrata, en-**trah**-tah, f., entrance ; income
entro, **en**-tro, adv. & prep., within
entusiasmare, en-too-ze'ahss-**mah**-ray, v., to
    throw into raptures
entusiasmo, en-too-ze'**ahss**-mo, m., enthusiasm
enumerare, ay-noo-may-**rah**-ray, v., to enumerate

enunciare, ay-noonn-**chah**-ray, v., to enunciate
epa, ay-pah, f., big belly
epatico, ay-**pah**-te-ko, a., livery
epidemia, ay-pe-day-**mee**-ah, f., epidemic
epigrafe, ay-pee-grah-fay, f., epigraph
epilessia, ay-pe-less-**see**-ah, f., epilepsy   [clude
epilogare, ay-pe-lo-**gah**-ray, v., to sum up ; to con-
episodio, ay-pe-zo-de'o, m., episode, incident
epistola, ay-**piss**-to-lah, f., epistle
epiteto, ay-pee-tay-to, m., epithet
epoca, **ay**-po-kah, f., epoch
eppure, ayp-**poo**-ray, conj., yet ; still
epurare, ay-poo-**rah**-ray, v., to purify ; to clarify
epurazione, ay-poo-rah-tse'**o**-nay, f., purification
equatore, ay-kwah-**tor**-ay, m., equator
equestre, ay-**kwess**-tray, a., equestrian
equinozio, ay-kwe-**no**-tse'o, m., equinox
equipaggiare, ay-kwe-pahd-**jah**-ray, v., to equip ;
  (naut) to man
equipaggio, ay-kwe-**pahd**-jo, m.,equipment ; crew
equità, ay-kwe-**tah**, f., equity
equivoco, ay-**kwee**-vo-ko, a.,* equivocal. m. mis-
equo°, **ay**-kwo, a., equitable, right, fair   [take
era, **ay**-rah, f., era
erario, ay-**rah**-re'o, m., public treasury
erba, **air**-bah, f., grass, herb   [balist
erbaiuolo, air-bah-e'oo-**o**-lo, m., greengrocer ; her-
erede, ay-**ray**-day, m. & f., heir
eredità, ay-ray-de-**tah**, f., inheritance
ereditare, ay-ray-de-**tah**-ray, v., to inherit
eremita, ay-ray-**mee**-tah, m., hermit
eremitaggio, ay-ray-me-**tahd**-jo, m., hermitage
eresia, ay-ray-**zee**-ah, f., heresy
eretico, ay-**ray** te-ko, m., heretic. a., *heretical
erezione, ay-ray-tse'**o**-nay, f., erection ; building
ergastolo, air-**gass**-to-lo, m., penitentiary ; prison
erica, ay-re-kah, f., heather ; fern
erigere, ay-**ree**-jay-ray, v., to erect, to build
erigersi, ay-re-**jair**-se, v., to assume the right
ermellino, air-mell-**lee**-no, m., ermine
ernia, air-ne'ah, f., hernia, rupture
eroe, ay-**ro**-ay, m., hero

eroismo, ay-ro-eess-mo, m., heroism
erompere, ay-rom-pay-ray, v., to burst **forth**
erpete, air-pay-tay, m., (med.) herpes
erpicare, air-pe-kah-ray, v., to harrow
erpice, air-pe-chay, m., harrow
errante, air-rahn-tay, a., wandering
errare, air-rah-ray, v., to err; to roam
errore, air-ro-ray, m., error, blunder
erta, air-tah, f., steep incline
erto*, air-to, a., steep; rising
erudito, ay-roo-dee-to, m., scholar. a.,* **learned**
eruttare, ay-root-tah-ray, v., to belch
eruzione, ay-roo-tse'o-nay, f., eruption
esagerare, ay-zah-jay-rah-ray, v., to exaggerate
esalare, ay-zah-lah-ray, v., to exhale
esalazione, ay-zah-lah-tse'o-nay, f., exhalation
esaltare, ay-zahl-tah-ray, v., to exalt
esame, ay-zah-may, m., examination
esaminare, ay-zah-me-nah-ray, v., to examine
esangue, ay-zahn-goo'ay, a., bloodless; almost dead
esanime, ay-zah-ne-may, a., inanimate
esasperare, ay-zahss-pay-rah-ray, v., to exasperate
esattezza, ay-zaht-tet-tsah, f., exactness, precision
esatto*, ay-zaht-to, a., exact; punctual
esattore, ay-zaht-tor-ay, m., collector
esaudire, ay-zah'oo-dee-ray, v., to grant [plete
esaurire, ay-zah'oo-ree-ray, v., to exhaust; to de-
esazione, ay-zah-tse'o-nay, f., exaction
esca, ess-kah, f., bait; food; tinder; decoy
esclamare, ess-klah-mah-ray, v., to exclaim
escludere, ess-kloo-day-ray, v., to exclude
esclusione, ess-kloo-ze'o-nay, f., exclusion [tate
escogitare, ess-ko-je-tah-ray, v., to devise; to medi-
escremento, ess-kray-men-to, m., excrement
escrescenza, ess-kray-shen-tsah, f., excrescence
escursione, ess-koohr-se'o-nay, f., excursion
esecrabile, ay-zay-krah-be-lay, a., execrable
esecrare, ay-zay-krah-ray, v., to execrate, to loathe
esecutivo*, ay-zay-koo-tee-vo, a., executive
esecutore, ay-zay-koo-tor-ay, m., executor, trustee
esecuzione, ay-zay-koo-tse'o-nay, f., execution;
performance

eseguire, ay-zay-goo'ee-ray, v., to execute ; to fulfil

esempio, ay-zem-pe'o, m., example

esemplare, ay-zem-plah-ray, m., specimen. a., **exesentare,** ay-zen-tah-ray, v., to exempt [emplary

esente, ay-zen-tay. a., exempt

esenzione, ay-zen-tse'O-nay, f., exemption ; privilege

esercente, ay-zair-chen-tay, m., tradesman

esercitare, ay-zair-che-tah-ray, v., to exercise

esercito, ay-zair-che-to, m., army

esercizio, ay-zair-chee-tse'o, m., exercise

esibire, ay-ze-bee-ray, v., to exhibit

esibizione, ay-ze-be-tse'O-nay, f., exhibition

esigenza, ay-ze-jen-tsah, f., exigency

esigere, ay-zee-jay-ray, v., to exact

esiguità, ay-ze-goo'e-tah, f., scantiness

esile, ay-ze-lay, a., slender ; thin ; weak

esiliare, ay-ze-le'ah-ray, v., to exile ; to relegate

esilio, ay-zee-le'o, m., exile

esistente, ay-ziss-ten-tay, a., existing, living

esistere, ay-ziss-tay-ray, v., to exist

esitante, ay-ze-tahn-tay, a., hesitating

esitare, ay-ze-tah-ray, v., to hesitate ; to sell

esito, ay-ze-to, m., issue ; success

esofago, ay-zo-fah-go, m., gullet

esonerare, ay-zo-nay-rah-ray, v., to exonerate

esorbitante, ay-zor-be-tahn-tay, a., exorbitant

esordire, ay-zor-dee-ray, v., to make a first appearance

esortare, ay-zor-tah-ray, v., to exhort

esoso, ay-zo-zo, a., greedy ; detestable

esotico, ay-zo-te-ko, a., exotic

espandere, ess-pahn-day-ray, v., to expand

espansione, ess-pahn-se'O-nay, f., expansion

espatriare, ess-pah-tre'ah-ray, v., to expatriate

espatriarsi, ess-pah-tre-ar-se, v., to emigrate

espellere, ess-pell-lay-ray, v., to expel

esperienza, ess-pay-re'en-tsah, f., experience

esperimentare, ess-pay-re-men-tah-ray, v., to experiment ; to try ; to test

esperto*, ess-pair-to, a., skilled, expert

espiare, ess-pe'ah-ray, v., to expiate, to atone for

espiazione, ess-pe'ah-tse'O-nay, f., atonement

espirare, ess-pe-rah-ray, v., to expire ; to exhale

esplicare, ess-ple-kah-ray, v., to explain

esplicito*, ess-plee-che-to, a., explicit

esplodere, ess-plo-day-ray, v., to explode

esplorare, ess-plo-rah-ray, v., to explore ; to sound

esploratore, ess-plo-rah-tor-ray, m., explorer

esplosione, ess-plo-ze'o-nay, f., explosion

esplosivo, ess-plo-zee-vo, m., explosive

esporre, ess-por-ray, v., to expose

esportare, ess-por-tah-ray, v., to export

esposizione, ess-po-ze-tse'o-nay, f., exhibition ; exposure ; explanation

espressione, ess-press-se'o-nay, f., expression ; elocution

espressivo*, ess-press-see-vo, a., expressive

espresso*, ess-press-so, a., express ; on purpose

esprimere, ess-pree-may-ray, v., to express

espropriare, ess-pro-pre'ah-ray, v., to evict

espugnare, ess-poo-n'yah-ray, v., to take by storm

espulsione, ess-pooll-se'o-nay, f., expulsion

espurgare, ess-poohr-gah-ray, v., to expurgate

essa, ess-sah, pron., she ; it ; herself ; that one

essendochè, ess-sen-do-kay, conj., since ; as ; considering

essenza, ess-sen-tsah, f., essence ; oil ; petrol

essere, ess-say-ray, v., to be. m., being

essicare, ess-se-kah-ray, v., to dry up ; to season

esso, ess-so, pron., he ; it ; him ; that one ; he himself, esst, m., east. a., eastern. adv., eastward [self

estasi, ess-tah-ze, f., ecstasy

estate, ess-tah-tay, f., summer

estendere, ess-ten-day-ray, v., to extend

estensivo*, ess-ten-see-vo, a., extensive

estenuare, ess-tay-noo'ah-ray, v., to extenuate

esteriore, ess-tay-re'o-ray, m., exterior. a., external

esterminare, ess-tair-me-nah-ray, v., to exterminate

esternare, ess-tair-nah-ray, v., to manifest

esterno, ess-tair-no, m., outside, exterior. a.,* external

estero, ess-tay-ro, a., foreign ; strange. all'estero, abroad

esteso, ess-**tay**-zo, a., large, vast. per —, in full

estimare, ess-te-**mah**-ray, v., to estimate ; to appraise

estimo, **ess**-te-mo, m., valuation

estinguere, ess-**tin**-goo'ay-ray, v., to extinguish

estirpare, ess-teer-**pah**-ray, v., to extirpate ; to estivo [weed

estivo, ess-**tee**-vo, a., of summer

estorcere, ess-**tor**-chay-ray, v., to extort

estorsione, ess-tor-se'**O**-nay, f., extortion

estradizione, ess-trah-de-tse'**O**-nay, f., extradition

estraneo, ess-**trah**-nay-o, m., stranger. a.,*strange

estrarre, ess-**trar**-ray, v., to extract ; to draw lots

estratto, ess-**traht**-to, m., extract ; synopsis

estrazione, ess-trah-tse'**O** - nay, f., extraction ; drawing

estremità, ess-tray-me-**tah**, f., extremity, end

estremo, ess-**tray**-mo, m., extremity. a.,*extreme

estuario, ess-too'ah-re'o, m., estuary

esuberante, ay-zoo-bay-**rahn**-tay, a., exuberant

esule, **ay**-zoo-lay, m., exile

esultare, ay-zooll-**tah**-ray, v., to exult

età, ay-**tah**, f., age ; period, century

etere, **ay**-tay-ray, m., ether ; air ; sky

eterno*, ay-**tair**-no, a., eternal

etichetta, ay-te-**ket**-tah, f., label ; etiquette

etico*, **ay**-te-ko, a., ethical ; consumptive

etisia, ay-te-zee-ah, f., consumption

ettaro, **ayt**-tah-ro, m., hectare

eucalitto, ay-oo-kah-**lit**-to, m., eucalyptus

evacuare, ay-vah-koo'**ah**-ray, v., to evacuate

evadere, ay-**vah**-day-ray, v., to evade

evangelo, ay-vahn-**jay**-lo, m., gospel

evaporare, ay-vah-po-**rah**-ray, v., to evaporate

evaso, ay-**vah**-zo, m., escaped convict

evenienza, ay - vay - ne'**en** - tsah, f., occurrence. all'—, if need be

evento, ay-**ven**-to, m., event

evincere, ay-**veen**-chay-ray, v., to evict

evitare, ay-ve-**tah**-ray, v., to avoid ; to escape

evizione, ay-ve-tse'**O**-nay, f., eviction

evo, **ay**-vo, m., age, period

evocare, ay-vo-**kah**-ray, v., to evoke

evoluto*, ay-vo-**loo**-to, a., modern ; transformed

evoluzione, ay-vo-loo-tse'o-nay, f., evolution

evviva, ayv-vee-vah, interj., hurrah !

eziandio, ay-tse'ahn-de-o, adv., even ; also ; yet

fa, fah, adv., ago

fabbisogno, fahb-be-zo-n'yo, m., the needful

fabbrica, fahb-bre-kah, f., works ; manufactory ; building

fabbricante, fahb-bre-**kahn**-tay, m., manufacturer ; maker ; builder

fabbricare, fahb-bre-**kah**-ray, v., to build ; to manufacture

fabbro, fahb-bro, m., blacksmith

faccenda, faht-chen-dah, f., business ; intrigue

facchinata, fahk-ke-nah-tah, f., hard toil ; rudeness

facchino, fahk-kee-no, m., porter ; uncouth fellow

faccia, faht-chah, f., face. in or di —, opposite. **faccia a faccia,** face to face

facciata, faht-chah-tah, f., facade

faceto*, fah-chay-to, a., facetious ; witty

facezia, fah-chay-tse'ah, f., jest ; witticism

facile, fah-che-lay, a., easy

facilitare, fah-che-le-tah-ray, v., to facilitate

facilmente, fah-chill-men-tay, adv., easily

facilone, fah-che-lo-nay, m., happy go lucky person

facinoroso, fah-che-no-ro-zo,a.,rebellious. m.,rioter

facoltà, fah-koll-tah, f., faculty

facoltativo*, fah-koll-tah-tee-vo, a., optional

facondia, fah-kon-de'ah, f., eloquence

faggio, fahd-jo, m., beech-tree

fagiano, fah-jah-no, m., pheasant

fagiolo, fah-jo-lo, m., kidney-bean

fagotto, fah-got-to, m., bundle ; (mus.) bassoon

faina, fah-ee-nah, f., polecat

falcato, fahl-kah-to, a., scythe shaped

falce, fahl-chay, f., scythe ; sickle

falciare, fahl-chah-ray, v., to mow   [chino

falciatrice, fahl-chah-tree-chay, f., mowing ma-

falciatura, fahl-chah-too-rah, f., mowing

falcidia, fahl-chee-de'ah, f., tare ; deduction

falco[ne], fahl-ko, m., hawk ; falcon

falda, fahl-dah, f., plait ; fold ; flake ; foot

falegname, fah-lay-n'**yah**-may, m., carpenter
falena, fah-**lay**-nah, f., moth
falla, **fahl**-lah, f., (naut.) leak
fallace, fahl-**lah**-chay, a., fallacious; deceitful
fallacia, fahl-**lah**-chah, f., fallacy; deceit
fallire, fahl-**lee**-ray, v., to fail; to go bankrupt
fallito, fahl-**lee**-to, m., bankrupt
fallo, **fahl**-lo, m., fault, error
falo, fah-lo, m., bonfire
falsare, fahl-**sah**-ray, v., to distort, to adulterate
falsariga, fahl-sah-**ree**-gah, f., black ruled paper
falsario, fahl-**sah**-re'o, m., forger
falsificare, fahl-se-fe-**kah**-ray, v.,to falsify, to forge
falsificatore, fahl-se-fe-kah-**tor**-ay, m., forger
falsità, fahl-se-**tah**, f., falsehood
falso, **fahl**-so, a.,* false, untrue. m., forgery
fama, **fah**-mah, f., fame, renown
fame, **fah**-may, f., hunger
famigerato, fah-me-jay-**rah**-to, a., notorious
famiglia, fah-**mee**-l'yah, f., family   [tive
famigliare, fah-me-l'**yah**-ray, a., familiar. m., rela-
famiglio, fah-**mee**-l'yo, m., man-servant
fanale, fah-**nah**-lay, m., lantern; lamp; light
fanciulla, fahn-**chool**-lah, f., young girl; maid
fanciullesco*, fahn-chool-**less**-ko, a., childish
fanciullezza, fahn-chool-**let**-tsah, f., childhood
fanciullo, fahn-**chool**-lo, m., young boy; infant
fandonia, fahn-do-ne'ah, f., preposterous lie
fanello, fah-**nel**-lo, m., linnet
fanfarone, fahn-fah-**ro**-nay, m., blusterer
fango, **fahn**-go, m., mud
fangoso, fahn-go-zo, a., muddy, miry
fannullone, fahn-nool-lo-nay, m., idler; wanton
fantaccino, fahn-taht-**chee**-no, m., foot-soldier
fantasma, fahn-**tahss**-mah, m., spectre, ghost
fantasticare, fahn-tahss-te-**kah**-ray, v.,to imagine
fante, **fahn**-tay, m., foot-soldier; (cards) jack
fanteria, fahn-tay-**ree**-ah, f., infantry
fantesca, fahn-**tess**-kah, f., servant-girl
fantino, fahn-**tee**-no, m., jockey
fantoccio, fahn-**tot**-cho, m., puppet; doll
farabutto, fah-rah-**boot**-to, m., blackguard

faraggine, fah-rahd-je-nay, f., medley

farcire, far-chee-ray, v., to stuff

fardello, far-dell-lo. m., bundle ; package

fare, fah-ray, v., to do, to make, to be. m., manner

faretra, fah-ray-trah, f., quiver

farfalla, far-fahl-lah, f., butterfly

farina, fah-ree-nah, f., flour ; meal

farinoso, fah-re-no-zo, a., floury ; mealy

farmacia, far-mah-chee-ah. f., chemist's shop

farmacista, far-mah-chiss-tah, m. & f., chemist

farmaco, far-mah-ko, m., drug ; remedy

farnetico, far-nay-te-ko, a.,* frenzied. m., craze

faro, fah-ro, m., lighthouse ; head-light

farsa, far-sah, f., farce

farsetto, far-set-to, m., waistcoat

fascetta, fah-shet-tah, f., corset ; small band

fascia, fah-she'ah, f., bandage ; band

fasciare, fah-she'ah-ray, v., to bandage

fasciatura, fah-she'ah-too-rah, f., bandage

fascicolo, fah-shee-ko-lo, m., magazine ; bundle

fascina, fah-shee-nah, f., faggot

fascino, fah-she-no, m., fascination, spell

fascio, fah-she'o, m., bundle ; sheaf

fascista, fah-shiss-tah, m. & f., fascist. a., fascist

fase, fah-zay, f., phase

fastello, fahss-tell-lo, m., faggot

fasti, fahss-te, m. pl., records

fastidio, fahss-tee-de'o, m., annoyance ; trouble

fasto, fahss-to, m., pomp

fastoso°, fahss-to-zo, a., ostentatious, pompous

fata, fah-tah, f., fairy

fatica, fah-tee-kah, f., fatigue ; hard work ; labour

faticare, fah-te-kah-ray, v., to tire ; to toil

faticoso°, fah-te-ko-zo, a., tiresome ; painful

fato, fah-to, m., fate, destiny

fattaccio, faht-taht-cho, m., wicked deed

fattibile, faht-tee-be-lay, a., feasible

fatto, faht-to, m., fact ; deed. p.p., made

fattore, faht-tor-ay, m., steward ; farmer ; creator

fattoria, faht-to-ree-ah, f., farm ; farm-house

fattorino, faht-to-ree-no, m., errand-boy

fattura, faht-too-rah, f., invoice ; bill ; work

fatturare, faht-too-rah-ray, v., to invoice; to debase
fatuo*, fah-too'o, a., conceited
fauci, fah'oo-che, f. pl., mouth of animal
fautore, fah'oo-tor-ay, m., patron, promoter
fava, fah-vah, f., broad bean
favella, fah-vell-lah, f., speech; language
favellare, fah-vell-lah-ray, v., to talk, to speak
favilla, fah-vill-lah, f., spark
favo, fah-vo, m., honey-comb
favola, fah-vo-lah, f., fable
favoleggiare, fah-vo-led-jah-ray, v., to fable
favoloso*, fah-vo-lo-zo, a., fabulous
favoreggiare, fah-vo-red-jah-ray, v., to abet
favorevole, fah-vo-ray-vo-lay, a., favourable
favorire, fah-vo-ree-ray, v., to favour
fazioso*, fah-tse'o-zo, a., rebellious
fazzoletto, faht-tso-let-to, m., handkerchief
febbraio, feb-brah-e'o, m., February
febbre, feb-bray, f., fever
febbricitante, feb-bre-che-tahn-tay, a., feverish
febbrile, feb-bree-lay, a., feverish
feccia, fet-chah, f., dregs, lees; rabble
feci, fay-che, f. pl., excrements; dregs
fecondo*, fay-kon-do, a., fruitful, fertile
fede, fay-day, f., faith
fedele, fay-day-lay, a., faithful
fedeltà, fay-dell-tah, f., fidelity
federa, fay-day-rah, f., pillow-case
fedine, fay-dee-nay, f. pl., whiskers
fegato, fay-gah-to, m., liver; (pop.) pluck
felce, fell-chay, f., fern, bracken
felice, fay-lee-chay, a., happy
felicitare, fay-le-che-tah-ray, v., to congratulate
felino*, fay-lee-no, a., feline
fellone*, fell-lo-nay, a., traitorous; perfidious
fellonia, fell-lo-nee-ah, f., treason; wickedness
felpa, fell-pah, f., plush; nappy material
feltro, fell-tro, m., felt
feluca, fay-loo-kah, f., cocked hat
felze, fel-tsay, m., gondola-cabin
femmina, fem-me-nah, f., female
femminile, fem-me-nee-lay, a., feminine

fendere, fen-day-ray, v., to cleave, to hew

fenditura, fen-de-too-rah, f., cleft ; slot

fenico, fay-ne-ko, a., acido —, carbolic acid

fenicottero, fay-ne-kot-tay-ro, m., flamingo

feretro, fay-ray-tro, m., coffin

feria, fay-re'ah, f., holiday

feriale, fay-re'ah-lay, a., daily

ferire, fay-ree-ray, v., to wound

ferita, fay-ree-tah, f., wound

ferito, fay-ree-to, m., wounded man

ferma, fair-mah, f., period of enlistment

fermaglio, fair-mah-l'yo, m., clasp, buckle

fermare, fair-mah-ray, v., to stop ; to fasten

fermata, fair-mah-tah, f., stop, halt

fermentare, fair-men-tah-ray, v., to ferment

fermento, fair men-to, m., ferment ; yeast

fermezza, fair-met-tsah, f., firmness ; steadiness

fermo, fair-mo, a.,* firm ; fast. interj., stop!
    — in posta, poste restante

feroce, fay-ro-chay, a., ferocious

ferraio, fair-rah-e'o, m., fabbro —, blacksmith

ferramenta, fair-rah-men-tah, f., ironmongery ;
    tools

ferrare, fair-rah-ray, v., to shoe ; to hoop with iron

ferrata, fair-rah-tah, a., strada—, railway

ferriera, fair-re'ay-rah, f., iron-works

ferro, fair-ro, m., iron. — di cavallo, horse-shoe

ferrovia, fair-ro-vee-ah, f., railway

ferroviere, fair-ro-ve'ay-ray, m., railway-man

fervere, fair-vay-ray, v., to be hot ; to boil

fervore, fair-vor-ay, m., fervour

fesso, fess-so, a., cracked ; split, cloven

fessura, fess-soo-rah, f., fissure ; crack

festa, fess-tah, f., holiday ; party ; festival

festeggiare, fess-ted jah-ray, v., to celebrate

festevole, fess-tay-vo-lay, a., festive, joyful

festino, fess-tee-no, m., banquet ; entertainment

festone, fess-to-nay, m., festoon

festoso⁴, fess-to-zo, a., festive ; merry

festuca, fess-too-kah, f., bit of straw ; sailing-boat

fetente, fay-ten tay, a., stinky

feticcio, fay-tit-cho, m., fetish

fetore, fay-tor-ay, m., stink

fetta, fet-tah, f., slice

fetuccia, fay-toot-chah, f., ribbon, tape

fiaba, fe'ah-bah, f., fairy-tale

fiacca, fe'ahk-kah, f., slackness

fiaccare, fe'ahk-kah-ray, v., to break; to tire out

fiacchezza, fe'ahk-ket-tsah, f., feebleness

fiacco*, fe'ahk-ko, a., weak; tired

fiaccola, fe'ahk-ko-lah, f., torch

fiala, fe'ah-lah, f., phial

fiamma, fe'ahm-mah, f., flame; (flag) pennon

fiammeggiare, fe'ahm-med-jah-ray, v., to flame; to shine

fiammifero, fe'ahm-mee-fay-ro, m., match

fiancheggiare, fe'ahn-ked-jah-ray [or fiancare, fe'ahn-kah-ray], v., to flank; to support

fianco, fe'ahn-ko, m., flank

fiasca, fe'ahss-kah, f., flask

fiasco, fe'ahss-ko, m., flask; (fig.) failure

fiatare, fe'ah-tah-ray, v., to breathe; to whisper

fiato, fe'ah-to, m., breath, respiration; (fig.) courage

fibbia, feeb-be'ah, f., buckle

fibra, fee-brah, f., fibre, thread; strength

fibroso*, fe-bro-zo, a., fibrous

ficcare, feek-kah-ray, v., to drive in; to poke

fico, fee-ko, m., fig; fig-tree

fidanzamento, fe-dahn-tsah-men-to, m., betrothal

fidanzarsi, fe-dahn-tsar-se, v., to become engaged

fidanzato, fe-dahn-tsah-to, a., betrothed. m., fiancé

fidarsi, fe-dar-se, v., to rely upon

fidato*, fe-dah-to, a., trustworthy

fido*, fee-do, a., faithful, true

fiducia, fe-doo-chah, f., trust; hope

fiele, fe'ay-lay, m., gall; jaundice; enmity

fieno, fe'ay-no, m., hay; fodder

fiera, fe'ay-rah, f., wild beast; fair

fiero*, fe'ay-ro, a., fierce; haughty

fievole, fe'ay-vo-lay, a., feeble

figgere, feed-jay-ray, v., to fix

figlia, fee-l'yah, f., daughter

figliare, fe-l'yah-ray, v., to bring forth young

figliastro, fe-l'yahss-tro, m., step-son

FIG 127 FIO

figlio, fee-l'yo, m., son   [godchild

figlioc[cio][cia], fe-l'yot-[cho][chah], m. & f.,

fignolo, fee-n'yo-lo, m., boil, furuncle

figura, fe-goo-rah, f., figure

figurare, fe-goo-rah-ray, v., to represent; to show

figurarsi, fe-goo-rar-se, v., to imagine

fila, fee-lah, f., row; file. far la —, to queue up

filanda, fe-lahn-dah, f., silk-spinning

filare, fe-lah-ray, v., to spin

filati, fe-lah-te, m. pl., spun yarns

filatoio, fe-lah-to-e'o, m., spinning-wheel

filatura, fe-lah-too-rah, f., spinning

filetto, fe-let-to, m., fillet; filament; stripe; snaffle

filiale, fe-le'ah-lay, f., branch. a., filial

filigrana, fe-le-grah-nah, f., filigree

film, film, m., film. — sonoro, talking film

filo, fee-lo, m., thread; wire; (knife) edge

filosofo, fe-lo-zo-fo, m., philosopher

filovia, fe-lo-vee-ah, f., cable-railway

filtrare, feel-trah-ray, v., to filter

filugello, fe-loo-jell-lo, m., silk-worm

filza, feel-tsah, f., string; series

finan[che][co], fe-nahn-[kay][ko], adv., even

finanza, fe-nahn-tsah, f., finance; revenue

finanziario*, fe-nahn-tse'ah-re'o, a., financial

finchè, feen-kay, conj., until; as long as

fine, fee-nay, m. & f., end, goal. a., fine; thin

finestra, fe-ness-trah, f., window   [ment

finezza, fe-net-tsah, f., fineness; acuteness; refine-

fingere, feen-jay-ray, v., to feign

finimento, fe-ne-men-to, m., harness; ornament

finimondo, fe-ne-mon-do, m., end of the world

finire, fe-nee-ray, v., to finish; to cease

finitezza, fe-ne-tet-tsah, f., finish; completion

fino, fee-no, a.,* fine; thin; subtle; artful. prep. &
    adv., till; until; as far as. — da, from

finocchio, fe-nock-ke'o, m., fennel

finora, fe-no-rah, adv., up till now, so far

finta, feen-tah, f., feint; sham

finto*, feen-to, a., feigned, sham

finzione, feen-tse'o-nay, f., fiction; deceit

fiocco, fe'ook-ko, m., tassel; snow-flake

fiocina, fe'o-che-nah, f., harpoon
fioco°, fe'o-ko, a., hoarse ; feeble, **faint**
fionda, fe'onn-dah, f., sling
floraia, fe'o-rah-e'ah, f., flower-girl ; **flower-stall**
fiordaliso, fe'or-dah-lee-zo, m., fleur-de-lis
fiore, fe'o-ray, m., flower ; bloom
fiorente, fe'o-ren-tay, a., blooming ; thriving
fioretto, fe'o-ret-to, m., foil ; little flower
fiori, fe'o-re, m. pl., (cards) clubs
fiorire, fe'o-ree-ray, v., to blossom ; **to prosper**
fioritura, fe'o-re-too-rah, f., bloom
fiorrancio, fe'or-rahn-cho, m., marigold
fiotto, fe'ot-to, m., wave, billow, flow
firma, feer-mah, f., signature
firmare, feer-mah-ray, v., to sign
firmatario, feer-mah-tah-re'o, m., signatory
fisarmonica, fe-zar-mo-ne-kah, f., accordion-like
    instrument
fischiare, fiss-ke'ah-ray, v., to whistle ; to hiss
fischietto, fiss-ke'et-to, m., small whistle
fischio, fiss-ke'o, m., whistle ; signal
fisco, fiss-ko, m., Treasury
fisica, fee-ze-kah, f., physic ; physics
fisico, fee-ze-ko, m., physicist. a., **physical**
fisime, fee-ze-may, f. pl., whims, moods
fis[s]o°, fee-zo, a., fixed ; firm ; stable
fissare, fiss-sah-ray, v., to fix, to settle
fitta, fit-tah, f., stitch in the side
fittaiuolo, fit-tah-e'oo-o-lo, m., tenant-farmer
fittizio°, fit-tee-tse'o, a., fictitious
fitto, fit-to, m., rent, hire. a.,° thick
fiumana, fe'oo-mah-nah, f., flooded **river**
fiume, fe'oo-may, m., river ; (fig.) **flow**
fiutare, fe'oo-tah-ray, v., to sniff
fiuto, fe'oo-to, m., sense of smell ; odour ; **scent**
flagello, flah-jell-lo, m., whip ; plague
flagrante, flah-grahn-tay, a., flagrant. **in —, in**
flauto, flah'oo-to, m., (mus.) flute   [the act
flebile, flay-be-lay, a., plaintive ; feeble
flemma, flem-mah, f., phlegm ; (fig.) **coolness**
flessibile, fless-see-be-lay, a., flexible
floscio°, flo-she'o, a., flabby

flotta, flot-tah, f., fleet

fluido, floo'e-do, m., fluid, a.,* liquid

fluire, floo'ee-ray, v., to flow ; to run

flusso, flooss-so, m., flux ; rising tide

flutto, floot-to, m., wave, billow

fluttuare, floot-too'ah-ray, v., to fluctuate

fluttuazione, floot-too'ah-tse'O-nay, f., fluctuation ; [wavering

foca, fo-kah, f., seal

focaccia, fo-kaht-chah, f., cake

focaia, fo-kah-e'ah, a., pietra —, flint

focatico, fo-kah-te-ko, m., special local tax

foce, fo-chay, f., mouth of river

fochista, fo-kiss-tah, m., stoker

focolare, fo-ko-lah-ray, m., hearth, fireplace

focoso*, fo-ko-zo, a., fiery

fodera, fo-day-rah, f., lining, case

foderare, fo-day-rah-ray, v., to line

fodero, fo-day-ro, m., scabbard ; sheath

foggia, fod-jah, f., vogue ; shape ; way

foglia, fo-l'yah, f., leaf ; tin-foil ; petal. **mangiar**
la —, to become suspicious

fogliame, fo-l'yah-may, m., foliage

foglio, fo-l'yo, m., sheet ; newspaper

fogna, fo-n'yah, f., sewer ; drain

fognatura, fo-n'yah-too-rah, f., sewers, drainage

folata, fo-lah-tah, f., gust ; flock of birds

folgorare, fol-go-rah-ray, v., to thunder ; to lighten

folgore, fol-gor-ay, f., lightning ; thunderbolt

folla, fol-lah, f., crowd ; quantity

folle, fol-lay, a., mad

folleggiare, fol-led-jah-ray, v., to fool about, to frolic

folletto, fol-let-to, m., imp, elf. **fuoco** —, will-
follia, fol-lee-ah, f., folly [o'-the-wisp

folto, fol-to, a.,* thick. m., thickness

fondaccio, fon-daht-cho, m., dregs

fondaco, fon-dah-ko, m., warehouse

fondamento, fon-dah-men-to, m., foundation

fondare, fon-dah-ray, v., to establish, to found

fondatore, fon-dah-tor-ay, m., founder

fondere, fon-day-ray, v., to melt ; to smelt ; to cast

fonderia, fon-day-ree-ah, f., foundry

fonditore, fon-de-tor-ay, m., founder ; smelter

fondo, fon-do, m., bottom ; landed property ; funds ; stock. a.,* deep

fonografo, fo-no-grah-fo, m., gramophone

fontana, fon-tah-nah, f., fountain

fonte, fon-tay, f., source. m., font

foraggio, fo-rahd-jo, m., forage

forare, fo-rah-ray, v., to pierce, to drill

forbici, for-be-che, f. pl., scissors

forbire, for-bee-ray, v., to polish ; to wipe

forca, for-kah, f., gibbet ; pitch-fork

forchetta, for-ket-tah, f., fork

forcuto, for-koo-to, a., forked ; cloven

foresta, fo-ress-tah, f., forest

forestie[re] [ra], fo-ress-te'ay-[ray] [rah], m. & f., foreigner ; stranger ; visitor. a., foreign ; strange

forfecchia, for-feck-ke'ah, f., earwig

forfora, for-fo-rah, f., dandruff

foriere, fo-re'ay-ray, m., quartermaster

forma, for-mah, f., form ; figure ; mould ; last

formaggio, for-mahd-jo, m., cheese

formale, for-mah-lay, a., formal   [bring up

formare, for-mah-ray, v., to form ; to shape ; to

formica, for-mee-kah, f., ant

formicaio, for-me-kah-e'o, m., ant-hill ; swarm

formidabile, for-me-dah-be-lay, a., formidable

formoso*, for-mo-zo, a., beautiful, handsome

fornace, for-nah-chay, f., furnace ; kiln

fornaio, for-nah-e'o, m., baker

fornello, for-nell-lo, m., stove ; kitchen-cooker

fornire, for-nee-ray, v., to furnish ; to supply

fornitore, for-ne-tor-ay, m., furnisher ; purveyor

forno, for-no, m., oven. alto —, blast furnace

foro, fo-ro, m., hole ; perforation ; bar ; courts ; for-

forra, for-rah, f., glen, dale ; ravine   [um

forse, for-say, adv., perhaps ; maybe

forsennato, for-sen-nah-to, a.,* uncontrolled tempered. m., raving lunatic

forte, for-tay, a., strong. m., fort ; strong point

fortezza, for-tet-tsah, f., strength ; fortress

fortificare, for-te-fe-kah-ray, v., to fortify

fortuito*, for-too-e-to, a., by chance

fortuna, for-too-nah, f., fortune ; luck ; wealth

foruncolo, fo-roonn-ko-lo, m., boil

forza, for-tsah, f., force ; strength ; **power**

forzare, for-tsah-ray, v., to force

forzato, for-tsah-to, m., convict ; **galley-slave**.
   p.p., compelled

forziere, for-tse'ay-ray, m., safe ; **iron-chest**

fosco*, foss-ko, a., gloomy ; dull

fosfato, foss-fah-to, m., phosphate

fosforo, foss-fo-ro, m., phosphorus

fossa, foss-sah, f., ditch ; grave

fossetta, foss-set-tah, f., dimple

fosso, foss-so, m., ditch ; moat [tograph

fotografia, fo-to-grah-fee-ah, f.,photography ; pho-
fotografo, fo-to-grah-fo, m., photographer

fra, frah, prep., between, amongst, within

fracassare, frah-kahss-sah-ray, v., to smash

fracasso, frah-kahss-so, m., din ; damage

fracidezza, frah-che-det-tsah, f., rottenness

fracido, frah-che-do, a., rotten ; dank ; **soaked**

fradicio*, frah-de-cho, a., soaked ; rotten

fragola, frah-go-lah, f., strawberry

fragore, frah-gor-ay, m., (noise) crash

fragranza, frah-grahn-tsah, f., fragrance [stand

fraintendere,frah-in-ten-day-ray, v.,to misunder-
fralezza, frah-let-tsah, f., frailty

frammassone, frahm-mahss-so-nay,m.,freemason

frammentario, frahm-men-tah-re'o, a., fragmen-
frammento, frahm-men-to, m., fragment [tary

frammischiare,frahm-miss-ke'ah-ray,v.,to mix up

frana, frah-nah, f., landslip

franchezza, frahn-ket-tsah, f., frankness

franchigia, frahn-kee-jah, f., in—, tax or duty free

franco, frahn-ko, a.,* frank ; free. m., franc

francobollo, frahn-ko-boll-lo, m., postage-stamp

frangere, frahn-jay-ray, v., to crush

frangia, frahn-jah, f., fringe

frantoio, frahn-to-e'o, m., olive-press

frantumare, frahn-too-mah-ray, v., to smash

frantumi, frahn-too-me, m. pl., fragments, **bits**

frapporsi, frahp-por-se, v., to interfere

frasario, frah-zah-re'o, m., phrase-book

frasca, frahss-kah, f., leafy bough ; foliage

frascame, frahss-**kah**-may, m., foliage

frase, frah-zay, f., phrase

frassino, frahss-se-no, m., ash-tree [indent

frastagliare, frahss-tah-le'**ah**-ray, v., to slash ; to

frastuono, frahss-too'o-no, m., uproar

frate, frah-tay, m., friar

fratellanza, frah-tell-**lahn**-tsah, f., fraternity

fratellastro, frah-tell-lahss-tro, m., step-brother

fratello, frah-**tell**-lo, m., brother

fraterno*, frah-**tair**-no, a., fraternal

fratta, fraht-tah, f., thicket

frattanto, fraht-**tahn**-to, adv., meanwhile

fratturare, fraht-too-**rah**-ray, v., to fracture

frazionario, frah-tse'o-**nah**-re'o, a., fractional

freccia, fret-chah, f., arrow

freddare, fred-**dah**-ray, v., to cool ; to shoot dead

freddezza, fred-**det**-tsah, f., coldness

freddo, **fred**-do, m., cold weather. a.,* cold ; cool

freddura, fred-**doo**-rah, f., cold wave ; chill

fregamento, fray-gah-**men**-to, m., rubbing

fregare, fray-**gah**-ray, v., to rub ; to cheat

fregata, fray-**gah**-tah, f., frigate ; rubbing

fregio, **fray**-jo, m., frieze ; trimming

fregola, **fray**-go-lah, f., spawning-season

fremere, **fray**-may-ray, v., to shake ; to thrill

frenare, fray-**nah**-ray, v., to restrain ; to brake

frenesia, fray-nay-**zee**-ah, f., frenzy

freno, **fray**-no, m., brake ; bit ; (fig.) control [cy

frequenza, fray-**kwen**-tsah, f., frequence ; frequen-

freschezza, frayss-**ket**-tsah, f., freshness ; coolness

fresco, **frayss**-ko, m., coolness. a.,* cool, fresh ;

fretta, frayt-tah, f., haste [new ; new-laid

frettoloso*, frayt-to-lo-zo, a., hasty

friabile, fre-ah-be-lay, a., crumbling

friggere, **freed**-jay-ray, v., to fry

friggitore, freed-je-**tor**-ay, m., fried food shop

frigido*, **free**-je-do, a., frigid

frigorifero, fre-go-ree-**fay**-ro, m., refrigerator

fringuello, freen-goo'**ell**-lo, m., chaffinch

frittata, freet-**tah**-tah, f., omelet

frittella, freet-**tell**-lah, f., pancake ; fritter

fritto, **freet**-to, a., fried ; (fig.) lost, "done for"

frivolezza, fre-vo-let-tsah, f., frivolity

frizione, fre-tse'o-nay, f.,friction ; (motoring) clutch

frizzante, freet-tsahn-tay, a., piquant

frizzare, freet-tsah-ray, v., to sting ; to sparkle

frizzo, freet-tso, m., joke ; sally ; pricking

frodare, fro-dah-ray, v., to defraud

frodatore, fro-dah-tor-ay, m., cheat, swindler

frode, fro-day, f., fraud ; fake

frodo, fro-do, m., cheat. **cacciar di —**, poaching

froge, fro-jay, f., (horse) nostrils

frollare, froi-lah-ray, v., to scramble ; to make tender ; to make a fluttering sound

frollo, frol-lo, a., tender

frombola, from-bo-lah, f., sling

fronda, fron-dah, f., leafy branch ; revolt

fronte, fron-tay, f., forehead ; (mil.) front

fronteggiare, fron-ted-jah-ray, v.,to face; to oppose

frontiera, fron-te'ay-rah, f., frontier

fronzoli, fron-dzo-le, m. pl., finery

frotta, frot-tah, f., troop

frottola, frot-to-lah, f., fable ; lie

frugare, froo-gah-ray, v., to search ; to rummage

fruire, froo'ee-ray, v., to enjoy ; to benefit

frullare, frool-lah-ray, v., to beat eggs ; to twirl

frullino, frool-lee-no, m., egg-beater ; small snipe

frumento, froo-men-to, m., wheat

frusta, frooss-tah, f., whip

frustagno, frooss-tah-n'yo, m., kind of corduroy

frustare, frooss-tah-ray, v., to whip

frutta, froot-tah, f., fruit

fruttare, froot-tah-ray, v., to fructify ; to yield

frutteto, froot-tay-to, m., orchard

frutto, froot-to, m., fruit ; profit

fu, foo, a., deceased, passed away, late

fucilare, foo-che-lah-ray, v., to shoot

fucilata, foo-che-lah-tah, f., gun-shot ; (mil.) fusil-

fucile, foo-chee-lay, m., gun ; rifle [lade

fucina, foo-chee-nah, f., forge ; smithy

fuga, foo-gah, f., flight ; leakage ; (mus.) fugue

fugare, foo-gah-ray, v., to put to flight

fuggire, food-jee-ray, v., to flee ; to avoid, to shun

fulgere, fool-jay-ray, v., to shine ; to glitter

fuliggine, foo-leed-je-nay, f., soot
fulmicotone, fool-me-ko-to-nay, m., gun-cotton
fulminare, fool-me-nah-ray, v., to strike by lightning ; (fig.) to crush
fulmine, fool-me-nay, m., lightning
fulvo*, fool-vo, a., tawny [stack
fumaiuolo, foo-mah-e'oo-o-lo, m., funnel, chimney
fumare, foo-mah-ray, v., to smoke ; (fig.) **to fume**
fumatore, foo-mah-tor-ay, m., smoker
fumo, foo-mo, m., smoke ; fume
funaiolo, foo-nah-e'o-lo, m., rope-maker
fune, foo-nay, f., rope
funebre, foo-nay-bray,a., funereal. **carro—**, hearse
funesto*, foo-ness-to, a., fatal ; distressing
fungere, foonn-jay-ray, v., to act for ; to perform
fungo, foonn-go, m., mushroom ; mould
funzionare, foonn-tse'o-nah-ray, v., to function
funzione, foonn-tse'o-nay, f., function ; service
fuochista, foo'o-kiss-tah, m., stoker
fuoco, foo'o-ko, m., fire ; focus. **—d'artificie**, fireworks
fuorchè, foo'or-kay, conj., except [works
fuori, foo'o-re, prep., out ; outside ; except
fuoruscito, foo'o-roo-shee-to, m., exile ; outlaw
fuorviare, foo'or-ve'ah-ray, v., to go or lead astray
furbaccione, foohr-baht-cho-nay, m., sly fellow
furberia, foohr-bay-ree-ah, f., artfulness
furbo, foohr-bo, a.,* sly ; subtile. m., rogue
furente, foo-ren-tay, a., furious
furetto, foo-ret-to, m., ferret
furfante, foohr-fahn-tay, m., rogue ; swindler
furfanteria, foohr-fahn-tay-ree-ah, f., swindling
furgone, foohr-go-nay, m., lorry ; van
furia, foo're'ah, f., fury ; hurry
furiere, foo-re'ay-ray, m., quarter-master
furore, foo-ro-ray, m., fury
furto, foohr-to, m., theft
fusa, foo-zah, **fare le —**, to purr
fuso, foo-zo, m., spindle ; shaft. a., cast ; **melted**
fusoliera, foo-zo-le'ay-rah, f., fuselage
fustigare, fooss-te-gah-ray, v., to whip
fusto, fooss-to, m., stem ; frame ; cask
futile, foo-te-lay, a., futile, trifling

gabbaminchioni, gahb-bah-min-ke'o-ne, **gabba-mondo,** gahb-bah-**mon**-do, m. & f., **swindler**

gabbano, gahb-bah-no, m., overcoat

gabbare, gahb-bah-ray, v., to deceive

gabbia, gahb-be'ah, f., cage ; topsail

gabbiano, gahb-be'ah-no, m., sea-gull

gabbo, gahb-bo, m., joke. **farsi —, to mock**

gabella, gah-bell-lah, f., duty ; excise

gabelliere, gah-bell-le'ay-ray, m., excise-officer

gabinetto, gah-be-**net**-to,m.,cabinet ; study ; closet

gaggia, gahd-jee-ah, f., acacia

gagliardetto, gah-l'yar-det-to, m., pennant

gagliardo°, gah-l'yar-do, a., sturdy, robust

gaglioffo, gah-l'yof-fo, m., lout ; (fam.) rogue

gaiezza, gah-e-ett-tsah, f., gaiety, merriment

gaio°, gah-e'o, a., gay

galantuomo, gah-lahn-too'o-mo, m., **honest man**

galateo, gah-lah-tay-o, m., education

galeotto, gah-lay-ot-to, m., convict

galera, gah-lay-rah, f., prison ; galley

galetta, gah-let-tah, f., ship-biscuit

galla, gahl-lah, f., gall ; oak-apple

galleggiare, gahl-led-jah-ray, v., to float

galleria, gahl-lay-ree-ah, f., gallery ; tunnel

gallina, gahl-lee-nah, f., hen

gallo, gahl-lo, m., cock

gallonare, gahl-lo-nah-ray, v., to lace

gallone, gahl-lo-nay, m., lace ; stripe ; **gallon**

galoppare, gah-lop-pah-ray, v., to gallop

galoppino, gah-lop-pee-no, m., messenger

galoscia, gah-lo-she'ah, f., **galosh** ; clog

gamba, gahm-bah, f., leg

gambale, gahm-bah-lay, m., legging

gambero, gahm-bay-ro, m., crayfish

gambo, gahm-bo, m., stalk ; stem

gamella, gah-mell-lah, f., mess-tin

gamma, gahm-mah, f., (mus.) gamut, **scale**

ganascia, gah-nah-she'ah, f., jaw

gancio, gahn-cho, m., hook, crook

ganghero, gahn-gay-ro, m., hinge

ganz[a] [o], gahn-tsah, f., m., mistress ; **lover**

gara, gah-rah, f., competition

garante, gah-rahn-tay, m., surety ; voucher

garanzia, gah-rahn-tsee-ah, f., guarantee, warranty

garbare, gar-bah-ray, v., to satisfy

garbato*, gar-bah-to, a., well-bred ; **amiable**

garbo, gar-bo, m., breeding ; manners

garbuglio, gar-boo-l'yo, m., jumble, medley

gareggiare, gah-red-jah-ray, v., to compete

garetta, gah-ret-tah, f., sentry-box

garetto, gah-ret-to, m., fetlock ; knuckle

gargarismo, gar-gah-reez-mo, m., gargle

garofano, gah-ro-fah-no, f., (flower) pink

garrire, gar-ree-ray, v., to warble ; to flap

garza, gar-dsah, f., gauze ; white heron

garzone, gar-tso-nay, m., waiter ; apprentice

gasolina, gah-zo-lee-nah, f., petrol

gatta, gaht-tah, f., she-cat

gattabuia, gaht-tah-boo-e'ah, f., prison, jail

gatto, gaht-to, m., tom-cat, cat

gaudente, gah'oo-den-tay, a., merry, cheerful

gaudio, gah'oo-de'o, m., joy, gladness, bliss

gavazzare, gah-vaht-tsah-ray, v., to carouse

gavitello, gah-ve-tell-lo, m., buoy

gazza, gaht-tsah, f., magpie ; (fig.) talker

gazzetta, gahd-dzet-tah, f., gazette

gelare, jay-lah-ray, v., to freeze ; to chill

gelata, jay-lah-tah, f., hoar-frost

gelato, jay-lah-to, m., ice-cream. a., frozen

gelo, jay-lo, m., frost ; ice

gelone, jay-lo-nay, m., chilblain

gelosia, jay-lo-zee-ah, f., jealousy ; venetian blind

geloso*, jay-lo-zo, a., jealous

gelso, jayl-so, m., mulberry-tree

gelsomino, jayl-so-mee-no, m., jasmine

gemelli, jay-mell-le, m. pl., cuff-links ; twins

gemere, jay-may-ray, v., to groan ; to bemoan

gemito, jay-me-to, m., moan ; lamentation

gemma, jaym-mah, f., gem, jewel ; (plant) shoot

generare, jay-nay-rah-ray, v., to generate ; to beget

generatrice, jay-nay-rah-tree-chay, f., generator.

  stazione —, power-station

genere, jay-nay-ray, m., kind ; gender

genero, jay-nay-ro, m., son-in-law

generoso°, jay-nay-ro-zo, a., generous
genetliaco, jay-net-lee-ah-ko, m., birthday
gengiva, jen-jee-vah, f., (teeth) gum
genio, jay-ne'o, m., genius ; talent
genitori, jay-ne-to-re, m. pl., parents
gennaio, jen-nah-e'o, m., January
gentaglia, jen-tah-l'yah, f., riffraff
gente, jen-tay, f., people, race
gentilezza, jen-te-let-tsah, f., kindness : politeness
gentiluomo, jen-te-loo'o-mo, m., gentleman
genuflettere, jay-noo-flet-tay-ray, v., to bend the
geranio, jay-rah-ne'o, m., geranium   [knee
gerarchia, jay-rar-kee-ah, f., hierarchy
gerente, jay-ren-tay, m., manager ; director
gerenza, jay-ren-tsah, f., management
gergo, jayr-go, m., slang
germe, jayr-may, m., germ
germoglio, jayr-mo-l'yo, m., sprout ; offshoot
gesso, jess-so, m., chalk ; plaster
gesta, jess-tah, f. pl., exploits, deeds
gestione, jess-te'o-nay, f., management
gestire, jess-tee-ray, v., to manage ; to gesticulate
gesto, jess-to, m., gesture, action ; sign
gettare, jet-tah-ray, v., to throw
getto, jet-to, m., jet ; throw ; shoot
gettone, jet-to-nay, m., (games) counter
gherminella, gayr-me-nell-lah, f., trick
ghermire, gayr-mee-ray, v., to claw ; to snatch
ghetta, gayt-tah, f., gaiter
ghiacciaia, ghe-aht-chah-e'ah, f., ice-safe
ghiacciaio, ghe-aht-chah-e'o, m., glacier
ghiacciare, ghe-aht-chah-ray, v., to freeze
ghiaccio, ghe-aht-cho, m., ice.   a., frozen
ghiaia, ghe-ah-e'ah, f., gravel ; shingle
ghianda, ghe-ahn-dah, f., acorn
ghiandaia, ghe-ahn-dah-e'ah, f., jay
ghiera, ghe-ay-rah, f., ferrule ; locking ring
ghigliottina, ghe-l'ye'ot-tee-nah, f., guillotine
ghignare, ghe-n'yah-ray, v., to grin
ghigno, ghe-n'yo, m., sneer ; grin ; ugly face
ghiotto°, ghe-ot-to, a., gluttonous
ghiottone, ghe-ot-to-nay, m., glutton

ghiribizzo, ghe-re-bit-tso, m., whim
ghirigoro, ghe-re-go-ro, m., flourish
ghirlanda, gheer-lahn-dah, f., garland
ghisa, ghee-zah, f., cast-iron
già, je'ah, adv., already; quite so; late
giacchè, je'ahk-kay, adv., since; seeing that
giaco[hett]a, je'ahk-[ket-t]ah, f., jacket
giacenza, je'ah-chen-tsah, f., demurrage
giacere, je'ah-chay-ray, v., (location) to lie
giaciglio, je'ah-chee-l'yo, m., pallet, rough bed
giacinto, je'ah-cheen-to, m., hyacinth
giaguaro, je'ah-goo'ah-ro, m., jaguar
giallo, je'ahl-lo, a., yellow
giammai, je'ahm-mah-e, adv., never
giara, je'ah-rah, f., jar; bowl
giardinaggio, je'ar-de-nahd-jo, m., gardening
giardiniera, je'ar-de-ne'ay-rah, f., flower-stand
giardiniere, je'ar-de-ne'ay-ray, m., gardener
giardino, je'ar-dee-no, m., garden. — d'infanzia, infants' school
giarrettiera, je'ar-ret-te'ay-rah, f., garter
giberna, je-bair-nah, f., cartridge-box
giglio, jee-l'yo, m., lily
gilè, je-lay, m., waistcoat
ginepraio, je-nay-prah-e'o, m., (fig.) muddle
ginepro, je-nay-pro, m., juniper; gin
gingillo, jeen-jeell-lo, m., toy; trifle
ginnasio, jeen-nah-ze-o, m., classical school
ginnastica, jeen-nahss-te-kah, f., gymnastics
ginnico, jeen-ne-ko, a., gymnastic
ginocchio, je-nock-ke'o, m., knee
ginocchioni, je-nock-ke'o-ne, adv., kneeling
giocare, je'o-kah-ray, v., to play; to jest
giocatore, je'o-kah-tor-ay, m., player; gambler
giocattolo, je'o-kaht-to-lo, m., toy, plaything
giocoliere, je'o-ko-le'ay-ray, m., juggler
giocondità, je'o-kon-de-tah, f., mirth, joy
giogo, je'o-go, m., yoke; ridge; mountain range
gioia, je'o-e'ah, f., joy; precious stone
gioielleria, je'o-e'ell-lay-ree-ah, f., jeweller's; jewels
gioielliere, je'o-e'ell-le'ay-ray, m., jeweller
gioiello, je'o-e'ell-lo, m., jewel

gioioso*, je'o-e'o-zo, a., joyful, merry

gioire, je'o-ee-ray, v., to rejoice

giornalaio, je'or-nah-lah-e'o, m., newsagent

giornale, je'or-nah-lay, m., newspaper ; diary

giornaliero, je'or-nah-le'ay-ro, m., journeyman. a., daily

giornata, je'or-nah-tah, f., day ; day's wage

giorno, je'or-no, m., day

giovamento, je'o-vah-men-to, m., benefit

giovane, je'o-vah-nay, m. & f., young man ; young woman ; youth ; lad. a., young ; youthful

giovanile, je'o-vah-nee-lay, a., juvenile

giovare, je'o-vah-ray, v., to help ; to assist

giovedì, je'o-vay-dee, m., Thursday

giovenca, je'o-ven-kah, f., heifer

giovenco, je'o-ven-ko, m., young bullock, steer

gioventù, je'o-ven-too, f., youth, youthfulness

giovevole, je'o-vay-vo-lay, a., profitable ; useful

gioviale, je'o-ve'ah-lay, a., jovial

giovinastro, je'o-ve-nahss-tro, m., dissolute lad

giovinezza, je'o-ve-net-tsah,f.,youth, youthfulness

girabile, je-rah-be-lay, a., turnable ; negotiable

girare, je-rah-ray, v., to turn round ; to endorse

girarrosto, je-rar-ross-to, m., turnjack, turnspit

girasole, je-rah-so-lay, m., sunflower

girata, je-rah-tah, f., turn ; endorsement

giratario, je-rah-tah-re'o, m., endorser ; transferee

giravolta, je-rah-voll-tah, f., turning ; evolution

girella, je-rell-lah, f., pulley-wheel ; weather-cock

girino, je-ree-no, m., tadpole

giro, jee-ro, m., circuit ; revolution ; stroll

gironzare, je-ron-tsah-ray, v., to dawdle

girovago, je-ro-vah-go, m., tramp, rover

gita, jee-tah, f., excursion

gitano [gitana], je-tah-no, m. [f.], gipsy

giù, je'oo, adv., down ; below ; downwards

giubba, je'oob-bah, f., jacket ; mane

giubilare, je'oo-be-lah-ray, v.,to rejoice; to pension

giubileo, je'oo-be-lay-o, m., jubilee

giudeo, je'oo-day-o, m., Jew. a., Jewish

giudicare, je'oo-de-kah-ray, v., to judge

giudice, je'oo-de-chay, m., judge ; umpire

giudizio, je'oo-dee-tse'o, m., common sense; judgment; opinion; court

giugno, je'oo-n'yo, m., June

giulivo*, je'oo-lee-vo, a., joyous

giullare, je'ool-lah-ray, m., minstrel

giumenta, je'oo-men-tah, f., mare

giuncati, je'oonn-kah-tah, f., curd, junket

giunchiglia, je'oonn-kee-l'yah, f., jonquil

giunco, je'oonn-ko, m., bulrush

giungere, je'oonn-jay-ray, v., to arrive; to reach

giunta, je'oonn-tah, f., overweight; seam; council.
per —, in addition to

giuntare, je'oonn-tah-ray, v., to join

giuntura, je'oonn-too-rah, f., joint

giuocare, je'oo-o-kah-ray, v., to play; to gamble

giuocatore, je'oo-o-kah-tor-ay, m., player; gambler

giuoco, je'oo-o-ko, m., play; game; sport

giuramento, je'oo-rah-men-to, m., oath

giurare, je'oo-rah-ray, v., to swear

giurato, je'oo-rah-to, m., juryman.   a., sworn

giuri, giuria, je'oo-ree, je'oo-ree-ah, m. & f., jury

giuridico*, je'oo-ree-de-ko, a., juridical

giurista, je'oo-riss-tah, m., lawyer; jurist

giusta, je'ooss-tah, prep., according to

giustezza, je'ooss-tet-tsah, f., accuracy; justness

giustizia, je'ooss-tee-tse'ah, f., justice

giustiziare, je'ooss-te-tse'ah-ray, v., to execute

giustiziere, je'ooss-te-tse'ay-ray, m., executioner

giusto*, je'ooss-to, a., just; right, exact

glabro, glah-bro, a., hairless

glaciale, glah-chah-lay, a., glacial, icy; frozen

glandula, glahn-doo-lah, f., gland

gli, l'yee, pron., to him; to it.   art., the

glicerina, gle-chay-ree-nah, f., glycerine

globo, glo-bo, m., globe; ball

gloria, glo-re'ah, f., glory

gloriarsi, glo-re'ar-se, v., to be proud of; to boast

gobba, gob-bah, f., hump

gobbo, gob-bo, m., hunchback

goccia, got-chah, f., drop

gocciolare, got-cho-lah-ray, v., to drip, to trickle

godere, go-day-ray, v., to enjoy; to rejoice

godimento, go-de-men-to, m., enjoyment, pleasure

goffaggine, gof-fahd-je-nay, f., clumsiness

goffo°, gof-fo, a., clumsy ; dull

gogna, go-n'yah, f., pillory

gola, go-lah, f., throat ; gorge

goletta, go-let-tah, f., schooner

golfo, gol-fo, m., gulf

goloso, go-lo-zo, m., glutton. a.,° gluttonous

gomena, go-may-nah, f., cable, hawser

gomitata, go-me-tah-tah, f., push with the elbow

gomito, go-me-to, m., elbow ; angle ; joint

gomitolo, go-mee-to-lo, m., ball of thread

gomma, gom-mah, f., gum ; rubber

gommoso, gom-mo-zo, a., gummy

gonfalone, gon-fah-lo-nay, m., standard

gonfiamento, gon-fe'ah-men-to, m., swelling

gonfiare, gon-fe'ah-ray, v., to inflate

gonfiezza, gon-fe'et-tsah, f., swelling

gonfio°, gon-fe'o, a., swollen ; inflated

gongolare, gon-go-lah-ray, v., to exult ; to chuckle

gonn[ell]a, gon-[nell-]ah, f., gown, skirt

gonzo, gon-dzo, a.,° stupid. m., ninny

gora, go-rah, f., mill-course

gorgheggiare, gor-ghed-jah-ray, v., to warble

gorgo, gor-go, m., whirlpool

gorgogliare, gor-go-l'yah-ray, v., to gurgle

gorgoglio, gor-go-l'yo, m., gurgling ; bubbling

gota, go-tah, f., cheek

gotta, got-tah, f., gout

gottoso, got-to-zo, a., gouty

governante, go-vair-nahn-tay, f., governess

governare, go-vair-nah-ray, v., to rule ; to steer

governo, go-vair-no, m., government ; steering

gozzo, got-tso, m., goitre ; crop

gozzovigliare, got-tso-ve-l'yah-ray, v., to revel

gracchiare, grahk-ke'ah-ray, v., to crow

gracidare, grah-che-dah-ray, v., to croak

gracile, grah-che-lay, a., delicate ; slim

gracilità, grah-che-le-tah, f., slenderness ; delicacy

gradassata, grah-dahss-sah-tah, f., blustering

gradasso, grah-dahss-so, m., bully, blusterer

gradevole, grah-day-vo-lay, a., pleasing

gradimento, grah-de-men-to, m., approval
gradinata, grah-de-nah-tah, f., flight of steps
gradino, grah-dee-no, m., step ; rung
gradire, grah-dee-ray, v., to appreciate ; **to please**
gradito°, grah-dee-to, a., pleasing
grado, grah-do, m., degree ; rank
graduare, grah-doo'ah-ray, v., to graduate
graduato, grah-doo'ah-to, m., non-com. officer
graffiare, grahf-fe'ah-ray, v., to scratch, to claw
graffio, grahf-fe'o, m., scratch ; grappling iron
gragnola, grah-n'yo-lah, f., hail
grammo, grahm-mo, m., gramme
granaio, grah-nah-e'o, m., granary ; barn
granata, grah-nah-tah, f., grenade ; broom
granato, grah-nah-to, m., garnet ; pomegranate
grancassa, grahn-kahss-sah, f., big drum
granchio, grahn-ke'o, m., crab ; cramp ; blunder
grande, grahn-day, a., great ; high ; big
grandinare, grahn-de-nah-ray, v., to hail
grandine, grahn-de-nay, f., hail
grandioso°, grahn-de'o-zo,a.,imposing ; sumptuous
granello, grah-nell-lo, m., grain ; seed ; pip ; **stone**
granfia, grahn-fee-ah, f., claw, paw, talon
granita, grah-nee-tah, f., iced sherbet **drink**
granito, grah-nee-to, m., granite
grano, grah-no, m., grain ; corn ; wheat ; trifle
granturco, grahn-toohr-ko,m.,maize, Indian corn
grappa, grahp-pah, f., brandy
grappolo, grahp-po-lo, m., bunch of grapes
grassezza, grahss-set-tsah, f., fatness ; abundance
grasso, grahss-so, m., fat ; grease, a.,**°**fat, plump
grassume, grahss-soo-may, m., grease ; filth
grata, grah-tah, f., grate ; grating
graticola, grah-tee-ko-lah, f., gridiron ; **grate**
gratificazione, grah-te-fe-kah-tse'o-nay, f., gratification ; gratuity ; bonus
gratitudine, grah-te-too-de-nay, f., gratitude
grato°, grah-to, a., grateful ; pleasing
grattacielo, graht-tah-chay-lo, m., skyscraper
grattare, graht-tah-ray, v., to scratch ; **to scrape**
grattugia, graht-too-jah, f., grater
gravame, grah-vah-may, m., tax ; burden ; **charge**

gravare, grah-**vah**-ray, v., to charge ; to burden

grave, grah-vay, a., grave ; heavy

gravezza, grah-**vet**-tsah, f., gloom ; importance

gravida, grah-ve-dah, a., pregnant

gravidanza, grah-ve-**dahn**-tsah, f., pregnancy

gravità, grah-ve-**tah**, f., gravity ; importance

gravitare, grah-ve-tah-ray, v., to gravitate

gravoso, grah-**vo**-zo, a., heavy ; burdensome

grazia, grah-**tse**-ah, f., grace ; favour

graziare, grah-**tse**'ah-ray, v., to pardon

grazie, grah-**tse**'ay, interj., thank you ! thanks !

grazioso*, grah-tse'**o**-zo, a., gracious ; gratuitous

gregario, gray-gah-re'o.a.,gregarious ; (mil.)private

gregge, gred-jay, m., herd, flock

greggio [grezzo], gred-jo, a., unpolished

grembiale[grembiule],grem-be'ah-lay,m.,apron

grembo, grem-bo, m., lap ; (fig.) bosom

gremire, gray-mee-ray, v., to stuff ; to crowd

greppia, grayp-pe'ah, f., manger

greppo, grayp-po, m., rocky ground

greto, gray-to, m., gravel river-bed

gretto*, gret-to, a., mean

gridare, gree-dah-ray, v., to cry out

grido, gree-do, m., cry, outcry ; shout ; **fame**

grigio, gree-jo, a., grey

griglia, gree-l'yah, f., grate ; grating

grilletto, greel-let-to, m., trigger ; small **cricket**

grillo, greel-lo, m., cricket ; (fig.) whim

grimaldello, gre-mahl-del-lo, m., skeleton-key

grinfia, green-fe'ah, f., claw ; paw ; talon

grinza, green-tsah, f., wrinkle ; furrow

grippe, greep-pay, m., influenza

gronda[ia], gron-dah, f., gutter

grondare, gron-dah-ray, v., to drip ; **to pour**

groppa, grop-pah, f., crupper ; buttock

grossa, gross-sah, f., gross

grossezza, gross-set-tsah, f., thickness

grossista, gross-siss-tah, m., wholesale **dealer**

grosso, gross-so, m., bulk. a.,* big ; thick

grossolano*, gross-so-lah-no, a., coarse

grotta, grot-tah, f., grotto ; cave

gru, grua, groo, groo-ah, f., crane ; (naut.) **davit**

gruccia, **groot**-chah, f., crutch
grufolare, groo-fo-lah-ray, v., to grub
grugnire, groo-n'yee-ray, v., to grunt
grugnito, groo-n'yee-to, m., grunting. grunt
grugno, groo-n'yo, m., snout. fare il —, to frown
grullo, **grool**-lo, m., dolt
grumo, **groo**-mo, m., clot
gruppare, groop-**pah**-ray, v., to group
gruppo, **groop**-po, m., group
gruzzolo, **groot**-tso-lo, m., hoard
guadagnare, goo'ah-dah-n'**yah**-ray, v., to earn ;
   to gain ; to win
guadagno, goo'ah **dah**-n'yo, m., gain ; profit
guadare, goo'ah-**dah**-ray, v., to ford
guado, goo'ah-do, m., ford
guai, goo'ah-e, interj., woe ! beware !
guaina, goo'ah-ee-nah, f., sheath
guaio, goo'ah-e'o, m., woe ; disaster
guaire, goo'ah-ee-ray, v., to howl
gualcire, goo'ahl-**chee**-ray, v., to rumple
guancia, goo'ahn-chah, f., cheek
guanciale, goo'ahn-**chah**-lay, m., pillow
guantaio, goo'ahn-tah-e'o, m.,glover ; glove-maker
guanto, goo'ahn-to, m., glove
guardare, goo'ar-**dah**-ray, v., to guard ; to look at
guardaroba, goo'ar-dah-**ro**-bah, f., wardrobe ;
   cloak-room
guardia, goo'ar-de'ah, f., guard ; sentry ; policeman
guardiamarina, goo'ar-de'ah-mah-**ree**-nah, m.,
   midshipman
guardiano, goo'ar-de'**ah**-no, m., warder: caretaker
guari, goo'ah-re, adv., not much ; at all
guaribile, goo'ah-**ree**-be-lay, a., curable
guarigione, goo'ah-re-jo-nay, f., recovery, cure
guarire, goo'ah-**ree**-ray, v., to cure ; to heal
guarnigione, goo'ar-ne-jo-nay, f., garrison
guarnire, goo'ar-**nee**-ray, v., to trim ; to furnish
guarnizione, goo'ar-ne-tse'o-nay, f., trimming
guastafeste, goo'ahss-tah-**fess**-tay, m.,wet blanket
guastare, goo'ahss-**tah**-ray, v., to spoil ; to waste
guasto, goo'ahss-to, a.,* spoilt ; rotten ; decayed
   wasted. m., damage ; havoc

guatare, goo'ah-tah-ray, v., to gaze at ; to spy

guazza, goo'aht-tsah, f., dew

guazzabuglio, goo'aht-tsah-boo-l'yo, m., muddle

guazzare, goo'aht-tsah-ray, v., to flounder

guazzetto, goo'aht-tset-to, m., stew ; sauce

guazzo, goo'aht-tso, m., puddle ; water-colour

guercio, goo'air-cho, a., squinting

guerra, goo'air-rah, f., war

guerriero, goo'air-re-ay-ro, m., warrior. a.,warlike

gufo, goo-fo, m., owl

guglia, goo-l'yah, f., spire

guida, goo'ee-dah, f., guide, conductor ; guide-book

guidare, goo'e-dah-ray, v., to guide, to lead

guiderdone, goo'e-dair-do-nay, m., reward

guinzaglio, goo'een-tsah-l'yo, m., leash

guisa, goo'ee-zah, f., way ; mode

guizzare, goo'eet-tsah-ray, v., to flash ; to wriggle

guscio, goo-she'o, m., shell, husk

gustare, gooss-tah-ray, v., to taste

gusto, gooss-to, m., taste ; (fig.) pleasure

gustoso*, gooss-to-zo, a., tasty ; pleasing

h.—As an initial letter the H is not now used in Italian, except to differentiate between o, ai, a, anno, and ho, hai, ha, hanno.

i, e, art., m. pl., the

iarda, e'ar-dah, f., yard

iattura, e'aht-too-rah, f., misfortune ; damage

Iddio, eed-dee-o, m., God

idea, e-day-ah, f., idea

ideare, e-day-ah-ray, v., to imagine, to conceive

identità, e-den-te-tah, f., identity

idillio, e-deel-le'o, m., idyll

idiota, e-de'o-tah, m. & f., idiot. a., stupid

idolatria, e-do-lah-tree-ah, f., idolatry

idoneità, e-do-nay-e-tah, f., ability ; fitness

idoneo*, e-do-nay-o, a., able, fit ; suitable

idraulica, e-drah'oo-le-kah, f., hydraulics

idropisia, e-dro-pe-see-ah, f., dropsy

iena, e'ay-nah, f., hyena

ieri, e'ay-re, adv., yesterday

iettatore, e'ayt-tah-**tor**-ay, m., bird of ill omen
iettatura, e'ayt-tah-**too**-rah, f., evil eye ; spell
igiene, e-je'ay-nay, f., hygiene, health
ignaro*, en-**yah**-ro, a., ignorant ; unknown
ignavo*, en-**yah**-vo, a., cowardly ; indolent
ignobile, en-**yo**-be-lay, a., ignoble ; low born
ignorare, en-yo-**rah**-ray, v., to ignore
ignoto*, en-**yo**-to, a., unknown
ignudo, en-**yoo**-do, m., nudity, a.,* naked
il, eel, art., m., the
ilare, ee-lah-ray, a., cheerful, joyous, gay
illanguidire, eel-lahn-goo'e-dee-ray, v.,to **languish**
illecito*, eel-lay-che-to, a., illicit
illeso, eel-lay-zo, a., safe, sound, unhurt
illibato*, eel-le-bah-to, a., pure, faultless
illimitato*, eel-le-me-tah-to, a., unlimited
illudere, eel-loo-day-ray, v., to deceive
illuminare, eel-loo-me-nah-ray, v., to light
illustrare, eel-looss-trah-ray, v., to illustrate
illustre, eel-**looss**-tray, a., illustrious
imbacuccare, im-bah-kook-**kah**-ray, v.,to wrap up
imbaldanzire, im-bahl-dahn-tsee-ray, v., to grow
   bold
imballaggio,im-bahl-**lahd**-jo,m.,packing; wrapper
imballare, im-bahl-**lah**-ray, v., to pack
imbalsamare, im-bahl-sah-**mah**-ray, v.,to embalm
imbandierare, im-bahn-de'ay-**rah**-ray,v.,to beflag
imbandire, im-bahn-**dee**-ray, v., to lay the table
imbarazzare, im-bah-raht-**tsah**-ray, v., to embarrass ; to hinder
imbarazzo, im-bah-**raht**-tso, m., embarrassment
imbarcatoio, im-bar-kah-to-e'o, m., landing-stage
imbarcazione, im-bar-kah-tse'o-nay, m., boat
imbarco, im-**bar**-ko,m.,embarkation ; landing-stage
imbastare, im-bah-**stah**-ray, v., to put on pack-
   saddle
imbastire, im-bah-**stee**-ray, v., to stitch up
imbattersi,im-baht-tair-se,v.,(fig.) to come **across**
imbattuto, im-baht-**too**-to, a., unbeaten
imbaulare, im-bah'oo-**lah**-ray, v., to pack
imbavagliare, im-bah-vah-l'**yah**-ray, v., to **gag**
imbecille, im-bay-**cheel**-lay, m. & f., imbecile

imbelle, im-bell-lay, a., faint-hearted

imbellettarsi, im-bell-let-tar-se, v., to make up

imbellire, im-bell-lee-ray, v., to beautify

imberbe, im-bair-bay, a., beardless

imbevere, im-bay-vay-ray, v., to absorb ; to imbibe

imbiancare, im-be'ahn-kah-ray, v., to whiten

imbizzarrirsi, im-bid-dzar-reer-se, v., to bolt ; to get excited

imboccare, im-bock-kah-ray, v., to enter into ; to spoon-feed ; (fig.) to prompt

imboscata, im-boss-kah-tah, f., ambush

imboscato, im-boss-kah-to, m., shirker

imboschito, im-boss-kee-to, a., woody

imbottigliare, im-bot-te-l'yah-ray, v., to bottle

imbottire, im-bot-tee-ray, v., to stuff, to pad

imbottitura, im-bot-te-too-rah, f., stuffing

imbrandire, im-brahn-dee-ray, v., to brandish

imbrattare, im-braht-tah-ray, v., to soil, to stain

imbrigliare, im-bre-l'yah-ray, v., to bridle ; to dam

imbrogliare, im-bro-l'yah-ray, v., to embroil ; to deceive

imbroglio, im-bro-l'yo, m., muddle ; fraud

imbroglione, im-bro-l'yo-nay, m., swindler

imbruglio, im-broo-l'yo, m., bundle

imbrunire, im-broo-nee-ray, v., to get dark

imbruttire, im-broot-tee-ray, v., to grow ugly

imbucare, im-boo-kah-ray, v., to post

imbucarsi, im-boo-kar-se, v., to hide oneself

imbuto, im-boo-to, m., funnel

imeneo, e-may-nay-o, m., wedlock

imitare, e-me-tah-ray, v., to imitate

immagazzinare, im-mah-gahd-dze-nah-ray, v., to store, to warehouse

immaginare, im-mah-je-nah-ray, v., to imagine

immagine, im-mah-je-nay, f., image

immancabile, im-mahn-kah-be-lay, a., unfailing

immane, im-mah-nay, a., huge

immantinente, im-mahn-te-nen-tay, adv., without delay

immedesimarsi, im-may-day-ze-mar-se, v., to identify with

immemore, in-may-mo-ray, a., unmindful

immergere, im-**mair**-jay-ray, **v.**, to submerge, to dip

immigrare, im-me-**grah**-ray, **v.**, to immigrate

immischiarsi, im-miss-ke'**ar**-se, **v.**, to meddle with

immiserire, im-me-zay-**ree**-ray, **v.**, to impoverish

immissione, im-miss-se'**o**-nay, **f.**, inlet

immolare, im-mo-**lah**-ray, **v.**, to sacrifice

immollare, im-mol-**lah**-ray, **v.**, to soak ; to moisten

immondezza, im-mon-**det**-tsah, **f.**, refuse, dirt

immondizia, im-mon-de-**tsee**-ah, **f.**, dirt, waste

immondo°, im-**mon**-do, **a.**, filthy

immoto°, im-**mo**-to, **a.**, unmoved

immutato°, im-moo-**tah**-to, **a.**, unaltered

imo, **ee**-mo, **a.**, lowest

impaccare, im-pahk-**kah**-ray, **v.**, to wrap up

impacciare, im-paht-**chah**-ray, **v.**, to embarrass ; to trouble ; to get in the way of

impaccio, im-**paht**-cho, **m.**, trouble ; impediment

impadronirsi, im-pah-dro-**neer**-se, **v.**, to get hold of

impagabile, im-pah-**gah**-be-lay, **a.**, priceless

impagliare, im-pah-l'**yah**-ray, **v.**, to stuff

impalato°, im-pah-**lah**-to, **a.**, impaled ; stiff

impalcatura, im-pahl-kah-**too**-rah, **f.**, scaffolding

impallidire, im-pahl-le-**dee**-ray, **v.**, to turn pale

impalmare, im-pahl-**mah**-ray, **v.**, to plight troth

impappinato°, im-pahp-pe-**nah**-to, **a.**, confused

imparare, im-pah-**rah**-ray, **v.**, to learn

impareggiabile, im-pah-red-**jah**-be-lay, **a.**, incomparable

imparentato, im-pah-ren-**tah**-to, **a.**, related

impari, im-**pah**-re, **a.**, odd, uneven

impartire, im-par-**tee**-ray, **v.**, to impart, to convey

impassibile, im-pahss-**see**-be-lay, **a.**, impassive

impastare, im-pahss-**tah**-ray, **v.**, to knead

impasticciare, im-pahss-tit-**chah**-ray, **v.**, to muddle up ; to smear

impasto, im-**pahss**-to, **m.**, mixing ; kneading

impastoiare, im-pahss-to-e'**ah**-ray, **v.**, to tether ; to put fetters on ; to hinder

impattare, im-paht-**tah**-ray, **v.**, to be quits

impaurire, im pah'oo-**ree**-ray, **v.**, to scare

impavido°, im-**pah**-ve-do, **a.**, intrepid, fearless

impazientirsi, im-pah-tse'en-**teer-se**, v., to lose patience

impazz[ire][are], im-paht-tsee-ray, v., to go mad ; to madden

impedire, im-pay-dee-ray, v., to impede

impegnare, im-pay-n'yah-ray, v., to pledge

impegno, im-pay-n'yo, m., pledge ; engagement

impellere, im-pel-lay-ray, v., to impel

impenetrabile, im-pay-nay-**trah-**be-lay, a., inscrutable. impenetrable

impensabile, im-pen-sah-be-lay, a., unthinkable

impensato*, im-pen-sah-to, a., unforeseen

impensierito, im-pen-se-ay-ree-to, a., worried

impepare, im-pay-**pah-**ray, v., to pepper

imperito*, im-pay-ree-to, a., unskilled

imperizia, im-pay-ree-tse'ah, f., inexperienced

impero, im-pay-ro, m., empire ; authority

imperocché, im-pay-rock-kay, conj., for, whereas

imperterrito*, im-pair-tair-re-to, a., fearless

impestare, im-pess-tah-ray, v., to infect ; to stink

impeto, im-pay-to, m., impetuosity, fury

impiantare, im-pe'ahn-tah-ray, v., to implant ; to found

impianto, im-pe'ahn-to, m., plant, installation

impiastricciare, im-pe'ahss-trit-chah-ray, v., to plaster ; to smear

impiastro, im-pe'ahss-tro, m., plaster ; poultice

impiccare, im-pick-kah-ray, v., to hang

impicciare, im-pit-chah-ray, v., to embarrass

impiccinire, im-pit-che-nee-ray, v., to grow smaller

impiccio, im-pit-cho, m., embarrassment

impiccolire, im-pick-ko-lee-ray, v., to lessen, to belittle

impiegare, im-pe'ay-gah-ray, v., to employ, to use

impiegato, im-pe'ay-gah-to, m., clerk, employee

impiego, im-pe'ay-go, m., situation, employment

impietosire, im-pe'ay-to-zee-ray, v., to move ; to pity

impietrare, im-pe'ay-trah-ray, v., to petrify

impigliare, im-pe-l'yah-ray, v., to entangle

impigrire, im-pe-gree-ray, v., to become indolent

impinguare, im-pin-goo'ah-ray, v., to fatten

impinzare, im-pin-tsah-ray, v., to gorge

impiombare, im-pe'om-bah-ray, v., to stop
impiombatura, im-pe'om-bah-too-rah, f., filling
implicare, im-ple-kah-ray, v., to implicate
impolverare, im-pol-vay-rah-ray, v., to make
 dusty ; to powder
imponente, im-po-nen-tay, a., imposing
impopolare, im-po-po-lah-ray, a., unpopular
imporre, im-por-ray, v., to impose
importare, im-por-tah-ray, v., to import ; to matter
importo, im-por-to, m., total amount, sum
importunare, im-por-too-nah-ray, v., to disturb
imposta, im-poss-tah, f., duty, tax ; shutter ; frame
impostare, im-poss-tah-ray, v., to post ; to lay
impostore, im-poss-tor-ay, m., impostor
impotente, im-po-ten-tay, a., powerless
impratichirsi, im-prah-te-keer-se, v., to practise
imprecare, im-pray-kah-ray, v., to curse
impregnare, im-pray-n'yah-ray, v., to impregnate
imprendere, im-pren-day-ray, v., to undertake
imprenditore, im-pren-de-tor-ay, m., contractor
impresa, im-pray-zah, f., undertaking
imprestito, im-press-te-to, m., loan. prendere
 a —, to borrow
impreveduto*, im-pray-vay-doo-to, a., unforeseen
imprevisto*, im-pray-viss-to, a., unexpected
imprigionamento, im-pre-jo-nah-men-to, m.,
 imprisonment
imprigionare, im-pre-jo-nah-ray, v., to imprison
imprimere, im-pree-may-ray, v., to impress ; to print
improbo*, im-pro-bo, a., wicked ; hard
improduttivo*, im-pro-doot-tee-vo, a., unproductive ; unprofitable
impronta, im-pron-tah, f., impression ; foot-print
improntare, im-pron-tah-ray, v., to mark
improperio, im-pro-pay-re'o, m., insult, abuse
impropizio*, im-pro-pee-tse'o, a., unfavourable
improvvisata, im-prov-ve-zah-tah, f., agreeable
 surprise
improvviso*, im-prov-vee-zo, a., sudden, unexpected
impugnare, im-poo-n'yah-ray, v., to seize ; to
 contest

impugnatura, im-poo-n'yah-too-rah, f., hilt; han-

impulso, im-pool-so, m., impulse [dle

impuntarsi, im-poonn-tar-se, v., to be obstinate

impuntato*, im-poonn-tah-to, a., stubborn

impuro*, im-poo-ro, a., impure

imputare, im-poo-tah-ray, v., to impute; to charge in, in, prep., in; into; on; upon; at; within

inabile, in-ah-be-lay, a., unfit; unable [able

inaccettabile, in-aht-chet-tah-be-lay, a., unaccept-

inadeguato*, in-ah-day-goo'ah-to, a., inadequate

inalberare, in-ahl-bay-rah-ray, v., (flag) to hoist

inalterabile, in-ahl-tay-rah-be-lay, a., unalterable

inalzare, in-ahl-tsah-ray, v., to raise

inamidare, in-ah-me-dah-ray, v., to starch

inanità, in-ah-ne-tah, f., inanity; futility

inapprezzabile, in-ahp-pred-dzah-be-lay, a., in-appreciable

inappuntabile, in-ahp-poonn-tah-be-lay, a., irre-proachable

inargentare, in-ar-gen-tah-ray, v., to silver-plate

inarrivabile, in-ar-re-vah-be-lay, a., inaccessible

inascoltato, in-ahss-kol-tah-to, a., unheeded

inaspettato*, in-ahss-pet-tah-to, a., unexpected

inasprire, in-ahss-pree-ray, v., to irritate

inatteso*, in-aht-tay-zo, a., unexpected

inattivo*, in-aht-tee-vo, a., inactive

inatto*, in-aht-to, a., inapt

inattuabile, in-aht-too'ah-be-lay, a., impracticable

inaudibile, in-ah'oo-dee-be-lay, a., inaudible

inaudito, in-ah'oo-dee-to, a., unheard of

incagliare, in-kah-l'yah-ray, v., to strand

incallire, in-kahl-lee-ray, v., to harden

incallito*, in-kahl-lee-to, a., callous, hardened

incalorire, in-kah-lo-ree-ray, v., to heat up

incalvire, in-kahl-vee-ray, v., to grow bald

incalzare, in-kahl-tsah-ray, v., to pursue

incamminare, in-kahm-me-nah-ray, v., to start

incantare, in-kahn-tah-ray, v., to enchant

incantevole, in-kahn-tay-vo-lay, a., enchanting

incanto, in-kahn-to, m., spell; auction

incanutire, in-kah-noo-tee-ray, v., to go grey

incapace, in-kah-pah-chay, a., incapable, unable

incapacità, in-kah-pah-che-tah, f., incapacity

incarcerare, in-kar-chay-rah-ray, v., to imprison

incarcerazione, in-kar-chay-rah-tse'o-nay, f., imprisonment

incaricare, in-kah-re-kah-ray, v., to entrust

incaricato, in-kah-re-kah-to, a., entrusted with

incarico, in-kah-re-ko, m., task ; charge

incartamento, in-kar-tah-men-to, m., file

incartare, in-kar-tah-ray, v., to wrap up in paper

incarto, in-kar-to, m., file ; outer covering

incassare, in-kahss-sah-ray, v., to collect; to cash; to pack in a case ; to set gems

incasso, in-kahss-so, m., taking   [enchase

incastrare, in-kahss-trah-ray, v., to wedge in ; to

incastro, in-kahss-tro, m., groove

incatenare, in-kah-tay-nah-ray, v., to chain

incatramare, in-kah-trah-mah-ray, v., to tar

incauto°, in-kah'oo-to, a., incautious

incavare, in-kah-vah-ray, v., to hollow

incavatura, in-kah-vah-too-rah, f., excavation

incavo, in-kah-vo, m., notch ; cavity

incendiare, in-chen-de'ah-ray, v., to set on fire

incendio, in-chen-de'o, m., conflagration

incenerire, in-chay-nay-ree-ray, v., to incinerate

incensare, in-chen-sah-ray, v., to incense

incenso, in-chen-so, m., incense

incentivo, in-chen-tee-vo, m., incentive

inceppare, in-chep-pah-ray, v., to hinder ; to jam

incerare, in-chay-rah-ray, v., to wax

incertezza, in-chair-tet-tsah, f., uncertainty

incerto°, in-chair-to, a., uncertain, unsettled

incessante, in-chess-sahn-tay, a., incessant

incettare, in-chet-tah-ray, v., to corner

inchiesta, in-ke'ess-tah, f., inquest ; inquiry

inchinarsi, in-ke-nar-se, v., to bow ; to submit

inchino, in-kee-no, m., bow, curtsy

inchiodare, in-ke'o-dah-ray, v., to nail, to nail up

inchiostro, in-ke'oss-tro, m., ink

inchiudere, in-ke'oo-day-ray, v., to include, to enclose

inchiuso, in-ke'oo-zo, a., enclosed, included

inciampare, in-chahm-pah-ray, v., to stumble

inciampo, in-chahm-po, m., stumble ; obstacle
incidente, in-che-den-tay, m., incident
incidenza, in-che-den-tsah, f., incidence, chance
incidere, in-chee-day-ray, v., to incise ; to engrave
incinta, in-chin-tah, a., pregnant
incipriarsi, in-che-pre'ar-se, v., to powder oneself
incirca, in-cheer-kah, prep., about
incisione, in-che-ze'o-nay, f., engraving ; incision
incisore, in-che-zor-ay, m., engraver
incitamento, in-che-tah-men-to, m., incitement
incitare, in-che-tah-ray, v., to incite
incitativo, in-che-tah-tee-vo, a., inciting
inciuccarsi, in-chook-kar-se, v., to get drunk
incivile, in-che-vee-lay, a., impolite
inclinare, in-kle-nah-ray, v., to incline ; to deviate
inclinevole, in-kle-nay-vo-lay,a.,inclined, disposed
inolito*, in-kle-to, a., famous
includere, in-kloo-day-ray,v.,to include ; to enclose
incluso*, in-kloo-zo, a., included ; enclosed
incoerente, in-ko-ay-ren-tay, a., incoherent
incollare, in-koll-lah-ray, v., to stick ; to glue
incoloro*, in-ko-lo-ro, a., colourless
incolpare, in-koll-pah-ray, v., to blame ; to accuse
incolto*, in-koll-to, a., uncultivated ; (fig.) rough
incolume, in-ko-loo-may, a., unharmed
incombente, in-kom-ben-tay, a., incumbent
incombenza, in-kom-ben-tsah, f., task ; errand
incombustibile, in-kom-booss-tee-be-lay, a., fire-proof
incomodare, in-ko-mo-dah-ray, v., to incommode ; to annoy
incomodo, in-ko-mo-do, m., inconvenience ; disturbance. a.,* inconvenient ; uncomfortable
incompiuto, in-kom-pe'oo-to, a., unfinished
incomportabile, in-kom-por-tah-be-lay, a., intolerable, insupportable
incomposto*, in-kom-poss-to, a., muddled ; ill-behaved
incomprensibile, in-kom-pren-see-be-lay, a., incomprehensible
inconcepibile, in-kon-chay-pee-be-lay, a., inconceivable

inconcusso*, in-kon-kooss-so, a., unshaken ; firm

inconsapevole, in-kon-sah-pay-vo-lay,a.,unaware

inconseguente, in-kon-say-goo'en-tay, a., inconsequent, inconclusive

inconsiderato*, in-kon-se-day-rah-to, a., inconsiderate

inconsistente, in-kon-siss-ten-tay, a.,inconsistent

inconsolabile, in-kon-so-lah-be-lay, a., inconsolable

inconsueto*, in-kon-soo'ay-to, a., unusual [able

inconsulto, in-kon-sooll-to, a., hasty, rash [ble

incontentabile, in-kon-ten-tah-be-lay, a., insatia-

incontrare, in-kon-trah-ray, v., to meet ; to befall

incontro, in-kon-tro, m., meeting ; (mil.) encounter. prep., against ; to meet

incoraggiamento, in-ko-rahd-jah-men-to, m., encouragement

incoraggiare, in-ko-rahd-jah-ray, v., to encourage

incorniciare, in-kor-ne-chah-ray, v., to frame

incoronare, in-ko-ro-nah-ray, v., to crown

incoronazione, in-ko-ro-nah-tse'o-nay, f., coronation

incorporare, in-kor-po-rah-ray, v., to incorporate

incorrere, in-kor-ray-ray, v., to incur

incorrettezza, in-kor-ret-tet-tsah, f., inaccuracy ; misdemeanour

incorrotto*, in-kor-rot-to, a., not corrupt, pure

incosciente, in-ko-she'en-tay, a., unconscious

incostante, in-koss-tahn-tay, a., inconstant

incostanza, in-koss-tahn-tsah, f., fickleness

incredibile, in-kray-dee-be-lay, a., incredible

incredulo*, in-kray-doo-lo, a., incredulous

incremento, in-kray-men-to, m., increment, rise

increspare, in-kress-pah-ray, v., to wrinkle ; to crisp, to wave the hair

incrociare, in-kro-chah-ray, v., to cross ; to cruise

incrociatore, in-kray-chah-tor-ay, m., cruiser

incrocio, in-kro-cho, m., crossing ; cross roads

incrollabile, in-krol-lah-be-lay, a., unshakable

incrostare, in-kross-tah-ray, v., to incrust

incrudelire, in-kroo-day-lee-ray, v., to be cruel

incruento*, in-kroo'en-to, a., bloodless

incubo, in-koo-bo, m., nightmare

incudine, in-**koo**-de-nay, f., anvil
inculcare, in-kool-**kah**-ray, v., to inculcate
incuorare, in-koo'o-**rah**-ray, v., to hearten
incurabile, in-koo-**rah**-be-lay, a., incurable
incurante, in-koo-**rahn**-tay, a., heedless
incuria, in-koo-re'ah, f., negligence, carelessness
incurvare, in-koohr-**vah**-ray, v., to bend
incustodito, in-kooss-to-dee-to, a., unguarded
incutere, in-**koo**-tay-ray, v., to induce
indaco, in-dah-ko, m., indigo   [gate
indagare, in-dah-**gah**-ray, v., to search, to investi-
indagine, in-**dah**-je-nay, f., research, enquiry
indarno, in-**dar**-no, adv., in vain
indebitarsi, in-day-be-**tar**-se, v., to run into debts
indebito°, in-**day**-be-to, a., undue; unjust
indebolire, in-day-bo-**lee**-ray, v., to enfeeble
indecente, in-day-**chen**-tay, a., indecent
indecenza, in-day-**chen**-tsah, f., indecency
indecisione, in-day-che-ze'**o**-nay, f., indecision
indeciso°, in-day-**chee**-zo, a., undecided
indefesso°, in-day-**fess**-so, a., untiring
indegnità, in-day-n'ye-**tah**, f., indignity, affront
indegno°, in-**day**-n'yo, a., unworthy, shameful
indemoniato, in-day-mo-ne'**ah**-to, a., possessed
  with the devil. m., one possessed
indenne, in-den-nay, a., undamaged
indennità, in-den-ne-**tah**, f., indemnity   [nify
indennizzare, in-den-nid-**dzah**-ray, v., to indem-
indentro, in-den-tro, prep., within; inwards
indesiderabile, in-day-ze-day-**rah**-be-lay, a., undesirable
indi, in-de, adv., thence; then; hereafter
indicare, in-de-**kah**-ray, v., to indicate, to direct
indicatore, in-de-kah-**tor**-ay, m., guide; directory; way-sign
indice, in-de-chay, m., index; forefinger
indicibile, in-de-**chee**-be-lay, a., unutterable
indietreggiare, in-de'ay-tred-**jah**-ray, v., to fall
  back; to shrink
indietro, in-de'**ay**-tro, adv., backwards; behind
indifeso, in-de-**fay**-zo, a., undefended
indigeno, in-dee-jay-no, a., native

indigente, in-de-jen-tay, a., poor. m. & f., **a needy person**

indigenza, in-de-jen-tsah, f., indigence

indigeribile, in-de-jay-ree-be-lay, a., indigestible

indigesto°, in-de-jess-to, a., indigestible

indire, in-dee-ray, v., to notify, to summon

indirizzare, in-de-rit-tsah-ray, v., to direct ; **to address** [dress

indirizzo, in-de-rit-tso, m., address ; way [dress

indiscreto°, in-diss-kray-to, a., indiscreet

indiscutibile, in-diss-koo-tee-be-lay, a., unquestionable

indisporre, in-diss-por-ray, v., to indispose

indisposto, in-diss-poss-to, a., indisposed

indisputabile, in-diss-poo-tah-be-lay, a., indisputable, evident

indissolubile, in-diss-so-loo-be-lay, a., indissoluble

indistruttibile, in-diss-troot-tee-be-lay, a., indestructible

indivia, in-dee-ve'ah, f., endive [structible

individuo, in-de-vee-doo'o, m., individual

indivisibile, in-de-ve-zee-be-lay, a., indivisible

indizio, in-dee-tse'o, m., indication

indolcire, in-dol-chee-ray, v., to sweeten

indole, in-do-lay, f., nature ; bent, disposition

indolenza, in-do-len-tsah, f., indolence

indomani, in-do-mah-ne, m., the next **day**

indomato, in-do-mah-to, a., untamed

indorare, in-do-rah-ray, v., to gild

indoratore, in-do-rah-tor-ay, m., gilder

indossare, in-doss-sah-ray, v., to don

indosso, in-doss-so, adv., on ; with [duced

indotto, in-dot-to, m., ignorant, illiterate. p.p., in-

indovinare, in-do-ve-nah-ray, v., to divine, to guess

indovinello, in-do-ve-nell-lo, m., riddle

indovino, in-do-vee-no, m., foreteller, diviner. a., prophetical

indovuto°, in-do-voo-to, a., undue, unjust

indubbio°, in-doob-be'o, a., undoubted

indugiare, in-doo-jah-ray, v., to delay ; **to defer**

indugio, in-doo-jo, m., delay ; hesitation

indulgere, in-dool-jay-ray, v., to pardon ; to indulge

indurire, in-doo-ree-ray, v., to harden, **to steel**

indurre, in-doohr-ray, v., **to induce**

indursi, in-doohr-se. v., to make up one's mind

industria, in-dooss-tre-ah, f., industry

industriale, in-dooss-tre-**ah**-lay, m., **industrialist,** a., industrial

inedia, in-ay-de'ah, f., need of food

inedito, in-ay-de-to, a., unpublished

inefficace, in-ef-fe-**kah**-chay, a., **ineffective**

ineguale, in-ay-goo'ah-lay, a., unequal ; **uneven**

inerente, in-ay-**ren**-tay, a., inherent

inerme, in-**air**-may, a., unarmed

inerzia, in-**air**-tse'ah, f., inertia

inesatto°, in-ay-**zaht**-to, a., inexact   [tible

inesauribile, in-ay-zah'oo-**ree**-be-lay, a.,inexhaus-

inescusabile, in-ess-koo-zah-be-lay,a.,inexcusable

ineseguibile, in-ay-zay-goo'ee-be-lay, a., not exe-
cutable

inesercitato, in-ay-zair-che-**tah**-to, a., untrained

inesigibile, in-ay-ze-jee-be-lay, a., not recoverable

inesorabile, in-ay-zo-**rah**-be-lay, a., inexorable

inesperto°, in-ess-**pair**-to, a., inexpert

inesplicabile°,in-ess-ple-**kah**-be-lay,a.,inexplicable

inesprimibile, in-ess-pre-**mee**-be-lay, a., inexpressible

inespugnabile, in-ess-poo-n'**yah**-be-lay,a.,impreg-

inettezza, in-et-**tet**-tsah, f., inaptness   [nable

inetto°, in-**et**-to, a., inapt ; unfit

inezia, in-**ay**-tse'ah, f., trifle

infamare, in-fah-**mah**-ray, v., to **defame, to slander**

infame, in-**fah**-may, a., infamous

infante, in-**fahn**-tay, m., infant

infarcire, in-far-**chee**-ray, v., to stuff

infardare, in-far-**dah**-ray, v., (burden) to **pack**

infarinare, in-fah-re-**nah**-ray, v., to flower

infarinatura, in-fah-re-nah-**too**-rah, f., smuttering

infastidire, in-fahss te-**dee**-ray, v., to annoy; to bore

infaticabile, in-fah-te-**kah**-be-lay, a., untiring

infatti, in-**faht**-te, adv., in fact ; indeed

infatuare, in-fah-too'**ah**-ray, v., to infatuate

infausto°, in-**fah'ooss**-to, a., of ill omen

infecondo°, in-fay-**kon**-do, a., barren

infelice, in-fay-**lee**-chay, a., miserable, **unhappy**

inferire, in-fay-**ree**-ray, v., to infer

infermeria, in-fair-may-ree-ah, f., infirmary
infermiera, in-fair-me'ay-rah, f., nurse
infermiere, in-fair-me'ay-ray, m., male nurse
infermo, in-fair-mo, a., sick ; invalid
inferno, in-fair-no, m., hell
inferocire, in-fay-ro-chee-ray, v., to infuriate
inferriata, in-fair-re'ah-tah, f., grating
infestare, in-fess-tah-ray, v., to infest
infesto*, in-fess-to, a., noxious, unhealthy
infettare, in-fet-tah-ray, v., to infect
infezione, in-fay-tse'o-nay, f., infection, contagion
infido*, in-fe-do, a., unfaithful ; unreliable
inferire, in-fe'ay-ree-ray, v., to rage ; to be cruel
infievolire, in-fe'ay-vo-lee-ray, v., to enfeeble
infiggere, in-feed-jay-ray, v., to drive in
infilare, in-fe-lah-ray, v., to thread, to string
infilata, in-fe-lah-tah, f., row, infilade
infilzare, in-feel-tsah-ray, v., to string ; to pierce
infimo*, in-fe-mo, a., lowest ; undermost, vilest
infine, in-fee-nay, adv., finally, at last
infingardo, in-feen-gar-do, a.,*idle. m., sluggard
infinito*, in-fe-nee-to, a., boundless, unlimited
infino, in-fee-no, prep., till, until ; as far as
infinocchiare, in-fe-nock-ke'ah-ray, v., to fool
inflorare, in-fe'o-rah-ray, v., to beflower
infliggere, in-fleed-jay-ray, v., to inflict, to impose
influenza, in-floo-en-tsah, f., influence ; influenza
influenzare, in-floo-en-tsah-ray, v., to influence
influsso, in-flooss-so, m., influx
infocare, in-fo-kah-ray, v., to inflame ; to heat
infondato*, in-fon-dah-to, a., unfounded
infondere, in-fon-day-ray, v., to infuse
informare, in-for-mah-ray, v., to inform
informe, in-for-may, a., shapeless ; imperfect
infornata, in-for-nah-tah, f., ovenfull
infortunio, in-for-too-ne'o, m., accident
inforzare, in-for-tsah-ray, v., to enforce
infossato*, in-foss-sah-to, a., sunken
infracidire, in-frah-che-dee-ray, v., to rot ; **to soak**
infradiciarsi, in-frah-de-char-se, v., to get **soaked**; to rot
infrangere, in-frahn-jay-ray, v., to infringe

infrazione, in-frah-tse'o-nay, f., infraction
infreddarsi, in-fred-dar-se, v., to catch cold
infreddatura, in-fred-dah-too-rah, f., chill
infrenare, in-fray-nah-ray, v., to restrain
infruttuoso*, in-froot-too'O-zo, a., fruitless
ingabbiare, in-gahb-be'ah-ray, v., to cage ; to jail
ingaggiare, in-gahd-jah-ray, v., to engage ; to enrol
ingannare, in-gahn-nah-ray, v., to deceive ; to trick
ingannatore, in-gahn-nah-tor-ay, m., deceiver
ingannevole, in-gahn-nay-vo-lay, a., deceitful
inganno, in-gahn-no, m., deceit ; trick ; (fig.) error
ingarbuglione, in-gar-boo-l'yo-nay, m., impostor;
    muddler
ingegnarsi, in-jay-n'yar-se, v., to strive one's best
ingegnere, in-jay-n'yay-ray, m., engineer
ingegno, in-jay-n'yo, m., skill ; artifice : genius
ingegnoso*, in-jay-n'yO-zo, a., ingenious ; witty
ingelosire, in-jay-lo-zee-ray, v., to feel jealous
ingenito*, in-jay-ne-to, a., innate ; inborn
ingente, in-jen-tay, a., huge   [noble
ingentilire, in-jen-te-lee-ray, v., to refine ; to en-
ingenuo*, in-jay-noo'o, a., ingenuous
ingerenza, in-jay-ren-tsah, f., interference ; charge
ingerirsi, in-jay-reer-se, v., to meddle
ingessare, in-jess-sah-ray, v., to plaster
inghiottire, in-ghe'ot-tee-ray, v., to gulp
ingiallire, in-jahl-lee-ray, v., to turn yellow
inginocchiarsi, in-je-nock-ke'ar-se, v., to kneel
inginocchiatoio, in-je-nock-ke'ah-to-e'o, m.,
    kneeling-stool
ingiù, in-joo, adv., downwards ; down
ingiungere, in-joonn-jay-ray, v., to enjoin
ingiunzione, in-joonn-tse'o-nay, f., injunction
ingiuria, in-joo-re'ah, f., injury ; offence
ingiuriare, in-joo-re'ah-ray, v., to insult ; to abuse
ingiustizia, in-jooss-tee-tse'ah, f., injustice, wrong
ingiusto*, in-jooss-to, a., unjust, wrongful
ingolare, in-go-lah-ray, v., to gulp down
ingolfarsi, in-gol-far-se, v., to be immersed in
ingombrare, in-gom-brah-ray, v., to encumber
ingombro, in-gom-bro, m., encumbrance
ingommare, in-gom-mah-ray, v., to gum

ingordigia, in-gor-dee-jah, f., greediness, **voracity**

ingordo°, in-gor-do, a., greedy

ingorgarsi, in-gor-gar-se, v., to be blocked

ingorgo, in-gor-go, m., stoppage   [gorge

ingozzare, in-got-tsah-ray, v., to forcibly feed; to

ingranaggio, in-grah-nahd-jo, m., gearing

ingrandire, in-grahn-dee-ray, v., to enlarge

ingrassare, in-grahss-sah-ray, v., to fatten

ingrasso, in-grahss-so, m., manure

ingraticciata, in-grah-tit-chah-tah, f., trellis

ingratitudine, in-grah-te-too-de-nay, f., ingrati-

ingrato°, in-grah-to, a., ungrateful   [tude

ingravidare, in-grah-ve-dah-ray, v., to make

    pregnant; to become pregnant

ingraziarsi, in-grah-tse'ar-se, v., to ingratiate

ingrediente, in-gray-de-en-tay, m., ingredient

ingresso, in-gress-so, m., entrance, entry

ingrossare, in-gross-sah-ray, v., to thicken

ingrosso, in-gross-so, adv., wholesale; in bulk

inguantarsi, in-goo'ahn-tar-se, v., to put on gloves

inguaribile, in-goo'ah-ree-be-lay, a., incurable

inguine, in-goo'e-nay, m., groin

iniettare, in-e-et-tah-ray, v., to inject

iniezione, in-e-ay-tse'o-nay, f., injection

inimicarsi, e-ne-me-kar-se, v., to make an enemy of

ininterrotto°, e-nin-tair-rot-to, a., uninterrupted

iniquo°, in-ee-koo'o, a., iniquitous, wicked

iniziale, in-e-tse'ah-lay, f., initial. a., initial

iniziare, in-e-tse'ah-ray, v., to initiate

inizio, in-ee-tse'o, m., beginning

innaffiare, in-nahf-fe'ah-ray, v., to water

innaffiatoio, in-nahf-fe'ah-to-e'o, m., watering-can

innaffiatrice, in-nahf-fe'ah-tree-chay, f., water-cart

innamorarsi, in-nah-mo-rar-se, v., to fall in love

innanzi, in-naan-tse, adv. & prep., before; above;

    in preference

innegabile, in-nay-gah-be-lay, a., undeniable

inneggiare, in-ned-jah-ray, v., to praise; to sing

    hymns

innestare, in-ness-tah-ray, v., to graft; to vaccinate

innesto, in-ness-to, m., graft; vaccination

inno, in-no, m., hymn; anthem

innocenza, in-no-chen-tsah, f., innocence
innocuo*, in-no koo'o, a., innocuous, harmless
innominato*, in-no-me-nah-to, a., nameless
innovare, in-no-vah-ray, v., to innovate [merable
innumerevole, in-noo-may-ray-vo-lay, a., innu-
inoculare, in-o-koo-lah-ray, v., to inoculate
inodoro*, in-o-do-ro, a., inodorous, scentless
inoltrare, in-oll-trah-ray, v., to forward on
inoltrarsi, in-oll trar-se, v., to advance further
inoltrato, in-oll-trah-to, a., late
inoltre, in-oll-tray, adv., besides, moreover
inoperoso*, in-o-pay-ro-zo, a., inactive ; idle
inopinato*, in-o-pe-nah-to, a., unexpected
inoppugnabile, in-op-poo-n'yah-be-lay, a., in-
controvertible
inorgoglirsi, in-or-go-l'yeer-se, v., to grow proud
inorridire, in-or-re-dee-ray, v., to horrify
inosservato*, in-oss-sair-vah-to, a., unnoticed
inquadrare, in-koo'ah-drah-ray, v., to frame ; to
form up
inquietudine, in-koo'e-ay-too-de-nay, f., uneasi-
inquilino, in-koo'e-lee-no, m., lodger ; tenant [ness
inquinare, in-koo'e-nah-ray, v., to infect, to taint
insaccare, in-sack-kah-ray, v., to put in a sack ; to
put in a bag ; (fig.) to make money
insalata, in-sah-lah-tah, f., salad
insalatiera, in-sah-lah-te'ay-rah, f., salad-bowl
insalubre, in-sah-loo-bray, a., unhealthy
insanabile, in-sah-nah-be-lay, a., incurable
insanguinato, in-sahn-goo'e-nah-to, a., blood-
insania, in-sah-ne'ah, f., insanity [stained
insano*, in-sah-no, a., insane ; unhealthy
insaponare, in-sah-po-nah-ray, v., to soap
insaputa, in-sah-poo-tah, f., all' — **di**, without
the knowledge of
inscindibile, in-shin-dee-be-lay, a., inseparable
inscrivere, in-skree-vay-ray, v., to inscribe ; to book
insecchire, in-seck-kee-ray, v., to dry up
insediamento, in-say-de'ah-men-to, m., installation, settling
insediare, in-say-de'ah-ray, v., to put in office
insegna, in-say-n'yah, f., ensign, standard

insegnamento, in-say-n'yah-men-to, m., teaching

insegnante, in-say-n'yahn-tay, m. & f., teacher

insegnare, in-say-n'yah-ray, v., to teach

inseguimento, in-say-goo'e-men-to, m., pursuit

inseguire, in-say-goo'ee-ray, v., to pursue

insenatura, in-say-nah-too-rah, f., creek

insensato*, in-sen-sah-to, a., foolish

insequestrabile, in-say-koo'ess-trah-be-lay, a., unsequestrable

inserire, in-say-ree-ray, v., to insert, to add

inservibile, in-sair-vee-be-lay, a., unserviceable

insetticida, in-set-te-chee-dah, m., insecticide

insetto, in-set-to, m., insect

insidia, in-see-de'ah, f., snare, artifice

insidioso*, in-se-de'o-zo, a., insidious

insieme, in-se-ay-may, adv., together ; at the same time. l'—, m., the whole ; the bulk

insigne, in-see-n'yay, a., renowned   [sion

insignorirsi, in-se-n'yo-reer-se, v., to gain posses-

insino, in-see-no, adv., till, until ; when

insinuare, in-se-noo'ah-ray, v., to insinuate

insipido*, in-see-pe-do, a., insipid, tasteless

insistere, in-siss-tay-ray, v., to insist, to persist

insocevole, in-so-chay-vo-lay, a., unsociable

insoddisfatto*, in-sod-diss-faht-to, a., dissatisfied

insofferente, in-soff-fay-ren-tay, a., intolerant

insolazione, in-so-lah-tse'o-nay, f., sunstroke

insolito*, in-so-le-to, a., unwonted ; rare

insolubile, in-so-loo-be-lay, a., insoluble

insolvenza, in-soll-ven-tsah, f., insolvency

insolvibile, in-soll-vee-be-lay, a., insolvent

insomma, in-som-mah, adv., in short ; altogether

insonne, in-son-nay, a., sleepless

insonnia, in-son-ne'ah, f., insomnia   [able

insopportabile, in-sop-por-tah-be-lay, a., unbear-

insorgere, in-sor-jay-ray, v., to revolt

insorto, in-sor-to, m., insurgent

insospettirsi, in-soss-pet-teer-se, v., to become suspicious

insostenibile, in-soss-tay-nee-be-lay, a., intolerable

insozzare, in-sot-tsah-ray, v., to soil

insperabile, in-spay-rah-be-lay, a., hopeless

insperato, in-spay-rah-to, a., unexpected
inspirare, in-spe-rah-ray, v., to inspire
instabile, in-stah-be-lay, a., unstable ; inconstant
installare, in-stahl-lah-ray, v., to install
installazione, in-stahl-lah-tse'o-nay, f., installation
insù, in-soo, adv., upwards ; above
insuccesso, in-soot-chess-so, m., unsuccessfulness
insufficiente, in-soof-fe-chen-tay, a., insufficient
insulare, in-soo-lah-ray, a., insular
insulso*, in-sool-so, a., vapid ; (fig.) silly
insultare, in-sool-tah-ray, v., to insult
insulto, in-sool-to, m., insult ; outrage
insurrezione, in-soor-ray-tse'o-nay, f., insurrection
intaccare, in-tahk-kah-ray, v., to notch
intagliare, in-tah-l'yah-ray, v., to incise ; to engrave
intagliatore, in-tah-l'yah-tor-ay, m., carver
intaglio, in-tah-l'yo, m., carving ; cut
intanto, in-tahn-to, adv., in the meantime
intarsio, in-tar-se'o, m., inlaid work, marquetry
intascare, in-tahss-kah-ray, v., to pocket
intatto, in-taht-to, a., intact
intavolare, in-tah-vo-lah-ray, v., to start, to
begin ; to line with wainscot
integrale, in-tay-grah-lay, a., integral, essential
integrità, in-tay-gre-tah, f., integrity
integro*, in-tay-gro, a., upright
intelaiatura, in-tay-lah-e'ah-too-rah, f., framework
intelletto, in-tell-let-to, m., intellect
intelligenza, in-tell-le-jen-tsah, f., intelligence
intelligibile, in-tell-le-jee-be-lay, a., intelligible
intemerato, in-tay-may-rah-to, a., undefiled, pure
intemperanza, in-tem-pay-rahn-tsah, f., intemperance
intemperie, in-tem-pay-re-ay, f. pl., inclemency
of the weather   [seur
intendente, in-ten-den-tay, m., steward ; connois-
intendere, in-ten-day-ray, v., to understand ;
to purpose
intendersi, in-ten-dair-se, v., to be in agreement
with ; to understand one another
intensità, in-ten-se-tah, f., intensity ; violence
intenso*, in-ten-so, a., intense

intento, in-ten-to, m., design, aim, intent

intenzionale, in-ten-tse'o-nah-lay, a., intentional

intercedere, in-tair-chay-day-ray, v., to intervene

interccessione, in-tair-chess-se'o-nay, f., inter-
cession

intercettare, in-tair-chet-tah-ray, v., to intercept

interdire, in-tair-dee-ray, v., to interdict

interdizione, in-tair-de-tse'o-nay, f., interdiction

interessante, in-tay-ress-sahn-tay, a., interesting

interessare, in-tay-ress-sah-ray, v., to interest

interessato*, in-tay-ress-sah-to, a., interested ;
greedy

interesse, in-tay-ress-say, m., interest ; advantage

interiore, in-tay-re'or-ay, a., inward ; internal

intermedio, in-tair-may-de'o, a., intermediate

intermezzo, in-tair-med-dzo, m., interval ; interlude

intermittente, in-tair-mit-ten-tay, a., intermittent

internazionale, in-tair-nah-tse'o-nah-lay, a., international

interno*, in-tair-no, a., internal ; inward ; interior

intero*, in-tay-ro, a., entire, all

interporre, in-tair-porr-ray, v., to interpose

interpretare, in-tair-pray-tah-ray, v., to interpret

interpretazione, in-tair-pray-tah-tse'o-nay, f., in-
terpretation

interprete, in-tair-pray-tay, m. & f., interpreter

interrare, in-tair-rah-ray, v., to bury

interrogare, in-tair-ro-gah-ray, v., to interrogate

interrogatorio, in-tair-ro-gah-tor-e'o, m., inter-
rogatory

interrogazione, in-tair-ro-gah-tse'o-nay, f., query,
interrogation

interrompere, in-tair-rom-pay-ray, v., to interrupt

interruzione, in-tair-roo-tse'o-nay, f., interruption ; (wireless) jamming

intervallo, in-tair-vahl-lo, m., interval

intervenire, in-tair-vay-nee-ray, v., to intervene ;
to attend

intervista, in-tair-viss-tah, f., interview

intervistare, in-tair-viss-tah-ray, v., to interview

intesa, in-tay-zah, f., accord, confidential agreement

intestato, in-tess-tah-to, a., intestate

intestino, in-tess-tee-no, m., intestine. **a., inside**

intiero⁰, in-te'ay-ro, a., whole

intimare, in-te-mah-ray, v., to summon

intimazione, in-te-mah-tse'o-nay, f., intimation : declaration

intimidire, in-te-me-dee-ray, v., to intimidate

intimità, in-te-me-tah, f., intimacy

intimo, in-te-mo, a., intimate, inmost

intimorire, in-te-mo-ree-ray, v., to frighten

intirizzire, in-te-rit-tsee-ray, v., to benumb

intitolare, in-te-to-lah-ray, v., to entitle ; to dedicate ; to give a name to

intollerabile, in-toll-lay-rah-be-lay, a., intolerable

intollerante, in-toll-lay-rahn-tay, a., intolerant

intolleranza, in-toll-lay-rahn-tsah, f., intolerance

intonacare, in-to-nah-kah-ray, v., to plaster

intonare, in-to-nah-ray, v., to intone ; to tune

intonazione, in-to-nah-tse'o-nay, f., intonation

intoppo, in-top-po, m., hindrance, obstruction

intorbidire, in-tor-be-dee-ray, v., to become turbid ; (fig.) to become gloomy

intorno, in-tor-no, prep., about, around

intortigliare, in-tor-te-l'yah-ray, v., to twist

intralciare, in-trahl-chah-ray, v., to disconcert ; to embroil [pose

intramezzare, in-trah-med-dzah-ray, v., to interpose

intransigente, in-trahn-ze-jen-tay, a., intransigent ; irreconciliable

intraprendere, in-trah-pren-day-ray, v., to undertake

intrattenere, in-traht-tay-nay-ray, v., to entertain

intrecciare, in-tret-chah-ray, v., to interweave

intreccio, in-tret-cho, m., plot ; intermingling

intrepido⁰, in-tray-pe-do, a., fearless, dauntless

intrigante, in-tre-gahn-tay, a., intriguing. m. & f., busybody

intrigare, in-tre-gah-ray, v., to plot

intrigo, in-tree-go, m., intrigue

intrinseco, in-trin-say-ko, a., intrinsic

introdurre, in-tro-doohr-ray, v., to introduce

introduzione, in-tro-doo-tse'o-nay, f., introduction

intromettersi, in-tro-met-tair-se, v., to meddle with, to interfere

intrudere, in-troo-day-ray, v., to intrude
intrusione, in-troo-ze'o-nay, f., intrusion
intruso, in-troo-zo, m., intruder
intuitivo*, in-too'e-tee-vo, a., intuitive
intuizione, in-too'e-tse'o-nay, f., intuition
inumanità, in-oo-mah-ne-tah, f., inhumanity
inumano*, in-oo-mah-no, a., inhuman; pitiless
inumare, in-oo-mah-ray, v., to inter
inumidire, in-oo-me-dee-ray, v., to moisten
inusitato*, in-oo-ze-tah-to, a.,unusual; out of date
inutile, in-oo-te-lay, a., useless; fruitless
inutilmente, in-oo-til-men-tay, adv., uselessly
invadere, in-vah-day-ray, v., to invade
invalido, in-vah-le-do,m.,invalid.a.,*invalid; feeble
invano, in-vah-no, adv., in vain, vainly
invariabile, in-vah-re-ah-be-lay,a.,invariable; firm
invasione, in-vah-ze'o-nay, f., invasion
invasore, in-vah-zor-ay, m., invader
invecchiare, in-vek-ke'ah-ray, v., to grow old
invece, in-vay-chay, adv., instead
inveire, in-vay-ee-ray, v., to inveigh
invendibile, in-ven-dee-be-lay, a., unsaleable
invendicato, in-ven-de-kah-to, p.p., unrevenged
inventare, in-ven-tah-ray, v., to invent
inventario, in-ven-tah-re'o, m., inventory, list
inventore, in-ven-tor-ay, m., inventor; contriver
invenzione, in-ven-tse'o-nay, f., invention ; (fig.) fib
invernale, in-vair-nah-lay, a., wintry, hibernal
inverniciare, in-vair-ne-chah-ray, v., to varnish
inverno, in-vair-no, m., winter; winter season
invero, in-vay-ro, adv., indeed; truly; in truth
inverosimile, in-vay-ro-see-me-lay, a., improbable
invertire, in-vair-tee-ray, v., to invert; to reverse
investigare, in-vess-te-gah-ray, v., to investigate
investire, in-vess-tee-ray, v., to invest; to assail
invetriare, in-vay-tre-ah-ray, v., to glaze
invettiva, in-vet-tee-vah, f., invective; insult
inviare, in-ve'ah-ray, v., to send, to transmit
inviato, in-ve'ah-to, m., envoy, messenger
invidia, in-vee-de'ah, f., envy
invidiabile, in-ve-de'ah-be-lay, a., enviable
invidiare, in-ve-de'ah-ray, v., to envy

invidioso*, in-ve-de'o-zo, a., envious, invidious
inviluppare, in-ve-loop-pah-ray, v., to wrap up
invincibile, in-vin-chee-be-lay, a., invincible
invio, in-vee-o, m., sending, conveyance
inviolabile, in-ve'o-lah-be-lay, a., inviolable
invisibile, in-ve-zee-be-lay, a., invisible
invitare, in-ve-tah-ray, v., to invite ; to screw up
invitato, in-ve-tah-to, m., guest
invito, in-vee-to, m., invitation
invocare, in-vo-kah-ray, v., to invoke, to call upon
involgere, in-voll-jay-ray, v., to wrap up ; to involve
involto, in-voll-to, m., parcel
involucro, in-vo-loo-kro, m., casing ; outer cover
invulnerabile, in-vooll-nay-rah-be-lay, a., invulnerable
inzaccherare, in-dzahk-kay-rah-ray, v., to get muddy, to be splashed with mud
inzuccherare, in-dzook-kay-rah-ray, v., to sugar
inzuppare, in-dzoop-pah-ray, v., to soak, to steep
io, ee-o, pron., I. **son —**, it is I
iodio, e'o-de-o, m., iodine
ioduro, e'o-doo-ro, m., iodide
ipnotismo, ip-no-teess-mo, m., hypnotism
ipocrita, e-po-kre-tah, m. & f., hypocrite
ipoteca, e-po-tay-kah, f., mortgage
ipotecare, e-po-tay-kah-ray, v., to mortgage
ipotesi, e-po-tay-ze, f., hypothesis
ippopotamo, ip-po-po-tah-mo, m., hippopotamus
ira, ee-rah, f., anger
irascibile, e-rah-shee-be-lay, a., irascible, irritable
irato*, e-rah-to, a., irate, angry ; incensed
iride, ee-re-day, f., iris ; rainbow
ironia, e-ro-nee'ah, f., irony
irradiare, eer-rah-de'ah-ray, v., to irradiate, to radiate [diate
irragionevole, eer-rah-jo-nay-vo-lay, a., unreasonable ; irrational
irreconciliabile, eer-ray-kon-che-le'ah-be-lay, a., irreconciliable
irrefragabile, eer-ray-frah-gah-be-lay, a., incontestable ; undeniable
irregolarità, eer-ray-go-lah-re-tah, f., irregularity
irremovibile, eer-ray-mo-vee-be-lay, a., immovable

irreparabile, eer-ray-pah-**rah**-be-lay, a., irreparable
irreprensibile, eer-ray-pren-**see**-be-lay, a., blameless
irresistibile, eer-ray-ziss-**tee**-be-lay, a., irresistible
irresoluto*, eer-ray-zo-**loo**-to, a., wavering, irresolute
irrevocabile, eer-ray-vo-**kah**-be-lay, a., irrevocable
irrigare, eer-re-**gah**-ray, v., to irrigate
irrigazione, eer-re-gah-tse-**O**-nay, f., irrigation
irrimediabile, eer-re-may-de-**ah**-be-lay, a., irremediable [diable
irritabile, eer-re-tah-be-lay, a., irritable
irritare, eer-re-**tah**-ray, v., to irritate
irriverente, eer-re-vay-**ren**-tay, a., irreverent
irrugginire, eer-rood-je-**nee**-ray, v., to rust
irruzione, eer-roo-tse-**O**-nay, f., irruption
irsuto, eer-**soo**-to, a., hairy, bristly
iscrizione, iss-kre-tse-**O**-nay, f., inscription, title
isola, **ee**-zo-lah, f., island [lation
isolamento, e-zo-lah-**men**-to, m., isolation; insu-
isolano, e-zo-**lah**-no, m., islander; insular
isolare, e-zo-**lah**-ray, v., to isolate; to insulate
isolato, e-zo-**lah**-to, m., separate block of houses
isolatore, e-zo-lah-**tor**-ay, m., insulator
ispettore, iss-pet-**tor**-ay, m., inspector
ispezionare, iss-pay-tse-o-**nah**-ray, v., to inspect
ispezione, iss-pay-tse-**O**-nay, f., inspection
ispirare, iss-pe-**rah**-ray, v., to inspire; to instil
ispirazione, iss-pe-rah-tse-**O**-nay, f., inspiration
istantaneo*, iss-tahn-**tah**-nay-o, a., instantaneous
istante, iss-**tahn**-tay, m., instant; moment
istanza, iss-**tahn**-tsah, f., petition; (law) instance
isterico*, iss-**tay**-re-ko, a., hysterical
istesso, iss-**tess**-so, a., the same, similar
istigare, iss-te-**gah**-ray, v., to instigate
istigazione, iss-te-gah-tse-**O**-nay, f., instigation
istintivo*, iss-tin-**tee**-vo, a., instinctive, natural
istinto, iss-**tin**-to, m., instinct
istituire, iss-te-too-**ee**-ray, v., to institute
istituto, iss-te-**too**-to, m., institute, college
istitutore, iss-te-too-**tor**-ay, m., tutor; founder
istitutrice, iss-te-too-**tree**-chay, f., governess
istituzione, iss-te-too-tse-**O**-nay, f., institution

istmo, eest-mo. m., isthmus
istoria, iss-to-re'ah, f., history ; story
istruire, iss-troo'ee-ray, v., to instruct
istruirsi, iss-troo-eer-se, v., to learn
istruito, iss-troo'ee-to, a., learned, informed
istruttivo*, iss-troot-tee-vo, a., instructive
istruzione, iss-troo-tse'o-nay, f., instruction
istupidire, iss-too-pe-dee-ray, v., to make stupid
iterare, e-tay-rah-ray, v., to iterate
itterizia, it-tay-ree-tse'ah, f., jaundice
iuniore, e'oo-ne'o-ray, a., junior, younger
iuta, e'oo-tah, f., jute
ivi, ee-ve, adv., there
izzare, it-tsah-ray, v., to anger

---

j & k.——— These letters do not occur at all in
modern Italian, either as initials or in the
body of words. "I" has been substituted
in words formerly commencing with "J."

---

la, lah, art., the. pron., her ; it
là, lah, adv., there ; yonder. **qua e —**, here and there
labbro, lahb-bro, m., lip ; border
labile, lah-be-lay, a., frail
laburista, lah-boo-riss-tah, m., labour supporter
lacca, lahk-kah, f., lacquer. **cera —**, sealing-wax
lacchè, lahk-kay, m., footman, lackey
laccio, laht-cho, m., noose ; (fig.) trap
lacerare, lah-chay-rah-ray, v., to lacerate ; to tear
lacrima, lah-kre-mah, f., tear
lacrimare, lah-kre-mah-ray, v., to shed tears
lacuna, lah-koo-nah, f., lagoon ; gap ; (fig.) need
laddove, lahd-do-vay, adv., whilst
ladro, lah-dro, m., thief. **— di strada**, highway-
ladrocinio, lah-dro-chee-ne'o, m., robbery [man
laggiù, lahd-joo, adv., yonder ; below
lagnanza [lagno], lah-n'yahn-tsah, f., complaint
lagnarsi, lah-n'yar-se, v., to complain ; to moan
lago, lah-go, m., lake
lagrima, lah-gre-mah, f., tear
lagrimoso*, lah-gre-mo-zo, a., tearful

laguna, lah-goo-nah, f., lagoon

laico, lah-e-ko, m., layman. a.,* secular

laido*, lah-e-do, a., hateful; obscene

lama, lah-mah, f., blade; metal-plate; moor

lambicco, lahm-beek-ko, m., still

lambire, lahm-bee-ray, v., to lick; to touch lightly

lamentare, lah-men-tah-ray, v., to lament

lamentarsi, lah-men-tar-se, v., complain

lamentevole, lah-men-tay-vo-lay, a., plaintive, sad

lamina, lah-me-nah, f., thin sheet of metal

lampada, lahm-pah-dah, f., lamp

lampadario, lahm-pah-dah-re'o, m., chandelier

lampone, lahm-po-nay, f., raspberry

lampreda, lahm-pray-dah, f., lamprey

lana, lah-nah, f., wool. buona —, (fig.) scamp

lancetta, lahn-chet-tah, f., lancet; hand of watch

lancia, lahn-chah, f., lance; launch

lanciare, lahn-chah-ray, v., to hurl; to launch

lanciere, lahn-chay-ray, m., lancer

lancio, lahn-cho, m., high jump, leap; bound

landa, lahn-dah, f., heath; prairie

laneria, lah-nay-ree-ah, f., woollen goods

languido*, lahn-goo'e-do, a., languid

languire, lahn-goo'ee-ray, v., to languish; to fade

languore, lahn-goo'o-ray, m., languor

lanoso, lah-no-zo, a., woolly; shaggy

lanterna, lahn-tair-nah, f., lantern

lanugine, lah-noo-je-nay, f., down; soft hair

lanuto, lah-noo-to, a., (see lanoso)

laonde, lah-on-day, adv., whereupon, wherefore

lapidare, lah-pe-dah-ray, v., to stone

lapide, lah-pe-day, f., grave-stone, stone-tablet

lapilli, lah-peel-le, m. pl., ashes from volcano

lapis, lah-piss, m., lead-pencil

lardo, lar-do, m., bacon; lard

larghezza, lar-ghet-tsah, f., breadth; generosity

largire, lar-jee-ray, v., to give liberally

largo*, lar-go, a., wide; lavish

laringe, lah-reen-jay, f., larynx, windpipe

lasciare, lah-she'ah-ray, v., to leave; to let

lascito, lah-she-to, m., legacy

lascivo*, lah-shee-vo, a., wanton, lewd

lassativo, lahss-sah-tee-vo, a., laxative
lassezza, lahss-set-tsah, f., lassitude, fatigue
lasso, lahss-so, a., tired; unhappy
lassù, lahss-soo, adv., up there
lastra, lahss-trah, f., sheet; paving stone
lastrico, lahss-tre-ko, m., pavement
latitante, lah-te-tahn-tay, a.,absconding; fugitive
latitudine, lah-te-too-de-nay, f., latitude; width
lato, lah-to, a., wide. m., side
latore, lah-tor-ay, m., bearer
latrare, lah-trah-ray, v., to bark
latrina, lah-tree-nah, f., public W.C.
latta, laht-tah, f., sheet-iron; can
lattaio, laht-tah-e'o, m., milkman
latte, laht-tay, m., milk. fiore di —, cream
latteo, laht-tay-o, a., milky
latteria, laht-tay-ree-ah, f., dairy-farm
lattuga, laht-too-gah, f., lettuce
laudano, lah'oo-dah-no, m., laudanum
laurearsi, lah'oo-ray-ar-se, v., to graduate
laureato, lah'oo-ray-ah-to, m., graduate
lauro, lah'oo-ro, m., laurel; (fig.) glory
lauto, lah'oo-to, a., splendid; sumptuous
lavabile, lah-vah-be-lay, a., washable
lavagna, lah-vah-n'yah, f., black-board; slate
lavamano, lah-vah-mah-no, m., washstand
lavanda, lah-vahn-dah, f., washing; lavender
lavandaia, lah-vahn-dah-e'ah, f., laundress
lavanderia, lah-vahn-day-ree-ah, f., laundry
lavare, lah-vah-ray, v., to wash; (fig.)to purify
lavatoio, lah-vah-to-e'o, m., lavatory; wash-house
lavorante, lah-vo-rahn-tay, m., worker; labourer
lavorare, lah-vo-rah-ray, v., to work; to toil
lavoro, lah-vo-ro, m., work; labour
le, lay, art., the. pron., them; her; to her
leale, lay-ah-lay, a., loyal, sincere, trusty
lealmente, lay-ahl-men-tay, adv.,loyally, faithfully
lealtà, lay-ahl-tah, f., loyalty, fidelity
lebbra, leb-brah, f., leprosy
lebbroso, leb-bro-zo, m., leper. a., leprous
leccare, leck-kah-ray, v., to lick; (fig.)to flatter
leccata, leck-kah-tah, f., licking; flattery

leccone, leck-ko-nay, m., glutton
leccornia, leck-kor-ne'ah, f., titbit
ledere, lay-day-ray, v., to injure
lega, lay-gah, f., league, union; alloy
legaccio, lay-gaht-cho, f., garter; (fig.) tie
legale, lay-gah-lay, a., lawful. m., lawyer
legalizzare, lay-gah-lit-tsah-ray, v., to legalize
legame, lay-gah-may, m., bond; chain
legare, lay-gah-ray, v., to bind; to tie; to bequeath
legatario, lay-gah-tah-re'o, m., legatee
legato, lay-gah-to, m., legacy; bequest
legatore, lay-gah-tor-ay, m., bookbinder
legatura, lay-gah-too-rah, f., binding
legazione, lay-gah-tse'o-nay, f., legation, **embassy**
legge, led-jay, f., law
leggenda, led-jen-dah, f., legend
leggere, led-jay-ray, v., to read
leggero, led-jay-ro, a., light, slight, nimble [tiness
leggiadria, led-jah-dree-ah, f., gracefulness, pret-
leggio, led-jee-o, m., desk; music-stand
legione, lay-je'o-nay, f., legion
legittimo, lay-jit-te-mo, a., legitimate, just
legnaiuolo, lay-n'yah-e'oo-O-lo, m.,carpenter, join-
legname, lay-n'yah-may, m., timber [er
legno, lay-n'yo, m., wood; branches; cab
legnoso, lay-n'yo-zo, a., woody
legume, lay-goo-may, m., vegetable
lei, lay-e, pron., she; her; you
lembo, lem-bo, m., border; edge
leniente, lay-ne'en-tay, a., lenient
lenire, lay-nee-ray, v., to soothe; to calm
lente, len-tay, f., lens; (leguminous) lentil
lentezza, len-ted-dzah, f., slowness, slackness
lenticchia, len-tick-ke'ah, f., lentil
lento, len-to, a., slow, tardy. adv., slowly
lenza, len-tsah, f., fishing-line
lenzuolo, len-tsoo'o-lo, m., bed-sheet; cover
leone, lay-o-nay, m., lion
leonessa, lay-o-ness-sah, f., lioness
leopardo, lay-o-par-do, m., leopard
lepre, lay-pray, m. & f., hare
lesina, lay-ze-nah, f., awl; (fig.) avarice

lesinare, lay-ze-nah-ray, v., to be niggardly

lessare, less-sah-ray, v., to boil; to stew

lessico, less-e-ko, m., lexicon

lesso, less-so, m., boiled meat. a., boiled

lesto*, less-to, a., quick, nimble, agile

letamare, lay-tah-mah-ray, v., to manure, to dung

letame, lay-tah-may, m., dung

letargo, lay-tar-go, m., lethargy; dullness

lettera, let-tay-rah, f., letter, type

letterale, let-tay-rah-lay, a., literal

letterario, let-tay-rah-re'o, a., literary [learned

letterato, let-tay-rah-to, m., a learned person. a.,

letteratura, let-tay-rah-too-rah, f., literature

lettiera, let-te-ay-rah, f., bedstead

lettiga, let-tee-gah, f., litter

letto, let-to, m., bed

lettore, let-tor-ay, m., reader

lettura, let-too-rah, f., reading

leva, lay-vah, f., lever; levy; conscription

levare, lay-vah-ray, v., to raise, to take off

levarsi, lay-var-se, v., to rise

levata, lay-vah-tah, f., rising; taking away

levatrice, lay-vah-tree-chay, f., midwife

levigare, lay-ve-gah-ray, v., to gloss, to smooth

levriere, lay-vre-ay-ray, m., greyhound

lezione, lay-tse'o-nay, f., lesson

li, le, art., the. pron., them. adv., there

libbra, lib-brah, f., (in weight) pound

libeccio, le-bet-cho, m., S.W. wind

libello, le-bell-lo, m., libel

libellula, le-bell-loo-lah, f., dragon-fly

liberare, le-bay-rah-ray, v., to free, to release

libero*, lee-hay-ro, a., free; liberated

libertà, le-bair-tah, f., liberty

libidine, le-bee-de-nay, f., wantonness

libraio, le-brah-e'o, m., bookseller

libreria, le-bray-ree-ah, f., bookseller's shop; library

libro, lee-bro, m., book

licenza, le-chen-tsah, f., licence; furlough [dismissal

licenziamento, le-chen-tse'ah-men-to, m., leave;

licenziare, 'e-chen-tse'ah-ray, v., to dismiss; to grant permission

licenzioso*, le-chen-tse'o-zo, a., licentious, dissolute
liceo, le-chay-o, m., lyceum
lichene, le-kay-nay, m., lichen
lido, lee-do, m., shore, beach
lieto*, le'ay-to, a., glad, merry
lieve, le'ay-vay, a., light, trifling. adv., lightly
lievitare, le'ay-ve-tah-ray, v., to leaven ; to ferment
lievito, le'ay-ve-to, m., yeast ; fermentation
lignaggio, le-n'yad-jo, m., lineage
lilla, [lila], lil-lah, f., lilac
lima, lee-mah, f., file ; (fruit) lime ; (fig.) false friend
limaccioso, le-maht-cho-so, a., muddy ; miry
limare, le-mah-ray, v., to file
limitare, le-me-tah-ray, v., to limit. m., threshold
limite, lee-me-tay, m., limit ; boundary
limonata, le-mo-nah-tah, f., lemonade
limone, le-mo-nay, m., lemon ; lemon-tree
limosina, le-mo-ze-nah, f., alms
limpido*, lim-pe-do, a., limpid
lince, lin-chay, f., lynx
lindo*, lin-do, a., smart, trim, tidy
linea, lee-nay-ah, f., line
lineamenti, le-nay-ah-men-te, m. pl., features
lineare, le-nay-ah-ray, v., to draw, to delineate
lingua, lin-goo'ah, f., tongue ; language [lumnious
linguacciuto, lin-goo'aht-choo-to, a., chatty ; ca-
linguaggio, lin-goo'ahd-jo, m., language
lino, lee-no, m., flax, to linen
linseme, lin-say-may, m., linseed
liquefare, le-kway-fah-ray, v., to liquify
liquidare, le-kwe-dah-ray, v., to liquidate ; to sell off
liquido*, lee-kwe-do, m., liquid. a.,* liquid, fluid
liquirizia, le-kwe-rit-tse'ah, f., liquorice
liquore, le-kwo-ray, m., liquor ; liqueur
lira, lee-rah, f., (coin) lira ; (mus.) lyre
lirico, lee-re-ko, a., lyric, lyrical
lisca, liss-kah, f., fish-bone [animal
lisciare, le-she-ah-ray, v., to polish ; to stroke an
liscio*, lee-she-o, a., smooth, glossy, sleek
liso, lee-zo, a., threadbare
lista, liss-tah, f., list
lite, lee-tay, f., law-suit ; contest

litigare, le-te-gah-ray. v., to litigate ; **to quarrel**
litigio, le-tee-jo, m., dispute ; quarrel
litro, lee-tro, m., litre
liuto, lee'oo-to, m., lute
livellare, le-vell-lah-ray, v., to level
livello, le-vell-lo, m., level
lividura, le-ve-doo-rah, f., bruise
livore, le-vo-ray, m., grudge
livrea, le-vray-ah, f., livery
lo, lo, art., the. pron., him ; it
locale, lo-kah-lay, a., local. m., room ; **premises**
locanda, lo-kahn-dah, f., inn ; family hotel
locare, lo-kah-ray, v., to let
locatore, lo-kah-tor-ay, m., lessor
locusta, lo-kooss-tah, f., locust
locuzione, lo-koo-tse'o-nay, f., **locution**
lodare, lo-dah-ray, v., to praise
lode, lo-day, f., praise
lodola, lo-do-lah, f., lark
loggia, lod-jah, f., lodge ; terrace ; open **gallery**
logorare, lo-go-rah-ray, v., to wear out
logoro*, lo-go-ro, a., worn out ; wasted
lombaggine, lom-bahd-je-nay, f., lumbago
lombata, lom-bah-tah, f., loin of meat
lombo, lom-bo, m., loin
lombrico, lom-bree-ko, m., worm
longanime, lon-gah-ne-may, a., patient
lontananza, lon-tah-nahn-tsah, f., distance
lontano*, lon-tah-no, a., far, remote
lontra, lon-trah, f., otter
loquace, lo-kwah-chay, a., loquacious
lordare, lor-dah-ray, v., to soil
lordo*, lor-do, a., dirty, foul. peso —, **gross weight**
lordura, lor-doo-rah, f., filth ; rubbish
loro, lo-ro, pron., they ; them ; their ; theirs
lotta, lot-tah, f., struggle ; wrestling match
lottare, lot-tah-ray, v., to strive ; to wrestle
lottatore, lot-tah-tor-ay, m., wrestler
lotto, lot-to, m., lot ; lottery
lozione, lo-tse'o-nay, f., lotion
lubrificare, loo-bre-fe-kah-ray, v., **to lubricate**
lucchetto, look-ket-to, m., padlock

luccicare, loot-che-**kah**-ray, v., to glitter ; to shine
luccio, loot-cho, m., pike
lucciola, loot-cho-lah, f., fire-fly ; glow-worm
luce, loo-chay, f., light ; day-light ; lamp
lucente, loo-**chen**-tay, a., shining, luminous
lucerna, loo-chair-nah, f., lamp
lucertola, loo-chair-to-lah, f., lizard
lucidare, loo-che-**dah**-ray, v., to polish
lucidezza, loo-che-det-tsah, f., brightness ; lucidity
lucido, loo-che-do, a.,* bright. m., shoe-polish
lucignolo, loo-che-n'yo-lo, m., wick
lucrare, loo-**krah**-ray, v., to earn
lucrativo, loo-krah-**tee**-vo, a., lucrative, paying
lucro, loo-kro, m., profit
ludibrio, loo-dee-bre-o, m., mockery, derision
luglio, loo l'yo, m., July
lugubre, loo-goo-bray, a., lugubrious, mournful
lui, loo-e, pron., him ; it ; he
lumaca, loo-**mah**-kah, f., snail ; (fig.) sluggard
lumaio, loo-**mah**-e'o, m., lamp-lighter
lume, loo-may, m., light ; (fig.) genius
lumiera, loo-me'ay-rah, f., bracket for candles
luminoso*, loo-me-no-zo, a., luminous
luna, loo-nah, f., moon ; (fig.) temper. — **di miele**, honeymoon
lunedì, loo-nay-dee, m., Monday
lunga, loonn-gah, f., strap ; length of time
lunghezza, loonn-get-tsah, f., length, duration
lungi, loonn-je, adv. & prep., far ; far off
lungo, loonn-go, a., long. prep., along
luogo, loo'o-go, m., place, room, dwelling
luogotenente, loo'o-go-tay-**nen**-tay, m., lieutenant
lupanare, loo-pah-nah-ray, m., brothel
lupo, loo-po, [**lupa**] [**loo-pah**] m., wolf [f., she-
luppolo, loop-po-lo, m., hop   wolf]
lurco, loohr-ko, a., gluttonous
lurido, loo-re-do, a., foul
lusco, looss-ko, a., short-sighted ; (fig.) heavy
lusinga, loo-sin-gah, f., flattery ; allurement
lusingare, loo-sin-**gah**-ray, v., to flatter ; to allure
lusso, looss-so, m., luxury
lussurioso*, looss-soo-re'o-zo, a., lustful, wanton

lustrare, looss-**trah**-ray, v., to polish
lustro, looss-tro, m., lustre ; gloss
lutto, loot-to, m., mourning ; sorrow

ma, mah, conj., but
macca, **mahk**-kah, f., abundance
macchia, **mahk**-ke'ah, f., stain
macchiare, mahk-ke'**ah**-ray, v., to stain, to spot
macchina, **mahk**-ke-nah, f., engine ; motor-car ;
  (fig) plot. — **da scrivere**, typewriter
macchinale, mahk-ke-**nah**-lay, a., mechanical
macchinare, mahk-ke-nah-ray, v., to plot ; to plan
macchinio, mahk-ke-nah-re'o, m., machinery
macchinista, mahk-ke-**niss**-tah, m., machinist
macellaio, mah-chayl-lah-e'o, m., butcher
macellare, mah-chayl-lah-ray, v., to slaughter
macello, mah-**chell**-lo, m., slaughter-house;
  (fig) massacre
macilento, mah-che-**len**-to, a., lean ; meagre
macina, **mah**-che-nah, f., mill-stone
macinamento, mah-che-nah-**men**-to, m.,grinding
macinare, mah-che-**nah**-ray, v., to grind, to mill
macinino, mah-che-**nee**-no, m., coffee or pepper-
macula, mah-**koo**-lah, f., blemish, spot   [mill
madama, mah-**dah**-mah, f., madam
madamigella, mah-dah-me-**jell**-lah, f.,young lady;
madido, mah-de-do, a., moist   [madam
madornale, mah-dor-**nah**-lay, a., great ; gross
madre, **mah**-dray, f., mother ; matrix
madreperla, mah-dray-**pair**-lah, f.,mother of pearl
madreselva, mah-dray-**sell**-vah, f., honeysuckle
madrevite, mah-dray-**vee**-tay, f., screw-nut
madrigna, mah-**dree**-n'yah, f., stepmother
madrina, mah-**dree**-nah, f., godmother
maestà, mah-**ess**-tah, f., majesty ; dignity
maestoso°, mah-ess-**to**-zo, a., majestic
maestra,mah-**ess**-trah,f.,school-mistress, governess
maestrale, mah-ess-**trah**-lay, m., N.W. wind
maestranza, mah-ess-**trahn**-dzah, f., guild
maestrare, mah-ess-**trah**-ray, v., to instruct
maestrevole, mah-ess-**tray**-vo-lay, a., masterly
maestria, mah-ess-**tree**-ah, f., mastery in art, etc.

maestro, mah-**ess**-tro, m., master ; composer.
  a., masterly ; experienced
maga, mah-gah, f., sorceress   [fruit
magagna, mah-gah-n'yah, f., defect ; rottenness in
magari, mah-gah-re, even so ! God grant !
magazzino, mah-gahd-dze-no, m., warehouse ;
  stores ; magazine
maggio, mahd-jo, m., May
maggioranza, mahd-jo-rahn-dzah, f., majority
maggiore, mahd-jor-ay, m., major. a., greater ;
maggiorenne, mahd-jo-ren-nay, a., of age   [elder
magia, mah-jee-ah, f., magic
magico*, mah-je-ko, a., magical ; enchanting
magistero, mah-jiss-tay-ro, m., mastery ; skill
magistrale, mah-jiss-trah-lay, a., magisterial,
  masterly, great
maglia, mah-l'yah, f., network ; mesh ; stitch
maglieria, mah-l'yay-re-ah, f., hosiery
maglio, mah-l'yo, m., mallet ; cricket-bat
magnanimo*, mah-n'yah-ne-mo,a., magnanimous
magnano, mah-n'yah-no, m., locksmith
magnete, mah-n'yay-tay, m., magnet
magnetico*, mah-n'yay-te-ko, a., magnetic
magnetizzare,mah-n'yay-tid-dzah-ray,v.,to magnetize ; to mesmerize
magnificare, mah-n'ye-fe-kah-ray, v., to magnify
magnificenza, mah-n'ye-fe-chen-tsah, f., magnificence
magnifico*, mah-n'yee-fe-ko, a., magnificent
magno, mah-n'yo, a., great ; grand
mago, mah-go, m., magician
magrezza, mah-gret-tsah, f., leanness
magro*, mah-gro, a., lean, thin
mai, mah-e, adv., ever ; never
maiale, mah-e'ah-lay, m., pig ; (pop.) dirty fellow
mais, mah-iss, m., maize
maiuscola, mah-e'ooss-ko-lah, f., capital letter
malaccorto*, mah-lahk-kor-to, a., uncouth ; inconsiderate
malacreanza,mah-lah-kray-ahn-tsah, f., bad man-
malandrino, mah-lahn-dree-no, m., ruffian [ners
malaticcio, mah-lah-tit-cho, a., delicate

malato, mah-lah-to, m., patient. a., unwell, ill

malattia, mah-laht-tee-ah, f., illness; disease

maldicente, mahl-de-chen-tay, a., slanderous

male, mah-lay, m., harm; sickness. adv., hardly

maledetto, mah-lay-det-to, interj., damn it!

maledire, mah-lay-dee-ray, v., to curse; to damn

malerba, mah-lair-bah, f., weed; (fig.) rascal

malevolo, mah-lay-vo-lo, a., malevolent

malfatto, mahl-faht-to, m.,misdeed. a.,misshapen

malgrado, mahl-grah-do, prep., in spite of

maligno, mah-lee-n'yo, a., malignant

malinconia, mah-lin-ko-nee-ah, f., melancholy

malinconico*, mah-lin-ko-ne-ko, a., melancholic

malincuore, mah-lin-koo'o-ray, adv., grudgingly

malinteso, mah-lin-tay-zo, m., misunderstanding.
a., misunderstood

malizia, mah-lee-tse'ah, f., malice; craftiness

malizioso*, mah-le-tse'o-zo, a., malicious   [ty

mallevadoria, mahl-lay-vah-do-ree-ah,f.,bail,sure-

malmenare, mahl-may-nah-ray, v., to ill-treat

malocchio, mahl-ock-ke'o, m., evil-eye

malora, mah-lo-rah, f., ruin; perdition. andare
in —, to go to the bad

malsano, mahl-sah-no, a., unwholesome

malsicuro, mahl-se-koo-ro, a., insecure; uncertain

maltrattare, mahl-traht-tah-ray, v., to ill-treat

malva, mahl-vah, f., mallow

malvagio, mahl-vah-jo, a., wicked. m., rogue

malversazione, mahl-vair-sah-tse'o-nay, f., em-
bezzlement

mammella,mahm-mel-lah,f.,teat; woman's breast

mammola, mahm-mo-lah, f., violet

manata, mah-nah-tah, f., handful

mancanza, mahn-kahn-tsah, f., want; defect

mancare, mahn-kah-ray, v.,to be in want of; to be
missing

manchevole, mahn-kay-vo-lay, a., defective

mancia, mahn-chah, f., tip, gratuity

mancino,mahn-che-no,m.,left hand. a.,left-handed

mandare, mahn-dah-ray, v., to send; to order

mandato,mahn-dah-to,m.,mandate; authorisation

mandorla, mahn-dor-lah, f., almond

mandra, mahn-drah, f., flock, herd

mandriano, mahn-dre-ah no, m., herdsman

maneggevole, mah-ned-jay-vo-lay, a., handy

maneggiare, mah-ned-**jah**-ray, v., to handle ; to touch

maneggio, mah-ned-jo, m., handling ; management ; administration ; riding-school

manesco*, mah-**ness**-ko, a., handy ; pugnacious

manette, mah-net-tay, f pl., handcuffs

manganare, mahn-gah-**nah**-ray, v., to mangle

mangano, mahn-gah-no, m., mangle

mangiabile, mahn-jah-be-lay, a., eatable   [der

mangiare, mahn-jah-ray, v., to eat ; (fig.) to squan-

mangime, mahn-jee-may, m., fodder

manica, mah-ne-kah, f., sleeve

manico, mah-ne-ko, m., handle

manicomio, mah-ne-**ko**-me'o, m., lunatic asylum

manicotto, mah-ne-**kot**-to, m., muff

maniera, mah ne'ay-rah, f., manner ; usage

manieroso*, mah-ne'ay-**ro**-zo, a., affected ; polite

manifattore, mah-ne-faht-**tor**-ay, m., manufacturer

manifattura, mah-ne-faht-**too**-rah, f., manufacture, make

manifestare, mah-ne-fess-**tah**-ray, v., to manifest

manifesto, mah-ne-**fess**-to, a.,* manifest, clear,
m., manifest ; poster

maniglia, mah-**nee**-l'yah, f., handle ; shackle

manipolo, mah-nee-po-lo, m., handful

maniscalco, mah-niss-**kahl**-ko, m., blacksmith

mano, mah-no, f., hand ; (at cards) the lead.
man —, little by little

manovale, mah-no-**vah**-lay, m., labourer

manovella, mah-no-**vell**-lah, f., (mech.) crank

manovra, mah-**no**-vrah, f., manœuvre ; drill

mansueto, mahn-soo-**ay**-to, a., meek

mantello, mahn-**tell**-lo, m., cloak

mantenere, mahn tay-**nay**-ray, v., to maintain

mantenimento, mahn-tay-ne-**men**-to, m., main-

manuale, mah-noo'ah-lay, a., manual   [tenance

manubrio, mah-**noo**-bre-o, m., handle-bar

manzo, mahn-dzo, m.,beef. **—arrosto,** roastbeef

maomettano, mah-o-met-**tah**-no, m., Mahometan

mappa, **mahp**-pah, f., map

maraviglia, mah-rah-**vee**-l'yah, f., marvel

maravigliarsi, mah-rah-ve-l'**yar**-se, v., to marvel at

maraviglioso, mah-rah-ve-l'**yo**-zo, a., marvellous

marca, **mar**-kah, f., mark. — **da bollo**, revenue-stamp. — **di fabbrica**, trade-mark.

marcare, mar-**kah**-ray, v., to mark ; to note down

marcatura, mar-kah-**too**-rah, f., marking

marchesa, mar-**kay**-zah, f., marchioness

marchese, mar **kay**-zay, m., marquis

marchio, **mar**-ke'o, m., mark, stamp

marcia, **mar** chah, f., march ; (med.) pus

marciapiede, mar-chah-pe'**ay**-day, m., pavement ;

marciare, mar-**chah**-ray, v., to march [foot-path

marcio, **mar**-cho, a., rotten ; crumbling

marcire, mar-**chee**-ray, v., to rot ; to fester

marco, **mar**-ko, m., (currency) German mark

mare, **mah**-ray, m., sea. **alto** —, high seas

marea, mah-**ray**-ah, f., tide ; ebb and flow

maresciallo, mah-ray-**shall**-lo, m., marshal

margherita, mar-ghay-**ree**-tah, f., daisy

margheritina, mar-ghay-re-**tee**-nah, f., daisy ;

margine, **mar**-je-nay, m., margin ; edge [beads

marina, mah-**ree**-nah, f., navy ; marine

marinaio, mah-re-nah-e'o, m., sailor, mariner

marinare, mah-re-nah-ray, v., to pickle

mariolo, mah-re'o-lo, m., swindler, thief

maritare, mah-re-**tah**-ray, v., to join in wedlock

maritarsi, mah-re-tar-se, v., to get married

marito, mah-**ree**-to, m., husband

marittimo, mah-**rit**-te-mo, a., maritime; sea...

marmellata, mar-mell-**lah**-tah, f., marmalade

marmitta, mar-**mit**-tah, f., stewing-pot

marmo, **mar**-mo, m., marble

marmocchio, mar-**mock**-ke'o, m., brat

maroso, mah-ro-so, m., billow, swamp

marra, **mar**-rah, f., hoe

marrone, mar-ro-nay, m., chestnut, chestnut-tree
a., (colour) brown

marsina, mar-**see**-nah, f., dress-jacket

martedi, mar-**tay**-dee, m., Tuesday

martellare, mar-tell-lah-ray, v., to hammer
martello, mar-tell-lo, m., hammer ; knocker
martinetto, mar-te-net-to, m., (tool) jack
martire, mar-te-ray, m., martyr
martirio, mar-tee-re'o, m., martyrdom
martora, mar-to-rah, f., marten
martoriare, mar-to-re'ah-ray, v., to torture
marziale, mar-tse'ah-lay, a., martial
marzo, mar-tso, m., March   [drel
mascalzone, mahss-kahl-tso-nay, m.,rogue, scoun-
mascella, mah-shel-lah, f., jaw, jawbone
maschera, mahss-kay-rah, f., mask
mascherare, mahss-kay-rah-ray, v., to mask ; to
   camouflage
mascherata, mahss-kay-rah-tah, f., masquerade
maschiezza,mahss-ke'et-tsah,f.,manliness; virility
maschile, mahss-kee-lay, a., male
maschio, mahss-ke'o, m., male   [robber
masnadiere, mahss-nah-de'ay-ray, m., highway-
massa, mahss-sah, f., mass ; pile
massacro, mahss-sah-kro, m., slaughter
massaggio, mahss-sahd-jo, m., massage
massaia, mahss-sah-e'ah, f., housewife
masseria, mahss-say-ree-ah, f., farm   [effects
masserizia, mahss-say-ree-tse'ah, f., household-
massiccio, mahss-sit-cho, a., massive
massima, mahss-se-mah, f., adage ; principle
massimo,mahss-se-mo, m.,maximum. a.,*greatest
masso, mahss-so, n., rock
massone, mahss-so-nay, m., freemason
masticare, mahss-te-kah-ray, v., to masticate
mastice, mahss-te-chay, m., rubber-solution ;
   china-cement
mastietto, mahss-te'et-to, m., hinge
mastino, mahss-tee-no, m., mastiff
mastro, mahss-tro, a., main. libro —, ledger
matassa, mah-tahss-sah, f., skein ; spool
materasso[a], mah-tay-rahss-so, m. [f.], mattress
materia, mah-tay-re'ah, f., matter
materno, mah-tair-no, a., maternal
matita, mah-tee-tah, f., pencil ; crayon
matrice, mah-tree-chay, f., mould ; womb

matrigna, mah-**tree**-n'yah, f., stepmother

matrimonio, mah-tre-**mo**-ne'o, m., matrimony

matrina, mah-**tree**-nah, f., godmother

matrona, mah-**tro**-nah, f., matron

mattana, maht-**tah**-nah, f., bad temper

mattare, maht-**tah**-ray, v., to kill : (chess) to mate

mattina, maht-**tee**-nah, f., morning

mattinata, maht-te-**nah**-tah, f., matinée

mattiniero, maht-te-ne'**ay**-ro, a., early rising

matto, matto, maht-to, a.,* mad. m., lunatic

mattone, maht-**to**-nay, m., brick

maturare, mah-too-**rah**-ray, v., to ripen

maturato*, mah-too-**rah**-to, a., ripe, mature ; due

maturo, mah-**too**-ro, a., ripe, mature

mazza, mazza, maht-tsah, f., stick ; club ; mace

mazzo, mazzo, maht-tso, m., bundle ; pack ; pile

me, may, pron., me

meccanicizzare, meck-kah-ne-chit-**tsah**-ray, v., to mechanize

meccanico, meck-**kah**-ne-ko, m., mechanic

medaglia, may-**dah**-l'yah, f., medal

medaglione, may-dah-l'**yo**-nay, m., medallion

medesimo, may-**day**-se-mo, pron. & a., same, self

media, may-**de**'ah, f., average ; proportion

mediante, may-de'**ahn**-tay, prep., by means of

mediatore, may-de'ah-**tor**-ay, m., intermediary ; broker

mediazione, may-de'ah-tse'**o**-nay, f., mediation ; brokerage

medicare, may-de-**kah**-ray, v., to heal ; to medicate

medicina, may-de-**chee**-nah, f., medicine

medico, may-**de**-ko, m., doctor

medio, may-**de**'o, a., middle ; medium

mediocre, may-de'**o**-kray, a., mediocre, middling

meditare, may-de-**tah**-ray, v., to meditate

megera, may-**jay**-rah, f., shrew ; vixen

meglio, may-l'yo, adv., better. m., best

mela, mela, may-lah, f., apple

melassa, may-**lahss**-sah, f., treacle ; molasses

mellone, mell-**lo**-nay, m., melon

melma, melma, mell-mah, f., mud

melo, melo, may-lo, m., apple-tree

melodìa, may-lo-dee-ah, f., melody
melodioso*, may-lo-de'o-zo, a., melodious
membrana, mem-brah-nah, f., membrane
membro, mem-bro, m., limb; member
membruto, mem-broo-to, a., stout-limbed
memorabile, may-mo-rah-be-lay, a., memorable
memore, may-mo-ray, a., mindful
memoria, may-mo-re'ah, f., memory; record
menare, may-nah-ray, v., to lead; to carry along
mendicante, men-de-kahn-tay, m., beggar
mendicare, men-de-kah-ray, v., to beg
mendicità, men-de-che-tah, f., mendicity, beggary
menestrello, may-ness-trel-lo, m., servant; mins-
meningite, may-nin-jee-tay, f., meningitis [trel
meno, may-no, adv., less. **per lo —**, at least
menomare, may-no-mah-ray, v., to lessen, to mi-
menomo, may-no-mo, a., smallest; least [nimise
mensa, men-sah, f., table; (mil.) mess
menta, men-tah, f., mint
mente, men-tay, f., mind; opinion. **imparare
a —**, to learn by heart
mentire, men-tee-ray, v., to lie
mentitore, men-te-tor-ay, m., liar
mento, men-to, m., chin
mentre, men-tray, adv., while
menzionare, men-tse'o-nah-ray, v., to mention
menzione, men-tse'o-nay, f., mention. **far —**,
to mention
menzogna, men-tso-n'yah, f., untruth, lie
meraviglia, may-rah-vee-l'yah, f., marvel [man
mercante, mair-kahn-tay, m., merchant; trades-
mercantile, mair-kahn-tee-lay, a., mercantile
mercanzia, mair-kahn-tsee-ah, f., goods, wares
mercato, mair-kah-to, m., market. **a buon —**, cheap
mercatura, mair-kah-too-rah, f., trading; trade
merce, mair-chay, f., merchandise; goods; wares
mercede, mair-chay-day, f., reward; pity
mercenario, mair-chay-nah-re'o, m., mercenary.
a.,* mercenary; venal
merceria, mair-chay-ree-ah, f., hosiery
merciaio, mair-chah-e'o, m., haberdasher
merciaiolo, mair-chah-e'o-lo, m., pedlar

mercoledì, mair-ko-lay-**dee**, m., Wednesday
mercurio, mair-**koo**-re'o, m., mercury
merenda, may-**ren**-dah, f., light afternoon meal
meretrice, may-ray-**tree**-chay, f., prostitute
meridiana, may-re-de'**ah**-nah, f., sun-dial
meridionale, may-re-de'o-**nah**-lay, a., southern
meriggio, may-**rid**-jo, m., midday
meringa, may-**rin**-gah, f., meringue
meritare, may-re-**tah**-ray, v., to merit ; **to gain**
merito, **may**-re-to, m., merit
merletto, mair-**let**-to, m., lace
merlo, **mair**-lo, m., blackbird
merlotto, mair-**lot**-to, m., simpleton
merluzzo, mair-**loot**-tso, m., cod-fish
mero*, **may**-ro, a., mere
mesata, may-**zah**-tah, f., a month's pay
mescere, **may**-shay-ray, v., to pour out
meschino*, mess-**kee**-no, a., mean ; miserly
mescita, **may**-she-tah, f., wine-bar ; snack-bar
mescitore, may-she-**tor**-ay, m., mixer
mescolanza, mess-ko-**lahn**-tsah, f., mixture
mescolare, mess-ko-**lah**-ray, v., to mix ; to shuffle
mese, **may**-zay, m., month
messa, **mess**-sah, f., mass ; stake
messaggero, mess-sahd-**jay**-ro, m., messenger
messe, **mess**-say, f., crop
mestare, mess-**tah**-ray, v., to stir
mestiere, mess-te'**ay**-ray, m., business, occupation
mesto*, **mess**-to, a., sad, melancholic
mesto[ia][lo], **mess**-to-lah, [f.] [m.], ladle
meta, **may**-tah, f., aim
metà, may-**tah**, f., half. **fare a —,** to go halves
metallo, may-**tahl**-lo, m., metal
meteora, may-**tay**-o-rah, f., meteor
meticcio, may-**tit**-cho, m., half-bred ; mongrel
metodo, **may**-to-do, m., method, rule
metraggio, may-**trahd**-jo, m., **a —,** by the metre
metrico*, **may**-tre-ko, a., metrical, metric
metro, **may**-tro, m., metre ; underground-railway
mettere, **met**-tay-ray, v., to put ; to place ; to invest
mezzaluna, med-dzah-**loo**-nah, f., crescent, half-moon

mezzana, med-dzah-nah, f., procuress

mezzanotte, med-dzah-not-tay, f., midnight [jug

mezzina, med-dzee-nah, f., metal or earthenware

mezzo, med-dzo, m., middle ; half ; way. a., half ; over-ripe fruit

mezzobusto, med-dzo-booss-to, m., half-bust

mezzogiorno, med-dzo-jor-no, m., noon ; south

mi, mee, pron., me ; to me ; myself

mi, mee, m., (mus.) mi, E

miagolare, me'ah-go-lah-ray, v., to mew

mica, mee-kah, f., crumb. adv., not at all, **not a bit**

miccio, mit-cho, m., donkey

microfono, me-kro-fo-no, m., microphone

midollo[la], me-doll-lo, m., marrow : the best

miele, me'ay-lay, m., honey. **luna di—,** honeymoon

mietere, me'ay-tay-ray, v., to reap ; to mow

mietitore, me'ay-te-tor-ay, m., harvester

mietitrice, me'ay-te-tree-chay, f., woman-**harvester** ; reaping-machine

migliaio, me-l'yah-e'o, m., a thousand

miglio, mee-l'yo, m., mile   [ration

miglioramento, me-l'yo-rah-**men**-to, m., amelio-

migliorare, me-l'yo-**rah**-ray, v., to improve

migliore, me-l'yor-ay, m. & f., best. a., better

mignatta, me-n'yaht-tah, f., leech   [som

mignolo, mee-n'yo-lo, m., little finger ; olive-blos-

migrare, me-grah-ray, v., to migrate

milione, me-le'o-nay, m., million

militare, me-le-tah-ray, m., soldier. **a.,** military

militesente, me-le-tay-sen-tay, **m.,** free from military service

mille, mil-lay, a., thousand

millepiedi, mil-lay-pe'ay-de, m., millepede

millesimo, mil-lay-ze-mo, a., thousandth

mimica, mee-me-kah. f., mimicry ; gesticulation

mina, mee-nah, f., mine

minaccia, me-naht-chah, f., threat

minacciare, me-naht-chah-ray, v., to threaten

minaccioso[2], me-naht-cho-zo, a., threatening

minare, me-nah-ray, v., to mine ; to undermine

minatore, me-nah-tor-ay, m., miner

minchionare, min-ke'o-**nah**-ray, v., to make fun of

minestra, me-**ness**-trah, f., vegetable soup
miniatura, me-ne'ah-**too**-rah, f., miniature
miniera, me-ne'**ay**-rah, f., mine ; pit
minimo, **mee**-ne-mo, m., the least ; minimum
minio, mee-ne'o. m., red oxide of lead
ministero, me-niss-**tay**-ro, m., ministry
ministro, me-**niss**-tro, m., minister ; representative
minore, me-**nor**-ay, a., minor ; under age ; less
minorenne, me-no-**ren**-nay, m. & f., person under
minugia, me-**noo**-jah, f., gut ; string   [age
minuscolo, me-**nooss**-ko-lo, a., small ; mean
minuta, me-**noo**-tah, f., rough draft
minuto, me-**noo**-to, a.,° very small. m., minute.
  al —, retail
mio, **mee**-o, pron., mine.   a., my
miope, mee-o-**pay,** a., short-sighted
miosotide, me'o-zo-te-day, f., forget-me-not
mira, **mee**-rah, f., aim, purpose ; (gun) sight
mirabile, me-**rah**-be-lay, a., wonderful
miracolo, me-**rah**-ko-lo, m., miracle ; prodigy
miracoloso°, me-rah-ko-lo-zo, a., miraculous
miraggio, me-**rahd**-jo, m., mirage, illusion
mirallegro, me-rahl-**lay**-gro, m., congratulation
mirare, me-**rah**-ray, v., to aim at ; to gaze at
mirra, **meer**-rah, f., myrrh
mirto, **meer**-to, m., myrtle-tree
miscellaneo, me-shell-**lah**-nay-o, a., miscellaneous
mischia, **miss**-ke'ah, f., hand to hand fight
mischiare, miss-ke'**ah**-ray, v., to mix ; to mingle
miscredenza, miss-kray-**den**-tsah, f., atheism ;
  disbelief
miscuglio, miss-**koo**-l'yo, m., mixture ; medley
miserabile, me-zay-rah-**be**-lay, m., poor ; wretch.
  a., miserable ; unfortunate ; needy
miseria, me-zay-re'ah, f., misery ; poverty
misericordia, me-zay-re-**kor**-de'ah, f., compassion
misericordioso°, me-zay-re-kor-de'o-zo, a., merciful
misfatto, miss-**faht**-to, m., crime ; wicked action
missione, miss-se'o-nay, f., mission ; delegation
misterioso°, miss-tay-re'o-zo, a., mysterious ; secret
mistero, miss-**tay**-ro, m., mystery ; secret

misto, miss-to, a., mixed
mistura, miss-too-rah, f., mixture
misura, me-zoo-rah, f., measure. extent ; **capacity**
misurare, me-zoo-rah-ray, v., to measure ; to consi-
misurino, me-zoo-ree-no, m., graduated glass [der
mite, mee-tay, a., mild ; gentle
mitezza, me-tet-tsah, f., mildness
mitigare, me-te-gah-ray, v., to mitigate ; **to alleviate**
mito, mee-to, m., myth
mitologia, me-to-lo-jee-ah, f., mythology
mitra, mee-trah, f., mitre
mitraglia, me-trah-l'yah, f., canister-shot
mitragliatrice, me-trah-l'yah tree-chay, f., ma-
mo, mo, (short for **modo**), see **modo** [chine-gun
mobile, mo-be-lay, m., piece of furniture. a., movable ; changeable
mobilia, mo-bee-le'ah, f., furniture
mobilitare, mo-be-le-tah-ray, v., **to mobilize**
moccio, mot-cho, m., mucus
moccolo, mock-ko-lo, m., **candle-tip**
moda, mo-dah, f., mode, vogue
modellare, mo-dell-lah-ray, v., to mould
modello, mo-dell-lo, m., model ; type ; **pattern**
moderare, mo-day-rah-ray, v., to moderate
moderato*, mo-day-rah-to, a., moderate ; sober
moderno*, mo-dair-no, a., modern, very latest
modestia, mo-dess-te'ah, f., modesty, unpreten-
tiousness
modesto*, mo-dess-to, a., modest ; **unpretentious**
modico*, mo-de-ko, a., moderate
modificare, mo-de-fe-kah-ray, v., **to modify**
modista, mo-diss-tah, f., milliner
modulo, mo-doo-lo, m., module ; form
modo, mo-do, m., manner ; method ; (gram.) mood
mogano, mo-gah-no, m., mahogany
moglie, mo-l'yay, f., wife
mole, mo-lay, f., big building ; hugeness
molestare, mo-less-tah-ray, v., to molest
molesto, mo-less-to, a., troublesome
molla, moll-lah, f., spring
mollare, moll-lah-ray, v., to slacken
molle, moll-lay, a., soft ; soaked. f. pl., **fire-tongs**

mollettiere, moll-let-te'ay-ray, f. pl., puttees

mollezza, moll-let-tsah, f., softness

mollificare, moll-le-fe-kah-ray, v., to mollify

molo, mo-lo, m., mole, pier ; wharf

molosso, mo-loss-so, m., mastiff

molteplice, moll-tay-ple-chay, a., manifold

moltiplicare, moll-te-ple-kah-ray, v., to multiply

moltitudine, moll-te-too-de-nay, f., multitude

molto, moll to, a., much adv., very. di —, by far

momentaneo*, mo-men-tah-nay-o, a., momentary

momento, mo-men-to, m., moment

monaca, mo-nah-kah, f., nun

monaco, mo-nah-ko, m., monk

monarca, mo-nar-kah, m., monarch

monarchia, mo-nar-kee-ah, f., monarchy

monastero, mo-nahss-tay-ro, m., monastery

moncherino, mon-kay-ree-no, m., (limb) stump

monco, mon-ko, a., one-handed ; maimed

mondano*, mon-dah-no, a., worldly ; mundane

mondare, mon-dah-ray, v., to peel ; to clean

mondo, mon-do, m., world ; mankind. a.,* clean

monellerie, mo-nell-lay-ree-ay, f. pl., pranks

monello, mo-nell-lo, m., urchin

moneta, mo-nay-tah, f., money, coinage.
 — spicciola, small change

monetare, mo-nay-tah-ray, v., to coin, to mint

monile, mo-nee-lay, m., personal ornaments ; jew-

monito, mo-ne-to, m., admonition [ellery

monta, mon-tah, f., stazione di —, stud

montaggio, mon-tahd-jo, m., assembling

montagna, mon-tah-n'yah, f., mountain

montagnoso, mon-tah-n'yo-zo, a., mountainous

montanaro, mon-tah-nah-ro, m., mountaineer

montare, mon-tah-ray, v., to mount ; to climb

monte, mon-tay, m., mount. —di pietà, pawn-shop

montone, mon-to-nay, m., ram ; mutton

montuoso, mon-too'o-zo, a., mountainous

montura, mon-too-rah, f., uniform

mora, mo-rah, f., mulberry ; negress

morale, mo-rah-lay, a., moral. m., morals

morbido, mor-be-do, a., soft ; mellow ; downy

morbillo, mor-beel-lo, m., measles

morbo, mor-bo, m., contagious disease

morboso*, mor-bo-zo, a., morbid

mordente, mor-den-tay, a., biting ; pungent

mordere, mor-day-ray, v., to bite

morfina, mor-fee-nah, f., morphia

moribondo, mo-re-bonn-do, a., moribund, dying

morire, mo-ree-ray, v., to die ; (light) to go out

mormorare, mor-mo-rah-ray, v., to murmur, to grumble

mormorio, mor-mo-ree-o, m., murmur ; muttering

moro, mo-ro, m., Moor ; negro ; mulberry-tree

morso, mor-zo, m., bite ; mouthful ; (bridle) bit

mortaio, mor-tah-e'o, m., mortar

mortale, mor-tah-lay, a., mortal ; human

mortalità, mor-tah-le-tah, f., mortality

morte, mor-tay, f., death

mortificare, mor-te-fe-kah-ray, v., to mortify

morto, mor-to, a., dead. m., dead body

mortorio, mor-to-re'o, m., funeral

mosaico, mo-zah'e-ko, m., mosaic

mosca, moss-kah, f., fly. — **cieca**, (game) blind-man's buff

moschea, moss-kay-ah, f., mosque

mossa, moss-sah, f., movement ; (at chess) move

mostarda, moss-tar-dah, f., mustard

mosto, moss-to, m., must ; apple or grape juice not fermented

mostra, moss-trah, f., display ; (crew) muster

mostrare, moss-trah-ray, v., to show ; to exhibit

mostro, moss-tro, m., monster

mostruoso*, moss-troo'o-zo, a., monstrous

mota, mo-tah, f., mud, mire

motivare, mo-te-vah-ray, v., to give a motive

motivo, mo-tee-vo, m., motive ; reason

moto, mo-to, m., motion ; tumult

motocicletta, mo-to-che-klet-tah, f., motor-cycle

motociclismo, mo-to-che-kliss-mo, m., motor-cycling

motociclista, mo-to-che-kliss-tah, m., motor-cyclist

motonave, mo-to-nah-vay, f., motor-ship

motore, mo-tor-ay, m., engine, motor

motorizzazione, mo-to-rid-dzah-tse'o-nay, f. motorization, mechanization

motteggiare, mot-ted-jah-ray, v., to jest ; to laugh

motteggio, mot-ted-jo, m.,joke ; jest ; mockery [at

motto, mot-to, m., motto ; epigram

movente, mo-ven-tay, m., motive ; incentive ; cause. a., active

movimento, mo-ve-men-to, m., movement

mozione, mo-tse'o-nay, f., motion

mozzo, mot-tso, m., cabin-boy ; stable-boy

mucca, mook-kah, f., milk cow

mucchio, mook-ke'o, m., heap ; mass

muco, moo-ko, m., mucus

mudare, moo-dah-ray, v., to moult

muffa, moof-fah, f., mould ; must

muffare, moof-fah-ray, v., to become musty

muffoso, moof-fo-zo, a., mouldy

mugghiare, moog-ghe'ah-ray, v., (see **muggire**)

muggine, mood-jee-nay, m., mullet

muggire, mood-jee-ray, v., to bellow ; to roar

mughetto, moo-get-to, m., lily of the valley

mugnaio, moo-n'yah-e'o, m., miller

mugolare, moo-go-lah-ray, v., to yelp ; to howl

mula, moo-lah, f., she-mule ; slipper

mulino, moo-lee-no, m., mill

mulo, moo-lo, m., mule

multa, mool-tah, f., (for an offence) fine

multare, mool-tah-ray, v., to fine

multiplicare, mool-te-ple-kah-ray, v., to multiply

mummia, moom-me'ah, f., mummy

mungere, moonn-jay-ray, v., to milk ; (fig.) to extort money

municipalità, moo-ne-che-pah-le-tah, f., municipality

municipio, moo-ne-chee-pe'o, m., municipality ; town-hall

munificenza, moo-ne-fe-chen-tsah, f.,munificence

munifico°, moo-nee-fe-ko, a., munificent, generous

munire, moo-nee-ray, v., to provide with

munizioni, moo-ne-tse'o-ne, f. pl., ammunition ; stores

muovere, moo'o-vay-ray, v., to move ; to persuade

muraglia, moo-rah-l'yah, f., wall
murale, moo-rah-lay, a., mural
murare, moo-rah-ray, v., to build a wall ; to wall up
muratore, moo-rah-tor-ay, m., bricklayer
muro, moo-ro, m., wall
muschio, mooss-ke'o, m., musk
musco, mooss-ko, m., moss
muscolare, mooss-ko-lah-ray, a., muscular
muscolo, mooss-ko-lo, m., muscle
museo, moo-zay-o, m., museum
museruola, moo-zay-roo'o-lah, f., muzzle
musica, moo-ze-kah, f., music
musico, moo-ze-ko, m., musician
muso, moo-zo, m., snout
musoliera, moo-zo-le'ay-rah, f., muzzle
mussolina, mooss-so-lee-nah, f., muslin
mustacchi, mooss-tahk-ke, m. pl., moustache
muta, moo-tah, f., change ; relief ; set ; team
mutabile, moo-tah-be-lay, a., variable, changing
mutande, moo-tahn-day, f. pl., drawers, pants
mutare, moo-tah-ray, v., to change
mutilare, moo-te-lah-ray, v., to mutilate
mutilato, moo-te-lah-to, a., disabled : mutilated
muto, moo-to, m., dumb. a., dumb ; (gram.) mute
mutuatario, moo-too'ah-tah-re'o, m., borrower
mutuo, moo-too-o, a., mutual. m., loan

nacchera, nahk-kay-rah, f., castanet ; kettle-drum ;
nafta, nahf-tah, f., naphta [rattle
nano, nah-no, m., dwarf
nappa, nahp-pah, f., tassel ; cockade ; puff
nappo, nahp-po, m., cup ; drinking-glass ; goblet
narciso, nar-chee-so, m., narcissus
narcotico, nar-ko-te-ko, m., narcotic, soporific
narici, nah-ree-che, f., nostrils
narrare, nar-rah-ray, v., to relate, to recite,
   to tell, to report
narratore, nar-rah-tor-ay, m., narrator, relator
nasale, nah-sah-lay, a., nasal
nascere, nah-shay-ray, v., to be born ; to rise
nascita, nah-she-tah, f., birth
nascondere, nah-skon-day-ray, v., to conceal

nascondersi, nah-skon-dair-se, v., to hide oneself
nascondiglio, nah-skon-dee-l'yo, m., hiding place
nascosto°, nah-skoss-to, a., hidden, private, secret
nasello, nah-zell-lo, m., whiting; door-catch; hake
naso, nah-zo, m., nose
naspo, nah-spo, m., reel; winder
nastro, nah-stro, m., ribbon
natale, nah-tah-lay, a., natal; native. m., Xmas-day
natica, nah-te-kah, f., buttock
nativo, nah-tee-vo, m., native
natura, nah-too-rah, f., nature; kind; temper
naturalizzare, nah-too-rah-lit-tsah-ray, v., to
naturalize
naufragare, nah'oo-frah-gah-ray, v., to be ship-
naufragio, nah'oo-frah-jo.m..shipwreck [wrecked
naufrago, nah'oo-frah-go, a. a wrecked person
nausea, nah'oo-zay-ah, f., nausea; loathing
nauseabondo, nah'oo-zay-ah-bon-do, a., nau-
seous; loathsome
nautica, nah'oo-te-kah, f., nautical science
navale, nah-vah-lay, a., naval
nave, nah-vay, f., ship; nave of a church
navigabile, nah-ve-gah-be-lay, a., navigable
navigatore, nah-ve-gah-tor-ay, m., navigator
navigazione, nah-ve-gah-tse'o-nay, f., navigation
navone, nah-vo-nay, m., turnip
nazionale, nah-tse'o-nah-lay, a., national
nazionalità, nah-tse'o-nah-le-tah, f., nationality
nazione, nah-tse'o-nay, f., nation; country of origin
ne, nay, pron., us; of it; from it; of them; from
them; some of it; etc. **nè...nè,** neither...nor
neanche, nay-ahn-kay, conj., not even
nebbia, nayb-be'ah, f., fog
nebbioso, nayb-be'o-zo, a., foggy; misty
nebuloso, nay-boo-lo-zo, a., cloudy, hazy
necessario°, nay-chess-sah-re'o, a., necessary
necessità, nay-chess-se-tah, f., necessity; need
necessitare, nay-chess-se-tah-ray, v., to need; to
nefando, nay-fahn-do, a., nefarious [force
nefasto, nay-fahss-to, a., unlucky
negamento, nay-gah-men-to, m., denial
negare, nay-gah-ray, v., to deny

negativa, nay-gah-tee-vah, f., negative ; denial
neghittoso*, nay-gheet-to-zo, a., lazy ; sluggish
negletto, nay-glet-to, a., careless
negligere, nay-glee-jay-ray, v., to neglect
negoziante, nay-go-tse'ahn-tay, m. & f., trader
negoziare, nay-go-tse'ah-ray, v., to negotiate
negozio, nay-go-tse'o, m., shop ; business ; trade
negriere, nay-gre'ay-ray, m., slave-driver
nembo, nem-bo, m., tempest ; shower
nemico, nay-mee-ko, m., enemy ; fiend. a., **inimi-**
cal, hostile, adverse
nemmeno, nem-may-no, adv., not even
nenia, nay-ne'ah, f., tedious song
neo, nay-o, m., mole, spot. a., new
neonato, nay-o-nah-to, m., new-born
neppure, nayp-poo-ray, adv., not even
nero, nay-ro, a., black ; negro. m., nigger
nervo, nair-vo, m., nerve ; sinew
nervosità, nair-vo-ze-tah, f., nervousness ; vigour
nervoso*, nair-vo-zo, a., nervous ; irritable ; strong
nespolo, nay-spo-lo, m., medlar-tree
nesso, ness-so, m., connection   [body
nessuno, ness-soo-no, a., no, not any. pron., no-
nettare, nayt-tah-ray, v., to clean, to cleanse
nettare, nayt-tah-ray, m., nectar
nettezza, nayt-tet-tsah, f., cleanliness ; neatness
netto*, **nayt**-to, a., clean ; pure ; net
neutrale, nay'oo-trah-lay, a., neutral ; indifferent
neutro, nay'oo-tro, a., neuter
neve, nay-vay, f., snow
nevicare, nay-ve-kah-ray, v., to snow
nevischio, nay-vee-ske'o, m., sleet, drizzling snow
nevoso, nay-vo-zo, a., snowy
nevralgia, nay-vrahl-jee-ah, f., neuralgia
nevrotico, nay-vro-te-ko, a., neurotic
nicchia, neek-ke'ah, f., niche
nicchio, neek-ke'o, m., recess ; shell
nichel, nee-kayl, m., nickel
nidiata, ne-de'ah-tah, f., bevy
nidificare, ne-de-fe-kah-ray, v., to make a nest
nido, nee-do, m., nest
niello, ne-el-lo, m., inlaid work on metal

niente, ne-en-tay, m., nothing

nientemeno, ne-en-tay-may-no, adv., no less : that's all !

nimicare, ne-me-kah-ray, v., to antagonize; to abhor

ninfea, neen-fay-ah, f., water-lily

ninnare, neen-nah-ray, v., to rock, to lull asleep

ninnolo, neen-no-lo, m., trifle, nothing of value

nipote, ne-po-tay, m. & f., nephew ; niece ; grand-child

nitidezza, ne-te-det-tsah, f., neatness [child

nitido*, nee-te-do, a., trim, elegant ; bright, clear

nitrato, ne-trah-to, m., nitrate

nitrire, ne-tree-ray, v., to neigh

nitrito, ne-tree-to, m., neighing

nitro, nee-tro, m., saltpetre

niuno, ne-oo-no, pron., nobody, no one

no, no, adv., no, not

nobile, no-be-lay, a., noble

nobilitare, no-be-le-tah-ray, v., to ennoble

nobiltà, no-beel-tah, f., nobility

nocca, nock-kah, f., knuckle

nocchiere, nock-ke'ay-ray, m., helmsman, pilot

nocchio, nock-ke'o, m., knot ; knob

nocciola, not-cho-lah, f., hazel-nut

nocciolo, not-cho-lo, m., kernel ; stone of a fruit

noce, no-chay, f., walnut

nocemoscata, no-chay-mo-skah-tah, f., nutmeg

nocivo*, no-chee-vo, a., noxious ; hurtful

nocumento, no-koo-men-to, m., harm ; damage

nodo, no-do, m., knot ; hitch. —**scorsoio**, slip-knot

nodoso, no-do-zo, a., knotted, gnarled

noi, no-e, pron., we

noia, no-e'ah, f., tediousness ; annoyance

noiare, no-e'ah-ray, v., to vex ; to molest ; to weary

noleggiare, no-led-jah-ray, v., to hire or to let a ship by contract

noleggio, no-led-jo, m., freight ; hire

nolo, no-lo, m., hire ; freight charges

nomare, no-mah-ray, v., to name

nome, no-may, m., name ; (gram.) noun

nomignolo, no-mee-n'yo-lo, m., nickname

nomina, no-me-nah, f., nomination

nominale, no-me-nah-lay, a., nominal

nominare, no-me-**nah**-ray, v., to nominate ; to call

non, non. adv., not

noncurante, non-koo-**rahn**-tay, a., careless

nonna, non-nah, f., grandmother

nonno, non-no, m., grandfather

nono, no-no, a., ninth [ding

nonostante, no-no-**stahn**-tay, adv., notwithstan-

nord, nord, m., north

nordico, nor-de-ko, a., northern

normale, nor-**mah**-lay, a., normal [ness

nostalgia, no-stahl-jee-ah, f., nostalgia, homesick-

nostrale, no-**strah**-lay, a., native, grown in one's own country

nostrano, no-**strah**-no, a., (see nostrale)

nostro, noss-tro, a. & pron., our ; ours

nota, no-tah, f., note ; sign ; list

notaio, no-tah-e'o, m., notary [swim

notare, no-**tah**-ray, v., to note ; to consider ; to

notariato, no-tah-re'**ah**-to, m., notary's office

notevole, no-tay-vo-lay, a., notable, worthy of note

notificare, no-te-fe-**kah**-ray, v., to notify

notificazione, no-te-fe-kah-tse'**o**-nay, f., notification, declaration

notizia, no-tee-tse'ah, f., news ; notice

noto°, no-to, a., noted ; evident

notorio°, no-**to**-re'o, a., notorious ; evident ; public

nottambulo, not-**tahm**-boo-lo, m., sleep-walker

notte, not-tay, f., night ; (fig.) darkness

nottola, not-to-lah, f., bat ; owl ; wooden latch

notturno, not-**toohr**-no, a., nocturnal

novanta, no-**vahn**-tah, a., ninety

novantesimo, no-vahn-**tay**-ze-mo, a., ninetieth

nove, no-vay, a., nine

novella, no-vell-lah, f., novel ; fable ; news

novellista, no-vell-lee-stah, m. & f., novelist ; story-writer

novello°, no-**vell**-lo, a., new, fresh, young

novembre, no-vem-bray, m., November

noverare, no-vay-**rah**-ray, v., to enumerate. to count

novero, no-vay-ro, m., number ; enumeration

novità, no-ve-tah, f., novelty ; news

novizio, no-**vee**-tse'o, m., novice ; apprentice

nozione, no-tse'o-nay, f., notion

nozze, not-tsay, f. pl., wedding, nuptials

nuoe, noo-bay, f., cloud

nuca, noo-kah, f., nape of the neck

nucleo, noo-klay-o, m., nucleus [possess

nudare, noo-dah-ray, v., to bare ; to undress ; to dis-

nudità, noo-de-tah, f., nudity

nudo*, noo-do, a., naked ; bare [matter

nulla, nooll-lah, m., nothing. non fa—, it does not

nullità, nooll-le-tah, f., nullity ; insignificance

nullo*, nooll-lo, a., null, useless, none

numerare, noo-may-rah-re, v., to number

numerico*, noo-may-re-ko, a., numerical

numero, noo-may-ro, m., number ; cypher

numeroso*, noo-may-ro-zo, a., numerous

nunziare, noonn-tse'ah-ray, v., (see annunziare)

nunzio, noonn-tse'o, m., papal ambassador

nuocere, noo'o-chay-ray, v., to hurt, to wrong

nuora, noo'o-rah, f., daughter-in-law

nuotare, noo'o-tah-ray, v., to swim

nuotatore, noo'o-tah-tor-ay, m., swimmer

nuova, noo'o-vah, f., news ; novelty

nuovo*, noo'o-vo, a., new

nutrice, noo-tree-chay, f., nurse ; wet-nurse

nutrimento, noo-tre-men-to, m., nourishment

nutrire, noo-tree-ray, v., to nourish ; to support

nutritivo, noo-tre-tee-vo, a., nourishing

nuvola, noo-vo-lah, f., cloud

nuvoloso, noo-vo-lo-zo, a., cloudy

nuziale, noo-tse'ah-lay, a., nuptial

O, o, conj., either, or

oasi, o-ah-ze, f., oasis

obbediente, ob-bay-de'en-tay, a., obedient

obbedienza, ob-bay-de'en-tsah, f., obedience

obbedire, ob-bay-dee-ray, v., to obey ; to submit

obbligare, ob-ble-gah-ray, v., to compel

obbligazione, ob-ble-gah-tse'o-nay, f., obligation

obbligo, ob-ble-go, m., duty ; bond

obblio, ob-blee-o, m., oblivion

obiettare, o-be'et-tah-ray, v., to object

obietto, o-be'et-to, m., object ; cause

obiezione, o-be'ay-tse'O-nay, f., objection, difficulty

obito, o-be-to, m., death

obliquo*, o-blee-kwo, a., oblique; **indirect**

oboe, o-bo-ay, m., oboe; oboist

oca, o-kah, f., goose

occasionare, ok-kah-ze'o-nah-ray, v., to cause

occasione, ok-kah-ze'O-nay, f., occasion

occaso, ok-**kah**-zo, m., west, occident

occhiaia, ok-ke'ah-e'ah, f., (eye) socket

occhiali, ok-ke'ah-le, m. pl., spectacles [gnette

occhialino, ok-ke'ah-lee-no, m., eye-glass; lor-

occhiata, ok-ke'ah-tah, f., glance

occhiello, ok-ke'el-lo, m., button-hole; **eyelet**

occhio, ok-ke'o, m., eye; bud

occidente, ot-che-den-tay, m., west

occorrente, ok-kor-ren-tay, m., the needful

occorrenza, ok-kor-ren-tsah, f., occurrence; circumstance

occorrere, ok-**kor**-ray-ray, v., to occur

occultare, ok-kool-tah-ray, v., to hide, to conceal

occulto*, ok-**kool**-to, a., occult; secret [ploy

occupare, ok-koo-**pah**-ray, v., to occupy; **to em-**

oceano, o-**chay**-ah-no, m., ocean

ocra, o-krah, f., ochre

oculatezza, o-koo-lah-**tet**-tsah, f., **cautiousness**

oculista, o-koo-lee-stah, m., oculist

odiare, o-de'ah-ray, v., to hate

odio, o-de'o, m., odium, dislike

odorare, o-do-rah-ray, v., to smell

odorato, o-do-rah-to, m., sense of smelling

odore, o-do-ray, m., scent, smell

offendere, of-fen-day-ray, v., to offend; **to injure**

offensivo*, of-fen-see-vo, a., offensive

offensore, of-fen-**sor**-ay, m., offender

offerire, of-fay-ree-ray, v., (see **offrire**)

offerta, of-fair-tah, f., offer, bid

offesa, of-**fay**-zah, f., offence

officiale, of-fe-chah-lay, m., official

officina, of-fe-chee-nah, f., workshop

officio, of-fee-cho, m., office; duty; function

officioso, of-fe-cho-zo, a., zealous; courteous;
  semi-official

offrire, of-free-ray, v., to offer, to tender
offuscare, of-fooss-kah-ray, v., to darken
oftalmia, of-tahl-mee-ah, f., ophthalmia
oggetto, od-jet-to, m., object
oggi, od-je, adv., to-day, this day, now
ogni, o-n'ye, a., each, every
Ognissanti, o-n'yeess-sahn-te, m., All Saints' Day
ognuno, o-n'yoo-no, pron., everyone
oliera, o-le'ay-rah, f., cruet-stand
olio, o-l'yo, m., oil
oliva, o-lee-vah, m., olive
olivastro, o-le-vah-stro, a., olive-coloured
olivo, o-lee-vo, m., olive-tree
olmo, ol-mo, m., elm
oltracciò, ol-traht-cho, adv., moreover
oltraggiare, ol-trahd-jah-ray, v., to outrage
oltraggio, ol-trahd-jo, m., outrage, offence
oltre, ol-tray, adv., far advanced, prep., beyond ;
  further
oltrepassare, ol-tray-pahss-sah-ray, v., to over-
  step, to surpass
omaggio, o-mahd-jo, m., homage, respect
omai, o-mah-e, adv., now ; from now on
ombelico, om-bay-lee-ko, m., navel
ombra, om-brah, f., shade, shadow, spectre
ombrellino, om-brell-lee-no, m., sunshade
ombrello, om-brell-lo, m., umbrella
ombroso*, om-bro-zo, a., shady ; sensitive
omero, o-may-ro, m., shoulder
omettere, o-met-tay-ray, v., to omit   [deress
omicida, o-me-chee-dah, m. & f., murderer ; mur-
omicidio, o-me-chee-de'o, m., murder ; man-
omo, o-mo, m., (see uomo)   [slaughter
oncia, on-chah, f., ounce ; (fig.) small quantity
onda, on-dah, f., wave, billow   [where
onde, ón-day, adv., whence, therefore, whereby,
ondeggiare, on-ded-jah-ray, v., to waver, to hesitate
ondulare, on-doo-lah-ray, v., to rock ; to wave
ondulato*, on-doo-lah-to, a., undulating ; wavy
oneroso*, o-nay-ro-zo, a., onerous, burdensome
onestà, o-nay-stah, f., honesty ; decency
onesto*, o-nay-sto, a., honest ; decent

onice, o-ne-chay. f., onyx
onorare, o-no-rah-ray, v., to honour
onorario, o-no-rah-re'o, m., fee. a., **honorary**
onore, o-no-ray, m., honour
onta, on-tah, f., shame; affront
ontano, on-tah-no, m., elder-tree; elder
onusto, o-nooss-to, a., heavy; burdened
opacità, o-pah-che-tah, f., opacity; **darkness**
opaco, o-pah-ko, a., opaque; **dark**
opale, o-pah-lay, f., opal
opera, o-pay-rah, f., opera; work. **mano d'—,**
   hand labour
operaio, o-pay-rah-e'o, m., workman
operare, o-pay-rah-ray, v., to operate; **to act**
operatore, o-pay-rah-tor-ay, m., operator
operazione, o-pay-rah-tse'o-nay, f., operation;
   business undertaking
operoso, o-pay-ro-zo, a., industrious; quick, brisk
opificio, o-pe-fee-cho, m., mill; factory
opimo, o-pee-mo, a., rich, fruitful
opinare, o-pe-nah-ray, v., to deem, to think
oppio, op-pe'o, m., opium
opponente, op-po-nen-tay, m. & f., opponent
opporre, op-por-ray, v., to oppose
opportuno*, op-por-too-no, a., opportune
opposizione, op-po-ze-tse'o-nay, f., opposition
opposto*, op-poss-to, a., opposite
oppressivo*, op-press-see-vo, a., oppressive
opprimere, op-pree-may-ray, v., to oppress
oppure, op-poo-ray, conj., or, or else
opuscolo, o-poo-sko-lo, m., pamphlet, leaflet
ora, o-rah, f., hour; time. adv., now, at this time.
   or —, just now
oracolo, o-rah-ko-lo, m., oracle
orafo, o-rah-fo, m., goldsmith
oragano, o-rah-gah-no, m., hurricane
orale, o-rah-lay, a., oral
oramai, o-rah-mah-e, adv., (see **ormai**)
orare, o-rah-ray, v., to pray
orario, o-rah-re'o, m., time-table. a., **hourly**
orata, o-rah-tah, f., gold-fish
oratore, o-rah-tor-ay, m., orator

orbe, or-bay, m., orb, world
orcio, or-cho, m., oil-jar
orco, or-ko, m., ogre
orda, or-dah, f., horde
ordigno, or-dee-n'yo, m., machine ; utensil
ordinamento, or-de-nah-men-to, m.,arrangement
ordinare, or-de-nah-ray, v., to arrange, to put in order ; (eccl.) to ordain
ordinario*, or-de-nah-re'o, a., ordinary
ordine, or-de-nay, m., order
ordire, or-de-ray, v., to plot
orecchiare, o-reck-ke'ah-ray, v., to listen
orecchino, o-reck-kee-no, m., ear-ring
orecchio, o-reck-ke'o, m., ear ; hearing
orefice, o-ray-fe-chay, m., goldsmith
orezzo, o-ret-tso, m., light breeze
orfano, or-fah-no, m., orphan
orfanotrofio, or-fah-no-tro-fe'o, m., orphanage
organino, or-gah-nee-no, m., street-organ
organizzare, or-gah-need-dzah-ray, v.,to organize
organo, or-gah-no, m., organ
orgia, or-jah, f., orgy
orgoglio, or-go-l'yo, m., pride
orgoglioso*, or-go-l'yo-zo, a., proud
orientale, o-re-en-tah-lay, a., oriental ; eastern
oriente, o-re-en-tay, m., orient ; east
originale, o-re-je-nah-lay, a., original ; first in order
originario, o-re-je-nah-re'o, a., native
origine, o-ree-je-nay, f., origin ; source
origliere, o-re-l'yay-ray, m., pillow
orina, o-ree-nah, f., urine
orinale, o-re-nah-lay, m., chamber-pot
orinatoio, o-re-nah-to-e'o, m., lavatory
ori[u]olo, o-re'o-lo, m., clock ; watch
orizzontale, o-rit-tson-tah-lay, a., horizontal
orizzonte, o-rit-tson-tay, m., horizon
orlare, or-lah-ray, v., to hem ; to border
orlatura, or-lah-too-rah, f., hem ; border
orlo, or-lo, m., hem ; border ; brim
orma, or-mah, f., trace ; footstep
ormai, or-mah-e, adv., now ; henceforth
ornamentare, or-nah-men-tah-ray, v.,to decorate

ornare, or-nah-ray, v., to adorn ; to embellish
orno, or-no, m., ash-tree ; wild ash   [sel
oro, o-ro, m., gold ; money ; riches. — **falso**, tin-
urologiaio, o-ro-lo-jah-e'o, m., watchmaker
orologio, o-ro-lo-je'o, m., watch ; clock. — **da polso**, wrist-watch
orpello, or-pel-lo, m., tinsel ; falsehood
orrendo°, or-ren-do, a., horrible ; dreadful
orribile, or-ree-be-lay, a., horrible ; horrid
orrore, or-ro-ray, m., horror ; dreadfulness ; **vileness**
orso, or-so, m., bear
orsù, or-soo, interj., come on ! buck up !
ortica, or-tee-kah, f., nettle
orticultore, or-te-kool-tor-ay, m., horticulturist
orto, or-to, m., kitchen-garden ; vegetable-garden
ortodosso°, or-to-doss-so, a., orthodox
ortolano, or-to-lah-no, m., kitchen-gardener
orzaiuolo, or-dzah-e'oo-o-lo, m., (eye-lid) **sty**
orzo, or-dzo, m., barley
osare, o-zah-ray, v., to dare
osceno°, o-shay-no, a., obscene
oscillare, o-sheel-lah-ray, v., to oscillate
oscillazione, o-sheel-lah-tse'o-nay, f., oscillation
oscurare, oss-koo-rah-ray, v., to darken
oscuro°, oss-koo-ro, a., dark, obscure, dull
ospedale, oss-pay-dah-lay, m., hospital
ospite, oss-pe-tay, m., host ; visitor, guest   [house
ospizio, oss-pee-tse'o, m., hospice, infirmary, alms-
ossame, oss-sah-may, m., number of bones
ossequio, oss-say-kwe-o, m., obsequiousness, re-verence
ossequioso°, oss-say-kwe'o-zo, a., obsequious
osservanza, oss-sair-vahn-tsah, f., observance
osservare, oss-sair-vah-ray, v., to observe
osservatore, oss-sair-vah-tor-ay, m., observer
osservatorio, oss-sair-vah-to-re'o, m., observatory
osservazione, oss-sair-vah-tse'o-nay, f., observation
ossidare, oss-se-dah-ray, v., to oxidize
ossigeno, oss-see-jay-no, m., oxygen
osso, oss-so, m., bone : (fruit) stone
ossuto, oss-soo-to, a., bony
ostacolo, oss-tah-ko-lo, m., obstacle

ostaggio, oss-**tahd**-jo, m., hostage
ostare, oss-**tah**-ray, v., to impede
oste, oss-**tay**, m., inn-keeper ; great army
ostentazione, oss-ten-tah-tse'**o**-nay, f., ostentation
osteria, oss-tay-**ree**-ah, f., hostelry, inn [house
ostessa, oss-**tess**-sah, f., landlady of inn or lodging-
ostia, oss-te-ah, f., Host ; altar-wafer ; wafer
ostile, oss-**tee**-lay, a., hostile, inimical
ostilità, oss-te-le-**tah**, f., hostility
ostinarsi, oss-te-**nar**-se, v., to persist obstinately
ostinato*, oss-te-**nah**-to, a., obstinate, pig-headed
ostinazione, oss-te-nah-tse'**o**-nay, f., obstinacy
ostrica, oss-tre-kah, f., oyster
ostruire, oss-troo-ee-ray, v., to obstruct, to hinder
ostruzione, oss-troo-tse'**o**-nay, f., obstruction
otre, o-tray, m., leather-bottle ; skin-sack (for liq-
ottagono, ot-**tah**-go-no, m., octagon [uids]
ottanta, ot-**tahn**-tah, a., eighty
ottantenne, ot-tahn-**ten**-nay,m. & f.,octogenarian
ottava, ot-**tah**-vah, f., (mus.) octave
ottavo, ot-**tah**-vo, a., eighth
ottemperare, ot-tem-pay-**rah**-ray, v., to comply
ottenere, ot-tay-**nay**-ray, v., to obtain
ottico, ot-te-ko, m., optician. a., optical, visual
ottimismo, ot-te-**miss**-mo, m., optimism
ottimo*, ot-te-mo, a., excellent ; perfect
otto, ot-to, a., eight
ottobre, ot-to-bray, m., October
ottone, ot-to-nay, m., brass, yellow copper
otturare, ot-too-**rah**-ray, v.,to block up ; (teeth) to
ottuso*, ot-**too**-zo, a., dense, stupid [stop
ovaio, o-**vah**-yo, m., egg-seller
ovaiolo, o-vah-**yo**-lo, m., egg-cup
ovale, o-**vah**-lay, a., oval, elliptical
ovatta, o-**vaht**-tah, f., wadding ; cotton-wool
ovattare, o-vaht-**tah**-ray, v., to pad
ove, o-vay, adv., where ; if ; inasmuch as
ovest, o-vest, m., west
ovile, o-**vee**-lay, m., sheep-pen
ovunque, o-**voonn**-kway, adv., everywhere
ovvero, ov-**vay**-ro, con., or ; in fact
ovviare, ov-ve'**ah**-ray, v., to obviate ; to hinder

ovvio, ov-ve'o, a., obvious
oziare, o-tse'ah-ray, v., to idle
ozio, o-tse'o, m., leisure, free time
ozioso*, o-tse'o-zo, a., indolent ; without occupation

pacato, pah-kah-to, a., staid, quiet
pacca, pahk-kah, f., a slap ; tap on the shoulder
pacchetto, pahk-ket-to, m., passenger and cargo ship
pacco, pahk-ko, m., pack, bundle
pace, pah-chay, f., peace [calm
pacificare, pah-che-fe-kah-ray, v., to pacify ; to
pacifico*, pah-chee-fe-ko, a., pacific, quiet
padella, pah-dell-lah, f., pan
padiglione, pah-de-l'yo-nay, m., pavilion ; tent
padre, pah-dray, m., father ; priest ; ancestor
padrigno, pah-dree-n'yo, m., stepfather
padrino, pah-dree-no, m., godfather
padrona, pah-dro-nah, f., mistress ; landlady
padrone, pah-dro-nay, m., master ; protector ; proprietor ; landlord
paesaggio, pah-ay-sahd-jo, m., landscape
paesano, pah-ay-zah-no, m., compatriot. a., rural
paese, pah-ay-zay, m., country ; home
paffuto, pahf-foo-to, a., plump
paga, pah-gah, f., salary
pagaia, pah-gah-e'ah, f., paddle
pagamento, pah-gah-men-to, m., payment
pagare, pah-gah-ray, v., to pay
paggio, pahd-jo, m., page or errand-boy
pagherò, pah-gay-ro, m., promissory note
pagina, pah-je-nah, f., page
paglia, pah-l'yah, f., straw ; chaff
pagnotta, pah-n'yot-tah, f., loaf
paio, pah-e'o, m., a pair of ...
pala, pah-lah, f., shovel ; oar-blade
palafitta, pah-lah-fit-tah-ray, v., to put up a fence
palafreniere, pah-lah-fray-ne'ay-ray, m., groom
palato, pah-lah-to, m., palate
palazzina, pah-laht-tsee-nah, f., suburban house
palazzo, pah-laht-tso, m., palace ; a grand house
palchetto, pahl-ket-to, m., (theatre) box

palco, **pahl**-ko, m., platform; (theatre) box.
— scenico, stage
palesare, pah-lay-**zah**-ray, v., to reveal
palese, pah-**lay**-zay, a., manifest
palestra, pah **less**-trah, f., gymnasium
paletta, pah-**let**-tah, f., small shovel
paletto, pah-**let**-to, m., bolt
palio, pah-**l'yo**, m., prize at a race; canopy
palizzata, pah-lit-**tsah**-tah, f., fence
palla, **pahl**-lah, f., ball; bullet
palliare, pahl-le'**ah**-ray, v., to palliate
pallido°, **pahl**-ie-do, a., pale
pallini, pahl-**lee**-ne, m. pl., small shot
pallone, pahl-lo-nay, m., balloon; large leather ball
pallore, pahl-**lor**-ay, f., palor
pallottola, pahl-**lot**-to-lah, f., pellet
palma, **pahl** mah, f., palm; palm-tree
palmo, **pahl**-mo, m., (measure) span of the hand
palo, **pah**-lo, m., pale; pole
palombaro, pah-lom-**bah**-ro, m., diver
palpare, pahl-**pah**-ray, v., to touch, to feel
palpebra, **pahl**-pay-brah, f., eye-lid
palpitare, pal-pe-**tah**-ray, v., to palpitate
palude, pah-**loo**-day, f., marsh
paludoso, pah-loo-**do**-zo, a., marshy
panattiera, pah-naht-te'**ay**-rah, f., bin for bread
panca, **pahn**-kah, f., bench, seat
pancia, **pahn**-chah, f., belly, paunch
panciotto, pahn-**chot**-to, m., waistcoat
pancone, pahn-**ko**-nay, m., bench, thick board
pane, **pah**-nay, m., bread; loaf of bread
panereccio, pah-nay-**ret**-cho, m., whitlow
panettiere, pah-net-te'**ay**-ray, m., baker
panico, **pah**-ne-ko, m., panic; ill-grounded fear
paniere, pah-ne'**ay**-ray, m., basket   [wich
panino, pah-**nee**-no, m., roll. — **gravido,** sand-
panna, **pahn**-nah, f., cream)
pannaiolo, pahn-nah-e'o-lo, m., clothier; draper
panno, **pahn**-no, m., cloth
pantaloni, pahn-tah-**lo**-ne, m. pl., trousers
pantano, pahn-**tah**-no, m., bog, swamp
pantera, pahn-**tay**-rah, f., panther

pantofola, pahn-to-fo-lah, f., house-slipper
Papa, pah-pah, m., Pope
papale, pah-pah-lay, a., papal
papavero, pah-pah-vay-ro, m., poppy
pappagallo, pahp-pah-gahl-lo, m., parrot
paracadute, pah-rah-kah-doo-tay, m., parachute
paracolpi, pah-rah-koll-pe, m., buffer
paradiso, pah-rah-dee-zo, m., paradise
paradosso, pah-rah-doss-so, m., paradox
parafango, pah-rah-fahn-go, m., mud-guard
parafulmine, pah-rah-fool-me-nay, m., lightning-
     conductor
parafuoco, pah-rah-foo'o-ko, m., fire-screen ; fender
paragonare, pah-rah-go-nah-ray, v., to compare
paragone, pah-rah-go-nay, m., comparison
paralisi, pah-rah-le-ze, f., paralysis
paralume, pah-rah-loo-may, m., lamp-shade
parapetto, pah-rah-pet-to, m., parapet ; breast-work
parapiglia, pah-rah-pee-l'yah, f., turmoil, hurly-
     burly
parare, pah-rah-ray, v., to decorate ; to parry
parata, pah-rah-tah, f., parade ; parrying
paravento, pah-rah-ven-to, m., wind-screen
parco, par-ko, m., park. a., moderate ; frugal
parecchi, pah-reck-ke, a., several
pareggiare, pah-red-jah-ray, v., to equalize
parentado, pah-ren-tah-do, m., relationship, rela-
parente, pah-ren-tay, m., relative   [tives
parentesi, pah-ren-tay-ze, f., parenthesis
parere, pah-ray-ray, m., opinion. v., to appear
parete, pah-ray-tay, f., wall
pargolo, par-go-lo, m., small child
pari, pah-re, m., peer. a., equal ; similar ; even
paria, pah-re'ah, m., pariah
parimenti, pah-re-men-te, adv., likewise
parità, pah-re-tah, f., parity, equality
parlamentare, par-lah-men-tah-ray, v., to parley
parlare, par-lah-ray, v., to speak, to discourse
parlatore, par-lah-tor-ay, m., orator ; talker
parola, pah-ro-lah, f., word
parrocchia, par-rock-ke'ah, f., parish ; parish
     church

parrocchiano, par-rock-ke'ah-no, m., parishioner

parroco, par-ro-ko. m., parson

parrucca, par-rook-kah. f., wig

parrucchiere, par-rook-ke'ay-ray. m.,hairdresser : wig-maker

parsimonia, par-se-mo-n'yah. f., parsimony

parte, par-tay. f., part ; (political, etc.) party. da —, on one side, aside. in —, in some degree, in part

partecipare, par-tay-che-pah-ray, v., to participate ; to share ; (knowledge) to impart

partenza, par-ten-tsah. f., departure, setting off

particella, par-te-chell-lah. f., particle, small part

particina, par-te-chee-nah. f., small part

participio, par-te-chee-pe'o, m., participle

particolare, par-te-ko-lah-ray, a., particular, private

partigiano, par-te-jah-no, m., partisan

partire, par-tee-ray, v., to depart ; to share

partita, par-tee-tah, f., departure ; game, match

partito, par-tee-to, m., party ; manner ; contract

partitura (or **partizione**), par-te-too-rah, f., division ; (mus.) score

parto, par-to, m., confinement ; parturition

partorire, par-to-ree-ray, v., to give birth to

parziale, par-tse'ah-lay, a., partial, biassed

pascere (or **pascolare**), pah-shay-ray, v., to graze

pascolo, pahss-ko-lo, m., pasture

Pasqua, pahss-kwah, f., Easter

passabile, pahss-sah-be-lay, a., tolerable, bearable

passaggio, pahss-sahd-jo, m., passage ; promenade

passante, pahss-sahn-tay, m., passer-by ; passenger

passare, pahss-sah-ray, v., to pass ; to sift ; to carry across

passatempo, pahss-sah-tem-po, m., pastime

passato, pahss-sah-to, a., passed. m., past

passeggiare, pahss-sed-jah-ray, v., to walk ; to go for a walk

passeggiata, pahss-sed-jah-tah, f., walk, stroll

passeggiere, pahss-sed-jay-ray, m., passer-by : passenger

passeggio, pahss-sed-jo, m., promenade

passero[tto], pahss-say-ro, m., sparrow

passionato*, pahss-se'o-**nah**-to, a., passionate

passione, pahss-se'**O**-nay, f., passion

passivo, pahss-**see**-vo, a.,* passive. m., liabilities

passo, **pahss**-so, m., step

pasta, **pahss**-tah, f., paste ; piece of pastry

pastello, pahss-**tell**-lo, m., coloured crayon

pasticca, pahss-**tick**-kah, f., pastille

pasticceria, pahss-tit-chay-**ree**-ah, f., pastry-cook's shop ; pastry

pasticciere, pahss-tit-**chay**-ray, m., pastry-cook

pasticcio, pahss-**tit**-cho, m., pie ; (fig.) mix up

pastinaca, pahss-te-**nah**-kah, f., parsnip

pasto, **pahss**-to, m., food ; meal

pastore, pahss-**tor**-ay, m., shepherd ; pastor

pastoso*, pahss-**to**-zo, a., soft ; sticky, tacky

pastura, pahss-**too**-rah, f., pasture

patata, pah-**tah**-tah, f., potato

patente, pah-**ten**-tay, f., patent. a., obvious

paterno*, pah-**tair**-no, a., fatherly

patetico*, pah-**tay**-te-ko, a., pathetic

patibolo, pah-**tee**-bo-lo, m., gallows

patire, pah-**tee**-ray, v., to suffer

patria, **pah**-tre-ah, f., mother country, home

patrigno, pah-**tree**-n'yo, m., stepfather

patrocinare, pah-tro-che-**nah**-ray, v., to patronize

patrocinio [or **patronato**], pah-tro-**chee**-ne'o, m., patronage

patrono, pah-**tro**-no, m., patron

pattinaggio, paht-te-**nahd**-jo, m., skating

pattinare, paht-te-**nah**-ray, v., to skate

pattini, **paht**-te-ne, m. pl., skates

patto, **paht**-to, m., agreement ; treaty ; bargain

pattuglia, paht-**too**-l'yah, f., patrol

pattugliare, paht-too-l'**yah**-ray, v., to patrol

pattuire, paht-too-ee-ray, v., to stipulate ; to agree

pattume, paht-**too**-may, m., sweepings

paura, pah'**oo**-rah, f., fear, dread

pauroso*, pah'oo-**ro**-zo, a., afraid

pausa, pah'**oo**-zah, f., pause

paventare, pah-ven-**tah**-ray, v., to be afraid of

pavimentare, pah-ve-men-**tah**-ray, v., to pave

pavimento, pah-ve-**men**-to, m., pavement ; floor

pavone, pah-vo-nay, m., peacock

paziente, pah-tse'en-tay, a., patient, enduring. m. & f., sick person

pazienza, pah-tse'en-tsah, f., patience; perseverance

pazzia, pant-tsee-ah, f., madness; mania

pazzo, pant-tso, a., mad, crazy

pecca, peck-kah, f., fault, error; vice

peccaminoso*, peck-kah-me-no-zo, a., criminal

peccare, peck-kah-ray, v., to sin

peccato, peck-kah-to, m., sin

peccatore, peck-kah-tor-ay, m., sinner

pecchia, peck-ke'ah, f., bee

pece, pay-chay, m., pitch; tar

pecora, pay-ko-rah, f., sheep; (fig.) blockhead

pecoraio, pay-ko-rah-e'o, m., shepherd

pecoro, pay-ko-ro, m., ram

pecunia, pay-koo-ne'ah, f., money

pedaggio, pay-dahd-jo, m., toll; tax

pedalare, pay-dah-lah-ray, v., to pedal

pedale, pay-dah-lay, m., pedal

pedante, pay-dahn-tay, m., pedant

pedata, pay-dah-tah, f., kick; foot-print

pedina, pay-dee-nah, f., (draughts) piece

pedinare, pay-de-nah-ray, v., to shadow, to follow [closely

pedino, pay-dee-no, m., (chess) pawn

pedone, pay-do-nay, m., pedestrian

peggio (or **peggiore**), ped-jo, a. & adv., worse. m., worst

peggiorare, ped-jo-rah-ray, v., to grow worse

pegno, pay-n'yo, m., pledge; forfeit

pelago, pay-lah-go, m., sea; large expanse of water

pelare, pay-lah-ray, v., to peel; to plume; to fleece

pelle, pell-lay, m., skin; leather

pellegrinaggio, peil-lay-gre-nahd-jo, m., pilgrimage; journey

pellegrino, pell-lay-gree-no, m., pilgrim

pelliccia, pell-lit-chah, f., fur[-coat]

pellicciaio, pell-lit-chah-e'o, m., furrier

pellicola, pell-lee-ko-lah, f., film; cuticle

pelo, pay-lo, m., hair; (cloth) nap. — **dell'acqua**, surface of the water

peloso*, pay-lo-zo, a., hairy; rough; hirsute

pena, pay-nah, f., pain ; punishment ; grief ; penalty

penalità, pay-nah-le-tah, f., penalty

penalizzare, pay-nah-lid-dzah-ray, v., (games) to penalize

penare, pay-nah-ray, v., to suffer

pendente, pen-den-tay, a., hanging. m., pendant

pendenza, pen-den-tsah, f., slope

pendere, pen-day-ray, v., to hang

pendio, pen-dee-o, m., slope

pendola, pen-do-lah, f., clock

pendolo, pen-do-lo, m., pendulum

pendone, pen-do-nay, m., festoon

penetrare, pay-nay-trah-ray, v., to penetrate

penetrazione, pay-nay-trah-tse'o-nay, f., penetration

penisola, pay-nee-zo-lah, f., peninsula

penitente, pay-ne-ten-tay, a., penitent

penitenza, pay-ne-ten-tsah, f., penitence

penitenziario, pay-ne-ten-tse'ah-re'o, m., penitentiary

penna, pen-nah, f., pen ; feather. — **stilografica,** fountain-pen. **dar di —,** to cancel

pennello, pen-nell-lo, m., paint-brush

pennone, pen-no-nay, m., banner ; streamer

penoso*, pay-no-zo, a., painful

pensare, pen-sah-ray, v., to think

pensiero, pen-se'ay-ro, m., thought

pensieroso*, pen-se'ay-ro-zo, a., thoughtful

pensionare, pen-se'o-nah-ray, v., to pension off

pensionario, pen-se'o-nah-re'o, m., pensioner

pensione, pen-se'o-nay, f., pension ; boarding-house ; boarding-school

Pentecoste, pen-tay-koss-tay, m., Whitsuntide

pentimento, pen-te-men-to, m., repentance

pentirsi, pen-teer-se, v., to repent

pentola, pen-to-lah, s., (for cookery) pot

penzolare, pen-tso-lah-ray, v., to dangle, to hang

pepe, pay-pay, m., pepper ; pepper-plant

peperone, pay-pay-ro-nay, m., pimento

pepiniera, pay-pe-ne'ay-rah, f., (flower) nursery

pepita, pay-pee-tah, f., (ore) nugget

per, pair, prep., for ; by ; through

pera, pay-rah, f., pear ; (of atomizer) bulb

percalle, pair-kahl-lay, m., cotton, cambric

percento, pair-chen-to, m., per cent.
percentuale, pair-chen-too'ah-lay, f., **percentage**
percepire, pair-chay-pee-ray, v., to perceive
percezione, pair-chay-tse'o-nay, f., perception
perchè, pair-kay, adv., why; wherefore. conj.,
   since. m., the why
perciò, pair-cho, conj., therefore
percorrere, pair-kor-ray-ray, v., to peruse; **to travel**
percuotere, pair-koo'o-tay-ray, v., to strike
perdere, pair-day-ray, v., to lose ; to spoil
perdigiorno, pair-de-jor-no, m., idler
perdita, pair-de-tah, f., loss ; waste
perditore, pair-de-tor-ay, m., loser
perdonabile, pair-do-nah-be-lay, a., pardonable
perdonare, pair-do-nah-ray, v., to pardon
perdono, pair-do-no, m., pardon   [out
perdurare, pair-doo-rah-ray, v., to endure, to hold
peregrinare, pay-ray-gre-nah-ray, v., to wander
perentorio*, pay-ren-to-re'o, a., peremptory
perfetto*, pair-fet-to, a., perfect, thorough
perfezionare, pair-fay-tse'o-nah-ray, v., to improve
perfezione, pair-fay-tse'o-nay, f., perfection
perfidia, pair-fee-de'ah, f., perfidy
perfido*, pair-fe-do, a., perfidious
perfino, pair-fee-no, adv., even ; as far as
perforare, pair-fo-rah-ray, v., to pierce
pergamena, pair-gah-may-nah, f., parchment
pergamo, pair-gah-mo, m., pulpit
pergola, pair-go-lah, f., arbour, bower
pericolo, pay-ree-ko-lo, m., danger
pericoloso*, pay-re-ko-lo-zo, a., dangerous
periodico, pay-re'o-de-ko, a.,periodical. m., period-
periodo, pay-ree-o-do, m., period   [ical
perire, pay-ree-ray, v., to perish
perito, pay-ree-to, a., experienced,   m., expert
perituro, pay-re-too-ro, a., perishable
perizia, pay-ree-tse'ah, f., skill ; survey
perla, pair-lah, f., pearl
perlustrare, pair-loo-strah-ray, v., to explore
permanente, pair-mah-nen-tay, a., permanent
permeare, pair-may-ah-ray, v., to permeate
permesso, pair-mess-so, m., permission, permit

permettere, pair-met-tay-ray, v., to permit ; **to grant leave**

permuta, pair-moo-tah, f., exchange   [to barter

permutare, pair-moo-tah-ray, v., to exchange ;

pernice, pair-nee-chay, f., partridge

pernicioso*, pair-ne-cho-zo, a., pernicious ; **deadly**

perno, pair-no, m., pivot

pernottare, pair-not-tah-ray, v., to pass the night

pero, pay-ro, m., pear-tree

peró, pay-**ro**, conj., therefore ; however

perocchè, pay-rock-**kay**, conj., because

perorare, pay-ro-rah-ray, v., to plead ; **to harangue**

perpetuare, pair-pay-too**'ah**-ray, v., to perpetuate

perpetuo*, pair-**pay**-too-o, a., perpetual

perplesso, pair-pless-so, a., perplexed

persecutore, pair-say-koo-**tor**-ay, m., persecutor

persecuzione, pair-say-koo-tse'**o**-nay, f., persecution

perseguire, pair-say-goo'ee-ray, v., (see perseguitare)

perseguitare, pair-say-goo'e-**tah**-ray, v., to pursue ; to persecute, to molest

perseveranza, pair-say-vay-**rah**-tsah, f., perseverance

perseverare, pair-say-vay-**rah**-ray, v., to persevere

persiana, pair-se-ah-nah, f., Venetian blind

persino, pair-**see**-no, adv., even ; also

persistenza, pair-siss-**ten**-tsah, f., persistence [nue

persistere, pair-siss-tay-ray, v., to persist, to conti-

persona, pair-**so**-nah, f., person, individual

personaggio, pair-so-**nahd**-jo, m., personage [nel

personale, pair-so-nah-lay, a., personal. m., person-

personalità, pair-so-nah-le-**tah**, f., personality

perspicace, pair-spe-**kah**-chay, a., shrewd, keen

perspicuo*, pair-**spee**-koo-o, a., clear

persuadere, pair-soo'ah-**day**-ray, v., to persuade ; to convince

persuasione, pair-soo'ah-ze'**o**-nay, f., persuasion

pertanto, pair-**tahn**-to, adv. & prep., therefore ; **in fact**

pertica, pair-te-kah, f., pole

pertinace, pair-te-**nah**-chay, a., obstinate

pertinenza, pair-te-nen-tsah, f., pertinence

pertugio, pair-too-jo, m., aperture, hole

perturbare, pair-toohr-bah-ray, v., to perturb

pervenire, pair-vay-nee-ray, v., to attain

perversità, pair-vair-se-tah, f., perversity

perverso*, pair-vair-so, a., perverse, depraved

pervertire, pair-vair-tee-ray, v., to pervert

pervinca, pair-vin-kah, f., (flower) periwinkle

pesante, pay-zahn-tay, a., heavy; oppressive

pesantezza, pay-zahn-tet-tsah, f., weight

pesare, pay-zah-ray, v., to weigh

pesca, pess-kah, f., peach; fishing

pescagione [or **pescaggio**], pess-kah-jo-nay, f., (naut.) draught

pescaia, pess-kah-e'ah, f., fish-pond; sluice, dam

pescare, pess-kah-ray, v., to fish

pescatore, pess-kah-tor-ay, m., fisherman, angler

pesce, pay-shay, m., fish

pescecane, pay-shay-kah-nay, m., shark; dogfish

pescheria, pess-kay-ree-ah, f., fish-market

pescivendolo, pay-she-ven-do-lo, m., fishmonger

pesco, pess-ko, m., peach-tree.—**noce**, nectarine-tree

peso, pay-zo, m., weight; load; Argentine money

pessimo*, pess-se-mo, a., very bad; worst

pesta, pess-tah, f., trodden path

pestare, pess-tah-ray, v., to pound; to tread

peste, pess-tay, f., pest, plague; stink

petalo, pay-tah-lo, m., petal

petizione, pay-te-tse'o-nay, f., petition

petrolio, pay-tro-le'o, m., petroleum

pettegola, pet-tay-go-lah, f., (woman) chatterbox

pettinare, pet-te-nah-ray, v., to comb

pettine, pet-te-nay, m., comb; scallop-shell

pettirosso, pet-te-ross-so, m., robin [red breast]

petto, pet-to, m., breast, chest

petulante, pay-too-lahn-tay, a., petulant; pert

pezza [or **pezzo**], pet-tsah, m., piece; part

pezzuola, pet-tsoo'o-lah, f., handkerchief

piacere, pe'ah-chay-ray, m., pleasure; favour. v., to please

piacevole, pe'ah-chay-vo-lay, a., agreeable

piaga, pe'ah-gah, f., sore; wound

piagare, pe'ah-gah-ray, v., to wound
pialla, pe'ahl-lah, f., carpenter's plane
piallare, pe'ahl-lah-ray, v., to plane
pianare, pe'ah-nah-ray, v., to level
pianeta, pe'ah-nay-tah, f., planet ; (eccl.) chasuble
piangere, pe'ahn-jay-ray, v., to weep
piano, pe'ah-no, m., floor ; flat country, plain.
　　a.,* level ; smooth.　adv., softly
pianoforte, pe'ah-no-for-tay, m., piano
pianta, pe'ahn-tah, f., plant ; plan ; (foot) sole
piantagione, pe'ahn-tah-jo-nay, f., plantation
piantare, pe'ahn-tah-ray, v., to plant
piantatore, pe'ahn-tah-tor-ay, m., planter
pianterreno, pe'ahn-tair-ray-no, m., ground-floor
pianto, pe'ahn-to, m., tears, weeping
pianura, pe'ah-noo-rah, f., plain
piatire, pe'ah-tee-ray, v., to contest ; to litigate
piattaforma, pe'ah-tah-for-mah, f., platform
piatto, pe'aht-to, m., plate ; dish.　a., flat
piazza, pe'aht-tsah, f., square ; market
pica, pee-kah, f., magpie
picca, pick-kah, f., pike ; dispute ; (cards) spade
piccare, pick-kah-ray, v., to prick ; to pique
picchiare, pick-ke'ah-ray, v., to knock ; to beat
picchio, pick-ke'o, m., woodpecker ; knock
picchiotto, pick-ke'ot-to, m., knocker
piccino, pit-chee-no, m., little boy.　a., small
piccionaia, pit-cho-nah-e'ah, f., pigeon-house ;
　　(fig.) gallery
piccione, pit-cho-nay, m., pigeon
picco, pick-ko, m., peak
piccolo, pick-ko-lo, a., little ; mean
piccone, pick-ko-nay, m., pick-axe
pidocchio, pe-dock-ke'o, m., louse
piede, pe'ay-day, m., foot
piedi, pe'ay-de, in—, standing
piedistallo, pe'ay-de-stahl-lo, m., pedestal
piega, pe'ay-gah, f., fold, crease ; wrinkle
piegare, pe'ay-gah-ray, v., to fold, to plait
pieghevole, pe'ay-gay-vo-lay, a., pliable ; tractable
piego, pe'ay-go, m., bundle of letters or papers
piena, pe'ay-nah, f., flood ; throng

pienezza, pe'ay-net-tsah, f., abundance

pieno°, pe'ay-no, a., full

pietà, pe'ay-tah, f., pity ; piety

pietanza, pe'ay-tahn-tsah, f., plate of meat

pietoso, pe'ay-to-zo, a., piteous

pietra, pe'ay-trah, f., stone. — di paragone, touchstone

pietrificare, pe'ay-tre-fe-kah-ray, v., to petrify

piffero, pif-fay-ro, m., fife ; fifer

pigiama, pe-jah-mah, m., pyjamas

pigiare, pe-jah-ray, v., to press ; to crush

pigio, pee-jo, m., crowd

pigionale, pe-jo-nah-lay, m. & f., lodger ; tenant

pigione, pe-jo-nay, f., rent

pigliare, pe-l'yah-ray, v., to take ; to seize

pigmeo, pig-may-o, m., dwarf, pigmy

pignone, pe-n'yo-nay, m., pinion   [gage

pignorare, pe-n'yo-rah-ray, v., to pledge ; to mort-

pignoratario, pe-n'yo-rah-tah-re'o, m., pawn-

pigolare, pe-go-lah-ray, v., to chirp   [broker

pigrizia, pe-gree-tse'ah, f., laziness

pigro°, pee-gro, a., lazy ; indolent

pila, pee-lah, f., pile ; vat

pilastro, pe-lahss-tro, m., pillar

pillola, pil-lo-lah, f., pill

pilota, pe-lo-tah, m., pilot

pilotaggio, pe-lo-tahd-jo, m., pilotage ; pilot's fee

pilotare, pe-lo-tah-ray, v., to pilot

pina [or pigna], pee-nah, f., fir-cone

pinacoteca, pe-nah-ko-tay-kah, f., picture-gallery

pingere, pin-jay-ray, v., to paint

pingue, pin-goo'ay, a., fat ; plump

pinna, pin-nah, f., fin of a fish

pino, pee-no, m., pine-tree

pinzare, pin-tsah-ray, v., to sting

pinzette, pin-tset-tay, f. pl., tweezers, pincers

pio°, pee-o, a., pious ; charitable

pioggia, pe'od-jah, f., rain

piombare, pe'om-bah-ray, v., to lead ; (teeth) to stop. —addosso, to assail

piombo, pe'om-bo, m., lead ; plummet. a —, perpen-

pioniere, pe'o-ne'ay-ray, m., pioneer   [dicular

pioppo, pe'op-po, m., poplar-tree
piota, pe'o-tah, f., (turf) sod
piovere, pe'o-vay-ray, v., to rain
piovigginare, pe'o-vid-je-nah-ray, v., to drizzle
piovoso, pe'o-vo-zo, a., rainy
pipa, pee-pah, f., pipe
pipata, pe-pah-tah, f., pipeful. **fare una —**, to smoke a pipeful
pipistrello, pe-pe-strell-lo, m., (mammal) bat
pira, pee-rah, f., pyre
pirata, pe-rah-tah, m., pirate, corsair
piroscafo, pe-ro-skah-fo, m., steamer, vessel
pisciare, pe-shah-ray, v., to urinate
piscina, pe-shee-nah, f., swimming-bath ; fish-pond
piselli, pe-zell-le, m. pl., green peas
pispigliare, piss-pe-l'yah-ray, v., to whisper
pistola, piss-to-lah, f., pistol
pistone, piss-to-nay, m., piston
pitoccare, pe-tock-kah-ray, v., to beg for money
pitocco, pe-tock-ko, m., beggar
pittore, pit-tor-ay, m., painter
pittoresco*, pit-to-ress-ko, a., picturesque
pittura, pit-too-rah, f., painting
più, pe'oo, adv., more. **al —**, at most
piuma, pe'oo-mah, f., plume
piumaggio, pe'oo-mahd-jo, m., plumage
piumoso, pe'oo-mo-zo, a., downy
piuttosto, pe'oot-toss-to, adv., rather, somewhat
piviere, pe-ve'ay-ray, m., plover
pizzicagnolo, pit-tse-kah-n'yo-lo.m.,pork-butcher
pizzicare, pit-tse-kah-ray, v., to pinch ; to tingle ; to itch ; to prick
pizzico, pit-tse-ko, m., pinch
placare, plah-kah-ray, v., to appease, to pacify
placca, plahk-kah, f., plate ; badge
placcare, plahk-kah-ray, v., to plate
placido*, plah-che-do, a., placid
plagiario, plah-jah-re'o, m., plagiarist
planare, plah-nah-ray, v., to glide, to plane
platano, plah-tah-no, m., plane-tree, plantan
platea, plah-tay-ah, f., (theatre) pit
platino, plah-te-no, m., platinum

plauso, plah-oo-zo, m., applause
plebe, play-bay, f., rabble ; common people
plebeo, play-bay-o, m., plebian. a.,* vulgar
plico, plee-ko, m., envelope with enclosures ; folder
pneumatico, pnay'oo-mah-te-ko, a., pneumatic. m., motor-tyre
po, pe. a. & adv., (see poco)
pocanzi, po-kahn-tse, adv., just now ; quite recently
pochino, po-kee-no, m., very very little, wee bit
poco, po-ko, a. & adv., little ; few. m., little
podestà, po-dess-tah, m., mayor. f., power
poema, po'ay-mah, m., poem
poesia, po'ay-zee-ah, f., poetry
poeta, po'ay-tah, m., poet
poetico*, po'ay-te-ko, a., poetic
poggiarsi, pod-jar-se, v., to lean, to rest
poggio, pod-jo, m., little hill, hillock
poi, po'e, adv., afterwards ; then ; next
poichè, po'e-kay, adv. & conj., since ; considering
polipo, po-le-po, m., polypus
politeama, po-le-tay-ah-mah, m., theatre where different varieties of shows are given, i.e., co-medy, vaudeville, etc.
politica, po-lee-te-kah, f., politics ; policy
politico, po-lee-te-ko, a.,* political. m., politician
polizia, po-le-tsee-ah, f., police
polizza, po-lit-tsah, f., policy; note. — di cam-bio, bill of exchange. — di carico, bill of lading
pollaio, poll-lah-e'o, m., coop ; poultry-yard
pollaiuolo, poll-lah-e'oo-o-lo, m., poulterer
pollame, poll-lah-may, m., poultry
pollastra, poll-lahss-trah, f., pullet
pollastro, poll-lahss-tro, m., chicken
pollice, poll-le-chay, m., thumb ; big toe ; inch
pollo, poll-lo, m., chicken ; hen
polmone, poll-mo-nay, m., lung
polmonite, poll-mo-nee-tay, f., pneumonia
polo, po-lo, m., pole
polpa, poll-pah, f., pulp ; flesh
polpaccio, poll-paht-cho, m., (leg) calf
polsino, poll-see-no, m., cuff
polso, poll-zo, m., pulse ; wrist ; (fig.) vigour

poltiglia, poll-tee-l'yah, f., pulp or pap ; slush
poltrona, poll-tro-nah, f., armchair
poltronaletto, poll-tro-nah-let-to, m., bed-armchair
poltrone, poll-tro-nay, m., poltroon [chair
polvere, poll-vay-ray, f., dust ; powder
polveriera, poll-vay-re'ay-rah, f., powder-factory
polverizzare, poll-vay-rid-dzah-ray, v., to pulverize [rize
polveroso*, poll-vay-ro-zo, a., dusty
pomario, po-mah-re'o, m., orchard
pomice, po-me-chay, f., pumice-stone
pomo, po-mo, m., apple ; apple-tree ; pommel
pomodoro, po-mo-do-ro, m., tomato
pompa, pom-pah, f., pomp ; pump
pompare, pom-pah-ray, v., to pump
pompelmo, pom-pell-mo, m., grapefruit
pompiere, pom-pe'ay-ray, m., fireman
pomposo*, pom-po-zo, a., pompous
ponce, pon-chay, m., (drink) punch
ponderare, pon-day-rah-ray, v., to ponder, to weigh
pondi, pon-de, m.pl., dysentery
ponente, po-nen-tay, m., west
ponte, pon-tay,! m., bridge ; deck ; landing stage
pontefice, pon-tay-fe-chay, m., Pope
ponticello, pon-te-chell-lo, m., small bridge
pontone, pon-to-nay, m., pontoon
popolaccio, po-po-laht-cho, m., populace
popolare, po-po-lah-ray, a., popular. v., to populate
popolazione, po-po-lah-tse'o-nay, f., population
popolo, po-po-lo, m., people
popoloso, po-po-lo-zo, a., populous, peopled
popone, po-po-nay, m., melon
poppa, pop-pah, f., woman's breast ; (naut.) stern
poppare, pop-pah-ray, v., to suck, to take the breast
porcellino, por-chell-lee-no, m., sucking-pig ;
porcheria, por-chay-ree-ah, f., filth [guinea-pig
porcile, por-chee-lay, m., pig-sty
porco, por-ko, m., pig. a., piggish [hog
porcospino, por-ko-spee-no, m., porcupine ; hedge-
porgere, por-jay-ray, v., to hand ; to reach ; to present
poro, po-ro, m., pore [sent
poroso, po-ro-zo, a., porous
porpora, por-po-rah, f., purple

porporino, por-po-**ree**-no, a., purple-coloured

porre, por-ray, v., to place, to put

porro, por-ro, m., leek; (med.) wart

porta, por-tah, f., door. —girevole, revolving door

portabandiera, por-tah-bahn-de'**ay**-rah, m., ensign-bearer

portabile, por-tah-be-lay, a., portable [wallet

portafogli, por-tah-fo-l'ye, m., portfolio; letter-case;

portalettere, por-tah-let-tay-ray, m., postman

portamantello, por-tah-mahn-**tell**-lo, m., hat and coat-stand

portamento, por-tah-**men**-to, m., deportment; conduct

portamonete, por-tah-mo-**nay**-tay, m., purse

portapenne, por-tah-pen-nay, m., pen-holder

portare, por-tah-ray, v., to carry, to bear; to bring

portasigari, por-tah-see-gah-re, m., cigar-case

portaspilli, por-tah-spil-le, m., pin-cushion

portata, por-tah-tah, f., range; course; ship's load

portatore, por-tah-**tor**-ay, m., bearer, carrier

portento, por-ten-to, m., marvel

portiere, por-te'**ay**-ray, m., door-keeper, porter

porto, por-to, m., port; postage; cost of carriage

portone, por-to-nay, m., gate; main door

porzione, por-tse'**o**-nay, f., portion; allowance

posa, po-zah, f., rest, repose; pause; pose

posamine, po-zah-mee-nay, m., mine-layer [stand

posaombrelli, po-zah-om-**brel**-le, m., umbrella-

posare, po-zah-ray, v., to rest; to place, to put

posata, po-zah-tah, f., cover=knife, fork, spoon,

posato*, po-zah-to, a., sedate; quiet [etc.

poscia, po-she'ah, adv., afterwards

poscritto, po-**skrit**-to, m., postscript [morrow

posdomani, poz-do-**mah**-ne, adv., the day after to-

positivo*, po-ze-**tee**-vo, a., positive, real

posizione, po-ze-tse'**o**-nay, f., position, place

pospasto, poss-**pahss**-to, m., dessert

posporre, poss-por-ray, v., to postpone

possedere, poss-say-**day**-ray, v., to possess

possessione, poss-sess-se'**o**-nay, f., possession

possesso, poss-**sess**-so, m., possession

possessore, poss-sess-**sor**-ay, m., owner, possessor

possibile, poss-see-be-lay, a., possible

possibilità, poss-se-be-le-tah, f., possibility

posta, poss-tah, f., post ; post-office ; (job) occupation. **a bella —,** intentionally

postale, poss-tah-lay, a., postal. **vaglia —,** f., money-order

postare, poss-tah-ray, v., to post ; to affix

posteggio, poss-ted-jo, m., car-park ; parking

posteri, poss-tay-re, m. pl., descendants

posteriore, poss-tay-re'or-ay, a., posterior ; later

posterità, poss-tay-re-tah, f., posterity

postino, poss-tee-no, m., postman   [placed

posto, poss-to, m., site, spot ; (job) position. p.p.

postribolo, poss-tree-bo-lo, m., brothel

potare, po-tah-ray, v., to prune

potassa, po-tahss-sah, f., potash

potente, po-ten-tay, a., potent, mighty

potenza, po-ten-tsah, f., power, potency

potere, po-tay-ray, m., power ; authority. v., to be able

poveretto [or **poverino**], po-vay-ret-to, m., un-fortunate one

povero, po-vay-ro, a.,° poor. m., poor man

povertà, po-vair-tah, f., poverty

pozione, po-tse'o-nay, f., (med.) potion

pozza, pot-tsah, f., puddle ; drain ; pool

pozzetta, pot-tset-tah, f., dimple in the cheeks

pozzo, pot-tso, m., well ; pit

pranzare, prahn-dzah-ray, v., to dine

pranzo, prahn-dzo, m., dinner

prateria, prah-tay-ree-ah, f., meadows

pratica, prah-te-kah, f., practice ; experience

praticabile, prah-te-kah-be-lay, a., practicable

praticare, prah-te-kah-ray, v., to practise

pratico°, prah-te-ko, a., practical ; experienced

prato, prah-to, m., meadow, pasture-land

pravità, prah-ve-tah, f., malice, wickedness

precario°, pray-kah-re'o, a., precarious

precauzione, pray-kah'oo-tse'o-nay, f., precaution

prece, pray-chay, f., prayer

precedente, pray-chay-den-tay, a., foregoing. m., precedent

precedenza, pray-chay-den-tsah, f., precedence
precedere, pray-chay-day-ray, v., to precede
precetto, pray-chet-to, m., precept
precettore, pray-chet-tor-ay, m., tutor, instructor
precipitare, pray-che-pe-tah-ray, v., to precipitate, to hurry
precipitato°, pray-che-pe-tah-to, p.p., precipitated
precipitoso°, pray-che-pe-to-zo, a., rash ; precipi-
precipizio, pray-che-pee-tse'o, m., precipice [tous
precipuo°, pray-chee-poo-o, a., principal, main
precisione, pray-che-ze'o-nay, f., precision
preciso°, pray-chee-zo, a., precise
preclaro°, pray-klah-ro, a., illustrious
precoce, pray-ko-chay, a., precocious, premature
preconizzare, pray-ko-nid-dzah-ray, v., to proclaim ; to extol
preda, pray-dah, f., prey ; booty ; pillage
predare, pray-dah-ray, v., to pillage
predetto, pray-det-to, a., aforesaid, foretold
predica, pray-de-kah, f., sermon ; censure
predicare, pray-de-kah-ray, v., to preach ; to censure
predicatore, pray-de-kah-tor-ay, m., preacher
prediletto, pray-de-let-to, a., preferred, favourite
predire, pray-dee-ray, v., to predict
predisporre, pray-diss-por-ray, v., to predispose
predominare, pray-do-me-nah-ray, v., to pre-
dominate
predone, pray-do-nay, m., pillager
prefazione, pray-fah-tse'o-nay, f., preface
preferenza, pray-fay-ren-tsah, f., preference
preferire, pray-fay-ree-ray, v., to prefer ; to choose
prefetto, pray-fet-to, m., prefect, governor
prefiggere, pray-feed-jay-ray, v., to arrange
beforehand
pregare, pray-gah-ray, v., to pray ; to request
pregevole, pray-jay-vo-lay, a., esteemed
preghiera, pray-ghe'ay-rah, f., prayer
pregio, pray-jo, m., value ; renown [damage
pregiudizio, pray-joo-dee-tse'o, m., prejudice ;
pregno, pra-n'yo, a., pregnant
pregustamento, pray-gooss-tah-men-to, m., fore-
prelevare, pray-lay-vah-ray, v., to deduct [taste

preliminare, pray-le-me-**nah**-ray, a., preliminary

premere, pray-**may**-ray, v., to urge; to press

premettere, pray-**met**-tay-ray, v., to put before

premiare, pray-me-**ah**-ray, v., to reward

premiato, pray-me-**ah**-to, m., prize-winner

premio, pray-me'o, m., prize; premium

premito, pray-me-to, m., pressure, pushing

premunire, pray-moo-**nee**-ray, v., to forewarn

premura, pray-moo-rah, f., haste; eagerness

prendere, pren-**day**-ray, v., to take; to seize

prendibile, pren-**dee**-be-lay, a., liable to be seized

prenditoria, pren-de-to-**ree**-ah, f., lottery-office

prenome, pray-**no**-may, m., Christian name

preoccupare, pray-ock-koo-**pah**-ray, v., to preoccupy

preparare, pray-pah-**rah**-ray, v., to prepare [tion

preparazione, pray-pah-rah-tse'**o**-nay, f., preparation

presa, pray-zah, f., taking; conquest; pinch of snuff

presagio, pray-zah-jo, m., omen, presage

presagire, pray-zah-**jee**-ray, v., to foretell, to presbite, press-be-tay, a., long-sighted [sage

presbite, press-be-tay, a., long-sighted [sage

presbiterio, press-be-**tay**-re'o, m., presbytery

prosciutto, pray-**shoot**-to, m., ham

prescrivere, pray-**skree**-vay-ray, v., to prescribe

prescrizione, pray-skre-tse'**o**-nay, f., prescription

presentare, pray-zen-**tah**-ray, v., to present; to tender; to introduce

presentazione, pray-zen-tah-tse'**o**-nay, f., presentation

presente, pray-zen-**tay**, m., present. a., present

presentimento, pray-zen-te-men-to, m., premonition

presentire, pray-zen-**tee**-ray, v., to presage, to foretell

presenza, pray-zen-tsah, f., presence [tell

presenziare, pray-zen-tse'**ah**-ray, v., to be present

presepio, pray-**zay**-pe'o, m., (biblical) manger

preservare, pray-zair-**vah**-ray, v., to preserve

preservazione, pray-zair-vah-tse'**o**-nay, f., preservation

preside, pray-se-day, m., principal of a school

presidente, pray-se-**den**-tay, m., president

presidenza, pray-se-**den**-tsah, f., presidency

presidio, pray-see-de'o, m., garrison

presiedere, pray-se'ay-day-ray, v., to preside

pressa, **press-**sah, f., press; crowd

pressante, press-sahn-tay, a., pressing

pressare, press-sah-ray, v., to press; to impel

pressione, press-se'o-nay, f., pressure

presso, **press-**so, prep., near; about

pressochè, press-so-kay, adv., almost

prestabilire, press-tah-be-lee-ray, v., to establish beforehand

prestante, press-tahn-tay, a., of beautiful appearance

prestare, press-tah-ray, v., to lend; to render submission

prestezza, press-tet-tsah, f., quickness, celerity

prestidigitazione, press-te-de-je-tah-tse'o-nay, f., conjuring

prestigiatore, press-te-jah-tor-ay, m., conjurer

prestigio, press-tee-jo, m., prestige; magic

prestito, **press-**te-to, m., loan

presto, **press-**to, a., quick; ready.   adv., at once; early; quickly

presumere, pray-**zoo-**may-ray, v., to presume

presuntuoso*, pray-zoonn-too'o-zo, a., presumptuous; arrogant

presunzione, pray-zoonn-tse'o-nay, f., presumption

prete, pray-tay, m., priest

pretendente, pray-ten-den-tay, m., pretender

pretendere, pray-ten-day-ray, v., to profess; to demand

pretenzione, pray-ten-tse'o-nay, f., claim, right

preterire, pray-tay-ree-ray, v., to disregard; to neglect

pretesa, pray-**tay-**zah, f., claim

pretesto, pray-**tess-**to, m., pretext; pretence

pretto, **pret-**to, a., pure

pretura, pray-too-rah, f., office of jurisdiction

prevalere, pray-vah-**lay-**ray, v., to prevail

prevaricare, pray-vah-re-**kah-**ray, v., to prevaricate

prevaricazione, pray-vah-re-kah-tse'o-nay, f., prevarication

prevedere, pray-vay-**day-**ray, v., to foresee

prevenire, pray-vay-nee-ray, v., to prevent ; to avoid ; to forewarn

preventivo, pray-ven-tee-vo, a.,* preventive. m., estimate

prevenuto, pray-vay-noo-to, m., accused

prevenzione, pray-ven-tse'o-nay, f., prevention

previdenza, pray-ve-den-tsah,f.,Providence ; fore-

previo°, pray-ve'o, a., previous [sight

previsione, pray-ve-ze'o-nay, f., prevision. — del tempo, weather forecast

prezioso°, pray-tse'o-zo, a., precious ; delicious

prezzare, pret-tsah-ray, v., to value, to appraise

prezzatore, pret-tsah-tor-ay, m., appraiser

prezzemolo, pret-tsay-mo-lo, m., parsley

prezzo, pret-tso, m., price, cost

prezzolare, pret-tso-lah-ray, v., to engage some-one for a mean task

priego, pre-ay-go, v., earnest prayer

prigione, pre-jo-nay, f., prison

prigionia, pre-jo-nee-ah, f., imprisonment [iero]

prigioniere[iero], pre-jo-ne'ay-ray, m., prisoner

prima, pree-mah, adv., before ; first

primario°, pre-mah-re'o, a., primary ; principal

primaticcio, pre-mah-tit-cho, a., early ; first

primavera, pre-mah-vay-rah, f., spring

primeggiare, pre-med-jah-ray, v., to be first ; to

primitivo°, pre-me-tee-vo, a., primitive [excel

primizia, pre-mee-tse'ah, f., first fruits

primo°, pree-mo, a., first ; principal

primogenito, pre-mo-jay-ne-to, m., first child

primola, pree-mo-lah, f., primrose. — rossa, scarlet pimpernel

principale, prin-che-pah-lay, a., principal, main. m., master, principal

principe, prin-che-pay, m., prince

principessa, prin-che-pess-sah, f., princess

principiante, prin-che-pe'ahn-tay, m., beginner

principiare, prin-che-pe'ah-ray, v., to begin

principio, prin-chee-pe'o, m., beginning ; origin ; principle

priore, pre-o-ray, m., prior [principle

prioria, pre-o-ree-ah, f., priory

priorita, pre-o-re-tah, f., priority

pristino*, priss-te-no, a., previous; former; old

privare, pre-vah-ray, v., to deprive

privativa, pre-vah-tee-vah, f., monopoly

privativo, pre-vah-tee-vo, a., (trading privilege) exclusive

privato, pre-**vah**-to, m., W.C. a.,* private

privazione, pre-vah-tse'o-nay, f., privation; need

privilegio, pre-ve-lay-jo, m., privilege

privo, pree-vo, a., deprived; destitute; lacking

pro, pro, m., advantage; good for. senza —, use-

probabile, pro-bah-be-lay, a., probable [less

probità, pro-be-tah, f., probity, integrity

problema, pro-blay-mah, m., problem, question

probo, pro-bo, a., honest; righteous

proboscide, pro-bo-she-day, f., snout; trunk

procacciare, pro-kaht-chah-ray, v., to procure by painstaking effort

procace, pro-kah-chay, a., impertinent; forward; cheeky

procedere, pro-chay-day-ray, v., to proceed

procedimento, pro-chay-de-men-to, m., proceed-

procedura, pro-chay-doo-rah, f., procedure [ing

procella, pro-chell-lah, f., tempest

processare, pro-chess-sah-ray, v., to prosecute

processione, pro-chess-se'o-nay, f., procession

processo, pro-chess-so, m., law-suit; process

proclama, pro-klah-mah, m., proclamation

proclamare, pro-klah-mah-ray, v., to proclaim

proclamazione, pro-klah-mah-tse'o-nay, f., pro-clamation

proclive, pro-klee-vay, a., inclined

procura, pro-koo-rah, f., power of attorney; proxy

procurare, pro-koo-rah-ray, v., to procure; to inquire into

procuratore, pro-koo-rah-tor-ay, m., attorney;

prode, pro-day, a., brave, gallant [proctor

prodezza, pro-det-tsah, f., prowess, gallantry

prodigare, pro-de-gah-ray, v., to squander, to la-

prodigio, pro-dee-jo, m., prodigy [vish

prodigioso*, pro-de-jo-zo, a., extraordinary, astonishing

prodigo, pro-de-go, a.,* lavish; prodigal. m., prodigal

prodotto, pro-dot-to, m., product ; production
produrre, pro-doohr-ray, v., to produce
produttore, pro-doot-tor-ay, m., producer [output
produzione, pro-doo-tse'o-nay, f., production, yield,
proemio, pro'ay-me'o, m., introduction
profanare, pro-fah-nah-ray, v., to profane
profano*, pro-fah-no, a., profane ; impious
proferire, pro-fay-ree-ray, v., to proffer ; to declare
professare, pro-fess-sah-ray, v., to profess ; to teach
professionale, pro-fess-se'o-nah-lay, a., profession-
professione, pro-fess-se'o-nay, f., profession   [al
profeta, pro-fay-tah, m., prophet
profetare, pro-fay-tah-ray, v., (see **profetizzare**)
profetico*, pro-fay-te-ko, a., prophetic
profetizzare, pro-fay-tid-dzah-ray, v., to prophesy
profezia, pro-fay-tsee-ah, f., prophecy
profferta, prof-fair-tah, f., offer
profilo, pro-fee-lo, m., profile ; side-face [vantage
profittare, pro-fit-tah-ray, v., to profit, to take ad-
profittevole, pro-fit-tay-vo-lay, a., profitable
profitto, pro-fit-to, m., profit ; advantage
profondare, pro-fon-dah-ray, v., to dig ; to deep-
        en ; to sink ; to penetrate
profondere, pro-fon-day-ray, v., to lavish
profondità, pro-fon-de-tah, f., depth
profondo*, pro-fon-do, a., profound, deep
profugo, pro-foo-go, m., refugee. a., exiled
profumare, pro-foo-mah-ray, v., to perfume
profumeria, pro-foo-may-ree-ah, f., perfumery
profumo, pro-foo-mo, m., perfume
profusione, pro-foo-ze'o-nay, f., profusion
profuso*, pro-foo-zo, a., profuse, abundant
progenie, pro-jay-ne-ay, f., progeny, offspring
progettare, pro-jet-tah-ray, v., to project, to plan
progetto, pro-jet-to, m., plan, project ; design
programma, pro-grahm-mah, m., programme
progredire, pro-gray-dee-ray, v., to progress
progressivo*, pro-gress-see-vo, a., progressive
progresso, pro-gress-so, m., progress
proibire, pro-e-bee-ray, v., to prohibit
proibizione, pro-e-be-tse'o-nay, f., prohibition
proiettare, pro-e'et-tah-ray, v., to project

proiettile, pro-e'et-te-lay, m., projectile [lamp
proiettore, pro-e'et-tor-ay, m., search-light ; head-
proiezione, pro-e'ay-tse'o-nay, f., projection
prole, pro-lay, f., offspring
prolifico*, pro-lee-fe-ko, a., prolific
prolisso*, pro-liss-so, a., prolix
prologo, pro-lo-go, m., prologue, introduction
prolungare, pro-loonn-gah-ray, v., to prolong
promessa, pro-mess-sah, f., promise
promettere, pro-met-tay-ray, v., to promise
promovere [or **promuovere**], pro-mo-vay-ray,
   v., to promote ; to incite
promozione, pro-mo-tse'o-nay, f., promotion
promulgare, pro-mool-gah-ray, v., to promulgate
prono, pro-no, a., prone, prone to
pronome, pro-no-may, m., pronoun
pronostico, pro-noss-te-ko, m., prognostic
prontezza, pron-tet-tsah, f., readiness ; prompti-
   tude ; quickness
pronto*, pron-to, a., prompt ; ready ; quick
prontuario, pron-too'ah-re'o, m., book of reference ; guide ; hand-book
pronunziare, pro-noonn-tse'ah-ray, v., to pronounce. — **un discorso,** to make a speech
propagare, pro-pah-gah-ray, v., to propagate
propensione, pro-pen-se'o-nay, f., propensity
propiziare, pro-pe-tse'ah-ray, v., to propitiate
propizio*, pro-pee-tse'o, a., favourable, suitable
proporre, pro-por-ray, v., to propose, to offer
proporzionale, pro-por-tse'o-nah-lay, a., pro-
   portional
proporzionato*, pro-por-tse'o-nah-to, a., propor-
   tionate ; adequate
proporzione, pro-por-tse'o-nay, f., proportion
proposito, pro-po-ze-to, m., purpose, design
proposta, pro-poss-tah, f., proposal
proprietà, pro-pre-ay-tah, f., property ; peculiarity ; estate
proprietario, pro-pre-ay-tah-re'o, m., proprietor
proprio*, pro-pre'o, a., own ; proper ; genuine
propulsare, pro-pool-sah-ray, v., to propel
propulsore, pro-pool-sor-ay, m., propeller

prora, pro-rah, f., prow, bow

proroga, pro-ro-gah, f., delay ; adjournment

prorogare, pro-ro-gah-ray, v., to delay ; to adjourn

prorompere, pro-rom-pay-ray, v., to burst out

prosa, pro-zah, f., prose

prosapia, pro-sah-pe'ah, f., lineage

prosatore, pro-sah-tor-ay, m., prosaist   [dry

prosciugare, pro-she'oo-gah-ray, v., to drain ; to

prosciutto, pro-she'oot-to, m., ham

proscritto, pro-skrit-to, m., outlaw

proscrivere, pro-skree-vay-ray, v., to proscribe

prosecuzione, pro-say-koo-tse'o-nay, f., prosecution

proseguire, pro-say-goo'ee-ray, v., to prosecute ;
     to pursue

prosperare, pross-pay-rah-ray, v., to prosper

prosperità, pross-pay-re-tah, f., prosperity

prospero*, pross-pay-ro, a., prosperous

prospettiva, pross-pet-tee-vah, f., perspective

prospetto, pross-pet-to, m., prospect ; pamphlet

prossimità, pross-se-me-tah, f., proximity

prossimo*, pross-se-mo, a., next. m., neighbour

prosternare, pross-tair-nah-ray, v., to prostrate

prostrazione, pross-trah-tse'o-nay, f., prostration

proteggere, pro-ted-jay-ray, v., to protect

protendere, pro-ten-day-ray, v., to stretch out

protervo, pro-tair-vo, a., arrogant

protesi, pro-tay-se, f., an artificial joint or part
     supplied for a defect of the body

protesta, pro-tess-tah, f., protest, protestation

protestare, pro-tess-tah-ray, v., to protest

protesto, pro-tess-to, m., protest

protettore, pro-tet-tor-ay, m., protector

protezione, pro-tay-tse'o-nay, f., protection

protrarre, pro-trar-ray, v., to protract

prova, pro-vah, f., trial ; proof ; experiment

provare, pro-vah-ray, v., to try ; to prove ; to feel

provenienza, pro-vay-ne'en-tsah, f., source

provenire, pro-vay-nee-ray, v., to arise ; to come

provento, pro-ven-to, m., income, earnings   [from

proverbio, pro-vair-be'o, m., proverb

provincia, pro-vin-chah, f., province

provocante, pro-vo-kahn-tay, a., provoking

provocare, pro-vo-kah-ray, v., to provoke

provocazione, pro-vo-kah-tse'o-nay, f., provocation

provvedere, prov-vay-day-ray, v., to provide ; to provide for ; to stock

provveditore, prov-vay-de-tor-ay, m., purveyor

provvidenza, prov-ve-den-tsah, f., providence

provvido°, prov-ve-do, a., provident

provvigione [or provvisione], prov-ve-jo-nay, f., provision ; pension ; commission

provvisorio*, prov-ve-zo-re'o, a., provisional

provvista, prov-viss-tah, f., provision ; purchase

provvisto, prov-viss-to, p.p., supplied ; stocked ; provided for

prua, proo-ah, f., prow

prudente, proo-den-tay, a., prudent

prudenza, proo-den-tsah, f., prudence

prudere, proo-day-ray, v., to itch

prugna, proo-n'yah, f., plum. — secca, prune

prugno, proo-n'yo, m., plum-tree

pruina, proo'ee-nah, f., hoar-frost

pruno, proo-no, m., briar ; bramble

prurigine, proo-ree-je-nay, f., mild itching

pruriginoso, proo-re-je-no-zo,a.,producing itching

prurito, proo-ree-to, m., itching

pseudonimo, psay'oo-do-ne-mo, m., pseudonym

psichico, psee-ke-ko, a., psychic

psicologia, pse-ko-lo-jee-ah, f., psychology

pubblicare, poob-ble-kah-ray, v., to publish

pubblicità, poob-ble-che-tah, f., publicity

pubblico, poob-ble-ko, m., public. a.,° public

pudico°, poo-dee-ko, a., chaste, pure ; modest

pudore, poo-dor-ay, m., chastity, purity

puerile, poo'ay-ree-lay, a., childish, puerile

pugnace, poo-n'yah-chay, a., pugnacious

pugnale, poo-n'yah-lay, m., dagger

pugnare, poo-n'yah-ray, v., to fight

pugno, poo-n'yo, m., fist ; handful ; cuff

pulce, pool-chay, f., flea

pulcella, pool-chell-lah, f., maiden

Pulcinella, pool-che-nell-lah, m., Punch ; clown

pulcino, pool-chee-no, m., young chicken

puledra, poo-lay-drah, f., filly

puledro, poo-lay-dro, m., colt

puleggia, poo-led-jah, f., pulley

pulire, poo-lee-ray, v., to clean ; to polish

pulitezza, poo-le-tet-tsah, f., cleanness ; neatness

pulito°, poo-lee-to, a., clean ; polished

pulizia, poo-le-tsee-ah, f., cleanliness

pullulare, pooll-loo-lah-ray, v., to be in large numbers ; to shoot out

pulpito, pooll-pe-to, m., pulpit

pulsare, pooll-sah-ray, v., to pulsate

pulsazione, pooll-sah-tse'o-nay, f., pulsation

pungere, poonn-jay-ray, v., to prick ; to sting

pungolo, poonn-go-lo, m., goad

punire, poo-nee-ray, v., to punish

punizione, poo-ne-tse'o-nay, f., punishment

punta, poonn-tah, f., point ; end ; (pain) stitch ; (nail) brad

puntare, poonn-tah-ray, v., to point

punteggiare, poonn-ted-jah-ray, v., to punctuate

punteggiatura, poonn-ted-jah-too-rah, f., punctuation

puntellare, poonn-tell-lah-ray, v., to prop up

punteruolo, poonn-tay-roo'o-lo, m., bodkin

punto, poonn-to, m., dot, point ; instant ; stitch. adv., no such thing, not at all

puntuale, poonn-too'ah-lay, a., punctual, timely

puntuazione, poonn-too'ah-tse'o-nay, f., punctuation

puntura, poonn-too-rah, f., puncture ; prick ; (spasm) stitch

punzone, poonn-tso-nay, m., puncheon ; (fist) punch

pupilla, poo-pill-lah, f., (eye) pupil

pupillo, poo-pill-lo, m., ward

purchè, poohr-kay, conj., provided ; if however

pure, poo-ray, conj., yet ; also ; however ; too ; if

purezza, poo-ret-tsah, f., purity

purgare, poohr-gah-ray, v., to purge

purgativo, poohr-gah-tee-vo, a., purgative

purgatorio, poohr-gah-tor-e'o, m., purgatory

purificare, poo-re-fe-kah-ray, v., to purify

purità, poo-re-tah, f., purity

puro, poo-ro, a., pure

purpureo, poohr-poo-ray-o, m., purple

pus, pooss, m., pus, matter

pustola, pooss-to-lah, f., pustule, pimple ; blister

putredine, poo-tray-de-nay, f., rottenness, putridity, corruption

putrefare, poo-tray-fah-ray, v., to putrify ; to decompose [pose

putrido, poo-tre-do, a., putrid ; decomposed

puttana, poot-tah-nah, f., prostitute

puzza [or puzzo], poot-tsah, f., stench, bad odour

puzzare, poot-tsah-ray, v., to stink

puzzolente, poot-tso-len-tay, a., stinking

qua, kwah, adv., here. — e là, here and there

quacquero [or quaccherro], kwahk-**kway**-ro, m., Quaker

quaderno, kwah-**dair**-no, m., copy-book ; part

quadrante, kwah-**drahn**-tay, m., quadrant ; face of a watch. — solare, sun-dial

quadrare, kwah-**drah**-ray, v., to square ; to agree ; to fit

quadrato, kwah-**drah**-to, m., square. a.,* square

quadrello, kwah-**drell**-lo, m., arrow ; cube ; tile

quadro, kwah-**dro**,m.,square ; picture ; (cards) diamonds. a., square

quaggiù, kwahd-**joo**, adv., here below

quaglia, kwah-l'yah, f., quail

quagliare, kwah-l'yah-ray, v., to curdle

qualche, **kwahl**-kay, pron., some ; any. —**volta**, sometimes

qualcheduno [or qualcuno], kwahl-kay-**doo**-no, pron., someone

qualcosa, kwahl-**ko**-zah, f., something

quale, **kwah**-lay, pron., which ; who ; what

qualificare, kwah-le-fe-kah-ray, v., to qualify

qualità, kwah-le-**tah**, f., quality, kind

qualmente, kwahl-**men**-tay, adv., how, as

qualora, kwah-**lor**-ah, adv., whenever

qual-sia [or -siasi], kwahl-**see**-ah, } pron., —
qual-sisia [or -sivoglia], kwahl-se-see-ah, } whatever, whatsoever

qualunque, kwah-**loonn**-kway. pron., what ; whatever

quando, kwahn-do, adv., when ; if [time that

quandochè, kwahn-do-**kay**, adv., as soon as, any

quantità, kwahn-te-tah, f., quantity

quanto, kwahn-to, adv., how much ; **how long** ;
  with regard to ; as for

quantochè, kwahn-to-**kay**, conj., as much as

quantunque, kwahn-**toonn**-kway, conj., though ;
  although

quaranta, kwah-**rahn**-tah, a., forty

quarantena, kwah-rahn-**tay**-nah, f., quarantine

quarantesimo, kwah-rahn-tay-ze-mo, a., fortieth

quaresima, kwah-**ray**-ze-mah, f., Lent

quartiere, kwahr-te'**ay**-ray, m., quarter ; lodging

quarto, kwahr-to, m., fourth ; quarter ; quart.
  a., fourth

quarzo, kwahr-tso, m., quartz

quasi, kwah-ze, adv., almost. **— che,** as if

quassù, kwahss-**soo**, adv., up here

quatto, kwaht-to, a., stealthily, softly. **se ne
  andò quatto quatto,** he took French leave

quattordici, kwaht-**tor**-de-che, a., fourteen

quattordicinale, kwaht-tor-de-che-nah-lay, a. &
  adv., fortnightly

quattrino, kwaht-**tree**-no, m., farthing

quattro, kwaht-tro, a., four

quegli, kway-l'ye, pron., he ; they ; that ; **those**

quei, kway-e, pron., they ; those

quercia, kwayr-chah, f., oak

querela, kway-**ray**-lah, f., complaint

querelante, kway-ray-**lahn**-tay, m. & f., **plaintiff.**
  a., querulous

querelare, kway-ray-lah-ray, v., to take proceedings

querelato, kway-ray-**lah**-to, m., defendant. a., accused

quesito, kway-**zee**-to, m., problem

questi, kwess-te, pron., he ; the latter   [tions

questionario, kwess-te'o-**nah**-re'o, m., list of ques-

questione, kwess-te'o-**nay**, f., quarrel ; question ;
  law-suit

questo, kwess-to, a. & pron., this

questore, kwess-**tor**-ay, m., **commissioner of police**

questura, kwess-**too**-rah, f., police-station

questurino, kwess-too-ree-no, m., policeman
quetare [or **quietare**], kway-tah-ray, v., to quiet; to appease
qui, kwee. adv., here. **di — a pochi giorni**, in a few days
quibus, kwee-booss, m., (pop.) money [tance
quietanza, kwe'ay-tahn-tsah, f., receipt; acquit-
quiete, kwe'ay-tay, f., quiet; stillness
quieto°, kwe'ay-to, a., quiet, tranquil
quinci, kwin-che, adv., hence
quindi, kwin-de, adv., hence; therefore
quindici, kwin-de-che, a., fifteen
quindicina, kwin-de-chee-nah, f., fortnight
quindicinale, kwin-de-che-nah-lay, a. & adv., (see **quattordicinale**)
quinta, kwin-tah, f., (mus.) fifth; (fig.) secretly
quintale, kwin-tah-lay, m., (metric) approximately two hundredweight
quinto, kwin-to, a., fifth
quivi, kwee-ve, adv., there
quota, kwo-tah, f., share, allotment, **quota**
quotare, kwo-tah-ray, v., to quote
quotidiano°, kwo-te-de'ah-no, a., daily

rabarbaro, rah-bar-bah-ro, m., rhubarb
rabbia, rahb-be'ah, f., hydrophobia; mania; fury
rabbino, rahb-bee-no, m., rabbi
rabbioso°, rahb-be'o-so, a., rabid; mad; angry
rabbonacciare, rahb-bo-naht-chah-ray, v., to lull
rabbonire, rahb-bo-nee-ray, v., to reconcile; to pacify
rabbrividire, rahb-bre-ve-dee-ray, v., to shudder
rabbuffamento, rahb-boof-fah-men-to, m., confusion, disorder
rabbuffo, rahb-boof-fo, m., rebuke
rabbuiare, rahb-boo-e'ah-ray, v., to darken
raccapezzare, rahk-kah-pet-tsah-ray, v., to find out by diligence
raccapitolare, rahk-kah-pe-to-lah-ray, v., to recapitulate; to repeat
raccapricciare, rahk-kah-prit-chah-ray, v., to tremble with fear; to be horrified

raccattare, rahk-kaht-tah-ray, v., to pick up

racchetare, rahk-kay-tah-ray, v., to tranquillize

racchetta, rahk-ket-tah, f., racket

raccogliere, rahk-ko-l'ye'ay-ray, v., to gather

raccoglitore, rahk ko-l'ye-tor-ay, m., collector

raccolta, rahk-koll-tah, f., collection; harvest

raccomandare, rahk-ko-mahn-dah-ray, v., to re-commend. — **una lettera**, to register a letter

raccomodare, rahk-ko-mo-dah-ray, v., to mend

raccontare, rahk-kon-tah-ray, v., to narrate

racconto, rahk-kon-to, m., story; account

raccorciare, rahk-kor-chah-ray, v., to shorten

raccordare, rahk-kor-dah-ray, v., to connect

raccordo, rahk-kor-do, m., connection

raccostare, rahk-ko-stah-ray, v., to bring near

rachitico, rah-kee-te-ko, a., rickety

rachitide, rah-kee-te-day, f., rickets

rada, rah-dah, f., (maritime) roadstead

radazza, rah-daht-tsah, f., mop

raddolare, rahd-do-lah-ray, v., (naut.) to repair

raddolcire, rahd-doll-chee-ray, v., to sweeten; to soften

raddoppiare, rahd-dop-pe'ah-ray, v., to redouble; to repeat

raddormentarsi, rahd-dor-men-tar-se, v., to fall asleep again

raddrizzare, rahd-drit-tsah-ray, v., to straighten

radere, rah-day-ray, v., to shave

radiante, rah-de'ahn-tay, a., radiant

radiare, rah-de'ah-ray, v., to erase; to radiate

radiatore, rah-de'ah-tor-ay, m., radiator

radica, rah-de-kah, f., briar

radicale, rah-de-kah-lay, a., radical, principal

radicare, rah-de-kah-ray, v., to take root

radice, rah-dee-chay, f., root

radio, rah-de'o, f., wireless-set. m., radium

radiogramma, rah-de'o-grahm-mah, m., radio-gram

radiotelegrafia, rah-de'o-tay-lay-grah-fee-ah, f., wireless-telegraphy

rado°, rah-do, a., sparse; thin. **di—**, rarely

radunanza, rah-doo-nahn-tsah, f., assembly

radunare, rah-doo-nah-ray, v., to assemble

raduno, rah-doo-no, m., assembly ; meeting ; appointment

radura, rah-doo-rah,f.,grass covered way in a wood

rafano, rah-fah-no, m., horse-radish

raffazzonare, rahf-faht-tso-nah-ray, v., to re-shape, to refashion

rafferma, rahf-fair-mah, f., confirmation ; re-enlistment

raffermare, rahf-fair-mah-ray, v., to confirm ; to strengthen ; to ratify

raffermo, rahf-fair-mo, a., confirmed ; stale

raffica, rahf-fe-kah, f., squall

raffigurare, rahf-fe-goo-rah-ray, v., to recognize

raffilare, rahf-fe-lah-ray, v., to sharpen ; to clip

raffinamento, rahf-fe-nah-men-to, m., refinement

raffinare, rahf-fe-nah-ray, v., to refine

rafforzare, rahf-for-tsah-ray, v., to re-inforce

raffreddare, rahf-fraid-dah-ray, v., to cool

raffreddore, rahf-fraid-dor-ay, m., cold

raffrenare, rahf-fray-nah-ray, v., to refrain

raffronto, rahf-fron-to, m., comparison

ragazza, rah-gaht-tsah, f., girl, maid

ragazzo, rah-gaht-tso, m., boy, lad

ragghiare, rahg-ghe'ah-ray, v., to bray

raggiante, rahd-jahn-tay, a., shining

raggiare, rahd-jah-ray, v., to radiate, to beam

raggio, rahd-jo, m., ray ; radius ; spoke

raggiramento, rahd-je-rah-men-to, m., winding ; (fig.) subterfuge

raggiro, rahd-jee-ro, m., trick ; subterfuge

raggiungere, rahd-djoonn-jay-ray, v., to overtake ; (fig.) to attain

raggiustare, rahd-joo-stah-ray, v., to re-adjust

raggomitolare, rahg-go-me-to-lah-ray, v., to agglomerate, to coil

raggranellare, rahg-grah-nell-lah-ray, v.,to glean, to put together bit by bit ; to heap up

ragguagliare, rahg-goo'ah-l'yah-ray, v., to level ; to equalize ; to inform minutely

ragguardevole, rahg-goo'ar-day-vo-lay, a., considerable ; remarkable

ragia, rah-jah, f., resin ; (fig.) fraud
ragionamento, rah-jo-nah-men-to, m., reasoning
ragionare, rah-jo-nah-ray, v., to reason ; to argue
ragione, rah-jo-nay, f., reason ; rate ; firm ; right
ragioneria, rah-jo-nay-ree-ah, f., accountancy
ragionevole, rah-jo-nay-vo-lay, a., reasonable
ragioniere, rah-jo-ne'ay-ray, m., accountant
ragliare, rah-l'yah-ray, v., to bray
ragna, rah-n'yah, f., spider's web ; (fig.) snare
ragnatela[lo], rah-n'yah-tay-lah, f.[m.], cobweb,
spider's web
ragno, rah-n'yo, m., spider
rallargamento, rahl-lar-gah-men-to, m., enlarg-
ing ; dilation
rallegrare,rahl-lay-grah-ray,v.,to rejoice; to divert
rallentare, rahl-len-tah-ray, v., to slow down
rallungare, rahl-loonn-gah-ray, v., to lengthen
ramaiolo, ramaiuolo, (see romaiolo)
ramanzina, rah-mahn-tsee-nah, f., reprimand
rame, rah-may, m., copper
ramificare, rah-me-fe-kah-ray, v., to ramify
rammarico, rahm-mah-re-ko, m., grief [to amass
rammassare, rahm-mahss-sah-ray, v., to gather ;
rammendare, rahm-men-dah-ray, v., to repair,
to mend
rammentare, rahm-men-tah-ray, v., to remind
rammollire, rahm-moll-lee-ray, v., to soften
ramo, rah-mo, m., branch, bough
ramolaccio, rah-mo-laht-cho, m., horse-radish
ramoscello, rah-mo-shell-lo, m., twig   [ber
rampicare, rahm-pe-kah-ray, v., to climb, to clam-
rampino, rahm-pee-no, m., hook
rampogna, rahm-po-n'yah, f., reproach, rebuke
rampognare, rahm-po-n'yah-ray, v., to reproach,
to rebuke
rampollo, rahm-poll-lo,m.,offspring ; young shoot
rampone, rahm-po-nay, m., harpoon
rana, rah-nah, f., frog   [ness
rancidezza, rahn-che-det-tsah, f., rancidity, rank-
rancido°, rahn-che-do, a., rancid, sour, musty
rancore, rahn-kor-ay, m., rancour ; grudge
randagio, rahn-dah-jo, m., wanderer. a., stray

randello, rahn-dell-lo, m., cudgel

rango, rahn-go, m., rank ; degree

rannicchiarsi, rahn-nick-ke'ar-se, v., to crouch, to cower

rannuvolare, rahn-noo-vo-lah-ray, v., to cloud ; to sadden

ranocchio[a], rah-nock-ke'o, m.[f.], small frog

rantolo, rahn-to-lo, m., (death) rattle

rapa, rah-pah, f., turnip ; blockhead

rapace, rah-pah-chay, a., rapacious

rapido[*], rah-pe-do, a., rapid, swift

rapimento, rah-pe-men-to, m., rape ; rapture

rapina, rah-pee-nah, f., robbery ; prey

rapire, rah-pee-ray, v., to rape ; to kidnap ; to charm

rappezzare, rahp-pet-tsah-ray, v., to patch up ; to arrange

rappiccinire, rahp-pit-che-nee-ray, v., to belittle ; to lessen

rapportare, rahp-por-tah-ray, v., to report ; to transfer

rapporto, rahp-por-to, m., report ; connection ; record

rappresaglia, rahp-pray-zah-l'yah, f., reprisals

rappresentante, rahp-pray-sen-tahn-tay, m., agent

rappresentare, rahp-pray-sen-tah-ray, v., to represent ; to act

rappresentazione, rahp-pray-sen-tah-tse'o-nay, f., performance

rarità, rah-re-tah, f., rarity ; curios

raro[*], rah-ro, a., rare

raschiare, rahss-ke'ah-ray, v., to scrape ; to scratch

raschiatura, rahss-ke'ah-too-rah, f., scraping ; scratch

rasentare, rah-zen-tah-ray, v., to graze ; to touch

rasente, rah-zen-tay, a., close to

raso, rah-zo, m., satin. a., shaved ; bare

rasoio, rah-zo-e'o, m., razor. — **di sicurezza**, safety-razor

raspa, rahss-pah, f., rasp

raspare, rahss-pah-ray, v., to rasp ; to rake

rassegna, rahss-say-n'yah, f., muster ; review

rassegnare, rahss-say-n'yah-ray, v., to resign ; to give up

rassegnazione, rahss-say-n'yah-tse'O-nay, f., resignation

rasserenare, rahss-say-ray-nah-ray, v., to clear up

rassettare, rahss-set-tah-ray, v., to adjust ; to tidy

rassicurare, rahss-se-koo-rah-ray, v., to re-assure

rassodare, rahss-so-dah-ray, v., to harden ; to strengthen

rassomiglianza, rahss-so-me-l'yahn-tsah, f., resemblance

rassomigliare, rahss-so-me-l'yah-ray, v., to resemble

rastrellare, rahss-trell-lah-ray, v., to rake [rack

rastrelliera, rahss-trell-le'ay-rah, f., rack

rastrello, rahss-trell-lo, m., rake

rata, rah-tah, f., rate ; instalment ; portion

ratificare, rah-te-fe-kah-ray, v., to ratify

rattacconare, raht-tahck-ko-nah-ray, v., to re-heel

rattemperare, raht-tem-pay-rah-ray, v., to mitigate

rattenere, raht-tay-nay-ray, v., to detain ; to restrain ; to recollect

rattizzare, raht-tit-tsah-ray, v., to poke the fire ; to excite

ratto, raht-to, m., rat ; rape

rattoppare, raht-top-pah-ray, v., to patch ; to mend ; to cobble

rattrappirsi, raht-trahp-peer-se, v., to shrink up ; to shrivel

rattristare, raht-triss-tah-ray, v., to grieve ; to afflict

raucedine, rah'oo-chay-de-nay, f., hoarseness

rauco*, rah'oo-ko, a., hoarse ; raucous

ravanello, rah-vah-nell-lo, m., radish

ravvedersi, rahv-vay-dair-se, v., to repent

ravviare, rahv-ve'ah-ray, v., to set or to straighten things again ; (hair) to tidy

ravvicinare, rahv-ve-che-nah-ray, v., to draw or bring near again ; (friendships, etc.) to tighten

ravvisare, rahv-ve-zah-ray, v., to recognize

ravvivamento, rahv-ve-vah-men-to, m., revival

ravvivare, rahv-ve-vah-ray, v., to revive

ravvolgere, rahv-vohl-jay-ray, v., to wrap up ; to involve

raziocinio, rah-tse'o-che-ne'o, m., reasoning power

razza, raht-tsah, f., race ; kind ; (fish) skate

razzia, raht-tsee-ah, f., raid

razzo, raht-tso, m., rocket ; ray ; spoke

razzolare, raht-tso-lah-ray, v., to scratch

re, ray, m., king ; (mus.) D

reagire, ray-ah-jee-ray, v., to react

reale, ray-ah-lay, a., royal ; real

realista, ray-ah-leess-tah, m. & f., royalist

realizzare, ray-ah-lid-dzah-ray, v., to realize

realtà, ray-ahl-tah, f., reality, truth, fact

reame, ray-ah-may, m., realm

reato, ray-ah-to, m., crime ; fault ; offence

reazione, ray-ah-tse'o-nay, f., reaction

recapitare, recapito, recapitolazione, (see under **ri . . .**)

recare, ray-kah-ray, v., to bring ; to cause ; to as-

recarsi, ray-kar-se, v., to betake oneself [cribe

recedere, ray-chay-day-ray, v., to recede ; to retire

recente, ray-chen-tay, a., recent, new

recere, ray-chay-ray, v., to vomit

recesso, ray-chess-so, m., recess

recezione, ray-chay-tse'o-nay, f., reception

recidere, ray-chee-day-ray, v., to cut off, to ampu-

recidiva, ray-che-dee-vah, f., relapse [tate

recinto, ray-chin-to, m., enclosure

recipe, ray-che-pay, m., recipe ; prescription

recipiente, ray-che-pe'en-tay, m., receptacle, container. a., capable

reciprocare, ray-che-pro-kah-ray, v., to reciprocate

reciproco*, ray-chee-pro-ko, a., mutual

recita, ray-che-tah, f., performance ; recitation

recitare, ray-che-tah-ray, v., to recite ; to perform

reclamare, ray-klah-mah-ray, v., to claim

reclamo, ray-klah-mo, m., claim

reclinare, ray-kle-nah-ray, v., to recline, to lean

reclusione, ray-kloo-ze'o-nay, f., penal servitude

recluso, ray-kloo-zo, m., convict

recluta, ray-kloo-tah, f., recruit ; recruiting

reclutare, ray-kloo-tah-ray, v., to recruit

recognizione, (see ricognizione)

recondito, ray-**kon**-de-to, a., hidden, recondite

recriminare, ray-kre-me-**nah**-ray, v., to recrim-
redattore, ray-daht-**tor**-ay, m., editor   [inate

redazione, ray-dah-tse'**o**-nay, f., newspaper-office ;
   wording

reddito, rayd-de-to, m., revenue, receipts

redenzione, ray-den-tse'**o**-nay, f., redemption

redificare, ray-de-fe-**kah**-ray, v., to rebuild

redigere, ray-**dee**-jay-ray, v., to edit ; to draw up

redimere, ray-**dee**-may-ray, v., to redeem

redine[a], ray-de-nay, f., rein

reduce, ray-**doo**-chay, a., returning. m., veteran

refe, ray-fay, m., thread

referire, (see riferire)

refezione, ray-fay-tse'**o**-nay, f., repast

refrattario, ray-fraht-tah-re'o, a., refractory,
   rebellious ; contrary ; stubborn

refrigerio, ray-fre-**jay**-re'o, m., consolation ; refreshment

regalare, ray-gah-**lah**-ray, v., to present ; to feast

regale, ray-**gah**-lay, a., royal

regalo, ray-**gah**-lo, m., present, gift

regenerare, (see rigenerare)

reggenza, red-**jen**-tsah, f., regency

reggere, red-jay-ray, v., to support ; to bear ;
   to prop ; to govern ; to hold out

reggia, red-jah, f., royal palace   [ment

reggimento, red-je-**men**-to, m., regiment ; govern-

regia, ray-**jee**-ah, f., excise ; state-monopoly

regime, ray-**jee**-may, m., government

regina, ray-**jee**-nah, f., queen

regione, ray-**jo**-nay, f., region ; county

registratore, ray-jiss-trah-**tor**-ay, m., registrar

registrazione [or **registratura**], ray-jiss-trah-
   tse'**o**-nay, f., recording in a book ; registration

registro, ray-**jiss**-tro, m., register

regnare, ray-n'**yah**-ray, v., to reign, to govern

regno, ray-n'yo, m., kingdom ; realm

regola, ray-go-lah, f., rule ; law ; statute

regolamento, ray-go-lah-**men**-to, m., regulation ;
   bye-law

regolare, ray-go-lah-ray, a., regular ; exact. v., **to**
   regulate : to govern ; to determine

reità, ray-e-tah, f., guilt ; crime

reiterare, ray-e-tay rah-ray, v., to reiterate

relativo*, ray-lah tee-vo, a., relative

relatore, ray-lah tor-ay, m., reporter   [report

relazione, ray-lah tse'o-nay, f., relation ; dealing ;

relegare, ray-lay-gah-ray, v., to relegate : to exile

relegazione, ray-lay-gah-tse'o-nay, f., banishment ;
   exile

religione, ray-le-jo-nay, f., religion ; worship

religioso[a], ray-le-jo-zo.a., pious. m., monk. f., nun

reliquia, ray-lee-kwe-ah, f., relic

reliquario, ray-le-kwe-ah-re'o, m., shrine for relics

remare, ray-mah-ray, v., to row

rematore, ray-mah-tor-ay, m., rower   [cence

reminiscenza, ray-me-ne-shen-tsah, f., reminis-

remissione, ray-miss-se'o-nay, f., release ; pardon ;

remo, ray-mo, m., oar   [mercy

rena, ray-nah, f., sand ; gravel

rendere, ren-day-ray, v., to render : to restore ; **to**
   produce

rendersi, ren-dair-se, v., to become ; to yield

rendita, ren-de-tah, f., rent ; revenue ; income ;

rene, ray-nay, m., kidney   [annuity

renitente, ray-ne-ten-tay, a., reluctant

renna, ren-nah, f., reindeer

renoso, ray-no-zo, a., sandy

reo, ray-o, m., culprit

reparto, ray-par-to, m., section ; unit

repellere, ray-pell-lay-ray, v., to repel ; **to repulse**

repentaglio, ray-pen-tah-l'yo, m., peril ; risk

repente, ray-pen-tay, a., sudden. **di —**, **suddenly**

repentino*, ray-pen-tee-no, a., sudden

reperibile, ray-pay-ree-be-lay, a., discoverable

repertorio, ray-pair tor-e'o, m., repertory ; index

replica, ray-ple-kah, f., reply ; retort

replicare, ray-ple-kah-ray, v., to reply ; to retort

reprimere, ray-pree-may-ray, v., to repress, to check

reprobo, ray-pro-bo, m., reprobate. a., dissolute

repudiare, ray-poo-de'ah-ray, v., to repudiate

repulsore, ray-pooll-sor-ay, m., buffer

reputare, ray-poo-tah-ray, v., to repute ; to consider

reputazione, ray-poo-tah-tse'O-nay, f., reputation. [fame

requie, ray-kwe-ay, f., peace, repose

requisito, ray-kwe-zee-to, m., requisite

resa, ray-zah, f., surrender

rescindere, ray-sheen-day-ray, v., to rescind

rescissione, ray-shiss-se'O-nay, f., rescission

rescritto, ray-skreet-to, m., edict, decree

reseda, ray-zay-dah, f., mignonette

reservare, ray-zair-vah-ray, v., to reserve

residente, ray-ze-den-tay, m. & f., resident

residuo, ray-zee-doo-o, m., residue. a., left over

resina, ray-ze-nah, f., resin [sition

resistenza, ray-ziss-ten-tsah, f., resistance ; oppo-

resistere, ray-ziss-tay-ray, v., to resist ; to oppose

resoconto, ray-zo-kon-to, m., report ; account ren-

respingere, ress-peen-jay-ray, v., to repel [dered

respirare, ress-pe-rah-ray, v., to breathe

respiro, ress-pee-ro, m., breath ; respite

ressa, ress-sah, f., throng

resta, ress-tah, f., fish-bone ; string of onions

restare, ress-tah-ray, v., to remain [repair

restaurare, ress-tah'oo-rah-ray, v., to restore ; to

restituire, ress-te-too'ee-ray, v., to give back

restituzione, ress-te-too-tse'O-nay, f., restitution

resto, ress-to, m., residue ; remainder ; (small money) change

restringere, ress-trin-jay-ray, v., to restrain ; to narrow

restrittivo*, ress-treet-tee-vo, a., restrictive [tion

restrizione, ress-tre-tse'O-nay, f., restriction ; limita-

retaggio, ray-tahd-jo, m., inheritance

retata, ray-tah-tah, f., (fish) haul ; (police) raid

rete, ray-tay, f., net ; network ; trap

retenzione, (see ritenzione)

reticella, ray-te-chell-lah, f., hair-net

reticente, ray-te-chen-tay, a., reticent

reticolato, ray-te-ko-lah-to, m., wire-paling ; barbed wire fence

retina, ray-tee-nah, f., retina ; gas-mantle

retribuire, ray-tre-boo'e-ray, v., to repay, to recompense

retro, ray-tro, a. & adv., back, behind ; afterwards. m., posterior

retrocarica, ray-tro-kah-re-kah, f., breech-loading

retrocedere, ray-tro-chay-day-ray, v., to go back ; to retire ; to reduce to the ranks

retrogrado, ray-tro-grah-do, a., retrograde ; backward person

retroguardia, ray-tro-goo'ar-de'ah, f., rear-guard

retta, ret-tah, f., straight line ; (food) board

rettangolo, ret-tahn-go-lo, m., rectangle. a., rectangular

rettifica, ret-tee-fe-kah, f., rectification

rettile, ret-te-lay, m., reptile

retto, ret-to, m., rectum. a.,* straight ; upright

rettore, ret-tor-ay, m., rector

rettorica, ret-to-re-kah, f., rhetoric

reumatismo, ray'oo-mah-tiss-mo, m., rheumatism

reverberare, (see **riverberare**)

reverenza, ray-vay-ren-tsah, f., reverence ; curtsy

revisione, ray-ve-ze'o-nay, f., revision ; examination

revisore, ray-ve-zor-ay, m., reviser ; censor. — di conti, auditor

revocare, ray-vo-kah-ray, v., to revoke

riabilitazione, re'ah-be-le-tah-tse'o-nay, f., rehabilitation

riaccostare, re'ahck-koss-tah-ray, v., to draw closer again

rialto, re'ahl-to, m., eminence. a., high

rialzare, re'ahl-tsah-ray, v., to raise again ; to lift

rialzista, re'ahl-tsiss-tah, m., (stock-exchange) bull

rialzo, re'ahl-tso, m., raising of prices ; prominence

riapparire, re'ahp-pah-ree-ray, v., to re-appear

riassumere, re'ahss-soo-may-ray, v., to resume ; to sum up

riaversi, re'ah-vair-se, v., to come to, to revive

ribadire, re-bah-dee-ray, v., to rivet ; to confirm

ribalta, re-bahl-tah, f., foot-light ; trap-door

ribalzare, re-bahl-tsah-ray, v., to rebound

ribalzo, re-bahl-tso, m., rebound ; jerk

ribassista, re-bahss-siss-tah, m., (on the stock-exchange) bear

ribasso, re-bahss-so, m., abatement ; rebate

ribattere, re-baht-tay-ray, v., to hit back again ; to disprove

ribellarsi, ré-bell-lar-se, v., to rebel

ribelle, re-bell-lay, a., rebellious. m. & f., rebel

ribellione, re-bell-le'o-nay, f., revolt

ribes, ree-bess, m., currant ; gooseberry

riboccare, re-bock-kah-ray, v., to overflow

ribollire, re-boll-lee-ray, v., to boil again (or up)

ribrezzo, re-bret-tso, m., repulsion ; shudder

ributtante, re-boot-tahn-tay, a., repulsive [back

ricacciare, re-kaht-chah-ray, v.,to repulse, to drive

ricaduta, re-kah-doo-tah, f., relapse

ricalcitrare, re-kahl-che-trah-ray, v., to be recalcitrant ; to be restive

ricamare, re-kah-mah-ray, v., to embroider

ricambiare, re-kahm-be'ah-ray, v., to reciprocate

ricambio, re-kahm-be'o, m., pezzi di —, spare

ricamo, re-kah-mo, m., embroidery [parts

ricapitare, re-kah-pe-tah-ray, v., to remit

ricapito, re-kah-pe-to, m.,address ; visiting-address

ricapitolare, re-kah-pe-to-lah-ray, v., to summarize ; to repeat

ricattare, re-kaht-tah-ray, v., to blackmail

ricavare, re-kah-vah-ray, v., to dig out ; to profit by

ricchezza, reek-ket-tsah, f., riches

riccio[lo], reet-cho, m.,curl ; hedgehog. a., curled

ricco*, reek-ko, a., rich ; fertile

ricerca, re-chair-kah, f., research, quest

ricercare, re-chair-kah-ray, v., to search ; to go in quest of

ricercato*, re-chair-kah-to, a.,in demand ; affected

ricetta, re-chet-tah, f., prescription ; recipe

ricettacolo,re-chet-tah-ko-lo,m.,receptacle ; niche

ricettare, re-chet-tah-ray, v., to receive ; to aid & abet to prescribe ; (stolen goods) to receive

ricettatore, re-chet-tah-tor-ay, m., (of stolen goods) receiver ; abettor

ricevere,re-chay-vay-ray,v.,to receive ; to entertain

ricevimento, re-chay-ve-men-to, m., reception

ricevitore, re-chay-ve-tor-ay, m., receiver

ricevuta, re-chay-voo-tah, f., receipt

ricezione, re-chay-tse'o-nay, f., reception

richiamare, re-ke'ah-mah-ray, v., to recall; to summon

richiamo, re-ke'ah-mo, m., call. uccello di —, decoy-bird

richiedere, re-ke'ay-day-ray, v., to request; to entreat; to ask again

richiesta, re-ke'ess-tah, f., request, demand

ricino, ree-che-no, m., ricinus; castor-oil [pense

ricompensare, re-kom-pen-sah-ray, v., to recom-

ricomprare, re-kom-prah-ray, v., to buy back; to redeem

riconciliare, re-kon-che-le'ah-ray, v., to reconcile

riconoscente, re-ko-no-shen-tay, a., grateful

riconoscenza, re-ko-no-shen-tsah, f., gratitude

riconoscere, re-ko-nO-shay-ray, v., to recognize

ricordanza, re-kor-dahn-tsah, f., recollection

ricordare, re-kor-dah-ray, v., to recollect

ricordo, re-kor-do, m., keepsake

ricorrente, re-kor-ren-tay, m. & f., petitioner

ricorrenza, re-kor-ren-tsah, f., repetition; anniversary

ricorrere, re-kor-ray-ray, v., to recur; to resort

ricorso, re-kor-so, m., appeal, claim

ricostituire, re-koss-te-too'ee-ray, v., to reconstitute

ricostruire, re-koss-troo'ee-ray, v., to reconstruct

ricotta, re-kot-tah, f., curd

ricoverare, re-ko-vay-rah-ray, v., to recover; to harbour

ricreare, re-kray-ah-ray, v., to recreate; to amuse

ricredere, re-kray-day-ray, v., to retract

ricucire, re-koo-chee-ray, v., to re-sew; to mend

ricuperare, re-koo-pay-rah-ray, v., to recover; to recuperate

ricupero, re-koo-pay-ro, m., recovery; salvage

ricurvo, re-koohr-vo, a., bent, curved

ricusare, re-koo-zah-ray, v., to refuse, to reject

ridere, ree-day-ray, v., to laugh

ridestare, re-day-stah-ray, v., to arouse again

ridicolo°, re-dee-ko-lo, a., ridiculous

ridotto, re-dot-to, m., redoubt; haunt

ridurre, re-doohr-ray, v., to reduce

riduzione, re-doo-tse'o-nay, f., reduction

riempiere, re'em-pe'ay-ray, v., to fill up; to replenish

riepilogare, re'ay-pe-lo-gah-ray, v., to abridge

riescire, re'ay-shee-ray, v., to succeed

rifacimento, re-fah-che-men-to, m., re-doing; re-building; compensation

rifare, re-fah-ray, v., to remake; to compensate

rifarsi, re-far-se, v., to restore one's losses or health

rifatto, re-faht-to, m., a new rich

riferimento, re-fay-re-men-to, m., reference

riferire, re-fay-ree-ray, v., to refer; to report

rifinire, re-fe-nee-ray, v., to finish off, to complete

rifiutare, re-fe'oo-tah-ray, v., to refuse

rifiuto, re-fe'oo-to, m., refusal; rubbish

riflessione, re-fless-se'o-nay, f., reflexion

riflettere, re-flet-tay-ray, v., to reflect

riflettore, re-flet-tor-ay, m., reflector; search-light

riflusso, re-flooss-so, m., ebb, reflux   [ments

rifocillare, re-fo-chill-lah-ray, v., to take refresh-

riforma, re-for-mah, f., reform

riformare, re-for-mah-ray, v., to reform; to declare unfit

rifornimento, re-for-ne-men-to, m., supply, pur-

rifreddi, re-fraid-de, m. pl., cold dishes   [veyance

rifuggire, re-food-jee-ray, v., to shrink from; to shirk

rifugio, re-foo-jo, m., refuge; shelter; dug-out

rifulgere, re-fooll-jay-ray, v., to shine

riga, ree-gah, f., line; stripe; ruler

rigagnolo, re-gah-n'yo-lo, m., streamlet; gutter

rigare, re-gah-ray, v., to rule; to draw

rigattiere, re-gaht-te'ay-ray, m., second-hand dealer

rigettare, re-jet-tah-ray, v., to reject; to vomit

rigetto, re-jet-to, m., refuse; refusal

rigidezza, re-je-det-tsah, f., rigidity; strictness

rigido*, ree-je-do, a., rigid; stern

rigirare, re-je-rah-ray, v., to turn about

rigoglioso*, re-go-l'yo-zo, a., flourishing; vigorous

rigonfiare, re-gon-fe'ah-ray, v., to swell up

rigore, re-go-ray, m., rigour; strictness

riguardare, re-goo'ar-dah-ray, v., to look upon; to examine

riguardo, re-goo'ar-do, m., regard ; care ; **respect**

riguardoso, re-goo'ar-do-zo, a., respectful

rigurgitare, re-goohr-je-tah-ray, v., to be **glutted** ; to overflow

rilasciare, re-lah-she'ah-ray, v., to let go ; to slacken ; to give

rilascio, re-lah-she'o, m., release ; consignment

rilassamento, re-lahss-sah-men-to, m., relaxation ; slackening

rilassare, re-lahss-sah-ray, v., to relax

rilegare, re-lay-gah-ray, v., to tie again ; to **relegate**

rilegatore, re-lay-gah-tor-ay, m., binder

rilento, re-len-to, adv., cautiously

rilevare, re-lay-vah-ray, v., to lift up ; to emphasize ; to relieve ; to sketch

rilucere, re-loo-chay-ray, v., to shine, to glitter

riluttante, re-loot-tahn-tay, a., reluctant

rima, ree-mah, f., rhyme

rimandare, re-mahn-dah-ray, v., to send back ; to discharge ; to emit

rimaneggiare, re-mah-ned-jah-ray, v., to handle again ; to adapt

rimanente, re-mah-nen-tay, m., remainder

rimanere, re-mah-nay-ray, v., to remain ; to abide

rimarchevole, re-mar-kay-vo-lay, a., remarkable

rimare, re-mah-ray, v., to rhyme

rimbalzare, reem-bahl-tsah-ray, v., to rebound

rimbeccare, reem-beck-kah-ray, v., to reply abrupt-

rimboccare, reem-bock-kah-ray, v., to turn up [ly

rimbombare, reem-bom-bah-ray, v., to roar ; to rumble

rimborsare, reem-bor-sah-ray, v., to reimburse

rimborso, reem-bor-so, m., reimbursement.
contro —, payment on delivery

rimediare, re-may-de'ah-ray, v., to remedy ; to cure

rimedio, re-may-de'o, m., remedy ; physic

rimembrare, re-mem-brah-ray, v., to remember

rimenare, re-may-nah-ray, v., to bring back ; to stir

rimescolare, re-mess-ko-lah-ray, v., to shake up ; to shuffle ; to blend

✝messa, re-mess-sah, f., remittance ; pardon ; ~oach-house. **auto —,** garage

rimettere, re-met-tay-ray, v., to replace; to remit; to pardon; to postpone

rimettersi, re-met-tair-se, v., to get well again; (weather) to get fine again

rimonta, re-mon-tah, f., repairing; (mil.) remount

rimondare, re-mon-dah-ray, v., to prune

rimorchiare, re-mor-ke'ah-ray, v., to tow

rimorchiatore, re-mor-ke'ah-tor-ay, m., tug

rimorso, re-mor-so, m., remorse

rimostranza, re-moss-trahn-tsah, f., expostulation

rimostrare, re-moss-trah-ray, v., to remonstrate

rimpatriare, reem-pah-tre-ah-ray, v., to repatriate

rimpetto, reem-pet-to, prep., opposite

rimpiangere, reem-pe'ahn-jay-ray, v., to lament; to regret

rimpianto, reem-pe'ahn-to, m., sorrow

rimpiazzare, reem-pe'aht-tsah-ray, v., to replace

rimproverare, reem-pro-vay-rah-ray, v., to reprove

rimprovero, reem-pro-vay-ro, m., reproach, reprimand

rimunerare, re-moo-nay-rah-ray, v., to remunerate

rimuovere, re-moo'o-vay-ray, v., to remove

rinascenza [or **rinascimento**], re-nah-shen-tsah, f., revival; rebirth

rincalzare, reen-kahl-tsah-ray, v., to tuck up; to be on the heels of; to earth up

rincarare, reen-kah-rah-ray, v., to make dearer

rinchiudere, reen-ke'oo-day-ray, v., to enclose; to shut in

rinchiuso, reen-ke'oo-zo, a., locked in; enclosed

rincontrare, reen-kon-trah-ray, v., to meet; to come across

rincontro, reen-kon-tro, m., meeting. **di —**, opposite

rincrescere, reen-kray-shay-ray, v., to be sorry

rinculare, reen-koo-lah-ray, v., to recoil

rinfacciare, reen-faht-chah-ray, v., to reproach

rinforzare, reen-for-tsah-ray, v., to reinforce; to strengthen

rinfrancare, reen-frahn-kah-ray, v., to fortify

rinfrescare, reen-fress-kah-ray, v., to cool; refresh

rinfresco, reen-**fress**-ko, m., refreshment
rinfusa, reen-**foo**-zah, adv., helter-skelter
ringalluzzirsi, reen-gahl-loot-**tseer**-se, v., (pop.) to put on airs
ringhiare, reen-ghe'**ah**-ray, v., to snarl, to growl
ringhiera, reen-ghe'**ay**-rah, f., pulpit ; railing
ringiovanire, reen-jo-vah-**nee**-ray, v., to rejuvenate
ringraziare, reen-grah-tse'**ah**-ray, v., to thank
rinnegare, reen-nay-**gah**-ray, v., to deny ; to reject
rinnegato, reen-nay-**gah**-to, m., renegade
rinnovabile, reen-no-**vah**-be-lay, a., renewable
rinnovamento, reen-no-vah-**men**-to, m., renewal ; rebirth
rinnovare, reen-no-**vah**-ray, v., to renovate
rinomanza, re-no-**mahn**-tsah, f., renown ; fame
rinsaldare, reen-sahl-**dah**-ray, v., to strengthen, to consolidate
rinserrare, reen-sair-**rah**-ray, v., to lock in ; to close
rintoccare, reen-tock-**kah**-ray, v., to toll   [up
rintocco, reen-**tock**-ko, m., tolling ; knell
rintracciare, reen-traht-**chah**-ray, v., to follow by tracks ; to look through the files, etc.
rintronare, reen-tro-**nah**-ray, v., to deafen [blunt
rintuzzare, reen-toot-**tsah**-ray, v., to repulse ; to
rinunzia, re-**noonn**-che'ah, f., renunciation
rinunziare, re-noonn-tse'**ah**-ray, v., to renounce ;

reen-vay-ne-**men**-to, m., find

-**nee**-ray, v., to find ; to come

v., to send back ; to dis-

rn ; postponement

v., to wrap up

canal

                                            [again

-ah-ray, v., to pacify

v., to pay again ; to re-

riparare, re-pah-**rah**-ray, v., to repair ; to remedy ; to shelter

riparo, re-**pah**-ro, m., shelter ; defence

ripartire, re-par-**tee**-ray, v., to leave again ; to allot

riparto, re-**par**-to, m., department ; apportionment

ripassare, re-pahss-**sah**-ray, v., to go over again ; to iron

ripensare, re-pen-**sah**-ray, v., to think over

riperc[u]otere, re-pair-ko-**tay**-ray, v., to echo, to repercuss

ripetere, re-**pay**-tay-ray, v., to repeat ; (study) to cram

ripetitore, re-pay-te-**tor**-ay, m., (crammer) coach

ripiano, re-pe-**ah**-no, m.,(staircase) landing ; terrace

ripido*, ree-pe-do, a., steep

ripiegare, re-pe-**ay**-**gah**-ray, v., to fold ; to retreat

ripiegarsi, re-pe-**ay**-**gar**-se, v., to bend ; to retreat

ripiego, re-pe-**ay**-go, m., expedient

ripieno, re-pe-**ay**-no, a.,* stuffed ; full. m., stuffing

ripigliare, re-pe-l'**yah**-ray, v., to retake ; to resume

riporre, re-**por**-ray, v., to replace ; to put away

riportare, re-por-**tah**-ray, v., to carry back ; to carry forward ; to report ; to win

riporto, re-**por**-to, m., amount brought forward

riposare, re-po-**zah**-ray, v., to replace ; to rest

riposo, re-**po**-zo, m., repose

ripostiglio, re-poss-**tee**-l'yo, m., recess

riprendere, re-**pren**-day-ray, v., to take back ; reprehend

ripresa, re-**pray**-zah, f., revival ; replay ; (sports) game or round

riprestinare, re-press-te-**nah**-ray, v., to to reinstate

riprodurre, re-pro-**doohr**-ray, v., to re to breed

riprova, re-**pro**-vah, f., rechecking ; e

riprovare, re-pro-**vah**-ray, v., to rep again

ripudiare, **riputare**, **riputazion**

ripugnare, re-poo-n'**yah**-ray, v., to

ripulsa, re-**pooll**-sah, f., repulse ;

risa, ree-zah, f.pl., laughing

risacca, re-zahck-kah, f., surf

risaia, re-zah-e'ah, f., rice-field

risalire, re-zah-lee-ray, v., to reclimb; **to go up** stream

risaltare, re-zahl-tah-ray, v., to rebound; to jut; to stand out

risalto, re-zahl-to, m., projection; jutting out

risanabile, re-sah-nah-be-lay, a., curable

risanamento, re-sah-nah-men-to, m., cure; slum-clearance

risanare, re-sah-nah-ray, v., to cure; (land) to reclaim

risaputo, re-sah-poo-to, m., common knowledge

risarcimento, re-zar-che-men-to, m., compensation

risarcire, re-zar-chee-ray, v., to indemnify; to restore

risata, re-zah-tah, f., laughter; derision [restore

riscaldamento, reess-kahl-dah-men-to, m., heating

riscaldare, reess-kahl-dah-ray, v., to warm

riscattare, reess-kaht-tah-ray, v., to redeem; to pay ransom

riscattatore, reess-kaht-tah-tor-ay, m., liberator

riscatto, reess-kaht-to, m., ransom; deliverance

rischiarare, reess-ke'ah-rah-ray, v., to clear; to illustrate

rischiare, reess-ke'ah-ray, v., to risk; to dare

rischio, reess-ke'o, m., risk, danger [some

rischioso°, reess-ke'o-zo, a., dangerous; venture-

risciacquare, re-she'ahck-kwah-ray, v., to rince

riscontrare, reess-kon-trah-ray, v., to compare; to answer; to audit

riscontro, reess-kon-tro, m., encounter; checking; answer

riscossa, reess-koss-sah, f., rescue, assistance

riscossione, reess-koss-se'o-nay, f., collection

riscuotere, reess-koo'o-tay-ray, v., to collect money; to reshake

riseccare, re-sayk-kah-ray, v., to dry up, to shrivel

risentimento, re-zen-te-men-to, m., resentment

risentire, re-zen-tee-ray, v., to feel; to resent

riserbo, re-zair-bo, m., reserve, discretion

riserva, re-zair-vah, f., reserve; reservation; guard

riservare, re-sair-vah-ray, v., to reserve

risibile, re-zee-be-lay, a., ludicrous

risico, ree-ze-ko, m., risk

risiedere, re-ze'ay-day-ray, v., to reside

risipola, re-zee-po-lah, m., erysipelas

risma, reess-mah, f., ream ; kind

riso, ree-zo, m., rice ; laughter

risolare, re-so-lah-ray, v., to resole

risoluto°, re-zo-loo-to, a., resolute

risolvere, re-soll-vay-ray, v., to resolve [solution

risolvimento, re-sol-ve-men-to, m., resolution ;

risonanza, re-so-nahn-tsah, f., resonance

risonare, re-so-nah-ray, v., to resound

risorgimento, re-zor-je-men-to, m., rebirth

risorsa, re-zor-sah, f., resource [save

risparmiare, reess-par-me'ah-ray, v., to spare ; to

risparmio, reess-par-me'o, m., saving ; savings

rispecchiare, reess-peck-ke'ah-ray, v., to mirror

rispettabile, reess-pet-tah-be-lay, a., respectable

rispettare, reess-pet-tah-ray, v., to respect

rispettoso°, reess-pet-to-zo, a., respectful

rispondere, reess-pon-day-ray, v., to respond

risposta, reess-poss-tah, f., reply ; parry & thrust

rissa, reess-sah, f., brawl

rissare, reess-sah-ray, v., to brawl

rissoso°, reess-so-zo, a., quarrelsome

ristabilire, reess-tah-be-lee-ray, v., to re-establish ;
to recover

ristagno, reess-tah-n'yo, m., stagnation ; stopping

ristampa, reess-tahm-pah, f., reprint

ristorare, reess-to-rah-ray, v., to restore

ristorazione, reess-to-rah-tse'o-nay, f., restoration

ristoro, reess-to-ro, m., comfort ; recreation ; refreshment

ristrettezza, reess-tret-tet-tsah, f., narrowness

ristretto°, reess-tret-to, a., restricted

ristringere, reess-trin-jay-ray, v., to restrict ; to

ristucco, reess-took-ko, (pop.) fed up [limit

risultare, re-zooll-tah-ray, v., to result ; to seem

risultato, re-zooll-tah-to, m., result

risvegliare, reess-vay-l'yah-ray, v., to awaken

risveglio, reess-vay-l'yo, m., awakening

ritagli, re-tah-l'ye. m. pl., scraps ; pieces

ritardare, re-tar-dah-ray, v., to retard

ritardatario, re-tar-dah-tah-re'o, m., late arrival ; straggler

ritardo, re-tar-do, m., delay

ritegno, re-tay-n'yo, m., self-control (or restraint)

ritemprare, re-tem-prah-ray, v., to retemper ; to strengthen

ritenere, re-tay-nay-ray, v., to retain ; to hinder

ritentare, re-ten-tah-ray, v., to attempt again

ritenuta, re-tay-noo-tah, f., stoppage

ritenuto*, re-tay-noo-to, a., retained, reserved

ritirare, re-te-rah-ray, v., to withdraw

ritirata, re-te-rah-tah, f., retreat ; W.C.

ritiro, re-tee-ro, m., retirement

ritmo, reet-mo, m., rythm

rito, ree-to, m., rite ; custom

ritoccare, re-tock-kah-ray, v., to retouch

ritorcere, re-tor-chay-ray, v., to retort ; to twist

ritornare, re-tor-nah-ray, v., to return [again

ritornello, re-tor-nell-lo, m., refrain

ritorno, re-tor-no, m., return

ritrarre, re-trar-ray, v., to draw back ; to depict

ritrarsi, re-trar-se, v., to retire ; to shelter

ritrattare, re-traht-tah-ray, v., to retract ; to depict ; to portray

ritratto, re-traht-to, m., portrait ; description

ritrosia, re-tro-zee-ah, f., prudery

ritroso*, re-tro-zo, a., wayward ; averse ; modest

ritrovare, re-tro-vah-ray, v., to recover ; to revisit ; to meet again

ritto*, rit-to, a., upright

riunire, re-oo-nee-ray, v., to reunite

riuscire, re-oo-shee-ray, v., to succeed

riuscita, re-oo-shee-tah, f., success

riva, ree-vah, f., bank ; sea-shore [compete

rivaleggiare, re-vah-led-jah-ray, v., to rival ; to

rivalersi, re-vah-lair-se, v., to recoup

rivalità, re-vah-le-tah, f., rivalry

rivangare, re-vahn-gah-ray, v., to dig up

rivedere, re-vay-day-ray, v., to see again ; to revise ; to review

rivelare, re-vay-lah-ray, v., to reveal

rivelazione, re-vay-lah-tse'o-nay, f., revelation

rivendere, re-ven-day-ray, v., to sell again

rivendicare, re-ven-de-kah-ray, v., to revendicate ; to revenge

rivendita, re-ven-de-tah, f., retail   [reflect

riverberare, re-vair-bay-rah-ray, v., (heat, etc.) to

riverenza, re-vay-ren-tsah, f., reverence

riverire, re-vay-ree-ray, v., to revere, to honour

riversare, re-vair-sah-ray, v., to overturn ; to pour out ; to reverse

riverso, re-vair-so, m., reverse ; reverse side ; ill-luck

rivestire, re-vess-tee-ray, v., to invest ; to dress again

rividibile, re-ve-dee-be-lay, a., temporarily unfit

riviera, re-ve'ay-rah, f., coast ; region bordering sea

rivincita, re-vin-che-tah, f., return game ; retali-

rivista, re-viss-tah, f., review   [ation

rivivere, re-vee-vay-ray, v., to revive

rivo, ree-vo, m., rivulet

rivolgere, re-voll-jay-ray, v., to revolve ; to ruminate ; to turn round

rivolta, re-voll-tah, f., revolt ; coat trimmings

rivoltare, re-voll-tah-ray, v., to turn over ; to revolt

rivoltella, re-voll-tell-lah, f., revolver

rivoltoso, re-voll-to-zo, a.,* riotous ; seditious. m., rioter ; rebel

rizzare, rit-tsah-ray, v., to put upright, to raise

roba, ro-bah, f., goods ; gown ; things ; stuff

robaccia, ro-baht-chah, f., rubbish ; rabble

robinetto, ro-be-net-to, m., tap

rocca, rock-kah, f., fortress ; reef

rocchetto, rock-ket-to, m., spool ; (eccl.) rochet

roccia, rot-chah, f., rock ; breakers

roccioso*, rot-cho-zo, a., rocky

roco*, ro-ko, a., hoarse

rodente, ro-den-tay, a.,gnawing ; biting. m., rodent

rodere, ro-day-ray, v., to gnaw ; to fret ; to eat

rodomonte, ro-do-mon-tay, m., bully   [away

rogare, ro-gah-ray, v., (legal) to draw up

rogatoria, ro-gah-tor-e'ah, f., (law) enquiry

rogito, ro-je-to, m., (law) deed

rogna, ro-n'yah, f., scab ; mange ; itch

rognone, ro-n'**yo**-nay, m., kidney

rognoso², ro-n'**yo**-zo, a., scabby ; **mangy**

rogo, ro-go, m., pyre ; stake

romanza, ro-**mahn**-tsah, f., romance

romanzo, ro-**mahn**-tso, m., novel

rombare, rom-bah-ray, v., to rumble ; **to boom**

rombo, rom-bo, m., rumbling ; boom ; turbot

romitaggio, ro-me-**tahd**-jo, m., hermitage

romito, ro-**mee**-to, a., solitary ; secluded. m., hermit

rompere, rom-pay-ray, v., to break, to snap ; **to crush**

rompicapo, rom-pe-**kah**-po, m., nuisance ; puzzle

rompicollo, rom-pe-**koll**-lo, m., reckless person

rompinoci, rom-pe-**no**-che, m., nut-cracker

rompiscatole, rom-piss-**kah**-to-lay, m., **bore**

rompitesta, rom-pe-**tess**-tah, m., puzzle

ronda, ron-dah, f., patrol ; round, beat

rondine, ron-de-nay, f., swallow

rondone, ron-**do**-nay, m., martin

ronfare, ron-fah-ray, v., to snore

ronzare, ron-**dzah**-ray, v., to buzz, to hum, **to drone**

ronzino, ron-**dzee**-no, m., worn-out horse

ronzio, ron-**dzee**-o, m., buzzing, droning

rosa, ro-zah, f., rose.   a., pink

rosaio, ro-zah-e'o, m., rose-bush ; rose-tree

roseto, ro-**zay**-to, m., rose-garden

rosicchiare, ro-zick-ke'**ah**-ray, v., to nibble

rosmarino, ross-mah-**ree**-no, m., rosemary

rosolare, ro-zo-lah-ray, v., to roast crisply

rosolia, ro-zo-lee-ah, f., measles

rosolio, ro-zo-l'yo, m., fruit-syrup

rospo, ross-po, m., toad

rossastro, ross-**sahss**-tro, a., reddish

rossignuolo (see **usignuolo**)

rosso², ross-so, a., red. — **d'uovo,** yolk of the egg

rossore, ross-**sor**-ay, m., blush ; redness

rosticceria, ross-tit-chay-**ree**-ah, f., shop for having meats, etc., cooked

rosto, ross-to, m., roast

rostro, ross-tro, m., beak ; rostrum ; (naut.) ram

rotabile, ro-tah-be-lay, a., for car traffic

rotaia, ro-tah-e'ah, f., rail, railway-track

rotare, ro-tah-ray, v., to rotate; to turn

rotazione, ro-tah-tse'o-nay, f., rotation, revolution

rotella, ro-tell-lah, f., little wheel; knee-cap

rotolare, ro-to-lah-ray, v., to roll; to wallow

rotolo, ro-to-lo, m., roll; scroll

rotondo°, ro-ton-do, a., round, circular

rotta, rot-tah, f., rout; breach; route, via. **in — per**, bound for

rottami, rot-tah-me, m. pl., fragments; wreckage

rotto°, rot-to, p.p. & a., broken; tired

rottura, rot-too-rah, f., rupture; breakage; breach; fracture

rotula, ro-too-lah, f., knee-cap

roventare, ro-ven-tah-ray, v., to make red-hot

rovente, ro-ven-tay, a., red-hot; fiery

rovesciamento, ro-vay-she'ah-men-to, m., overthrow; upsetting; capsizing

rovesciare, ro-vay-she'ah-ray, v., to overthrow; to upset; to spill; to capsize; to reverse

rovescio°, ro-vay-she'o, m., reverse side; misfortune; downpour; overthrow

roveto, ro-vay-to, m., thorny shrub

rovina, ro-vee-nah, f., ruin; downfall; havoc

rovinare, ro-ve-nah-ray, v., to ruin; to lay waste

rovinoso°, ro-ve-no-zo, a., ruinous; devastating

rovistare, ro-viss-tah-ray, v., to rummage

rovo, ro-vo, m., bramble

rozza, rot-tsah, a., worn-out horse

rozzo°, rod-dzo, a., rough; rugged; uncouth

rubare, roo-bah-ray, v., to rob; to steal

ruberia, roo-bay-ree-ah, f., robbery; larceny

rubicondo°, roo-be-kon-do, a., ruddy, rubicund

rubinetto°, roo-be-net-to, m., tap

rubino, roo-bee-no, m., ruby

rude, roo-day, a., rude

ruderi, roo-day-re, m. pl., ruins

ruffiano, roo-fe'ah-no, m., procurer

ruga, roo-gah, f., wrinkle; ripple

ruggine, rood-je-nay, f., rust; blight; **(fig.)** feud

rugginoso°, rood-je-no-zo, a., rusty

ruggire, rood-jee-ray, v., to roar

ruggito, rood-jee-to, m., roar, roaring

rugiada, roo-jah-dah, f., dew

rugosità, roo-go-ze-tah, f., wrinkled state ; rough-[ness

rugoso°, roo-go-zo, a., wrinkled ; furrowed

rullare, rooll-lah-ray, v., to roll ; (drum) **to roll**

rullio, rooll-lee-o, m., rolling ; tossing

rullo, rooll-lo, m., roller ; roll ; ninepin

rum, room, m., rum

ruminare, roo-me-nah-ray, v., to ruminate ; to muse

rumore, roo-mor-ay, m., noise ; rumour

rumoreggiare, roo-mo-red jah-ray, v., to rumble

rumoroso°, roo-mor-o-zo, a., noisy

ruolo, roo'o-lo, m., roll ; list

ruota, roo'o-tah, f., wheel ; (fig.) **far la —, to court**

rupe, roo-pay, f., rock ; cliff

rurale, roo-rah-lay, a., rural

ruscello, roo-shell-lo, m., rivulet ; streamlet

russare, rooss-sah-ray, v., to snore

rustico, rooss-te-ko, a.,° rustic. m., peasant

rutilante, roo-te-lahn-tay, a., beaming, gleaming

ruttare, root-tah-ray, v., to belch

ruvidezza, roo-ve-det-tsah, f., coarseness

ruvido°, roo-ve-do, a., rough, rugged

ruzzolare, root-tso-lah-ray, v., to tumble down ; to roll over

ruzzoloni, root-tso-lo-ne, adv., rolling down (or over)

sabato, sah-bah-to, m., Saturday

sabaudo=savoiardo, sah-bah'oo-do, a., of Savoy

sabbia, sahb-be'ah, f., sand

sabbioso, sahb-be'o-zo, a., sandy

sacca, sahk kah, f., bag, wallet, satchel

saccente, saht-chen-tay, m. & f., would-be-wise person

saccheggiare, sahk-ked-jah-ray, v., to plunder

saccheggio, sahk-ked-jo, m., sack, plunder

sacchetto, sahk-ket to, m., small bag

sacco, sahk-ko, m., sack ; pillage

saccoccia, sahk-kot-chah, f., pocket

sacerdote, sah-chair-do-tay, m., priest

sacerdozio, sah-chair-do-tse'o, m., priesthood

sacramentare, sah-krah-men-tah-ray, v., to administer sacraments ; to swear

sacramento, sah-krah-**men**-to, m., sacrament holy communion. interj., damn !

sacrare, sah-**krah**-ray, v., to consecrate [suary

sacrario, sah-**krah**-re'o, m., sacristy, shrine, os-

sacrificare, sah-kre-fe-**kah**-ray, v., to sacrifice

sacripante, sah-kre-**pahn**-tay, m., blusterer

sacro°, **sah**-kro, a., sacred

saetta, sah-et-tah, f., arrow ; lightning

sagace, sah-**gah**-chay, a., keen, shrewd

saggezza, sahd-jet-tsah, f., wisdom

saggiare, sahd-**jah**-ray, v., to assay [a..° wise

saggio, **sahd**-jo, m., essay ; sample ; wise man.

sagoma, **sah**-go-mah, f., outline ; mould

sagra, **sah**-grah, f., religious festival

sagrestano, sah-gress-**tah**-no,m.,sacristan; **sexton**

sagrestia, sah-gress-**tee**-ah, f., sacristy

saia, sah-e'ah, f., serge

saio, sah-e'o, m., cassock

sala, **sah**-lah, f., hall ; drawing-room

salamoia, sah-lah-**mo**-e'ah, f., brine

salamelecchi, sah-lah-may-**leck**-ke, m.pl.,salaams

salare, sah-**lah**-ray, v., to salt. — **la scuola, to** play truant

salariato, sah-lah-re'**ah**-to, a., hired

salassare, sah-lahss-**sah**-ray, v., to bleed

salato°, sah-**lah**-to, a., salted ; dear ; painful

salcio, **sahl**-cho. m., willow

saldare, sahl-**dah**-ray, v., to solder ; to settle

saldatura, sahl-dah-**toohr**-ah, f., solder

saldezza, sahl-**det**-tsah, f., firmness

saldo, **sahl**-do, a.,° sound ; solid. m., **balance**

sale, sah-lay, m.,° salt ; (fig.) sense

salice, **sah**-le-chay, m., willow

saliera, sah-le'**ay**-rah, f., salt-cellar

salina, sah-**lee**-nah, f., salt-works

salire, sah-**lee**-ray, v., to ascend ; to climb

saliscendi, sah-le-**shen**-de, m., latch ; lift

salita, sah-**lee**-tah, f., ascent ; acclivity

salma, **sahl**-mah, f., corpse

salmastro, sahl-**mahss**-tro, a., saltish ; **swampy**

salmo, **sahl**-mo, m., psalm

salmone, sahl-**mo**-nay, m., salmon

salnitro, sahl-nee-tro, m., saltpetre
salone, sah-lo-nay, m., saloon
salotto, sah-lot-to, m., sitting-room
salpare, sahl-pah-ray, v., to weigh anchor
salsa, **sahl-sah**, f., sauce ; seasoning
salsiccia, sahl-sit-chah, f., sausage
salsiera, sahl-se'ay-rah, f., sauce-dish
saltare, sahl-tah-ray, v., to jump ; to dance
saltellare, sahl-tell-lah-ray, v., to gambol
salterello, sahl-tay-rell-lo, m., gambol, hop
saltimbanco, sahl-tim-bahn-ko, m., mountebank
salto, sahl-to, m., jump. — **mortale**, m., somersault
saltuariamente, sahl-too'ah-re'ah-men-tay, adv., occasionally
salumi, sah-loo-me, m. pl., salted meats, etc.
salumiere, sah-loo-me'ay-ray, m., pork-butcher
salutare, sah-loo-tah-ray, v., to salute. a., healthy
salute, sah-loo-tay, f., health ; safety. interj., hallo !
saluto, sah-loo-to, m., salute ; greeting
salva, **sahl-vah**, f., volley. —**danaio**, m., money-
salvagente, sahl-vah-jen-tay, m., life-belt [box
salvamento, sahl-vah-men-to, m., rescue
salvare, sahl-vah-ray, v., to rescue
salvatore, sahl-vah-tor-ay, m., Saviour ; **rescuer**
salve, sahl-vay, interj., hallo ! farewell !
salvezza, sahl-vet-tsah, f., safety
salvia, **sahl**-ve'ah, f., sage
salvietta, sahl-ve'et-tah, f., napkin
salvo, **sahl**-vo, a., safe ; excepting
sambuco, sahm-boo-ko, m., elder-tree
sampogna, sahm-po-n'yah, f., reed ; flageolet
san (for **santo**), sahn, a., saint
sanabile, sah-nah-be-lay, a., curable
sanare, sah-nah-ray, v., to heal
sangue, sahn-goo'ay, m., blood ; race [pudding
sanguinaccio, sahn-goo'e-naht-cho, m., black-
sanguinare, sahn-goo'e-nah-ray, v., to bleed
sanguisuga, sahn-goo'e-soo-gah, f., leech
sanità, sah-ne-tah, f., health ; salubrity
sano*, sah-no, a., healthy ; just
santarello, sahn-tah-rell-lo, m., little saint

santificare, sahn-te-fe-**kah**-ray, v., to sanctify

santissimo, sahn-**tiss**-se-mo. m., Holy Sacrament

santità, sahn-te-**tah**, f., sanctity

santo, **sahn**-to. a.,° holy. m., saint

santocchio, sahn-**tock**-ke'o. m., hypocrite

santolo[a], **sahn**-to-lo,m.[f.], god-father [mother]

sanzionare, sahn-tse'o-**nah**-ray, v., to sanction

sapere, sah-**pay**-ray, m., knowledge. v., to know; to smell

sapiente, sah-pe-**en**-tay, a., learned. m., sage

sapienza, sah-pe-**en**-tsah, f., wisdom

sapone, sah-**po**-nay, m., soap

saponetta, sah-po-**net**-tah, f., toilet-soap

sapore, sah-**por**-ay, m., savour

saporito°, sah-po-**ree**-to, a., savoury ; (fig.) saucy

sarchiare, sar-ke'**ah**-ray, v., to weed

sarchiatura, sar-ke'ah-**toohr**-ah, f., weeding

sarda, **sar**-dah, f., cornelian

sardella, sar-**dell**-lah, f., pilchard

sargia, **sar**-jah, f., serge

sariga, sah-**ree**-gah, f., opossum

sarta, **sar**-tah, f., dressmaker

sartiame, sar-te'**ah**-may, m., rigging

sarto, **sar**-to, m., tailor

sartoria, sar-to-**ree**-ah, f., tailor's shop

sasso, **sahss**-so, m., pebble ; rock

sassofono, sahss-**so**-fo-no, m., saxophone

sassoso, sahss-**so**-zo, a., stony

satirico°, sah-**tee**-re-ko, a., satirical

satollare, sah-**toll**-**lah**-ray, v., to satiate

sauro, **sah**'oo-ro, a., chestnut. m., horse

saviezza, sah-ve'**et**-tsah, f., wisdom

savio°, **sah**-ve'o, a., wise ; learned

saziare, sah-tse'**ah**-ray, v., to satiate

sazio°, **sah**-tse'o, a., satiated, full

sbaccellare, zbaht-chell-**lah**-ray, v., to shell

sbadato°, zbah-**dah**-to, a., careless

sbadigliare, zbah-de-l'**yah**-ray, v., to yawn   [der

sbagliare, zbah-l'**yah**-ray, v., to mistake ; to blun-

sballare, zbahl-**lah**-ray, v., to unpack ; to brag

sbalordire, zbah-lor-**dee**-ray, v., to astonish, to amaze

sbalzare, zbahl-**tsah**-ray, v., to overturn; to bounce

sbalzo, zbahl-tso, m., bound, leap

sbancare, zbahn-**kah**-ray, v., to beat the bank

sbandare, zbahn-dah-ray, v., to disband; to scatter

sbandire, zbahn-dee-ray, v., to banish

sbaragliare, zbah-rah-l'yah-ray, v., to rout

sbarazzare, zbah-raht-**tsah**-ray, v., to clear; to rid

sbarbarsi, zbar-bar-se, v., to shave

sbarbato, zbar-bah-to, a., without beard

sbarcare, zbar-**kah**-ray, v., to disembark

sbarcatoio, zbar-kah-to-e'o, m., landing-place

sbarco, zbar-ko, m., landing; unloading

sbarra, zbar-rah, f., bar; rail

sbarrare, zbar-rah-ray, v., to bar; to fasten

sbatacchiare, zbah-tahk-ke'ah-ray, v., to bang

sbattere, zbaht-tay-ray, v., to beat; to bang; to whisk

sbevazzare, zbay-vaht-**tsah**-ray, v., to tipple

sbiadire, zbe'ah-dee-ray, v., to fade

sbieco, zbe'ay-ko, a., aslant

sbigottire, zbe-got-tee-ray, v., to dismay

sbilancio, zbe-lahn-cho, m., deficit

sbilenco, zbe-len-ko, a., crooked

sbirciare, zbeer-chah-ray, v., to peep; to leer

sbirro, zbeer-ro, m., "cop"=policeman [wishes

sbizzarrirsi, zbeet-tsar-reer-se, v., to gratify one's

sboccare, zbock-kah-ray, v., to flow into; to over-

sboccato°, zbock-kah-to, a., foul-mouthed [flow

sbocciare, zbot-chah-ray, v., to open; to blossom

sbocco, zbock-ko, m., outlet; river-mouth

sbocconcellare, zbock-kon-chell-lah-ray, v., to

sbollire, zboll-lee-ray, v., to cool down [nibble

sbornia, zbor-ne'ah, f., drunkenness

sborsamento, zbor-zah-men-to, m., disbursement

sborsare, zbor-sah-ray, v., to disburse

sbottonare, zbot-to-nah-ray, v., to unbutton

sbozzare, zbot-tsah-ray, v., to sketch; to outline

sbraitare, zbrah'e-tah-ray, v., to vociferate

sbranare, zbrah-nah-ray, v., to tear to pieces

sbravazzare, zbrah-vaht-tsah-ray, v., to swagger

sbriciolare, zbre-cho-lah-ray, v., to crumble

sbrigare, zbre-**gah**-ray, v., to execute speedily

sbrigativo*, zbre-gah-tee-vo, a., expeditious

sbrogliare, zbro-l'yah-ray, v., to disentangle

sbruffare, zbroof-fah-ray, v., to besprinkle, to splash

sbucciare, zboot-chah-ray, v., to peel; to skin

sbudellare, zboo-del-lah-ray, v., to disembowel

sbuffare, zboof-fah-ray, v., to puff; to snort

scabro*, skah-bro, a., rough, wild

scabroso*, skah-bro-zo, a., rough; (fig.) delicate

scacchi, skahk-ke, m. pl., chess

scacchiera, skahk-ke'ay-rah, f., chess-board

scacciare, skaht-chah-ray, v., to drive out

scacco, skahk-ko, m., check

scadente, skah-den-tay, a., falling due

scadenza, skah-den-tsah, f., due date; expiry

scadere, skah-day-ray, v., to fall due

scafandro, skah-fahn-dro, m., diving-suit

scaffale, skahf-fah-lay, m., bookshelf

scafo, skah-fo, m., hulk, hull

scaglia, skah-l'yah, f., chip; (fish) scale

scagliare, skah-l'yah-ray, v., to hurl

scagliarsi, skah-l'yar-se, v., to attack

scaglione, skah-l'yo-nay, m., echelon

scala, skah-lah, f., stairs; ladder

scalare, skah-lah-ray, v., to escalade; to lower

scaldabagno, skahl-dah-bah-n'yo, m., geyser

scaldaletto, skahl-dah-let-to, m., bed-warmer

scaldare, skahl-dah-ray, v., to heat; to excite

scalino, skah-lee-no, m., step; rung

scalo, skah-lo, m., port of call

scalpello, skahl-pell-lo, m., scalpel; chisel

scalpitare, skahl-pe-tah-ray, v., to stamp

scalpore, skahl-por-ay, m., noise; fuss; ado

scaltro*, skahl-tro, a., cunning

scalzare, skahl-tsar-ay, v., to take off shoes

scalzo*, skahl-tso, a., barefooted   [mistake

scambiare, skahm-be'ah-ray, v., to exchange; to

scambio, skahm-be'o, m., exchange, barter

scampagnata, skahm-pah-n'yah-tah, f., country outing

scampanare, skahm-pah-nah-ray, v., to peal

scampanio, skahm-pah-nee-o, m., (bells) peal

scampare, skahm-pah-ray, v., to escape, to bolt

scampo, skahm-po, m., escape ; safety

scampolo, skahm-po-lo, m., remnant

scanalare, skah-nah-lah-ray, v., to flute [scratch

scancellare, skahn-chell-lah-ray, v., to erase ; to

scandagliare, skahn-dah-l'yah-ray, v., to sound

scandalizzare, skahn-dah-lid-dzah-ray, v., to scandalize

scannare, skahn-nah-ray, v., to slit the throat

scanno, skahn-no, m., chair ; pew ; bench

scansare, skahn-sah-ray, v., to shirk ; to shun

scapestrato, skah-pess-trah-to, m., scamp

scapito, skah-pe-to, m., detriment

scapola, skah-po-lah, f., shoulder-blade

scapolo, skah-po-lo, m., bachelor

scappare, skahp-pah-ray, v., to decamp

scappata, skahp-pah-tah, f., flight ; escapade

scappatoia, skahp-pah-to-e'ah, f., dodge

scappellarsi, skahp-pell-lar-se, v., to raise hat

scappellotto, skahp-pell-lot-to, m., smack on head

scarabocchiare, skah-rah-bock-ke'ah-ray, v., to scrawl

scarafaggio, skah-rah-fahd-jo, m., cockroach

scaramuccia, skah-rah-moot-chah, f., skirmish

scaraventare, skah-rah-ven-tah-ray, v., to hurl

scarcerare, skar-chay-rah-ray, v., to release from

scarica, skah-re-kah, f., volley ; discharge [prison

scaricare, skah-re-kah-ray, v., to discharge ; to

scarno*, skar-no, a., thin, wasted   [relieve

scarpa, skar-pah, f., shoe

scarso*, skar-so, a., short, lacking

scartafaccio, skar-tah-faht-cho, m., note-book

scartare, skar-tah-ray, v., to discard

scarto, skar-to, m., waste ; jerk

scartoccio, skar-tot-cho, m., paper-cornet

scassinare, skahss-se-nah-ray, v., to break open

scatenare, skah-tay-nah-ray, v., to unchain

scatola, skah-to-lah, f., box

scattare, skaht-tah-ray, v., to spring up ; to flare up

scaturire, skah-too-ree-ray, v., to gush

scavalcare, skah-too-vahl-kah-ray, v., to be thrown off a horse ; to jump over ; to skip

scavare, skah-vah-ray, v., to dig ; to hollow

scavo, skah-vo, m., excavation
scegliere, shay-l'yay-ray, v., to choose
scellerato*, shell-lay-rah-to, a., perfidious
scelta, shell-tah, f., choice ; option
scelto*, shell-to, a., chosen ; refined
scemare, shav-mah-ray, v., to lessen
scemo, shay-mo, a., simple-minded
scempio, shem-pe'o, m., simpleton ; **havoc**
scena, shay-nah, f., stage ; scenery
scenario, shay-nah-re'o, m., scenery ; decoration
scendere, shen-day-ray, v., to descend ; to alight
scendiletto, shen-de-let-to, m., bed-side rug
scernere, shair-nay-ray, v., to discern ; to choose
scesa, shay-zah, f., declivity
scettico, shet-te-ko, a.,* sceptical, m., sceptic
scettro, shet-tro, m., sceptre
sceverare, shay-vay-rah-ray, v., to sever
scevro, shay-vro, a., free from ...
scheda, skay-dah, f., slip of paper ; card
scheggia, sked-jah, f., splinter ; chip
scheggiare, sked-jah-ray, v., to chip ; to splinter
scheletro, skay-lay-tro, m., skeleton
schema, skay-mah, m., scheme ; plan
scherma, skair-mah, f., fencing
schermire, skair-mee-ray, v., to fence ; to avoid
schermo, skair-mo, m., screen
schernire, skair-nee-ray, v., to scorn ; to scoff at
scherno, skair-no, m., scorn ; sneer
scherzare, skair-tsah-ray, v., to joke ; to trifle with
scherzevole, skair-tsay-vo-lay, a., playful ; merry
scherzo, skair-tso, m., joke ; fun
schiaccianoci, ske'aht-chah-no-che, m., nut-cracker
schiacciare, ske'aht-chah-ray, v., to crush ; to humiliate
schiaffeggiare, ske'ahf-fed-jah-ray, v., to slap, to smack
schiaffo, ske'ahf-fo, m., box on the ear ; insult
schiamazzo, ske'ah-maht-tso, m., cackling racket
schiantare, ske'ahn-tah-ray, v., to rend ; to break up
schianto, ske'ahn-to, m., crash ; great sorrow
schiarire, ske'ah-ree-ray, v., to clear up
schiattare, ske'aht-tah-ray, v., to burst ; to explode

schiavitù, ske'ah-ve-too, f., slavery
schiavo, ske'ah-vo, m., slave. a., enslaved
schiena, ske'ay-nah, f., (body) back
schiera, ske'ay-rah, f., company ; rank and file
schierare, ske'ay-rah-ray, v., to array
schietto°, ske'et-to, a., frank, sincere ; pure
schifezza, ske-fet-tsah, f., filth ; loathing
schifiltà, ske-fill-tah, f., squeamishness
schifiltoso°, ske-fill-to-zo, a., difficult to please
schifo, **skee**-fo, m., loathing ; rowing-boat
schifoso°, ske-fo-zo, a., loathsome
schioccare, ske'ock-kah-ray, v., (sound) to crack
schioppo, ske'op-po, m., gun, shot-gun
schiudere, ske'oo-day-ray, v., to reveal ; to open
schiuma, ske'oo-mah, f., foam, froth ; scum
schiumare, ske'oo-mah-ray, v., to foam ; to skim
schivare, ske-vah-ray, v., to shun ; to despise
schivo°, **skee**-vo, a., reserved ; modest
schizzare, skit-tsah-ray, v., to pop out ; to
  sketch ; to gush
schizzettare, skit-tset-tah-ray, v., to syringe
schizzetto, skit-**tset**-to, m., syringe
schizzo, skit-tso, m., splash ; sketch
scia, she'ah, f., (ship's) wake
sciabola, she'ah-bo-lah, f., sabre
sciacallo, she'ah-kahl-lo, m., jackal
sciacquare, she'ahk-kwah-ray, v., to rinse ; to wash
sciagura, she'ah-goo-rah, f., misfortune, calamity
scialacquare, she'ah-lahk-**kwah**-ray, v., to
  squander
scialacquatore, she'ah-lahk-kwah-tor-ay, m.,
scialbo°, she'ahl-bo, a., sallow   [spendthrift
scialle, she'ahl-lay, m., shawl
scialuppa, she'ah-loop-pah, f., boat, launch
sciamare, she'ah-mah-ray, v., to swarm
sciame, she'ah-may, m., swarm ; (fig.) crowd
sciampagna, she'ahm-pah-n'yah, m., champagne
sciarpa, she'ar-pah, f., scarf
sciatica, she'ah-te-kah, f., sciatica
scibile, **shee**-be-lay, m., all-knowledge
sciente, she'en-tay, a., aware ; learned
scienza, she'en-tsah, f., science ; knowledge

scilinguare, she-lin-goo'ah-ray, v., to stammer
scimmia, shim-me'ah. f., monkey
scimmiottare, shim-me'ot-tah-ray, v., to ape
scimunito, she-moo-nee-to, a., silly
scindere, sheen-day-ray, v., to separate
scintillare, sheen-till-lah-ray, v., to scintillate
sciocchezza, she'ock-ket-tsah, f., stupidity
sciocco, she'ock-ko, a.,* stupid. m., fool
sciogliere, she'o-l'yay-ray, v., to untie; to set
free; to dissolve
scioglimento, she'o-l'ye-men-to, m., dissolution
sciolta, she'ol-tah, f., diarrhœa
sciolto*, she'ol-to, a., loose; nimble; melted
scioperare, she'o-pay-rah-ray, v., to strike
sciopero, she'o-pay-ro, m. strike
scipido*, shee-pe-do, a., insipid, dull, flat
sciroppo, she-rop-po, m., syrup
sciugare, she'oo-gah-ray, v., to dry
sciupare, she'oo-pah-ray, v., to waste, to spoil
sciupio, she'oo-pee-o, m., waste, dissipation
scivolare, she-vo-lah-ray, v., to slip; to slide
scoccare, skock-kah-ray, v., to shoot; to strike
scodella, sko-dell-lah, f., bowl
scoglio, sko-l'yo, m., reef, rock; cliff
scoiattolo, sko'e-aht-to-lo, m., squirrel
scolare, sko-lah-ray, v., to drain; to drip; to strain
scolaro (or **scolare**), sko-lah-ro, m., pupil
scolatoio, sko-lah-to-e'o, m., drain; sink; strainer
scolo, sko-lo, m., drain; flow; (med.) discharge
scolorire, sko-lo-ree-ray, v., to fade; to tarnish
scolpare, skoll-pah-ray, v., to excuse; to justify
scolpire, skoll-pee-ray, v., to carve; to engrave; to
scombro, **skom**-bro, m., mackerel [sculpture
scommessa, skom-mess-sah, f., wager; stake
scommettere, skom-met-tay-ray, v., to bet
scomodare, sko-mo-dah-ray, v., to trouble
scomodo, **sko**-mo-do, m., inconvenience; pain.
a.,* incommodious; troublesome
scomparire, skom-pah-ree-ray, v., to vanish [ing
scomparsa, skom-par-sah, f., disappearance; miss-
scompigliare, skom-pe-l'yah-ray, v., to upset; to
muddle

scompiglio, skom-pee-l'yo, m., disorder ; confusion

scomposto², skom-**poss**-to, a., unbecoming

scomunicare, sko-moo-ne-**kah**-ray, v., excommunicate

sconcertare, skon-chair-**tah**-ray, v., to disconcert

sconcerto, skon-**chair**-to, m., perturbation

sconcio, **skon**-cho, a., indecent ; unbecoming

sconfessare, skon-fess-**sah**-ray, v., to disavow

sconfiggere, skon-**fid**-jay-ray, v., to rout ; to discomfit

sconfinato, skon-fe-**nah**-to, a., without limits

sconfitta, skon-**fit**-tah, f., rout ; discomfiture

sconfortante, skon-for-**tahn**-tay, a., discomforting

sconforto, skon-**for**-to, m., discomfort [avoid

scongiurare, skon-joo-**rah**-ray, v., to beseech ; to

sconnesso², skon-**ness**-so, a., loose ; desultory

sconoscere, sko-**no**-shay-ray, v., to ignore ; to be ungrateful

sconosciuto², sko-no-**shoo**-to, a., unknown

sconquassare, skon-kwahss-**sah**-ray, v., to shatter

sconsigliare, skon-se-l'yah-ray, v., to dissuade

sconsigliato², skon-se-l'**yah**-to, a., rash

sconsolato², skon-so-**lah**-to, a., disconsolate

scontare, skon-**tah**-ray, v., to discount ; to expiate

scontentare, skon-ten-**tah**-ray, v., to displease

scontentezza, skon-ten-**tet**-tsah, f., discontent

sconto, **skon**-to, m., discount

scontrino, skon-**tree**-no, m., voucher

scontro, **skon**-tro, m., clash ; collision

scontroso, skon-**tro**-so, a., cantankerous

sconvenevole, skon-vay-**nay**-vo-lay, a., improper

sconvolgere, skon-**voll**-jay-ray, v., to convulse

scopa, **sko**-pah, f., broom ; birch

scopare, sko-**pah**-ray, v., to sweep

scoperta, sko-**pair**-tah, f., discovery ; disclosure

scoperto, sko-**pair**-to, m., open air. a.,² open

scopo, **sko**-po, m., object ; scope

scoppiare, skop-pe'**ah**-ray, v., to burst [rattle

scoppiettare, skop-pe'et-**tah**-ray, v., to crackle ; to

scoppio, **skop**-pe'o, m., explosion ; burst

scoprire, sko-**pree**-ray, v., to discover ; to unveil : to reveal

scoraggiamento, sko-rahd-jah-**men**-to, m., discouragement

scoraggiare, sko-rahd-**jah**-ray, v., to discourage

scorazzare, sko-raht-**tsah**-ray, v., to run about; [to raid

scorbuto, skor-**boo**-to, m., scurvy

scorciare, skor-**chah**-rav, v., to shorten

scorciatoia, skor-chah-to-e'ah, f., short-cut

scorgere, skor-**jay**-ray, v., to perceive

scoria, sko-re'ah, f., dross; slag   [fill

scorpacciata, skor-paht-**chah**-tah, f., filling one's

scorrere, skor-**ray**-ray, v., to glide; to flow; to glance over

scorreria, skor-ray-**ree**-ah, f., inroad; intrusion

scorretto°, skor-**ret**-to, a., faulty

scorrevolezza, skor-ray-vo-**let**-tsah, f., fluency; smooth running

scorribanda, skor-re-**bahn**-dah, f., incursion

scorsa, skor-sah, f., glaɔing over

scorso, skor-so, p.p., past

scorsoio, skor-so-e'o, a., nodo—, (noose) loop

scortare, skor-**tah**-ray, v., to escort

scortecciare, skor-tet-**chah**-ray, v., (strip) to bark

scortese, skor-**tay**-zay, a., impolite

scortesia, scortay-**zee**-ah, f., impoliteness

scorticare, shor-te-**kah**-ray, v., to skin

scorza, skor-tsah, f., bark; rind

scoscendere, sko-**shen**-day-ray, v., to break off [to slope

scosceso°, sko-**shay**-zo, a., steep; broken

scossa, skoss-sah, f., shake; jerk

scostare, skoss-**tah**-ray, v., to push aside

scostumatezza, skoss-too-mah-**tet**-tsah, f., licentiousness

scotennare, sko-ten-**nah**-ray, v., to scalp

scottare, skot-**tah**-ray, v., to scald; (fig.) to sting

scotto, skot-to, m., bill

scovare, sko-**vah**-ray, v., to ferret out

scranna, skrahn-nah, f., stool; bench

screanzato°, skray-ahn-**tsah**-to, a., ill-bred

screditare, skray-de-**tah**-ray, v., to discredit

screpolare, skray-po-**lah**-ray, v., to crack; to chap

screpolatura, skray-po-lah-**too**-rah, f., crevice

screziato, skray-tse'ah-to, a., variegated

scribacchiare, skre-bahk-ke'ah-ray, v., to scribble

scricchiolare, skrik-ke'o-lah-ray, v., to creak

scricciolo, **skrit**-cho-lo, m., wren

scrigno, **skree**-n'yo, m., safe ; casket

scriminatura, skre-me-nah-**too**-rah, f., hair-parting

scritto, **skrit**-to, m., writing ; deed

scrittoio, skrit-to-e'o, m., writing-desk

scrittore, skrit-**tor**-ay, m., writer

scrittura, skrit-**too**-rah, f., handwriting ; entry ;
   scripture ; artist's engagement

scrivania, skre-vah-**nee**-ah, f., writing-desk

scrivano, skre-**vah**-no, m., clerk

scrivere, **skree**-vay-ray, v., to write   [sponge

scroccare, skrock-**kah**-ray, v., to swindle ; to

scroccone, skrock-**ko**-nay, m., sharper ; sponger

scrofa, **skro**-fah, f., sow

scrollare, skroll-**lah**-ray, v., to shake off

scrollo, **skroll**-lo, m., shaking off

scrosciare, skro-she'**ah**-ray, v., to patter ; to pour

scroscio, **skro**-she'o, m., clatter ; downpour

scrostare, skro-**stah**-ray, v., to scrape off

scrupolo, **skroo**-po-lo, m., scruple

scrutare, skroo-**tah**-ray, v., to scrutinize

scucire, skoo-**chee**-ray, v., to unstitch

scuderia, skoo day-**ree**-ah, f., stable ; stud

scudiere, skoo-de'**ay**-ray, m., groom ; equerry

scudiscio, skoo-dee-she'o, m., riding-whip

scudo, **skoo**-do, m., shield ; coin

scuffia, **skoof**-fe'ah, f., cap

scufflotto, skoof-fe'**ot**-to, m., box on the ears

scugnizzo, skoo-n'**yeet**-tso, m., urchin

sculacciare, skoo-laht-**chah**-ray, v., to spank

scultore, skooll-**tor**-ay, m., sculptor

scuola, skoo'o lah, f., school ; doctrine

scuotere, skoo'o-tay-ray, v., to shake ; to jerk

scure, **skoo**-ray, f., axe

scuro, **skoo**-ro, a.,° dim, gloomy. m., darkness

scusa, **skoo**-zah, f., excuse

scusare, skoo-**zah**-ray, v., to excuse

sdaziare, zdah-tse ah-ray, v., to clear goods

sdebitarsi, zday-be-**tar**-se, v., to meet obligations

sdegnare, zday-n'**yah**-ray, v., to disdain

sdegnato*, zday-n'yah-to, a., indignant

sdegno, zday-n'yo, m., indignation ; contempt

sdoganare, zdo-gah-**nah**-ray, v., to clear goods

sdraiarsi, zdrah-e'ar-se, v., to sprawl

sdrucciolare, zdrooht-cho-lah-ray, v., to slip

sdrucciolevole, zdrooht-cho-lay-vo-lay,a.,slippery

se, say, conj., if, whether [themselves

sè, say, pron., one's self ; himself ; herself ; itself ;

sebbene, seb-bay-nay, conj., although, though

secca, seck-kah, f., shoal ; sandbank ; drought

seccare, seck-**kah**-ray, v., to dry ; to tease ; to bore

seccarsi, seck-**kar**-se, v., to trouble oneself

seccatore, seck-kah-**tor**-ay, m., bore ; nuisance

seccatura, seck-kah-**too**-rah, f., annoyance

secchio[a], seck-ke'o, m. [f.], bucket ; scuttle

secco*, seck-ko, a., dry ; withered ; flabby

seco, say-ko, pron., with him ; with her ; with them

secolare, say-ko-**lah**-ray, m., layman. a., profane,

secolo, say-ko-lo, m., century ; age [secular

secondare,say-kon-**dah**-ray,v.,to second ; to favour

secondo, say-**kon**-do, a., second. m., second.
prep., according to. adv., it depends

secrezione, say-kray-tse'o-nay, f., secretion

sedano, say-dah-no, m., celery

sede, say-day,f.,seat ; abode ; head office :[Holy]See

sedere, say-**day**-ray, v., to sit down. m., seat, pos-

sedia, say-de'ah, f. ,chair [terior

sedicente, say-de-**chen**-tay, a., so-called

sedicesimo, say-de-**chay**-ze-mo, a., sixteenth

sedici, say-de-che, a., sixteen

sedile, say-**dee**-lay, m., seat, bench

seducente, say-doo-**chen**-tay, a., enticing

sedurre, say-**doohr**-ray, v., to seduce ; to corrupt

seduta, say-**doo**-tah, f., sitting ; meeting

sega, say-gah, f., saw

segale, say-gah-lay, f., rye

segare, say-**gah**-ray, v., to saw ; to cut ; to mow

seggio, sed-jo, m., chair ; seat

seggiolone, sed-jo-lo-nay, m., easy-chair

segheria, say-gay-ree ah, f., saw-mill

segnalare, say-n'yah-**lah**-ray, v., to signal ; **to no-**
tify ; to signalize

segnalibro, say-n'yah-lee-bro, m., book-mark
segnare, say-n'yah-ray, v., to mark, to score
segno, say-n'yo, m., sign ; mark
sego, say-go, m., tallow   [tiveness
segretezza, say-gray-tet-tsah, f., secrecy ; secre-
seguace, say-goo'ah-chay, m., follower, adherent
segugio, say-goo-jo, m., blood-hound
seguire, say-goo'ee-ray, v., to follow ; to carry on
seguitare, say-goo'e-tah-ray, v., to follow ; to
    persevere
seguito, say-goo'e-to, m., retinue ; continuation
sei, say-e, a., six
selciare, sell-chah-ray, v., to pave
selciato, sell-chah-to, m., pavement
sella, sell-lah, f., saddle
sellaio, sell-lah-e'o, m., saddler
sellare, sell-lah-ray, v., to saddle
selva, sell-vah, f., wood ; forest
selvaggina, sell-vahd-jee-nah, f., (animals) game
selvaggio, sell-vahd-jo, a., *savage ; wild. m..savage
sembiante, sem-be'ahn-tay, m., appearance ;
    outlook
sembrare, sem-brah-ray, v., to seem ; to look like
seme, say-may, m., seed. grain ; (fig.) germ
semenza, say-men-tsah, f., seed
semenzaio, say-men-tsah-e'o, m., (plants) nursery
semestre, say-mess-tray, m., half-year
semicupio, say-me-koo-pe'o, m., hip-bath
semidio, say-me-dee-o, m., demi-god   [chet
semiminima, say-me-mee-ne-mah, f., (mus.) crot-
seminare, say-me-nah-ray, v., to sow ; to scatter
seminatore, say-me-nah-tor-ay, m., sower
semola, say-mo-lah, f., bran
sempiterno, sem-pe-tair-no, a., everlasting
semplice, sem-ple-chay, a., simple ; pure ; single
semplicità, sem-ple-che-tah, f., simplicity
sempre, sem-pray, adv., always
senape, say-nah-pay, m., mustard
senno, sen-no, m., sense, wisdom
seno, say-no, m., bosom ; womb ; small bay
sensale, sen-sah-lay, m., broker ; agent
sensato*, sen-sah-to, a., sensible

senseria, sen-say-ree ah, f., brokerage ; agency
sensibile, sen-see-be-lay, a., sensitive ; perceptible
senso, sen-so, m., sense ; feeling. — **unico**, one way street
sentenza, sen-ten-tsah, f., (law) sentence
sentiero, sen-te'ay-ro, m., path
sentina, sen-tee-nah, f., bilge ; cesspool
sentinella, sen-te-nell-lah, f., sentry, sentinel
sentire, s n-tee-ray, v., to hear ; to feel ; to smell
sentore, sen-tor-ay, m., smell ; indication
senza, sen-tsah, prep., without. **senz' altro,** unfailingly ; instantly, directly
separare, say-pah-rah-ray, v., to separate
sepolcro, say-poll-kro, m., sepulchre
sepoltura, say-poll-too-rah, f., burial
seppellire, sep-pell-lee-ray, v., to bury
seppia, sep-pe'ah, f., cuttle-fish ; sepia
sequela, say-kway-lah, f., sequel ; series
sequestrare, say-kwess-trah-ray, v., to sequestrate
sera, say-rah, f., evening
serata, say-rah-tah, f., benefit evening
serbare, sair-bah-ray, v., to keep ; to reserve
serbatoio, sair-bah-to-e'o, m., reservoir
serenità, say-ray-ne-tah, f., serenity
serico°, say-re-ko, a., silken
serie, say-re-ay, f., series ; order
serietà, say-re-ay-tah, f., seriousness
serotino, say-ro-tee-no, a., tardy, late
serpe[nte], sair-pay, m., serpent, snake
serpeggiare, sair-ped-jah-ray, v., to wind ; to creep
serpigine, sair-pee-je-nay, f., ringworm
serra, sair-rah, f., gorge ; green-house ; crush
serrare, sair-rah-ray, v., to lock ; to bolt
serrata, sair-rah-tah, f., lock-out
serratura, sair-rah-too-rah, f., lock
serto, sair-to, m., garland
serva, sair-vah, f., servant-maid
servaggio, sair-vahd-jo, m., bondage
servente, sair-ven-tay, m., male-nurse
servire, sair-vee-ray, v., to serve
servitore, sair-ve-tor-ay, m., servant ; valet
servitù, sair-ve-too, f., bondage ; service

servizio, sair-vee-tse'o, m., service ; favour

servo, sair vo. m., servant ; valet ; slave

sessanta, sess-sahn-tah, a., sixty

sessantesimo, sess-sahn-**tay**-ze-mo, a., sixtieth

sesso, sess-so, m., sex

sestante, sess-**tahn**-tay, m., sextant

sesto, sess-to, a., sixth

seta, say-tah, f., silk

setaceo, say-tah-chay-o, a., silky

sete, say-tay, f., thirst ; (fig.) longing

seteria, say-tay-ree-ah, f., silken goods

setola, say-to-lah, f., bristle ; horse-hair

setoloso, say-to-lo-zo, a., hairy

setta, set-tah, f., sect ; league ; gang

settanta, set-**tahn**-tah, a., seventy

settantesimo, set-tahn-**tay**-ze-mo, a., seventieth

sette, set-tay, a., seven

settembre, set-tem-bray, m., September

settentrionale, set-ten-tre'o-**nah**-lay,a.,northerly

settimana, set-te-**mah**-nah, f., week

settimo, set-te-mo, a., seventh

settore, set-tor-ay, m., sector

sevizia, say-**vee**-tse'ah, f., ill-treatment

sezione, say-tse'o-nay, f., section ; portion

sfaccendato, sfaht-chen-**dah**-to, a., idle ; **useless**

sfacciatezza, sfaht-chah-tet-tsah, f., brazenness

sfacciato°, sfaht-**chah**-to, a., impudent ; shameless

sfacimento, sfah-che-**men**-to, m.,ruin, breaking-up

sfaldare, sfahl-**dah**-ray, v., to slice ; to slip

sfalsare, sfahl-sah-ray, v., to misrepresent

sfamare, sfah-**mah**-ray, v., to still hunger

sfare, sfah-ray, v., to undo

sfarinare, sfah-re-**nah**-ray, v., to pulverize ; to mill

sfarzo, sfar-tso, m., pomp ; magnificence

sfatare, sfah-**tah**-ray, v., to deprive ; to dispel

sfatto, sfaht-to, p. p., undone, broken

sfavillare,sfah-vill-**lah**-ray,v.,to sparkle ; to twinkle

sfavorevole, sfah-vo-**ray**-vo-lay, a., unfavourable

sfegatato, sfay-gah-**tah**-to, a., impassioned

sfera, sfay-rah, f., sphere, globe, world

sferrare, sfair-**rah**-ray, v., to unfetter ; **to unshoe** ;
to strike ; to kick

I—10

sferza, sfair-tsah, f., whip, lash
sferzare, sfair-tsah-ray, v., to whip
sfiatare, sfe'ah-tah-ray, v., to puff ; to leak
sfiatato, sfe'ah-tah-to, a., out of breath
sfibbiare, sfeeb-be'ah-ray, v., to unbuckle ; to speak [out
sfida, sfee-dah, f., challenge ; defiance
sfidare, sfe-dah-ray, v., to challenge ; to defy
sfiducia, sfe-doo-chah, f., mistrust
sfiduciato, sfe-doo-chah-to, a., downhearted
sfigurare, sfe-goo-rah-ray, v., to disfigure
sfilata, sfe-lah-tah, f., (mil.) review
sfinge, sfin-jay, f., sphinx
sfinire, sfe-nee-ray, v., to weaken ; to exhaust
sfinito, sfe-nee-to, a., exhausted
sfiorare, sfe'o-rah-ray, v., to skim
sfiorire, sfe'o-ree-ray, v., to wither
sfoderare, sfo-day-rah-ray, v., to unsheathe
sfogare, sfo-gah-ray, v., to give vent to ; to exhale
sfogatoio, sfo-gah-to-e'o, m., vent ; outlet
sfoggiare, sfod-jah-ray, v., to parade ; to show off
sfoggio, sfod-jo, m., pomp ; show
sfogliare, sfo-l'yah-ray, v., to read hastily ; to strip
sfogo, sfo-go, m., rash ; (wrath, affection) outflow
sfollare, sfoll-lah-ray, v., to swarm out ; to clear
sfondare, sfon-dah-ray, v., to stave in
sformare, sfor-mah-ray, v., to deform ; to mutilate
sfornito, sfor-nee-to, a., deprived
sfortuna, sfor-too-nah, f., misfortune
sfortunato, sfor-too-nah-to, a., unfortunate, un- [lucky
sforzare, sfor-tsah-ray, v., to force
sforzarsi, sfor-tsar-se, v., to endeavour
sforzo, sfor-zo, m., endeavour ; exertion
sfracellare, sfrah-chell-lah-ray, v., to shatter
sfrattare, sfraht-tah-ray, v., to evict
sfregiare, sfray-jah-ray, v., to disfigure ; to slash
sfregio, sfray-jo, m., gash ; affront ; damage
sfrenato, sfray-nah-to, a., unrestrained
sfrondare, sfron-dah-ray, v., to strip of ...
sfrontatezza, sfron-tah-tet-tsah, f., effrontery
sfrontato, sfron-tah-to, a., cheeky
sfruttare, sfroot-tah-ray, v., to exploit
sfuggire, sfood-jee-ray, v., to escape ; to shun

sfumare, sfoo-mah-ray, v., to evaporate

sfumatura, sfoo-mah-too-rah, f., hue, shading

sfuriata, sfoo-re'ah-tah, f., a fit of rage

sgabello, zgah-bell-lo, m., stool

sganciare, zgahn-chah-ray, v., to unhook

sgangherato°, zgahn-gay-rah-to, a., tottering

sgarbato°, zgar-bah-to, a., uncivil

sgarbo, zgar-bo, m., (disrespect) slight   [away

sgattaiolare, zgaht-tah-e'o-lah-ray, v., to steal

sgelare, zjay-lah-ray, v., to thaw

sgelo, z'ay-lo, m., thaw

sghembo, zghem-bo, a., crooked; aslant

sghignazzare, zghe-n'yaht-tsah-ray, v., to laugh
   loudly; to scoff

sgobbare, zgob-bah-ray, v., to toil; to slave

sgocciolare, zgot-cho-lah-ray, v., to drip

sgolarsi, zgo-lar-se, v., to make oneself hoarse

sgomberare, zgom-bay-rah-ray, v., to remove; to

sgombero, zgom-bay-ro, m., removal   [evacuate

sgombro, zgom-bro, m., mackerel; clearing

sgomentare, zgo-men-tah-ray, v., to terrify

sgomento, zgo-men-to, m., dismay

sgonfiare, zgon-fe'ah-ray, v., to deflate; to reduce

sgorgare, zgor-gah-ray, v., to stream out

sgorgo, zgor-go, m., outflow

sgovernare, zgo-vair-nah-ray, v., to misgovern

sgozzare, zgot-tsah-ray, v., to slit the throat

sgradevole, zgrah-day-vo-lay, a., unpleasant

sgraffio, zgrahf-fe'o, m., scratch

sgranare, zgrah-nah-ray, v., (peas, etc.) to shell

sgranchire, zgrahn-kee-ray, v., to stretch

sgravare, zgrah-vah-ray, v., to unburden, to relieve

sgravarsi, zgrah-var-se, v., to give birth

sgravio, zgrah-ve'o, m., relief

sgraziato°, zgrah-tse'ah-to, a., awkward, clumsy

sgretolare, zgray-to-lah-ray, v., to grind

sgridare, zgre-dah-ray, v., to scold; to reprimand

sgridata, zgre-dah-tah, f., scolding

sgrovigliare, zgro-ve-l'yah-ray, v., to disentangle

sguainare, zgoo'ah-e-nah-ray, v., to unsheathe

sgualcire, zgoo'ahl-chee-ray, v., to rumple

sguardo, zgoo'ar-do, m., look, glance

sguazzare, zgoo'aht-tsah-ray, v., to feast ; to wallow

sguisciare, zgoo'e-she'ah-ray, v., to creep away

sgusciare, zgoo-she'ah-ray, v., to shell ; to steal out

si, se, adv., yes. pron., one ; oneself, etc.

sia ... sia, se-ah ... see-ah, conj., either ... or

sibilare, se-be-lah-ray, v., to hiss

sibilo, see-be-lo, m., hiss, hissing

sicario, se-kah-re'o, m., hired assassin

sicchè, sick-kay, adv., so ; thus ; therefore

siccità, sit-che-tah, f., drought ; dryness

siccome, sick ko-may, conj., since ; as ; on

sicurezza, se-koo-ret-tsah, f., security ; safety

sicuro°, se-koo-ro, a., sure, safe, firm. adv., certainly

sicurtà, se-koohr-tah, f., security ; assurance : bail

siderurgia, se-day-roohr-jee-ah, f., iron and steel

sidro, see-dro, m., cider   [industry

siepe, se'ay-pay, f., hedge

siero, se'ay-ro, m., serum

sigillare, se-jil-lah-ray, v., to seal ; to stop up

sigillo, se-jil-lo, m., seal, stamp, mark

sigla, see-glah, f., monogram

signora, se-n'yor-ah, f., lady ; madam ; Mrs.

signore, se-n'yor-ay, m., gentleman ; sir ; Mr.

signoreggiare, se-n'yor-ed-jah-ray, v., to rule over

signorile, se-n'yor-ee-lay, a., lordly ; noble

signorina, se-n'yor-ee-nah, f., Miss ; young lady

sillaba, seel-lah-bah, f., syllable

sillabare, seel-lah-bah-ray, v., to spell

silurante, se-loo-rahn-tay, f., torpedo-boat

siluro, se-loo-ro, m., torpedo   [wild

silvano [or silvestre], seel-vah-no, a., woody ;

silvicultura, seel-ve-kool-too-rah, f., forestry

simile, see-me-lay, a., like   m., fellow

simpatico°, seem-pah-te-ko, a., nice ; sympathetic

simpatizzare, seem-pah-tid-dzah-ray, v., to sym-

simposio, seem po-zt'o, m., grand banquet [pathize

simulacro, se-moo-lah-kro, m., effigy ; sham

simulare, se-moo-lah-ray, v., to sham

sincerarsi, seen-chay-rar-se, v., to assure oneself

sincero°, seen-chay-ro, a., sincere   [cise

sindacare, seen-dah-kah-ray, v., to audit ; to criti-

sindacato, seen-dah-kah-to, m., syndicate

sindaco, seen-dah-ko. m., mayor ; syndic

sinfonia, seen-fo-nee-ah. f., symphony [hiccough

singhiozzare, seen-ghe'ot-tsah-ray, v., to sob ; to

singhiozzo, seen-ghe'ot-tso. m., sob ; hiccough

singolo, seen-go-lo. a., single ; each

sinistra, se-niss-trah. f., left ; left-hand

sinistro, se-niss-tro. a.,* left ; sinister. m., disaster

sino, see-no. prep., till ; as far as ; whilst

sintassi, seen-tahss-se. f., syntax

sintomo, seen-to-mo. m., symptom. sign

sinuoso*, se-noo'o-zo. a., sinuous ; winding

sipario, se-pah-re'o. m., curtain

sirena, se-ray-nah. f., mermaid ; siren

siringa, se-reen-gah. f., syringe ; syringa

siringare, se-reen-gah-ray, v., to syringe

siroppo, se-rop-po. m., syrup

sistema, siss-tay-mah. m., system ; arrangement

sitibondo, se-te-bon-do. a., very thirsty

sito, see-to. m., site ; spot ; location

slacciare, zlaht-chah-ray, v., to unlace

slanciarsi, zlahn-char-se, v., to pounce upon

slancio, zlahn-cho. m., impulse ; impetus

sleale, zlay'ah-lay. a., disloyal ; treacherous

slealtà, zlay'ahl-tah. f., treachery ; disloyalty

slegare, zlay-gah-ray. v., to untie ; to loosen

slitta, zlit-tah. f., sledge

slittare, zlit-tah-ray. v., to sleigh ; to skid

slittamento, zlit-tah-men-to. m., skidding

slogare, zlo-gah-ray. v., to sprain ; to dislodge

slogatura, zlo-gah-too-rah. f., dislocation ; sprain

sloggiare, zlod-jah-ray. v., to evict ; to move

smagliante, zmah-l'yahn-tay. a., brilliant ; gleaming ; enticing

smagliare, zmah-l'yah-ray. v., to unknit ; to spar-

smagrire, zmah-gree-ray. v., to get thin [kle

smaltare, zmahl-tah-ray. v., to enamel

smaltire, zmahl-tee-ray. v., to sleep off drink effects ; to sell off

smalto, zmahl-to. m., enamel

smanceria, zmahn-chay-ree-ah. f., affected ways

smania, zmah-ne'ah. f., rage ; desire

smaniare, zmah-n'yah-ray. v., to rave

smanioso*, zmah-ne'O-zo. a., eager ; furious

smantellare, zmahn-tell-lah-ray, v., to dismantle

smargiasso, zmar-jahss-so, m., blusterer

smarrire, zmar-ree-ray, v., to lose, to mislay

smarrirsi, zmar-reer-se, v., to lose oneself ; to lose courage

smarrito*, zmar-ree-to, a., lost ; misled ; **stray** ; confused

smascherare, zmahss-kay-rah-ray, v., to unmask

smembrare, zmem-brah-ray, v., to dismember

smemorato, zmay-mo-rah-to, m., poor of memory

smentire, zmen-tee-ray, v., to belie ; to refute

smentita, zmen-tee-tah, f., denial

smeraldo, zmay-rahl-do, m., emerald

smerciare, zmair-chah-ray, v., to sell out

smercio, zmair-cho, m., sale

smeriglio, zmay-ree-l'yo, m., emery paper

smettere, zmet-tay-ray, v., to discontinue

smilzo*, zmeel-tso. a., lean ; poor

sminuire, zme-noo'ee-ray, v., to diminish

sminuzzare, zme-noot-tsah-ray, v., to mince

smistare, zme-stah-ray, v., to sort out ; to shunt

smisurato*, zme-zoo-rah-to, a., unbounded ; huge

smobigliato, zmo-be-l'yah-to, a., unfurnished

smoderato*, zmo-day-rah-to, a., immoderate

smontare, zmon-tah-ray, v., to dismount ; to alight

smorfia, zmor-fe'ah, f., wry-face

smorfioso*, zmor-fe'O-zo, a., affected

smorto, zmor-to, a., ashy-pale

smozzare, zmot-tsah-ray, v., to lop off

smungere, zmoonn-jay-ray, v., to sponge upon

smunto, zmoonn-to, a., ill-nourished

smuovere, zmoo'O-vay-ray, v., to move with effort

smuzzare, zmoot-tsah-ray, v., to round ; to blunt

snaturato*, znah-too-rah-to, a.,adulterated ; cruel

snellezza, znell-let-tsah, f., slenderness

snello*, znell-lo, a., slender ; nimble

snidare, zne-dah-ray, v.,to go nesting ; to drive out

snervare, znair-vah-ray, v., to unnerve

snodare, zno-dah-ray, v., to unknot ; to loosen

snudare, znoo-dah-ray, v., to denude

soavità, so'ah-ve-tah, f., gentleness ; mildness

sobborgo, sob-bor-go, m., suburb
sobillare, so-bill-lah-ray, v., to instigate
socchiudere, sock-ke'oo-day-ray, v., to half shut
soccorrere, sock-kor-ray-ray, v., to succour
soccorso, sock-kor-so, m., succour, help
socievole, so-chay-vo-lay, a., sociable
socio, so-cho, m., partner; member
sodalizio, so-dah-lit-tse'o, m., brotherhood [tory
soddisfacente, sod-diss-fah-chen-tay, a., satisfac-
soddisfare, sod-diss-fah-ray, v., to satisfy; to gratify
soddisfatto, sod-diss-faht-to, a., satisfied
sodo°, so-do, a., sound; sturdy; compact
sofferente, sof-fay-ren-tay, a., suffering
sofferenza, sof-fay-ren-tsah, f., pain; sorrow
soffiare, sof-fe'ah-ray, v., to blow; to breathe
soffice, sof-fe-chay, a., soft, springy
soffietto, sof-fe'et-to, m., bellows
soffio, sof-fe'o, m., breath; blowing
soffitta, sof-fit-tah, f., attic
soffitto, sof-fit-to, m., ceiling
soffocare, sof-fo-kah-ray, v., to suffocate
soffriggere, sof-freed-jay-ray, v., to fry slowly
soffrire, sof-free-ray, v., to suffer
soggetto, sod-jet-to, m., subject. a., liable
soggezione, sod-jay-tse'o-nay, f., subjection
sogghignare, sog-ghe-n'yah-ray, v., to grin
sogghigno, sog-ghe-n'yo, m., grin; sick smile
soggiogare, sod-jo-gah-ray, v., to subjugate
soggiornare, sod-jor-nah-ray, v., to sojourn
soglia, so-l'yah, f., threshold; (fish) sole
sogliola, so-l'yo-lah, f., (fish) sole
sognare, so-n'yah-ray, v., to dream   [the least
sogno, so-n'yo, m., dream. neppur per —, not in
solatìo, so-lah-te'o, a., sunny
solcare, soll-kah-ray, v., to furrow
solco, soll-ko, m., furrow; track; wrinkle
soldato, soll-dah-to, m., soldier
soldo, soll-do, m., pay; half-penny
sole, so-lay, m., sun; sunshine
solenne, so-len-nay, a., solemn; splendid
solere, so-lay-ray, v., to be used to
solerte, so-lair-tay, a., industrious

soletto, so-let-to, a., all alone

solfo, soll-fo, m., sulphur; brimstone

solingo, so-lin-go, a., solitary

solino, so-lee-no, m., collar

solito°, so-le-to, a., accustomed; habitual; ordinary

solitudine, so-le-too-de-nay, f., solitude

sollazzare, soll-lah'-tsah-ray, v.,to amuse; to cheer

sollecito°, soll-lay-che-to, a., solicitous; quick

solleticare, soll-lav-te-kah-ray, v., to tickle; to

solletico, soll-lay-te-ko, m., tickling [flatter

sollevare, soll-lay-vah-ray, v., to raise; to ease

sollievo, soll-le'ay-vo, m., relief

solo°, so-lo, a., alone. adv., only

solvibile, soll-vee-be-lay, a., soluble

solvibilità, soll-ve-be-le-tah, f., solvency

soma, so-mah, f., burden

somaro, so-mah-ro, m., beast of burden; donkey

somiglianza, so-me-l'yahn-tsah, f., likeness

somigliare, so-me-l'yah-ray, v., to be like

somma, som-mah, f., sum; amount; summit

sommare, som-mah-ray, v., to sum up

sommario, som-mah-re'o, m., summary

sommergere, som-mair-jay-ray, v., to submerge

sommergibile, som-mair-jee-be-lay, m., submarine

sommesso°, som-mess-so, a., subdued; humble

somministrare, som-me-niss-trah-ray, v., to sup-

sommità, som-me-tah, f., summit; top [ply

sommo, som-mo, a.,° supreme. m., top

sommossa, som-moss-sah, f., riot

sonaglio, so-nah-l'yo, m., little bell; rattle

sonare, so-nah-ray, v., to ring, to play

sonda, son-dah, f., sounding instrument

soreria, so-nay-ree ah, f., (bell, etc.) striking device

sonnacchioso, son-nack-ke'o-zo, a., sleepy

sonnecchiare, son-neck-ke'ah-ray, v., to doze

sonnellino, son-nell-lee-no, m., nap; slumber

sonno, son-no, m., sleep

sonoro°, so-no-ro, a., sonorous, resounding

sontuoso°, son-too'o-zo, a., sumptuous [justice

soperchieria, so-pair-ke'ay-ree-ah, f., fraud; in-

sopore, so-po-ray, m., torpor

soppiantare, sop-pe'ahn-tah-ray, v., to supplant

soppiatto, sop-pe'aht-to, adv., di —, stealthily

sopportare, sop-por-tah-ray, v., to support

sopprimere, sop-pree-may-ray, v., to suppress

sopra, so prah, prep., on ; above : over ; besides

soprabito, so-prah-be-to, m., overcoat

sopraccennato, so-praht-chen-nah-to, a., above-mentioned

sopraffare, so-prahf-fah-ray, v., to overcome

sopraggiungere, so-prahd-joonn-jay-ray, v., to arrive suddenly ; to supervene

sopraluogo, so-prah-loo'o-go, m., inspection visit

soprannome, so-prahn-no-may, m., surname, nick-

soprappiù, so-prahl,p-pe'oo, m., surplus [name

soprascarpa, so-prah-skar-pah, f., galosh

soprascritta, so-prah-skrit-tah, f., address ; shop-sign

soprassedere, so-prahss-say-day-ray, v., to put off

sopratutto, so-prah-toot-to, adv., above all

sopravvanzare, so-phrav-vahn-tsah-ray, v., to overtake [vene

sopravvenire, so-prahv-vay-nee-ray, v., to super-

sopravvento, so-prahv-ven-to, m., windward ; advantage

sopravvivere, so-prahv-vee-vay-ray, v., to survive

soprintendere, so-prin-ten-day-ray, v., to supervise

sorbetto, sor-bet-to, m., ice-cream ; sherbet

sorbire, sor-bee-ray, v., to sip

sorcio, sor-cho, m., rat : mouse

sordità, sor-de-tah, f., deafness

sordo°, sor-do, a., deaf ; (fig.) dense

sorella, so-rell-lah, f., sister ; nun

sorellastra, so-rell-lahss-trah, f., step-sister

sorgente, sor-jen-tay, f., spring : origin

sorgere, sor-jay-ray, v., to rise : to issue [water

sorgivo, sor-jee-vo, a., acqua sorgiva, f., spring-

sormontare, sor-mon-tah-ray, v., to surmount

sornione, sor-ne'o-nay, m., sneak

sorpassare, sor-pahss-sah-ray, v., to surpass

sorprendente, sor-pren-den-tay, a., surprising

sorprendere, sor-pren-day-ray, v., to surprise

sorpresa, sor-pray-zah, f., surprise [up

sorreggere, sor-red-jay-ray, v., to uphold ; to prop

sorridere, sor-**ree**-day-ray, v., to smile
sorriso, sor-**ree**-zo, m., smile
sorseggiare, sor-sed-**jah**-ray, v., to sip
sorso, sor-so, m., sip ; draught
sorta, sor-tah, f., sort ; manner
sorte, sor-tay, f., luck ; destiny ; lot   [allot
sorteggiare, sor-ted-**jah**-ray, v., to draw lots ; to
sortilegio, sor-te-**lay**-jo, m., sorcery
sortire, sor-**tee**-ray, v., to go out ; to draw lots
sortita, sor-**tee**-tah, f., exit ; (mil.) sally
sorvegliare, sor-vay-l'**yah**-ray, v., to oversee
sorvolare, sor-vo-**lah**-ray, v., to fly over
sosia, so-ze'ah, m., (person) double
sospendere, soss-**pen**-day-ray, v., to suspend
sospettare, soss-pet-**tah**-ray, v., to suspect
sospetto, soss-**pet**-to, m., suspicion. a.,° suspected
sospingere, soss-**pin**-jay-ray, v., to push
sospirare, soss-pe-**rah**-ray, v., to sigh
sospiro, soss-**pee**-ro, m., sigh
sossopra, soss-**so**-prah, adv., upside-down
sosta, soss-tah, f., stop ; rest ; pause
sostantivo, soss-tahn-**tee**-vo, m., substantive
sostanza, soss-**tahn**-tsah, f., substance
sostare, soss-**tah**-ray, v., to stop ; to suspend
sostegno, soss-**tay**-n'yo, m., support ; prop
sostenere, soss-tay-**nay**-ray, v., to sustain ; to bear
sostituire, soss-te-too'ee-ray, v., to substitute
sottocoppa, sot-to-**kop**-pah, f., saucer
sottana, sot-tah-nah, f., petticoat ; cassock
sotterramento, sot-tair-rah-men-to,m.,interment
sotterraneo°, sot-tair-rah-nay-o, a., underground
sotterrare, sot-tair-**rah**-ray, v., to bury
sottigliezza, sot-te-l'**yay**-tsah, f., subtlety
sottile, sot-**tee**-lay, a., thin ; subtle   [to hint
sottintendere, sot-tin-**ten**-day-ray, v., to infer ;
sotto, sot-to, prep., under ; below. adv., beneath
sottolineare, sot-to-le-nay-**ah**-ray, v., to underline
sottomano, sot-to-**mah**-no, adv., underhand
sottomarino, sot-to-mah-**ree**-no, m., submarine
sottomettere, sot-to-**met**-tay-ray, v., to submit
sottoscrivere, sot-to-**skree**-vay-ray, v., to sub-
    scribe

sottoscrizione, sot-to-skre-tse'o-nay, f., subscrip-
sottosopra, sot-to-so-prah, adv., topsy-turvy [tion
sottostare, sot-to-stah-ray, v., to undergo
sottosuolo, sot-to-soo'o-lo, m., subsoil
sottrarre, sot-trar-ray, v., to subtract ; to deduce
sovente, so-ven-tay, adv., frequently
soverchiare, so-vair-ke'ah-ray, v., to overcome
soverchio*, so-vair-ke'o, a., superfluous
sovrano, so-vrah-no, m., sovereign
sovrapporre, so-vrahp-por-ray, v., superimpose
sovrumano, sov-vroo-mah-no, a., superhuman
sovvenire, sov-vay-nee-ray, v., to assist ; to remind
sovvenirsi, sov-vay-neer-se, v., to recollect
sovvenzione, sov-ven-tse'o-nay, f., subsidy
sovvertire, sov-vair-tee-ray, v., to overthrow
sozzare, sod-dzah-ray, v., to foul ; to sully
sozzo*, sod-dzo, a., filthy ; perverted
sozzura, sod-dzoo-rah, f., filth, foulness
spaccamonti, spahk-kah-mon-te, m., bragger
spaccare, spahk-kah-ray, v., to hew ; to cleave
spaccatura, spahk-kah-too-rah, f., fissure ; cleft
spacciare, spaht-chah-ray, v., to dispose of
spaccio, spaht-cho, m., shop ; despatch
spacco, spahk-ko, m., crack ; cleft
spaccone, spahk-ko-nay, m., braggart
spada, spah-dah, f., sword ; (cards) spade
spadroneggiare, spah-dro-ned-jah-ray, v., to domi-
spago, spah-go, m., twine [neer
spalancare, spah-lahn-kah-ray, v., to open wide
spalla, spahl-lah, f., shoulder ; back
spalliera, spahl-l'yay-rah, f., back of a seat
spallina, spahl-lee-nah, f., (mil.) shoulder-strap
spandere, spahn-day-ray, v., to shed ; to diffuse
sparare, spah-rah-ray, v., to shoot
sparecchiare, spah-reck-ke'ah-ray, v., to clear
spargere, spahr-jay-ray, v., to spread ; to scatter
spargimento, spahr-je-men-to-m., shedding ; scat-
sparire, spah-ree-ray, v., to disappear [tering
sparlare, spahr-lah-ray, v., to speak badly of
sparpagliare, spahr-pah-l'yah-ray, v., to scatter
sparso*, spahr-so, p.p., scattered
spartire, spahr-tee-ray, v., to share ; to allot

sparuto*, spah-**roo**-to, a., wan, thin

sparviere, spahr-ve'**ay**-ray, m., hawk

spasimare, spah-ze-**mah**-ray, v., to suffer **agonies**

spasimo, spah-ze-mo, m., spasm

spassare, spahss-**sah**-ray, v., to have fun

spasseggiare, spahss-sed-jah-ray, v., to have a stroll

spassionato*, spahss-se'o-nah-to, a., dispassionate ; unbiassed

spasso, **spahss**-so, m., amusement ; sport

spatriare, spah-tre'**ah**-ray, v., to expatriate

spauracchio, spah'oo-**rahk**-ke'o, m., scare-crow

spaurire, spah'oo-**ree**-ray, v., to scare

spavaldo, spah-**vahl**-do, m., boaster

spaventare, spah-ven-**tah**-ray, v., to frighten

spaventevole, spah-ven-**tay**-vo-lay, a., frightful

spavento, spah-**ven**-to, m., scare, dread

spazio, **spah**-tse'o, m., space, room

spazioso*, spah-tse'**o**-zo, a., spacious ; wide

spazzacamino, spaht-tsah-kah-**mee**-no, m., chimney-sweep

spazzare, spaht-**tsah**-ray, v., to sweep [ney-sweep

spazzatura, spaht-tsah-**too**-rah, f., sweepings ;

spazzino, spaht-**tsee**-no, m., sweeper [rubbish

spazzola, **spaht**-tso-lah, f., brush

spazzolino, spaht-tso-**lee**-no, m., tooth-brush

specchiare, spayk-ke'**ah**-ray, v., to reflect

specchio, **spayk**-ke'o, m., mirror

specialità, spay-chah-le-**tah**, f., speciality

specie, **spay**-chay, f., species ; kind

specificare, spay-che-fe-**kah**-ray, v., to specify

specula, **spay**-koo-lah, f., observatory

spedire, spay-**dee**-ray, v., to dispatch ; to hasten

speditezza, spay-de-**tet**-tsah, f., quickness

spedizioniere, spay-de-tse'o-ne'**ay**-ray, m., forwarding agent

spegnare, spay-n'**yah**-ray, v., to redeem [lay

spegnere, **spay**-n'yay-ray, v., to extinguish ; to allay

spegnimento, spay-n'ye-**men**-to, m., extinguishing ; quenching

spelare, spay-**lah**-ray, v., to skin ; to peel ; **to pluck**

spelonca, spay-**lon**-kah, f., den, cavern

spendere, **spen**-day-ray, v., to spend

spendereccio, spen-day-**ret**-cho, m., spendthrift

spennare, spen-nah-ray, v., to pluck ; to fleece
spensierato°, spen-se'ay-rah-to, a., thoughtless
spento, spen-to, a., put out ; dying ; extinct
spenzolare, spen-tso-lah-ray, v., to dangle
speranza, spay-rahn-tsah, f., hope
sperare, spay-rah-ray, v., to hope
spergiuro, spair-joo-ro, m., perjury
sperimentare, spay-re-men-tah-ray, v., to experi-
sperone, spay-ro-nay, m., spur [ment
sperperare, spair-pay-rah-ray, v., to fritter away
sperpero, spair-pay-ro, m., squandering
spesa, spay-zah, f., purchase ; cost
spesso°, spess-so, a., thick adv., frequently
spessore, spess-sor-ay, m., thickness
spettabile, spet-tah-be-lay, a., estimable
spettacolo, spet-tah-ko-lo, m., performance
spettare, spet-tah-ray, v., to pertain to
spettatore, spet-tah-tor-ay, m., spectator
spettrale, spet-trah-lay, a., spectral
spettro, spet-tro, m. ghost
speziale, spay-tse'ah-lay, m., apothecary
spezie, spay-tse-ay, f. pl., spices
spezieria, spay-tse-ay-ree-ah, f., pharmacy
spezzare, spet-tsah-ray, v., to break
spia, spee-ah, f., spy
spiacente, spe'ah-chen-tay, a., displeasing [sorry
spiacere, spe'ah-chay-ray, v., to displease ; to be
spiacevole, spe'ah-chay-vo-lay, a., unpleasant
spiaggia, spe'ahd-jah, f., beach
spianare, spe'ah-nah-ray, v., to level
spianata, spe'ah-nah-tah, f., plain ; clearing
spiantare, spe'ahn-tah-ray, v., to uproot
spiare, spe'ah-ray, v., to spy, to watch
spiccante, speek kahn-tay, a., striking
spiccare, speek-kah-ray, v., to pluck ; to detach
spicchio, speek ke'o, m., (of fruit) slice
spicciare, speet-chah-ray, v., to hasten
spiccioli, speet-cho-le, m. pl., small change
spiegamento, spe'ay-gah-men-to, m., display
spiegare, spe'ay-gah-ray, v., to explain ; to unfold
spiegativo, spe'ay-gah tee-vo, a., explanatory
spiegazione, spe'ay-gah-tse'o-nay, f., explanation

spiegazzare, spe'ay-gaht-tsah-ray, v., to rumple, to ruffle

spietato*, spe'ay-tah-to, a., cruel, unmerciful

spiga, spee-gah, f., ear of corn

spigolare, spe-go-lah-ray, v., to glean

spillare, spil-lah-ray, v., (cask) to tap

spillo, spil-lo, m., pin

spilorcio, spe-lor-cho, a., stingy. m., miser

spina, spee-nah, f., thorn ; (fish) bone

spineto, spe-nay-to, m., thorny growth

spingere, speen-jay-ray, v., to push

spino, spee-no, m., thorn

spinta, speen-tah, f., push

spione, spe-o-nay, m., spy

spira, spee-rah, f., spire ; coil

spirare, spe-rah-ray, v., to breathe ; to expire

spirito, spee-re-to, m., spirit ; mind ; wit

spiritoso*, spe-re-to-zo, a., witty

spizzico, spit-tse-ko, adv., a —, gradually

splendere, splen-day-ray, v., to sparkle ; to dazzle

spoglia, spo-l'yah, f., booty ; corpse

spogliare, spo-l'yah-ray, v., to spoil ; to undress ;

spola, spo-lah, f., weaver's shuttle   [to fleece

spoletta, spo-let-tah, f., fuse

spolpare, spoll-pah-ray, v., to strip meat off bone

spolverare, spoll-vay-rah-ray, v., to dust

spolverizzare, spoll-vay-rid-dzah-ray, v., to spray

sponda, spon-dah, f., shore, strand

sponsali, spon-sah-le, m. pl., nuptials

spopolare, spo-po-lah-ray, v., to depopulate

spoppare, spop-pah-ray, v., to wean

sporcaccione, spor-kaht-cho-nay, m., indecent man

sporcare, spor-kah-ray, v., to soil, to foul

sporcizia, spor-chee-tse'ah, f., filth ; rubbish

sporco*, spor-ko, a., filthy ; untidy

sporgere, spor-jay-ray, v., to jut [or lean] out

sporta, spor-tah, f., basket

sportello, spor-tell-lo, m., car-door ; small window

sposa, spo-zah, f., bride ; wife

sposalizio, spo-zah-lee-tse'o, m., wedding

sposare, spo-zah-ray, v., to wed

sposo, spo-zo, m., husband ; bridegroom

spossatezza, sposs-sah-**tet**-tsah, f., weariness

spossessare, sposs-sess-**sah**-ray, v., to deprive

spostare, sposs-**tah**-ray, v., to displace

spotestare, spo-tess-**tah**-ray, v., to deprive of power

sprazzo, spraht-tso, m., (light) beam

sprecare, spray-**kah**-ray, v., to waste

sprecone, spray-**ko**-nay, m., waster

spregiare, spray-**jah**-ray, v., to despise, to contemn

spregio, spray-jo, m., disdain ; slight

spremere, spray-**may**-ray, v., to squeeze

sprezzabile, spret-**tsah**-be-lay, a., contemptible

sprezzante, spret-**tsahn**-tay, a., contemptuous

sprezzare, spret-**tsah**-ray, v., to despise

sprezzo, spret-tso, m., contempt

sprigionare, spre-jo-**nah**-ray, v., to set free

sprigionarsi, spre-jo-**nar**-se, v., to escape

sprizzare, spreet-**tsah**-ray, v., to spray ; to spout

sprofondare, spro-fon-**dah**-ray, v., to sink

spronare, spro-**nah**-ray, v., to spur

sprone, spro-nay, m., spur

sproporzionato*, spro-por-tse'o-**nah**-to, a., out of proportion

sproposito, spro-**po**-ze-to, m., error, slip

sprovvisto, sprov-**viss**-to, a., deprived

spruzzare, sproot-**tsah**-ray, v., to spout, to sprinkle

spruzzo, sproot-tso, m., spray

spudoratezza, spoo-do-rah-**tet**-tsah, f., impudence

spugna, spoo-n'yah, f., sponge

spuma, spoo-mah, f., foam, froth, sparkle

spuntare, spoonn-**tah**-ray, v., to dawn ; to blunt ; to get the advantage

spuntato, spoonn-**tah**-to, a., blunt

spuntino, spoonn-**tee**-no, m., (food) snack

spurgare, spoohr-**gah**-ray, v., to expurgate

sputare, spoo-**tah**-ray, v., to spit

sputo, spoo-to, m., spittle

squadra, skwah-drah, f., fleet ; squad ; team

squadrare, skwah-**drah**-ray, v., to " size up "

squadrista, skwah-**driss**-tah, m., fascist from

squagliarsi, skwah-l'yar-se, v., to melt   [choice

squalo, skwah-lo, m., shark

squama, skwah-mah, f., scale

squarcio, skwar-cho, m., rent, gash
squartare, skwar-tah ray, v., to quarter ; to rip
squilibrato, skwe-le-brah-to, m., crazy person
squilibrio, skwe-lee-bre-o, m., bad balance
squilla, skweel lah, f., small bell
squillare, skweel-lah-ray, v., to sound
squisito, skwe-zee-to, a., exquisite [root
sradicare, zrah-de kah ray, v., to eradicate ; to up-
sregolato, zray-go-lah-to, a., badly regulated
stabile, stah-be-lay, a., firm, m., premises
stabilimento, stah-be-le-men-to, m., factory ; concern
stabilire, stah-be-lee-ray, v., to establish ; to fix ; to
staccare, stahk-kah-ray, v., to detach [assign
stacciare, staht-chah-ray, v., to sift
staccio, staht-cho, m., sieve
stadio, stah-de'o, m., stadium ; stage
staffa, stahf-fah, f., stirrup
staffilare, stahf-fe-lah-ray, v., to whip ; to lash
staffile, stahf-fee-lay, m., whip [ture
stagionare, stah-jo-nah-ray, v., to season ; to ma-
stagione, stah-jo-nay, f., season
stagnare, stah-n'yah-ray, v., to stagnate ; to tin ;
stagno, stah-n'yo, m., pond ; tin [to stop
staio, stah-e'o, m., bushel
stalla, stahl-lah, f., stable
stalliere, stahl-le'ay-ray, m., groom
stallo, stahl-lo, m., stall ; stable [morning
stamane [stamattina], stah-mah-nay, adv., this
stampa, stahm-pah,f.,print ; press ; printed matter
stampare, stahm-pah-ray, v., to print ; to stamp
stampella, stahm-pell-lah, f., crutch
stampo, stahm-po, m., matrix ; mould
stancare, stahn-kah-ray, v., to tire ; to weary
stanchezza, stahn-ket-tsah, f., tiredness
stan'o, stahn-ko, a., tired
stanga, stahn-gah, f., pole ; bar ; shaft
stangare, stahn-gah-ray, v., to bar [pieces
stanghetta, stahn-ghet-tah, f., (spectacles) side
stanotte, stah-not-tay, adv., to-night
stante, stahn-tay, conj., since ; as
stantio, stahn-tee-o, a., stale ; rancid

stantuffo, stahn-toof-fo, m., piston
stanza, stahn-tsah, f., room ; apartment
stanziare, stahn-tse'ah-ray, v., to allot
stappare, stahp-pah-ray, v., to uncork
stare, stah-ray, v., to be : to stand ; to stay : to suit ;
                                    [to fit
starna, star-nah, f., grouse
starnutare, star-noo-tah-ray, v., to sneeze
stasera, stah-say-rah, adv., this evening
statista, stah tiss-tah, m., statesman
stato, stah-to, m., state ; rank ; quality
statuire, stah-too'ee-ray, v., to decree
statura, stah-too-rah, f., height ; figure
statuto, stah-too-to, m., statute ; charter
stazionario, stah-tse'o-nah-re'o, a., stationary
stazza, staht-tsah, f., gauge ; tonnage
stazzare, staht-tsah-ray, v., to gauge
stecca, stek-kah, f., stick ; ruler ; cue
stecchino, stek-kee-no, m., tooth-pick
steccconata, stek-ko-nah-tah, f., paling
stella, stell-lah, f., star
stelo, stay-lo, m., stem ; stalk
stemma, stem-mah, m., coat of arms
stendere, sten-day-ray, v., to extend ; to compose
stenodattilografa, stay-no-daht-te-lo-grah-fah, f.,
      shorthand-typist
stentare, sten-tah-ray, v., to be in want ; to strug-
stento, sten-to, m., want   [gle
sterco, stair-ko, m., dung
sterminare, stair-me-nah-ray, v., to exterminate
sterminio, stair-mee-ne'o, m., extermination
stesso, stess-so, a. & pron., self ; the same
stia, stee-ah, f., hen-coop
stile, stee-lay, m., style ; poniard
stilettare, ste-let-tah-ray, v., to stab
stilla, still-lah, f., drop
stillare, still-lah-ray, v., to drip ; to percolate
stima, stee-mah, f., esteem ; appraisement
stimatore, ste-mah-tor-ay, m., appraiser
stimolo, stee-mo-lo, m., stimulus ; incitement
stinco, stin-ko, m., shin
stingere, stin-jay-ray, v., to fade
stipettaio, ste-pet-tah-e'o, m., cabinet-maker

stipulare, ste-poo-lah-ray, v., to stipulate
stiracchiare, ste-rahk-ke'ah-ray, v., to cavil ; to
stirare, ste-rah-ray, v., to iron ; to stretch [haggle
stirpe, steer-pay, f., lineage
stitichezza, ste-te-ket-tsah, f., constipation
stiva, stee-vah, f., (ship) hold
stivale, ste-vah-lay, m., boot
stivaloni, ste-vah-lo-ne, m. pl., top-boots
stivare, ste-vah-ray, v., to stow ; to pack tightly ;
stizza, steet-tsah, f., anger [to pile up
stizzirsi, steet-tseer-se, v., to be vexed
stoccata, stock-kah-tah, f., stab ; thrust
stoffa, stoff-fah, f., cloth, material
stogliere, sto-l'yay-ray, v., to divert ; to dissuade
stolidezza, sto-le-det-tsah, f., stupidity
stomachevole, sto-mah-kay-vo-lay, a., disgusting
stonare, sto-nah-ray, v., to be out of tune
stonatura, sto-nah-too-rah, f., not in harmony
stoppa, stop-pah, f., tow ; padding
stoppia, stop-pe'ah, f., stubble
stoppino, stop-pee-no, m., wick
storcere, stor-chay-ray, v., to twist
stordire, stor-dee-ray, v., to stun ; to dumbfound
storia, sto-re'ah, f., history ; tale
storione, sto-re'o-nay, m., sturgeon
stormire, stor-mee-ray, v., (leaves) to rustle
stormo, stor-mo, m., flock ; flutter
stornare, stor-nah-ray, v., to turn aside ; to advise
 against ; to cancel
stornello, stor-nell-lo, m., starling ; refrain
storpiare, stor-pe'ah-ray, v., to disable
storpio, stor-pe'o, m., lame person ; cripple
storta, stor-tah, f., sprain
storto[6], stor-to, a., distorted ; crooked
stoviglie, sto-vee-l'yay, f. pl., crockery
strabiliante, strah-be-l'yahn-tay, a., bewildering
strabismo, strah-biss-mo, m., squinting
straccare, strahk-kah-ray, v., to tire out
stracciare, straht-chah-ray, v., to tear ; to crumple
straccio, straht-cho, m., rag ; tear
straccione, straht-cho-nay, m., a down and out
stracco[*], strahk-ko, a., tired

stracotto, strah-**kot**-to, a., overdone

strada, strah-dah, f., road. — **maestra**, main road

stradone, strah-**do**-nay, m., avenue, drive

strage, strah-jay, f., shamble ; (fam.) a big quantity

stralciare, strahl-**chah**-ray, v., to extract

stralunare, strah-loo-**nah**-ray, v., to roll eyes

stramazzare, strah-maht-**tsah**-ray, v., to fall heavily

stramberia, strahm-bay-**ree**-ah, f., eccentricity

strame, strah-may, m., manure

stranezza, strah-**net**-tsah, f., oddity ; freak

straniero, strah-ne'**ay**-ro, m., stranger, foreigner

strano°, strah-no, a., strange ; unusual [abuse

strapazzare, strah-paht-**tsah**-ray, v., to rebuke ; to

strapazzo, strah-**paht**-tso, m., toil ; ill-usage

strappare, strahp-**pah**-ray, v., to snatch ; to wrench

strappo, strahp-po, m., tear ; snatch

straripare, strah-re-**pah**-ray, v., to overflow

strasciare, strah-she-**kah**-ray, v., to drag ; to drawl

strascico, strah-she-ko, m., (gown) train ; after

strascinare, strah-she-**nah**-ray, v., to drag [effects

strato, strah-to, m., stratum ; layer

stravagante, strah-vah-**gahn**-tay, a., eccentric

stravolgere, strah-**voll**-jay-ray, v., to perturb ; to distort

straziare, strah-tse'**ah**-ray, v., to torture ; to tear ; to

strazio, strah-**tse**'o, m., torture ; affliction [harass

strega, stray-gah, f., witch ; sorceress

stregare, stray-**gah**-ray, v., to bewitch

stregone, stray-**go**-nay, m., wizard

stremare, stray-**mah**-ray, v., to exhaust

stremo, stray-mo, m., end, limit

strenna, stren-nah, f., New Year's present

strepitare, stray-pe-**tah**-ray, v., to cause a din

strepito, stray-pe-to, m., din

stretta, stret-tah, f., grip ; seizure ; defile

strettezza, stret-**tet**-tsah, f., narrowness ; lack

stretto, stret-to, a.,° narrow ; close. m., straits

strettoia, stret-to-e'ah, f., press ; coercion

stria, stree-ah, f., fluting ; streak

stridere, stree-day-ray, v., to shriek

strido, stree-do, m., shriek ; trill

strigare, stre-gah-ray, v., to unriddle
strigliare, stre-l'yah-ray, v., to groom
strillare, streel-lah-ray, v., to scream, to bawl
strillo, streel-lo, m., cry, scream
strimpellare, streem-pell-lah-ray, v., to strum
stringa, streen-gah, f., (shoes, etc.) lace
stringere, streen-jay-ray, v., to press; to grasp; to bind; to conclude
stringersi, streen-jair-se, v., to shrug; to shrink
striscia, stree-she'ah, f., stripe; band; ray; strop
strisciare, stre-she'ah-ray, v., to creep; to crawl; to flatter
ctritolare, stre-to-lah-ray, v., to crush; to mince
strizzare, street-tsah-ray, v., — l'occhio, to wink
strofa, stro-fah, f., strophe; refrain
strofinaccio, stro-fe-naht-cho, m., duster
strofinare, stro-fe-nah-ray, v., to rub
stropicciare, stro-pit-chah-ray, v., to rub down
strozza, strot-tsah, f., throat
strozzare, strot-tsah-ray, v., to throttle
strozzino, strot-tsee-no, m., moneylender   [troy
struggere, strood-jay-ray, v., to consume; to des-
struggersi, strood-jair-se, v., to pine after
strutto, stroot-to, m., lard
struttura, stroot-too-rah, f., structure
struzzo, stroot-tso, m., ostrich
studiare, stoo-de'ah-ray, v., to study
stufa, stoo-fah, f., stove; hot-house
stufare, stoo-fah-ray, v., to stew; to tire
stufato, stoo-fah-to, m., stew
stufo, stoo-fo, a., fed up
stuoia, stoo'o-e'ah, f., mat
stuolo, stoo'o-lo, m., a large number
stupire, stoo-pee-ray, v., to astonish, to surprise
stuprare, stoo-prah-ray, v., to violate
sturare, stoo-rah-ray, v., to uncork
stuzzicadenti, stoot-tse-kah-den-te, m., tooth-pick
stuzzicare, stoot-tse-kah-ray, v., to tickle; to tease
su, soo, adv & prep., up; over; on; above; about
subbuglio, soob-boo-l'yo, m., turmoil
subdolo, soob-do-lo, a., crafty; deceitful
subire, soo-bee-ray, v., to undergo

subitaneo*, soo-be-**tah**-nay-o, a., sudden [at once
subito*, soo-be-to, a., unexpected adv., suddenly ;
subornare, soo-bor-**nah**-ray, v., to suborn
succedere, soot-**chay**-day-ray, v., to succeed ; to
succhiare, sook-ke'**ah**-ray, v., to suck; to sip [happen
succhiello, sook-ke'**el**-lo, m., gimlet
succo, **sook**-ko, m., juice ; sap
succursale, sook-koor-sah-**lay**, f., (business) branch
sud, sood, m., south
sudare, soo-**dah**-ray, v., to sweat ; (fig.) to work
sudario, soo-dah-re'o, m., shroud   [hard
suddetto, sood-**det**-to, a., above-mentioned
sudditanza, sood-de-**tahn**-tsah, f., national status
suddito, **sood**-de-to, m., subject
sudicio*, soo-de-cho, a., slovenly ; filthy
sudore, soo-**dor**-ay, m., sweat ; (fig.) toil
sufficiente, soof-fe-**chen**-tay, adv., sufficient
suffisso, soof-**fiss**-so, m., suffix
suffragio, soof-**frah**-jo, m., suffrage ; support ;
suffuso, soof-**foo**-zo, a., suffused   [prayer
suggellare, sood-jell-**lah**-ray, v., to seal
suggello, sood-**jell**-lo, m., seal ; token   [prompt
suggerire, sood-jay-**ree**-ray, v., to suggest ; to
suggeritore, sood-jay-re-**tor**-ay, m., prompter
sughero, **soo**-gay-ro, m., cork
sugna, soo-n'yah, f., grease, tallow
sugo, **soo**-go, m., gravy ; juice ; (fig.) object
sugoso*, soo-**go**-zo, a., succulent, juicy
suicidarsi, soo'e-che-**dar**-se, v., to commit suicide
suicidio, soo'e-**chee**-de-o, m., suicide
sulfureo, sool-foo-ray-o, a., sulphureous
sullodato, sool-lo-**dah**-to, a., above-mentioned
sunto, **soonn**-to, m., synopsis
suntuoso*, soonn-too'**o**-zo, a., sumptuous
suo, **soo**-o, pron., his ; her ; its
suocera, soo-o-**chay**-rah, f., mother-in-law
suocero, soo-o-**chay**-ro, m., father-in-law
suola, soo-o-lah, f., (foot, shoe, etc.) sole
suolo, soo-o-lo, m., soil ; floor   [sound
suonare, soo-o-**nah**-ray, v., to ring ; to play ; to
suono, soo-o-no, m., sound ; tune
suora, soo-o-rah, f., nun

superare, soo-pay-**rah**-ray, v., to overcome ; to sur-
superbia, soo-**pair**-be'ah, f., pride ; arrogance [pass
superbo*, soo-**pair**-bo, a., superb ; proud
superficiale, soo-pair-fe-**chah**-lay, a., superficial ;
superficie, soo-pair-**fee**-chay, f., surface [light
suppellettile, soop-pell-**let**-te-lay, m., utensil
supplica, **soop**-ple-kah, f., request ; entreaty [treat
supplicare, soop-ple-**kah**-ray, v., to petition ; to en-
supplire, soop-**plee**-ray, v., to substitute
supplizio, soop-plee-tse'o, m., torture ; agony ; rack
supporre, soop-**por**-ray, v., to suppose
suppurare, soop-poo-**rah**-ray, v., (pus)to discharge ;
supremo*, soo-**pray**-mo, a., supreme [to gather
suscettibile, soo-shet-**tee**-be-lay, a., susceptible
suscitare, soo-she-**tah**-ray, v., to raise
susina, soo-**zee**-nah, f., plum
susino, soo-**zee**-no, m., plum-tree
susseguente, sooss-say-goo'**en**-tay, a., subsequent,
sussidio, sooss-**see**-de'o, m., subsidy ; allowance [consecutive
sussistere, sooss-**siss**-tay-ray, v., to subsist [prise
sussultare, sooss-sool-**tah**-ray, v., to start, to sur-
sussulto, sooss-**sool**-to, m., start ; startle ; quake
sussurrare, sooss-soohr-**rah**-ray, v., to whisper ;
to mutter
sussurr[i]o, sooss-**soohr**-ro, m., murmur ; hum
svagare, zvah-**gah**-ray, v., to distract ; to entertain
svago, **zvah**-go, m., pastime
svaligiare, zvah-le-**jah**-ray, v., to steal ; to plunder
svalutare, zvah-loo-**tah**-ray, v., to devalue ; to be-
svanire, zvah-**nee**-ray, v., to vanish [little
svantaggio, zvahn-**tahd**-jo, m., disadvantage
svaporare, zvah-po-**rah**-ray, v., to evaporate
svariare, zvah-re'**ah**-ray, v., to vary
svarione, zvah-re'**o**-nay, m., blunder ; misprint
svecchiare, zvayk-ke'**ah**-ray, v., to rejuvenate
sveglia, zvay-l'yah, f., alarm-clock
svegliare, zvay-l'**yah**-ray, v., to rouse [awake
svegliarsi, zvay-l'**yar**-se, v., (cease sleeping) to
sveglio, zvay-l'yo, a., awake ; smart
svelare, zvay-**lah**-ray, v., to unveil, to disclose
svellere, zvell-**lay**-ray, v., to pull out ; to pluck
svelto*, zvell-to, a., slim ; brisk ; nimble

svenare, zvay-nah-ray, v., (to drain of) to bleed
svendere, zven-day-ray, v., to sell off
svendita, zven-de-tah, f., clearance sale
svenimento, zvay-ne-men-to, m., fainting fit
svenire, zvay-nee-ray, v., to faint
sventare, zven-tah-ray, v., to foil, to frustrate
sventato*, zven-tah-to, a., baffled ; thoughtless
sventolare, zven-to-lah-ray, v., to air ; to fan ; to winnow
sventrare, zven-trah-ray, v., to disembowel
sventura, zven-too-rah, f., misfortune [happy
sventurato*, zven-too-rah-to, a., unfortunate ; un-
svenuto, zvay-noo-to, a., fainted
svergognare, zvair-go-n'yah-ray, v., to put to
    shame ; to disgrace [cheeky
svergognato*, zvair-go-n'yah-to,a., brazen-faced ;
svernare, zvair-nah-ray,v.,to hibernate, to winter
svestire, zvess-tee-ray, v., to undress [habit
svezzare, zvet-tsah-ray, v., to wean ; to loose the
sviare, zve'ah-ray, v., to go astray ; to parry a blow
sviarsi, zve'ar-se, v., to diverge ; to err
svignarsela, zve-n'yar-say-lah, v., to creep away ;
    to be off
sviluppare, zve-loop-pah-ray, v., to spread out ; to
sviluppo, zve-loop-po. m., development [develop
svincolare, zvin-ko-lah-ray, v., to free from
svisare, zve-zah-ray, v., to misrepresent
svista, zviss-tah, f., oversight
svitare, zve-tah-ray, v., to unscrew
svogliato*, zvo-l'yah-to, a., reluctant, averse
svolazzare, zvo-laht-tsah-ray, v., to flutter
svolgere, zvoll-jay-ray, v., to unfold ; to unroll
svolta, zvoll-tah, f., a turning
svoltare, zvoll-tah-ray, v., to turn ; to unroll
sv[u]otare, zvo-tah-ray, v., to empty

tabaccaio, tah-bahk-kah-e'o, m., tobacconist
tabacchiera, tah-bahk-kee-ay-rah, f., snuff-box
tabella, tah-bell-lah, f., tablet ; list ; label
tacca, tahk-kah, f., cut ; notch ; defect
taccagno*, tahk-kah-n'yo, a., mean ; sordid
tacchino, tahk-kee-no, m., turkey

taccia, taht-chah, f., charge; blemish
tacciare, taht-chah-ray, v., to charge; to accuse
tacco, tahk-ko, m., heel
taccuino, tahk-koo'e-no, m., pocket-case or diary
tacere, tah-chay-ray, v., to keep silent. m., silence
tacito*, tah-che-to, a., silent, taciturn
tafano, tah-fah-no, m., borse-fly
tafferuglio, tahf-fay-roo-l'yo, m., scrimmage
taglia, tah-l'yah, f., size; figure; ransom
tagliaborse, tah-l'yah-bor-say, m., pickpocket
tagliacarte, tah-l'yah-kar-tay, m., paper-knife
taglialegna, tah-l'yah-lay-n'yah, m., wood-cutter
tagliando, tah-l'yahn-do, m., coupon
tagliare, tah-l'yah-ray, v., to cut; (tree) to fell
tagliatore, tah-l'yah-tor-ay, m., cutter
tagliente, tah-l'yen-tay, a., sharp, keen
taglio, tah-l'yo, m., cut; edge; (meat) joint
taglione, tah-l'yo-nay, m., tit for tat   [shred
tagliuzzare, tah-l'yoot-tsah-ray, v., to mince; to
tait, tah-eet, m., morning-coat
talamo, tah-lah-mo, m., bridal bed   [as
talchè, tahl-kay, conj., therefore; such as; as soon
tale, tah-lay, a., such; alike
talloncino, tahl-lon-chee-no, m., counterfoil; cou-
tallone, tahl-lo-nay, m., heel   [pon
talmente, tahl-men-tay, adv., so; so much
talora, tah-lor-ah, adv., sometimes
talpa, tahl-pah, f., mole; (fig.) blockhead
taluno, tah-loo-no, pron., some; somebody
talvolta, tahl-vol-tah, adv., sometimes
tambureggiare, tahm-boo-red-jah-ray, v., to drum
tamburo, tahm-boo-ro, m., drum; drummer
tampone, tahm-po-nay, m., blotter; (med.) wad
tana, tah-nah, f., den; cave; lair
tanaglie, tah-nah-l'yay, f pl., pincers
tanfo, tahn-fo, m., musty smell
tantino, tahn-tee-no, m., a wee bit, a little
tanto, tahn-to, a., so much, as much. adv., so
tapino, tah-pee-no, m., a poor "devil"   [much
tappa, tahp-pah, f., stopping-place; lap
tappare, tahp-pah-ray, v., to cork; to plug
tappeto, tahp-pay-to, m., carpet

tappezzeria, tahp-pet-tsay-**ree**-ah, f., tapestry ; upholstery

tappezziere, tahp-pet-tse'**ay**-ray. m., upholsterer

tappo, tahp-po, m., stopper

tara, tah-rah, f., tare ; hereditary fault

tarchiato°, tar-ke'**ah**-to, a., sturdy

tardare, tar-**dah**-ray, v., to retard

tardo°, tar-do, a., late ; dull ; slow

tarlato, tar-**lah**-to, a., rotten

tarlo, tar-lo, m., wood-worm

tarma, tar-mah, f., moth

tartagliare, tar-tah-l'**yah**-ray, v., to stammer

tartaruga, tar-tah-**roo**-gah, f., tortoise, turtle

tartassare, tar-tahss-**sah**-ray, v., to ill-use

tartufo, tar-**too**-fo, m., truffle ; (fig.) idiot

tasca, tahss-kah, f., pocket

tassa, tahss-sah, f., tax ; duty

tassare, tahss-**sah**-ray, v., to tax ; to rate

tassativo°, tahss-sah-**tee**-vo, a., peremptory

tasso, tahss-so, m., badger ; interest ; yew-tree

tastare, tahss-**tah**-ray, v., to touch ; to taste ; to taste

tastiera, tahss-te'**ay**-rah, f., key-board   [sound

tasto, tahss-to, m., taste ; (mus.) key

tatto, taht-to, m., tact ; sense of touch

tavola, tah-vo-lah, f., table ; index ; list ; plank [floor

tavolato, tah-vo-**lah**-to, m., wainscot ; panelling ;

tavoletta, tah-vo-**let**-tah, f., tablet

tavoliere, tah-vo-le'**ay**-ray, m., chess-board ; plateau

tavolozza, tah-vo-**lot**-tsah, f., palette

tazza, taht-tsah; f., cup

te, tay, pron., thee

tè, tay, m., tea

teatro, tay-**ah**-tro, m., theatre

teco, tay-ko, pron., with thee

tedesco, tay-**dess**-ko, a., German

tediare, tay-de'**ah**-ray, v., to weary

tegame, tay-**gah**-may, m., frying-pan

tegola, tay-go-lah, f., tile

teiera, tay-**yay**-rah, f., tea-pot

tela, tay-lah, f., canvas ; trap ; web

tela incerata, tay-lah in-chay-**rah**-tah, f., oilskin ; tarpaulin

telaio, tay-lah-e'o, m., loom ; frame

telefonata, tay-lay-fo-nah-tah, f., **telephone-call.**
— **interurbana**, trunk-call

telone, tay-lo-nay, m., large curtain

tema, tay-mah, m., theme ; task, f., fear

temerario°, tay-may-rah-re'o, a., dare-devil

temere, tay-may-ray, v., to fear

tempaccio, tem-paht-cho, m., very bad weather

tempera, tem-pay-rah, f., tempering ; distemper ;
toning

temperare, tem-pay-rah-ray, v., to **moderate ;**
to temper ; to weaken

temperino, tem-pay-ree-no, m., penknife

tempestivo°, tem-pess-tee-vo, a., timely

tempia, tem-pe'ah, f., temple

tempio, tem-pe'o, m., temple ; church

tempo, tem-po, m., time ; weather

temporale, tem-po-rah-lay, a., temporal, m., storm

temporaneo°, tem-po-rah-nay-o, a., temporary

temporeggiare, tem-po-red-jah-ray, v., to tem-

tempra, tem-prah, f., temper ; character   [porize

tenace, tay-nah-chay, a., tenacious ; tacky

tenacità, tay-nah-che-tah, f., tenacity

tenaglia, tay-nah-l'yah, f., pincers

tenda, ten-dah, f., tent ; awning ; curtain

tendere, ten-day-ray, v., to stretch ; to aim for ; to

tendina, ten-dee-nah, f., window-blind   [guard

tendine, ten-de-nay, m., tendon, sinew

tenebre, tay-nay-bray, f. pl., darkness

tenebroso°, tay-nay-bro-zo, a., dark ; confused

tenente, tay-nen-tay, m., lieutenant

tenere, tay-nay-ray, v., to hold ; to believe

tenerezza, tay-nay-ret-tsah, f., tenderness

tenero°, tay-nay-ro, a., tender, delicate

tenia, tay-ne'ah, m., tape-worm

tenitore, tay-ne-tor-ay, m., owner ; keeper

tenore, tay-nor-ay, m., tenor ; meaning

tentare, ten-tah-ray, v., to tempt ; to try

tentoni, ten-to-ne, adv., a —, groping

tenue°, tay-noo'ay, a., thin ; slender

tenuta, tay-noo-tah, f., behaviour ; uniform ; **estate**

teoria, tay-o-ree-ah, f., theory

teppa, tayp-pah, f., rabble

teppista, tayp-piss-tah, m., ruffian [shilly-shally

tergiversare, tair-je-vair-sah-ray, v., to shift ; to

tergo, tair-go, m., back. adv., **a —,** behind

termine, tair-me-nay, m., term ; limit ; end ; word ; terminus

termosifone, tair-mo-se-fo-nay, m., radiator

terra, tair-rah, f., earth ; country ; estate

terraglia, tair-rah-l'yah, f., pottery ; crockery

terrazziere, tair-raht-tse'ay-ray, m., navvy

terremoto, tair-ray-mo-to, m., earthquake

terreno, tair-ray-no, a., worldly. m., land ; ground

terriccio, tair-rit-cho, m., mould

terzeruolo, tair-tsay-roo'o-lo, m., (naut.) reef

terzo, tair-tso, a., third

teschio, tess-ke'o, m., skull

tesoreria, tay-zo-ray-ree-ah, f., treasury

tesoro, tay-zo-ro, m., treasure ; (fig.) riches [card

tessera, tess-say-rah, f., season-ticket ; member's

tesserato, tess-say-rah-to, a., ticket-holder ; mem-

tessere, tess-say-ray, v., to weave [ber

tessile, tess-se-lay, a., textile

tessitore, tess-se-tor-ay, f., weaver

tessitura, tess-se-too-rah, f., weaving ; tissue

tessuto, tess-soo-to, m., material, cloth

testa, tess-tah, f., head ; sense

testardo, tess-tar-do, a., pig-headed

testare, tess-tah-ray, v., to bequeath, to will

teste, tess-tay, m. & f., witness

teste, tess-tay, adv., just now

testificare, tess-te-fe-kah-ray, v., to testify [dence

testimonianza, tess-te-mo-ne'ahn-tsah, f., evi-

testimoniare, tess-te-mo-ne'ah-ray, v., to testify

testimonio, tess-te-mo-ne'o, m., witness ; testimony

testo, tess-to, m., text

testuggine, tess-tood-je-nay, f., tortoise ; turtle

tetro, tay-tro, a., gloomy ; bleak

tetta, tet-tah, f., breast ; teat

tettare, tet-tah-ray, v., to suck

tetto, tet-to, m., roof ; (fig.) shelter

tettoia, tet-to-e'ah, f., shed

ti, tee, pron., thou ; thee

tibia, tee-be'ah, f., shin-bone
ticchio, teek-ke'o, m., whim
tifo, tee-fo, m., typhus
tifoso, te-fo-zo, m., (enthusiast) sports-**fan**
tiglio, tee-l'yo, m., lime-tree
tiglioso, te-l'yo-zo, a., tough
tigna, tee-n'yah, f., scab
tign[u]ola, te-n'yo-lah, f., moth
tigre, tee-gray, m. & f., tiger, tigress
timbrare, teem-**brah**-ray, v., to stamp
timbro, teem-bro, m., stamp
timo, tee-mo, m., thyme
timone, te-mo-nay, m., rudder ; helm ; shaft
timoneggiare, te-mo-ned-**jah**-ray, v., to steer
timoniere, te-mo-ne'**ay**-ray, m., helmsman
timore, te-mo-ray, m., fear
tingere, tin-jay-ray, v., to dye ; to stain
tino, tee-no, m., vat, tub
tinozza, te-not-tsah, f., hip-bath ; bucket
tinta, tin-tah, f., dye ; colour, shade, hue
tintinnio, tin-tin-nee-o, m., tinkling
tintore, tin-tor-ay, m., dyer
tintoria, tin-to-ree-ah, f., dye-works
tipo, tee-po, m., type, model
tipografo, te-po-grah-fo, m., printer
tiraggio, te-rahd-jo, m., draught   [nize
tiranneggiare, te-rahn-ned-**jah**-ray, v., to tyran-
tiranno, te-**rahn**-no, m., tyrant
tirare, te-rah-ray, v., to pull : to print ; to throw :
    to shoot. — **calci,** to kick
tirata, te-rah-tah, f., pull ; tedious speech
tirato°, te-rah-to, a., drawn ; (fig.) mean
tiratura, te-rah-too-rah, f., edition, issue
tirchio, teer-ke'o, a., stingy
tirella, te-rel-lah, f., (strap) trace
tiretto, te-ret-to, m., drawer   [action
tiro, tee-ro, m., pull : hurl ; shot ; range ; mean
tirocinio, te-ro-chee-ne'o, m., apprenticeship
tisi, tee-ze, f., consumption
tisico, tee-ze-ko, a., consumptive   [to assay
titolare, te-to-lah-ray, m., principal. v., to name ;
titoli, tee-to-le, m. pl., (stocks) bonds

titolo, tee-to-lo, m., title ; token : pretext : (precious metal) fineness

titubare, te-too-bah-ray, v., to hesitate

tizzo, tit-tso, m., fire-brand [to occur

toccare, tock-kah-ray, v., to touch ; to have to :

tocco, tock-ko, m., touch ; stroke

togliere, to-l'yay-ray, v., to take away : to take off

tolda, toll-dah, f., deck

tolleranza, toll-lay-rahn-tsah, f., tolerance

tollerare, toll-lay-rah-ray, v., to endure

tomaio, to-mah-e'o, m., upper leather

tomba, tom-bah, f., tomb, vault

tombola, tom-bo-lah, f., lottery ; tumble

tomo, to-mo, m., volume

tondo, ton-do, a.,* round. m., dish

tonfo, ton-fo, m., thud, plop

tonnellaggio, ton-nell-lahd-jo, m., tonnage

tonnellata, ton-nell-lah-tah, f., ton

tonno, ton-no, m., tunny-fish

tono, to-no, m., tone ; tune. darsi del —, to make oneself important

topo, to-po, m., rat ; mouse

toppa, top-pah, f., lock ; patch

torace, to-rah-chay, m., chest

torba, tor-bah, f., peat

torbido°, tor-be-do, a., turbid

torcere, tor-chay-ray, v., to twist

torchio, tor-ke'o, m., press

torcia, tor-chah, f., torch

torcicollo, tor-che-kol-lo, m., stiff-neck

torcitura, tor-che-too-rah, f., twist

tordo, tor-do, m., thrush

torlo, tor-lo, m., yolk

tornaconto, tor-nah-kon-to, m., profit

tornare, tor-nah-ray, v., to turn ; to return

torneo, tor-nay-o, m., tournament

tornio, tor-ne'o, m., lathe

tornitore, tor-ne-tor-ay, m., turner

toro, to-ro, m., bull

torpedine, tor-pay-de-nay, f., torpedo

torpediniera, tor-pay-de-ne'ay-rah, f., torpedo-boat

torpedone, tor-pay-do-nay, m., motor-coach

torpido, tor-pe-do, a., torpid
torre, tor-ray, f., tower
torrefare, tor-ray-fah-ray, v., to torrefy, **to roast**
torreggiare, tor-red-jah-ray, v., **to tower**
torretta, tor-ret-tah, f., turret
torso, tor-so, m., trunk; stump; **core**
torta, tor-tah, f., cake; twist
torto, tor-to, m., wrong; fault
tortora, tor-to-rah, f., turtle-dove
torturare, tor-too-**rah**-ray, v., to torture
torvo*, tor-vo, a., surly
tosare, to-zah-ray, v., to shear, to clip
tosone, to-zo-nay, m., fleece
tosse, toss-say, f., cough
tossire, toss-see-ray, v., to cough
tostare, toss-tah-ray, v., to toast; to roast
tosto, toss-to, adv., soon. a., brazen. —**che**, adv.,
tovaglia, to-vah-l'yah, f., table-cloth [as soon as
tovagliolo, to-vah-l'yo-lo, m., napkin
tozzo, tot-tso, m., morsel. a., stocky
**tra, trah, prep., among; with; between
trabalzare, trah-bahl-**tsah**-ray, v., to jolt
trabalzone, trah-bahl-**tso**-nay, m., jolt
traboccare, trah-bock-kah-ray, v., to overflow
trabocchetto, trah-bock-**ket**-to, m., trap, pitfall
tracannare, trah-kahn-**nah**-ray, v., to swill
traccia, traht-chah, f., trace; mark; footprint
tracciare, traht-**chah**-ray, v., to trace
trachea, trah-**kay**-ah, f., windpipe
tracollare, trah-kol-lah-ray, v., to collapse
tracollo, trah-**kol**-lo, m., ruin, collapse
tracotanza, trah-ko-**tahn**-tsah, f., arrogance
tradimento, trah-de-**men**-to, m., treason
tradire, trah-dee-ray, v., to betray
traditore, trah-de-tor-ay, m., traitor
traducibile, trah-doo-**chee**-be-lay, a., translatable
tradurre, trah-**doohr**-ray, v., to translate
traente, trah-en-tay, m., (bill) drawer
trafelato*, trah-fay-**lah**-to, a., out of breath
trafficare, trahf-fe-**kah**-ray, v., to trade; to deal in
traffico, trahf-fe-ko, m., traffic; trade
trafiggere, trah-**fld**-jay-ray, v., to transfix

trafiletto, trah-fe-let-to, m., news paragraph
trafitta, trah-fit-tah, f., stab ; puncture ; seizure
traforare, trah-fo-rah-ray, v., to pierce ; to fret
traforo, trah-fo-ro, m., tunnel ; fret work
trafugare, trah-foo-gah-ray, v., to run away with
traghettare, trah-ghet-tah-ray, v., to ferry
traghetto, trah-ghet-to, m., ferry
tragittare, trah-jit-tah-ray, v., to cross
tragitto, trah-jit-to, m., crossing, passage
traguardo, trah-goo'ar-do, m., level ; winning-post
trainare, trah-e-nah-ray, v., to haul
traino, trah-e-no, m., trailer ; sledge
tralasciare, trah-lah-she'ah-ray, v., to cease; to omit
traliccio, trah-lit-cho, m., sack-cloth
tralignare, trah-le-n'yah-ray, v., to degenerate
trama, trah-mah, f., weft ; texture ; plot
tramaglio, trah-mah-l'yo, m., trammel
tramandare, trah-mahn-dah-ray, v., to transmit
tramare, trah-mah-ray, v., to plot ; to weave
trambusto, trahm-booss-to, m., hubbub ; confusion
tramite, trah-me-tay, m., way. per il —, through
tramontana, trah-mon-tah-nah, f., north
tramontare, trah-mon-tah-ray, v., to set, to sink
tramonto, trah-mon-to, m., setting ; fall
tramortire, trah-mor-tee-ray, v., to stun
trampoli, trahm-po-le, m. pl., stilts
tramutare, trah-moo-tah-ray, v., to transmute
tramvia, trahm-vee-ah, f., tram
tranello, trah-nell-lo, m., trick ; snare ; fraud
trangugiare, trahn-goo-jah-ray, v., to gulp
tranquillo*, trahn-kwill-lo, a., still ; calm
transazione, trahn-zah-tse'o-nay, f., transaction
transigere, trahn-see-jay-ray, v., to transact
trapanare, trah-pah-nah-ray, v., to drill
trapassare, trah-pahss-sah-ray, v., to pass away ; to pierce
trapasso, trah-pahss-so, m., transition ; transfer ; death
trapelare, trah-pay-lah-ray, v., to trickle through
trapiantare, trah-pe'ahn-tah-ray, v., to transplant
trappola, trahp-po-lah, f., pitfall ; ambush

trappolare, trahp-po-**lah**-ray, v., to ensnare; to dupe

trapunta, trah-**poonn**-tah, f., quilt

trapuntare, trah-poonn-**tah**-ray, v., to quilt; to embroider [

trarre, **trahr**-ray, v., to draw; to reap

trasalire, trah-sah-**lee**-ray, v., to startle

trasandato*, trah-sahn-**dah**-to, a., neglected

trasbordare, trahss-bor-**dah**-ray, v., to tranship

trascendere, trah-**shen**-day-ray, v., to exceed

trascinare, trah-she-**nah**-ray, v., to drag; to haul

trascorrere, trahss-**kor**-ray-ray, v., to elapse; (time) to spend

trascorso, trahss-**kor**-so, a., gone by. m., mistake

trascrivere, trahss-**kree**-vay-ray, v., to transcribe

trascurare, trahss-koo-**rah**-ray, v., to neglect; to overlook

trasferire, trahss-fay-**ree**-ray, v., to transfer

trasformare, trahss-for-**mah**-ray, v., to transform

trasgredire, trahss-gray-**dee**-ray, v., to trespass; to infringe

traslocare, trahss-lo-**kah**-ray, v., to displace; to remove [

trasloco, trahss-lo-ko, m., removal

trasognato*, trah-so-n'yah-to, a., absent-minded

trasparenza, trahss-pah-**ren**-tsah, f., transparency

traspirare, trahss-pe-**rah**-ray, v., to transpire; to perspire

traspirazione, trahss-pe-rah-tse'**o**-nay, f., perspiration

trasporre, trahss-**por**-ray, v., to transpose; to trespass

trasportare, trahss-por-**tah**-ray, v., to transport; to transfer [

trassato, trahss-**sah**-to, m., drawee

trastullarsi, trahss-tooll-**lar**-se, v., to play

trastullo, trahss-**tooll**-lo, m., toy; game

trasvolare, trahss-vo-**lah**-ray, v., to fly across

tratta, **traht**-tah, f., pull; draft; trawl; slavery

trattabile, traht-**tah**-be-lay, a., tractable

trattamento, traht-tah-**men**-to, m., treatment; feast; management

trattare, traht-**tah**-ray, v., to treat; to handle; to deal in [

trattario, traht-**tah**-re'o, m., drawee

trattativa, traht-tah-**tee**-vah, f., negotiation

trattato, traht-**tah**-to, m., treatise; treaty

trattenere, traht-tay-**nay**-ray, v., to detain ; to amuse

trattenimento, traht-tay-ne-**men**-to, m., entertainment

tratto, traht-to, m., distance ; tract ; quotation.
ad un —, adv., all at once

trattore, traht-**tor**-ay, m., inn-keeper

trattoria, traht-to-**ree**-ah, f., inn

travaglio, trah-**vah**-l'yo, m., work ; labour

travasare, trah-vah-**zah**-ray, v., to decant

trave, trah-vay, f., beam

travedere, trah-vay-**day**-ray, v., to see not clearly

traversa, trah-**vair**-sah, f., side-street ; sleeper

traversare, trah-vair-**sah**-ray, v., to traverse

traverso, trah-**vair**-so, a., oblique ; adverse

travestimento, trah-vess-te-**men**-to, m., disguise

travestire, trah-vess-**tee**-ray, v., to disguise

traviare, trah-ve-**ah**-ray, v., to mislead

travisare, trah-ve-**zah**-ray, v., to misinterpret

travolgere, trah-**vol**-jay-ray, v., to upset ; to carry [away

trazione, trah-tse'**o**-nay, f., traction

tre, tray, a., three

trebbiare, treb-be'**ah**-ray, v., to thresh

treccia, tret-chah, f., plait

tredicesimo, tray-de-**chay**-ze-mo, a., thirteenth

tredici, tray-de-che, a., thirteen

tregua, tray-goo'ah, f., truce ; respite

tremare, tray-**mah**-ray, v., to shiver ; to quake

tremarella, tray-mah-**rell**-lah, f., fear

trementina, tray-men-**tee**-nah, f., turpentine

tremito, tray-me-to, m., shiver ; tremor

tremolio, tray-mo-**lee**-o, m., quiver, shaking

treno, tray-no, m., train

trenta, tren-tah, a., thirty

trentesimo, tren-**tay**-ze-mo, a., thirtieth

trepidare, tray-pe-**dah**-ray, v., to shake

tresca, tress-kah, f., intrigue

tribolare, tre-bo-**lah**-ray, v., to torment ; (fig.) to [slave

tribordo, tre-**bor**-do, m., starboard

tribù, tre-**boo**, f., tribe

tricheco, tre-**kay**-ko, m., walrus

triciclo, tre-**chee**-klo, m., tricycle

trifoglio, tre-fo-l'yo, m., clover
trigesimo, tre-**jay**-ze-mo, a., thirtieth
triglia, tre-l'yah, f., red mullet
trillo, trill-lo, m., trill ; (mus.) quaver
trimestre, tre-**mess**-tray, m., (3 months) **quarter**
trina, tree-nah, f., point-lace
trincare, trin-**kah**-ray, v., to drink gaily
trincea, trin-**chay**-ah, f., trench
trincerare, trin-chay-**rah**-ray, v., to entrench
trinchetto, trin-**ket**-to, m., foresail
trinciare, trin-chah-ray, v., to carve ; **to slice**
trionfare, tre-on-**fah**-ray, v., to triumph
triplice, tree-ple-chay, a., triple
triplo, tree-plo, a., threefold
trippa, trip-pah, f., (fam.) belly
tripudio, tre-**poo**-de'o, m., rejoicing
triste, triss-tay, a., sad ; dismal
tristo*, triss-to, a., pale ; wicked
tritare, tre-**tah**-ray, v., to mince
trivella, tre-**vell**-lah, f., (tool) drill
trivellare, tre-vell-**lah**-ray, v., to bore
trivello, tre-**vell**-lo, m., gimlet
trivio, tree-ve'o, m., three streets meeting ; **brothel**
trofeo, tro-**fay**-o, m., trophy
troia, tro-e'ah, f., sow ; (fig.) loose woman
tromba, trom-bah, f., trumpet
troncare, tron-**kah**-ray, v., to sever ; to cease
tronco, tron-ko, m., trunk ; bust
tronfio*, tron-fe'o, a., bombastic
trono, tro-no, m., throne
troppo, trop-po, a., too. adv., too much
trota, tro-tah, f., trout
trottare, trot-**tah**-ray, v., to trot ; to run
trottata, trot-**tah**-tah, f., trot ; run ; ride
trotto, trot-to, m., trot
trottola, trot-to-lah, f., top
trovare, tro-**vah**-ray, v., to find ; to invent ; **to**
meet ; to call on
trovatello, tro-vah-**tell**-lo, m., foundling
trovatore, tro-vah-tor-ay, m., finder ; minstrel
truccatura, trook-kah-**too**-rah, f., make up ; fake
trucco, trook-ko, m. disguise ; trick ; billiards

truce, troo-chay, a., fierce, murderous
trucidare, troo-che-**dah**-ray, v., to slay
trucioli, troo-cho-le, m. pl., shavings
truffa, troof-fah, f., swindling
truffare, troof-**fah**-ray, v., to swindle
trufferia, troof-fay-**ree**-ah, f., trickery
truppa, troop-pah, f., troop ; band ; **troupe**
tu, too, pron., thou
tubo, too-bo, m., tube, pipe ; hose
tuffare, toof-**fah**-ray, v., to dip ; to dive in
tuffo, toof-fo, m., dip, plunge
tugurio, too-**goo**-re'o, m., hovel, attic
tumulare, too-moo-**lah**-ray, v., to inter
tumulo, too-moo-lo, m., tomb
tuo, too-o, pron., thy, thine
tuonare, too'o-**nah**-ray, v., to thunder
tuono, too'o-no, m., thunder
turacciolo, too-**raht**-cho-lo, m., cork
turare, too-**rah**-ray, v., to cork ; to plug ; **to gag** ; to choke up
turba, toohr-bah, f., multitude, mob
turbamento, toohr-bah-**men**-to, m., confusion
turbare, toohr-**bah**-ray, v., to perturb
turbinare, toohr-be-**nah**-ray, v., to whirl
turbine [turbinio], toohr-be-nay, m., whirlwind
turchese, toohr-**kay**-say, f., turquoise
turchino, toohr-**kee**-no, a., sky-blue
turpe, toohr-pay, a., vile   [ances
turpiloquio, toohr-pe-lo-**kwe**-o, m., noxious utter-
tutela, too-**tay**-lah, f., guardianship ; tutelage
tutore [tutrice], too-**tor**-ay, m. [f.], guardian
tuttavia, toot-tah-**vee**-ah, adv., yet ; nevertheless
tutto, toot-to, a., all ; entire
tuttora, toot-**tor**-ah, adv., yet

ubbia, oobb-**bee**-ah, f., mania ; hobby
ubbidire, oobb-be-**dee**-ray, v., to obey
ubbriacare, oobb-bre-ah-**kah**-ray, v., to make **or** get tipsy
ubbriachezza [ubbriacatura], oobb-bre-ah-**ket**-tsah, f., drunkenness
ubertà, oo-bair-**tah**, f., fruitfulness

uccello, oot-**chell**-lo, m., bird; chicken
uccidere, oot-**chee**-day-ray, v., to kill; **to murder**
uccisione, oot-che-ze'**O**-nay, f., slaughter
uccisore, oot-che-**zo**-ray, m., slayer
udibile, oo-**dee**-be-lay, a., audible
udienza, oo-de-en-tsah, f., audience; **sitting**
udire, oo-**dee**-ray, v., to hear
udito, oo-**dee**-to, m., hearing
uditorio, oo-de-tor-e'o, m., audience
udizione, oo-de-tse'**o**-nay, f., audition
ufficiale, oof-fe-**chah**-lay, a., official. m., officer;
    functionary
ufficio [uffizio], oof-**fee**-cho, m., office; **duty**
uggia, **ood**-jah, f., annoyance
uggioso°, ood-**jo**-zo, a., sullen; gloomy; tiresome
uguaglianza, oo-goo'ah-l'**yahn**-tsah, f., equality
uguagliare, oo-goo'ah-l'**yah**-ray, v., to equal
uliva, oo-**lee**-vah, f., olive
ulivo, oo-**lee**-vo, m., olive-tree
ultimare, ool-te-**mah**-ray, v., to finish
ultimo°, **ool**-te-mo, a., last; lowest; furthest
ululare, oo-loo-**lah**-ray, v., to howl
umettare, oo-met-**tah**-ray, v., to moisten
umile, **oo**-me-lay, a., humble, modest
umiliare, oo-me-l'**yah**-ray, v., to humiliate
umore, oo-**mor**-ay, m., humour; temper
unanime, oo-**nah**-ne-may, a., unanimous
uncinare, oonn-che-**nah**-ray, v., to hook; **to grap-**
uncino, oonn-**chee**-no, m., hook; clasp   [ple
undecimo, oonn-**day**-che-mo, a., eleventh
undici, oonn-**de**-che, a., eleven
ungere, oonn-**jay**-ray, v., to oil; to smear
unghia, oonn-ghah, f., nail; claw; hoof
unguento, oonn-goo'**en**-to, m., ointment
unico°, **oo**-ne-ko, a., unique; sole
unificare, oo-ne-fe-**kah**-ray, v., to unify
uniformare, oo-ne-for-**mah**-ray, v., to conform
unione, oo-ne'**o**-nay, f., union; link
unire, oo-**nee**-ray, v., to unite; to connect
unito°, oo-**nee**-to, a., united; compact; **even**
uno, **oo**-no, a., one; a *or* an. m., somebody
unto, oonn-to, a.,* greasy. m., grease

untuoso*, oonn-too-o-zo, a., greasy ; smeary : oily
uomo, oo'o-mo, m., man ; husband ; individual
uopo, oo'o-po, m., need, want
uosa, oo'o-zah, f., spat ; gaiter
uovo, oo'o-vo, m., egg. — sodo, hard-boiled egg
uragano, oo-rah-gah-no, m., hurricane
urbano*, oohr-bah-no, a., urbane ; civil
urgere, oohr-jay-ray, v., to urge
urina, oo-ree-nah, f., urine
urlare, oohr-lah-ray, v., to howl ; to shout
urlo, oohr-lo, m., yell
urna, oohr-nah, f., urn ; ballot-box
urtare, oohr-tah-ray, v., to bump against
urto, oohr-to, m., shock ; bump
usanza, oo-zahn-tsah, f., custom, habit
usare, oo-zah-ray, v., to use ; to be used to
usato*, oo-zah-to, a., used ; second-hand
usciere, oo-she'ay-ray, m., bailiff ; beadle ; usher
uscio, oo-she'o, m., door
uscire, oo-shee-ray, v., to go out
uscita, oo-shee-tah, f., issue ; exit
usignuolo, oo-ze-n'yoo'o-lo, m., nightingale
uso, oo-zo, m., habit, practice
usura, oo-zoo-rah, f., usury
usurpare, oo-zoohr-pah-ray, v., to usurp
utensile, oo-ten-se-lay, m., implement ; utensil
utile, oo-te-lay, a., useful, profitable
utilizzare, oo-te-lid-dzah-ray, v., to utilize
uva, oo-vah, f., grape. — passa, raisin.
— spina, gooseberry.

vacanza, vah-kahn-tsah, f., holidays ; vacancy
vacare, vah-kah-ray, v., to vacate, to give up
vacca, vahk-kah, f., cow
vaccinare, vaht-che-nah-ray, v., to vaccinate
vaccino, vaht-chee-no, m., vaccine
vacillare, vah-chill-lah-ray, v., to vacillate, to sway
vacuo, vah-koo'o, a., void, empty. m., vacuum
vagabondare, vah-gah-bon-dah-ray, v., to tramp ;
to loaf about
vagamente, vah-gah-men-tay, adv., vaguely ;
elegantly

vagare, vah-gah-ray, v., to ramble

vagheggiare, vah-ghed-jah-ray, v., to desire ; to ogle

vaghezza, vah-ghet-tsah, f., prettiness ; grace ; pleasure

vagire, vah-jee-ray, v., to whimper

vaglia, vah-l'yah, f., renown. **—postale,** money-order

vagliare, vah-l'yah-ray, v., to sift ; to select

vaglio, vah-l'yo, m., sieve

vago*, vah-go, a., vague ; pretty ; cosy

vagone, vah-go-nay, m., waggon ; van ; truck

vainiglia, vah'e-nee-l'yah, f., vanilla

vaiolo, vah-e'o-lo, m., small-pox

valanga, vah-lahn-gah, f., avalanche

valente, vah-len-tay, a., valiant ; clever

valentia, vah-len-tee-ah, f., cleverness ; bravery

valere, vah-lay-ray, v., to be worth

valevole, vah-lay-vo-lay, a., worthy

valicare, vah-le-kah-ray, v., to cross ; to wade through

valico, vah-le-ko, m., pass ; gap

valido*, vah-le-do, a., valid ; lawful ; healthy

valigia, vah-lee-jah, f., suit-case ; mail

vallata, vahll-lah-tah, f., wide valley

valle, vahll-lay, f., valley, glen, dale

valletto, vahll-let-to, m., valet

valore, vah-lor-ay, m., value ; bravery ; cost

valuta, vah-loo-tah, f., currency, value

valutare, vah-loo-tah-ray, v., to value, to appraise

valvola, vahll-vo-lah, f., valve

valzer, vahll-zair, m., waltz

vampa, vahm-pah, f., flame ; (fig.) passion

vaneggiare, vah-ned-jah-ray, v., to rave

vanga, vahn-gah, f., spade

vangare, vahn-gah-ray, v., to dig, to till

vangelo, vahn-jay-lo, m., Gospel

vano*, vah-no, a., vain, futile

vantaggiare, vahn-tahd-jah-ray, v., to further ; to favour

vantaggio, vahn-tahd-jo, m., advantage ; behalf

vantare, vahn-tah-ray, v., to praise ; to boast of

vantarsi, vahn-tar-se, v., to boast ; to strut

vanto, vahn-to, m., boast ; honour ; fame

vaporare, vah-po-**rah**-ray, v., to evaporate ; **to let off steam**

vapore, vah-**por**-ay, m., vapour, steam ; **steamer**

varare, vah-**rah**-ray, v., to launch

varcare, vahr-**kah**-ray, v., to cross over

variato*, vah-re'**ah**-to, a., varied ; different

varice, vah-**ree**-chay, f., varicose vein

vario°, vah-re'o, a., varied ; various

variopinto, vah-re'o-**pin**-to, a., mottled, **variegated**

varo, vah-ro, m., launching

vasaio, vah-**zah**-e'o, m., potter ; dealer in china

vasca, vahss-kah, f., basin ; bath ; tank

vascello, vah-**shell**-lo, m., ship ; warship ; vessel

vasellame, vah-zell-**lah**-may, m., crockery, china

vaso, vah-zo, m., pot ; vase

vassallo, vahss-**sahll**-lo, m., vassal

vassoio, vahss-**so**-e'o, m., tray ; shallow dish

vasto°, vahss-to, a., vast ; ample ; roomy

vaticinare, vah-te-che-**nah**-ray, v., to foretell

ve, vay, pron., you. adv., there

vecchiezza, vek-ke'**et**-tsah, f., old age

vecchio, **vek**-ke'o, a., old, antique ; second-hand. m., old man

vecchiume, vek-ke'**oo**-may, m., discarded utensils ; rags

vece, vay-chay, f., place ; part

vedere, vay-**day**-ray, v., to see ; to look at ; to see to

vedetta, vay-**det**-tah, f., outpost ; sentinel ; watch

vedova, vay-do-vah, f., widow

vedovo, vay-do-vo, m., widower

veduta, vay-**doo**-tah, f., view

veemente, vay-ay-**men**-tay, a., vehement

vegetale, vay-jay-**tah**-lay, m., vegetable

vegeto*, vay-jay-to, a., healthy ; fertile

veggente, ved-**jen**-tay, m., seer

veglia, vay-l'yah, f., eve ; vigil ; **evening party ;** sleeplessness ; brink

vegliardo, vay-l'**yar**-do, m., venerable old man

vegliare, vay-l'**yah**-ray, v., to keep awake ; to be vigilant

veglione, vay-l'**yo**-nay, m., fancy dress ball

veicolo, vay-ee-ko-lo, m., vehicle
vela, vay-lah, f., sail ; sailing-ship
velare, vay-lah-ray, v., to veil ; to disguise
veleggiare, vay-led-jah-ray, v., to sail
veleno, vay-lay-no m., poison ; infection
veletta, vay-let-tah, f., veil
veliere[o], vay-l'yay-ray, m., sailing-ship
velivolo, vay-lee-vo-lo, m., flying machine
velleità, vel-lay-e-tah, f., impotent wish
vello, vell-lo, m., fleece
velloso, vell-lo-zo, a., shaggy
velluto, vell-loo-to, m., velvet
velo, vay-lo, m., veil ; film ; pretence
veloce, vay-lo-chay, a., swift ; express ; nimble
velocimetro, vay-lo-chee-may-tro, m., speedometer
veltro, vell-tro, m., greyhound
vena, vay-nah, f., vein ; grain ; luck ; leaning
vendemmia, ven-dem-me'ah, f., vintage
vendere, ven-day-ray, v., to sell
vendibile, ven-dee-be-lay, a., saleable
vendicare, ven-de-kah-ray, v., to vindicate
vendita, ven-de-tah, f., sale
venditore [venditrice], ven-de-tor-ay, m. [f.],
salesman [saleswoman], vendor
venerare, vay-nay-rah-ray, v., to venerate
venerdì, vay-nair-dee, m., Friday
venia, vay-ne'ah, f., pardon ; leave
venire, vay-nee-ray, v., to come ; to occur
ventaglio, ven-tah-l'yo, m., fan
ventata, ven-tah-tah, f., (wind) gust
ventesimo, ven-tay-ze-mo, a., twentieth
venti, ven-te, a., twenty
ventilare, ven-te-lah-ray, v., to ventilate
vento, ven-to, m., wind ; draught ; conceit
ventola, ven-to-lah, f., fan
ventre, ven-tray, m., belly, abdomen
ventura, ven-too-rah, f., chance, luck
venturo, ven-too-ro, a., future ; coming
venustà, vay-nooss-tah, f., comeliness
venuta, vay-noo-tah, f., arrival
verace, vay-rah-chay, a., veracious

veramente, vay-rah-**men**-tay, adv., truly; really

verbigrazia, vair-be-**grah**-tse'ah, adv., for instance

verbo, vair-bo, m., verb; word

verde, vair-day, a., green; fresh. m., green; vigour. **esser al —**, to be broke

verderame, vair-day-**rah**-may, m., verdigris

verdetto, vair-**det**-to, m., verdict; judgment

verdura, vair-**doo**-rah, f., verdure; greens; prime

verecondia, vay-ray-**kon**-de'ah, f., shyness; reserve

verga, vair-gah, f., rod; wand; ingot

vergare, vair-**gah**-ray, v., to flog; to draw up

verghetta, vair-**ghet**-tah, f., rod; twig; cane

vergine, vair-je-nay, f., virgin

vergogna, vair-go-n'yah, f., shame; shyness

veridicità, vay-re-de-che-**tah**, f., truth

verificatore, vay-re-fe-kah-**tor**-ay, m., inspector

veritiero*, vay-re-te'ay-ro, a., truthful; true

verme, vair-may, m., worm

vermicelli, vair-me-**chell**-le, m. pl., vermicelli

vermiglio, vair-mee-l'yo, m., vermilion

vernice, vair-nee-chay, f., varnish; paint; polish

verniciare, vair-ne-**chah**-ray, v., to varnish; to polish

vero*, vay-ro, a., true; real

verosimile, vay-ro-see-me-lay, a., likely

verricello, vair-re-**chell**-lo, m., winch

verruca, vair-**roo**-kah, f., wart

versamento, vair-sah-**men**-to, m., payment; shedding

versante, vair-**sahn**-tay, m., watershed; slope

versare, vair-**sah**-ray, v., to pour; to spill; to pay

versato*, vair-**sa**-to, a., spilled; paid; expert

verso, vair-so, m., verse; way. prep., towards

vertere, vair-tay-ray, v., to refer to

vertice, vair-te-chay, m., tip, peak

vertigine, vair-tee-je-nay, f., dizziness

veruno, vay-**roo**-no, pron., nobody; not one

verziere, vair-dze'ay-ray, m., kitchen-garden

verzura, vair-**dzoo**-rah, f., greens

vescica, vay-**shee**-kah, f., bladder; blister

vescicante, vay-she-**kahn**-tay, m., mustard plaster

vescovado, vess-ko-**vah**-do, m., bishopric
vescovile, vess-ko-**vee**-lay, a., episcopal
vescovo, **vess**-ko-vo, m., bishop
vespa, **vess**-pah, f., wasp
vespaio, vess-**pah**-e'o, m., wasps' nest
vespasiano, vess-pah-ze'**ah**-no, m., urinal
vespri, **vess**-pre, m. pl., vespers
vessare, vess-**sah**-ray, v., to vex ; to harrass
vessillo, vess-**sill**-lo, m., flag, banner, standard
vestaglia, vess-tah-l'yah, f., overalls
veste, **vess**-tay, f., coat ; dress ; disguise ; excuse ; role
vestiario, vess-te-**ah**-re'o, m., trousseau ; outfit ;
  cloak-room
vestimenti, vess-te-**men**-te, m. pl., garments
vestire, vess-**tee**-ray, v., to dress. m., clothing
vestito, vess-**tee**-to, m., dress ; suit
veterinario, vay-tay-re-**nah**-re'o, m., veterinary
vetraio, vay-**trah**-e'o, m., glazier
vetreria, vay-tray-**ree**-ah, m., glass-ware
vetrina, vay-**tree**-nah, f., shop-window
vetro, **vay**-tro, m., glass
vetta, **vet**-tah, f., peak, top ; spire
vettovaglie, vet-to-**vah**-l'yay, f. pl., victuals
vettura, vet-**too**-rah, f., cab ; car ; freight
vetturino, vet-too-**ree**-no, m., cabman
vetustà, vay-tooss-**tah**, f., ancientness
vetusto°, vay-**tooss**-to, a., very old
vezzeggiare, vet-tsed-**jah**-ray, v., to fondle
vezzo, **vet**-tso, m., caress ; charm ; way ; necklace
vezzoso°, vet-**tso**-zo, a., nice ; graceful
vi, vee, adv., there. pron., you
via, **vee**-ah, f., street ; way. adv., away, out.
  interj., come !
viabilità, ve'ah-be-le-**tah**, f., road conditions
viadotto, ve'ah-**dot**-to, m., viaduct
viaggiare, ve'ahd-**jah**-ray, v., to travel
viaggiatore, ve'ahd-jah-**tor**-ay, m., traveller
viaggio, ve'**ahd**-jo, m., voyage ; journey
viale, ve'**ah**-lay, m., avenue ; drive
viandante, ve'ahn-**dahn**-tay, m., wayfarer
viavai, ve'ah-**vah**-e, m., bustling

vibrare, ve-brah-ray, v., to vibrate ; to jar ; to sling ; to give

vicario, ve-kah-re'o, m., vicar

vicenda, ve-chen-dah, f., happening ; change

viceré, ve-c..ay-ray, m., viceroy

vicinanza, ve-c..c-nahn-tsah, f., proximity

vicinato, ve-che-nah-to, m., neighbourhood ; neighbours

vicino, ve-chee-no, m., neighbour. a.,* near. adv., near

vicolo, vee-ko-lo, m., lane ; alley

vidimare, ve-de-mah-ray, v., to authenticate

vieppiù, ve'ayp-pe'oo, adv., much more

vie.are, ve'ay-tah-ray, v., to prohibit

vieto*, ve'ay-to, a., out-of-date ; forbidden

vigente, ve-jen-tay, a., existing

vigere, vee-jay-ray, v., to be in force

vigesimo, ve-jay-ze-mo, a., twentieth

vigilare, ve-je-lah-ray, v., to watch ; to watch over

vigile, vee-je-lay, a., vigilant. m., policeman

vigilia, ve-jee-le'ah, f., eve ; vigil

vigliacco, ve-l'yahk-ko, a.,* cowardly ; vile. m., coward

vigna [**vigneto**], vee-n'yah, f., vineyard

vigore, ve-gor-ay, m., vigour

vile, vee-lay, a., vile, contemptible

vilipendere, ve-le-pen-day-ray, v., to abuse

villa, **vill**-lah, m., rural or suburban residence

villaggio, vill-lahd-jo, m., village

villania, vill-lah-nee-ah, f., abuse

villano, vill-lah-no, a.,* ill-bred. uncouth. m., yokel, rustic

villanzone, vill-lahn-tso-nay, m., uncouth person

villeggiante, vill-led-jahn-tay, m., holiday-maker

villino, vill-lee-no, m., cottage

villoso*, vill-lo-zo, a., hairy ; shaggy

viltà, vill-tah, f., cowardice ; vileness

vimine, vee-me-nay, m., cane ; twig

vi..aio, ve-nah-e'o, m., wine-merchant

vincente, vin-chen-tay, m., the winner

vin.ere, vin-chay-ray, v., to vanquish ; to win

vincita, vi..-che-tah, f., gain, winnings ; win

vincitore, vin-che-**tor**-ay, m., conqueror ; winner
vincolare, vin-ko-**lah**-ray, v., to bind legally ; to tie
vincolo, **vin**-ko-lo, m., bond ; link
vino, **vee**-no, m., wine
violaciocca, ve'o-lah-**chock**-kah, f., wallflower
violare, ve'o-**lah**-ray, v., to violate
violentare, ve'o-len-**tah**-ray, v., to force ; to ill-use
violento, ve'o-**len**-to, a., violent ; impetuous
violetto, ve'o-**let**-to, m., violet colour
violino, ve'o-**lee**-no, m., fiddle
viottola, ve'**ot**-to-lah, f., path
vipera, **vee**-pay-rah, f., viper
viraggio, ve-**rahd**-jo, m., developing ; veering
virare, ve-**rah**-ray, v., to veer
virgola, **veer**-go-lah, f., comma
virgolette, veer-go-**let**-tay, f. pl., quotation marks
virgulto, veer-**gool**-to, m., shoot, sucker
virile, ve-**ree**-lay, a., virile
virilmente, ve-rill-**men**-tay, adv., manly
virtù, veer-**too**, f., virtue
virtuoso*, veer-too'**o**-zo, a., virtuous
visceri, **vee**-shay-re, m., entrails
vischio, **viss**-ke'o, m., mistletoe ; bird-lime snare
visconte, viss-**kon**-tay, m., viscount
visibile, ve-**zee**-be-lay, a., visible
visiera, ve-ze'**ay**-rah, f., eye-shade ; mask
visione, ve-ze'**o**-nay, f., vision
visitare, ve-ze-**tah**-ray, v., to visit ; to examine
visitatore, ve-ze-tah-**tor**-ay, m., visitor
viso, **vee**-zo, m., face ; appearance
vispo*, **viss**-po, a., lively, nimble
vista, **viss**-tah, f., view ; eyesight
visto, **viss**-to, m., visa
vistoso*, viss-**to**-zo, a., showy
vita, **vee**-tah, f., life ; waist ; existence
vitalizio, ve-tah-lee-**tse**'o, m., life-annuity
vite, **vee**-tay, f., vine ; screw
vitello, ve-**tell**-lo, m., calf ; veal
viticoltore, ve-te-koll-**tor**-ay, m., vine-cultivator
vittima, **vit**-te-mah, f., victim
vitto, **vit**-to, m., food
vittoria, vit-**tor**-e'ah, f., victory

vittorioso, vit-to-re'O-zo, a., victorious, triumphant

vituperare, ve-too-pay-rah-ray, v., to vituperate, to abuse

vituperoso*, ve-too-pay-ro-zo, a., shameful ; abusive

viuzza, ve'oot-tsah, f., narrow street

viva, vee-vah, interj., hurrah ! long live !

vivacchiare, ve-vahk-ke'ah-ray, v., to live poorly

vivace, vc-vah-chay, a., lively, sprightly

vivacità, ve-vah-che-**tah**, f., vivacity, briskness

vivamente, ve-vah-men-tay, adv., vividly ; gaily

vivanda, ve-**vahn**-dah, f., food ; dish

vivandiere, ve-vahn-de'**ay**-ray, m., victualler, caterer

vivente, ve-ven-tay, a., living

vivere, vee-vay-ray, v., to live ; to subsist. m., existence

viveri, vee-vay-re, m. pl., victuals

vivezza, ve-vet-tsah, f., liveliness, vivacity ; vividity

vivificare, ve-ve-fe-kah-ray, v., to imbue with life

vivo*, vee-vo, a., lively, alert

viziare, ve-tse'ah-ray, v., to vitiate

vizio, vee-tse'o, m., vice ; blemish

vizioso, ve-tse'o-zo, a., corrupted ; vicious

vizzo, vit-tso, a., withered ; wizened

vocabolario, vo-kah-bo-lah-re'o, m., vocabulary ; dictionary

vocabolo, vo-**kah**-bo-lo, m., word ; expression

vocale, vo-kah-lay, a., vocal. f., vowel

vocazione, vo-kah-tse'o-nay, f., vocation

voce, vo-chay, f., voice

vociferare, vo-che-fay-**rah**-ray, v., to vociferate

voga, vo-gah, f., vogue ; rowing

vogare, vo-gah-ray, v., to row

voglia, vo-l'yah, f., wish, will, fancy

voglioso*, vo-l'yo-zo, a., eager

voi, vo-e, pron., you

volante, vo-lahn-tay, a., flying ; loose. m., steering-wheel

volare, vo-lah-ray, v., to fly

volatile, vo-lah-te-lay, a., volatile. m., bird

volatilizzare, vo-lah-te-lid-dzah-ray, v., to volatilize

volentieri, vo-len-te'ay-re, adv., willingly

volere, vo-lay-ray, v., to will; to want. m., desire

volgare, voll-gah-ray, a., vulgar

volgarità, voll-gah-re-tah, f., vulgarity

volgere, voll-jay-ray, v., to turn; to bend; to roll

volgo, voll-go, m., people; mob; low class

volo, vo-lo, m., flight

volontà, vo-lon-tah, f., will

volontario, vo-lon-tah-re'o, a.,* voluntary; spontaneous. m., volunteer

volpe, voll-pay, f., fox

volpino*, voll-pee-no, a., foxy, sly, artful

volta, voll-tah, f., turn; time; vault

voltare, voll-tah-ray, v., to turn; to turn round; to revolve

volteggiare, voll-ted-jah-ray, v., to vault; to hover; to fly about

volto, voll-to, m., face; mien; arch

volubile, vo-loo-be-lay, a., voluble

volume, vo-loo-may, m., volume; mass

voluminoso*, vo-loo-me-no-zo, a., voluminous

voluttà, vo-loot-tah, f., lust

voluttuoso*, vo-loot-too-o-zo, a., voluptuous

vomero, vo-may-ro, m., ploughshare

vomitare, vo-me-tah-ray, v., to vomit

vorace, vo-rah-chay, a., voracious

voracità, vo-rah-che-tah, f., greediness

voragine, vo-rah-je-nay, f., abyss, ravine

vortice, vor-te-chay, m., vortex; whirl

vostro, voss-tro, a., your. pron., yours

votante, vo-tahn-tay, m., voter

votare, vo-tah-ray, v., to vote

votarsi, vo-tar-se, v., to devote oneself

voto, vo-to, m., vote; solemn promise

vulcano, vooll-kah-no, m., volcano

vulcanico, vooll-kah-ne-ko, a., volcanic

vulnerabile, vooll-nay-rah-be-lay, a., vulnerable

vulnerare, vooll-nay-rah-ray, v., to injure

vuotare, voo'o-tah-ray, v., to empty

vuoto, voo'o-to, a., empty ; inane. m., vacuum ; naught ; vanity

---

w, x, y.—These letters do not occur in Italian (foreign words excepted) either as initials or otherwise. S is used instead of X, and I instead of Y.

---

zacchera, tsahk-kay-rah, f., spot of mud
zaffare, tsahf-fah-ray, v., to stop up
zafferano, tsahf-fay-rah-no, m., saffron
zaffiro, tsahf-fee-ro, m., sapphire
zaffo, tsahf-fo, m., wad, plug
zagaglia, tsah-gah-l'yah, f., javelin
zaino, tsah-e-no, m., knapsack
zampa, tsahm-pah, f., paw
zampare, tsahm-pah-ray, v., to paw
zampillare, tsahm-pill-lah-ray, v., (fluid) to jet
zampillo, tsahm-pill-lo, m., jet
zampogna, tsahm-po-n'yah, f., bag-pipe
zangola, tsahn-go-lah, f., churn ; vat
zangolare, tsahn-go-lah-ray, v., to churn
zanna, tsahn-nah, f., tusk ; fang
zanzara, tsahn-tsah-rah, f., gnat
zanzariera, tsahn-tsah-re'ay-rah, f., mosquito-net
zappa, tsahp-pah, f., hoe ; spade
zappare, tsahp-pah-ray, v., to till ; to sap
zappatore, tsahp-pah-tor-ay, m., sapper
zatta, tsaht-tah, f., raft
zattera, tsaht-tay-rah, f., raft
zavorra, tsah-vor-rah, f., ballast
zebra, tsay-brah, f., zebra
zecca, tsek-kah, f., (parasite) tick ; (money) mint
zeffiro, tsef-fe-ro, m., zephyr
zelante, tsay-lahn-tay, a., zealous
zelo, tsay lo, m., zeal
zenzero, tsen-tsay-ro, m., ginger
zeppo, tsep-po, a., full to the brim ; overcrowded
zerbinotto, tsair-be-not-to, m., coxcomb ; fop
zia, tsee-ah, f., aunt
zibaldone, tse-bahl-do-nay, m., medley

zibellino, tse-bell-lee-no, m., sable

zigrino, tse-gree-no, m., shagreen

zimarra, tse-mar-rah, f., gown

zimbello, tsim-bell-lo, m., decoy ; object of ridicule

zinco, tsin-ko, m., zinc

zingaro, tsin-gah-ro, m., gipsy

zio, tsee-o, m., uncle

zitella, tse-tell-lah, f., spinster, young woman

zitellona, tse-tell-lo-nah, f., old maid

zittire, tsit-tee-ray, v., to hush

zitto, tsit-to, a.,* silent ; still. interj., shut up !

zizzania, tsit-tsah-ne'ah, f., discord

zoccolo, tsock-ko-lo, m., wooden shoe ; hoof ; pedestal ; (fig.) simpleton

zolfanello, tsoll-fah-nell-lo, m., sulphur-match

zolfare, tsoll-fah-ray, v., to spray with sulphur

zolfino, tsoll-fee-no, m., sulphur-match

zolfo, tsoll-fo, m., sulphur

zolla, tsoll-lah, f., lump

zona, tso-nah, f., zone

zoologico, tso-o-lo-je-ko, a., zoological

zoppicare, tsop-pe-kah-ray, v., to limp ; to walk lamely

zoppo, tsop-po, a.,* lame ; faulty. m., lame person

zotico, tso-te-ko, m., boorish ; uncouth

zucca, tsook-kah, f., pumpkin

zuccata, tsook-kah-tah, f., thrust with the head

zuccherare, tsook-kay-rah-ray, v., to sweeten

zuccherino, tsook-kay-ree-no, m., bon-bon, candy

zucchero, tsook-kay-ro, m., sugar

zuccheroso, tsook-kay-ro-so, a., sugary

zucchetto, tsook-ket-to, m., skull-cap ; small pumpkin

zuccone, tsook-ko-nay, m., dense fellow ; big pumpkin

zuffa, tsoof-fah, f., fray, scuffle

zufolare, tsoo-fo-lah-ray, v., to whistle

zuppa, tsoop-pah, f., soup ; a mix up

zuppiera, tsoop-pe'ay-rah, f., tureen

zurlare, tsoor-lah-ray, v., to jest, to ridicule

DIZIONARIO
INGLESE-ITALIANO
(ENGLISH-ITALIAN DICTIONARY)

(Per la spiegazione della pronuncia figurata si leggano attentamente le pagine x., xii., e xiii.)

a, ei. art., un, uno, una

abaft, a-baaft', adv., (naut.) poppa, marcia indietro

abandon. a-ban'-dn, v., abbandonare

abandoned, a-ban'-dond, a., abbandonato

abase, a-beis', v., abbassare, umiliare, degradare

abash, a-bash', v., turbare, sconcertare, svergognare

abate, a-beit', v., (weather) calmare ; (price) abbas-   [sare

abbot, ab'-ot, n., abate m.

abbreviate, a-brii'-vi-eit, v., abbreviare

abdicate, ab'-di-keit, v., abdicare

abdomen, ab-dou'-men, n., addome m.

abduction, ab-dŏk'-shon, n., rapimento **m.**

abet, a-bet', v., istigare ; tener mano a

abeyance, a-bei'-ans, n., sospeso m.

abhor, ab-hoor', v., aborrire

abhorrent, ab-hor'-ent, a., ripugnante

abide, a-baid', v., dimorare ; **— by,** aderire

ability, a-bil'-i-ti, n., abilità f.

ab ect, ab'-chekt, a., abbietto

ablaze, a-bleis', adv., infiammato, in fiamme

able, ei'-bl, a., abile ; **to be —,** potere

ably, ei'-bli, adv., abilmente

abnormal*, ab-noor'-mal, a., anormale ; (mis-   shapen) deforme

aboard, a-boord', adv., a bordo

abode, a-boud', n., dimora f., abitazione f.

abolish, a-bol'-ish, v., abolire ; sopprimere

abominable, a-bom'-in-a-bl, a., abbominevole

aboriginal, ab-o-rich'-in-al, a., aborigeno

abortion, a-boor'-shon, n., aborto m.

abound, *a*-baund', v., abbondare

about, *a*-baut', adv., circa ; verso ; intorno ; quasi ; vicino ; a rispetto di ; (ship) pronto ; (— to do) sul punto di

above, *a*-bŏv', adv., su, sopra, al di sopra

abrasion, *a*-brei'-shon, n., abrasione f., scortica-

abreast, *a*-brest', adv., di fronte   [tura f.

abridge, *a*-brich', v., abbreviare, riassumere

abroad, *a*-brood', adv., all'estero

abrupt*, *a*-brŏpt', a., brusco ; (steep) scosceso

abscess, ab'-ses, n., ascesso m.

abscond, ab-skond', v., nascondirsi

absence, ab'-sens, n., assenza f.

absent, ab'-sent, a., assente. v., (— oneself) assentarsi : — -minded, a., distratto

absentee, ab-sen-tii', n., assente m. & f.

absolute*, ab'-so-liuut, a., assoluto

absolve, ab-solv',v.,assolvere ; — from,assolvere da

absorb, ab-soorb', v., assorbire

abstain, ab-stein', v., astenersi

abstainer, ab-stein'-*a*, n., astemio m.

abstemious*, ab-stii'-mi-os, a., astemio, sobrio

abstinence, ab'-sti-nens, n., astinenza f.

abstract, ab-strakt', v., astrarre

abstract, ab'-strakt, n., estratto m., compendio m.
a., astratto

absurd*, ab-sĕrd', a., assurdo

abundant, *a*-bŏn'-dant, a., abbondante

abuse, *a*-biuus', v., abusare ; (affront) ingiuriare

abuse, *a*-biuus', n., abuso m. ; (affront) ingiuria f.

abusive*, *a*-biuus-iv, a., abusivo

abyss, *a*-bis', n., abisso m.

acacia, *a*-kei'-shi-*a*, n., acacia f., gaggia f.

academy, *a*-kad'-e-mi, n., accademia f.

accede, ak'-siid, v., accedere

accelerate, ak-sel'-*er*-eit, v., accelerare

accent, ak'-sent, n., accento m.

accent, ak-sent', v., accentare

accentuate, ak-sent'-iu-eit, v., accentuare

accept, ak-sept', v., accettare ; —ance, n., accettazione f. ; —or, accettante m.

access, ak'-ses, n., accesso m. ; entrata f.

accession, ak-ses'-shon, n., accessione f.

accessory, ak'-ses-so-ri, n., accessorio m. ; (person) complice m. & f.

accident, ak'-si-dent, n., accidente m.

accidental*, ak-si-den'-tl, a., accidentale

acclaim, a-kleim', v., acclamare

accommodate, a-kom'-o-deit, v., accomodare ; (lodge) alloggiare ; (lend) prestare

accommodation, a-kom-o-dei'-shon, n., accomodamento m. ; (lodging, shelter) alloggio m.

accompaniment, a-kŏm'-pa-ni-ment, n., accompagnamento m.

accompanist, a-kŏm'-pa-nist, n., accompagnatore m., accompagnatrice f.

accompany, a-kŏm'-pa-ni, v., accompagnare

accomplice, a-kom'-plis, n., complice m. & f.

accomplish, a-kom'-plish, v., compiere ; (purpose) venir a capo di ; —ment, n., compimento m.; (performance) effettuazione f.; —ments, doti f.pl.

accord, a-koord', n., accordo m., gradimento m. v., accordare ; in —ance with, d'accordo con ; of one's own —, di propria volontà ; —ing to, prep., secondo ; in armonia con : —ingly, adv., in conseguenza ; conformemente

accordion, a-koor'-di-on, n., armonica f.

accost, a-kost', v., accostare

account, a-kaunt', n., (bill) conto m. ; (explanation) rapporto m.; on —, in conto...; on no —, in nessun modo ; — for, v., (responsibility) rendere conto di ; —able, a., responsabile

accountant, a-kaunt-ant, n., ragioniere m.

accrue, a-kruu', v., accumulare ; provenire

accumulate, a-kiuu'-miu-leit, v., accumulare

accuracy, ak'-iu-ra-si, n., accuratezza f.

accurate*, ak'-iu-reit, a., accurato, esatto

accursed, a-kerst, a., maledetto

accuse, a-kiuus', v., accusare

accustom, a-kŏs'-tm, v., accostumare

ace, eis, n., asso m.

ache, eik, n., dolore m. v., far male

achieve, a-chiiv', v., eseguire ; (success) conseguire

achievement, *a*-chiiv'-ment, n., (attainment) conseguimento m. ; (performance) fatto m.

acid, as'-id, n., acido m. a., acido

acidity, *a*-sid'-i-ti, n., acidità f.

acknowledge, ak-nol'-ech, v., riconoscere ; (receipt) accusare

acknowledgment, ak-nol'-ech-ment, n., ricognizione f. ; (receipt) ricevuta f.

acme, ak'-mi, n., apogeo m. ; cima f.

acorn, ei'-koorn, n., ghianda f.

acoustics, *a*-kus'-tiks, n., acustica f.

acquaint, *a*-kueint'. v., avvertire ; (familiarize) far conoscere ; **—ance,** n., conoscenza f. ; (person) conoscente m. & f.

acquiesce, a-kui-es', v., accondiscendere

acquiescence, a-kui-es'-ans, n., consenso m.

acquire, *a*-kuair', v., acquistare, conseguire

acquisition, ak-kui-si'-shon, n., acquisto m.

acquit, *a*-kuit', v., scaricare, (law) prosciogliere

acquittal, *a*-kuit'-l, n., assoluzione f.

acre, ei'-kr, n., acro m.

acrid, ak'-rid, a., acre

across, *a*-kros', adv., attraverso. prep., a traverso

act, akt, n., azione f. ; (of a play) atto m. ; (law) legge f. v., agire ; (in a theatre) recitare

action, ak'-shon, n., azione f.; (law) processo m.; (war) combattimento m.

active*, ak'-tiv, a., attivo

activity, ak-tiv'-i-ti, n., attività f.

actor, ak'-ta, n., attore m.

actress, ak'-tres, n., attrice f.

actual*, ak'-tiu-al, a., attuale ; reale

actuate, ak'-tiu-eit, v., incitare ; mettere in azione

acumen, *a*-kiuu'-men, n., acume m.

acute, *a*-kiuut'. a., acuto

acuteness, *a*-kiuut'-nes, n., acutezza f.

adage, ad'ich, n., adagio m.

adamant, ad'-*a*-mant, a., duro come un diamante

adapt, *a*-dapt', v., adattare

adaptation, *a*-dap-tei'-shon, n., adattamento m.

add, ad, v., aggiungere ; (sum) addizionare

adder, ad'-*a*, n., (serpent) aspide f.

addicted, *a*-dikt'-id. a., dedito

addition, *a*-di'-shon. n., addizione f.

additional, *a*-di'-shon-l. a., aggiunto

addle, ad'-l. a., (egg) guasto ; (mind) confuso

address, *a*-dres'. v., indirizzare ; (orally) **far un**
discorso. n., indirizzo m. ; discorso m.

adduce, *a*-diuus', v., addurre

adequacy, ad'-i-kua-si. n., adeguamento m.

adequate, ad'-i-kuet. a., adeguato

adhere, ad-hiir'. v., aderire

adherence, ad-hiir'-ens. n., aderenza f. ; (loy
alty) adesione f

adherent, ad-hiir'-ent. n.,partigiano m. a., aderente

adhesive, ad-hii'-siv. a., adesivo n., adesivo m.

adjacent, a-chei'-sent. a., adiacente

adjoin, *a* choin', v.,aggiungere ; (to be next to) esser

adjoining, *a*-choin'-ing. a., vicino   [attiguo

adjourn, *a*-chërn'. v., aggiornare

adjournment, *a*-chërn'-ment. n., rinvio m.

adjudge, *a*-chöch', v., aggiudicare

adjunct, a'-chön-kt.a., aggiunto. n., accessorio m.

adjust, *a*-chöst', v., aggiustare ; (mech.) regolare

adjustment, *a*-chöst'-ment. n., aggiustamento m.

adjutant, a'-chu-tant. n., aiutante m

administer, ad-min'-is-ta, v., amministrare

admirable, ad'-mi-ra-bl. a., ammirevole

admiral, ad'-mi-ral. n., ammiraglio m.

admire, ad-mair', v., ammirare

admission, ad-mi'-shon. n., ammissione f., entrata f.

admit, ad-mit'. v., ammettere ; fare entrare

admittance, ad-mit'-ans, n., ammissione f.,
entrata f.

admonish, ad-mon'-ish. v., ammonire

admonition, ad-mo-ni'-shon. n., ammonizione f.

ado, *a*-duu', n., scalpore m.; (noise) agitazione f.

adopt, *a*-dopt', v., adottare

adore, *a*-door', v., adorare

adorn, *a*-doorn', v., adornare

adornment, *a*-doorn'-ment, n., adornamento m.

adrift, *a*-drift', adv., (sea) alla deriva ; (lost) in per-

adroit°, *a* droit'. a., destro   [dizione

adulate, ad'-iu-leit. v., adulare

adulation, ad-iu-lei'-shon. n., adulazione f.

adult, a-dŏlt', n., adulto m. a., adulto

adulterate, a-dŏl'-te-reit, v., adulterare; falsificare

adultery, a-dŏl'-te-ri, n., adulterio m.

advance, ad-vaans', v., avanzare ; (prices) aumentare ; (lend) anticipare. n., (progress) progresso m. ; (money) anticipo m. ; (prices) aumento m. ; in —, anticipatamente

advancement, ad-vaans'-ment, n., promozione f. ; progresso m. ; anticipo m.

advantage, ad-vaan'-tich, n., vantaggio m.

advantageous°, ad-vaan-tei'-chos, a., vantaggioso

advent, ad'-vent, n., avvento m.

adventitious, ad-ven-tish'-os, a., avventizio

adventure, ad-ven'-cha, n., avventura f.

adventurer, ad-ven'-cha-ra, n., avventuriere m.

adventurous, ad-ven'-cha-ros, a., avventuroso

adversary, ad'-ver-sa-ri, n., avversario m.

adverse°, ad'-vèrs, a., avverso ; contrario

advert, ad-vèrt', v., alludere

advertise, ad'-ver-tais, v., annunziare

advertisement, ad-vèr'-tis-ment, n., annunzio m.

advertiser, ad-vèr'-tais-a, n., inserzionista m. & f.

advice, ad-vais', n., consiglio m. ; avviso m.

advisability, ad-vais'-a-bil-i-ti, n., saggezza f.

advisable, ad-vais'-a-bl, a., saggio ; opportuno

advise, ad-vais', v., consigliare ; (inform) avvisare ; ill —d, mal avvisato ; well —d, ben avvisato

adviser, ad-vais'-a, n., consigliere m.

advocacy, ad'-vo-ka-si, n., patrocinio m.

advocate, ad'-vo-keit, n., avvocato m. v., difendere

aerated, ei'-e-rei-tid, a., gassoso

aerial, ei'-ri-al, n., (radio) antenna f. a., aereo

aerodrome, e'-er-o-droum, n., aeroporto m.

aeroplane, e'-er-o-plein, n., aereo m., velivolo m.

afar, a-faar', adv., lontano, lungi, da lontano

affable, af'-a-bl, a., affabile, cortese

affably, af'-a-bli, adv., affabilmente

affair, a-fèr', n., affare m.

affect, a-fekt', v., toccare ; (move) commuovere ; (pretend) affettare ; —ing, a., commovente

affected, a-fek'-tid, a., affettato; (moved) commosso

affection, *a*-fek'-shon, n., affezione f.

affectionate*, *a*-fek'-shon-eit, a., affezionato

affianced, *a*-fai'-anst, a., fidanzato

affidavit, *a*-fi-dei'-vit, n., dichiarazione giurata f.

affiliate, *a*-fil'-i-eit, v., affiliare

affinity, *a*-fin'-i-ti, n., affinità f.

affirm, *a*-fĕrm', v., affermare

affirmation, *a*-fĕr-mei'-shon, n., affermazione f.

affirmative*, *a*-fĕrm'-at-iv, a., affermativo. n., affermativa f.

affix, *a*-fiks', v., affiggere ; (mark) apporre

afflict, *a*-flikt', v., affliggere

affliction, *a*-flik'-shon, n., afflizione f.

affluence, af'-lu-ens, n., (wealth) opulenza f.

affluent, af'-lu-ent, a., abbondante ; (rich) ricco

afford, *a*-foord', v.,(means) permettere ; (grant) dare

affray, *a*-frei', n., rissa f.

affright, *a*-frait', v., spaventare

affront, *a*-frŏnt', n., affronto m. v., oltraggiare

aflame, *a*-fleim', a., in fuoco

afloat, *a*-flout'. a. & adv., a galla, galleggiante

aforesaid, *a*-foor'-sed, a., suddetto

afraid, *a*-freid', a., spaventato ; to be — of, aver paura di

afresh, *a*-fresh', adv., di nuovo

aft, aaft, adv., a poppa ; indietro

after, aaft'-*a*, prep., dopo. adv., secondo ; dopo

afternoon, aaft'-*er*-nuun, n., dopo mezzogiorno m.

afterthought, aaft'-*er*-Zoot, n., riflessione f.

afterwards, aaft'-*er*-uerds, adv., in seguito

again, *a*-ghein', adv., nuovamente ; ripetutamente

against, *a*-gheinst', prep., contro

age, eich, n., età f.; (period) epoca f.; to be of —, essere maggiorenne ; —d, a., vecchio

agency, ei'-chen-si.n.,agenzia f.; (fig.) intervento m.

agent, ei'-chent, n., agente m., reppresentante m.

aggravate, ag'-ra-veit, v., aggravare

aggregate, ag'-ri-gheit, v., aggregare. a., aggregato. n., aggregato m.

aggression, *a*-gre'-shon, n., aggressione f.

aggressive, *a*-gres'-iv, a., aggressivo

aggrieve, *a*-griiv', v., affliggere

aghast, *a-gaast'*, a., sbigottito

agile, a'chail, a., agile

agitate, a'chi-teit, v., (shake) agitare ; (mental) turbare ; (stir up strife) eccitare

agitation, a-chi tei'-shon, n., agitazione f. ; turbamento m. ; (strife) turbolenza f.

ago, *a gou'*, a., fa ; **long—**, adv., molto tempo fa

agonize, ag'-o-nais, v., agonizzare

agonizing ag'-o-nais ing, a., agonizzante

agony, ag'-o-ni, n., agonia f

agree, *a-grii'* v., convenire ; **— to**, essere d'accordo ; **—able**, a., gradevole ; **—ment**, n., accordo m.; (contract) contratto m.

agricultural, a-gri-kŏl'-cha-ral, a., agricolo

agriculture, a-gri-kŏl'-cha, n., agricoltura f.

aground, *a* graund', a., incagliato, arenato

ague, e'-ghiu, n., febbre intermittente f.

ahead, a-hed', adv., avanti ; in testa

aid, eid, n., aiuto m. v., aiutare

aigret, ei'-gret, n., pennacchio m.

ail, eil, v., soffrire ; **—ing**, a., sofferente

ailment, eil'-ment, n., male m., pena f.

aim, eim, n., (arms) mira f. ; (object) scopo m. v., mirare

aimless, eim'-les, a., senza scopo

air, er, n., aria f. ; (mien) cera f. ; (tune) aria f. v., (clothes) arieggiare ; **—conditioning**, n., condizionamento dell'aria m. ; **—gun**, fucile ad aria compressa m.; **—ily**, adv., leggermente ; **—ing**, n., ventilazione f ; **—port**, aeroporto m. ; **—ship**, dirigibile m.; **—tight**, a., ermetico: impenetrabile all'aria ; **—y**, arioso

aisle, ail, n., navata f.

ajar, *a*-chaar', a., socchiuso

akimbo, a-kim'-bou, adv., appoggiato sui fianchi

akin, a-kin', a., imparentato

alabaster, al'-a-baas-ta, n., alabastro m.

alacrity, a-lak'-ri-ti, n., alacrità f.

alarm, *a*-laarm', v., allarmare n., allarme m. ; **—clock**, sveglia f ; **—ing**, a., allarmante

album, al'-bum, n., album m.

alcohol, al'-ko-hol, n., alcool m.

alert, *a-lert'*, a., vigilante, all'erta ; **on the —**, all'erta ; **—ness**, n., vigilanza f. ; (nimbleness) prontezza f.

alias, ei'-li-as. adv., altrimenti. n., nome supposto m.

alibi, al'-i-bai, n., alibi m.

alien, eil'-i-en, n., straniero m. **a.**, straniero

alienate, ei'-li-en-eit, v., alienare

alight, *a-lait'*, a., acceso ; in fiamme. v., scendere

alike, *a-laik'*, a & adv., simile

alive, *a-laiv'*, a. & adv., vivo, vivente

all, ool. a., tutto, tutta ; tutti, tutte ; ogni. adv., completamente ; perfettamente ; **— along**, adv., lungo ; **— right**, sta bene ; **— the more**, tanto più : **not at —**, niente affatto

allay, *a-lei'*, v., mitigare ; calmare

allege, *a-lech'*, v., allegare

alleged, *a-lech'-d*, a., allegato

allegiance, *a-lii'-chi-ans*, n., fedeltà f.

alleviate, *a-li'-vi-eit*, v., alleviare

alley, al'-i, n., vicolo m. ; **blind —**, via senza uscita f.

alliance, *a-lai'-ans*, n., alleanza f.

allied, *a-laid'*, a., alleato ; affine

allot, *a-lot'*, v., assegnare

allotment, *a-lot'-ment*, n., assegno m. ; (ground) pezzo di terra m.

allow, *a-lau'*, v., permettere ; concedere ; assegnare

allowance, *a-lau'-ans*, n., permesso m. ; (monetary) assegno m. ; (rebate) sconto m. ; **to make —ance**, v., tener in conto

alloy, *a-loi'*, n., lega f.

allude, *a-liuud'*, v., alludere

allure, *a-liur'*, v., attrarre ; (tempt) sedurre

alluring, *a-liur'-ing*, a., attraente

allusion, *a-liuu'-shon*, n., allusione f.

ally, *a-lai'*, n., alleato m. v., congiungere

Almighty, ool-mai'-ti, n., onnipotente m.

almond, aa'-mond, n., mandorla f.

almost, ool'-moust. adv., quasi

alms, aams, n., elemosina f. ; **—house**, ospizio dei poveri m.

aloft, *a-loft'*, adv., sopra, in alto

alone, a-loun', adv., solo

along, a-long', adv. & prep., lungo

alongside, a-long'-said, adv., attraccato

aloof, a-luuf', adv., alla larga ; keep —, v. tenersi a parte

aloud, a-laud', adv., ad alta voce

already, ool-red'-i, adv., già

also, ool'-sou, conj., anche ; ugualmente

altar, ool'-ta, n., altare m.

alter, ool'-ta, v., mutare

alteration, ool-tĕr-ei'-shon, n., mutamento m.

alternate, ool'-tĕr'-neit, a., alterno ; on—days, ogni due giorni

alternative, ool-tĕr'-na-tiv, n., alternativa f.

although, ool-Dou', conj., quantunque, sebbene

altitude, al'-ti-tiuud, n., altitudine f.

altogether, ool-tog-eD'-a, adv., interamente

alum, al'-am, n., allume m.

aluminium, al-iu-mini'-i-am, n., alluminio m.

always, ool'-ues, adv., sempre

amass, a-mas', v., ammassare

amateur, am-a-ter',n.,amatore m.;dilettante m. & f.

amaze, a-meis', v., stupire

amazement, a-meis'-ment, n., stupore m.

ambassador, am-bas'-a-da, n., ambasciatore m.

amber, am'-br, n., ambra f.

ambiguity, am-bi-ghiu'-i-ti, n., ambiguità f.

ambiguous*, am-bi'-ghiu-os, a., ambiguo

ambition, am-bi'-shon, n., ambizione f.

ambitious*, am-bi'-shos, a., ambizioso

ambulance, am'-biu-lans, n., ambulanza f.

ambuscade, am-bus-keid', n., imboscata f.

ambush, am'-bush, n., imboscata f. v., imboscare

ameliorate, a-mii'-lior-eit, v., migliorare

amenable, a-mii'-na-bl, a., responsabile

amend, a-mend', v., emendare ; (correct) correggere

amendment, a-mend'-ment, n.,ammendamento m.

amends, a-mends', make —, v., riparare

amethyst, am'-i-Zist, n., ametista f.

amiable, ei'-mi-a-bl, a., amabile

amicable, am'-i-ka-bl, a., amichevole

amid(st), a-mid(st)', prep., fra, tra, in mezzo

amidships, a-mid'-ships, adv., a mezza nave

amiss, *a*-mis', a., scompigliato. adv., **a sproposito**; **take —**, v., prendere a male

amity, am'-i-ti, n., amicizia f.

ammonia, *a*-mou'-ni-*a*, n., ammoniaca f.

ammunition, am-iu-ni'-shon, n., munizione f.

amnesty, am'-nes-ti, n., amnistia f.

among(st), *a*-mŏng(st)', prep., tra, fra

amorous, am'-*or*-os, a., amoroso

amount, *a*-maunt', v., ammontare. n., importo m.

ample, am'-pl, a., ampio, vasto

amplify, am'-pli-fai, v., amplificare

amputate, am'-piu-teit, v., (med.) amputare

amuck, *a*-mŏk', **run —**, v., andare all' impazzata

amuse, *a*-miuus', v., divertire

amusement, *a*-miuus'-ment, n., divertimento m., trastullo m.

amusing°, *a*-miuus'-ing, a., dilettevole

an, an, art., un, uno, una

anæmia, *a*n-iim'-i*a*, n., anemia f.

anæsthetic, an-es-Zet'-ik, n., anestetico m.

analogous, *a*-nal'-og-os, a., analogo

analysis, *a*-nal'-i-sis, n., analisi f.

analyze, an'-*a*-lais, v., analizzare

anarchy, an'-ar-ki, n., anarchia f.

ancestor, an'-ses-tr, n., antenato m.

ancestry, an'-ses-tri, n., antenati m.pl.; lignaggio m.

anchor, ang'-ka, n., ancora f. v., ancorare

anchorage, ang'-ker-eich, n., ancoraggio m.

anchovy, an-chou'-vi, n., alice f.

ancient°, ein'-shent, a., antico

and, and, conj., e, ed

anew, *a*-niuu', adv., nuovamente, daccapo

angel, ein'-chel, n., angelo m.

anger, ang'-ga, n., collera f., ira f. v., adirare, incollerire

angina, an-chai'-na, n., angina f.

angle, ang'-gl.n., angolo m. v., (fish)pescare **alla lenza**

angler, ang'-gla, n., pescatore alla lenza m.

angling, ang'-gling, n., pesca colla lenza f.

angry; ang'-gri, a., adirato; (enraged) stizzito

anguish, ang'-guish, n., angoscia f., ambascia f.

animal, an'-i-mal, n., animale m. a., animale

animate, an'-i-meit. v., animare ; ravvivare

animated, an'-i-mei-tid, a., animato

animation, an-i-mei'-shon, n., animazione **f.**

animosity, an-i-mou'-si-ti, n., animosità **f.**

aniseed, an'-i-siid, n., anice **m.**

ankle, ang'-kl, n., caviglia **f.**

annals, an'-als, n., pl., annali **m. pl.**

annex, a-neks', a., annesso. v., annettere

annihilate, a-nai'-hil-eit, v., annientare

anniversary, a-ni-ver'-sa-ri, n., anniversario **m.**

annotate, an'-oo-teit. v., annotare

announce, a-nauns'. v., annunziare

announcement, a-nauns'-ment, n., annunzio **m.**

announcer, a-nauns'-a, n., annunciatore **m.**

annoy, a-noi', v., annoiare ; molestare ; **—ing,**
a., noioso

annoyance, a-noi'-ans, n., noia **f.**

annual*, an'-iu-al, a., annuo, annuale

annuity, a-niuu'-i-ti, n., annualità **f.**

annul, a-nöl', v., annullare

annulment, a-nöl'-ment, n., annullamento **m.** ;
abrogazione **f.**

anoint, a noint', v., ungere

anomalous*, a-nom'-a-los, a., anomalo

anonymous*, a-non'-i-mos, a., anonimo

another, a-nöD'-r, a. & pron., un altro

answer, aan'-sr, n., risposta **f.** v., rispondere

answerable, aan'-ser-a-bl, a., responsabile

ant, ant, n., formica **f.**

antagonist, an-tag'-o-nist, n., antagonista **m. & f.**

antecedent, an-ti-sii'-dent, a., antecedente

antecedents, an-ti-sii'-dents.n.pl.,antecedenti **m.pl.**

antedate, an-ti-deit, v., antidatare

antediluvian, an-ti-di-luu'-vi-an, a., antidiluviano

antelope, an'-ti-loup, n., antilope **f.**

anterior, an-ti'-ri-or, a., anteriore

anteroom, an'-ti-ruum, n., anticamera **f.**

anthem, an'-Zem, n., cantico **m.** : **National —,**
inno nazionale **m.**

anthracite, an'-Zra-sait, n., antracite **f.**

anthrax, an'-Zraks, n., carbonchio **m.**

anticipate, an-tis'-i-peit, v., anticipare

anticipation, an-tis-i-pei'-shon, n., anticipazione f.; **in —,** adv., anticipatamente

antics, an'-tiks, n. pl., sgambetti m. pl.

antidote, an'-ti-dout, n., antidoto m.

antipathy, an-tip'-a-Zi, n., antipatia f.

Antipodes, an-tip'-o-diis, n. pl., antipodi m. pl.

antiquarian, an-ti-kuei'-ri-an, n., antiquario m.

antiquated, an'-ti-kueit-id, a., antiquato

antique, an-tiik', a., antico. n., antichità f.

antiseptic, an-ti-sep'-tik, n., antisettico m.

antlers, ant'-las, n. pl., corna di cervo f. pl.

anvil, an'-vil, n., incudine f.

anxiety, ang-sai'-i-ti, n., ansietà f.

anxious*, ang-shos, a., ansioso

any, en'-i, a., (any one) qualunque ; (some) del, dello, della, degli, delle, dei ; (every) ogni ; **not —,** non ne

anybody, en'-i-bo-di, pron., chiunque

anyhow, en'-i-hau, conj., comunque

anything, en'-i-Zing, pron., qualunque cosa ; (something) qualche cosa

anyway, en'-i-uei, adv., **in qualunque modo ;** in ogni modo

anywhere, en'-i-uer, adv., ovunque

apart, a-paart', adv., a parte

apartment, a-paart'-ment, n., stanza f. ; **camera f.**

apartments, a-paart'-ments, n. pl., stanze f. pl.

apathy, ap'-a-Zi, n., apatia f.

ape, eip, n., scimmia f.

aperient, a-pii'-ri-ent, n., purgante m.

aperture, ap'-er-cha, n., apertura f.

apex, ei'-peks, n., apice m.

apiece, a-piis', adv., al pezzo ; a ciascuno

apish, eip-ish, a., scimmiesco

apologize, a-pol'-o-chais, v., scusarsi, far le scuse

apology, a-pol'-o-chi, n., scusa f., apologia f.

apoplexy, a'-po-pleks-i, n., apoplessia f.

apostle, a-pos'-l, n., apostolo m.

apostrophe, a-pos'-tro-ie, n., (gram.) apostrofe f.

apothecary, a-poZ'-i-ka-ri, n., farmacista m. ; spe- [ziale m.

appal, a-pool', v., sbigottire

appalling, a-pool'-ing, a., spaventevole

apparatus, ap-*a*-rei'-tos, n., apparecchio **m**.

apparel, *a*-par'-*el*, n., vestimento m.

apparent[*], *a*-pei'-rent. a., apparente

apparition, ap-*a*-ri'-shon, n., apparizione f.

appeal, *a*-piil', n., appello m. v., appellarsi; — **to**, (like) attrarre

appear, *a*-piir', v., apparire; (seem) sembrare

appearance, *a*-piir'-ans, n., apparizione f.; (in public) debutto m.; (looks, figure) aspetto m.

appease, *a*-piis', v., placare, calmare

appellant, *a*-pel'-ant, n., (law) appellante m. & f.

append, *a*-pend', v., appendere

appendage, *a*-pend'-ich, n., aggiunta f., annesso m.

appendicitis, *a*-pend-i-sai'-tis, n., appendicite f.

appendix, *a*-pen'-diks, n., appendice f.

appertain, ap-*er*-tein', v., appartenere

appetite, ap'-i-tait, n., appetito m.

appetizer, ap'-i-tais-*a*, n., aperitivo **m**.

appetizing, ap'-i-tais-ing, a., appetitoso

applaud, *a*-plood', v., applaudire

applause, *a*-ploos', n., applauso m.

apple, ap'-*el*, n., mela f.; — **tree**, melo **m**.

appliance, *a*-plai'-ans, n., apparecchio **m**.

applicant, ap'-li-kant, n., candidato m.; (petitioner) postulante **m**.

application, ap-li-kei'-shon, n., (use) applicazione f.; (request) richiesta f.

apply, *a*-plai', v., (use) applicare; (as candidate) richiedere; — **to**, (turn to) dirigersi

appoint, *a*-point', v., designare

appointment, *a*-point'-ment, n., (meeting) appuntamento m.; (post) impiego m.

apportion, *a*-poor'-shon, v., ripartire

apportionment, *a*-poor'-shon-ment, n., ripartizione f.

apposite, ap'-o-sit, a., a proposito

appraise, *a*-pres', v., apprezzare

appraisement, *a*-pres'-ment, n., stima f.

appraiser, *a*-pres'-*a*, n., stimatore m.

appreciable, *a*-prii'-shi-*a*-bl, a., apprezzabile

appreciate, *a*-prii'-shi-eit, v., apprezzare; (price) aumentare di valore

appreciation, *a*-prii-shi-ei′-shon, n., apprezzamento m.

apprehend, ap′-ri-hend, v., (fear) temere ; (seize) sequestrare ; (understand) comprendere

apprehension, ap-ri-hen′-shon, n.,(fear)timore m.; (arrest) arresto m. ; (ideas) concezione f.

apprehensive*, ap-ri-hen′-siv, a., apprensivo

apprentice, *a*-pren′-tis, n., praticante m.

apprenticeship, *a*-pren′-tis-ship, n., tirocinio m

apprise, *a*-prais′, v., apprendere

approach, *a*-prooch′, v., avvicinare

approbation, ap-ro-bei′-shon, n., approvazione f.

appropriate, *a*-proo′-pri-eit, v., appropriarsi. a.,* conveniente

appropriateness, *a*-proo′-pri-eit-nes, n., convenienza f.

approval, *a*-pruu′-val, n., approvazione f.

approve, *a*-pruuv′, v., approvare

approximate, *a*-proks′-i-meit, a.,* prossimo. v., avvicinarsi

appurtenance, *a*-per′-ten-ans, n., pertinenza f.

apricot, ei′-pri-kot, n., albicocca f.

April, ei′-pril, n., aprile m.

apron, ei′-pron, n., grembiale m.

apse, aps, n., abside f.

apt, apt, a., atto, soggetto

aptitude, ap′-ti-tiuud, n., attitudine f.

aqueduct, ak′-ui-dŏkt, n., acquedotto **m**.

aqueous, ei′-kui-os, a., acquoso

aquiline, ak′-uil-in, a., aquilino

arable, ar′-a-bl, a., arabile

arbiter, aar′-bit-*a*, n., arbitro m.

arbitrary, aar′-bi-tra-ri, a., arbitrario

arbitrate, aar′-bi-treit, v., arbitrare

arbitration, aar-bi-trei′-shon, n., arbitraggio **m**.

arbour, aar′-ba, n., pergola f.

arc, aark, n., arco m.; —**lamp**, lampada ad arco f.

arcade, aark′-eid, n., arcata f., galleria f.

arch, aarch, n., volta f., arco m.

archbishop, aarch-bish′-op, n., arcivescovo m.

archdeacon, aarch-dii′-kn, n., arcidiacono m.

archduke, aarch-diuuk′, n., arciduca m.

archer, aarch'-*a,* n., arciere m.

archery, aarch'-*a*-ri, n., tiro all'arco m.

archetype, aar'-ki-taip, n., archetipo m.

architect, aar'-ki-tekt, n., architetto m.

archives, aar'-kaiv*s*, n. pl., archivi m. pl.

archway, aarch'-uei, n., sotto passaggio **m.**

arctic, aark'-tik, a., artico

ardent°, aar'-dent, a., ardente

ardour, aar'-*da,* n., ardore m.

arduous°, aar'-diu-os, a., arduo

area, e'-ri-*a,* n., area f. ; (basement yard) cortile **m.**

arena, a-rii'-na, n., arena f.

argue, aar'-ghiu*u,* v., discutere ; (discuss) dibattere

argument, aar'-ghiu-ment, n., argomento m. ;
disputa f.

aright, a-rait', adv., dritto ; bene

arise, a-rais', v., provenire ; (revolt) levarsi

aristocracy, ar-is-tok'-ra-si, n., aristocrazia f.

aristocratic, ar-is-tok-rat'-ik, a., aristocratico

arithmetic, a-riZ'-met-ik, n., aritmetica f.

ark, aark, n., arca f

arm, aarm, n., braccio m. ; (weapon) arma f.
v., armare

armament, aar'-ma-ment, n., armamento m.

armchair, aarm'-cher, n., poltrona f.

armistice, aar'-mis-tis, n., armistizio m.

armlet, aarm'-let, n., bracciale m.

armour, aar'-ma, n., armatura f. v., corazzare

armoured, a-*a*-merd, a., corazzato

armoury, aar'-mor-i, n., armeria f. ; arsenale **m.** ;
armatura f.

armpit, aarm'-pit, n., ascella f.

arms, aarm*s,* n. pl., (mil.) armi f. pl. ; coat of —,
stemma m., blasone m.

army, aar'-mi, n., esercito m.

aromatic, ar-o-mat'-ik, a., aromatico

around, a-raund', adv., intorno. prep., attorno

arouse, a-raus', v., eccitare ; (awaken) svegliare

arrange, a-*a*einch', v., ordinare, apprestare

arrant°, ar'-ant, a., di prima riga

array, a-rei', v., disporre ; (bedeck) rivestire.
n., ordine m. ; (dress) apparato **m.**

arrears, a-rirs', n. pl., arretrati m. pl.

arrest, a-rest'. v., arrestare ; (step) fermare. n., arresto m.

arrival, a-rai'-val. n., arrivo m.

arrive, a-raiv'. v., arrivare ; (aim) pervenire

arrogance, a'-ro-gans, n., arroganza f.

arrogant*, a'-ro-gant. a., arrogante

arrow, a'-rou. n., freccia f., strale m.

arsenal, aar'-sen-l. n., arsenale m.

arsenic, aar'-sen-ik, n., arsenico m.

arson, aar'-son. n., incendio doloso m.

art, aart. n., arte f. ; (cunning) artificio m.

arterial, aar-tii'-ri-al. —**road,** n., strada di gran traffico f. ; strada nazionale f.

artery, aar'-ter-i. n., arteria f.

artful*, aart'-ful, a., (sly) scaltro

artichoke, aar'-ti-chouk. n., carciofo m.

article, aar'-ti-kl. n., articolo m.

articulate, aar-tik'-iu-leit. v., articolare

artifice, aar'-ti-fis n., astuzia f.

artificial*, aar-ti-fish'-al. a., artificiale, artificioso

artillery, aar-til'-ri, n., artiglieria f.

artisan, aar-ti-san', n., artigiano m.

artist, aart'-ist. n., artista m. & f.

artistic, aar-tis'-tik. a., artistico

as, as. conj., come, anche ; fin. che ; — **for,** in quanto a ; — **if,** come se ; — **soon as,** tostochè ; — **though,** come se ; — **to,** in quanto a ; — **well,** egualmente ; — **yet,** finora

asbestos, as-bes'-tos. n., asbesto m., amianto m.

ascend, a-send'. v., ascendere

ascent, a-sent'. n., ascensione f. ; salita f.

ascertain, a-sa-tein'. v., assicurarsi

ascribe, as-kraib'. v., attribuire

ash, ash. n., cenere f. ; (tree) frassino m. ; —**pan,** cassa delle ceneri f. ; —**tray,** porta cenere m.

ashamed, a-sheimd'. a., contuso, vergognoso

ashore, a-shor'. adv., a terra ; (aground) arenato

aside, a-said'. adv., in disparte

ask, aask. v., domandare ; (beg) pregare ; (invite) invitare

askew, *a-skiuu'*, adv., di traverso

asleep, *a-sliip'*, a., addormentato ; **to be —**, v., essere addormentato ; **to fall —**, addormentarsi

asparagus, *as-par'-a-gos*, n., asparago m.

aspect, *as'-pekt*, n., aspetto m.

aspen, *asp'-n*, n., tremula f.   a., (fig.) tremante

aspersion, *as-per'-shon*, n., (sprinkling) aspersione f. ; (calumny) diffamazione f.

asphyxia, *as-fiks'-ia*, n., asfissia f.

aspirate, *as'-pi-reit*, v., aspirare

aspire, *as-pair'*, **— after**, v., ambire

ass, *as*, n., asino m.

assail, *a-seil'*, v., assalire ; **—ant**, n., assalitore m.

assassinate, *a-sas'-si-neit*, v., assassinare

assault, *a-soolt'*, n., assalto m.   v., assaltare

assay, *a-sei'*, v., saggiare. n., saggio m.

assemble, *a-sem'-bl*, v., radunare ; (persons, animals) radunarsi

assembly, *a-sem'-bli*, n., assemblea f.

assent, *a-sent'*, v., assentire. n., consenso m.

assert, *a-sert'* v., sostenere.; **—ion**, n., asserzione f.

assess, *a-ses'*, v., tassare ; valutare

assessment, *a-ses'-ment*, n., valutazione f.

assets, *a'-sets*, n. pl., (personal) beni m. pl. ; (commercial) attivo m.

assiduous*, *a-sid'-iu-os*, a., assiduo

assign, *a-sain'*, v., assegnare

assignee, *as-si-nii'*, n., cessionario m.

assignment, *a-sain'-ment*, n., assegnamento m.

assist, *a-sist'*, v., assistere; **—ance**, n., assistenza f.

assistant, *a-sist'-ant*, n., assistente m. & f. ; (shop) commesso m., commessa f.

assize, *a-sais'*, n., corte d'Assise f.

associate, *a-sou'-shi-eit*, v., associare. n., socio m.; complice m. & f.   a. associato

association, *a-sou-si-e'-shon*, n., società f.

assort, *a-soort'*, v., assortire

assortment, *a-soort'-ment*, n., assortimento m.

assuage, *a-sueich'*, v., placare

assume, *a-siuum'*, v., supporre

assuming, *a-siuum'-ing*, a., presuntuoso ; **— that**, posto che

assumption, *a*-sŏmp'-shon, n., presunzione f.; assunzione f.

assurance, *a*-shur'-ans, n., assicurazione f.

assure, *a*-shur', v., assicurare

asterisk, as'-tėr-risk, n., asterisco m.

astern, *a*-stėrn', adv., (naut.) indietro

asthma, as'-ma, n., asma f.

astir, *a*-stėr', adv., in moto

astonish, as-ton'-ish, v., sorprendere

astound, as-taund', v., sbalordire

astray, *a*-strei', go —, v., fuorviarsi; lead —, traviare

astride, *a*-straid', adv., a cavalcioni

astronomer, as-tron'-o-ma, n., astronomo m.

astute, as-tiut', a., astuto, fino

astuteness, as-tiut'-nes, n., astutezza f.

asunder, *a*-sŏn'-da, adv., in parti; a parte

asylum, *a*-sai'-lom, n., asilo m.; (mental) manicomio m.

at, at, prep., a, in, con, dentro, presso, da; — home, n., (fig.) ricevimento privato m.; — once, adv., immediatamente; — times, alle volte

athlete, aZ'-liit, n., atleta m. & f.

athwart, *a*-Zuoort', adv. & prep., di traverso

atom, at'-om, n., atomo m.

atone, *a*-toun', v., espiare; —ment, n., espiazione f.

atrocious, *a*-trou'-shos, a., atroce

atrophy, at'-ro-fi, n., atrofia f.

attach, *a*-tach', v., attaccare; annettere; —able, a., attaccabile; —ment, n., attaccamento m.; (legal) sequestro m.

attack, *a*-tak', n., attacco m. v., attaccare; aggredire

attain, *a*-tein', v., (acquire) conseguire; (reach) pervenire; —ment, n., conseguimento m.; —ments, (talents) talento m.

attempt, *a*-tempt', v., provare; (risk) tentare. n., tentativo m.; (attack) attentato m.

attend, *a*-tend', v., attendere; (to be present) assistere a; —ance, n., servizio m.

attendant, *a*-tend'-ant, n., assistente m. & f.; (shop) commesso m., commessa f.; (keeper) guardiano m. a., relativo

attention, *a*-ten'-shon. n., attenzione f.

attest, *a*-test'. v., testimoniare

attic. at'-ick, n., soffitta f.

attire, *a* tair'. v., vestire ; adornarsi. n., vestito m.

attitude, a'-ti-tiuud. n., attitudine f.

attorney, *a*-tér'-ni. n., procuratore m. : **power of —**, procura f.

attract, *a*-trakt'. v., attrarre ; —ion, n., attrazione f. : —ive, a., attrattivo

attribute, *a*-trib'-iut. v., attribuire. n., attributo m.

auburn, oo'-bérn. a., castagno

auction, ook'-shon. v. vendere all'asta. n., asta f.; incanto m. ; —eer, banditore all'asta m.

audacious*, oo-dei'-shos, a., audace

audacity, oo-das'-i-ti. n., audacia f.

audible, oo' di-bl, a., udibile

audience, oo'-di-ens, n., (assembly) uditorio m.

audit, oo'-dit, v., verificare. n., revisione f.

auditor, oo'-dit-or. n., revisore di conti m. : (hearer) uditore m.

augment, oogh'-ment. v., aumentare

augur, oo'-ga. n., augurio m. v., presagire

August, oo-gost, n., agosto m.

august, oo-gost'. a., augusto

aunt. amt. n., zia f.

auspicious*, oos-pi'-shos. a., propizio

austere*, oos-tir'. a., austero

authentic, oo-Zen'-tik. a., autentico

author, oo' Za. n., autore m.

authorise, oo'-Zor-ais, v., autorizzare

authoritative*, oo-Zor'-i-ta-tiv. a., autorizzato

authority, oo Zor'-i-ti. n., autorità f.

autocar, oo'-to-kaar. n., autocarro m.

automatic, oo-to-mat'-ik. a., automatico

autumn, oo'-tom. n., autunno m.

auxiliary, oogh-sil'-i-a-ri, a., ausiliario

avail. *a*-veil'. n., vantaggio m. v., servirsi : **— one-self of**, approfittare

available. *a*-veil'-*a*-bl. a., utile ; disponibile

avalanche, av'-*a*-laanch, n., valanga f.

avaricious*, av-*a*-ri'-shos. a., avaro

avenge, *a*-vench'. v., vendicare

avenue, av'-e-niuu, n., viale m.

average, av'-a-rich, a., medio. n., media f.

averse*, a-vèrs', a., avverso, opposto

aversion, a-vèr'-shon, n., avversione f.

avert, a-vèrt', v., evitare ; stornare

aviary, ei'-vi-a-ri, n., uccelliera f.

aviation, ei-vi-ei'-shon, n., aviazione f.

avidity, a-vid'-i-ti, n., avidità f.

avocation, av-o-kei'-shon, n., occupazione f.

avoid, a-void', v., evitare ; (elude) sottrarsi

avoidance, a-void'-ans, n., scampo m. ; annullazione f.

avow, a-vau', v., confessare

avowal, a-vau'-al, n., confessione f.

await, a-ueit', v., aspettare

awake, awaken, a-ueik', a-ueik'-n, a., sveglio. v., svegliarsi ; (arouse) svegliare

awakening, a-ueik'-ning, n., risveglio m.

award, a-uoord', n., decisione f. v., aggiudicare ; (prize) dare

aware, a-uer', a., conscio ; attento

away, a-uei', adv., via, fuori, assente. **far —**, molto lontano

awe, oo, n., rispetto m. ; terrore m.

awful°, oo'-ful, a., spaventevole

awhile, a-uail', adv., per un certo tempo

awkward, ook'-uerd, a., imbarazzante ; (clumsy) goffo

awkwardness, ook'-uerd-nes, n., goffaggine f.

awl, ool, n., lesina f.

awning, oon'-ing, n., tenda f.

awry, a-rai', a. & adv., di traverso ; a sghembo

axe, aks, n., ascia f., scure f., mannaia f.

axle, aks'-l, n., asse m.

azure, a'-sher, n., azzurro m. a., azzurro

babble, bab'-bl, v., balbettare

baby, bei'-bi, n., bimbo m., bambino m.

bachelor, bach'-el-a, n., celibe m.

back, bak, n., dorso m. v., (support) appoggiare ; (wager) scommettere a. adv., indietro ; (return) di ritorno

backbone, bak'-boun, n., (anatomy) spina dorsale f. ; (fig.) forza f.

background, bak'-graound, n., sfondo m.

backseat, bak'-siit, n., posto di dietro m. (fig.) posto secondario m.

backslide, bak'-slaid, v., rinunciare ; declinare

backward, bak'-uard, a., tardivo ; retrogrado

backwards, bak'-uards, adv., in dietro

backwater, bak'-uoo-ta, n., risacca f.

bacon, bei'-kn, n., lardo m.

bad, bad, a., cattivo ; —**ness**, n., cattiveria f.

badge, bach, n., distintivo m.

badger, bach'-a, n., tasso m. v., tormentare

baffle, baf'-l, v., sventare

bag, bagh, n., sacco m. ; **hand —**, borsetta f., sacco a mano m.

baggage, bagh'-ich, n., bagaglio m.

bagpipe, bagh'-paip, n., cornamusa f.

bail, beil, n., cauzione f. ; — **out**, v., farsi garante ; **on —**, in libertà contro cauzione

bailiff, bei'-lif, n., usciere m.

bait, beit, n., esca f. v., adescare

baize, beis, n., baietta f.

bake, beik, v., cuocere nel forno

bakelite, beik'-ër-lait, n., galalite f.

baker, beik'-a, n., fornaio m.

bakery, beik'-er-i, n., panetteria f.

balance, bal'-ans, n., equilibrio m. ; (scales) bilancia f. ; (commercial) saldo di conto m. v., bilanciare, saldare ; — **sheet**, n., bilancio m.

balcony, bal'-ko-ni, n., balcone m. ; (theatre) loggione m.

bald*, boold, a., calvo ; (fig.) nudo

baldness, boold'-nes, n., calvizie f. ; (fig.) nudità f.

bale, beil, n., balla f. v., imballare ; (naut.) vuotare

baleful*, beil'-ful, a., funesto ; malevolo

balk, baulk, book, v., contrariare

ball, bool, n., palla f. ; (billiard) biglia f. ; (dance) ballo m.

ballast, bal'-ast, n., (road, etc.) ghiaia f.; (naut.) zavorra f. v., zavorrare

ballet, bal'-e, n., balletto m.

balloon, b*a*-luun', n., ballone m.

ballot, bal'-*ot*, n., scrutinio m.; **(second ballot) bal-**
lottaggio m. v., ballottare

balm, baam, n., balsamo m.

balsam, bool'-sam, n., balsamo m.

baluster, bal'-*os*-t*a*, n., balustrata f.

bamboo, bam-buu', n., (cane) bambù m.

bamboozle, bam-buu'-s*l*, v., corbellare, **ingannare**

ban, ban, n., bando m. v., bandire

banana, b*a*-naa'-na, n., banana f.

band, band, n., benda f., fascia f.; (music) **banda f.;**
(gang) banda f.

bandage, band'-ich, n., benda f.

bandbox, band'-boks, n., scatola di cartone f.

bandmaster, band'-maas-t*a*, n., maestro di banda m.

bandy (legged), ban'-di, a., colle gambe storte,
sbilenco

bane, bein, n., peste f.

baneful°, bein'-f*u*l, a., velenoso

bang, bengh, n., colpo m. v., sbattere

banish, ban'-ish, v., bandire

banister, ban'-is-t*a*, n., ringhiera f.

bank, bengk, n., banca f.; (river, etc.) **argine m.;**
(seat) banco m.

bank-book, bengk'-buk, n., libretto di banca m.

banker, bengk'-*a*, n., banchiere m.

bank-holiday, bengk-hol'-i-de, n., festa legale f.

bank-note, bengk'-n*o*ut, n., biglietto di banca m.

bankrupt, bengk'-röpt, n., fallito m. a., fallito

bankruptcy, bengk'-röpt-si, n., bancarotta f.

banner, ban'-*a*, n., bandiera f.

banquet, bang'-ku*e*t, n., banchetto m.

banter, ban'-t*a*, n., scherzo m., baia f. v., burlare

baptism, bap'-ti*s*m, n., battesimo m.

bar, baar, v., sbarrare, n., (drinks) bar m.; (horizontal) sbarra f.; (metal) sbarra f.; (mus.) battuta f.; (law) foro m.

barb, baarb, n., punta f.

barbarian, baar-be'-ri-*a*n, n., barbaro m. a., bar-

barbarity, baar-ba'-i-ti, n., barbarie f. [baro

barbed, baarbd, a., spinoso

barber, baar'-b*a*, n., barbiere m.

bard, baard, n., bardo m.
bare, ber, a., nudo. v., spogliare ; —**faced**, a., sfacciato ;—**footed**, scalzo :—**headed**, a capo scoperto
barely, ber'-li, adv., appena
bareness, ber'-nes, n., nudità f.
bargain, baar'-ghin, n., occasione f. v., mercanteggiare
barge, baarch, n., barca f.
bark, baark, v., abbaiare. n., abbaiamento m. ; (tree) corteccia f.
barley, baar'-li, n., orzo m.
barmaid, baar'-meid, n., cameriera di bar f.
barn, baarn, n., cascina f. ; granaio m.
barometer, ba-rom'-it-a, n., barometro m.
baron, bar'-on, n., barone m.
baroness, bar'-on-es, n., baronessa f.
barracks, bar'-aks, n. pl., caserma f.
barrel, bar'-el, n., barile m. ; (gun) canna f.
barren, bar'-en, a., sterile ; (land) arido
barrier, bar'-i-a, n., barriera f.
barrister, bar'-is-ta, n., avvocato m.
barrow, bar'-ou, n., carretino m. ; **wheel—**, carriuola f.
barter, baar'-ta, v., barattare. n., scambio m.
base, beis, v., basare. n., base f. ; (pedestal) basamento m. a., basso, vile
baseless, beis'-les, a., senza fondamento
basement, beis'-ment, n., sottosuolo m.
baseness, beis'-nes, n., bassezza f.
bashful°, bash'-ful, a., pudico
bashfulness, bash'-ful-nes, n., verecondia f.
basin, bei'-sn, n., bacinella f. ; (wash) catinella f.
basis, bei'-sis, n., fondamento m.
bask, baask, v., scaldarsi
basket, baas'-kit, n., cesta f., canestro m.
bass, beis, n., (voice, music) basso m.
bassoon, ba-suun', n., fagotto m.
bastard, bas'-tard, n., bastardo m. a., bastardo
baste, beist, v., inumidire
bat, bat, n., pipistrello m. ; (sport) mazza f.
batch, bach, n., (bread) infornata f. ; (articles, etc.) mucchio m.

bath, baaZ, n., bagno m. : — -**chair**, poltrona a ruote f. ; — -**room**, stanza da bagno f. ; **shower**- —, doccia f.

bathe, beiD, v., bagnarsi ; —**r**, n., bagnante m. & f.

batten, bat'-n, n., asse di legno m. v., assicurare con assi

batter, bat'-a, n., pasta da friggere f. v., buttar giù

battle, bat'-l, n., battaglia f. v., combattere

battleship, bat'-l-ship, n., corazzata f.

bawl, bool, v., urlare

bay, bei, n., (geographical) baia f. : (horse) baio m. v., abbaiare ; — -**tree**, n., alloro m.

bayonet, be'-on-et, n., baionetta f.

be, bii, v., essere, stare : esistere

beach, biich, n., spiaggia f. v., dare alla spiaggia

beacon, bii'-kon, n., fanale m.

bead, biid, n., (glass) perla f. ; (drop) goccia f.

beadle, bii'-dl, n., bidello m.

beagle, bii'-gul, n., (hound) bassotto m.

beak, biik, n., becco m.

beam, biim, n., trave f. ; (light) raggio m.

beaming, biim'-ing, a., raggiante

bean, biin, n., fagiuolo m.

bear, ber, n., orso m. ; (speculator) ribassista m. v., (endure) sopportare ; (produce) produrre ; —**able**, a., sopportabile ; —**er**, n., portatore m. ; (mech.) supporto m. ; —**ing**, (behaviour) contegno m. ; (mech.) cuscinetto m. ; —**ings**, (location) orientamento m.

beard, biird, n., barba f. ; —**ed**, a., barbuto

beardless, bird'-les, a., imberbe

beast, biist, n., bestia f.

beastly, biist'-li, adv. & a., bestiale

beat, biit, n., colpo m. ; (pulse) pulsazione f. ; (music) battuta f. v., battere

beautiful°, biuu'-ti-ful, a., bello

beautify, biuu'-ti-fai, v., abbellire

beauty, biuu'-ti, n., bellezza f., beltà f. ; grazia f. ; — -**spot**, (mole) neo m. ; (country) bel punto m.

beaver, bii'-va, n., castoro m.

becalm, bi-kaam', v., calmare ; (naut.) rimanere in bonaccia

because, bi-koos′, conj., perchè ; — **of,** in causa di

beckon, bek′-n, v., far segno

become, bi-kŏm′, v., divenire

becoming*, bi-kŏm′-ing, a., (conduct) conveniente (dress) che sta bene

bed, bed, n., letto m. :   **flower** —, aiuola f. ; — **ding,** biancheria da letto f. ; — **pan,** orinale da letto m. ; — **ridden,** a., costretto a letto

bedeck, bi-dek′, v., ornarsi

bedew, bi-diuu′, v., umettare

bedroom, bed′-ruum, n., stanza da letto f.

bedstead, bed′-sted, n., lettiera f.

bee, bii, n., ape f. ; — **hive,** alveare **m.**

beech, biich, n., faggio m.

beef, biif, n., carne di bue f. ; — **steak,** bistecca f.

beer, bir, n., birra f.

beet, biit, n., bietola f. ; — **root,** barbabietola f.

beetle, bii′-tl, n.,scarabeo m.; **black** —, scarafaggio [m.

befall, bi-fool′, v., accadere

befitting, bi-fit′-ing, a., confacente

before, bi-for′, prep., davanti a. adv., prima, **avanti**

beforehand, bi-for′-hand, adv., in anticipo

befoul, bi-faul′, v., imbrattare

befriend, bi-frend′, v., proteggere ; trattare d'amico

beg, begh, v., (request, etc.) pregare ; (alms) mendicare ; — **ging,** n., (alms) accattonaggio m.

beget, bi-ghet′, v., procreare

beggar, beg′-a, n., mendicante m. & f.

begin, bi-ghin′, v., principiare

beginner, bi-ghin′-a, n., principiante **m.**

beginning, bi-ghin′-ing, n., principio m.

begone ! bi-goon′, interj., vattene !

begrime, bi-graim′, v., annerire

begrudge, bi-grŏch′, v., dare a malincuore

beguile, bi-gail′, v., ingannare

behalf, be-haaf′, n., interesse m. ; **on** — **of,** in favore di

behave, bi-heiv′, v., contenersi

behaviour, bi-heiv′-ia, n., contegno m.

behead, bi-hed′, v., decapitare

behind, bi-haind′, prep., dietro. adv., dopo ; **indietro**

behindhand, bi-haind′-hand. a., in ritardo

behold, bi-hould', v., guardare, mirare. interj., ecco !

behove, bi-houv', v., convenire

being, bii'-ing, n., esistenza f. ; (human) essere m.

belabour, bi-lei'-ba, v., (thrash) bastonare

belated, bi-lei'-tid, a., ritardato ; sorpreso dalla notte

belch, belch, v., eruttare ; (vulg.) ruttare

beleaguer, bi-lii'-ga, v., assediare

belfry, bel'-fri, n., campanile a torre m.

belie, bi-lai', v., smentire

belief, bi-liif', n., credenza f.

believable, bi-liiv'-a-bl, a., credibile

believe, bi-liiv', v., credere

believer, bi-liiv'-a, n., credente m. & f.

belittle, bi-lit'-l, v., impiccolire

bell, bel, n., campana f. ; campanello m. ; sonaglio m.

belligerent, bel-ich'-e-rent, a., belligerante

bellow, bel'-ou, n., muggito m. v., muggire

bellows, bel'-ous, n. pl., soffietto m.

belly, bel'-i, n., ventre m.

belong, bi-long', v., appartenere

belongings, bi-long'-ings, n. pl., cose f. pl. ; indumenti m. pl.

beloved, bi-lŏv'-id, a., diletto

below, bi-lou', prep., al di sotto di.   adv. giù ; laggiù ; quaggiù

belt, belt, n., cintura f. ; (mech.) cinghia f. v., cingere

bemoan, bi-moun', v., gemere ; lamentarsi di

bench, bench, n., banco m. ; (law) corte di giustizia f.

bend, bend, n., curva f. ; (road, etc.) svolta f. v., curvare

beneath, bi-niiZ', prep., sotto ; indegno di.   adv. sotto ; giù

benediction, ben-i-dik'-shon, n., (eccl.) benedizione f.

benefactor, ben-i-fak'-ta, n., benefattore m.

benefice, ben'-i-fis, n., beneficio m.

beneficence, ben-ef'-i-sens, n., beneficenza f.

beneficial*, ben-i-fi'-shal, a., salutare ; vantaggioso

beneficiary, ben-i-fi'-sha-ri, n., beneficiario m.

benefit, ben'-i-fit, n., profitto m. v., trarre profitto da

benevolence, bi-nev'-o-lens, n., beneficenza f. ; bontà f.

benevolent*, bi-nev'-o-lent, a., benefico

benign*, bi-nain', a., benigno

benignant, bi-nig'-nant. a., benevolente

bent, bent, n., (fig.) inclinazione f.

benumb, bi-nŏm', v., intorpidire

benzine, ben'-siin, n., benzina f.

bequeath, bi-kuiiZ', v., lsgare

bequest, bi-kuest', n., legato m.

bereave, bi-riiv', v., privare

bereavement, bi-riiv' ment, n., perdita f.

berry, be'-ri. n., bacca f ; (coffee) grano m.

berth, bërZ, n. (cabin) cabina f ; (on train) **cuc**cetta f ; (anchorage) luogo d'ancoraggio **m.**; (position) posto m., impiego m.

beseech, bi-siich', v., supplicare

beset, bi-set', v., assediare ; importunare

beside, bi-said', prep., presso di ; fuori di

besides, bi-saids', adv., in oltre ; d'altronde

besiege, bi-siich', v., assediare

besmear, bi-smir', v., imbrattare, sporcare

besotted, bi-sot'-id, a., abbrutito

bespangle, bi-spang'-gol, v., coprire di lustrini

bespatter, bi-spat'-a, v., infangare

bespeak, bi-spiik', v., comandare ; ritenere

besprinkle, bi-spring-kl, v., spruzzare, innaffiare ; (strew) spargere

best, best. a., migliore. adv., il meglio. v., avere il vantaggio su

bestial*, bes'-ti-al, a., bestiale

bestir (oneself), bi-stër'. v., muoversi

bestow, bi-stou', v., concedere, dare

bestowal, bi-stou'-al, n., conferimento m.

bestrew, bi-struu', v., spargere

bet, het, n., scommessa f. v., scommettere

betake (oneself), bi-teik', v., recarsi

betoken, bi-tou'-kn, v., annunciare

betray, bi-trei', v., tradire

betrayal, bi trei'-al, n., tradimento m.

betroth, bi-trouD', v., fidanzarsi

betrothal, bi-tloD'-al, n., fidanzamento m.

better, bet'-a.a., migliore adv., meglio v., migliorare

better, bettor, bet'-a, n., (gambler) scommettitore m.

betterment, bet'-er-ment. n., miglioramento m.

betting, bet'-ing. n., scommesse f. pl.

between, bi-tuïin'. prep., fra. adv., in mezzo a

bevel, bev'-l. v., smussare ; diamantare

beverage, bev'-er-ich. n., bevanda f.

bevy, bev'-i. n., brigata f.

bewail, bi-ueil', v., rimpiangere

beware, bi-uer', v., guardarsi. interj., attenzione !

bewilder, bi-uil'-da, v., sbalordire

bewilderment, bi-uil'-der-ment, n., sbalordimento m.

bewitch, bi-uich', v., stregare ; (fig.) affascinare

beyond, bi-iond', adv., al di là di

bias, bai'-as, n., prevenzione f. v., influire

bible, bai'-bl. n., Bibbia f.

bibulous, bib'-iu-los, a., spugnoso

bicker, bik'-a, v., accattare brighe

bickering, bik'-er-ing. n., litigio m.

bicycle, bai'-si-kl. n., bicicletta f. v., andare in bicicletta

bid, bid. n., (at a sale) offerta f. v., offrire ; (order) comandare

bidder, bid'-a. n., offerente m. & f.

bidding, bid'-ing. n., offerte f. pl.

bide, baid, v., aspettare ; sopportare ; (abide) stare

bier, bir. n., bara f.

big, bigh. a., grande ; vasto ; importante

bigness, bigh'-nes. n., grandezza f. ; grossezza f.

bigot, big'-ot. n., fanatico m. ; (pious) bigotto m.

bigoted, big'-ot-id. a., bigotto

bilberry, bil'-be-ri. n., mirtillo m.

bile, bail. n., bile f.

bilious, bil'-i-os. a., bilioso

bilk, bilk. v., gabbare

bill, bil. n., conto m. ; (of exchange) cambiale f. ; (poster) annunzio m. ; (parliament) progetto di legge m. ; (bird) becco m. ; — of fare, lista delle vivande f.

billet, bil'-et. n., alloggio m. v., alloggiare

billiards, bil'-iards, n. pl., biliardo m.

bin, bin. n., (wine) nicchia da vino f.; (refuse) cassa della spazzatura f.

bind, baind, v., legare ; (books) rilegare ; (vow) obbligarsi ; (fetter) legare ; — **up,** bendare

binding, baind'-ing, n., (books) rilegatura f.

binoculars, bi-nok'-iu-lers, n. pl., binoccolo m.

biography, bai-ogh'-ra-fi, n., biografia f.

biplane, bai'-plein, n., biplano m.

birch, berch, n., (tree) betulla f. ; (rod) verga f. v., vergare

bird, berd, n., uccello m. ; —**'s-eye view,** vista a volo d'uccello f.

birth, berZ, n., nascita f.

birthday, berZ'-dei, n., compleanno m.

birth-mark, berZ'-maark, n., voglia f.

birthplace, berZ'-pleis, n., luogo di nascita m.

birthrate, berZ'-reit, n., natalità f.

biscuit, bis'-kit, n., biscotto m.

bishop, bish'-op, n., vescovo m. ; (chess) alfiere m.

bit, bit, n., pochino m. ; (horse) morso m.

bitch, bich, n., cagna f.

bite, bait, n., morso m. ; (mouthful) morso m. v., mordere

biting, bait'-ing, a., mordente ; (wind) pungente

bitter, bit'-a, a., amaro

bitterness, bit'-a-nes, n., amarezza f.

black, blak, n., negro m., nero m. a., nero ; (gloomy) lugubre. v., annerire ; (polish) lustrare

blackbeetle, blak'-bii-tl, n., scarafaggio m.

blackberry, blak'-be-ri, n., mora di spino f.

blackbird, blak'-berd, n., merlo m.

blackcurrant, blak'-kor-ent, n., ribes nero m.

blacken, blak'-en, v., annerire ; (fig.) denigrare

blackguard, bla'-gard, n., mascalzone m.

blacking, blak'-ing, n., cera da scarpe f.

blacklead, blak'-led, n., grafite f. ; (pencil) matita f.

blackleg, blak'-leg, n., (fig.) crumiro m.

blackmail, blak'-meil, n., ricatto m. v., ricattare

blackmailer, blak'-meil-a, n., ricattatore m.

blacksmith, blak'-smiZ, n., maniscalco m.

blackthorn, blak'-Zoorn, n., pruno selvatico m.

bladder, blad'-a, n., vescica f.

blade, bleid, n., lama f. ; (grass) foglia f. ; (oar) pala f.

blame, bleim, n., biasimo m. v., biasimare

blameless°, bleim'-les, a., irreprensibile ; **innocente**

blanch, blaanch, v., impallidire

bland, bland, a., blando

blandishment, blan'-dish-ment, n., lusinga f.

blank, blangk, n., (lottery) bianco m. a., (vacant) vacante ; (page) bianco ; (shot) a salve

blanket, blang'-ket, n., coperta f.

blare, bler, n., squillo m. ; (fig.) **muggito m.** v., squillare

blaspheme, blas-fiim', v., bestemmiare

blasphemy, blas'-fi-mi, n., bestemmia f.

blast, blaast, v., (explode) far saltare ; (fig.) maledire. n., (gust) raffica f. ; (trumpet) suono m.

blatant, blei-tant, a., schiamazzante

blaze, bleis, v., avvampare. n., fiamma f. ; (conflagration) braciere m. ; — **of light**, baleno m.

bleach, bliich, v., imbiancare

bleak, bliik, a., (raw) freddo ; (bare) desolato

bleat, bliit, v., belare

bleed, bliid, v., sanguinare ; salassare [m.

bleeding, bliid'-ing, n., perdita di sangue f. ; salasso

blemish, blem'-ish, n., macchia f. v., macchiare

blend, blend, v., mescolare. n., mescolanza f.

bless, bles, v., benedire ; —**ed**, a., benedetto

blessing, bles'-ing, n., benedizione f.

blight, blait, n., (plant) peste f. v., guastare

blind, blaind, a., cieco. v., accecare. n., (window) cortina f. ; (venetian) persiana f.

blindfold, blaind'-fould, v., bendare gli occhi

blindman, blaind'-man, n., cieco m.

blindness, blaind'-nes, n., cecità f.

blink, blingk, v., battere le palpebre

blinkers, bling-kers, n., (horse) paraocchi m. pl.

bliss, blis, n., felicità f. ; —**ful**, a., felice

blister, blis'-ta, n., vescica f. v., far vesciche

blithe°, blaiD, a., gaio

blizzard, blis'-ard, n., tormenta di neve f.

bloat, blout, v., gonfiare

bloater, blout'-a, n., aringa affumicata f.

block, blok, v., bloccare. n., (wood) ceppo m. ; (traffic) blocco m. ; —**head**, stupido m.

blockade, blok-eid, n., (naut.) blocco m.

blood, blŏd, n., sangue m. ; **—hound**, cane segugio m ; **—shed**, spargimento di sangue m.;
—shot, a., iniettato di sangue ; **—thirsty**, san-
guinario ; **—y**, insanguinato

bloom, bluum, v., fiorire   n., fiore m.

blooming, bluum'-ing, n., fioritura f.   a., in fiori

blossom, blos'-om, n., fiore m.   v., fiorire

blot, blot, v., macchiare ; (dry) asciugare.
n., (ink) sgorbio m ; (blemish) macchia f. ;
—ting-paper, carta asciugante f.

blotch, bloch, n., macchia f. ; (pimple) pustola f.
v., macchiare

blouse, blaus, n., blusa f.

blow, blou, n., pugno m. ; colpo m.; (trumpet) soffio m.   v., soffiare ; soffiarsi ;   **— up**, (tyres
etc.) gonfiare ; (explode) far saltare

blowpipe, blou'-paip, n., canna da vetraio f.;
(welding) canna da saldare f.

blubber, blŏb'-a, n., grasso di balena m.   v., pia-
gnucolare

bludgeon, bloch'-en, n., randello m.

blue, bluu, n., turchino m., azzurro m.   a., turchino, azzurro ; **—stocking**, n., (fig.) saccentona f.

bluebell, bluu'-bel, n., campanella f.

bluff, blaff, n., montatura f   v., gettar fumo agli occhi

bluish, bluu'-ish, a., azzurrognolo

blunder, blŏn'-da, n., equivoco m.   v., cadere in
equivoco

blunt, blŏnt, a., ottuso.   v., ottundere

bluntness, blŏnt'-nes, n., ottusità f.

blur, blër, v., annebbiare.   n., macchia f.

blurt, blërt, v., parlare a sproposito

blush, blŏsh, n., rossore m.   v., arrossire

bluster, blŏs'-ta, v., far lo spavaldo ; **—er**, n., spavaldo m.; **—ing**, a., spavaldo ; (gusty) strepitoso

boar, bor, n., verro m. ; **wild —**, cinghiale m.

board, bord, n., asse f. ; tavola f. ; (directors) consiglio direttivo m. ; (food) vitto m., (naut.) bordo m.   v., foderare di tavole ; **notice—**, n., tavola per gli annunzi f. ; **—er**, pensionante m. &
f. ; **—ing-house**, pensione f. ; **—ing-school**,
collegio m.

boast, boust. v., vantarsi. n., vanteria f.

boaster, boust'-a. n., millantatore m.

boat, bout. n., battello m. ; (rowing) barca f.; **motor- —**, motoscafo m.. **steam- —**, vapore m.

boat-hook, bout'-huk. n., gancio d'approdo m.

boating, bout'-ing. n., canottaggio m.

boatman, bout'-man. n., barcaiuolo m.

boatswain, bou'-sn. n., nostromo m.

bob, bob. v., pendolare : **— about**, fiottare

bobbin, bob'-in. n., rocchetto m. ; spola f.

bode, boud. v., presagire

bodice, bod'-is. n., giubbettino m.

bodily, bod'-i-li. a., corporeo. adv., interamente ; di peso

bodkin, bod'-kin. n., punteruolo m.

body, bod'-i. n., corpo m. ; (corpse) cadavere m.

bog, bogh. n., pantano m. ; **—gy**, a., pantanoso

bogey, bou'-ghi. n., (children's) uomo nero m.

bogie, bou'-ghi. n., (mech.) carrello girevole m.

boil, boil. v., bollire. n., (med.) foruncolo m.

boiler, boil'-a. n., caldaia f.

boisterous, boist'-er-os. a., impetuoso

bold*, bould. a., ardito

boldness, bould'-nes. n., ardimento m.

bolster, boul'-sta. n., capezzale m. : **—up**, v., sostenere

bolt, boult. v., dar i catenacci ; (horse) prendere la mano. n., catenaccio m. ; (lightning) fulmine m.

bomb, bom. n., bomba f. v., bombardare

bombard, bom-baard'. v., bombardare

bombastic, bom-bas'-tik. a., ampolloso

bond, bond. n., (obligation) obbligazione f. ; (tie) legame m. ; (stock) buono del tesoro m., obbligazione f. ; **in —**, (customs) nei magazzini generali m. pl.

bondage, bon'-dich. n., servitù f.

bone, boun. n., osso m. ; (fish) spina di pesce f.

bonfire, bon'-fair. n., falò m.

bonnet, bon'-et. n., berretta f. ; (car) cofano m.

bonus, bou'-nus. n., premio m., gratificazione f.

bony, bou'-ni. a., ossuto

book, buk. n., libro m. v., entrare nei libri ; prenotare, riservare

bookbinder, buk'-baind-*a*, n., rilegatore di libri **m**
book-case, buk'-keis, n., libreria f.
booking-office, buk'-ing-of-is, n., ufficio biglietti **m.**
book-keeper, buk'-kiip-*a*, n., contabile **m.**
book-keeping, buk'-kiip-ing, n., contabilità f.
book-mark, buk'-maark, n., segnalibri **m.**
bookseller, buk'-sel-*a*, n., libraio **m.**
bookshop, buk'-shop, n., libreria f., libraio **m.**
bookstall, buk'-stool, n., chiosco di giornali **m.**
bookworm, buk'-uerm, n., (fig.) topo di biblioteca **m.**
boom, buum, n., (commercial) ripresa vivace f. ;
    (spar) scopamare **m.** ; (noise) **rombo m.,** rim-
    bombo **m.** v., (trade) andare a gonfie vele ;
    (noise) rombare
boon, buun, n., grazia f., **manna f.**
boor, bur, n., (fig.) villano m.
boorish*, bur'-ish, a., villano
boot, buut, n., stivale m. ; **—maker,** calzolaio **m.**
booth, buuD, n., baracca f.
booty, buu'-ti, n., bottino m.
border, boor'-da, n., (ornamental edge) **orlo m.** ;
    (frontier) frontiera f. v., orlare
bordering, boor'-der-ing, a., confinare ; (fig.) vicino
bore, bor, v., perforare ; (weary) annoiare.
    n., (gun) calibro m. ; (person) seccatore **m.**
born, boorn, a., nato
borough, bör'-*o*, n., borgo **m.**
borrow, bor'-ou, v., prendere a prestito
bosom, bu'-*som*, n., seno **m.**
botanist, bot'-*an*-ist, n., botanico **m.**
botany, bot'-*a*-ni, n., botanica f.
both, bouZ, a., ambedue
bother, boD'-*a*, v., seccare. n., seccatura f.
bottle, bot'-*el*, v., imbottigliare. n., bottiglia f.
bottom, bot'-om, n., fondo **m.**
bottomless, bot'-om-les, a., senza fondo
bough, bau, n., ramo m.
bounce, bauns, v., rimbalzare. n., balzo m.
bound, baund. v., limitare ; (jump) saltare.
    n., (jump) balzo m. ; **— for,** a., in rotta per **;**
    — to, (obliged) tenuto
boundary, baun'-da-ri, n., confine **m.**

bountiful*, baun'-ti-ful, a., generoso

bounty, baun'-ti, n., liberalità f.; sussidio m.

bouquet, bu'-kei, n., mazzo di fiori m.; aroma m.

bout, baut, n., assalto m.

bow, bou, n., (archery) arco m.; (violin) archetto m.; (tie, knot) nodo m.

bow, bau, v.,inchinarsi. n., inchino m.; (ship) prua f.

bowels, bau'-els, n. pl., budella f. pl.

bowl, bool, n., scodella f.; vaso m.; (ball) boccia f. v., giuocare alle boccie

box, boks, v., (fight) far a pugni. n., scatola f.; (chest) cassa f.; (theatre) palco m.; (snuff, etc.) tabacchiera f.; — **on the ears**, schiaffo m.

boxer, boks'-a, n., pugilatore m.

boxing, boks'-ing, n., pugilato m.

boy, boi, n., ragazzo m.; —**hood**, fanciullezza f.

boycott, boi'-kot, v., boicottare. n., boicottaggio m.

brace, breis, v., legare; (health) fortificare. n., (mech.) braccio di antenna m.; (two) paio m.

bracelet, breis'-let, n., braccialetto m.

braces, brei'-ses, n. pl., bretelle f. pl.

bracing, breis'-ing, a., fortificante

bracken, brak'-n, n., felce f.

bracket, brak'-et, v., abbracciare. n., mensola f.; (parenthesis) parentesi f.

brackish, brak'-ish, a., salmastro

brag, bragh, v., millantare

braggart, brag'-aart, n., millantatore m.

braid, breid, n., treccia f.; (dress) guarnizione f. v., intrecciare

brain, brein, n., (substance) cervello m.; (mind) intelletto m.

braise, breis, v., stufare

brake, breik, n., freno m. v., frenare

bramble, bram'-bl, n., rovo m.

bran, bran, n., crusca f.

branch, braanch, n., ramo m.; (commercial) succursale f.; — **off**, v., ramificare

brand, brand, n., marca f.; (fire) ferro da marchiare m. v., marchiare

brandish, bran'-dish, v., brandire

brandy, bran'-di, n., acquavite f.

brass, braas, n., ottone m.

bravado, bra-vaa'-dou, n., smargiassata f.

brave*, breiv, a., valoroso

bravery, breiv'-er-i, n., valore m.

bravo! braa'-vou, interj., bravo!

brawl, brool, v., schiamazzare. n., schiamazzo m.

brawn, broon, n., salame di porco m.; muscolo m.

brawny, broo'-ni, a., tarchiato

bray, brei, v., (donkey) ragliare

brazen, brei'-sen, a., sfacciato

brazier, brei'-sia, n., braciere m.

Brazil-nut, bre-sil'-nŏt, n., noce del Brasile f.

breach, briich, n., rottura f.; infrazione f.; abuso m.

bread, bred, n., pane m.

breadth, bredZ, n., larghezza f.; altezza f.

break, breik, v., rompere; (law)violare; (smash) spezzare. n., rottura f.; (pause) pausa f.

breakage, breik'-ich, n., rottura f.; guasti m. pl.

breakdown, breik'-daun, n., interruzione f.; (health) esaurimento m.

breakers, breik'-ers, n. pl., (wave) cavalloni m. pl.; (naut.) scogli m pl.

breakfast, brek'-fast, v., far colazione. n., prima colazione f.

breakwater, breik'-uoo-ta, n., frangionde m.

bream, briim, n., reina f.

breast, brest, n., petto m.; seno m.

breastbone, brest'-boun, n., sterno m.

breastplate, brest'-pleit, n., corazza f.

breath, breZ, n., respiro m., fiato m.

breathe, briiD, v., respirare

breathless, breZ'-les, a., senza fiato

bred, bred, a., (well) ben educato

breech, briich, n., (gun) culatta f.

breeches, briich'-is, n pl., calzoni m. pl.

breed, briid, v., produrre. n., razza f.

breeder, briid'-a, n., allevatore m.

breeding, briid'-ing, n., educazione f.; (stock) allevamento m.

breeze, briis, n., brezza f.

breezy, brii'-si, a., fresco

brethren, breD'-ren, n. pl., confratelli m. pl.

brevet, bre'-vet, n., brevetto m.

brevity, brev'-i-ti, n., brevità f.

brew, bruu, v., fabbricar birra

brewer, bruu'-a, n., birraio m.

brewery, bruu'-ar-i, n., fabbrica di birra f.

briar, brai'-a, n., (wood) radica f.; (bramble) rovo m.

bribe, braib, v., corrompere : n., denaro di corruzione m.

bribery, brai'-ber-i, n., corruzione f.

brick, brik, n., mattone m.

bricklayer, brik'-lei-a, n., muratore m.

bridal, brai'-dl, a., nuziale

bride, braid, n., sposa f.; **—groom**, sposo m.; **—smaid**, damigella d'onore f.

bridge, brich, n., ponte m. v., gettar un ponte sopra

bridle, brai'-dl, n., briglia f. v., imbrigliare

brief, briif, a.,* breve v., avvisare. n., causa f.

brig, brigh, n., brigantino m.

brigade, bri-gheid', n., brigata f.

brigadier, brig-a-diir', n., generale di brigata m.

bright°, brait, a., chiaro ; (lively) vivace

brighten, brait'-n, v., rischiarare ; (enliven) animare

brightness, brait'-nes, n., chiarezza f. ; (mind) vivacità f.

brill, bril, n., rombo m.

brilliancy, bril'-ian-si, n., splendore m.

brilliant, bril'-iant, n., brillante m. a.,* brillante

brim, brim, n., orlo m. ; (hat) falda f. ; **— over**, v., traboccare

brimstone, brim'-stoun, n., solfo m.

brindled, brin'-dlid, a., macchiato

brine, brain, n., salamoia f. v., marinare

bring, bring, v., portare, recare ; **— forward**, (accounts) riportare ; **— in**, (receipts) produrre ; **— up**, (educate) allevare

brink, bringk, n., orlo m.

briny, brai'-ni, a., salmastro

brisk, brisk, a., agile ; (lively) **vispo**

brisket, brisk'-et, n., petto m.

briskness, brisk'-nes, n., agilità f. ; vivacità f.

bristle, bris'-l, n., setola f. v., arricciare : levarsi

bristling, bris'-ling, a., rizzantesi

brittle, brit'-el, a., fragile

brittleness, brit'-el-nes, n., fragilità f.

broach, brooch, n., spiedo m. v., (— a subject) intavolare

broad°, brood, a., largo, ampio

broadcast, brood'-kaast, n., (radio) radio diffusione f. v., diffondere

brocade, bro-keid', n., broccato m.

brogue, brough, n., accento m.

broil, broil, v., arrostire. n., (quarrel) rissa f.

broker, brou'-ka, n., sensale m.; (receiver) usciere m.; **stock-—**, agente di cambio m.

brokerage, brou'-ker-ich, n., senseria f.

bromide, brou'-maid, n., bromuro m.

bronchitis, brong-kai'-tis, n., bronchite f.

bronze, brons, n., bronzo m. v., bronzare; (tan) abbronzare

brooch, brooch, n., spilla f.

brood, bruud, n., covata f. v., covare

brook, bruk, n., ruscello m. v., tollerare

broom, bruum, n., scopa f.; (plant) ginestra f.

broth, brooZ, n., brodo m.

brothel, broD'-el, n., bordello m.

brother, broD'-a, n., fratello m.; — -in-law, cognato m.

brotherhood, broD'-er-huud, n., fraternità f.

brotherly, broD'-er-li, a., fraterno

brow, brau, n., sopracciglio m.; (fig.) fronte f.

browbeat, brau'-biit, v., mirare altezzosamente

brown, braun, a., bruno. v., abbrunire

brownish, braun'-ish, a., brunastro

browse, braus, v., pascolare

bruise, bruus, n., contusione f. v., contundere

brunette, bru-net', n., brunetta f.

brunt, brönt, n., urto m.

brush, brösh, n., spazzola f.; (paint) pennello m. v., spazzolare; (sweep) spazzare

brushwood, brösh'-uud, n., cespuglio m.

brusque, brösk, a., brusco

Brussels sprouts, brös-els-srauts', n. pl., cavoli di Brusselle m. pl.

brutal,* bruu'-tl, a., brutale

brutality, bruu-tal'-i-ti, n., brutalità f.

brutalize, bruu'-tal-ais, v., imbestialirsi

brute, bruut, n., bruto m.

bubble, bŏb'-l, n., bolla f. v., bollire

buck, bŏk, n., (deer) daino m. a., maschio

bucket, bŏk'-et, n., secchia f.

buckle, bŏk'-l, n., fibbia f. v., affibbiare

buckskin, bŏk'-skin, n., pelle di daino f.

buckwheat, bŏk'-uiit, n., saggina f.

bud, bŏd, n., germoglio m. ; (flower) bottone **m.**
v., germogliare

budge, bŏch, v., muoversi

budget, bŏch'-et, n., bilancio m.

buff, bŏf, a., color camoscio

buffalo, bŏf'-a-lou, n., buffalo m.

buffer, bŏf'-a, n., (railway) para urti m.

buffet, buf'-e, n., (refreshment) buffet m., **bar m.;**
(sideboard) credenza f.

buffet, bŏf'-it, v., abbattere

buffoon, bo-fuun', n., buffone m.

bug, bŏgh, n., cimice f. ; —bear, spauracchio **m.**

bugle, biuu'-gol, n., (mil.) cornetta f.

build, bild, v., edificare, costruire

builder, bild'-a, n., costruttore m.

building, bild'-ing, n., edifizio m.

bulb, bŏlb, n., bulbo m. ; (lamp) lampadina f.

bulge, bŏlch, v., curvarsi, n., gonfiatura f.

bulk, bŏlk, n., volume m.; in —, in massa

bulky, bŏlk'-i, a., massiccio

bull, bul, n., toro m.; (stock-exchange) rialzista m.;
—'s eye, (target) barilozzo m.

bulldog, bul'-dogh, n., mastino m.

bullet, bul'-et, n., palla f.

bulletin, bul'-i-tin, n., bollettino m.

bullfinch, bul'-finch, n., monachino **m.**

bullion, bul'-ion, n., verga f.

bullock, bul'-ok, n., bue m.

bully, bul'-i, n., bravaccio m. v., malmenare

bulrush, bul'-rŏsh, n., giunco m.

bulwark, bul'-uerk, n., (rampart) baluardo m.,
bastione m.; (naut.) murata f.; (fig.) baluardo m.

bump, bŏmp, n., colpo m. ; (swelling) bozza f.
   v., percuotere

bumper, bŏm'-pa, n., (glass) bicchiere ricolmo m.;
   (for motor-cars) para urti m.

bumpkin, bŏmp'-kin, n., villano m.

bumptious, bŏmp'-shŏs, a., arrogante

bunch, bŏnch, v., legare in fascio. n. mazzo m. ;
   — of grapes, grappolo d'uva m.

bundle, bŏn'-dl, n., pacco m.; (of wood) fastello m.
   v., impacchettare

bung, bŏng, n., tappo m.;—hole, buco di botte m.

bungalow, bŏng'-ga-lou, n., bangalò m.

bungle, bŏng'-gol, v., guastare. n., pasticcio m.

bungler, bŏng'-gla, n., guastamestieri m.

bunion, bŏn'-ion, n., bonione m.

bunker, bŏng'-ka, n., (coal) stiva da carbone f.

bunkum, bŏng'-kom, n., chiacchiera f.

bunting, bŏn'-ting n., (cloth) tessuto da bandiere m.

buoy, boi, n., boa f.

buoyancy, boi'-an-si, n., galleggiabilità f.

buoyant, boi'-ant, a., galleggiante

burden, bĕr'-dn, n., carico m. v., caricare

burdensome, bĕr'-den-som, a., pesante

bureau, biu'-rou, n., ufficio m. ; scrittoio m.

bureaucracy, biu-ro'-kra-si, n., burocrazia f.

burgess, bĕr'-ches, n., borghese m.

burgh, bĕrgh, (see **borough**)

burglar, bĕr'-gla, n., svaligiatore m.

burglary, bĕr'-gla-ri, n., svaligiamento m.

burial, be'-ri-al, n., seppellimento m.

burial-ground, be'-ri-al-graund, n., camposanto m.

burlesque, ber-lesk', n., burla f.

burly, bĕr'-li, a., corpulento

burn, bĕrn, v., bruciare ; (arson) **incendiare**.
   n., bruciatura f. ; (brook) rivolo m.

burner, bĕrn'-a, n., becco di gaz m.

burnish, bĕrn'-ish, v., brunire. n., imbrunitura f.

burrow, bŏr'-ou, v., scavare una tana

bursar, bĕr'-sa, n., (school) economo m.

burst, bĕrst, v., scoppiare ; (crack) screpolarsi

bury, ber'-i, v., seppellire ; (conceal) sotterrare

bus, bŏs, n., autobus m.

bush, bush, n., cespuglio m.

bushel, bŭsh'-l, n., staio m.

bushy, bush'-i, a., cespuglioso

business, bĭs'-nes, n., affari m.pl.; occupazione f.

business-like, bĭs'-nes-laik, a., pratico

bust, bŏst, n., busto m.

bustle, bŏst'-l, n., trambusto m. v., menare scalpore

busy, bĭs'-i, a., affaccendato; (place) movimentato. v., (oneself) affaccendarsi

busybody, bĭs'-i-bod-i, n., faccendone m.

but, bŏt, conj. & prep., ma; che. adv., se non, solamente, fuorchè

butcher, buch'-a, n., macellaio m. v., macellare

butler, bŏt'-la, n., maggiordomo m.

butt, bŏt, n., estremità f.; (gun) calcio m.; (cask) tino m. v., colpire colla testa

butter, bŏt'-a, n., burro m.

buttercup, bŏt'-er-kŏp, n., bottone d'oro m.

butter-dish, bŏt'-er-dish, n., piatto da burro m.

butterfly, bŏt'-er-flai, n., farfalla f.

buttock, bŏt'-ok, n., natica f.

button, bŏt'-n, n., bottone m. v., abbottonare

button-hole, bŏt'-n-houl, n., occhiello m.

buttress, bŏt'-res, n., contrafforte m.; sostegno m. v., puntellare

butts, bŏts, n. pl., posizione dei bersagli f.

buxom*, bŏk'-som, a., (woman) gagliarda

buy, bai, v., comprare

buyer, bai'-a, n., compratore m.

buzz, bŏs, n., ronzio m. v., ronzare

buzzard, bŏs'-erd, n., bozzago m.

by, bai, prep., da, di, a; presso di. adv., vicino di; con; per

by-law, bai'-loo, n., regolamento m.

bystander, bai'-stan-da, n., spettatore m.

byway, bai'-uei, n., strada fuori mano f.

byword, bai'-uĕrd, n., detto comune m.

cab, kab, n., (motor) auto di piazza f.; (horses) vettura f.

cabal, ka-bal', n., cabala f. v., incabolare

cabbage, kab'-ich, n., cavolo m.

cabin, kab'-in, n., cabina f.; (hut) capanna f.
cabinet, kab'-in-et, n., gabinetto m.
cabinet-maker, kab'-in-et-meik-a, n., ebanista m.
cable, kei'-bl, n., cavo m.; (naut.) gomena f.
    v., telegrafare
cablegram, kei'-bl-gram, n., cablogramma m.
cabman, kab'-man, n., cocchiere m.; (taxi) autista m.
cackle, kak'-l, n., chiacchiera f. v., chiocciare
cad, kad, n., facchino m.
caddy, kad'-i, n., scatola da tè f.
cadge, kach, v., mendicare ; —r, n., mendicante m.
cage, keich, n., gabbia f. v., ingabbiare
cajole, ka-choul', v., lusingare
cake, keik, n., torta f.; (soap) tavoletta f.
calabash, kal'-a-bash, n., zucca f.
calamitous*, ka-lam'-i-tos, a., calamitoso
calamity, ka-lam'-i-ti, n., calamità f.
calcine, kal'-sin, v., calcinare
calculate, kal'-kiu-leit, v., calcolare
caldron, kool'-dron, n., calderone m.
calendar, kal'-en-da, n., calendario m.
calf, kaaf, n., vitello m.; (leg) polpaccio m.
calico, kal'-i-kou, n., tela di cotone f.
call, kool. v., chiamare ; (name) chiamarsi ;
    (visit) visitare
callous*, kal'-os, a., (unfeeling) indurito
calm, kaam, n., calma f. a.,* calmo. v., calmare
calmness, kaam'-nes, n., calma f.
calumniate, ka-lŏm'-ni-eit, v., calunniare
calumny, kal'-om-ni, n., calunnia f.
cambric, keim'-brik, n., batista f.
camel, kam'-l, n., cammello m.
cameo, kam'-i-ou, n., cammeo m.
camera, kam'-er-a, n., macchina fotografica f.;
    in —, a porte chiuse
camisole, kam'-i-soul, n., camicetta f.
camomile, kam'-o-mail, n., camomilla f.
camp, kamp, v., accampare. n., campo m.;
    —-bed, letto da campo m.; —-stool, sedia
    da campo f.
campaign, kam-pein', n., campagna f.

camphor, kam'-*fer*, n., canfora f.

can, kan, n., brocca f. v., (preserve) mettere in iscatola

can, kan, v., (to be able) potere ; (to know) sapere

canal, ka-nal', n., canale m.

canary, ka-neh'-ri, n., canarino m.

cancel, kan'-sl, v., cancellare

cancer, kan'-sa, n., cancro m.

candid*, kan'-did, a., candido, franco

candidate, kan'-di-deit, n., candidato m.

candied, kan'-did, a., candito

candle, kan'-dl, n., candela f.

candlestick, kan'-del-stik, n., candeliere m.

candour, kan'-da, n., candore m.

candy, kan'-di, n., dolci canditi m. pl.

cane, kein, n., bastone m. v., bastonare

canine, ka'-nain, a., canino ; n., canino m.

canister, kan'-is-ta, n., scatola f.

canker, kang'-ka, n., canchero m.

cannibal, kan'-i-bl, n., cannibale m. & f.

cannon, kan'-on, n., cannone m.; (billiards) carambola f.

canoe, ka-nuu', n., canoa f.

canon, kan'-on, n., (ecclesiastical law) canone m. ; (title) canonico m.

canopy, kan'-o-pi, n., baldacchino m.

cant, kant, n., simulazione f.; —ing, a., sornione

cantankerous, kan-tang'-ker-os, a., bisbetico

canteen, kan-tiin', n., cantina f.

canter, kan'-ta, n., piccolo galoppo m. v., andare al piccolo galoppo

canvas, kan'-vas, n., canavaccio m.

canvass, kan'-vas, v., (votes, etc.) sollecitare

cap, kap, n., berretto m.

capable, kei'-pa-bl, a., capace

capacity, ka-pa'-si-ti, n., capacità f.

cape, keip, n., capo m. ; (cover) mantello m.

caper, kei'-pa, n., (pickle) cappero m.

capital, kap'-i-tl, n., (money) capitale m.; (city) capitale f. ; (letter) lettera maiuscola f.

capitulate, ka-pi'-tiu-leit, v., capitolare

capon, kei'-pn, n., cappone m.

capricious*, ka-prish'-os, a., capriccioso

capsize, kap-saiz', v., capovolgere

capstan, kap'-stan, n., (naut.) argano m.

capsule, kap'-siul, n., capsula f.

captain, kap'-tin, n., capitano m. v., capitanare

captive, kap-tiv, n., prigioniero m.; captivo m.

captivity, kap-tiv'-i-ti, n., prigionia f.

capture, kap'-chur, n., cattura f. v., catturare

car, kaar, n., carro m.: auto f.: (aero) navicella f.

caramel, kar'-a-mel, n., caramella f.

carat, kar'-at, n., carato m.

caravan, kar'-a-van, n., carovana f.

caraway, kar'-a-uei, n., carvi m. pl.

carbide, kaar'-baid, n., carburo m.

carbine, kaar'-bain, n., carabina f.

carbolic, kaar-bol'-ik, n., acido fenico m.

carbon, kaar'-bon, n., carbonio m.; — **paper**, carta carbone f.

carbuncle, kaar'-bong-kl, n., carbonchio m.

carburettor, kaar'-ba-ret-a, n., carburatore m.

carcase, carcass, kaar'-kas, n., carcassa f.

card, kaard, n., biglietto da visita m.: (playing) carta f.; — **case**, scatola per biglietti da visita f.

cardboard, kaard'-bord, n., cartone m.; — **box**, scatola di cartone f.

cardinal, kaar'-di-nal, n., cardinale m.

care, ker, n., attenzione f.; (anxiety) affanno m.; (tending) cura f.: **take** — ! interj., attenzione ! **take** — **of**, v., aver cura di ; — **for**, piacere; c/o, presso

career, ka-riir', n., carriera f.

careful*, ker'-ful, a., attento

careless*, ker'-les, a., disattento ; negletto

carelessness, ker'-les-nes, n., negligenza f.

caress, ka-res', n., carezza f. v., accarezzare

caretaker, ker'-tei-ka, n., guardiano m.

cargo, kaar'-gou, n., carico m.

caricature, kar'-i-ka-chur, n., caricatura f. v., caricaturare

carmine, kaar'-main, n., carminio m.

carnage, kaar'-nich, n., carneficina f.

carnal°, kaar'-nal. a., carnale

carnation, kaar-nei'-shon, n., garofano m.

carnival, kaar'-ni-vl, n., carnevale m.

carol, kar'-ol, n., (Xmas) cantico di Natale m.

carp, kaarp, n., (fish) carpa f. v., cavillare

carpenter, kaar'-pen-ta, n., falegname m.

carpet, kaar'-pet, n., tappeto m.

carriage, kar'-ich, n., carrozza f.; (train) vettura f.;
(freight) trasporto m.; (deportment) portamento m.

carrier, kar'-i-a, n., agenzia di trasporti f.; (on
car, cycle, etc.) porta bagaglio m.; — -pigeon,
piccione viaggiatore m.

carrion, kar'-i-on, n., carogna f.

carrot, kar'-ot, n., carota f.

carry, kar'-i, v., portare; — on, (fig.) continuare

cart, kaart, n., carretto m. v., trasportare

cartage, kaar'-tich, n., vettura f.

carter, kaar'-ta, n., carrettiere m.

cartload, kaart'-loud, n., carrettata f.

cartoon, kaar-tuun', n., caricatura f.

cartridge, kaar'-trich, n., cartuccia f.

carve, kaarv, v., intagliare; (meat) tagliare

carving, kaarv'-ing, n., intaglio m.

cascade, kas-keid', n., cascata f.

case, keis, n., caso m.; (box) cassa f.; (cigarette) scatola da sigarette f.; (wallet) portafoglio m.;
(spectacle, jewel) astuccio m.; (watch) cassa f.;
(law) processo m.; in —, in caso

casement, keis'-ment, n., finestra f.

cash, kash, n., denaro m.; (ready money) contanti m pl. v., incassare

cash-book, kash'-buk, n., libro di cassa m.

cash-box, kash'-boks, n., cassetta dei denari f.

cashier, kash'-ir, n., cassiere m. v., (mil.) radiare

cashmere, kash'-mir, n., cascimira f.

cask, kaask, n., barile m.

casket, kaas'-ket, n., scrigno m., cofanetto m.

cassock, kas'-ok, n., camice m.

cast, kaast, n., (throw) lancio m.; (theatre) distribuzione delle parti f.; (metal) forma di fusione f.
v., (throw) gettare; (metal) fondere; — -iron,
n., ghisa f.

castanet, kas'-ta-net, n., nacchere f. pl.
caste, kaast, n., casta f.
castigate, kas'-ti-gheit, v., castigare
castle, kaa'-sl, n., castello m.; (chess) **torre f.** v., arroccare
castor, kaas'-tor, n., (furniture bearings) rotella f.
castor-oil, kaas'-tor-oil, n., olio di ricino m.
casual*, kash'-iu-al, a., casuale
casualties, kash'-iu-al-tes, n.pl., (mil.) perdite f.pl.
casualty, kash'-iu-al-ti, n., accidente m.
cat, kat, n., gatto m.
catalogue, kat'-a-logh, n., catalogo m. v., catalogare
catarrh, ka-taar', n., catarro m.
catastrophe, ka-tas'-tro-fi, n., catastrofe f.
catch, kach, v., prendere; (seize) cogliere, pigliare; — up, raggiungere. n., presa f.; (door) nottolino m.
catching, kach'-ing, a., contagioso
catchword, kach'-uërd, n., parola di riferimento f.
category, kat'-i-gor-i, n., categoria f.
cater, kei'-ta, v., provvedere
caterer, kei'-ter-a, n., provveditore m.
caterpillar, kat'-er-pil-a, n., bruco m.
cathedral, ka-Zii'-dral, n., cattedrale f.
catholic, kaZ'-o-lik, n., cattolico m. a., cattolico
cattle, kat'-l, n., bestiame m.
cauliflower, ko'-li-flau-er, n., cavolfiori m.
caulk, kook, v., calafatare
cause, koos, n., causa f. v., causare
causeway, koos'-uei, n., diga f.; marciapiede m.
caustic, koos'-tik, n., caustico m. a., caustico
cauterize, koo'-ter-ais, v., cauterizzare
caution, koo'-shon, n., cautela f.; prudenza f. v., avvertire
cautious*, koo'-shos, a., cauto
cavalier, kav-a-lir', n., cavaliere m.
cavalry, kav'-al-ri, n., cavalleria f.
cave, keiv, n., caverna f.
cavernous, kav'-ern-os, a., cavernoso
cavil, kav'-il, v., cavillare
cavity, kav'-i-ti, n., cavità f.; (tooth) buco m.
caw, koo, v., gracchiare

Cayenne pepper, kei-en' pep'-*a*, n., **pepe di** Caienna m.

cease, siis, v., cessare

ceaseless*, siis'-les, a., incessante

cedar, siil'-*da*, n., cedro m.

cede, siid, v., cedere

ceiling, siil'-ing, n., soffitto m.

celebrate, sel'-i-breit, v., celebrare

celebrated, sel'-i-breit-id, a., celebre

celerity, si-ler'-i-ti, n., celerità f.

celery, sel'-*e*-ri, n., sedano m.

celestial, si-les'-ti-*a*l, a., celeste

celibacy, sel'-i-*ba*-si, n., celibato m.

cell, sel, n., cella f.

cellar, sel'-*a*, n., cantina f.

celluloid, sel'-iu-loid, n., celluloide f.

cement, si-ment', n., cemento m. ; (for crockery, etc.) mastice m. v., cementare

cemetery, sem'-i-ta-ri, n., cimitero m.

censor, sen'-*sor*, n., censore m.

censorship, sen'-sor-ship, n., censura f.

census, sen'-sos, n., censimento m.

cent, sent, n., cento m. ; (coin) centesimo m.

centenary, sen'-ti-ner-i, n., centenario m.

central, sen'-tral, a., centrale

central-heating, sen'-tral-hii'-ting, n., riscaldamento centrale m.

centralize, sen'-tral-ais, v., centralizzare

centre, sen'-tr, n., centro m.

century, sen'-cher-i, n., secolo m.

ceramics, ser-am'-iks, n., ceramica f.

ceremonious*, ser-i-mou'-ni-os, a., cerimonioso

ceremony, ser-i-mou'-ni, n., cerimonia f. ; (rite) cerimoniale m.

certain*, ser'-tin, a., certo

certainty, ser'-tin-ti, n., certezza f.

certificate, ser-tif'-i-keit, n., certificato m.

certify, ser'-ti-fai, v., certificare, attestare

certitude, ser'-ti-tiuud, n., certezza f.

cessation, ses-sei'-shon, n., cessazione f.

cession, se'-shon, n., cessione f.

cesspool, ses'-puul, n., cesso m.

chafe, cheif. v., (rub) riscaldare : (wear) logorare ; (fret) irritarsi

chaff, chaaf. n., pula f.; (banter) beffa f. v., deridere

chaffinch, chaf'-inch. n., fringuello m.

chafing-dish, cheif'-ing-dish. n., scaldavivande m.

chain, chein. n., catena f.; — up. v., incatenare

chair, cher. n., sedia f.

chairman, cher'-man. n., presidente m.

chaise, sheis. n., calesse m.

chalice, chal'-is. n., calice m.

chalk, chook. n., gesso m. v., ingessare

challenge, chal'-inch. n., sfida f. v., sfidare

chamber, cheim'-ber. n., camera f.;—pot, orinale m.

chamberlain, cheim'-ber-lin. n., ciambellano m.

chambermaid, cheim'-ber-meid. n., cameriera f.

chambers, cheim'-bers. n. pl., (office) studio legale m.

chamois, sham'-oi. n., camoscio m.

champagne, sham-pein'. n., sciampagna f.; — -glass, coppa da sciampagna f.

champion, cham'-pi-on. n., campione m.

chance, chaans. n., occasione f.; fortuna f. a., casuale. v., arrischiare

chancel, chaan'-sl. n., coro m.

chancellor, chaan'-se-lor. n., cancelliere m.

chancery, chaan'-se-ri. n., cancelleria f.

chandelier, shan-di-lir'. n., candelabro m.

change, cheinch. n., (small money) moneta spicciola f.; (alteration) cambiamento m. v., cambiare

changeable, chein'-cha-bl. a., variabile

changeless, cheinch'-les. a., immutabile

channel, chan'-l. v., scavare. n., canale m.; (sea) braccio di mare m.; **the English —**, la Manica f.

chant, chaant. n., cantico m. v., cantare

chaos, kei'-os. n., caos m.

chaotic, kei-ot'-ik. a., caotico

chap, chap. n., screpolatura f.; (fellow) ragazzo m. v., screpolare

chapel, chap'-l. n., cappella f.

chaperon, shap'-er-oun. n., accompagnatrice f.

chaplain, chap'-lin. n., cappellano m.

chaplet, chap'-let, n., rosario m. ; (wreath) ghirlanda f.

chapter, chap'-ta, n., capitolo m.

char, chaar, v., carbonizzare ; (clean) far servizi

character, kar'-ak-ta, n., carattere m.

charcoal, chaar'-koul, n., carbone di legna m.

charge, chaardsh, n., prezzo m. ; accusa f. ; (attack) carica f. ; (load) carico m. v., domandare ; accusare ; caricare ; to be in —, essere incaricato

charily, che'-ri-li, adv., frugalmente

chariot, che'-i-ot, n., carro m.

charitable, char'-it-a-bl, a., caritatevole .

charity, char'-i-ti, n., carità f.

charm, chaarm, n., amuleto m. ; fascino m. v., affascinare ; (tame) incantare

charming*, chaar'-ming, a., affascinante

charnel-house, chaar'-nel-haus, n., ossario m.

chart, chaart, n., carta marina f.

charter, chaar'-ta, v., (ship) noleggiare. n., (grant) brevetto m.

charwoman, chaar'-uu-man, n., donna a giornata f.

chary, che'-ri, a., cauto ; economo

chase, cheis, n., caccia f. v., cacciare ; (pursue) inseguire

chasm, kasm, n., abisso m.

chaste*, cheist, a., casto

chasten, cheis'-n, v., castigare ; (humble) sottomettere

chastise, chas-tais', v., castigare

chastity, chas'-ti-ti, n., castità f.

chasuble, chas'-iu-bl, n., pianeta f.

chat, chat, n., chiacchera f. v., chiacchierare

chattel, chat'-l, n., bene m.

chatter, chat'-a, n., chiacchierio m. v., cianciare ; (teeth) battere i denti

chatter-box, chat'-a-boks, n., chiacchierone m.

chauffeur, shoof'-ér, n., chauffeur m., conduttore d'automobile m.

cheap*, chiip, a., a buon mercato

cheapen, chiip'-n, v., diminuire di prezzo

I—13

cheapness, chiip'-nes, n., buon mercato m.

cheat, chiit, n., truffatore m. v., truffare

cheating, chiit'-ing, n., trufferia f.

check, chek, n., (restraint) freno m.; (chess) scacco m.; (verification) verifica f.; (pattern) quadretto m. v., (stop) arrestare ; (restrain) frenare ; (verify) verificare

checkmate, chek'-meit, n., **scacco matto** m. v., dar scacco matto

cheek, chiik, n., guancia f.; (impudence) sfacciatezza f. v., essere sfacciato

cheer, chir, n., allegrezza f.; (applause) acclamazione f. v., acclamare ; (brighten) allegrare

cheerful*, chir'-ful, a., allegro

cheerless*, chir'-les, a., triste

cheese, chiis, n., formaggio m.

chemical, kem'-i-kl, n., prodotto chimico m. a.,* chimico

chemise, shi-miis', n., camicia da donna f.

chemist, kem'-ist, n., chimico m.; (shop) farmacista m.

chemistry, kem'-ist-ri, n., chimica f.

cheque, chek, n., assegno m.

cheque-book, chek'-buk, n., libro di assegni m.

cherish, cher'-ish, v., amare ; accarezzare

cherry, cher'-i, n., ciliegia f.

cherub, cher'-ob, n., cherubino m.

chess, ches, n., scacchi m. pl.

chest, chest, n., petto m.; (trunk) cofano m.; (box) cassa f.; — **of drawers,** cassettone m.

chestnut, ches'-nöt, n., castagna f.

chew, chuu, v., masticare ; (cattle) ruminare

chicken, chik'-n, n., pollo m.; —**-pox,** varicella f.

chide, chaid, v., rimproverare

chief, chiif, n., capo m. a., principale

chiefly, chiif'-li, adv., principalmente

chilblain, chil'-blein, n., gelone m.

child, chaild, n., fanciullo m.

childish*, chaild -ish, a., bambinesco

childlike, chaild'-laik, a., come un bambino

chill, chil, n., infreddatura f. v., raffreddare

chilly, chil'-i, a., freddo

chime, chaim, n., scampanio m. v., risuonare

chimney, chim'-ni, n., caminetto m.; (lamp) tubo m.

chimney-sweep, chim'-ni-suiip, n., spazzacamino m.

chin, chin, n., mento m.

china, chai'-na, n., porcellana f.

chink, chingk, n., crepaccio m. v., tintinnare

chintz, chints, n., cretone di Persia m.

chip, chip, n., scheggia f. v., scheggiare

chiropodist, kai-rop'-od-ist, n., curacalli m.

chirp, chĕrp, n., cinguettio m. v., cinguettare

chisel, chis'-l, n., scalpello m.

chivalrous, shiv'-al-ros, a., cavalleresco

chive, chaiv, n., cipollina f.

chlorine, kloo'-rain, n., cloro m.

chloroform, kloo'-ro-form, n., cloroformio m.

chocolate, chok'-o-leit, n., cioccolata f.

choice, chois, n., scelta f. a., scelto

choir, kuair, n., coro m.

choke, chouk, v., soffocare ; — up, ostruire

choler, kol'-a, n., collera f.; —ic, a., collerico

cholera, kol'-er-a, n., colera m.

choose, chuus, v., scegliere

chop, chop, n., costoletta f. v., tagliare

chopper, chop'-a, n., coltellaccio m.

choral, ko'-ral, a., corale

chord, koord, n., (mus.) corda f.

chorister, kor'-is-ta, n., corista m. & f.

chorus, ko'-ros, n., coro m.

Christ, kraist, n., Cristo m.

christen, kris'-n, v., battezzare

christening, kris'-ning, n., battesimo m.

Christianity, kris-ti-an'-i-ti, n., Cristianità f.

Christmas, kris'-mas, n., Natale m. ; — -box, regalo di Natale m.; — -tree, albero di Natale m.

chronic, kron'-ik, a., cronico

chronicle, kron'-ik-l, n., cronaca f.

chrysanthemum, kri-san'-zi-mom, n., crisantemo m.

chubby, chŏb'-i, a., paffuto

chuck, chŏk, v., chiocciare

chuckle, chŏk'-l, n., (laugh) risatina. f. v., ridacchiare

chum, chŏm, n., compare m.

chunk, chŏngk, n., grossa fetta f.

church, chêrch, n., chiesa f.

churchyard, chêrch'-iaard, n., camposanto m.

churl, chêrl, n., mascalzone m.

churlish, chêrl'-ish, a., bisbetico, grossolano

churn, chêrn, n., zangola f. v., battere

cider, sai'-da, n., sidro m.

cigar, si-gaar', n., sigaro m.

cigarette, sig-a-ret', n., sigaretta f.

cinder, sin'-da, n., brace f.

cinema, sin'-e-ma, n., cinematografo m.

cinnamon, sin'-na-mon, n., cannella f.

cipher, sai-fa, n., cifra f.

circle, sêr'-k!, n., cerchio m. v., circolare

circlet, sêr'-klet, n., cerchietto m.

circuit, sêr'-kit, n., circuito m.

circuitous°, sêr-kiu'-it-os, a., tortuoso ; indiretto

circular, sêr'-kiu-lar, n., circolare f. a., circolare

circulate, sêr'-kiu-leit, v., circolare ; **circulating library**, n., biblioteca circolante f.

circumcise, sêr'-kom-sais, v., circoncidere

circumference, sêr-kŏm'-fer-ens, n., circonferenza f.

circumflex, sêr'-kom-fleks, a., circonflesso

circumscribe, sêr'-kom-skraib, v., circoscrivere

circumspect, sêr'-kom-spekt, a., circospetto

circumstance, sêr'-kom-stans, n., circostanza f.

circumstantial, sêr'-kom-stan-shal, a., circostanziale ; **—evidence**, n., testimonianze accessorie f.pl.

circumvent, sêr-kom-vent', v., raggirare

circus, sêr'-kos, n., circo m.; place) piazza rotonda f.

cistern, sis'-têrn, n., cisterna f.

citadel, -it'-a-del, n., cittadella f.

cite, -ait, v., citare

citizen, sit'-i-sen, n., cittadino m.

citizenship, sit'-i-sen-ship, n., cittadinanza f.

citron, sit'-ron, n., cedro m.

city, sit'-i, n., città f.

civil°, siv'-il, a., civile ; (urban) urbano ; (polite) corte e

civilian, siv-il'-ian, n., borghese m. & f.

civilisation, siv-il-ai-*sei*'-shon, n., civiltà f.

civility, siv-il'-i-ti, n., urbanità f.

claim, kleim, n., rivendicazione f.; (commercial) reclamo m.; (mine) diritto minerario m.; (demand) pretensione f. v., reclamare; pretendere

claimant, kleim'-ant, n., pretendente m. & f.

clamber, klam'-ba, v., arrampicarsi

clamorous⁎, klam'-or-os, a., clamoroso

clamour, klam'-*er*, n., clamore m.

clamp, klamp, n., rampone m. v., ramponare

clan, klan, n., tribù scozzese f.

clandestine, klan-des'-tin, a., clandestino

clang, klang, n., clangore m. v., far clangore

clank, klangk, v., tintinnare

clap, klap, v., applaudire. n., battuta di mani f.; (thunder) colpo m.

clapping, klap'-ing, n., applauso m.

clap-trap, klap'-trap, n., freddure f. pl.

claret, klar'-et, n., vino di Bordò m.

clarify, klar'-i-fai, v., chiarificare

clarinet, klar'-i-net, n., clarinetto m.

clash, klash, n., cozzo m., urto m. v., cozzare

clasp, klaasp, v., abbracciare. n., (catch) fermaglio m.

class, klaas, n., classe f. v., classificare

classify, klas'-i-fai, v., classificare

clatter, klat'-*a*, n., strepito m. v., strepitare

clause, kloos, n., clausola f.

claw, kloo, n., artiglio m.; (lobster, etc.) pinza f. v., graffiare

clay, klei, n., creta f.; —**ey**, a., argilloso

clean, kliin, v., pulire. a.,⁎ pulito

cleaning, kliin'-ing, n., pulizia f.

cleanliness, klen'-li-nes, n., pulitezza f.

cleanse, klens, v., purificare

clear, klir, a.,⁎ chiaro, puro ;(profit) netto. v., ordinare; (table) sparecchiare; (sky) schiarire; (customs) svincolare

clearness, klir'-nes, n., chiarezza f.

cleave, kliiv, v., fendere; (cling) aderire

cleft, kleft, n., fenditura f.

clematis, klem'-*a*-tis, n., clematite f.

clemency, klem'-en-si, n., clemenza f.

clench, klench, v., serrare
clergy, klĕr'-chi, n., clero m.
clergyman, klĕr'-chi-man, n., sacerdote m.
clerical, kler'-ik-l, a., d'ufficio ; (eccl.) clericale ;
— **error**, n., errore di trascrizione m.
clerk, klaark, n., impiegato m.
clever*, klev'-a, a., intelligente ; abile
cleverness, klev'-er-nes, n., abilità f.
click, klik, n., scricchiolio m.
client, klai'-ent, n., cliente m. & f.
clientele, klai'-ent-l, n., clientela f.
cliff, klif, n., scogliera f.
climate, klai'-met, n., clima m.
climax, klai'-maks, n., colmo m.
climb, klaim, n., ascesa f. v., salire ; (mountain) arrampicarsi
climber, klaim'-a, n., arrampicatore m.
clinch, klinch, n., presa f. v., tener in pugno
cling, kling, v., aggrapparsi
clink, klingk, n., tintinnio m. v., tintinnare
clip, klip, n., fermo m. ; molla f. v., (hair, etc.) tagliare ; (animals) tosare
cloak, klouk, n., mantello m. v., (fig.) favorire ;
(fig.) nascondere
cloak-room, klouk'-ruum, n., guardaroba m. ;
(railway) deposito bagagli m.
clock, klok, n., pendola f. ; alarm —, sveglia f.
clockwork, klok'-uĕrk, n., movimento d'orologio m.
clod, klod, n., zolla f.
clog, klogh, n., zoccolo m. ; — up, v., ostruire
cloister, klois'-ta, n., chiostro m.
close, klous, n., chiusura f. v., chiudere.
a., (weather) chiuso
closet, klos'-et, n., gabinetto m.
closure, klou'-shur, n., chiusura f.
clot, klot, n., grumo m. v., coagulare
cloth, kloZ, n., tessuto m.
clothe, klouD, v., vestire
clothes, klouDs, n., pl., abiti m., pl ; (bed) biancheria di letto f. ; — brush, spazzola da vestiti f.
clothier, klouD'-ia, n., negozio di vestiti m.
clothing, klouD'-ing, n., abbigliamento m.

cloud, klaud, n., nube f. v., annuvolarsi
cloudless, klaud'-les, a., **senza nubi**
cloudy, klaud'-i, a., nuvoloso ; (fig.) torbido
clout, klaut, n., (cloth) cencio m.; (smack) **scappaccione m.**
clove, klouv, n., chiodo di garofano m.
cloven, klouv'-n, a., forcuto
clover, klou'-va, n., trifoglio m. ; **to be in —**, v., essere nell'abbondanza
clown, klaun, n., pagliaccio m.; (lout) buffone m.
club, klôb, n., circolo m. ; (stick) clava f.; (cards) bastoni m. pl.
cluck, klôk, v., chiocciare
clue, kluu, n., indicazione f.
clump, klômp, n., ceppo m. ; (trees, etc.) gruppo m.
clumsiness, klôm'-si-nes, n., goffaggine f.
clumsy, klôm'-si, a., goffo
cluster, klôs'-ta, n., (grapes) grappolo m. ; (group) gruppo m. ; (roses) mazzo m. v., aggrupparsi
clutch, klôch, n., stretta f.; (motor) frizione f. v., afferrare
coach, kouch, n., diligenza f.; autocorriera f.; (tutor) ripetitore m. ; (sport) allenatore m. v., dar ripetizione
coachman, kouch'-man, n., cocchiere m.
coagulate, kou-a'-ghiu-leit, v., coagulare
coal, koul, n., carbone m. v., far carbone
coal-cellar, koul'-sel-a, n., carbonaia f.
coalition, ko-a-li'-shon, n., coalizione f.
coal-mine, koul'-main, n., miniera di carbone f.
coal-scuttle, koul'-skôt-l, n., secchio da carbone m.
coarse*, kours, a., grossolano
coarseness, kours'-nes, n., ruvidezza f.
coast, koust, n., costa f. v., costeggiare
coast-guard, koust'-gaard, n., guardacoste m.
coat, kout, n., abito m. ; (overcoat) soprabito m.; (animal) pelliccia f. ; (paint) mano f.; **— of arms**, stemma f.
coating, kout'-ing, n., strato m.
coax, kouks, v., blandire
cob, kob, n., (pony) cavallino m.

cobbler, kob'-la, n., ciabattino m.

cobweb, kob'-ueb, n., telaragna f.

cocaine, koo'-ka-in, n., cocaina f.

cochineal, koch'-i-nil, n., cocciniglia f.

cock, kok, n., (bird) gallo m.; (tap) **rubinetto m.** v., (gun) levare il grilletto; (ears) rizzare

cockade, ko-keid', n., coccarda f.

cockerel, kok'-er-el, n., galletto m.

cockle, kok'-l, n., gongola f.; (corn) **loglio m.**

cockroach, kok'-rouch, n., scarafaggio m.

cocoa, kou'-kou, n., cacao m.

cocoa-nut, kou'-kou-nŏt, n., noce di cocco f.

cocoon, ko-kuun', n., bozzolo m.

cod, kod, n., merluzzo m.; — **liver oil**, olio di merluzzo m.

coddle, kod'-l, v., (pamper) vezzeggiare

code, koud, n., codice m.

codicil, kod'-i-sil, n., codicillo m.

coerce, kou-ĕrs', v., costringere

coffee, kof'-i, n., caffè m.

coffee-pot, kof'-i-pot, n., caffettiera f.

coffer, kof'-a, n., cofano m.

coffers, kof'-ers, n. pl., cassa f.

coffin, kof'-in, n., bara f.

cog, kogh, n., dente f.; — **-wheel**, ruota dentata f.

cogitate, koch'-i-teit, v., meditare

cognac, koun'-iak, n., cognac m.

cognate, kogh'-neit, a., cognato

cognizance, kogh'-ni-sans, n., conoscenza f.; riconoscenza f.

cognizant, kogh'-ni-sant, a., conoscitore

coherence, kou-hi'-rens, n., coerenza f.

coherent, kou-hi'-rent, a., coerente; connesso

cohesion, kou-hi'-shon, n., coesione f.

cohesive*, kou-hi'-siv, a., coesivo

coil, koil, n., rotolo m.; (electric) **bobina f.** v., arrotolare

coin, koin, n., moneta f. v., coniare

coincide, kou-in-said', v., coincidere

coke, kouk, n., coke m.

colander, kol'-en-da, n., colatoio m.

cold, kould, n., freddo m. ; (head) **raffreddore** m. a., freddo

colic, kol'-ik, n., colica f.

collaborate, ko-lab'-o-reit, v., collaborare

collapse, ko-laps', n., crollo m. v., crollare

collar, kol'-er, n., collo m. ; (dog) collare m.

collar-bone, kol'-er-boun, n., clavicola f.

collate, ko-leit', v., collazionare

collateral*, ko-lat'-er-al, a., collaterale

collation, ko-lei'-shon, n., colazione f.

colleague, kol'-iigh, n., collega m. & f.

collect, ko-lekt', v., raccogliere ; riunire

collected, ko-lek'-tid, a., raccolto ; placido

collection, ko-lek'-shon, n., raccolta f. ; complesso m.

collective*, ko-lek'-tiv, a., collettivo

collector, ko-lek'-ta, n., collezionista m. & f. ; (revenue) esattore m.

college, kol'-ich, n., collegio m. ; (university) collegio universitario m.

collide, ko-laid', v., urtarsi

collier, kol'-ia, n., minatore m. ; (naut.) nave carboniera f.

colliery, kol'-ier-i, n., miniera di carbone f.

collision, ko-li-shon, n., collisione f.

collop, kol'-op, n., fetta f.

colloquial, ko-lou'-kui-al, a., familiare

collusion, ko-luu'-shon, n., collusione f.

colon, kou'-lon, n., due punti m. pl.

colonel, ker'-nel, n., colonnello m.

colonist, kol'-on-ist, n., colono m.

colonnade, ko-lon-eid', n., colonnato m.

colony, kol'-o-ni, n., colonia f.

colossal, ko-los'-l, a., colossale

colour, kol'-a, n., colore m. v., colorare

colouring, kol'-er-ing, n., tinta f.

colt, koult, n., puledro m.

column, kol'-om, n., colonna f.

coma, kou'-ma, n., (med.) coma m.

comb, koum, n., (for hair) pettine m. ; (bird) cresta f. ; (honey) favo m. v., pettinare

combat, kom'-bat, n., combattimento m. v., combattere

combatant, kom'-ba-tant, n., combattente m.

combative[2], kom'-ba-tiv, a., battagliero

combination, kom-bi-nei'-shon, n., combinazione f.

combine, kŏm-bain', v., combinare. n., alleanza f.

combustion, kom-bŏst'-ion, n., combustione f.

come, kŏm, v., venire; — **down**, scendere;
— **in**, entrare; — **off**, distaccarsi; — **out**,
uscire; — **up**, ascendere, salire

comedian, ko-mii'-di-an, n., commediante m. & f.

comedy, kom'-i-di, n., commedia f.

comet, kom'-et, n., cometa f.

comfort, kŏm'-fort, n., benessere m.; consolazione f.; (relief) alleviamento m. v., confortare

comfortable, kŏm'-fort-a-bl, a., confortevole

comic, kom'-ik, a., comico

coming, kŏm'-ing, a., prossimo. n., venuta f.

comma, kom'-a, n., virgola f.

command, ko-maand', n., comando m.; (knowledge) padronanza f. v., comandare

commander, ko-maand'-a, n., comandante m.;
(navy) capitano di fregata m.

commandment, ko-maand'-ment, n., comanda-
mento m.

commemorate, kom-em'-o-reit, v., commemorare

commence, ko-mens', v., cominciare, principiare

commencement, ko-mens'-ment, n., principio m.

commend, ko-mend', v., raccomandare; (praise) lodare

commendation, ko-men-dei'-shon, n., elogio m.

comment, kom'-ent, n., commento m.

comment, ko-ment', v., commentare

commerce, kom'-ĕrs, n., commercio m.

commercial, kom-ĕr'-shal, a., commerciale

commiserate, ko-mis'-ĕr-eit, v., commiserare

commission, ko-mish'-on, v., delegare; (naut.) armare. n., (percentage) commissione f.; (order) ordine m.; (mil.) grado d'ufficiale m.; (brokerage) provvigione f.

commissionaire, ko-mish-on-ĕr', n., commesso
alla porta m.

commit, ko-mit', v., (bind) impegnarsi; (crime,
fault) commettere; (prison) imprigionare

committee, ko-mit'-i, n., comitato m.

commodious*, ko-moud'-i-os, a., comodo

commodity, ko-mod'-i-ti, n., comodità f.

commodore, kom'-o-dor, n., commodoro m.

common, kom'-on, a.,* (usual) comune ; (universal) generale ; (vulgar) volgare. n., (public ground) terreno municipale m.

commoner, kom'-on-a, n., persona del popolo f.

commonplace, kom'-on-pleis, a., banale ; trito

Commons, kom'-ons, n.pl., (House of —) Camera dei Comuni f.

commonwealth, kom'-on-uelz, n., federazione di stati f.

commotion, ko-mou'-shon, n., commozione f.

commune, ko-miuun', v., conferire

communicate, ko-miuu'-ni-keit, v., comunicare

communication, ko-miuu-ni-kei'-shon, n., comunicazione f.

Communion, ko-miuu'-nion, n., (eccl.) comunione f.

community, ko-miuu'-ni-ti, n., comunità f.

compact*, kom-pakt', a., compatto

companion, kom-pan'-ion, n., compagno m.

companionship, kom-pan'-ion-ship, n., compagnia f. ; società f.

company, kŏm'-pa-ni, n., compagnia f. ; società f.

comparative*, kom-par-a-tiv, a., comparativo

compare, kom-per', v., paragonare

comparison, kom-par'-is-n, n., paragone m.

compartment, kom-paart'-ment, n., scompartimento m.

compass, kŏm'-pas, n., (magnetic) bussola f. ; (range) portata f. ; (a pair of) —es, pl., compassi m. pl.

compassionate*, kom-pa'-shon-eit, a., compassionevole

compel, kom-pel', v., costringere

compensate, kom'-pen-seit, v., compensare

compensation, kom-pen-sei'-shon, n., compensazione f.

compete, kom-piit', v., competere ; concorrere

competence, kom'-pi-tens, n., competenza f.

competition, kom-pi-ti′-shon, n., concorrenza f.: (games, etc.) concorso m.

competitor, kom-pet′-i-tσ, n., competitore m.; (comn̄ercial) concorrente m.

compile, kom-pail′, v., compilare

complacent°, kom-plei′-sent, a., compiacente

complain, kom-plein′, v., lagnarsi

complaint, kom-pleint′, n., lagnanza f.

complement, kom′-ple-ment, n., complemento m.

complete, kom-plijt′, v., completare. a., completo

completion, kom-plij′-shon, n., compimento m.

complex, kom′-pleks, a., complesso

complexion, kom-plek′-shon, n., carnagione f.

compliance, kom-plai′-σns, n., accordo m.; consenso m.

compliant°, kom-plai′-σnt, a., sommesso

complicate, kom′-pli-keit, v., complicare

compliment, kom-pli-ment′, v., complimentare. n., complimento m.

comply (with), kom-plai′, v., condiscendere

component, kom-pou′-nent, n., componente m.

compose, kom-pous′, v., comporre; calmare

composer, kom-pou′-sσ, n., compositore m.

composite, kom′-po-sit, a., composto

composition, kom-po-si′-shon, n., composizione f.

compositor, kom-po′-si-ter, n., compositore m.

composure, kom-pou′-shσr, n., compostezza f.

compound, kom′-paund, n., miscuglio m.; (enclosure) recinto m. v., comporre. a., composto; — **fracture,** n., frattura complicata f.; — **interest,** interesse composto m.

comprehend, kom-pri-hend′, v., comprendere

comprehension, kom - pri - hen′ - shon, n., comprensione f.

compress, kom′-pres, n., compressa f. v., comprimere

comprise, kom-prais′, v., comprendere

compromise, kom′-pro-mais, n., compromesso m. v., compromettere

compulsion, kom-pöl′-shon, n., coercizione f.

compulsory, kom-pöl′-so-ri, a., obbligatorio

compunction, kom-pöngk′-shon, n., compunzione f.

compute, kom-piuut', v., computare

comrade, kom-reid', n., camerata m. & f.

concave, kon-keiv', a., concavo

conceal, kon-siil', v., nascondere

concealment, kon-siil'-ment, n., segretezza f. ; (place) nascondiglio m.

concede, kon-siid', v., concedere

conceit, kon-siit', n., presunzione f. ; albagia f.

conceited°, kon-sii'-tid, a., presuntuoso

conceive, kon-siiv', v., concepire

concentrate, kon'-sen-treit, v., concentrare

conception, kon-sep'-shon, n., (idea) concetto m. ; (med.) concezione f.

concern, kon-sërn', n., (affair) affare m. ; (firm) azienda f. ; (disquiet) ansietà f. v., concernere ; to be —ed, (anxious) essere ansioso

concert, kon'-sërt, n., concerto m.

concession, kon-sesh'-on, n., concessione f.

conciliate, kon-sil'-i-eit, v., conciliare

concise°, kon-sais', a., conciso

conclude, kon-kluud', v., concludere

conclusion, kon-kluu'-shon, n., conclusione f.

conclusive°, kon-kluu'-siv, a., conclusivo

concoct, kon-kokt', v., elaborare ; preparare

concord, kon'-koord, n., concordia f.

concrete, kon'-kriit, n., calcestruzzo m. a., concreto

concur, kon-kër', v., concorrere

concurrence, kon-kör'-ens, n., concorso m.

concussion, kon-kösh'-on, n., concussione f.

condemn, kon-dem', v., condannare

condense, kon-dens', v., condensare

condescend, kon-di-send', v., condiscendere

condescension, kon-di-sen'-shon, n., condiscendenza f.

condiment, kon'-di-ment, n., condimento m.

condition, kon-di'-shon, n., condizione f.

conditional°, kon-di'-shon-al, a., condizionale

condole, kon-doul', v., condolersi

condolence, kon-dou'-lens, n., condoglianza f.

condone, kon-doun', v., condonare

conducive, kon-diuu'-siv, a., contributivo

conduct, kon'-dokt, n., (behaviour) condotta f.

conduct, kon-dŏkt', v., condurre ; (music) dirigere
conductor, kon-dŏkt'-*a*, n., (guide) conduttore m. ;
　(bus) controllore m. ; (music) direttore m.
conduit, kŏn'-dit, n., condotto m.
cone, koun, n., cono m. ; (fir-tree, etc.) pigna f.
confectioner, kon-fek'-sho-n*a*, n., confettiere m. ;
　(shop) pasticceria f.
confectionery, kon-fek'-sho-n*a*-ri, n., (sweet-
　meats) confetture f. pl.
confederate, kon-fed'-*er*-eit, n., confederato m. ;
　compare m.
confederation, kon-fed-*er*-ei'-shon, n., confedera-
　zione f.
confer, kon-fĕr', v., conferire
confess, kon-fes', v., confessare
confession, kon-fesh'-on, n., confessione f.
confide, kon-faid', v., confidare
confidence, kon'-fi-d*ens*, n., confidenza f.
confident*, kon'-fi-dent, a., certo
confidential*, kon-fi-den'-shal, a., confidenziale
confine, kon-fain', v., limitare ; (lock-up) relegare
confinement, kon-fain'-ment, n., (lying-in) parto m. ;
　(prison) detenzione f.
confirm, kon-fĕrm', v., confermare ; cresimare
confirmation, kon-fĕr-mei'-shon, n., conferma-
　zione f. ; (eccl.) cresima f.
confiscate, kon'-fis-keit, v., confiscare
conflagration, kon-fla-grei'-shon, n., incendio m.
conflict, kon'-flikt, n., conflitto m. v., confliggere
conflicting, kon-flikt'-ing, a., contraddittorio
conform, kon-fōorm', v., conformarsi
conformable, kon-fōor'-ma-bl, a., conforme
confound, kon-faund', v., confondere
confront, kon-frŏnt', v., (oppose) confrontare ;
　(face) affrontare
confuse, kon-fiuus', v., confondere
confusion, kon-fiuu'-shon, n., confusione f.
confute, kon-fiuut', v., confutare
congeal, kon-chiil', v., congelare
congenial, kon-chii'-ni-*al*, a., simpatico
congenital, kon-chen'-i-tl, a., congenito
congest, kon-chest', v., congestionare

congestion, kon-chest'-ion, n., congestione f.

congratulate, kon-grat'-iu-leit, v., felicitare

congratulation, kon-grat-iu-lei'-shon, n., congratulazione f.

congregate, kong'-gri-gheit, v., congregare

congregation, kong-gri-ghei'-shon, n., congregazione f.

congress, kong'-gress, n., congresso m.

conjecture, kon-chek'-chur, n., congettura f. v., congetturare

conjugal, kon'-chu-gal, a., coniugale

conjunction, kon-chŏnk'-shon, n., congiunzione f.

conjure, kŏn'-chur, v., far giuochi di prestigio; congiurare

conjurer, kŏn'-chur-a, n., prestigiatore f.

connect, ko-nekt', v., connettere

connection, ko-nek'-shon, n., **connessione** f.; (train, etc.) coincidenza f.

connive (at), ko-naiv', v., aver connivenza

connoisseur, kon-is-ĕr', n., conoscitore m.

conquer, kong'-ker, v., conquistare

conqueror, kong'-ker-a, n., conquistatore m.

conquest, kong'-kuest, n., conquista f.

conscience, kon'-shens, n., coscienza f.

conscientious*, kon-shi'-en-shos, a., coscienzioso

conscious*, kon'-shos, a., conscio

consciousness, kon'-shos-nes, n., conoscenza f.

conscript, kon'-skript, n., coscritto m.

consecrate, kon'-si-kreit, v., consacrare

consecutive*, kon-sek'-iu-tiv, a., consecutivo

consent, kon-sent', n., consentimento m. v., acconsentire

consequence, kon'-si-kuens, n., conseguenza f.

consequential, kon-si-kuen-shal, a., conseguente; (affectation) importante

consequently, kon'-si-kuent-li, adv., conseguentemente

conservative, kon-sĕr'-va-tiv, a., conservativo

conservatory, kon-sĕr'-va-to-ri, n., serra f.

conserve, kon-sĕrv', v., conservare. n., conserva f.

consider, kon-sid'-a, v., considerare

considerable, kon-sid'-er-a-bl, a., considerevole

considerate, kon-sid'-er-eit, a., pieno di considerazione

consideration, kon-sid-er-ei'-shon, n., (deliberation) riflessione f. ; (head) considerazione f.

considering, kon-sid'-er-ing, prep., considerato

consign, kon-sain', v., consegnare

consignee, kon-sain-ii', n., consegnatario m.

consignment, kon-sain'-ment, n., consegna f.

consignor, kon-sain'-a, n., speditore m.

consist (of), kon-sist', v., consistere

consistency, kon-sis'-ten-si, n., consistenza f.

consistent*, kon-sis'-tent, a., consistente

consolation, kon-so-lei'-shon, n., consolazione f.

console, kon-soul', v., consolare

consoler, kon-soul'-a, n., consolatore m.

consolidate, kon-sol'-i-deit, v., consolidare

consols, kon'-sols, n. pl., consolidati m. pl.

consonant, kon'-so-nant, n., consonante f.

consort, kon'-soort, n., consorte m. & f.

consort, kon-soort', v., unirsi

conspicuous*, kon-spik'-iu-os, a., (striking) evidente ; (distinguished) rimarchevole

conspiracy, kon-spir'-a-si, n., cospirazione f.

conspirator, kon-spir'-ei-ta, n., cospiratore m.

conspire, kon-spair', v., cospirare

constable, kön'-sta-bl, n., poliziotto m.

constabulary, kon-stab'-iu-la-ri, n., pubblica sicurezza f.

constancy, kon'-stan-si, n., costanza f.

constant*, kon'-stant, a., costante

constipation, kon-sti-pei'-shon, n., stitichezza f.

constituency, kon-stit'-iu-en-si, n., collegio elettorale m.

constituent, kon-stit'-iu-ent, n., costituente m. ; elettore m.

constitute, kon'-sti-tiuut, v., costituire

constitution, kon-sti-tiuu'-shon, n., costituzione f.

constrain, kon-strein', v., costringere

constraint, kon-streint', n., costringimento m.

constriction, kon-strik'-shon, n., costrizione f.

construct, kons-trökt', v., costruire

construction, kons-strök'-shon, n., **costruzione f.**

construe, kon'-struu. v., costrurre ; interpretare

consul, kon'-sul, n., console m.

consulate, kon'-siul-eit, n., consolato m.

consult, kon-sölt', v., consultare

consultation, kon-sul-tei'-shon, n., consulto m.

consume, kon-siuum', v., consumare

consumer, kon-siuu'-ma, n., consumatore m.

consummate, kon'-som-eit, v., consumare

consummation, kon-som-ei'-shon, n., consumazione f.

consumption, kon-söm'-shon, n., (use) consumo m. ; (med.) tisi f.

consumptive, kon-söm'-tiv, a., tisico

contact, kon'-takt, n., contatto m.

contagious, kon-tei'-chos, a., contagioso

contain, kon-tein', v., contenere

contaminate, kon-tam'-i-neit, v., contaminare

contemplate, kon'-tem-pleit, v., contemplare

contemporary, kon-tem'-po-ra-ri, a., contemporaneo. n., coetaneo m.

contempt, kon-temt', n., sprezzo m.

contemptible, kon-tem'-ti-bl, a., sprezzabile

contend, kon-tend', v., combattere ; (maintain) sostenere

content, kon-tent', a., contento. v., accontentare

contention, kon-ten'-shon, n., affermazione f.

contentious, kon-ten'-shos, a., contenzioso

contentment, kon-tent'-ment, n., contentezza f.

contents, kon-tents', n. pl., contenuto m.

contest, kon-test', v., contestare. n., contesa f.

contiguous*, kon-ti-ghiu'-os, a., contiguo

continent, kon'-ti-nent, n., continente m.

contingency, kon-tin'-chen-si, n., contingenza f.

contingent*, kon-tin'-chent, a., contingente

continual*, kon-tin'-iu-al, a., continuo

continuation, kon-tin-iu-ei'-shon, n., continuazione f.

continue, kon-tin'-iuu, v., continuare

continuous*, kon-tin'-iu-os, a., continuo

contortion, kon-toor'-shon, n., contorsione f.

contraband, kon'-tra-band, n., contrabbando m

contract, kon'-trakt, n., contratto m.

contract, kon-trakt′, v., contrarre: — **for**, contrattare

contraction, kon-trak′-shon, n., contrazione f.

contractor, kon-trak′-ta, n., fornitore **m.**; (builder) imprenditore m.

contradict, kon-tra-dikt′, v., contradire

contradiction, kon-tra-dik′-shon, n., contradizione f.

contrary, kon′-tra-ri, n., contrario m. a., contrario

contrast, kon′-trast, n., contrasto m.

contrast, kon-trast′, v., contrastare

contravene, kon-tra-viin′, v., contravvenire

contravention, kon-tra-ven′-shon, n., contravvenzione f.

contribute, kon-trib′-iut, v., contribuire

contribution, kon-trib-iuu′-shon, n., contribuzione f.

contrite, kon′-trait, a., contrito

contrivance, kon-trai′-vens, n., dispositivo m.

contrive, kon-traiv′, v., inventare ; trovare

control, kon-troul′, v., controllare. n., controllo m.; (feelings) comando m.

controller, kon-troul′-a, n., controllore m.; ispettore m.: (director) dirigente m. & f.

controversial, kon-tro-ver′-shal, a., controverso

controversy, kon′-tro-ver-si, n., controversia f.

conundrum, ko-nön′-drom, n., enigma m.

convalescence, kon-va-les′-ens, n., convalescenza f.

convalescent, kon-va-les′-ent, a., convalescente

convenience, kon-vii′-ni-ens, n., convenienza f.; (lavatory) gabinetto m.

convenient*, kon-vii′-ni-ent, a., conveniente

convent, kon′-vent, n., convento m.

convention, kon-ven′-shon, n., convenzione f.

converge, kon-verch′, v., convergere

conversant, kon′-ver-sant, a., famigliarizzato

conversation, kon-ver-sei′-shon, n., conversazione f.

converse, kon-vers′, v., conversare

conversion, kon-ver′-shon, n., conversione f.

convert, kon′-vert, n., convertito m.

convert, kon-vert′, v., convertire

convex, kon′-veks, a., convesso

convey, kon-vei', v., trasportare ; (impart) esprimere
conveyance, kon-vei'-ans, n., trasporto m. ;
vettura f. ; **deed of —**, atto traslativo m.
convict, kon'-vikt, n., forzato m. v., condannare
conviction, kon-vik'-shon, n., condanna f. ;
(belief) convincimento m.
convince, kon-vins', v., convincere
convivial, kon-viv'-i-al, a., gioviale, festevole
convoke, kon-vok', v., convocare
convoy, kon'-voi, n., convoglio m. v., scortare,
convogliare
convulse, kon-vols', v., andare in convulsione ;
(fig.) contorcersi
convulsion, kon-vŏl'-shon, n., convulsione f.
cony, kou'-ni, n., (fur) (pelliccia di) coniglio m.
coo, kuu, v., tubare
cooing, kuu'-ing, n., il tubare m.
cook, kuk, n., cuoco m. ; cuoca f. v. cucinare
cookery, kuk'-er-i, n., cucina f.
cool, kuul, a., fresco ; calmo. v., raffreddare
coolness, kuul'-nes, n., freschezza f.; (nerve) sangue freddo m.
coop, kuup, n., stia f. ; **— up**, v., ingabbiare
cooper, kuu'-pa, n., bottaio m.
co-operate, kou-op'-er-eit, v., cooperare
cope, koup, **— with**, v., far fronte a
copious*, kou'-pi-os, a., copioso
copper, kop'-a, n., rame m. ; (coin) moneta di
rame f.; (boiler) caldaia f. a., di rame
coppice, copse, kop'-is, kops, n., bosco ceduo m.
copy, kop'-i, n., copia f. v., copiare
copy-book, kop'-i-buk, n., quaderno m.
copyright, kop'-i-rait, n., diritto d'autore m.
coquetry, kou'-ket-ri, n., civetteria f.
coral, kor'-al, n., corallo m.
cord, koord, n., corda f. v., incordare
cordial, koor'-di-al, a.,* cordiale. n., cordiale m.
corduroy, koor-diu-roi', n., frustagno m.
core, kor, n., torso m. ; (fig.) il più profondo
co-respondent, kou-ri-spon'-dent, n., adultero m.
cork, koork, n., sughero m. ; (bottle) turacciolo m
v., tappare

corkscrew, koork'-skruu, n., cavatappi m.

cormorant, koor'-mo-rant, n., marangone **m.**

corn, koorn, n., grano m.; (foot) callo m.

cornelian, koor-nii'-li-an, n., cornalina f.

corner, koor'-na, n., angolo m.

cornflower, koorn'-flau-a, n., fioraliso **m.**

cornice, koor'-nis, n., cornice f.

coronation, ko-ro-nei'-shon, n., incoronazione f.

coroner, kor'-o-na, n., =giudice istruttore m.

coronet, kor'-o-net, n., corona nobiliare m.

corporal, koor'-po-ral, n., caporale m. a., corporale

corporation, koor-po-rei'-shon, n., corpulenza f.; (city) corporazione f.

corps, kor, n., corpo m.

corpse, koorps, n., cadavere m.

corpulency, koor'-piu-len-si, n., corpulenza f.

corpulent, koor'-piu-lent, a., corpulento

corpuscle, koor'-pos-l, n., corpuscolo m.

correct, ko-rekt', a.,*corretto; esatto. v.,correggere

corrective, ko-rek'-tiv, n., correttivo m. a., correttivo

correctness, ko-rekt'-nes, n., correttezza f.

correspond, kor-i-spond', v., corrispondere

correspondence, kor-i-spon'-dens, n., corrispondenza f.

correspondent, kor-i-spon'-dent, n., corrispondente m. & f.

corridor, kor'-i-door, n., corridoio m.; — -train, treno intercomunicante m.

corroborate, ko-rob'-o-reit, v., corroborare

corroboration, ko-rob-o-rei'-shon, n., corroborazione f.

corrode, ko-roud', v., corrodere

corrosive, kor-o'-siv, n., corrosivo m. a., corrosivo

corrugated, kor'-u-ghei-tid, a.,ondulato ; —-iron, n., lamiera ondulata f.; — -paper, cartone ondulato m.

corrupt, ko-ropt', v., corrompere. a.,*corrotto

corruption, ko-rop'-shon, n., corruzione f.

corsair, koor'-ser, n., corsaro m.

corset, koor'-set, n., busto m.

cortege, koor'-tesh, n., corteggio m.

cost, kost, n., prezzo m.; costo m.; (expense) spesa f. v., costare ; —s, n.pl., spese f.pl.; —ly, a., costoso

costermonger, kos'-ter-mŏng-ga, n., mercante ambulante m.

costive, kos'-tiv, a., stitico

costume, kos'-tiuum, n., costume m.

cosy, kou-si, a., confortevole. n., copriteiera m.

cot, kot, n., (child's) culla f.

cottage, kot'-ich, n., casetta campestre f.

cotton, kot'-n, n., cotone m.; (sewing) filo di cotone m.

cotton-wool, kot'-n-uul, n., bambagia f.; cotone idrofilo m.

couch, kauch, n., divano m.

cough, kof, n., tosse f. v., tossire

council, kaun'-sil, n., consiglio m.

councillor, kaun'-sil-a, n., consigliere m.

counsel, kaun'-sl, v., consigliare. n., (law) consulente legale m.

count, kaunt, n., (title) conte m.

count, kaunt, v., contare. n., conto m.; —ing-house, ufficio di contabilità m.; —less, a., innumerevole

countenance, kaun'-te-nans, n., contegno m. v., (tolerate) scusare ; (favour) favorire

counter, kaun'-ta, n., banco m.; (games) gettone m. adv., contro

counteract, kaun-ter-akt', v., contrariare ; neutralizzare ; (frustrate) sventare

counterbalance, kaun-ter-bal'-ans, v., contrabbilanciare

counterfeit, kaun'-ter-fiit, n., falsificazione f. a., falso. v., falsificare

counterfoil, kaun'-ter-foil, n., matrice f.

countermand, kaun-ter-maand', v., contrordinare

counterpane, kaun'-ter-pein, n., coltrice f.

counterpart, kaun'-ter-paart, n., controparte f.

countersign, kaun'-ter-sain, v., controfirmare. n., contrassegno m. ; (mil.) parola d'ordine f.

countess, kaun'-tes, n., contessa f.

country, kŏn'-tri, n., (rural) campagna f.; (state) paese m.

countryman, kŏn'-tri-man, n., campagnuolo m.; (compatriot) concittadino m.

county, kaun'-ti, n., contea f.

couple, kŏp'-l, n., coppia f.; (pair) **paio m.** v., accoppiare; (wagons) attaccare

courage, kŏr'-ich, n., coraggio m.

courageous*, ko-rei'-chos, a., coraggioso

course, kors, n., (throughout) corso m.; (tuition) corso m.; (race) campo di corse m.; (ship, etc.) rotta f.; (meals) piatto m.; (river) corso m.; **of —**, adv., naturalmente

court, kort, v., corteggiare. n., (royal) corte f.; (law) tribunale m.; **— -martial**, tribunale di guerra m.

courteous*, kĕr'-ti-os, a., cortese

courtesy, kĕr'-ti-si, n., cortesia f.

courtier, kor'-ti-a, n., cortigiano m.

courtship, kort'-ship, n., (wooing) corte f.

courtyard, kort'-iaard, n., cortile m.

cousin, kŏs'-n, n., cugino m.

cove, kouv, n., (geology) seno m., cala f.

covenant, kŏv'-i-nant, n., convenzione f.; patto m. v., stipulare

cover, kŏv'-a, n., copertina f.; (lid) coperchio **m.;** (shelter) rifugio m. v., coprire

covet, kŏv'-et, v., agognare

cow, kau, n., vacca f.

coward, kau'-uerd, n., codardo m.

cowardice, kau'-uer-dis, n., codardia f.

cower, kau'-a, v., rannicchiarsi

cowl, kaul, n., cappuccio m.; (chimney) cappuccio per fumaiolo m.

cowslip, kau'-slip, n., cuculo m.

coxcomb, koks'-koum, n., cresta di gallo f.; (fig.) vanaglorioso m.

coxswain, kok'-sn, n., timoniere **m.**

coy, koi, a., modesto

crab, krab, n., granchio m.

crab-apple, krab-ap'-el, n., **mela selvatica f.**

crack, krak, v., schioppiettare; (whip) schioccare; (fissure) fendersi; (nuts) schiacciare. n., fessura f.; spaccatura f.; (noise) strepito m.

cracker, krak'-*a*, n., (fireworks) salterello m. ; (Xmas) petardo m. ; (nut) schiaccianoci m.

crackle, krak'-l, v., crepitare

cradle, krei'-dl, n., (crib) culla f. ; (carrier) cesta f.

craft, kraaft, n., (trade) mestiere m. ; (naut.) bastimento m. ; (cunning) furberia f.

craftsman, kraafts'-*man*, n., artigiano m.

crafty, kraaf'-ti, a., astuto

crag, kragh, n., roccione m.

cram, kram, v., stipare ; (coach) istruire in fretta

cramp, kramp, n., crampo m. v., rannicchiare

cranberry, kran'-*be*-ri, n., mortella f.

crane, krein, n., gru f. ; (bird) gru f.

crank, krank, n., (mech.) manovella f. v., girare la manovella

crape, kreip, n., crespo m.

crash, krash, v., (collide) schiacciarsi ; (break) rompere ; (aero) schiacciarsi. n., collisione f. ; (noise) fracasso m. ; (financial) crac m.

crater, kreit'-*a*, n., cratere m.

crave, kreiv, v., implorare ; — **for**, desiderare ardentemente

craving, krei'-ving, n., brama f.

crawl, krool, n., strascinio m. v., strisciare

crayfish, krei'-fish, n., gambero fluviale m. ; (sea) aragosta f.

crayon, kre-on, n., pastello m.

craze, kreis, n., (fashion) smania f.

crazy, krei'-si, a., pazzo ; (structure) debole

creak, kriik, v., scricchiolare

cream, kriim, n., crema f.

creamy, krii'-mi, a., di crema

crease, kriis, v., spiegazzare. n., piega f.

create, kri-eit', v., creare

creature, krii'-chur, n., creatura f.

credentials, kri-den'-shals, n.pl., credenziali f.pl.

credible, kred'-i-bl, a., credibile

credit, kred'-it, n., credito m. v., accreditare

creditable, kred'-i-ta-bl, a., credibile

creditor, kred'-i-*ta*, n., creditore m.

credulous*, kred'-iu-los, a., credulo

creed, kriid, n., credo m.

creek, kriik, n., fiumiciattolo m.

creep, kriip, v., strisciare

creeper, kri'-*pa*, n., (plant) arrampicante m.

cremate, kri-meit', v., cremare

cremation, kri-mei'-shon, n., cremazione f.

creole, kri'-oul, n., creolo m.

crescent, kres'-ent, n., mezzaluna f.

cress, kres, n., crescione m.

crest, krest, n., (hill, bird) cresta f.; (heraldry) insegna araldica f.; — **-fallen**, a., abbattuto

crevice, krev'-is, n., crepaccio m.

crew, kruu, n., (naut.) equipaggio m.

crick, krik, n., crampo m.; (neck) torcicollo m.

cricket, krik'-*et*, n., grillo m.; (game) cricket m.

crime, kraim, n., delitto m.

criminal, krim'-i-n*al*, n., delinquente m. & f. a.,* criminale

crimson, krim'-*son*, a., cremisi

cringe, krinch, — to, v., abbassarsi

crinkle, kring'-kl, n., ruga f. v., arrugare

cripple, krip'-l, n., storpio m. v., storpiare

crisis, krai'-sis, n., crisi f.

crisp, krisp, a., croccante

criterion, krai-ti'-ri-on, n., criterio m.

critical*, krit'-i-k*al*, a., critico

criticism, krit'-i-si*sm*, n., critica f.

criticize, krit'-i-sais, v., criticare

croak, krouk, v., (frog) gracidare; (crow) gracchiare

crochet, krou'-she, v., lavorare all'uncinetto. n.,uncinetto m.

crockery, krok'-*er*-i, n., vasellame m.

crocodile, krok'-*o*-dail, n., coccodrillo m.

crocus, krou'-kos, n., croco m.

crook, kruk, n., uncino m.; (rogue) truffatore m.

crooked*, kru'-kid, a., curvato; (nose) adunco; (fig.) disonesto

crop, krop, n., raccolto m.; (throat) gozzo m. v., (hair) tosare

cross, kros, n., croce f. a., (vexed) arrabbiato v., farsi la croce; (step) attraversare; — **out**, cancellare; — **-examine**, sottoporre a interrogatorio

crossing, kros'-ing, n., passaggio m.
cross-road, kros'-roud, n., incrocio m.
crotchet, krot'-shit, n., (music) semiminima
crouch, krauch, v., rannicchiarsi
crow, krou, n., corvo m. v., (cock) cantare
crowbar, krou'-baar, n., leva f.
crowd, kraud, n., (quantity) mucchio **m.**; (throng) folla f. v., affollare
crown, kraun, v., coronare. n., corona f. ; (top part of the head) cima f.
crucible, kruu'-si-bel, n., crogiuolo m.
crucifix, kruu'-si-fiks, n., crocifisso m.
crucify, kruu'-si-fai, v., crocifiggere
crude*, kruud, a., crudo
cruel*, kruu'-el, a., crudele
cruelty, kruu'-el-ti, n., crudeltà f.
cruet, kruu'-et, n., oliera f.
cruise, kruus, n., crociera f. v., incrociare
cruiser, kruu'-sa, n., incrociatore m.
crumb, kröm, n., mollica f.
crumble, kröm'-bl, v., sbriciolarsi
crumple, kröm'-pl, v., sgualcire
crunch, krönch, v., crocchiare
crush, krösh, n., ressa f. v., serrarsi ; (grapes, olives) spremere ; (pound) schiacciare
crust, kröst, n., crosta f. v., incrostare
crusty, krös'-ti, a., ben cotto
crutch, kröch, n., gruccia f.
cry, krai, n., grido m. v., (call) gridare ; (weep) piangere
cryptic, krip'-tik, a., sibillino ; occulto
crystal, kris'-tl, n., cristallo m.
cub, köb, n., (lion) leoncello m.; (bear) orsacchio **m.**
cube, kiuub, n., cubo m.
cuckoo, ku'-kuu, n., cuculo m.
cucumber, kiuu'-köm-ba, n., cetriolo **m.**
cuddle, köd'-l, v., accarezzare
cudgel, köch'-l, n., randello m. v., bastonare
cue, kiuu, n., replica f. ; (billiards) stecca f.
cuff, köf, n., polsino m.
culinary, kiuu'-li-na-ri, a., culinario
culminate, köl'-mi-neit, v., culminare

culpable, kŭl′-pa-bl, a., colpevole

culprit, kŭl′-prit, n., colpevole m.

cultivate, kŭl′-ti-veit, v., coltivare

culture, kŭl′-chur, n., cultura f.

cumbersome, kŭm′-ber-som, a., ingombrante

cunning, kŭn′-ing, a., astuto. n., astuzia f.

cup, kŭp, n., tazza f.; (trophy) coppa f.

cupboard, kŭb′-erd, n., armadio m.

cupola, kiuu′-po-la, n., cupola f.

cur, kĕr, n., cagnaccio m.; (fig.) basso individuo m.

curate, kiu′-reit, n., curato m.

curb, kĕrb, n., orlo m.; (horse) morso rigido m.
v., frenare

curd, kĕrd, n., latte quagliato m.

curdle, kĕr′-dl, v., rappigliare

cure, kiur, n., cura f. v., curare; (meat, etc.) affumicare

curfew, kĕr′-fiuu, n., coprifuoco m.

curiosity, kiu-ri-os′-i-ti, n., curiosità f.

curious*, kiu′-ri-os, a., (inquisitive) curioso; (peculiar) strano

curl, kĕrl, n., riccio m. v., arricciare

currant, kŏr′-ant, n., (dried) uva passa f.; **black—**, ribes nero m.; **red—**, ribes rosso m.

currency, kŏr′-en-si, n., valuta f., moneta f.

current, kŏr′-ent, n., corrente f. a., corrente

curse, kĕrs, n., maledizione f. v., maledire

cursory, kĕr′-so-ri, a., frettoloso

curt*, kĕrt, a., breve; secco

curtail, ker-teil′, v., raccorciare

curtailment, ker-teil′-ment, n., raccorciamento m.

curtain, kĕr′-tin, n., cortina f.

curtsy, kĕrt′-si, n., inchino m. v., inchinarsi

curve, kĕrv, n., curva f. v., incurvarsi

cushion, kush′-on, n., cuscino m.

custard, kŏs′-terd, n., crema dolce f.

custody, kŏs′-to-di, n., prigione f.; (care) guardia f.

custom, kŏs′-tom, n., costume m.; (trade) clientela f.; **—house**, dogana f.; **—s-duty**, diritto di dogana m.

customary, kŏs′-tom-a-ri, a., abituale

customer, kŏs′-tom-a, n., cliente m. & f.

cut, kŏt, n., taglio m.   v., tagliare ; (snub) **schivare ;**
— **off**, tagliare fuori
cuticle, kiuu'-ti-kl, n., pellicina f.
cutlass, kŏt'-las, n., coltellaccio m.
cutler, kŏt'-la, n., coltellinaio m.
cutlery, kŏt'-ler-i, n., coltelleria f.
cutlet, kŏt'-let, n., costoletta f.
cutter, kŏt'-a, n., (tailor) tagliatore m. ; (ship) cutter m.
cuttle-fish, kŏt'-l-fish, n., seppia f.
cyclamen, sik-la-men, n., ciclamino m.
cycle, sai'-kl, n., bicicletta f. ; (time) ciclo m.
cylinder, sil'-in-da, n., cilindro m.
cynical*, sin'-i-kl, a., cinico
cypress, sai'-pres, n., cipresso m.

dabble, dab'-l, v., occuparsi ; (shares) speculare
dabbler, dab'-la, n., dilettante m. ; speculatore m.
daffodil, daf'-o-dil, n., asfodelo m.
dagger, dag'-a, n., pugnale m.
dahlia, de'-li-a, n., dalia f.
daily, dei'-li, a., ogni giorno ; quotidiano ; **giornaliero**
dainty, dein'-ti, a., delicato ; elegante
dairy, dei'-ri, n., latteria f.
daisy, dei'-si, n., margaritina f.
dale, deil, n., valle f.
dally, dal'-i, v., perder tempo
dam, dam, n., diga f.   v., sbarrare
damage, dam'-ich, n., danno m.   v., **danneggiare**
damask, dam'-ask, n., damasco m.   a., damascato
damn, dem, v., dannare.   interj., maledetto !
damnation, dem-nei'-shon, n., dannazione f.
damp, demp, n., umidità f.   a., umido
dance, daans, n., danza f.   v., danzare
dancer, daans'-a, n., ballerino m.
dandelion, dan'-di-lai-on, n., dente di leone m.
dandruff, dan'-drof, n., forfora f.
danger, dein'-chur, n., pericolo m.
dangerous*, dein'-cher-os, a., pericoloso
dangle, dang'-gol, v., dondolare
dapper, dap'-a, a., vivace ; lindo
dare, der, v., osare

daring°, deʹ-ring, a., ardito

dark, daark, a., oscuro ; fosco

darkness, daarkʹ-nes, n., oscurità f.

darling, daarʹ-ling, n., diletto m. a., caro

darn, daarn, v., rammendare

darning-wool, daarʹ-ning-uul, n., lana da rammendare f.

dart, daart, n., dardo m. v., dardeggiare

dash, dash, n., (short line) lineetta f. v., (throw) lanciare ; (rush) precipitare

dashing°, dashʹ-ing, a., focoso

dastard, dasʹ-tard, n., vile m. & f.

dastardly, dasʹ-tard-li, a., codardo

data, deiʹ-ta, n.pl., dati m.pl.

date, deit, n., data f. ; (fruit) dattero m. v., datare

daughter, dooʹ-ta, n., figlia f.; — -in-law, nuora f.

dauntless°, doontʹ-les, a., indomito

dawdle, dooʹ-dl, v., girondolare

dawn, doon, n., alba f. v., albeggiare

day, dei, n., giorno m.

daybreak, deiʹ-breik, n., aurora f.

daylight, deiʹ-lait, n., luce del giorno f.

dazzle, dasʹ-l, v., abbagliare

deacon, diiʹ-kn, n., diacono m.

dead, ded, a., morto

deaden, dedʹ-n, v., ammortire

deadlock, dedʹ-lok, n., via senza uscita f.

deadly, dedʹ-li, a., mortale

deaf, def, a., sordo

deafen, defʹ-n, v., assordire

deafness, defʹ-nes, n., sordità f.

deal, diil, n., (business) negozio m.; (quantity) quantità f.; (wood) legno d'abete m. v., (trade) commerciare ; (trade or act) trattare ; (cards) distribuire

dealer, diilʹ-a, n., negoziante m.; (cards) distributore m.

dean, diin, n., decano m.

dear°, dir, a., caro

dearth, dӗrZ, n., carestia f.

death, deZ, n., morte f.

debar, di-baarʹ, v., escludere

debase, di-beis', v., avvilire ; degradare

debate, di-beit', n., dibattimento m. v., dibattere

debater, di-bei'-ta, n., oratore m.

debauch, di-booch', n., stravizio m.

debauchery, di-boo'-cher-i, n., dissolutezza f.

debenture, di-ben'-chur, n., obbligazione f.

debit, deb'-it, n., debito m. v., addebitare

debt, det. n., debito m.

debtor, det'-a, n., debitore m.

decadence, di-kei'-dens, n., decadenza f.

decamp, di-kamp', v., levar il campo ; (flee) fuggire

decant, di-kant', v., travasare

decanter, di-kan'-ta, n., caraffa f.

decapitate, di-kap'-i-teit, v., decapitare

decay, di-kei', n., (decline, ruin) decadenza f. ;
(tooth) carie f. v., (rot) guastarsi ; (teeth) ca-
riarsi

decease, di-siis', n., decesso m.

deceased, di-siist', a., defunto

deceit, di-siit', n., (cunning) inganno m. ; (false-
ness) soperchieria f.

deceitful*, di-siit'-ful, a., perfido

deceive, di-siiv', v., ingannare ; (illusion) illudere

December, di-sem'-ba, n., dicembre m.

decency, dii'-sen-si, n., decenza f.

decennial, di-sen'-i-al, a., decennio

decent*, dii'-sent, a., decente ; (nice) onesto

deception, di-sep'-shon, n., inganno m. ; (illusion) illusione f.

deceptive, di-sep'-tiv, a., ingannevole

decide, di-said', v., decidere

decided, di-sai'-did, a., deciso

decimal, des'-i-mal, a., decimale. n., decimale m.

decipher, di-sai'-fa, v., decifrare

decision, di-si'-shon, n., decisione f

decisive*, di-sai'-siv, a., decisivo

deck, dek, n., ponte m. ; coperta f. v., abbellire

declaim, di-kleim', v., declamare

declaration, dek-la-rei'-shon, n., dichiarazione f.

declare, di-kler', v., dichiarare

declension, di-klen'-shon, n., declinazione f.

decline, di-klain', n., diminuzione f.; (values) discesa f.; (ground) declivio m.; (deterioration) decadenza f. v., deteriorare; (reject) rifiutare; (grammar) declinare

decompose, di-kom-pous', v., decomporre

decorate, dek'-o-reit, v., decorare

decoration, dek-o-rei'-shon, n., decorazione f.

decorous*, di-ko'-ros, a., decoroso

decoy, di-koi', n., esca f.; (bird) richiamo m.

decrease, dii'-kriis, n., diminuzione f.

decrease, di-kriis', v., diminuire

decree, di-krii', n., decreto m. v., decretare

decry, di-krai', v., denigrare

dedicate, ded'-i-keit, v., dedicare

deduce, di-diuus', v., dedurre

deduct, di-dŏkt', v., sottrarre

deduction, di-dŏk'-shon, n., deduzione f.

deed, diid, n., atto m.; (law) titolo m.

deem, diim, v., stimare

deep*, diip, a., profondo

deepen, diip'-n, v., approfondire

deer, dir, n., daino m.; (red) cervo m.

deface, di-feis', v., disfigurare

defamation, def-a-mei'-shon, n., diffamazione f.

defame, di-feim', v., diffamare

default, di-foolt', n., (business) mancanza di pagamento f.; (law) contumacia f. v., mancare agli impegni; (law) essere contumace

defaulter, di-fool'-ta, n., moroso m.; (law) contumace m. & f.

defeat, di-fiit', n., disfatta f. v., sconfiggere

defect, di-fekt', n., difetto m.

defective*, di-fek'-tiv, a., difettoso

defence, di-fens', n., difesa f.

defenceless, di-fens'-les, a., indifeso

defend, di-fend', v., difendere

defendant, di-fen'-dant, n., convenuto m.

defender, di-fen'-da, n., difensore m.

defensible, di-fen'-si-bl, a., scusabile

defensive, di-fen'-siv, n., difensiva f.

defer, di-fĕr', v., differire

deferential*, def-er-en'-shal, a., rispettoso

defiance, di-fai′-*a*ns, n., sfida f.

deficiency, di-fish′-*en*-si, n., deficienza f.

deficient, di-fish′-ent, a., deficiente

deficit, def′-i-sit, n., ammanco m.

defile, di-fail′, n., stretta f. v., macchiare

define, di-fain′, v., definire

definite*, def′-i-nit, a., definitivo

definition, def-i-ni′-shon, n., definizione f.

deflect, di-flekt′, v., deviare

deflection, di-flek′-shon, n., deviazione f.

deform, di-foorm′, v., deformare

defraud, di-frood′, v., defraudare

defray, di-frei′, v., pagare

deft*, deft, a., destro ; (clever) abile

defunct, di-fŏngkt′, a., defunto

defy, di-fai′, v., provocare ; (challenge) sfidare

degenerate, di-chen′-er-et, a., degenerato. v., degenerare

degradation, deg-ra-dei′-shon, n., degradazione f.

degrade, di-greid′, v., degradare

degree, di-grii′, n., grado m.

deign, dein, v., degnare

deject, di-chekt′, v., deprimere

dejection, di-chek′-shon, n., abbattimento m.

delay, di-lei′, n., indugio m. ; (late) ritardo m. v., indugiare ; ritardare

delectable, di-lek′-ta-bl, a., dilettevole

delegate, del′-i-gheit, n., delegato m. v., delegare

delete, di-liit′, v., cancellare

deleterious, di-li-ti′-ri-os, a., deleterio

deletion, de-lii′-shon, n., cancellazione f.

deliberate, di-lib′-er-eit, a.,* deliberato. v., deliberare

delicacy, del′-i-ka-si, n., delicatezza f. ; (food) leccornia f.

delicate*, del′-i-keit, a., delicato

delicious*, di-lish′-os, a., delizioso

delight, de-lait′, n., piacere m. v., dilettare

delightful*, de-lait′-ful, a., dilettevole

delineate, di-lin′-i-eit, v., delineare

delinquent, di-ling′-kuent, n., delinquente m. & f.

delirious, di-lir′-i-os, to be —, v., essere delirante

delirium, di-lir'-l-om, n., delirio m.

deliver, di-liv'-a,v.,(goods) consegnare ; (letters) distribuire ; (set free) liberare ; (speech) fare ; (note) rimettere

delivery, di-liv'-er-l, n., (goods) consegna f.; (letters) distribuzione f.; (deliverance) liberazione f.

delude, di-liuud', v., deludere

delusion, di-liuu'-shon, n., delusione f.

delve, delv, v., scavare : approfondire

demand, di-maand', n., domanda f. v., domandare

demean, di-miin', v., (oneself) abbassarsi

demeanour, di-mii'-ner, n., condotta f.

demented, di-men'-tid, a., demente

demise, di-mais', n., decesso m. ; legato m. v., decedere : legare

democratic, dem-o-krat'-ik, a., democratico

demolish, di-mol'-ish, v., demolire

demon, dii'-mon, n., demonio m.

demonstrate, di-mon'-streit, v., dimostrare

demoralize, di-mor'-a-lais, v., demoralizzare

demur, di-mër', v., esitare

demure*, di'-miuur, a., contegnoso

demurrage, di-mör'-ich, n., diritto di stallia m.

den, den, n., covo m.

denial, di-nai'-al, n., negazione f.

denizen, den'-i-șn, n., abitante m. & f.

denomination, di-nom-i-nei'-shon, n., culto m.; setta f.

denote, di-nout', v., denotare

denounce, de-nauns', v., denunziare

dense*, dens, a., denso

density, dens'-i-ti, n., densità f.

dent, dent, n., ammaccatura f.; (notch) tacca f. v., ammaccare

dentist, den'-tist, n., dentista m. & f.

dentistry, den'-tist-ri, n., odontoiatria f.

denude, di-niuud', v., denudare

deny, di-nai', v., negare : (deprive) privarsi

deodorizer, di-ou'-der-ai-sa, n., disodorante m.

depart, di-paart', v., partire

department, di-paart'-ment, n., dipartimento m.

departure, di-paar'-chur, n., partenza f.; — **platform**, imbarcatoio m.

depend, di-pend', v., dipendere; — **upon**, contare su

dependant, di-pen'-dant, a., dipendente

depict, di-pikt', v., dipingere

deplete, di-pliit', v., esaurire

depletion, di-plii'-shon, n., esaurimento m.

deplore, di-plor', v., deplorare

deport, di-port', v., deportare

deportment, di-port'-ment, n., contegno m.

depose, di-pous', v., deporre

deposit, di-pos'-it, n., deposito m. v., depositare

depositor, di-pos'-i-ta, n., depositante m.

depository, di-pos'-i-to-ri, n., deposito m.

depot, di'-pou, n., deposito m.; stazione ferroviaria f.; sede reggimentale f.; centro di reclutamento m.

deprave, di-preiv', v., depravare

deprecate, dep'-ri-keit, v., deprecare

depreciate, di-prii'-shi-eit, v., deprezzare

depredation, di-pri-dei'-shon, n., depredazione f.

depress, di-pres', v., deprimere

depression, di-pre'-shon, n., depressione f.; (feelings) abbattimento m.

deprivation, dep-ri-vei'-shon, n., privazione f.

deprive, di-praiv', v., privare; spogliare; (law) interdire

depth, depZ, n., profondità f.

deputy, dep'-iu-ti, n., deputato m.; sostituto m.

derailment, di-reil'-ment, n., deragliamento m.

derange, di-reinch', v., scompigliare

derangement, di-reinch'-ment, n., sconcerto m.

derelict, der'-i-likt, n., (naut.) scafo alla deriva m. a., abbandonato

deride, di-raid', v., deridere

derisive*, di-ral'-siv, a., derisivo

derive, di-raiv', v., derivare; dedurre

descend, di-send', v., discendere; (morally) abbassarsi

descendant, di-sen'-dant, n., discendente m. & f.

descent, di-sent', n., discesa f.; origine f.

describe, di-skraib', v., descrivere

description, di-skrip'-shon, n., descrizione f.; sorte f.

desecrate, des'-i-kreit, v., profanare

desert, des'-ĕrt, n., deserto m.

desert, di-sĕrt', v., disertare

deserter, di-sĕr'-ta, n., (mil.) disertore m.

desertion, di-sĕr'-shon, n., diserzione f.

deserve, di-sĕrv', v., meritare

deserving, di-sĕr'-ving, a., meritevole

design, di-sain', v., disegnare; (intention) proporsi. n., disegno m.; (pattern) motivo m.

designate, de'-sigh-neit, v., designare

designer, di-sai'-na, n., disegnatore m.

designing, di-sai'-ning, a., faccendiere. n., progetto m.

desirable, di-sai'-ra-bl, a., desiderabile

desire, di-sair', n., desiderio m.; (craving) voglia f. v., desiderare

desirous, di-sai'-ros, a., desideroso

desist, di-sist', v., desistere

desk, desk, n., scrittoio m.; (school) banco m.

desolate*, des'-o-leit, a., desolato

despair, di-sper', n., disperazione f. v., disperare

despatch, dis-pach', n., (sending) spedizione f.; (message) dispaccio m. v., spedire

desperate*, des'-per-eit, a., disperato; (reckless) forsennato

despicable, des'-pi-ka-bl, a., sprezzabile

despise, di-spais', v., sdegnare

despite, di-spait', prep., a dispetto; malgrado

despoil, di-spoil', v., spogliare

despondent, di-spon'-dent, a., scoraggiato

despot, des'-pot, n., despota m.

dessert, di-sĕrt', n., frutta f. pl.

destination, des-ti-nei'-shon, n., destinazione f.

destine, des'-tin, v., destinare

destiny, des'-ti-ni, n., destino m.

destitute, des'-ti-tiuut, a., bisognoso

destitution, des-ti-tiuu'-shon, n., indigenza f.

destroy, di-stroi', v., distruggere

destruction, dis-trŏk'-shon, n., distruzione f.

destructive, dis-trŏk'-tiv, a., distruttivo
desultory, des'-ol-to-ri, a., sconnesso, disordinato
detach, di-tach', v., staccarsi
detachable, di-tach'-a-bl, a., staccabile
detail, dii'-teil, n., dettaglio m.
detail, di-teil', v., (mil.) distaccare
detain, di-tein', v., trattenere ; (prison) tenere in prigione
detect, di-tekt', v., scorgere ; notare
detective, di-tek'-tiv, n., agente investigativo m.
detention, di-ten'-shon, n., detenzione f.
deter, di-tĕr', v., dissuadere
deteriorate, di-ti'-ri-o-reit, v., deteriorare
determine, di-tĕr'-min, v., determinare
detest, di-test', v., detestare
dethrone, di-ʒroun', v., detronizzare
detonation, di-to-nei'-shon, n., detonazione f.
detour, di-tuur', n., giro m.
detract, di-trakt', v., denigrare ; (value) detrarre
detrimental*, det-ri-men'-tal, a., nocivo
deuce, diuus, n., (cards) due m.; (tennis) parità f.
devastate, dev'-as-teit, v., devastare
develop, di-vel'-op, v., sviluppare
development, di-vel'-op-ment, n., sviluppo m.
deviate, dii'-vi-eit, v., deviare
device, di-vais', n., espediente m. ; (plan) trovata f.
devil, dev'-l, n., diavolo m.
devilry, dev'-il-ri, n., diavoleria f.
devise, di-vais', v., ideare ; (law) legare
devoid, di-void', a., privo
devote, di-vout', v., dedicare ; consacrarsi
devour, di-vaur', v., divorare
devout*, di-vaut', a., devoto
dew, diuu, n., rugiada f.
dexterous*, deks'-ter-os, a., destro
diabetes, dai-a-bii'-tis, n., diabete m.
diabolical*, dai-a-bol'-i-kal, a., diabolico
diagnose, dai'-agh-nous, v., fare la diagnosi
diagonal, dai-agh'-o-nal, a., diagonale
diagram, dai'-a-gram, n., diagramma m.
dial, dai'-al, n., quadrante m. v., (telephone) formare

dialect, dai'-*a*-lekt, n., dialetto m.

dialogue, dai'-*a*-logh, n., dialogo m.

diameter, dai-am'-i-t*a*, n., diametro m.

diamond, dai'-*a*-mond, n., diamante m.; (cards) quadri m. pl.

diarrhœa, dai-*a*-rii'-*a*, n., diarrea f.

diary, dai'-*a*-ri, n., diario m.; (pocket) agenda f.

dice, dais, n. pl., dadi m. pl.

dictate, dik'-teit, v., dettare

dictionary, dik'-shon-*a*-ri, n., dizionario m.

die, dai, v., morire. n., (stamp) conio m.; (gaming) dado m.

diet, dai'-*e*t, n., dieta f. v., stare a dieta

differ, dif'-*a*, v., differire; (disagree) non convenire

difference, dif'-*e*r-ens, n., differenza f.

different*, dif'-*e*r-ent, a., differente

difficult, dif'-ik-*e*lt, a., difficile

difficulty, dif'-ik-*e*lt-i, n., difficoltà f.

diffident, dif'-id-ent, a., diffidente; timido

diffuse, dif-iuus', v., diffondere. a., diffuso

dig, digh, v., scavare; — up, strappare

digest, di-chest', v., digerire

digestion, di-ches'-tion, n., digestione f.

dignified, digh'-ni-faid, a., dignitoso

dignitary, digh'-ni-ta-ri, n., dignatario m.

dignity, digh'-ni-ti, n., dignità f.

digression, di-gresh'-*on*, n., digressione f.

dike, daik, n., diga f.

dilapidated, di-lap'-i-dei-tid, a., devastato

dilapidation, di-lap-i-dei'-shon, n., dilapidazione f.

dilate, di-leit', v., dilatare

dilatory, dil'-*a*-t*o*-ri, a., dilatorio; tardo

dilemma, di-lem'-m*a*, n., dilemma m.

diligence, dil'-i-chens, n., diligenza f.

diligent*, dil'-i-chent, a., diligente

dilute, di-liuut', v., diluire

dim, dim, a., fosco. v., (darken) oscurarsi

dimension, di-men'-shon, n., dimensione f.

diminish, di-min'-ish, v., diminuire

dimple, dim'-p*e*l, n., fossetta f.

din, din, n., frastuono m. v., intronare

dine, dain, v., pranzare

dingy, din′-chi, a., sporco ; (faded) sbiadito

dining-car, dain′-ing-kaar, n., vagone restorante m.

dining-room, dain′-ing-ruum, n., sala da pranzo f.

dinner, din′-a, n., pranzo m.

dip, dip, n., depressione f. ; (plunge) tuffo m. v., abbassarsi ; tuffare ; (flag) ammainare ; — into, immergere

diphtheria, dif-Zii′-ri-a, n., difterite f.

diplomacy, di-plou′-ma-si, n., diplomazia f.

dire, dair, a., terribile ; tremendo

direct, di-rekt′, a.,* diritto. v., dirigere ; (address) indirizzare

direction, di-rek′-shon, n., direzione f.

directly, di-rekt′-li, adv., subito. conj., tostochè

director, di-rek′-ta, n., direttore m. ; dirigente m.

directory, di-rek′-to-ri, n., guida f.

dirigible, di′-ri-chi-bl, a., dirigibile

dirt, dĕrt, n., sporcizia f. ; immondizia f.

dirty, dĕr′-ti, a., sporco

disability, dis-a-bil′-i-ti, n., incapacità f.

disable, dis-ei′-bl, v., inabilitare ; (mech.) mettere fuori di servizio

disabuse, dis-a-biuus′, v., disingannare

disadvantage, dis-ad-vaan′-tich, n., svantaggio m.

disagree, dis-a-grii′, v., dissentire

disagreeable, dis-a-grii′-a-bl, a., sgradevole

disallow, dis-a-lau′, v., rifiutare ; negare

disappear, dis-a-pir′, v., sparire

disappearance, dis-a-pi′-rans, n., scomparsa f.

disappoint, dis-a-point′, v., deludere

disappointment, dis-a-point′-ment, n., delusione f.

disapprove, dis-a-pruuv′, v., disapprovare

disarm, dis-aarm′, v., disarmare

disaster, dis-aas′-ta, n., disastro m.

disastrous*, dis-aas′-tros, a., disastroso

disavow, dis-a-vau′, v., ritrattare ; smentire

disbelieve, dis-bi-liiv′, v., non credere

disburse, dis-bĕrs′, v., sborsare

disc, disk, n., disco m.

discard, dis-kaard′, v., scartare

discern, di-sĕrn′, v., discernere

discerning, di-sĕr′-ning, a., penetrante ; **oculato**

discharge, dis-chaarch', n., (dismissal) licenziamento m. ; (outflow, gun) scarica f. ; (mil. etc.) congedo m. ; (med.) suppurazione f. v., (cargo) scaricare ; (fulfil) adempire ; (med.) suppurare ; (acquit) assolvere

disciple, dis-ai'-pl, n., discepolo m.

discipline, dis'-i-plin, n., disciplina f.

disclaim, dis-kleim', v., negare ; ripudiare

disclose, dis-klous', v., rivelare

disclosure, dis-klou-shur, n., rivelazione f.

discolour, dis-kol'-a, v., scolorare

discomfort, dis-kŏm'-fort, n., sconforto m.

disconnect, dis-ko-nekt', v., sconnettere

discontent, dis-kon-tent', n., scontentezza f.

discontented, dis-kon-ten'-tid, a., insoddisfatto

discontinue, dis-kon-tin'-iuu, v., (cease) cessare ; (defer) rimandare ; (interrupt) interrompere

discord, dis-koord', n., disaccordo m.

discount, dis'-kaunt, n., sconto m. v., scontare ; at a —, sotto la pari

discourage, dis-kŏr'-ich, v., scoraggiare

discourse, dis-kors', n., discorso m. v., discorrere

discourteous, dis-kŏr'-ti-os, a., scortese

discover, dis-kŏv'-a, v., scoprire

discovery, dis-kŏv'-er-i, n., scoperta f.

discreet*, dis-kriit', a., discreto

discrepancy, dis-krep'-ans-i, n., differenza f.

discriminate, dis-krim'-i-neit, v., distinguere

discuss, dis-kŏs', v., discutere

discussion, dis-kŏsh'-n, n., discussione f.

disdain, dis-dein', n., sdegno m. v., sdegnare

disdainful*, dis-dein'-ful, a., sdegnoso

disease, di-siis', n., malattia f.

diseased, di-siisd', a., ammalato

disengaged, dis-en-gheichd', a., libero

disentangle, dis-en-tang'-gol, v., districare

disfavour, dis-fei'-va, n., sfavore m.

disfigure, dis-fi'-gher, v., sfigurare

disgrace, dis-greis', n., disgrazia f. v., disonorare

disguise, dis-gais', n., (make up, costumes) travestimento m. v., travestire ; (camouflage) mascherare

disgust, dis-gŏst', n., disgusto m. v., disgustare

dish, dish, n., piatto m.; (meals) pietanza f.;
— -cloth, strofinaccio m.; — up, v., servire

dishearten, dis-haar'-tn, v., scoraggiare

dishevelled, di-shev'-eld, a., scarmigliato

dishonest*, di-son'-ist, a., disonesto

dishonour, di-son'-a, n., disonore m. v., disonorare

disillusion, dis-il-liuu'-shon, v., disilludere

disinclination, dis-in-klin-ei'-shon, n., avversione f.

disinfect, dis-in-fekt', v., disinfettare

disinherit, dis-in-her'-it, v., diseredare

disjointed, dis-choin'-tid, a., (fig.) sconnesso

dislike, dis-laik', n., avversione f. v., non amare

dislocate, dis'-lo-keit, v., slogare

disloyal, dis-lo'-ial, a., sleale

dismal*, dis'-mal, a., triste, cupo

dismay, dis-mei', n., sgomento m. v., costernare

dismiss, dis-mis', v., licenziare

dismount, dis-maunt', v., smontare

disobedient*, dis-o-bii'-di-ent, a., disobbidiente

disobey, dis-o-bei', v., disobbidire

disorder, dis-oor'-da, n., disordine m. v., disordinare

disown, dis-oun', v., sconfessare

disparage, dis-par'-ich, v., denigrare

dispatch, dis-pach', (see **despatch**)

dispel, dis-pel', v., cacciare; dissipare

dispensary, dis-pen'-ser-i, n., dispensario m.

dispensation, dis-pen-sei'-shon, n., distribuzione f.;
(eccl.) dispensa f.

disperse, dis-pěrs', v., disperdere

display, dis-plei', n., spettacolo m.; (commercial) mostra f. v., (exhibit) mettere in mostra

displease, dis-pliis', v., dispiacere

displeasure, dis-plesh'-ur, n., scontento m.

disposal, dis-pou-sal, n., disposizione f.; (sale) vendita f.

dispose (of), dis-pous', v., disporre

disposed, dis-pousd', a., (minded) disposto

disprove, dis-pruuv', v., confutare

disputable, dis'-piu-ta-bl, a., discutibile

dispute, dis-piuut', n., disputa f. v., disputare

disqualify, dis-kuo'-li-fai, v., squalificare

disquiet, dis-kuai'-et, n., inquietudine f.   v., inquietare

disregard, dis-ri-gaard', n., indifferenza f.; trascuranza f.   v., trascurare

disrepute, dis-ri-piuut', n., discredito m.

disrespect, dis-ri-spekt', n., irriverenza f.

disrespectful, dis-ri-spekt'-ful, a., irriverente

dissatisfy, di-sat'-is-fai, v., scontentare

dissect, di-sekt', v., analizzare; (med.) sezionare

dissent, di-sent', v., dissentire. n., dissenso m.

dissimilar, di-sim'-i-lar, a., dissimile

dissipate, dis'-i-peit, v., dissipare

dissociate, di-sou'-shi-eit, v., separare

dissolute*, dis'-o-liuut, a., dissoluto

dissolve, di-solv', v., dissolvere

dissuade, di-sueid', v., dissuadere

distance, dis'-tans, n., distanza f.

distant*, dis'-tant, a., distante

distaste, dis-teist', n., avversione f.

distasteful, dis-teist'-ful, a., sgradevole

distemper, dis-tem'-pa, n., (paint) colore diluito m.; (dog) cimurro m.   v., dipingere a colore diluito

distend, dis-tend', v., dilatare

distil, dis-til', v., distillare

distinct*, dis-tingkt', a., distinto

distinction, dis-tingh'-shon, n., distinzione f.

distinguish, dis-tin'-guish, v., distinguere

distort, dis-toort', v., storcere; (fig.) snaturare

distract, dis-trakt', v., distrarre; rendere pazzo

distraction, dis-trak'-shon, n., distrazione f.

distrain, dis-trein', v., pignorare

distress, dis-tress', n., pena f.; (naut.) pericolo m.   v., desolare

distressing, dis-tres'-ing, a., doloroso

distribute, dis-trib'-iuut, v., distribuire

district, dis'-trikt, n., distretto m.

distrust, dis-tröst', n., sfiducia f.   v., diffidare

disturb, dis-tërb', v., disturbare

disturbance, dis-tër'-bans, n., disturbo m.; (mob) disordine m.

disuse, dis-iuus', n., disuso m.

ditch, dich, n., fosso m.

ditto, dit'-to, adv., idem

dive, daiv, n., tuffo m. v., **tuffarsi**

diver, daiv'-a, n., palombaro m.

diverge, di-věrch', v., divergere

divers(e), dai-věrs', a., diverso

diversion, di-věr'-shon, n., diversione f.; distrazione f.

divert, dai-věrt', v., divergere

divest, di-vest', v., svestirsi ; (deprive) spogliare

divide, di-vaid', v., dividere ; (distribute) spartire

divine*, di-vain', a., divino

division, di-vi'-shon, n., divisione f.

divorce, di-vors', n., divorzio m. v., divorziare

divulge, di-vŏlch', v., divulgare

dizzy, dis'-i, a., stordito ; vertiginoso

do, duu, v., fare ; essere abbastanza

docile, doo'-sail, a., docile

dock, dok, n., bacino m. v., entrare in bacino

dockyard, dok'-iaard, n., cantiere marittimo m.

doctor, dok'-ta, n., dottore m. v., curare ; (wines, etc.) fatturare

doctrine, dok'-trin, n., dottrina f.

document, dok'-iu-ment, n., documento m

dodge, doch, v., schivare. n., artificio m.

dog, dogh, n., cane m.

dogged*, dogh'-id, a., ostinato

dole, doul, n., sussidio m. v., distribuire

doleful*, doul'-ful, a., dolente

doll, dol, n., bambola f.

dome, doum, n., duomo m.; cupola f.

domestic, do-mes'-tik, n., domestico m. a., domestico

domesticated, do-mes-ti-kei'-tid, a., casalingo

domicile, dom'-i-sail, n., domicilio m.

dominate, dom'-i-neit, v., dominare

domineer, dom-i-niir', v., tiranneggiare

donation, do-nei'-shon, n., donazione f.

donkey, dong-ki, n., ciuco m., somaro m.

donor, do'-na, n., donatore m.

doom, duum, n., (fate) perdizione f. v., condannare

doomsday, duums'-dei, n., giorno del giudizio m.

door, dor, n., porta f.

door-keeper, dor'-kiip-*a*, n., portinaio m.

door-knocker, dor'-nok-*a*, n., battacchio **m.**

door-mat, dor'-mat, n., nettapiedi m.

dormitory, dor'-mi-to-ri, n., dormitorio **m.**

dose, dous, n., dose f.

dot, dot, n., punto m. v., mettere i punti

double, dŏb'-l, a. & adv., doppio. n., doppio m. ; (likeness) sosia m. v., raddoppiare

doubt, daut, n., dubbio m. v., dubitare

doubtful*, daut'-ful, a., dubbioso

douche, dush, n., doccia f.

dough, dou, n., pasta f.

dove, dŏv, n., colomba f. ; — -**cot**, colombaia f.

dowager, dau'-*e*-cha, n., vedova f.

down, daun, adv. & prep., giù, abbasso. n., piu mino m.

downcast, daun'-kaast, a., abbattuto

downfall, daun'-fool, n., caduta f., rovina f.

downhill, daun'-hil, a. & adv., in discesa

downpour, daun'-por, n., acquazzone m.

downstairs, daun'-sters, adv., abbasso

downwards, daun'-uerds, adv., in giù

dowry, dau'-ri, n., dote f.

doze, dous, n., sonnolino m. v., sonnecchiare

dozen, dŏs'-n, n., dozzina f.

drab, drab, a., grigio bruno. n., sporcacciona f.

draft, draaft, n., (money) cambiale f. ; (sketch) schizzo **m.** ; (writing) brutta copia f. v., redigere

drag, dragh, v., tirare ; trascinare ; dragare. n., draga f.

dragon, drag-*on*, n., dragone m. ; — -**fly**, libellula f.

dragoon, dra-guun', n., (mil.) dragone m.

drain, drein, n., fogna f. ; (land) canale di pro- sciugamento m. v., prosciugare

drainage, drein'-ich, n., fognatura **f.**

drake, dreik, n., anitra maschio m.

drama, draam'-*a*, n., dramma m.

dramatic, dra-ma'-tik, a., drammatico

draper, drei'-pa, n., (store) negozio di **drapperie m.**

drastic, dras'-tik, a., energico ; (law) draconiano

draught, draaft, n., (air) corrente d'aria f.;
  (drink) sorso m.; (sketch) disegno m., abbozzo **m.**;
  (ship) tiraggio m.; — **board**, scacchiera f.
draughts, draafts, n.pl., giuoco di dama m.
draughtsman, draafts'-man, n., disegnatore **m.**
draw, droo, n., (lottery) estrazione f.; (game) partita nulla f. v., (pull) tirare; (drag) trascinare;
  (sketch) disegnare; (liquids) spillare; (money) ritirare; (bill) trarre
drawback, droo'-bak, n., svantaggio **m.**
drawee, droo-ii, n., trassato m.
drawer, droo'-a,   n., (furniture) **cassetto m.**;
  (bill) traente **m.**
drawers, droo'-ers, n.pl., (apparel) mutandine f.pl.
drawing, droo'-ing, n., tiraggio m.; (sketch) disegno m.; —**room**, salotto m.
drawl, drool, n., pronuncia affettata f. v., parlare
  affettatamente
dread, dred, n., paura f. v., aver paura
dreadful[*], dred'-ful, a., spaventevole
dream, driim, n., sogno m. v., **sognare**
dreary, dri'-ri, a., lugubre
dredge, drech, v., dragare
dredger, drech'-a, n., cavafango m.
dregs, dreghs, n., sedimento m.; (fig.) feccia f.
drench, drench, v., inzuppare
dress, dres, n., veste f., **abito m.** v., vestirsi;
  (wounds) fasciare
dressing, dres'-ing, n., (med.) fasciatura f.;
  (culinary) condimento m.; —**case**, necessario
  da viaggio m.; —**gown**, veste da camera f.;
  —**room**, gabinetto di toeletta m.
dressmaker, dres'-meik-a, n., sarta f.
dribble, drib'-l, v., (drop) gocciolare; (saliva) bavare
drift, drift, n., (naut.) deriva f.; (snow, etc.) turbine di neve m.; (tendency) scopo m. v., andare
  alla deriva
drill, dril, v., (mil.) fare esercizi; (bore) perforare;
  n., (mil.) esercizio m.; (tool) perforatrice f.
drink, dringk, n., bibita f. v., bere
drip, drip, n., **goccia f.** v., gocciolare
dripping, drip'-ing, n., (fat) grasso d'arrosto **m.**

drive, draiv, n., (outing) scarrozzata f.; (approach) viale m. v., condurre

driver, draiv'-*a*, n., (engine) macchinista m.; (taxi) autista m. & f.; (horse) cocchiere m.

drizzle, dris'-l, n., pioggerella f.

droll, drôul, a., comico

drone, drôun, n., calabrone m. v., ronzare

droop, drûup, v., lasciar cadere; (plants) appassirsi

drop, drop, n., caduta f.; (liquid) **goccia** f. v., cadere; (let fall) lasciar cadere

dropsy, drop'-si, n., idropisia f.

drought, draut, n., siccità f.

drove, drôuv, n., (cattle) mandra f.

drown, draun, v., annegare; (to **cause**) **annegare**

drowsy, drau'-si, a., sonnolento

drudge, drôch, v., sgobbare

drudgery, drôch'-er-i, n., lavoro faticoso m.

drug, drôgh, n., droga f. v., narcotizzare

druggist, drô'-ghist, n., droghiere m.

drum, drôm, n., tamburo m. v., suonare il tamburo

drummer, drôm'-*a*, n., tamburino m.

drunk, drôngk, a., ubbriaco

drunkard, drông'-kard, n., beone m.

drunkenness, drông'-ken-nes, n., **ubbriachezza** f.

dry, drai, a.,* secco. v., seccare

dryness, drai'-nes, n., siccità f.

dubious*, diuu'-bi-os, a., dubbio

duchess, dôch'-es, n., duchessa f.

duck, dôk, n., anitra f. v., (bend) curvarsi

due, diuu, n., (share) parte f.; (rights) diritto m. a. & adv., (owing) dovuto; (mature) scaduto

duel, diuu'-el, n., duello m. v., battersi in duello

dues, diuus, n. pl., (toll. etc.) diritti m. pl.

duet, diu-et', n., duetto m.

duke, diuuk, n., duca m.

dull, dôl, a., (mind) ottuso; (markets) inattivo; (weather) triste; (metals, colours) opaco

duly (received), diuu'-li, adv., regolarmente

dumb, dôm, a., muto

dumbfound, dôm-faund', v., confondere

dummy, dôm'-i, n., (lay figure) manichino m.; (sham) imitazione f.; (cards) **quarta mano** f.

dump, dŏmp, n., deposito m.
dumping, dŏmp'-ing, n., dumping m.
dumpling, dŏmp'-ling, n., bodino m.
dung, dŏngh, n., sterco m.
dungeon, dŏn'-chen, n., segreta f.
dupe, diuup, n., babbeo m. v., abbindolare
duplicate, diuu'-pli-keit, n., duplicato m. a., duplicato. v., (imitate, typing) duplicare
durable, diu'-ra-bl, a., durevole
duration, diu-rei'-shon, n., durata f.
during, diu'-ring, prep., durante
dusk, dŏsk, n., oscurità f.
dusky, dŏs'-ki, a., oscuro ; bruno
dust, dŏst, n., polvere f. v., spolverare
dustbin, dŏst'-bin, n., recipiente della spazzatura m.
duster, dŏs'-ta, n., strofinaccio m.
dustman, dŏst'-man, n., spazzino m.
dutiful*, diuu'-ti-ful, a., rispettoso
duty, diuu'-ti, n., dovere m. ; (custom) diritto m.. dazio m. ; (officials) funzione f.
dwarf, duoorf, n., nano m. v., rimpiccolire
dwell, duel, v., abitare ; — upon, insistere
dweller, duel'-a, n., abitante m. & f.
dwelling, duel'-ing, n., abitazione f.
dwindle, duin'-dl, v., diminuire
dye, dai, n., tintura f. v., tingere ; — -works, n. pl., tintoria f.
dynamite, din'-a-mait, n., dinamite f.
dynamo, dain'-a-mou, n., dinamo f.
dysentery, dis'-n-tri, n., dissenteria f.

each, iich, a. & pron., ogni ; ciascuno, ciascuna ; — other, l'un l'altro, l'un l'altra
eager*, ii'-ga, a.,(keen) desideroso ; (desire) ardente
eagerness, ii'-gher-nes, n., avidità f. ; ardore m.
eagle, ii'-gol, n., aquila f.
ear, ir, n., orecchio m. ; (corn) spiga f. ; — -ring, orecchino m.
earl, ĕrl, n., conte m.
early, ĕr'-li, a. & adv., mattiniero ; di buon'ora
earn, ĕrn, v., guadagnare ; meritare
earnest*, ĕr'-nest, a., serio

earnings, ĕr′-ninghs, n. pl., guadagni m. pl.

earth, ĕrZ, n., terra f.   v., (electricity) porre contatto a terra

earthenware, ĕrZ′-n-ueir, n., ceramica f.

earthly, ĕrZ′-li, a., terreno ; terrestre

earthquake, ĕrZ′-kueik, n., terremoto m.

earwig, ir′-uigh, n., forbicina f.

ease, iis, n., (comfort) agio m.; (relief) sollievo m.; (facility) facilità f.   v., alleviare ; facilitare ; at one's —, a proprio agio

easel, ii′-sl, n., cavalletto m.

easily, ii′-si-li, adv., facilmente

east, iist, n., est m.

Easter, iis′-ta, n., Pasqua f.

easterly, iis′-tĕr-li, a., di levante

eastern, iis′-tĕrn, a., orientale

easy, ii′-si, a., facile ; — chair, n., seggiolone m.

eat, iit, v., mangiare ; (worms, etc.) rodere ; (corrode) corrodere

eatable, ii′-ta-bl, a., mangiabile

eatables, ii′-ta-bls, n. pl., commestibili m. pl.

eavesdropper, iivs′-drop-a, n., ascoltatore di nascosto m.

ebb, eb, n., riflusso m.   v., rifluire

ebony, eb′-o-ni, n., ebano m.

eccentric, ek-sen′-trik, a., eccentrico

echo, ck′-ou, n., eco m.   v., far eco

eclipse, i-klips′, n., eclissi f. ; eclissare

economise, i-kon′-o-mais, v., economizzare

economy, i-kon′-o-mi, n., economia f.

ecstasy, ek′-sta-si, n., estasi f.

eddy, ed′-i, n., turbine m. ; gorgo m.

edge, ech, n., (knife) filo m. ; (brink) orlo m.   v., (sharpen) dar il filo ; (border) orlare

edible, ed′-i-bl, a., commestibile

edify, ed′-i-fai, v., edificare

edit, ed′-it, v., pubblicare

edition, ed′-i-shon, n., edizione f.

editor, ed′-i-ta, n., editore m.

editorial, ed-i-to′-ri-al, a., d'editore

educate, ed′-iu-keit, v., istruire ; (rear) educare

eel, iil, n., anguilla f

efface, ef-eis', v., cancellare
effect, ef-ekt', n., effetto m. v., effettuare
effective*, ef-ek'-tiv, a., effettivo
effectual*, ef-ek'-tiu-al, a., efficace
effeminate, ef-em'-i-neit, a., effeminato
effervescent, ef-er-ves'-ent, a., effervescente
efficacious*, ef-i-kei'-shos, a., efficace
efficiency, ef-ish'-en-si, n., efficienza f.
efficient, ef-ish'-ent, a., (person) efficiente
effort, ef'-ort, n., sforzo m.
effrontery, ef-rant'-er-i, n., sfrontatezza f.
effusive*, ef-iuu'-siv, a., espansivo
egg, egh, n., uovo m.; — cup, porta uovo m.
egotism, eg'-ou-tism, n., egoismo m.
egress, i-gres', n., uscita f.
eiderdown, ai'-der-daun, n., (quilt) piumino m.
eight, eit, a., otto
eighteen, ei'-tiin, a., diciotto
eighteenth, ei'-tiinΣ, a., diciottesimo
eighth, eitZ, a., ottavo
eighty, ei'-ti, a., ottanta
either, ai'-Da, pron., l'uno o l'altro. a., ogni.
   conj., sia ... sia ; o ... o ...
eject, i-ohekt', v., espellere
elaborate, i-lab'-o-reit, v., elaborare. a., elaborato;
   (detailed) complicato
elapse, i-laps', v., trascorrere
elastic, i-las'-tik, n., elastico m. a., elastico
elate, i-leit', v., esaltare
elbow, el'-bou, n., gomito m. v., dar gomitate
elder, el'-da, n., maggiore m. & f.; primogenito m.;
   (tree) sambuco m.; —ly, a., attempato
eldest, el'-dest, n., maggiore m. & f.; primogenito m.;
   a., maggiore
elect, i-lekt', a., eletto. v., eleggere
election, i-lek-shon, n., elezione f.
electric(al), i-lek'-trik(-l), a., elettrico
electrician, i-lek-trish'-an, n., elettricista m.
electricity, i-lek-tri'-si-ti, n., elettricità f.
electrify, i-lek'-tri-fai, v., (railway) elettrificare
electro-plate, i-lek'-tro-pleit, v., galvanizzare.
   n., oggetti argentati m. pl.

elegance, el'-i-gans, n., eleganza f.
elegant*, el'-i-gant, a., elegante
element, el'-i-ment, n., elemento m.
elementary, el-i-men'-ta-ri, a., elementare
elephant, el'-i-fant, n., elefante m.
elevate, el'-i-veit, v., elevare
eleven, il-ev'-n, a., undici ; —th, undecimo
elf, elf, n., folletto m.
elicit, il-is'-it, v., far scaturire
eligible, el'-i-chi-bl, a., eligibile
eliminate, il-im'-i-neit, v., eliminare
elite, e-liit', n., fiore m.
elk, elk, n., alce m.
ell, el, n., (measure) auna f.
elm, elm, n., olmo m.
elongate, ii-longh'-eit, v., allungare
elope, i-loup', v., scappare
elopement, i-loup'-ment, n., fuga f.
eloquent*, el'-o-kuent, a., eloquente
else, els, a., altro. adv., altrimenti
elsewhere, els'-huer, adv., altrove
elucidate, i-liuu'-si-deit, v., elucidare
elude, i-liuud', v., eludere
elusive, i-liuu'-siv, a., ingannevole
emaciate, i-mei'-shi-eit, v., dimagrare
emanate, em'-a-neit, v., emanare
emancipate, i-man'-si-peit, v., emancipare
embalm, em-baam', v., imbalsamare
embankment, em-bangk'-ment, n., banchina f. ;
  (railway, road) scarpata f.
embark, em-baark', v., imbarcare
embarrass, em-bar'-as, v., imbarazzare
embarrassment, em-bar'-as-ment, n., imbarazzo m.
embassy, em'-bas-i, n., ambasciata f.
embellish, em-bel'-ish, v., abbellire
embers, em'-bers, n. pl., braci f. pl.
embezzle, em-bes'-l, v., prevaricare
embitter, em-bit'-a, v., (fig.) inasprire
embody, em-bod'-i, v., includere ; personificare
embolden, em-boul'-dn, v., inardire
embrace, em-breis', v., abbracciare
embrocation, em-bro-kei'-shon, n., embrocazione f.

embroider, em-broi'-d*a*, v., ricamare

embroidery, em-broi'-der-i, n., ricamo **m**.

embroil, em-broil', v., imbrogliare

emerald, em'-*e*-rald, n., smeraldo **m**.

emerge, i-merch', v., emergere

emergency, i-mer'-chen-si, n., bisogno urgente **m**.

emetic, i-met'-ik, n., emetico m.

emigrant, em'-i-grant, n., emigrante m. & f.

emigrate, em'-i-greit, v., emigrare

eminence, em'-in-ens, n., eminenza f.

eminent, em'-in-ent, a., eminente

emissary, em'-is-*a*-ri, n., emissario m.

emit, i-mit', v., emettere

emotion, i-mou'-shon, n., emozione f.

emotional, i-mou'-shon-*al*, a., impressionabile

emperor, em'-per-*a*, n., imperatore m.

emphasis, em'-fa-sis, n., enfasi f.

emphasize, em'-fa-sais, v., accentuare

emphatic, em-fat'-ik, a., enfatico

empire, em'-pair, n., impero m.

employ, em-ploi', v., impiegare

employer, em-ploi'-*a*, n., datore di lavoro m.

employment, em-ploi'-ment, n., impiego m.

empower, em-pau'-*a*, v., autorizzare

empress, em'-pres, n., imperatrice f.

empty, em'-ti, a., vuoto

emulate, em'-iu-leit, v., emulare

emulation, em-iu-lei'-shon, n., emulazione f.

enable, en-ei'-bl, v., metter in grado di

enact, en-akt', v., promulgare ; (theatre) rappresentare

enamel, en-am'-l, n., smalto m. v., smaltare

enamoured, en-am'-erd, a., innamorato

encamp, en-kamp', v., accamparsi

enchant, en-chaant', v., incantare

enchantment, en-chaant'-ment, n., incanto m.

encircle, en-ser'-kl, v., circondare

enclose, en-klous', v., accludere

enclosure, en-klou'-shur, n., (letter) allegato m.: (fence) recinto m.

encompass, en-kŏm'-pas, v., recingere

encore, ang-koor', interj., bis !

encounter, *en*-kaun'-ta, n., incontro m.; (enemy) scontro m. v., incontrare

encourage, *en*-kŏr'-ich, v., incoraggiare

encroachment, *en*-krouch'-ment, n., usurpazione f.; abuso m.

encumber, *en*-kom'-ba, v., ingombrare; (property) gravare

encumbrance, *en*-kŏm'-brans, n., (burden) carico m.

encyclopædia, *en*-sai-klo-pii'-di-a, n., enciclopedia f.

end, end, n., fine f.; (aim) fine m. v., finire

endanger, *en*-dein'-cha, v., mettere in pericolo

endear, *en*-dir', v., render caro

endearment, *en*-dir'-ment, n., tenerezza f.

endeavour, *en*-dev'-a, n., sforzo m. v., sforzarsi

endive, *en'*-div, n., indivia f.

endless°, end'-les, a., senza fine

endorse, *en*-doors', v., girare; (approve) appoggiare

endorsement, *en*-doors'-ment, n., girata f.; (approval) appoggio m.

endow, *en*-dau', v., dotare

endurance, *en*-diur'-ans, n., tolleranza f.

endure, *en*-diur', v., sopportare

enema, *en'*-i-ma, n., clistere m.

enemy, *en'*-i-mi, n., nemico m.

energetic, *en*-er-chet'-ik, a., energico

energy, *en'*-er-chi, n., energia f.

enervate, *en'*-er-veit, v., snervare

enfeeble, *en*-fii'-bl, v., debilitare

enfilade, *en*-fi-leid', v., infilare

enforce, *en*-fors', v., rafforzare

engage, *en*-gheich', v., occupare; (employ) impiegare; (reserve) riservare; (enemy) attaccare; (bind) obbligare

engaged, *en*-gheichd', a., occupato; fidanzato

engagement, *en*-gheich'-ment, n., (appointment) appuntamento m.; (betrothal) fidanzamento m.; (combat) combattimento m.

engaging, *en*-ghei'-ching, a., attraente

engender, *en*-chen'-da, v., generare

engine, *en'*-chin, n., macchina f.; motore m.

engineer, en-chi-nir´, n., ingegnere m.; — **corps,** (mil.) genio m.

engineering, en-chi-nir´-ing, n., ingegneria f.

engrave, en-greiv´, v., intagliare

engross, en-grous´, v., (absorbed) assorbirsi ; (document) far copia legale

engulf, en-gŏlf´, v., ingolfare

enhance, en-haans´, v., aumentare ; far risaltare

enjoin, en-choin´, v., ingiungere

enjoy, en-choi´, v., (like) godere ; — **oneself,** divertirsi

enjoyment, en-choi´-ment, n., soddisfazione f.; (delight) godimento m.

enlarge, en-laarch´, v., ingrandire

enlargement, en-laarch´-ment, n., ingrandimento m.

enlighten, en-lai´-tn, v., rendere edotto

enlist, en-list´, v., guadagnare ; (mil.) arruolarsi

enliven, en-lai´-vn, v., dar vita

enmity, en´-mi-ti, n., inimicizia f.

ennoble, en-ou´-bl, v., nobilitare

enormous*, i-noor´-mos, a., enorme

enough, i-nŏf´, adv., abbastanza

enquire, en-kuair´, (see inquire)

enrage, en-reich´, v., far arrabbiare

enrapture, en-rap´-chur, v., estasiare

enrich, en-rich´, v., arricchire

enrol, en-roul´, v., registrare ; classificare ; (mil.) arruolare

ensign, en´-sain, n., (flag) bandiera f.; (naval flag) bandiera di poppa f. ; (rank) portabandiera m.

enslave, en-sleiv´, v., rendere schiavo

ensnare, en-snĕr´, v., accalappiare

ensue, en-siuu´, v., derivare

entail, en-teil´, v., involvere ; (law) sostituire

entangle, en-tangh´-l, v., imbrogliare

enter, en´-ta, v., entrare ; — **up,** registrare

enterprise, en´-ter-prais, n., impresa f.

entertain, en-ter-tein´, v., intrattenere ; considerare

entertainment, en-ter-tein-ment, n., spettacolo m. ; trattenimento m.

enthusiasm, *en*-Ziuu'-*s*i-a*s*m, n., entusiasmo m.

entice, *en*-tais', v., allettare

entire*, *en*-tair', a., intero

entitle, *en*-tai'-tl, v., dar diritto ; intitolare

entomb, *en*-tuum', v., seppellire

entrance, *en*'-trans, n., entrata f.

entrance, *en*-traans', v., incantare

entreat, *en*-triit', v., supplicare

entrench, *en*-trench', v., trincerarsi

entrust, *en*-tröst', v., affidare

entry, *en*'-tri,n.,ingresso m.; (record) registrazione f.

entwine, *en*-tuain', v., intrecciare ; torcere

enumerate, i-niuu'-*mer*-eit, v., enumerare

envelop*, *en*-vel'-op, v., avviluppare

envelope, *en*'-vel-op, n., busta f.

envious*, *en*'-vi-o*s*, a., invidioso

environs, *en*-vai'-ron*s*, n. pl., dintorni m. pl.

envoy, *en*'-voi, n., inviato m.

envy, *en*'-vi, n., invidia f. v., invidiare

epicure, *ep*'-i-kiur, n., epicuro m.

epidemic, ep-i-dem'-ik, n., epidemia f. a., epidemico

episode, *ep*'-i-soud, n., episodio m.

epistle, *ep*-is'-l, n., epistola f.

epoch, ii'-pok, n., epoca f.

equal, ii'-ku*al*, n., eguale m. & f. a.,* eguale

equality, i-kuol'-i-ti, n., eguaglianza f.

equalize, ii'-kuol-ai*s*, v., eguagliare

equator, i-kuei'-ta, n., equatore m.

equerry, ek'-u*e*-ri n., scudiero m.

equilibrium, i-kui-lib'-ri-*o*m, n., equilibrio m.

equip, i-kuip', v., equipaggiare

equitable, ek'-ui-*ta*-bl, a., (just) giusto ; (fair) equanime

equity, ek-ui-ti, n., equità f.

equivalent, i-kui'-*va*-lent, a., equivalente

era, i'-*ra*, n., era f.

eradicate, i-rad'-i-keit, v., sradicare

erase, i-rei*s*', v., raschiare ; cancellare

eraser, i-rei*s*'-*a*, n., raschietto m.

erect, i-rekt', v., erigere. a., eretto

ermine, ĕr'-min, n., ermellino m.

err, ĕr, v., errare

errand, er'-and, n., commissione f.; — -boy, fattorino m.

erratic, er-ra'-tik, a., indeciso

erroneous*, e-rou'-ni-os, a., erroneo

error, er'-or, n., errore m.

eruption, i-rŏp'-shon, n., eruzione f.

escape, es-keip', v., scampare

escort, es-koort', v., scortare. n., scorta f.

especially, es-pesh'-al-i, adv., specialmente

essay, es'-ei, n., saggio m. v., tentare

essential*, es-en'-shal, a., essenziale

establish, es-tab'-lish, v., fondare

establishment, es-tab'-lish-ment, n., istituzione f.

estate, es-teit', n., (land) proprietà f.; (possession) beni m. pl.; (status) classe f.

esteem, es-tiim', n., stima f. v., stimare

estimate, es'-ti-meit, n., (costs) stima f.; (appraisement) valutazione f. v., stimare

estrange, es-treinch', v., alienare

etching, ech'-ing, n., incisione all'acqua forte f.

eternal*, i-ter'-nal, a., eterno

eternity, i-ter'-ni-ti, n., eternità f.

ether, ii'-Zer, n., etere m.

euphony, iuu'-fo-ni, n., eufonia f.

evacuate, i-vak'-iu-eit, v., evacuare

evade, i-veid', v., evadere

evaporate, i-vap'-or-eit, v., evaporare

evasive*, i-vei'-siv, a., evasivo

eve, iiv, n., vigilia f.

even, ii'-vn, a., (level) liscio; (land) piano; (mood) calmo; (numbers) pari. adv., perfino; (what is more) anche

evening, iiv'-ning, n., sera f.; — -dress, abito da sera m.; (tails) marsina f.; (ladies') veste da sera f.

evensong, ii'-ven-song, n., servizio serale m.

event, i-vent', n., avvenimento m.

eventful, i-vent'-ful, a., pieno d'incidenti

eventually, i-ven'-tiu-al-i, adv., finalmente

ever, ev'-a, adv., sempre; (at any time) mai

everlasting*, ev-er-laas'-ting, a., eterno

evermore, ev'-er-mor, adv., per sempre

every, ev'-ri, a. & pron., ogni ; ognuno

everybody, —one, ev'-ri-bod-i, —uŏn, a., ognuno

everything, ev'-ri-Zing, a., tutto, ogni cosa

everywhere, ev'-ri-huer, adv., dappertutto

evict, i-vikt', v., evincere

eviction, i-vik'-shon, n., evizione f.

evidence, ev'-i-dens, n., (proof) evidenza f.; (testimony) testimonianza f.; **furnish —**, v., testimoniare

evident*, ev'-i-dent, a., evidente

evil, ii'-vl, n., male m. a., cattivo

evince, i-vins', v., manifestare

evoke, i-vouk', v., evocare

evolve, i-volv', v., svolgere

ewe, iuu, n., pecora f.

exact, egh-sakt', a.,* esatto. v., esigere

exacting, egh-sakt'-ing, a., esigente

exactitude, egh-sakt'-ti-tiuud, n., esattezza f.

exaggerate, egh-sach'-er-eit, v., esagerare

exaggeration, egh-sach-er-ei'-shon, n., esagera-zione f.

exalt, egh-soolt', v., esaltare

examination, egh-sam-i-nei'-shon, n., esame m. ; (search, etc.) ispezione f.; (legal) interrogatorio m.

examine, egh-sam'-in, v., esaminare

example, egh-saam'-pl, n., esempio m.

exasperate, egh-sas-per-eit, v., esasperare

excavate, eks-ka-veit, v., scavare

exceed, ek-siid', v., eccedere

exceedingly, ek-sii'-ding-li, adv., straordinaria-mente

excel, ek-sel', v., eccellere

excellent*, ek'-sel-ent, a., eccellente

except, ek'-sept, prep., eccetto. v., eccettuare

exception, ek-sep'-shon, n., eccezione f.; **take —**, v., obbiettare

exceptional*, ek-sep'-shon-al, a., eccezionale

excerpt, ek'-serpt, n., estratto m.

excess, ek-ses', n., eccesso m.; (surplus) eccedenza f.

excessive*, ek-ses'-iv, a., eccessivo

exchange, eks-cheinch', n., cambio m. ; (telephone) centralino telefonico m.

exchequer, eks-chek′-*a*, n., tesoro pubblico m.

excise, ek-sais′, n., dazio m.

excitable, ek-sait′-*a*-bl, a., eccitabile

excite, ek-sait′, v., eccitare

excitement, ek-sait′-ment, n., eccitazione f.

exciting, ek-sai′-ting, a., eccitante

exclaim, eks-kleim′, v., esclamare

exclamation, eks-kla-mei′-shon, n., esclamazione f.

exclude, eks-kluud′, v., escludere

exclusive*, eks-kluu′-siv, a., esclusivo

excruciating, eks-kruu′-shi-ei-ting, a., atroce

exculpate, eks-köl′-peit, v., scolpare

excursion, eks-kër′-shon, n., gita f.

excuse, eks-kiuus′, v., scusare

excuse, eks-kiuus′, n., scusa f.

execute, ek′-si-kiuut, v., (perform) eseguire ; (put to death) mettere a morte

executioner, ek-si-kiuu′-shon-*a*, n., giustiziere m.

executor, ek-sek′-iu-t*a*, n., esecutore m.

exempt, egh-*s*empt′, v., esentare

exemption, egh-*s*emp′-shon, n., esenzione f.

exercise, eks′-*er*-sais, n., esercizio m.   v., esercitarsi ; (mil.) far esercizi

exert, egh-*s*ërt′, v., sforzarsi

exertion, egh-*s*ër′-shon, n., sforzo m.

exhale, eks-heil′, v., esalare

exhaust, egh-*s*oost′, v., esaurire.   n., (mech.) scappamento m.

exhaustive*, egh-*s*oost′-iv, a., esauriente

exhibit, egh-*s*ib′-it, n., oggetto esposto m.   v., mostrare ; esporre

exhibition, eks-i-bish′-*on*, n., esposizione f.; esibizione f.

exhilarate, egh-*s*il′-*a*-reit, v., ricreare

exhilarating, egh-*s*il′-*a*-rei-ting, a., invigorante

exhort, egh-*s*oort′, v., esortare

exigency, ek′-si-*ch*en-si, n., esigenza f.

exile, ek′-sail, n., esilio m. ; (person) esiliato m.   v., esiliare

exist, egh-*s*ist′, v., esistere

existence, egh-*s*is′-tens, n., **esistenza f.**

exit, ek′-sit, n., uscita f.

exodus, ek'-*so*-dus, n., esodo m.

exonerate, egh-*s*on'-*e*r-eit, v., esonerare ; (acquit) assolvere

exorbitant*, ek-*s*oor'-bi-t*a*nt, a., esorbitante

expand, eks-pand', v., espandere

expansion, eks-pan'-shon, n., espansione f.

expect, eks-pekt', v., aspettare ; (believe) credere

expectation, eks-pek-tei'-shon, n., aspettazione f.

expectorate, eks-pek'-to-reit, v., espettorare

expedient, eks-pii'-di-*e*nt, n., espediente m.

expedite, eks'-*p*i-dait, v., affrettare, accelerare

expel, eks-pel', v., espellere

expend, eks'-pend, v., spendere ; (use up) usare

expenditure, eks-pen'-di-ch*u*r, n., spesa f.

expense, eks-pens', n., spesa f.

expensive*, eks-pen'-siv, a., costoso

experience, eks-pi'-ri-*e*ns, n., esperienza f. v., esperimentare

experiment, eks-per'-i-m*e*nt, n., esperimento m. v., esperimentare

expert, eks-p*e*rt', n., perito m. a., perito

expire, eks-pair', v., (to die) spirare ; (time) terminare

explain, eks-plein', v., spiegare

explanation, eks-pla-nei'-shon, n., spiegazione f.

explicit*, eks-plis'-it, a., esplicito

explode, eks-ploud', v., esplodere

exploit, eks-ploit', n., bell'impresa f. v., sfruttare

explore, eks-plor', v., esplorare

export, eks-p*o*rt', v., esportare. n., esportazione f.

expose, eks-pou*s*', v., esporre ; (disclose) smascherare

expostulate, eks-pos'-tiu-leit, v., rimostrare

exposure, eks-pou-sh*u*r, n., (disclosure, etc.) smascheramento m. ; (photography) esposizione f.

expound, eks-paund', v., spiegare

express, eks-pres', n., espresso m. a.,* espresso

expression, eks-presh'-*o*n, n., espressione f.

expulsion, eks-p*o*l'-shon, n., espulsione f.

expunge, eks-p*o*nch', v., cancellare

exquisite*, eks'-kui-*s*it, a., squisito

extempore, eks-tem'-*p*o-ri, a., improvviso

extend, eks-tend', v., estendere

extensive*, eks-ten'-siv, a., vasto

extent, eks-tent', n., estensione f.

extenuating, eks-ten'-iu-eit-ing, a., attenuante

exterior, eks-ti'-ri-a, n., esteriore m. a.,* esterno

exterminate, eks-tĕr'-mi-neit, v., sterminare

external, eks-tĕr'-nal, a., esterno

extinct, eks-ting-kt, a., estinto

extinguish, eks-tingh'-uish, v., estinguere

extort, eks-toort', v., estorcere

extortion, eks-toor'-shon, n., estorsione f.

extra, eks'-tra, n., extra m. a., extra

extract, eks-tract', v., estrarre. n., estratto m.

extraordinary, eks-tra-oor'-di-na-ri, a., straordinario

extravagant*, eks-trav'-a-gant, a., stravagante ; costoso ; (exaggerated) esagerato

extreme, eks-triim', a., estremo

extremely, eks-triim'-li, adv., estremamente

extricate, eks'-tri-keit, v., estricare

eye, ai, n., occhio m. ; —glass, monocolo m. ; —glasses, occhiali m.pl. ; —witness, testimonio oculare m.

eyeball, ai'-bool, n., globo dell'occhio m.

eyebrow, ai'-brau, n., sopracciglio m.

eyelash, ai'-lash, n., ciglio m.

eyelet, ai'-let, n., occhiello m.

eyelid, ai'-lid, n., palpebra f.

eyesight, ai'-sait, n., vista f.

fable, fei'-bel, n., favola f. v., favoleggiare

fabric, fab'-rik, n., tessuto m.; (edifice) fabbrica f.

fabrication, fab-ri-kei'-shon, n., fabbricazione f.

fabulous*, fab'-iu-los, a., favoloso

facade, fa-sad', n., facciata f.

face, feis, n., faccia f. ; (clock) quadrante m. v., affrontare ; —cream, n., crema per la faccia f.

facetious*, fa-sii'-shos, a., faceto

facilitate, fa-sil'-i-teit, v., facilitare

facsimile, fack-sim'-i-lii, n., facsimile m.

fact, fakt, n., fatto m.

factory, fak'-to-ri, n., fabbrica f.

faculty, fak'-*ul*-ti, n., facoltà f.

fade, feid, v., appassire ; (colour) scolorire

faggot, fag'-ot, n., fastello m.

fail, feil, v., (omit) mancare ; (miscarry) fallire ; (exam.) essere riprovato ; (bankrupt) fallire ; **without —,** senza fallo

failure, feil'-*lur*, n., fallimento m. ; fiasco m.

faint, feint, v., svenire. a.,* leggero ; debole. n., svenimento m.

fair, fer, n., fiera f. a.,* bello ; (just) giusto ; (hair) biondo

fairness, fer'-nes, n., bellezza f. ; giustizia f. ; lealtà [f.

fairy, fe'-ri, n., fata f.

faith, feiZ, n., fede f.

faithful°, feiZ'-*ful*, a., fedele

faithless, feiZ'-les, a., infedele

falcon, fool'-kn, n., falco m.

fall, fool, n., caduta f. v., cadere

fallacy, fal'-*a*-si, n., fallacia f.

false°, fools, a., falso

falsehood, fools'-hud, n., falsità f.

falsification°,fool-si-fi-kei'-shon,n.,falsificazione f.

falsify, fool'-si-fai, v., falsificare

falter, fool-*ta*, v., (stagger) esitare ; (speech) balbettare

fame, feim, n., fama f.

famed, feimd, a., famoso

familiar°, *fa*-mil'-*ia*, a., familiare

family, fam'-i-li, n., famiglia f.

famine, fam'-in, n., carestia f.

famish, fam'-ish, v., affamare

famous°, fei'-mos, a., famoso

fan, fan, n., ventaglio m.; (electric) ventilatore m. v., sventolare

fanatic, *fa*-nat'-ik, n., fanatico m. a., fanatico

fancy, fan'-si, n., fantasia f.; (desire) capriccio m. v., immaginare ; avere voglia di

fancy-dress, fan'-si-dres, n., abito da maschera m.

fang, fangh, n., zanna f. ; (snake) dente m.

fantastic, fan-tas'-tik, a., fantastico

fantasy, fan'-*ta*-si, n., fantasia f.

far, faar, a. & adv., lontano

farce, faars, n., farsa f.

fare, fer, n., (boat, train) prezzo del viaggio m.; (bus, taxi) prezzo della corsa m.; (food) vitto m.

farewell, fer'-uel, n., congedo m. interj., addio!

farm, faarm, n., fattoria f. v., coltivare un podere

farmer, faar'-ma, n., agricoltore m.

farrier, far'-i-a, n., maniscalco m.

farther, faar'-Da, adv., più lontano; inoltre

fascinate, fas'-in-eit, v., affascinare

fashion, fash'-on, n., moda f. v., foggiare; in —, alla moda

fashionable, fash'-on-a-bl, a., di moda

fast, faast, a., rapido; (firm, fixed, tight) saldo; (colour) forte. n., digiuno m. v., digiunare

fasten, faas'-n, v., abbottonare; fissare; (close) chiu- [dere

fastidious*, fas-tid'-i-os, a., schizzinoso

fat, fat, n., grasso m. a., grasso

fatal*, fei'-tl, a., fatale

fatality, fat-al'-i-ti, n., fatalità f.

fate, feit, n., fato m.

fated, fei'-tid, a., destinato [cero m.

father, faa'-Da, n., padre m.; —-in-law, suo-

fatherly, faa'-Der-li, a., paterno

fathom, faD'-om, n., (naut.) braccio m. v., scan- dagliare

fatigue, fa-tigh', n., fatica f.; (mil.) servizio di fa- tica m. v., affaticare

fatten, fat'-n, v., ingrassare

fault, foolt, n., errore m.; difetto m.; (blame, cause) colpa f.

faultless*, foolt'-less, a., senza difetto

faulty, fool'-ti, a., difettoso

favour, fei'-va, n., favore m.; (letter) pregiata f. v., favorire

favourable, fei'-vor-a-bl, a., favorevole

favourite, fei'-vor-it, n., favorito m. a., favorito

fawn, foon, n., daino m. v., far moine. a., fulvo

fear, fir, n., paura f. v., temere

fearful*, fir'-ful, a., terribile; timoroso

fearless*, fir'-les, a., intrepido

feasible, fii'-si-bl, a., fattibile [giare

feast, fiist, n., festa f.; banchetto m. v., resteg-

feat, fiit. n., azione f.; (performance) prova f.; (exploit) bell'impresa f.

feather, feD'-er, n., penna f.; piuma f.

feathers, feD'-ers, n. pl., piume f. pl.; penne f. pl.

feature, fii'-chur, n., caratteristica f.

features, fii'-churs, n. pl., (face) fattezze f. pl.

February, feb'-ru-a-ri, n., febbraio m.

federal, fed'-er-al, a., federale

federation, fed-er-ei'-shon, n., federazione f.

fee, fii, n., onorario m.

feeble, fii'-bl, a., debole

feed, fiid, v., nutrire ; (cattle) pascere. n., pascolo m.

feel, fiil, v., sentire ; (touch) tastare. n., tatto m.

feeler, fii'-la, n., (insects) antenna f.

feeling, fii'-ling. n., senso m.; sentimento m. a., sentire [sibile

feign, fein, v., fingere

feint, feint, n., finta f.

fell, fel. v., abbattere

fellow, fel'-ou, n., membro m.; (pop.) camerata m.

fellowship, fel'-ou-ship, n., associazione f.; (pop.) compagnia f.

felony, fel'-o-ni, n., crimine m.

felt, felt, n., feltro m.

female, fii'-meil, a., femminile. n., femmina f.

feminine, fem'-i-nin, a., femminino

fen, fen, n., maremma f.; (bog) pantano m.

fence, fens, n., steccato m. v., rinchiudere ; (combat) tirare di scherma

fender, fen'-da. n., (hearth) paracenere f.; (ship) parabordo m.

ferment, fer'-ment. v., fermentare

fern, fern, n., felce f.

ferocious*, fi-rou'-shos, a., feroce

ferret, fer'-et, n., furetto m. v., frugare

ferrule, fer'-ul, n., ghiera f.

ferry, fer'-i, n., traghetto m. v., traghettare

fertile, fer'-tail, a., fertile

fertilize, fer'-ti-lais, v., fertilizzare

fervent*, fer'-vent, a., fervido

fester, fes'-ta, v., suppurare

festival, fes'-ti-vl, n., festa f.

festive, fes'-tiv, a., festivo

festoon, fes-tuun', n., festone m. v., **inghirlandare**

fetch, fech, v., portare ; (call for) andare **a cercare**

fetter, fet'-er, v., incatenare

fetters, fet'ers, n.pl., catene f.pl.

feud, fiuud, n., feudo m.

feudal, fiuu'-dl, a., feudale

fever, fii'-va, n., febbre f.

feverish, fii'-ver-ish, a., febbricitante

few, fiuu, a., pochi ; **a —**, alcuni, alcune

fibre, fai'-ba, n., fibra f.

fickle, fik'-l, a., incostante

fiction, fik'-shon, n., finzione f.; (book) romanzo m.

fictitious°, fik-ti'-shos, a., fittizio, falso

fidelity, fi-del'-i-ti, n., fedeltà f.

fidget, fich'-et, n., irrequietezza f. v., agitarsi

fidgety, fich'-et-i, a., irrequieto

field, fiild, n., campo m.:— **-glass**, cannocchiale **m.**; **—-marshal**, maresciallo di campo **m.**

fiend, fiind, n., diavolo m.

fiendish, fiind'-ish, a., diabolico

fierce, firs, a., fiero ; (stern) feroce

fiery, fai'-er-i, a., ardente ; (temper) **focoso**

fife, faif, n., piffero m.

fifteen, fif'-tiin, a., quindici

fifteenth, fif'-tiinZ, a., quindicesimo

fifth, fifZ, a., quinto. —, (one fifth) un quinto **m.**

fiftieth, fif'-ti-iZ, a., cinquantesimo

fifty, fif'-ti, a., cinquanta

fig, figh, n., fico m. ; **—-tree**, albero del fico **m.**

fight, fait, n., combattimento m. v., **combattere**

figure, fi'-gher, n., figura f.; (number) cifra f. v., figurare ; **—-head**, n., (ship) scultura di prora f.

filbert, fil'-bert, n., avellana f.

filch, filch, v., scroccare

file, fail, n., (tool) lima f.; (mil.) fila f.; (office) dossier m. v., limare ; (letters, etc.) classificare

filigree, fil'-i-grii, n., filagrana f.

fill, fil, v., riempire : (teeth) piombare. n., **sazietà f.**

filly, fil'-i, n., puledra f.

film, film, v., filmare. n., pellicola f. ; **sound —**, pellicola sonora f.

filter, fil'-ta, n., filtro m. v., **filtrare**

filth, filz, n., sporcizia f.

filthy, filz′-i, a., sporco

fin, fin, n., pinna f.

final°, fai′-nal, a., decisivo ; (last) finale

finance, fi-nans′, n., finanza f. v., finanziare

financial, fi-nan′-shal, a., finanziario

finch, finch, n., fringuello m.

find, faind, v., trovare ; (law) dichiarare. n., trovata f. ; scoperta f.

fine, fain, n., ammenda f. a.,° bello. v., multare

finery, fain′-er-i, n., ornamento m.

finger, fing′-ga, n., dito m. v., toccare

finish, fin′-ish, v., finire ; (cease) terminare. n., fine f. ; (goods) finitezza f.

fir, fĕr, n., abete m. ; — -cone, pigna f.

fire, fair, v., incendiare ; (shoot) tirare. n., fuoco m. ; (conflagration) incendio m.; — -alarm, allarme d'incendio m. ; — -brigade, corpo dei pompieri m. ; — -engine, pompa d'incendio f. ; — -escape, scala d'incendio f.; — -exit, uscita in caso d'incendio f.

firefly, fair′-flai, n., lucciola f.   [chista m.

fireman, fair′-man, n., pompiere m.; (stoker) fuofireplace, fair′-pleis, n., caminetto m.

fireplace, fair′-pleis, n., caminetto m.

fireproof, fair′-pruuf, a., a prova di fuoco

fireworks, fair′-uĕrks, n.pl., fuochi d'artificio m.pl.

firm, fĕrm, n., ditta f. a., solido ; risoluto

first, fĕrst, a., primo. adv., dapprima

firth, fĕrz, n., estuario m.

fish, fish, n., pesce m. v., pescare ; — -bone, n., spina di pesce f. ; — -hook, amo m.

fisherman, fish′-er-man, n., pescatore m.

fishing, fish′-ing, n., pesca f. ; — -rod, canna da pesca f.

fishmonger, fish′-mong-ga, n., pescivendolo m.

fissure, fish′-ur, n., fessura f.

fist, fist, n., pugno m.

fistula, fis′-tiu-la, n., fistola f.

fit, fit, n., convulsione f. a., conveniente. v., aggiustare ; (clothes) stare bene

fittings, fit′-ings, n.pl., accessori m.pl.

five, faiv, a., cinque

fix, fiks, v., fissare. n., (fig.) imbarazzo **m.**

fixture, fiks'-*chur*, n., infisso m.

flabby, flab'-i, a., flacido

flag, flagh, n., bandiera f. ; (flower) **giaggiolo m.**
v., imbandierare ; (languish) languire ; — **-ship,**
n., nave ammiraglia f. ; **—-staff,** albero di ban-

flagon, flag'-*on*, n., fiasco m.   [diera **m.**

flagrant°, flei'-*grant*, a., flagrante

flake, fleik, n., scaglia f. ; (snow) **fiocco m.**

flaky, flei'-ki, a., (pastry) frollo

flame, fleim, n., fiamma f.   v., fiammeggiare

flaming, flei'-ming, a., fiammeggiante

flange, flanch, n., orlo m. ; (wheel) flangia **f.**

flank, flangk, n., fianco m.   v., fiancheggiare

flannel, flan'-l, n., flanella f.

flap, flap, n., (table, etc.) ribalta f.; (pocket) **falda f.**
v., (wings) battere le ali

flare, fler, n., bagliore m.   v., fiammeggiare

flash, flash, v., lampeggiare. n., baleno m., **lam-**
po m. ; —**-light,** luce al magnesio f.

flashy, flash'-i, a., chiassoso

flask, flaask, n., fiaschetta f.

flat, flat, a.,° piano ; (market) debole ; (drink) **stantio.**
n., appartamento m. ; (music) bimmolle **m.**

flatten, flat'-n, v., livellare

flatter, flat'-*a*, v., adulare

flattering, flat'-*er*-ing, a., adulatorio

flattery, flat'-*er*-i, n., adulazione f.

flavour, flei'-*va*, v., condire. n., sapore m., **gusto m.**

flaw, floo, n., difetto m.

flax, flaks, n., lino m.

flea, flii, n., pulce f.

flee, flii, v., fuggire

fleece, fliis, n., vello **m.**   v., (fig.) spogliare

fleet, fliit, n., flotta f.   a., rapido, lesto

flesh, flesh, n., carne f.

flexible, fleks'-i-bl, a., flessibile

flicker, flik'-*a*, n., tremolio m.   v., tremolare

flight, flait, n., volo m.; fuga f.; (stairs) **gradinata f.**

flimsy, flim'-si, a., leggiero

finch, flinch, v., sbigottirsi

fling, flingh, v., scagliare

flint, flint, n., selce f. ; (fire) pietra focaia f.

flippant*, flip'-ant, a., petulante ; disinvolto

flirt, flĕrt, n., civetta f. v., civettare

float, flout, n., (raft) zattera f. ; (angler's) flotta-toio m. v., flottare ; (ship) galleggiare ; (a company, etc.) lanciare

flock, flok, n., (cattle) **gregge m.** ; (birds) stormo m. v., adunarsi

flog, flogh, v., sferzare

flood, flŏd, n., inondazione f. ; (tide) flusso m. v., inondare

floor, flor, n., pavimento m. ; (storey) **piano m.** v., pavimentare ; (fig.) atterrare

florid*, flor'-id, a., fiorito ; florido

florist, flor'-ist, n., fiorista m. & f.

floss, flos, n., bavella f.

flour, flaur, n., farina f.

flourish, flŏr'-ish, n., ostentazione f.; (trumpet) fan-fara f.; (pen) tratto di penna m. v., fiorire; prosperare ; brandire

flout, flaut, v., beffarsi

flow, flou, n., corrente f. ; (blood) **flusso m.** v., scorrere

flower, flau'-a, n., fiore m. v., fiorire

fluctuate, flŏk'-tiu-eit, v., fluttuare

flue, fluu, n., gola di camino f.

fluency, fluu'-en-si, n., correntezza f.

fluent*, fluu'-ent, a., corrente

fluffy, flŏf'-i, a., lanuginoso

fluid, fluu'-id, n., fluido m. a., fluido

fluke, fluuk, n., (chance) colpo di fortuna m.

flurry, flŏr'-i, n., trambusto m. v., agitare

flush, flŏsh, n., rossore m. v., (redden) arrossire; (rinse) lavar giù. a., a livello di

fluster, flŏs'-ta, n., agitazione f. v., perturbare

flute, fluut, n., (mus.) flauto m.

fluted, fluu'-tid, a., (grooved) scanalato

flutter, flŏt'-a, n., battito m. v., palpitare ; bat-tere le ali

fly, flai, v., volare ; (flag) flottare. n., mosca f.; — -leaf, foglio di guardia m. ; — -wheel, volante m.

foal, fool, n., puledro m. v., fogliare

foam, foum, n., schiuma f. v., schiumare

fob, fob, n., taschino d'orologio m.; **f.o.b. = free on board**, adv., franco a bordo

focus, fou′-kos, n., fuoco m. v., (optics) **centrare**; (camera) mettere in fuoco

fodder, fod′-a, n., foraggio m. v., foraggiare

foe, fou, n., nemico m.

fog, fogh, n., nebbia f.; **—-horn**, **corno da nebbia** m.

foggy, fo′-ghi, a., nebbioso

foil, foil, n., (fencing) fioretto m.; (metal) **foglia f.** v., sventare

foist, foist, v., spacciare; (fig.) insinuare

fold, fould, n., (clothes, etc.) piega f.; (sheep) **ovile m.** v., piegare; (arms) incrociare

foliage, fou′-li-ich, n., fogliame m.

folk, fouk, n., gente f.

follow, fol′-ou, v., seguire; (fig.) susseguire

follower, fol′-ou-a, n., seguace m.; (adorer) **adoratore** m.; (disciple) discepolo m.

folly, fol′-i, n., follia f.; (stupidity) **sciocchezza f.**

foment, fou-ment′, v., fomentare

fomentation, fou-men-tei′-shon, n., (med.) fomento m.

fond, fond, a.,° affettuoso; **to be — of**, v., **amare**

fondle, fon′-dl, v., carezzare

fondness, fond′-nes, n., tenerezza f.

font, font, n., fonte f.; fonte battesimale **m. & f.**

food, fuud, n., cibo m.; (beasts) foraggio **m.**

fool, fuul, n., sciocco m. v., gabbare

foolhardy, fuul′-haar-di, a., temerario

foolish°, fuul′-ish. a., sciocco

foot, fut, n., piede m.; **—-board**, **(train, cars,** etc.) predellino m.

football, fut′-bool, n., palla da calcio **f.;** (game) giuoco del calcio m.

footman, fut′-man, n., lacchè m.

footpath, fut′-paaZ, n., sentiero **m.;** (**pavement**) marciapiedi m.

footprint, fut′-print, n., impronta di piede **f.**

footstep, fut′-step, n., passo m.

footstool, fut'-stuul, n., posapiedi m.

fop, fop, n., zerbinotto m.

for, for, prep., per; durante. conj., poichè

forage, for'-ich, n., foraggio m. v., foraggiare

forbear, for-ber', v., tollerare; (refrain) astenersi

forbearance, for-ber'-ans, n., tolleranza f.

forbearing, for-ber'-ing, a., tollerante

forbid, for-bid', v., proibire; interdire

forbidding, for-bid'-ing, a., repulsivo

force, fors, n., forza f.; violenza f. v., forzare

forceful, fors'-ful, a., forte; determinato

forceps, for'-seps, n., forcipe m.

forcible, fors'-i-bl, a., violento

ford, ford, n., guado m. v., guadare

fore, for, a., anteriore. adv., anteriormente. n., davanti m.

forearm, for'-aarm, n., avambraccio m.

forebode, for-boud', v., presagire

foreboding, for-boud'-ing, n., presagio m.

forecast, for'-kaast, v., prevedere. n., (weather, etc.) previsione f.

forecastle, for'-kaas-l, n., castello di prua m.

foreclose, for-klous', v., operare un sequestro ipotecario

foredoom, for-duum', v., predestinare

forefathers, for'-faa-Ders, n. pl., antenati m. pl.

forefinger, for'-fing-ga, n., indice m.

forego, for-gou', v., rinunciare

foregoing, for-gou'-ing, a., precedente

foregone, for-gon', a., preconcetto

foreground, for'-graund, n., primo piano m.

forehead, for'-hed, n., fronte f.

foreign, for'-in, a., straniero

foreigner, for'-i-na, n., straniero m.

foreman, for'-man, n., capomastro m.; (jury) capo m.

foremost, for'-moust, a., primo; il più avanzato

forenamed, for'-neimd, a., sunnominato

forenoon, for'-nuun, n., mattinata f.

forerunner, for-rŏn'-a, n., precursore m.

foresee, for-sii', v., prevedere

foresight, for'-sait, n., previdenza f.

forest, for'-est, n., foresta f.

forestall, for-stool', v., prevenire

forester, for'-es-ta, n., guardaboschi m.

foretaste, for'-teist, n., pregustazione f.

foretell, for-tel', v., predire

forethought, for'-Zoot, n., previdenza f.; pre-meditazione f.

forewarn, for-uoorn', v., avvertire

forfeit, for'-fit, v., perdere. n., multa f.; confisca f.

forge, forch, n., fucina f. v., fucinare; (falsify) fal-

forger, forch'-a, n., falsario m. [sificare

forgery, forch'-er-i, n., falsificazione f.

forget, for-ghet', v., dimenticare; —me-not, n., (flower) miosotide f.

forgetful, for-ghet'-ful, a., dimentico

forgetfulness, for-ghet'-ful-nes, n.,dimenticanza f.

forgive, for-ghiv', v., perdonare

forgiveness, for-ghiv'-nes, n., perdono m.

fork, foork, n., forchetta f.; (road) biforcazione f. v., biforcarsi

forlorn, for-loorn', a., abbandonato; disperato

form, foorm, n., (shape) forma f.; (manners) ma-niera f.; (seat) banco m.; (a form to fill up) for-mulario m.;(class) classe f. v., formare; formarsi

formal*, foor'-mal, a., formale; cerimonioso

formality, foorm-al'-i-ti, n., formalità f.

formation, foor-mei'-shon, n., formazione f.

former, foor'-ma, a., antico; primo, quegli

formerly, foor'-mer-li, adv., una volta [quello

forsake, for-seik', v., abbandonare

forswear, for-suer', v., abiurare

fort, fort, n., forte m.

forth, forZ, adv., avanti; fuori

forthcoming, forZ-kŏm'-ing, a., prossimo

forthwith, forZ'-uiD, adv., immediatamente

fortieth, foor'-ti-iZ, n., quarantesimo

fortification, for-ti-fi-kei'-shon, n., fortificazione

fortify, foor'-ti-fai, v., fortificare; rinforzare [f.

fortitude, foor'-ti-tiuud, n., forza d'animo f.

fortnight, fort'-nait, n., quindicina f.

fortress, for'-tres, n., fortezza f.

fortuitous*, foor-tiuu'-i-tos, a., fortuito

fortunate*, foor'-tiu-net, a., fortunato

fortune, foor'-tiun, n., fortuna f. ; (luck) sorte f.

forty, foor'-ti, a., quaranta

forward, foor'-uard, adv., avanti. v., spedire

forwardness, foor'-uard-nes, n., precocità f. ; (pertness) arditezza f.

fossil, fos'-l, n., fossile m.

foster, fost'-a, v., nutrire ;   incoraggiare ; — -**parents,** n. pl., genitori adottivi m. pl.

foul, faul, a., basso ; sporco ; osceno. v., intorbidire ; (ship) urtare

found, faund, v., fondare ; (metal) fondere

foundation, faun-dei'-shon, n., fondamento m. ; fondazione f.

founder, faun'-da, n., fondatore m. ; (metal) fonditore m.

foundling, faund'-ling, n., trovatello m.

foundry, faun'-dri, n., fonderia f.

fountain, faun'-tin, n., fontana f. ; — -**pen,** penna

four, for, a., quattro   [stilografica f.

fourfold, for'-fould, a., quadruplo

fourteen, for'-tiin, a., quattordici

fourth, forZ, n., il quarto m.

fourthly, forZ'-li, adv., in quarto luogo

fowl, faul, n., pollo m. ; (poultry) pollame m.

fox, foks, n., volpe f. ; — -**terrier,** cane volpino m.

foxglove, foks'-ghlöv, n., digitale f.

fraction, frak'-shon, n., frammento m. ; (mathematical) frazione f.

fracture, frak'-chur, n., frattura f. v., fratturare

fragile, frach'-il, a., fragile

fragment, fragh'-ment, n., frammento m.

fragrance, frei'-grans, n., fragranza f.

fragrant°, frei'-grant, a., fragrante

frail, freil, a., fragile ; (health) debole

frame, freim, n., struttura f. ; (picture) cornice f. v., incorniciare

framework, freim'-uĕrk, n., armatura f. ; (pannelling, etc.) intelaiatura f.

franchise, fran'-chais, n., franchigia f.

frank, frangk, a., franco

frankness, frangk'-nes, n., franchezza f.

frantic, fran'-tik, a., frenetico

fraternal*, fra-těr′-nal, a., fraterno

fraud, frood, n., frode f.

fraudulent°, froo′-diu-lent, a., fraudolento

fray, frei, v., logorarsi. n., (scuffle) rissa f.

freak, friik, n., ghiribizzo m.

freakish, friik′-ish, a., bizzarro [gini

freckle, frek′-l, n., lentiggine f. v., coprirsi di lentig-

free, frii, v., liberare. a.,* libero ; gratis ; — **trade**, n., libero scambio m.

freedom, frii′-dom, n., libertà f.

freemason, frii′-mei-son, n., frammassone m.

freeze, friis, v., gelare ; congelare

freezing, frii′-sing, n., gelo m. ; congelazione f. a., ghiacciato

freight, freit, n., carico m.; (cost) nolo m. v., no-

frenzy, fren′-si, n., frenesia f. [leggiare

frequency, frii′-kuen-si, n., frequenza f.

frequent°, frii′-kuent, a., frequente

frequent°, fri-kuent′, v., frequentare

fresh*, fresh, a., fresco

freshness, fresh′-nes, n., freschezza f.

fret, fret, v., agitarsi ; — **-saw**, n., sega da tra- foro f. ; — **-work**, lavoro di traforo m.

fretful*, fret′-ful, a., irrequieto

friar*, frai′-a, n., frate m.

friary, frai′-er-i, n., confraternità f.

friction, frik′-shon, n., attrito m.; (massage) frizione f.

Friday, frai′-di, n., venerdì m.

friend, frend, n., amico m.; —**liness**, amicizia f.; —**ly**, a., amico ; amichevole ; —**ship**, n., amicizia f.

fright, frait, n., spavento m.; —**en**, v., spaventare

frightful*, frait′-ful, a., pauroso, spaventevole

frigid°, frich′-id, a., frigido ; (fig.) glaciale

frill, fril, n., trina f. v., increspare

fringe, frinch, n., frangia f. ; (edge) orlo m. v., frangiare ; orlare

frisky, frisk′-i, a., vivace ; (horse) focoso

fritter, frit′-a, n., (sweet) frittella f. ; — **away**, v., sciupare

frivolous°, friv′-ol-os, a., frivolo

frizzle, friz′-l, v., arricciare ; (cook) friggere

fro, frou, **to and —**, adv., avanti ed indietro, quà e là

frock, frok, n., veste f. ; (monk's) veste talare f.

frog, frogh, n., rana f. ; (small) ranocchia f.

frolic, frol'-ik, n., scherzo m. ; capestreria f. v., saltellare

from, from, prep., da, per, da parte di, secondo

front, front, n., davanti m. ; fronte f. ; (building) facciata f. ; in —, davanti

frontier, fron'-tir, n., frontiera f.

frost, frost, n., gelo m. ; — **bitten**, a., congelato

frosty, fros'-ti, a., glaciale

froth, froZ, n., spuma f. v., schiumare

frown, fraun, n., cipiglio m. v., aggrottar le ciglia

frugal*, fruu'-gol, a., frugale

fruit, fruut, n., frutto m.

fruiterer, fruu'-ter-a, n., fruttivendolo m.

fruitful, fruut'-ful, a., fruttuoso ; fruttifero ; fertile

fruition, fru-ish'-on, n., godimento m.

fruitless*, fruut'-les, a., sterile ; (fig.) infruttuoso

frustrate, fros-treit', v., sventare

fry, frai, v., friggere

fuchsia, fiuu'-shi-a, n., fucsia f.

fuel, fiu'-el, n., combustibile m.

fugitive, fiuu'-chi-tiv, n., fuggiasco **m.**

fugue, fiuugh, n., fuga f.

fulcrum, fŏl'-krom, n., fulcro m.

fulfil, ful-fil', v., compiere

fulfilment, ful-fil'-ment, n., compimento **m.** ; (duties, etc.) adempimento m.

full, ful, a., pieno

fulness, ful'-nes, n., pienezza f. ; abbondanza f.

fulsome, ful'-som, a., disgustoso ; servile

fume, fiuum, n., vapore m. v., (rage) fumare

fumigate, fiu'-mi-geit, v., affumicare

fun, fŏn, n., divertimento m. ; (joke) scherzo m.

function, fŏngk'-shon, n., funzione f. v., funzionare

functionary, fŏngk'-shon-a-ri, n., funzionario m.

fund, fŏnd, n., fondo m. ; —**s**, pl., capitale m.

fundamental*, fŏnd-a-men'-tl, a., fondamentale

funeral, fiuu'-ner-al, n., funerale m.

funnel, fŏn'-l, n., imbuto m. ; (engine, steamer) ciminiera f.

funny, fŏn'-i, a., divertente ; (person) buffo

fur, fĕr, n., pelliccia f.

furbish, fĕr'-bish, v., forbire

furious*, fiuu'-ri-os, a., furioso

furlong, fĕr'-long, n., stadio m.

furlough, fĕr'-lou, n., licenza f.　[forno m.

furnace, fĕr'-nis, n., fornace f.; blast --, alto

furnish, fĕr'-nish, v., ammobiliare ; fornire

furniture, fĕr'-ni-chur, n., mobilia f.

furrier, far'-i-a, n., pellicciaio m.

furrow, far'-ou, n., solco m. v., solcare

further, fĕr'-Da, a., più lontano ; altro.　adv., di
più ; al di là.　v., avanzare ; promuovere

furtherance, fĕr'-Der-ans, n., avanzamento m.

furtive*, fĕr'-tiv, a., furtivo

fury, fiu'-ri, n., furia f.

fuse, fiuus, n., (slow match) miccia f.; (time) spoletta f.; (electric) valvola f.　v., fondersi

fuss, fŏs, n., scalpore m.　v., far cerimonie

fustian, fŏs'-tian, n., fustagno m.

fustiness, fŏs'-ti-nes, n., odore di muffa m.

fusty, fŏs'-ti, a., muffito

futile, fiuu'-tail, a., futile

future, fiuu'-chur, n., futuro m.　a., futuro

gable, ghei'-bl, n., frontone m.

gadfly, gad'-flai, n., tafano m.

gaff, gaf, n., rampone m.; (naut.) gaffa f.

gag, gagh, n., bavaglio m.; (stage) improvvisazione f.
v., imbavagliare ; (stage) improvvisare

gaiety, ghe'-i-ti, n., gaiezza f.

gaily, ghei'-li, adv., gaiamente

gain, ghein, n., guadagno m.　v., (win) guadagnare ;
(obtain) ottenere ; (watch) avanzare

gait, gheit, n., andatura f.; passo m.

gaiter, ghei'-ta, n., ghetta f.

galaxy, gal'-ak-si, n., (astronomical) galassia f.;
(assembly) riunione di persone f.

gale, gheil, n., burrasca f.

gall, gool, n., (bile) bile f.; (nut) galla f.　v., irritare

gallant*, gal'-ant, a., galante ; (heroic) prode

gallantry, gal'-ant-ri, n., (courage) prodezza f.;
(manners) galanteria f.

gallery, gal'-_er_-i, n., loggione m.; (mine) **galleria** f.

galling, gool'-ing, a., crucciante

gallon, gal'-_on_, n., gallone m.

gallop, gal'-_op_, n., galoppo m. v., **galoppare**

gallows, gal'-_ous_, n. pl., patibolo m.

galore, ga-lor', adv., in abbondanza

galoshes, ga-losh'-_os_, n. pl., galosce f. pl.

galvanism, gal'-van-i_sm_, n., galvanismo m.

gamble, gam'-bl, v., giuocare

gambler, gam'-bla, n., giuocatore m.; giuocatrice f.

gambol, gam'-bl, n., salto m. v., sgambettare

game, gheim, n., giuoco m.; (animals) selvaggina f.;
—**keeper,** guardia caccia m.

gaming-house, ghei'-ming-_haus_, n., bisca f.

gammon, gam'-_on_, n., prosciutto m.; (humbug) chiacchiere f. pl.

gamut, gam'-_ut_, n., gamma f.

gander, gan'-da, n., oca maschio m.

gang, gangh, n., squadra f.; (robbers, etc.) banda f.

gangway, gangh'-_uei_, n., (passage) corridoio m.;
(ship's) passerella di sbarco f.

gaol, cheil, n., carcere m.

gap, gap, n., spaccatura f.; breccia f.

gape, gheip, v., guardare colla bocca aperta;
(open) spalancare

garage, ga-rash', n., rimessa d'automobile f.

garb, gaarb, n., abbigliamento m.

garbage, gaarb'-ich, n., rifiuti m. pl.

garden, gaar'-dn, n., giardino m.; (kitchen) orto m.

gardener, gaard'-na, n., giardiniere m.

gardening, gaard'-ning, n., giardinaggio m.

gargle, gaar'-gol, n., gargarismo m. v., gargarizzare

garish, ghe'-rish, a., vistoso

garland, gaar'-_land_, n., ghirlanda f. v., inghirlandare

garlic, gaar'-lik, n., aglio m.

garment, gaar'-_ment_, n., abito m.

garnish, gaar'-nish, n., guarnizione f. v., **guarnire**

garret, gar'-_et_, n., soffitta f.

garrison, gar'-i-_son_, n., guarnigione f.

garrulity, ga-riuu'-li-ti, n., garrulità f.

garrulous, gar'-iu-_los_, a., garrulo

garter, gaar'-_ta_, n., giarrettiera f.

gas, gas, n., gas m.: — **-burner**, becco di gas m.; — **-meter**, contatore a gas m.; — **works**, pl., officina del gas f.

gaseous, ghei'-si-os, a., gassoso

gash, gash, n., sfregio m. v., sfregiare

gasp, gaasp, n., anelito m. v., ansimare

gastric, gas'-trik, a., gastrico

gate, gheit, n., cancello m.

gather, gaD'-a, v., raccogliere; (people) riunirsi

gathering, gaD'-er-ing,n.,riunione f.; (med.) ascesso

gaudy, goo'-di, a., sfarzoso [m.

gauge, gheich, n., (size) misura f.; (tool) calibro m.; (rails) scartamento m. v., misurare; calibrare; (fig.) stimare

gaunt, goont, a., smunto

gauntlet, goont'-let, n., guanto lungo m.; (challenge) guanto di sfida m.

gauze, goos, n., garza f.; (wire) rete metallica f.

gawky, goo'-ki, a., goffo

gay, ghei, a., gaio [fisso m.

gaze, gheis, v., guardare fissamente. n., sguardo

gazelle, ga-sel', n., gazzella f.

gazette, ga-set', n., gazzetta f.; (official) giornale ufficiale m. v., pubblicare nella gazzetta ufficiale

gear, ghir, n., (mech.) ingranaggio m.; — **-box**, scatola dei cambi f.

gelatine, chel'-a-tin, n., gelatina f.

gelding, ghel'-ding, n., cavallo castrato m.

gem, chem, n., gemma f.

gender, chen'-da, n., genere m. [rale

general,chen'-er-al,n.,(officer) generale m. a.,gene-

generalize, chen'-er-a-lais, v., generalizzare

generally, chen'-er-a-li, adv., generalmente

generate, chen'-er-eit, v., generare

generation, chen'-er-ei-shon, n., generazione f.; produzione f.

generosity, chen-er-os'-i-ti, n., generosità f.

generous°, chen'-er-os, a., generoso

genial°, chii'-ni-al, a., (kindly) geniale

genitive, chen'-i-tiv, n., genitivo m.

genius, chii'-ni-os, n., genio m.

genteel, chen-tiil', a., distinto

Gentile, chen'-tail, n., gentile m.

gentility, chen-til'-i-ti, n., gentilezza f.

gentle, chen'-tl, a., gentile, amabile

gentleman, chen'-tl-man, n., gentiluomo m.

gentleness, chen'-tl-nes, n., gentilezza f.

gently, chent'-li, adv., gentilmente, quietamente

genuine, chen'-iu-in, a., genuino

genuineness, chen'-iu-in-nes, n., genuinità f.; pu- [rità f.

geography, chi-ogh'-ra-fi, n., geografia f.

geology, chi-ol'-o-chi, n., geologia f.

geometry, chi-om'-e-tri, n., geometria f.

geranium, chi-rei'-ni-om, n., geranio m.

germ, cherm, n., germe m.

germinate, cher'-mi-neit, v., germinare

gesticulate, ches-tik'-iu-leit, v., gesticolare

gesture, ches'-chur, n., gesto m.

get, ghet, v.,(obtain) procurare, ottenere ; (earn) gua- dagnare ; (fetch) andare a prendere ; (induce) in- durre ; (reach) giungere ; (become) diventare ; — **back,** (receive back) ricuperare ; — **down,** (fetch) calare ; (descend) discendere ; — **in,** far entrare ; (step in) entrare ; — **off,** (alight) scen- dere da ; (free) liberarsi ; — **on,** salire su ; (progress) progredire ; — **out,** sortire ; pubbli- care ; — **up,** levarsi

geyser, ghii'-sa, n., stufa a gas f.

ghastly, gaast'-li, a., orrido ; (pale) lugubre

gherkin, gher'-kin, n., cetrolino m.

ghost, goust, n., spettro m.

ghostly, goust'-li, a., spettrale

giant, chai'-ant, n., gigante m.

giantess, chai'-ant-es, n., donna gigante f.

gibberish, ghib'-er-ish, n., linguaggio sconnesso m.

gibbet, chib'-et, n., patibolo m.

gibe, chaib, n., scherno m. v., burlarsi

giblets, chib'-lets, n. pl., frattaglie f. pl.

giddiness, ghid'-i-nes, n., vertigine f.

giddy, ghid-i, a., stordito ; vertiginoso

gift, ghift, n., dono m.

gifted, ghif'-tid, a., dotato

gigantic, chai-gan'-tik, a., gigantesco [damente

giggle, ghigh'-l, n., riso stupido m. v., ridere stupi-

gild, ghild, v., dorare ; —ing, n., doratura f.

gills, ghils, n. pl., branchie f. pl.

gilt, ghilt, a., dorato. n., doratura f.

gimlet, ghim'-let. n., succhiello m.

gin, chin, n., ginepro m. ; (snare) trappola f.

ginger, chin'-cha. n., zenzero m. ; —bread, pan pepato m.

gipsy, chip'-si, n., zingaro m. a., zingaresco

giraffe, chi-raaf', n., giraffa f.

gird, ghërd, v., cingere ; (horse) cinghiare ; (mock) motteggiare

girder, ghër'-da, n., trave f.

girdle, ghër'-dl, n., cintura f. v., cinturare

girl, ghërl, n., ragazza f. ; fanciulla f.

girlhood, ghërl'-hud, n., adolescenza f.

girth, ghërZ, n., (belly-band) cinghia f. ; (circumference) contorno m.

gist, chist, n., punto principale m.

give, ghiv, v., dare ; (present) donare ; —back, restituire ; —in, cedere ; —up, rinunciare a ; abbandonare

giver, ghiv'-a, n., donatore m.

gizzard, ghis'-erd, n., ventriglio d'uccello m.

glacier, glas'-si-a, n., ghiacciaio m.

glad°, ghlad, a., lieto ; contento

gladden, ghlad'-n, v., allietare

glade, ghleid, n., radura f.

glance, ghlaans, n., occhiata f. ; —at, v., mirare ; —off, deviare

gland, ghland, n., glandola f.

glanders, ghlan'-ders, n. pl., (horse) morva f.

glare, ghler, n., bagliore m. ; (stare) sguardo feroce m. v., abbagliare ; (stare) guardare fissamente

glaring°, ghler'-ing, a., abbagliante ; manifesto

glass, ghlaas, n., vetro m. ; (mirror) specchio m. ; (tumbler) bicchiere m. ; —es, (spectacles) occhiali m.pl. ; —ware, vetrerie f.pl. ; —works, vetreria f. ; —y, a., vitreo ; (smooth) cristallino

glaze, ghleis, n., smaltatura f. v., smaltare

glazier, ghlei'-sha, n., vetraio m.

gleam, ghliim, n., barlume m. ; (ray) raggio m. v., luccicare ; brillare

glean, ghliin, v., spigolare

gleaner, ghliin'-*a*, n., spigolatore m.

glee, ghlii, n., gioia f.

glen, ghlen, n., valletta f.

glib², ghlib, a., sciolto

glide, ghlaid, v., scivolare ; planare

glider, ghlai'-*da*, n., (aircraft) velivolo m.

glimmer, ghlim'-*a*, n., luccicore m. v., rischiarare debolmente

glimpse, ghlimps, n., occhiata f. v., dare un'occhiata

glint, ghlint, n., scintillio m. v., scintillare

glisten, ghlis'-n, v., brillare ; rilucere

glitter, ghlit'-*a*, n., sfavillio m. v., sfavillare

gloat, ghlout, v., covare cogli occhi ; godersi di

globe, ghloub, n., globo m. : (sphere) sfera f.

globular, ghloub'-iu-*la*, a., sferico

gloom, ghluum, n., oscurità f.; (dismal) tristezza f.

gloomy, ghluu'-mi, a., oscuro ; (person) triste

glorify, ghlo'-ri-fai, v., glorificare

glorious², ghlo'-ri-*os*, a., glorioso ; magnifico

glory, ghlo'-ri, n., gloria f. ; — in, v., gloriarsi di

gloss, ghlos, n., lustro m. ; — over, v., lustrare

glossy, ghlos'-i, a., lucente

glove, ghlóv, n., guanto m.

glover, ghlóv'-*a*, n., guantaio m.   [rossire

glow, ghlou, n., ardore m.; bagliore m. v., ardere ; ar-

glue, ghluu, n., colla forte f. v., incollare

glum, ghlóm, a., cupo

glut, ghlót, n., (market) pletora f. v., innondare

glutton, ghlót'-n, n., ghiottone m.

gnarled, naarld, a., nodoso

gnash, nash, v., digrignare

gnashing, nash'-ing, n., (teeth) digrignamento m.

gnat, nat, n., zanzara f.

gnaw, noo, v., rodere

go, gou, v., andare ; — away, andare via ; (journey) partire ; — back, ritornare , — down, discendere ; (sink) affondare ; — for, andare a prendere ; (attack) lanciarsi contro ; — off, (depart) partire ; (abscond) scappare ; (guns, etc.) sparare ; — out, uscire ; estinguirsi ; — up, salire ; — without, far a meno di

goad, goud, n., pungolo m. v., pungolare

goal, goul, n., (football) porta f. ; (object) **meta f.**

goat, gout, n., capra f. ; **he— —**, caprone m., becco m.

gobble, gob'-l, v., trangugiare

gobbler, gob'-la, n., (person) goloso m.

goblet, gob'-let, n., coppa f.

goblin, gob'-lin, n., folletto m.

God, god, n., Dio m. ; **—child**, figlioccio m. ; **—father**, padrino m. ; **— —fearing**, a., timoroso di Dio ; **—less**, empio ; **—liness**, n., pietà f. ; **—ly**, a., pietoso ; **—mother**, n., madrina f. ; **—send**, fortuna inattesa f.

god, god, n., idolo m.

goddess, god'-es, n., dea f.

goggle-eyed, gogh'-ol-aid, a., occhi protuberanti

goggles, gogh'-ols, n. pl., occhiali da neve m. pl.

goitre, goi'-ta, n., gozzo m.

gold, gould, n., oro m. ; **—en**, a., d'oro ; **—finch**, n., cardellino m. ; **—fish**, orata f. ; **— —leaf**, foglio d'oro m. ; **—smith**, orefice m.

golf, golf, n., golf m.

golfer, golf'-a, n., giuocatore di golf m.

golf-links, golf'-lingks, n. pl., campo di golf m.

gong, gongh, n., gong m.

gonorrhœa, gon-o-ri'-a, n., gonorrea f.

good, gud, a., buono. adv., bene. n., bene m. ; (use) vantaggio m. ; **— —bye!** interj., arrivederci ! addio ! **—morning!** **—day!** **—afternoon!** = buon giorno ! **—evening!** buona sera ! **—night!** buona notte !

Good Friday, gud frai'-di, n., venerdì santo m.

good-natured, gud-nei'-churd, a., buono

goodness, gud'-nes, n., bontà f.

goods, gudṣ, n. pl., merci f. pl.

good-will, gud'-uil, n., buona volontà f. ; (business) clientela f., buona uscita f.

goose, guuṣ, n., oca f.

gooseberry, guuṣ'-be-ri, n., ribes m.

gore, gor, n., (blood) sangue congelato **m.** v., ferire colle corna

gorge, goorch, n., (ravine) gola f. v., (feed) satollare

gorgeous*, goor'-chos, a., magnifico ; sontuoso

gorilla, go-ril′-*a*, n., gorilla m.

gorse, goors, n., ginestra f.

gosling, gos′-ling, n., oca giovine f.

gospel, gos′-pl, n., vangelo m.

gossamer, gos′-*a-ma*, n., filo della Madonna m.

gossip, gos′-ip, v., ciarlare. n., ciarla f.; (person) ciar- gouge, gauch, v., scalpellare; strappare   [lona f.

gout, gaut, n., gotta f.; —**y**, a., gottoso

govern, gŏv′-*ern*, v., governare

governess, gŏv′-*ern*-es, n., governante f.

government, gŏv′-*ern*-ment, n., governo m.

governor, gŏv′-*ern*-*a*, n., (province) governatore m.; (bank, etc.) direttore generale m.; (mech.) regolatore m.

gown, gaun, n., veste f., sottana f.; (official) toga f.

grab, grab, v., impugnare. n., strappo m.; (mech.) braccio di presa m.

grace, greis, n., grazia f.; —**ful***, a., grazioso; —**fulness**, n., graziosità f.; —**less**, a., sgarbato

gracious*, grei′-shos, a., grazioso

gradation, gra-dei′-shon, n., gradazione f.

grade, greid, n., grado m.; rango m. v., graduare

gradient, grei′-di-ent, n., china f.

gradual*, grad′-iu-*al*, a., graduale

graduate, grad′-iu-eit, v., (intervals, spacing) graduare; (university) laurearsi. n., laureato m.

graft, graaft, n., innesto m.; (fig.) corruzione f. v., innestare

grain, grein, n., (cereal, measure) grano m.; (sand) granellino m.; (wood) vena f.; (paint) venatura f. v., dar la venatura

grammar, gram′-*a*, n., grammatica f.

granary, gran′-*a*-ri, n., granaio m.

grand*, grand, a., grande ; —**child**, n., nipotino m.; —**daughter**, nipotina f.; —**father**, nonno m.; —**mother**, nonna f.; —**son**, nipotino m.

grange, greinch, n., masseria f.

grant, graant, n., concessione f.; (gift) dono m. v., accordare

grape, greip, n., uva f.; —**fruit**, pompeimo m.; — -**shot**, mitraglia f.; — -**sugar**, zucchero d'uva m.

grapple, grap'-l, n., (hook) grappino m. v., **aggrappare** ; — **with**, (fig.) maneggiare

grasp, graasp, n., stretta f. v., afferrare ; (mentally) comprendere ; —**ing**, a., avido

grass, graas, n., erba f. ; (lawn) radura verde f.

grasshopper, graas'-hop-*a*, n., cavalletta f.

grassy, grass'-i, a., erboso

grate, greit, v., grattugiare ; (brakes, wheels, etc.) stridere. n., griglia f. ; — **upon**, v., stridere

gnateful*, greit'-ful, a., grato, riconoscente

gratefulness, greit'-ful-nes, n., gratitudine f.

gratification, grat-i-fi-kei'-shon, n., gratificazione f.

gratify, grat'-i-fai, v., gratificare

gratifying, grat'-i-fai-ing, a., gradevole

grating, grei'-ting, n., griglia f. a., (noise) lacerante

gratis, grei'-tis, adv., gratis

gratitude, grat'-i-tiuud, n., gratitudine f.

gratuitous*, gra-tiuu'-i-tos, a., gratuito ; (unwarranted) senza provocazione

gratuity, gra-tiuu'-i-ti, n., gratificazione f. ; (tip) mancia f.

grave, greiv, n., fossa f. a.,* grave, serio ; — -**digger**, n., becchino m. ; — -**stone**, lapide f. ; — -**yard**, cimitero m., campo santo m.

gravel, grav'-l, n., ghiaia f.

gravitate, grav'-i-teit, v., gravitare

gravity, grav'-i-ti, n., gravità f.

gravy, grei'-vi, n., sugo m.

gray, grei, a., grigio

graze, greis, v., (feed) pascere ; (slight rub) rasentare

grease, griis, n., grasso m. v., ungere

greasy*, grii'-si,a.,grasso, unto ; (road)sdrucciolevole

great*, greit, a., grande, grandioso ; (renowned) celebre, rinomato

greatness, greit'-nes, n., grandezza f.

greed, griid, n., ingordigia f. ; (avarice) avidità f. ; —**ily**, adv., ingordamente ; avidamente ; —**iness**, n., ingordigia f. ; avidità f. ; —**y**, a., ingordo ; avido

green, griin, n., verde m. a., verde. v., verdeggiare

greengage, griin'-gheich, n., susina f.

greengrocer, griin'-grou-s*a*, n., erbivendolo m.

greenhouse, griin'-haus, n., serra f.

greenish, griin'-ish, a., verdastro

greens, griin*s*, n. pl., erbaggi m. pl.

greet, griit, v., salutare; **—ing**, n., saluto m.

grenade, gre-neid', n., granata f.

grey, grei, a., grigio

greyhound, grei'-haund, n., levriere m.

grief, griif, n., dolore m.

grievance, grii'-*vans*, n., motivo di lagnanza **m.**

grieve, griiv, v., addolorare; (vex) vessare

grievous*, grii'-*vos*, a., penoso; grave

grill, gril, n., graticola f. v., arrostire

grim*, grim, a., orribile; (fierce) brutto, feroce

grimace, gri-meis', n., smorfia f.

grime, graim, n., (dirt) sudiciume m.; (soot) nero m.

grin, grin, n., smorfia f. v., ridere sardonicamente

grind, graind, v., tritare, macinare; (sharpen) affilare

grinder, grain'-*da*, n., affilatore m.; (cereals) mulino m.; (coffee, pepper, etc.) macinino **m.**

grip, grip, n., stretta f. v., stringere

gripe, graip, v., dare male di ventre

gripes, graips, n. pl., male di ventre **m.**

grisly, gris'-li, a., orribile

grist, grist, n., grano da macinare m.

grit, grit, n., granello di terra m.; **—ty**, a., sabbioso

groan, groun, n., gemito m. v., gemere

groats, grouts, n. pl., tritello di avena m.

grocer, grou'-*sa*, n., biadaiuolo m.

grocery, grou'-*sa*-ri, n., derrate coloniali f. pl.; **— store**, magazzino di derrate coloniali m.

grog, grogh, n., ponce m.

groggy, grogh'-i, a., barcollante

groin, groin, n., inguine m.; (arch) sesto **m.**

groom, gruum, n., stalliere m.

groove, gruuv, n., scanalatura f. v., scanalare

grope, group, v., brancolare

gross, grous, a.,* (thick, coarse) grossolano; (naut.) lordo. n., (12 dozen) grossa f.; **— weight**, peso lordo m.

ground, graund, v., (naut.) arenare. n., suolo m.; **—-floor**, pianterreno m.; **—work**, fondamento m.

groundless*, graund'-les, a., infondato

grounds, graunds, n. pl., (park) terre f. pl.

group, gruup, n., gruppo m. v., aggruppare

grouse, graus, n., francolino m. v., (fig.) brontolare

grovel, grov'-l, v., strisciare

grow, grou, v., crescere ; coltivare ; —n up, a., adulto

grower, grou'-a, n., coltivatore m.

growl, graul, n., brontolio m. v., ringhiare

growth, grouZn, n., tumore m.; (increase) aumento m.

grub, gröb, n., bruco m.

grudge, gröch, n., rancore m. v., invidiare ; dar a malincuore

gruel, gruu'-el, n., minestra d'avena f.

gruesome, gruu'-som, a., orripilante

gruff, gröf, a., arcigno

grumble, gröm'-bl, v., borbottare, mormorare

grumbler, gröm'-bla, n., brontolone m.

grunt, grönt, v., grugnire. n., grugnito m.

guarantee, ga-ran-tii', n., garanzia f.; (bail) cauzione f. v., garantire

guard, gaard, n., guardia f.; (railway) capo treno m.; (machine) misura di sicurezza f. ; (corps) guardia f. v., sorvegliare ; proteggere

guarded, gaar'-did, a., circospetto

guardian, gaar'-di-an, n., guardiano m.; (trustee) tutore m.

guess, ghes, v., indovinare

guesswork, ghes'-uërk, n., supposizione f.

guest, ghest, n., ospite m.; invitato m.

guidance, gai'-dens, n., guida f.

guide, gaid, v., guidare. n., guida f.

guild, ghild, n., corporazione f.   [genuo

guile, gail, n., astuzia f.; artificio m.; —less, a., in-

guilt, ghilt, n., colpa f.; —y, a., colpevole

guinea, ghin'-i, n., ghinea f.; —-fowl, faraona f.; —-pig, porco d'India m.

guise, gais, n., guisa f.

guitar, ghi'-taar, n., chitarra f.

gulf, gölf, n., golfo m.; abisso m.

gull, göl, n., gabbiano m. v., (fig.) ingannare

gullet, göl'-et, n., esofago m.

gulp, gölp, v., inghiottire. n., tranguciata f.

gum, göm, v., ingommare. n., gomma f.

gums, gŏm**s**, n. pl., (teeth) gengive f. pl.

gun, gŏn, n., fucile m.; (cannon) cannone m.;
— —**powder,** polvere da cannone f.

gunner, gŏn'-a, n., cannoniere m.

gunsmith, gŏn'-smiZ, n., armaiuolo m.

gurgle, ghĕr'-gol, v., gorgogliare. n., gorgoglio m.

gush, gŏsh, n., getto m. v., sgorgare

gust, gŏst, n., raffica f.

gut, gŏt, n., budello m.

gutter, gŏt'-a, n., rigagnolo m.; (roof) grondaia f.

guy, gai, n., (effigy) fantoccio m.

gymnasium, chim-nei'-si-om, n., palestra f.

gymnastics, chim-na**s**'-tiks, n.pl., ginnastica f.

gypsy, chip'-si, n., zingaro m.

N.B.—La lettera " H " deve sempre aspirarsi
distintamente salvo in alcune parole marcate §.

haberdasher, hab'-er-dash-a, n., merciaio m.

habit, hab'-it, n., abitudine f.; abito m.

habitable, hab'-it-a-bl, a., abitabile

habitual,§ ha-bit'-iu-al, a., abituale

hack, hak, v., sminuzzare. n., cavallo da nolo m.

hackneyed, hak'-nid, a., banale

haddock, had'-ok, n., baccalà m.

hag, hagh, n., furia f.

haggard§, hagh'-ard, a., sparuto

haggle, hagh'-l, v., stiracchiare

hail, heil, n., (frozen rain) grandine f. v., salutare;
(call) chiamare. interj., salve! salute!

hair, her, n., capello m.; — —**brush,** spazzola da
capelli f.; — —**dresser,** parrucchiere m.;
— —**pin,** forcina per capelli f.

hairy, he'-ri, a., peloso; capelluto

hake, heik, n., specie di merluzzo f.

hale, heil, a., robusto; (healthy) sano

half, haaf, n., metà f. a., mezzo

halibut, hal'-i-bŏt, n., passera f.

hall, hool, n., sala f.; (entry) vestibolo m.; — —**mark,**
marchio di saggio m.; — —**porter,** portiere m.

hallow, hal'-ou, v., santificare [f.

hallucination, ha-liu-si-nei'-shon, n., allucinazione

halo, hei′-lou, n., aureola f. ; (moon, etc.) alone m.

halt, hoolt, n., fermata f. v., **fermare, fermarsi.** interj., alt ! ferma !

halter, hool′-ta, n., cavezza f.

halve, haav, v., dimezzare

ham, ham, n., prosciutto m.

hamlet, ham′-let, n., borgo m.

hammer, ham′-a, n., martello m. v., **martellare**

hammock, ham′-ok, n., amaca f.

hamper, ham′-pa, n., cesta f. v., imbarazzare

hand, hand, n., mano f.; (clock) lancetta f. v., dare, rimettere; — -**bag,** n., sacco a mano m. ; — -**bill,** foglio di pubblicità m.; — -**book,** manuale m. ; — -**cuff,** manette f. pl. ; —**ful,** manata f.; — -**made,** a., fatto a mano ; — -**rail,** n., guidamano m.

handkerchief, hang′-ker-chiif, n., fazzoletto m.

handle, han′-dl, n., manico m.; (knob) maniglia f. v., maneggiare

handsome*, han′-som, a., bello

handy, han′-di, a., comodo ; (near by) sotto mano ; (able) destro

hang, hangh, v., (strangle) impiccare ; — **up,** appendere

hangar, hangh′-er, n., rimessa f. [dere

hangman, hangh′-man, n., boia m.

hanker, hang′-ka, v., bramare

happen, hap′-n, v., avvenire, accadere

happily, hap′-i-li, adv., felicemente

happiness, hap′-i-nes, n., felicità f.

happy, hap′-i, a., contento ; (joyful) felice

harangue, ha-rangh′, n., arringa f. v., arringare

harass, har′-as, v., tormentare

harbinger, haar′-bin-cha, n., foriero m.

harbour, haar′-ba, n., (naut.) porto m.; (shelter) rifugio m. v., albergare

hard, haard, a., duro ; difficile ; (character) aspro

harden, haar′-den, v., indurire

hardihood, haard′-i-hud, n., arditezza f.; vigore m.

hardly, haard′-li, adv., appena

hardness, haard′-nes, n., durezza f.

hardship, haard′-ship, n., (affliction) privazione f.; (injury) pena f. ; (exertion) strapazzo m.

hardware, haard'-uer, n., chincaglieria f.
hardy, haar'-di, a., vigoroso ; intrepido
hare, her, n., lepre f. ; — -**lip**, labbro leporino m.
harlequin, haar'-li-kuin, n., arlecchino m.
harlot, haar'-lot, n., puttana f.
harm, haarm, n., male m. v., far torto ; —**ful***, a., dannoso, nocivo ; —**less***, innocuo
harmonious, haar-mou'-ni-os, a., armonioso
harmonize, haar'-mon-ais, v., armonizzare
harness, haar'-nes, n., equipaggiamento m. ; (animal) bardatura f. v., bardare ; (to a cart) attaccare ; (forces) utilizzare
harp, haarp, n., arpa f.
harpoon, haar-puun', n., fiocina f. v., ramponare
harrow, har'-ou, n., erpice m. v., erpicare ; (feelings) tormentare
harsh, haarsh, a., aspro ; (colour) stridente
hart, haart, n., cervo con ramificazioni m.
harvest, haar'-vest, n., raccolto m. v., raccogliere
hash, hash, n., carne tritata f. ; (chaos) pasticcio m.
hassock, has'-sok, n., inginocchiatoio m.
haste, heist, n., fretta f.
hasten, hei'-sn, v., affrettare
hastily, heis'-ti-li, adv., affrettatamente
hat, hat, n., cappello m.; —-**box**, scatola da cappelli f. ; —-**brush**, spazzola da cappelli f. ; —-**pin**, spillo da cappello m. ; —-**stand**, porta cappelli m. ; —**ter**, cappellaio m.
hatch, hach, v., covare. n., (naut.) boccaporto m.
hatchet, hach'-et, n., accetta f.
hate, heit, n., odio m. v., odiare
hateful*, heit'-ful, a., odioso
hatred, hei'-tred, n., odio m.
haughtiness, hoo'-ti-nes, n., alterigia f.
haughty, hoo'-ti, a., altiero ; superbo
haul, hool, v., tirare ; (tow, drag) rimorchiare. n., tirata f. ; (catch) retata f.
haunch, hoonch, n., anca f. ; (meat) coscia f.
haunt, hoont, v., perseguitare ; (frequent) importunare. n., ritrovo m. ; (animals) tana f.
have, hav. v., avere ; (cause) fare
haven, hei'-vn, n., porto m. ; (fig.) rifugio m.

haversack, hav'-er-sak. n., bisaccia f.

havoc, hav'-ok, n., guasto m.; rovina f.

hawk, hook, n., falco m. v., rivendere al minuto

hawker, hoo'-ka, n., rivenditore ambulante m.

hawthorn, hoo'-zoorn, n., biancospino m.

hay, hei, n., fieno m.; — **fever**, febbre del fieno f.; — **-loft**, fienile m.; — **-making**, falciatura del fieno f.; — **-rick**, mucchio di fieno m.

hazard, haz'-erd, n., caso m.; rischio m. v., azzardare; —**ous°**, a., azzardoso

haze, heis, n., bruma f.

hazel, hei'-sl, n., nocciuolo m. a., nocciuola, castagno; — **-nut**, n., nocciuola f.

hazy, hei'-si, a., brumoso; (mental) fosco

he, hii, pron., egli, lui, colui, quegli, quello

head, hed, n., testa f. capo m.; (main) principale m., centrale m.; (chief) capo m.; (forefront) testa f.; — **-ache**, male di testa m.; — **-ing**, titolo m.; — **-lamp**, (motor's) faro m.; — **-land**, promontorio m.; — **-long**, adv., a capofitto; — **-master**, n., direttore di scuola m.; — **-quarters**, pl., sede principale f.; (mil.) quartiere generale m.; — **-strong**, a., testardo; — **-waiter**, n., capo cameriere m.; — **-way**, progresso m.

heady, hed'-i, a., inebriante

heal, hiil, v., guarire, sanare; — **ing**, a., curativo. n., guarigione f.

health, helZ, n., salute f.; — **-y**, a., sano, salutare

heap, hiip, n., mucchio m. v., ammucchiare

hear, hir, v., sentire, udire; — **er**, n., uditore m.; — **ing**, (sense) udito m.; (court) udienza f.

hearsay, hir'-sei, n., diceria f., sentito dire m.

hearse, hĕrs, n., carro funebre m.

heart, haart, n., cuore m.; (vegetable) centro m.; (cards) cuori m.pl.; — **-broken**, a., desolato; — **-burn**, n., acidezza di stomaco f.; — **-ily**, adv., cordialmente; di gusto; — **-less**, a., senza cuore

hearth, haarZ, n., focolare m.

heat, hiit, n., calore m. v., scaldare

heater, hiit'-a. n., calorifero m.

heating, hiit'-ing. n., riscaldamento m.

heath, hiiZ, n., landa f.

heathen, hii'-Den, n., pagano m.

heather, heD'-a, n., erica f.

heave, hiiv, v., alzare ; (naut.) trarre ; (naut.) mettersi in panna ; (sigh) trarre un sospiro

heaven, hev'-n, n., cielo m.

heavenly, hev'-n-li, a., celestiale, celestino

heaviness, hev'-i-nes, n., pesantezza f.

heavy, hev'-i, a., pesante

hedge, hech, n., siepe f. ; **—hog,** riccio m.

heed, hiid, v., dar retta a, far attenzione a. n., attenzione f.; **—ful,** a., attento ; vigilante ; **—less,** disattento ; incurante

heel, hiil, n., calcagno m. ; (shoe) tacco m.

hefty, hef'-ti, a., forte

heifer, hef'-a, n., giovenca f.

height, hait, n., altura f.

heighten, hai'-ten, v., rialzare ; (fig.) esaltare

heinous°, hei'-nos, a., odioso

§ **heir,** er, n., erede m. ; **—ess,** erede f.

§ **heirloom,** er'-lüm, n., eredità familiare f.

hell, hel, n., inferno m. ; **—ish,** a., infernale [m.

helm, helm, n., (wheel) timone m.;**—sman,** timoniere

helmet, hel'-met, n., elmetto m.

help, help, n., aiuto m. interj., aiuto ! v., aiutare ; servire ; (stand by) in soccorso

helper, hel'-pa, n., aiutante m.

helpful, help'-ful, a., utile

helpless, help'-les, a., impotente

hem, hem, n., orlo m. v., orlare ; **—in,** cingere

hemisphere, hem'-is-fir, n., emisfero m.

hemlock, hem'-lok, n., cicuta f.

hemorrhage, he'-mor-ech, n., emorragia f.

hemp, hemp, n., canapa f.

hen, hen, n., gallina f. ; (female bird) femmina f. ; **—roost,** posatoio m.

hence, hens, adv., di qua, di qui, di là ; (thus) così, per cui, quindi

henceforth, hens'-forZ, adv., d'ora innanzi

her, hër, pron., lei ; le ; suo, sua, suoi, sue

heraldry, her'-al-dri, n., araldica f.

herb, hërb, n., erba f.

herbalist, hër'-bal-ist, n., erborista m. & f.

herd, hĕrd, n., gregge m., mandria f., armento m. v., attruppare

herdsman, hĕrds'-man, n., mandriano m.

here, hir, adv., qui, qua, di qua ; —**about**, qui presso ; —**after**, n., altra vita f. adv., in avvenire ; —**by**, con ciò ; colla presente ; —**in**, incluso, accluso ; —**of**, di questo, di cui :—**on**, a questo proposito, su ciò ; —**to**, a ciò, a cui ; —**tofore**, precedentemente ; —**upon**, su ciò ; quindi ; —**with**, qui accluso, colla presente

hereditary, hi-red'-i-ta-ri, a., ereditario

heresy, her'-i-si, n., eresia f.

heretic, her'-i-tik, n., eretico m.

hermetic(al), her-met'-ik(al), a., ermetico

hermit, hĕr'-mit, n., eremita m. & f.

hermitage, hĕr'-mit-ich, n., eremitaggio m.

hernia, hĕr'-nia, n., ernia f.

hero, hi'-rou, n., eroe m. ; —**ic**, a., eroico

heroine, hi'-ro-in, n., eroina f.

heroism, hi'-ro-izm, n., eroismo m.

herring, her'-ing, n., aringa f.

hers, hĕrs, pron., il suo, la sua, i suoi, le sue, di lei

herself, hĕr-self', pron., ella stessa, lei medesima

hesitate, hes'-i-teit, v., esitare

hesitation, hes-i-tei'-shon, n., esitazione f.

hew, hiuu, v., spaccare

hiccough, hik'-op, n., singulto m.

hide, haid, n., pelle f.; cuoio m. v., nascondere

hideous*, hid'-i-os, a., orrendo ; odioso

hiding, hai'-ding, n., (beating) percosse f. pl. ; —**place**, nascondiglio m.

high, hai, a., alto ; (food) frollo ; —**est**, altissimo ; il più alto ; —**lander**, n., montanaro m.

highness, hai'-nes, n., Altezza f.

highway, hai'-uei, n., strada nazionale f.

hilarity, hi-lar'-i-ti, n., ilarità f.

hill, hil, n., collina f. ; (road) salita f.

hilly, hil'-i, a., collinoso

hilt, hilt, n., impugnatura f.

him, him, pron., lo, lui, gli, quello, quegli

himself, him-self', pron., egli stesso, lui medesimo

hind, haind, a., posteriore n., (deer) cerva f.

hinder, hin'-d*a*, v., impedire

hindermost, hain'-*der*-m*o*ust, a., ultimo   [m.

hindrance, hin'-dr*a*ns, n., ostacolo m., impedimento

hinge, hinch, n., cerniera f., ganghero m., cardine m.

hint, hint, n., cenno m. v., accennare

hip, hip, n., anca f.

hire, hair, v., noleggiare. n., nolo m.

his, his, pron., suo, sua, suoi, sue

hiss, his, v., sibilare. n., sibilo m.

historian, his-tou'-ri-*a*n, n., storico m.

historic(al), his-tor'-ik(*a*l), a., storico

history, his'-to-ri, n., storia f.

hit, hit, n., colpo m. v., colpire

hitch, hich, n., (obstacle) intoppo m.; (naut.) nodo m.
  v., (pull up) tirare su ; (hook on, etc.) attaccare

hither, hiD'-*a*, adv., qua ; —**to,** finora

hive, haiv, n., alveare m.

hoar, hor, a., bianco ; — **-frost,** n., brina f. [m.

hoard, hoord, v., accumulare. n., cumulo m., tesoro

hoarding, hoord'-ing, n., (enclosure) steccato m.

hoarse*, hors, a., rauco

hoary, hor'-i, a., grigio, bianco

hoax, houks, n., burla f. v., mistificare

hobble, hob'-l, v., zoppicare

hobby, ..ob'-i, n., passatempo favorito m.

hock, hok, n., vino del Reno m.; (leg) garretto m.

hoe, hou, n., zappa f. v., zappare

hog, hogh, n., maiale m., porco m.

hogshead, hogs'-hed, n., botte f.   [cello m.

hoist, hoist, v., alzare ; (flags) issare. n., (mech.) verri-

hold, hould, n., presa f.; (power) potere m. ;
  (ship) stiva f. v., tenere ; (contain) contenere ; (possess) possedere ; — **back,** trattenere ; —**er,** n.,
  presa f.; (receptacle) recipiente m., ricettacolo m.;
  (owner) possessore m., titolare m. ; — **good,** v.,
  essere buono, essere valido ; —**ing,** (tenure) podere m.; (share) partecipazione f. ; — **on,** v., tener
  fermo ; — **over,** posporre

hole, houl, n., buco m.

holiday, hol'-i-dei, n., giorno di riposo m. ; (bank
  holiday) giorno festivo m.

holidays, hol'-i-deis, n. pl., vacanze f. pl.

holiness, hol'-i-nes, n., santità f.

hollow, hol'-ou, n., buco m. **a.**, **vuoto**; (sound) sordo. v., scavare

holly, hol'-i, n., agrifoglio m.

holy, hou'-li, a., santo; — **water, n., acqua** santa f.; — **week,** settimana santa f.

homage, hom'-ich, n., omaggio m.

home, houm. n., (abode) casa f.; (family) focolaio domestico m.; (homeland) patria f.; **at —, in** casa; —**less,** a., senza tetto; —**ly,** intimo, casalingo, familiare; (to be) —**sick,** (essere) nostalgico; —**ward,** adv., verso casa, di ritorno; —**ward bound,** di ritorno

homœopathic, hou-mi-o-paZ'-ik, a., omeopatico

hone, houn, n., pietra da affilare f. v., affilare

§ **honest°**, on'-est, a., onesto, probo

§ **honesty**, on'-est-i, n., onestà f.

honey, hŏn'-i, n., miele m.; —**moon, luna di** miele f.; —**suckle,** caprifoglio m.

§ **honorary**, on'-or-a-ri, a., onorario

§ **honour**, on'-er, n., onore m. v., onorare

§ **honourable**, on'-er-a-bl, a., onorevole; (upright) giusto

hood, hud, n., cappuccio m.; (motor) cappotta f.

hoodwink, hud'-uingk, v., (fig.) accalappiare

hoof, huf, n., zoccolo m.

hook, huk, n., gancio m.; (fishing) amo m. v., agganciare; (catch) prendere all'amo; —**s and eyes,** n. pl., ganci ed occhielli m. pl.

hoop, hup, n., cerchio m.

hoot, huut, n., (owl) ululo m. v., ululare; (motor horn) suonare la tromba; — at, (hiss) dar la baia

hop, hop, n., (jump) balzo m.; (plant) luppolo m. v., (jump) saltellare ; (frisk) saltare ; (gather) raccogliere luppoli

hope, houp, n., speranza f. v., sperare

hopeful, houp'-ful, a., pieno di speranze

hopeless°, houp'-les, a., disperato ; senza **speranza**

horizon, ho-rai'-son, n., orizzonte m.

horizontal, ho-ri-son'-tal, a., orizzontale

horn, hoorn, n., corno m.; (motor) tromba f.

hornet, hoor'-net, n., calabrone m.

horrible, hor'-i-bl, a., orrido

horrid°, hor'-id, a., orrendo

horrify, hor'-i-fai, v., spaventare

horror, hor'-or, n., orrore m.

horse, hoors, n., cavallo m.; (clothes) cavalletto m.;   **—back** (on), adv., a cavallo;   **—hair,** n., crine di cavallo m.;   **—man,** cavaliere m.;   **—power,** cavalli vapore m.pl.;   cavalli di forza m.pl.;**—radish,** ramolaccio m.; **—shoe,** ferro da cavallo m.

hose, hoos, n., (stockings) calza f.; (socks) calzettino m.; (rubber tube) tubo di gomma m.

hosier, hou'-sher, n., bottega di maglierie f.

hosiery, hou'-sher-i, n., maglierie f.pl.

hospitable, hos'-pi-ta-bl, a., ospitale

hospital, hos'-pi-tl, n., ospedale m.

host, houst, n., oste m.; (social) ospite **m.;** (army) oste f.; (eccl.) ostia f.

hostage, hos'-tech, n., ostaggio m.

hostelry, hos'-tel-ri, n., osteria f.

hostess, hous'-tes, n., ostessa f.; (social) ospite f.

hostile, hos'-tail, a., ostile

hot°, hot, a., caldo; (condiment) **piccante**

hotel, ho-tel', n., albergo m.

hothouse, hot'-haus, n., serra f.   [tare

hound, haund, n., cane da caccia m.   v., persegui-

§ hour, auer, n., ora f.; **—ly,** adv., di ora in ora

house, haus, n., casa f.;   **—agent,** agente di case m.;   **—hold,** famiglia f. a., domestico;   **—keeper,** n., governante f.; massaia f.;**—maid,** domestica f.;   **— of Commons,** Camera di Comuni f.

hovel, hov'-l, n., tugurio m., casupola f.

hover, hov'-a, v., volteggiare, sorvolare

how, hau, adv., come;   **—ever,** conj., tuttavia;   **— far** ? quanto lontano ?   **—much** ? quanto ? quanta ?   **— many** ? quanti ? quante ?

howl, haul, n., guaito m.   v., guaire

hub, höb, n., mozzo m.; (fig.) centro **m.**

huddle, höd'-l, v., raggomitolare

hue, hiuu, n., colore m.; (shade) tinta f.   [zione **m.**

hue and cry, hiuu and krai, n., grido di riprova-

hug, hŏgh, v., abbracciare

huge, hiuch, a., enorme, immenso

hulk, hŏlk, n., (naut.) ossatura f.

hull, hŏl, n., (naut.) scafo m.

hum, hŏm, n., ronzio m. v., ronzare; (voice, etc.) cantarellare

human*, hiuu'-man, a., umano

humane*, hiu-mein', a., umano

humanity, hiu-man'-i-ti, n., umanità f.

humble, hŏm'-bl, a., umile. v., umiliare

humidity, hiu-mid'-i-ti, n., umidità f.

humiliate, hiu-mil'-i-eit, v., umiliare

humiliation, hiu-mi-li-ei'-shon, n., umiliazione f.

humorous, hiuu'-mer-os, a., umoristico; spiritoso

humour, hiuu'-ma, n., (temper) umore m.; (wit) spirito m. v., compiacere

hunch, hŏnch, n., gobba f.

hunchback, hŏnch'-bak, n., gobbo m.

hundred, hŏn'-dred, a., cento; —th, centesimo. n., centesimo m.; —weight, mezzo quintale m.

hunger, hŏn'-ga, n., fame f. v., affamare

hungry, hŏn'-gri, a., affamato

hunt, hŏnt, n., caccia f. v., cacciare

hunter, hŏn'-ta, n., cacciatore m.

hurdle, hŏr'-dl, n., siepe f.; ostacolo m.

hurl, hĕrl, v., scagliare

hurricane, hŏr'-i-kan, n., uragano m.

hurry, hŏr'-i, n., fretta f. v., affrettare

hurt, hĕrt, v., far torto; (pain) far male. n., male m.; (feelings) torto m.

hurtful*, hĕrt'-ful, a., nocivo; offensivo

husband, hŏs'-band, n., marito m., sposo m.

hush! hŏsh, interj., zitto! —up, v., mettere a tacere

husk, hŏsk, n., guaina f., guscio m., baccello m. v., sbucciare

husky, hŏs'-ki, a., (voice) rauco

hustle, hŏs'-l, v., affrettarsi; (jostle) urtare, spingere

hut, hŏt, n., capanna f.

hutch, hŏch, n., (rabbit) conigliera f.

hyacinth, hai'-a-sinZ, n., giacinto m.

hydrant, hai'-drant, n., idrante m.

hydraulic, hai-drou'-lik, a., idraulico

hydro, hai'-dro. **—gen,** n., idrogeno m.; **—pathic,** istituto idropatico m.; **—phobia,** idrofobia f.; **—plane,** idroplano m.

hygienic, hai-chi-en'-ik, a., igienico

hymn, him, n., inno m.

hyphen, hai'-fen, n., lineetta f.

hypocrisy, hi-po'-kri-si, n., ipocrisia f.

hypocrite, hip-o-krit', n., ipocrita m. & f.

hysterical, his-ter'-i-kal, a., isterico

I, ai, pron., io

ice, ais, n., ghiaccio m.; **—berg,** montagna di ghiaccio f.; **—bound,** a., serrato dal ghiaccio; **—-cream,** n., gelato m.

icicle, ais'-i-kl, n., ghiacciuolo m.

icy, ais'-i, a., diaccio

idea, ai-dii'-a, n., idea f.

ideal, ai-dii'-al, n., ideale m. a., ideale

idealize, ai-dii'-a-lais, v., idealizzare

identical*, ai-den'-ti-kl, a., identico

identify, ai-den'-ti-fai, v., identificare

identity, ai-den'-ti-ti, n., identità f.

idiom, id'-i-om, n., idiotismo m.

idiot, id'-i-ot, n., idiota m. & f.

idiotic, id-i-ot'-ik, a., idiota

idle, ai'-dl, a., pigro; ozioso; inattivo; (fig.) inutile. v., oziare; **—ness,** n., ozio m.

idler, aid'-la, n., poltrone m., bighellone m.

idol, ai'-dol, n., idolo m.; **—ize,** v., idolatrare

idyll, ai'-dil, n., idillio m.; **—ic,** a., idillico

if, if, conj., se; **even —,** persino se

ignite, igh-nait', v., accendere; infiammarsi

ignition, igh-ni'-shon, n., accensione f.

ignoble, igh-nou'-bl, a., ignobile; (mean) meschino

ignominious, igh-no-min'-i-os, a., ignominioso

ignominy, igh'-no-min-i, n., ignominia f.

ignorance, igh'-nor-ans, n., ignoranza f.

ignore, igh-nor', v., ignorare

ill, il, a., malato; **—ness,** n., malattia f.; **to be —,** v., essere ammalato; (sick) star male

illegal*, il-lii'-gal, a., illegale

illegible, il-lech'-i-bl, a., illeggibile

illegitimate*, il-lech-it'-i-met, a., illegittimo

illiterate, il-li'-těr-et, a., illetterato

illogical*, il-loch'-i-kl, a., illogico

illuminate*, il-liuu'-mi-neit, v., illuminare [f.

illumination, il-liuu-mi-nei'-shon, n., illuminazione

illusion, il-liuu'-shon, n., illusione f.

illusory, il-liuu'-so-ri, a., illusorio

illustrate, il'-lus-treit, v., illustrare

illustration, il-lus-trei'-shon, n., illustrazione f.

illustrious*, il-lŏs'-tri-os, a., illustre

image, im'-ich, n., immagine f. [f.

imagination, i-mach-in-ei'-shon, n., immaginazione

imagine, i-mach'-in, v., immaginarsi

imbecile, im'-bi-sail, n., imbecille m. & f.

imbibe, im-baib', v., imbevere; (absorb) **assorbire**

imbue, im-biuu', v., imbevere

imitate, im'-i-teit, v., imitare

immaculate*, im-mak'-lu-let, a., immacolato

immaterial*, im-ma-tii'-ri-al, a., immateriale

immature, im-ma-tiur', a., immaturo

immeasurable, im-mesh'-u-ra-bl, a., smisurato

immediate*, im-mii'-di-et, a., immediato

immense*, im-mens', a., immenso

immensity, im-mens'-i-ti, n., immensità f.

immerse, im-měrs', v., immergere

immigrant, im'-mi-grant, n., immigrante m. & f.

immigrate, im'-mi-greit, v., immigrare

imminent, im'-mi-nent, a., imminente

immoderate, im-mod'-er-et, a., immoderato

immodest*, im-mod'-ist, a., immodesto; **indecente**

immoral*, im-mor'-al, a., immorale

immortal*, im-moor'-tal, a., immortale

immortalize, im-moor'-tal-ais, v., immortalare

immovable*, im-muu'-va-bl, a., immobile

immune, im-miuun', a., immune

immunity, im-miuu'-ni-ti, n., immunità f.

immure, im-miur', v., rinchiudere

imp, imp, n., folletto m.; (little rascal) demonietto m.

impact, im'-pakt, n., impatto m.; scontro m.

impair, im-per', v., deteriorare, guastare; diminuire

impale, im-peil', v., impalare

impart, im-paart', v., impartire; **comunicare**

impartial*, im-paar'-shal, a., imparziale   [cabile
impassable, im-pass'-a-bl, a., impassabile, imprati-
impassive, im-pas'-iv, a., impassibile
impatience, im-pei'-shens, n., impazienza f.
impatient, im-pei'-shent, a., impaziente
impeach, im-piich', v., accusare; attaccare
impeachment, im-piich'-ment, n., accusa f.
impecunious, im-pi-kiuu'-ni-os, a., senza denari
impede, im-piid', v., impedire
impediment, im-ped'-i-ment, n., impedimento m.
impel, im-pel', v., impellere
impending, im-pen'-ding, a., imminente
imperative, im-per'-a-tiv, n.,(gram.)imperativo m.
    a., imperativo; (urgent) pressante
imperfect, im-per'-fekt, n., imperfetto m. a.,* im-
    perfetto; (defective) difettoso
imperfection, im-per-fek'-shon, n., imperfezione f.
imperial*, im-pi'-ri-al, a., imperiale
imperil, im-per'-il, v., arrischiare
imperishable, im-per'-i-sha-bl, a., imperituro
impersonate, im-per'-son-eit, v., personificare;
    impersonare
impertinence, im-per'-ti-nens, n., impertinenza f.
impertinent*, im-per'-ti-nent, a., impertinente
impervious, im-per'-vi-os, a., impervio
impetuous*, im-pet'-iu-os, a., impetuoso
impetus, im'-pi-tos, n., impeto m.
impiety, im-pai'-et-i, n., empietà f.
impious*, im'-pi-os, a., empio
implant, im-plaant', v., impiantare; (fig.) inculcare
implement, im'-pli-ment, n., attrezzo m.
implicate, im'-pli-keit, v., implicare
implicit*, im-plis'-it, a., implicito
implore, im-plor', v., implorare
imply, im-plai', v., implicare; (suggest) insinuare
impolite*, im-po-lait', a., scortese
import, im'-port, v., importare. n., importazione f.;
    — duty, tassa d'importazione f.; — er, impor-
    tatore m.
importance, im-por'-tans, n., importanza f.
important, im-por'-tant, a., importante
importune, im-por-tiuun', v., importunare

impose, im-pous', v., imporre ; — **upon,** abusare di

imposing, im-pous'-ing. a., imponente

imposition, im-po-si'-shon, n., imposizione f.

impossibility, im-pos-i-bil'-i-ti, n., impossibilità f.

impossible, im-pos'-i-bl, a., impossibile

impostor, im-pos'-ta, n., impostore m.

impotent, im'-po-tent, a., impotente

impound, im-paund', v., porre sotto **sequestro** provvisorio

impoverish, im-pov'-er-ish, v., impoverire

impracticable, im-prak'-ti-ka-bl, a., impraticabile

imprecation, im-pri-kei'-shon, n., imprecazione f.

impregnable, im-pregh'-na-bl, a., inespugnabile

impregnate, im-pregh'-neit, v., impregnare

impress, im-pres', v., imprimere. n., impressione f.; impronta f. ; —**ion,** impressione f.

impressive, im-pres'-iv, a., impressionante

imprint, im-print', n., stampato m.; impronta f.; frontespizio m. v., stampare

imprison, im-pris'-n, v., imprigionare [mento m.

imprisonment, im-pris'-n-ment, n., imprigiona-

improbable, im-prob'-a-bl, a., improbabile

improper, im-prop'-a, a., improprio ; sconveniente

impropriety, im-pro-prai'-i-ti, n., sconvenienza f.

improve, im-pruuv', v., migliorare ; abbellire

improvement, im-pruuv'-ment, n., miglioramento

improvident, im-prov'-i-dent, a.,imprevidente [m.

imprudent*, im-prud'-dent, a., imprudente

impudence, im'-piu-dens, n., impudenza f.

impudent, im'-piu-dent, a., impudente

impulse, im'-pöls, n., impulso m.

impure, im-piur', a., impuro ; (morally) impudico

impurity, im-piu'-ri-ti, n., impurità f.

impute, im-piuut', v., imputare

in, in, prep., a. adv., dentro

inability, in-a-bil'-i-ti, n., inabilità f.

inaccessible, in-ak-ses'-i-bl, a., inaccessibile

inaccuracy, in-ak'-iu-ra-si, n., inesattezza f.

inaccurate*, in-ak'-iu-ret, a., erroneo, poco **esatto**

inadequate*, in-ad'-i-kuet, a., inadeguato

inadvertent*, in-ad-vėr'-tent, a., disattento

inane, i-nein', a., vano ; futile

inanimate, i-nan'-i-met, a., inanimato
inapt, i-napt', a., improprio; disadatto
inasmuch, i-nas-mŏch', conj., per quanto ; **poichè**
inaudible, i-noo'-di-bl, a., inaudibile
inaugurate, i-noo'-ghiu-reit, v., inaugurare
inborn, **inbred**, in'-boorn, in'-bred, a., innato ;
   congenito
incalculable, in-kal'-kiu-la-bl, a., incalcolabile
incapable, in-kei'-pa-bl, a., incapace
incapacitate, in-ka-pas'-i-teit, v., inabilitare
incapacity, in-ka-pas'-i-ti, n., incapacità f.
incarnation, in-kar-nei'-shon, n., incarnazione f.
incautious*, in-koo'-shos, a., incauto
incense, in'-sens, n., incenso m.
incense, in-sens', v., irritare ; (incite) provocare
incentive, in-sen'-tiv, n., incentivo m.
incessant*, in-ses'-ant, a., incessante
inch, inch, n., pollice m.
incident, in-si-dent', n., incidente m.
incidental*, in-si-den'-tal, a., fortuito
incision, in-si'-shon, n., incisione f.
incite, in-sait', v., incitare
incivility, in-si-vil'-i-ti, n., inciviltà f.
inclination, in-kli-nei'-shon, n., inclinazione f.
incline, in-klain', n., (slope) pendio m. v., **incli-**
   nare ; inclinarsi
include, in-kluud', v., includere
inclusive, in-kluu'-siv, a., incluso
incoherent, in-ko-hi'-rent, a., incoerente
income, in'-kom, n., rendita f. ; — **-tax**, imposta
   sul reddito f.
incoming, in'-kŏm-ing, a., in arrivo ; (new) entrante
incommode, in-kom-oud', v., incomodare
incommodious, in-kom-ou'-di-os, a., incomodo
incomparable, in-kom'-pa-ra-bl, a., incomparabile
incompatible, in-kom-pat'-i-bl, a., incompatibile
incompetent, in-kom'-pi-tent, a., incompetente
incomplete*, in-kom-pliit', a., incompleto
incomprehensible, in-kom-pri-hen'-si-bl, a., incomprensibile
inconceivable, in-kon-sii'-va-bl, a., inconcepibile
inconclusive*, in-kon-kluu'-siv, a., inconcludente

incongruous, in-kong'-gru-*os*, a., incongruo   [bile
inconsiderable, in-kon-si'-dĕr-*a*-bl, a., inconsidera-
inconsiderate, in-kon-si'-dĕr-*et*, a., senza riguardo,
   sconsiderato
inconsistent, in-kon-sis'-*tent*, a., inconsistente
inconsolable, in-kon-sol'-*a*-bl, a., inconsolabile
inconstant*, in-kon'-stant, a., incostante
inconvenience, in-kon-vii'-ni-ens, v., dare incomodo, incomodare. n., sconvenienza f.
inconvenient, in-kon-vii'-ni-ent, a., sconveniente,
   incomodo
incorporate, in-kor'-po-reit, v., incorporare
incorrect*, in-ko-rekt', a., scorretto, erroneo
incorrigible, in-kor'-i-chi-bl, a., incorreggibile
increase, in-kriis', v., aumentare. n., aumento m
incredible, in-kred'-i-bl, a., incredibile
incredulous, in-kred'-iu-lus, a., incredulo
incriminate, in-krim'-i-neit, v., incriminare
inculcate, in-kŏl'-keit, v., inculcare
incumbent (on), in-kŏm'-bent, a., **dovere di**
incur, in-kĕr', v., incorrere
incurable, in-kiu'-ra-bl, a., incurabile   [gato
indebted, in-det'-id, a., indebitato ; (obliged) obbli-
indecent, in-dii'-sent, a., indecente
indecision, in-di-si'-shon, n., indecisione f.
indecisive*, in-di-sai'-siv, a., indeciso
indecorous, in-di-kou'-ros, a., indecoroso
indeed, in-diid', adv., in vero, davvero, realmente,
   in verità
indefatigable, in-di-fat'-i-ga-bl, a., infaticabile
indefensible, in-di-fen'-si-bl, a., insostenibile ; senza
indefinite, in-def'-i-nit, a., indefinito   [scuse
indelible, in-del'-i-bl, a., indelibile
indelicate, in-del'-i-keit, a., indelicato
indemnify, in-dem'-ni-fai, v., indennizzare
indemnity, in-dem'-ni-ti, n., indennità f.
independence, in-di-pen'-dens, n., indipendenza f.
independent, in-di-pen'-dent, a., indipendente
indescribable, in-di-skrai'-ba-bl, a., indescrivibile
indestructible, in-di-strŏk'-ti-bl, a., indistruttibile
index, in'-deks, n., indice m. v., rubricare
index-finger, in-deks-fing'-ga, n., indice m.

India-rubber, in-di-a-rŏb′-a, n., gomma f.
indicate, in′-di-keit, v., indicare. mostrare
indication, in-di-kei′-shon, n., indicazione f.
indicator, in′-di-kei-ta, n., indicatore m.
indict, in-dait′, v., accusare, denunziare
indifference, in-dif′-er-ens, n., indifferenza f.
indifferent°, in-dif′-er-ent, a., indifferente
indigestible, in-di-ches′-ti-bl, a., indigeribile
indigestion, in-di-ches′-tion. n., indigestione f.
indignant°, in-digh′-nant, a., indignato, sdegnato
indignity, in-digh′-ni-ti, n., indegnità f.
indigo, in′-di-go, n., indaco m.
indirect°, in-di-rekt′, a., indiretto
indiscreet°, in-dis-kriit′, a., indiscreto
indiscriminate, in-di-vid′-krim′-i-net, a., senza distin-
    zione, a caso ; —ly, adv., indistintamente, a caso
indispensable, in-dis-pen′-sa-bl, a., indispensabile
indisposed, in-dis-pousd′, a., indisposto
indisposition, in-dis-pou-sish′-on,n.,indisposizione
indisputable, in-dis-piu′-ta-bl, a., indiscutibile [f.
indistinct°, in-dis-tingkt′, a., indistinto ; confuso
indistinguishable, in-dis-ting-gui′-sha-bl, a., in-
    distinguibile
indite, in-dait′, v., redigere [viduo m.
individual, in-di-vid′-iu-al, a., individuale. n.,indi-
indolent°, in′-do-lent, a., indolente
indoors, in-doors′, adv., in casa
induce, in-diuus′, v., indurre
inducement, in-diuus′-ment, n., stimolo m.
indulge, in-dŏlch′, v., indulgere, abbandonarsi
indulgent°, in-dŏl′-chent, a., indulgente, benevolo
industrial, in-dos′-tri-al, a., industriale
industrious°, in-dos′-tri-os, a.,industrioso, diligente
industry, in′-dos-tri, n., industria f.
inebriated, in-ii′-bri-ei-tid, a., inebbriato
ineffective, in-ef-ek′-tiv, a., inefficace, vano
inefficient, in-ef-fish′-ent, a., inefficace ; (per-
    son) incapace
inept, i-nept′, a., inetto ; (stupid) assurdo
inequality, in-i-kuŏl′-i-ti, n., ineguaglianza f.; disu-
inert, in-ërt′, a., inerte [guaglianza f.
inestimable, in-es′-ti-ma-bl, a., inestimabile

inevitable, in-ev′-i-ta-bl, a., inevitabile
inexact, in-egh-ᴢakt′, a., inesatto
inexcusable, in-eks-kiuu′-ᴢa-bl, a., imperdonabile
inexhaustible, in-egh-ᴢoos′-ti-bl, a., inesauribile
inexpedient*, in-eks-pii′-di-ent, a., inopportuno
inexpensive*, in-eks-pen′-siv, a., economico, poco costoso
inexperience, in-eks-pi′-ri-ens, n., inesperienza f.:
  —d, a., inesperto, senza esperienza
inexplicable, in-eks′-pli-ka-bl, a., inesplicabile
inexpressible, in-eks-pres′-si-bl, a., inesprimibile
infallible, in-fal′-i-bl, a., infallibile
infamous*, in′-fa-mos, a., infame
infamy, in′-fa-mi, n., infamia f., bassezza f.
infancy, in′-fan-si, n., infanzia f.
infant, in′-fant, n., infante m., bambino m.:
  (law) minorenne m. & f.
infantry, in′-fan-tri, n., fanteria f.
infatuation, in-fat-iu-ei′-shon, n., esaltazione f.;
  (pop.) cotta f.
infect, in-fekt′, v., infettare
infectious, in-fek′-shos, a., contagioso, infettivo
infer, in-fĕr′, v., arguire, inferire
inference, in′-fĕr-ens, n., deduzione f., conclusione f.
inferior*, in-fi′-ri-or, a., inferiore
infernal, in-fĕr′-nal, a., infernale
infest, in-fest′, v., infestare; (molest) molestare
infidel, in′-fi-del, a., infedele. n., infedele m.
infinite*, in′-fi-nit, a., infinito
infirm, in-fĕrm′, a., infermo; (feeble) debole
infirmary, in-fĕrm′-a-ri, n., infermeria f.
inflame, in-fleim′, v., infiammare
inflammable, in-flam′-a-bl, a., infiammabile
inflammation, in-fla-mei′-shon, n., infiammazione f.
inflate, in-fleit′, v., enfiare; gonfiare; (tyres) gonfiare; (prices) aumentare
inflexible, in-fleks′-i-bl, a., inflessibile
inflict, in-flikt′, v., infliggere
inflow, in′-flou, n., influsso m.; afflusso m.
influence, in′-flu-ens, v., influire. n., influenza f.
influential, in-flu-en′-shal, a., influente
influenza, in-flu-en′-ᴢa, n., influenza f.

influx, in'-flŏks, n., flusso m., influsso m.

inform, in-foorm', v., informare, avvisare

informal, in-foor'-mal, a., informe

information, in-for-mei'-shon, n., informazione f.; (news) notizia f.

infrequent, in-frii'-kuent, a., raro, non comune

infringe, in-frinch', v., infrangere, violare ; (law) trasgredire : —**ment**, n., infrazione f.; trasgressione f.

infuriate, in-fiuu'-ri-eit, v., rendere furioso

infuse, in-fiuus', v., infondere ; (tea, etc.) mettere in infusione

ingenious°, in-chii'-ni-os, a., ingegnoso

ingenuity, in-chin-iuu'-i-ti, n., ingegnosità f.

ingot, in'-got, n., verga f., barra f.

ingrained, in-greind', a., impregnato : inveterato

ingratiate (oneself), in-grei'-shi-eit, v., ingraziarsi

ingratitude, in-grat'-i-tiuud, n., ingratitudine f.

ingredient, in-grii'-di-ent, n., ingrediente m.

ingrowing, in'-grou-ing, a., incarnato

inhabit, in-hab'-it, v., abitare, dimorare

inhabitable, in-hab'-it-a-bl, a., abitabile

inhabitant, in-hab'-it-ant, n., abitante m., residente m.

inhale, in-heil', v., inalare [dente m.

inherent°, in-hi'-rent, a., inerente

inherit, in-her'-it, v., ereditare

inheritance, in-her'-it-ans, n., eredità f.

inhospitable, in-hos-pi'-ta-bl, a., inospitale

inhuman, in-hiuu'-man, a., disumano

iniquitous, in-ik'-ui-tos, a., iniquo, perfido

initial, in-ish'al, n., iniziale f. a., iniziale

initiate, i-nish'-i-eit, v., iniziare

inject, in-chekt', v., iniettare

injection, in-chek'-shon, n., iniezione f.

injudicious°, in-chiu-dish'-os, a., imprudente, senza giudizio

injunction, in-chongk'-shon, n., (advice) ingiunzione f. ; (law) mandato m.

injure, in'-chiur, v., ferire ; (fig.) nuocere

injurious°, in-chiu-ri-os, a., pernicioso ; nocivo ; (fig.) diffamatorio

injury, in'-cher-i, n., ferita f., danno m.; (fig.) ingiuria f.

injustice, in-chos'-tis, n., ingiustizia f. [ria f.

ink, ingk, n., inchiostro m.: —stand, calamaio m.

inlaid, in-leid', a., intarsiato

inland, in'-land, n., interno m. a., interno

inlet, in-let', n., entrata f. ; (geographical) piccola insenatura f.

inmate, in'-meit, n., inquilino m.; pensionante m. & f. ; ricoverato m.; degente m. & f.

inmost, in'-moust, a., il più interno ; il più intimo

inn, in, n., locanda f. ; —-keeper, locandiere m., trattore m.

inner, in'-a, a., interno ; segreto

innocent*, in'-o-sent, a., innocente

innocuous, in-o'-kiu-os, a., innocuo

innovation, in-no-vei'-shon, n., innovazione f.

innumerable, in-iu'-mer-a-bl, a., innumerevole

inoculate, in-ok'-iu-leit, v., inoculare

inoffensive, in-o-fen'-siv, a., inoffensivo

inopportune, in-o'-por-tiuun, a., inopportuno [f.

inquest, in'-kuest, n., (coroner's) inchiesta giudiziaria

inquire, in-kuair', v., informarsi ; indagare

inquiry, in-kuai'-ri, n., informazione f.: indagine f.; (law) inchiesta f.:—-office, ufficio informazioni m

inquisition, in-kuis-ish'-on, n., inquisizione f.

inquisitive*, in-kuis'-it-iv, a., curioso, indiscreto : indagatore

inroad, in'-roud, n., incursione f. ; usurpazione f.

insane*, in-sein', a., demente, insano ; (fig.)insensato

insanity, in-san'-i-ti, n., demenza f.

insatiable, in-sei'-shi-a-bl, a., insaziabile

inscribe, in-skraib', v., inscrivere

inscription, in-skrip'-shon, n., iscrizione f.

insect, in'-sekt, n., insetto m.

insecure, in-si-kiur', a., insicuro, poco solido

insensible, in-sen'-si-bl, a., insensibile ; (unconscious) svenuto

inseparable, in-sep'-a-ra-bl, a., inseparabile

insert, in-sert', v., inserire ; —ion, n., inserzione f.

inside, in'-said, adv., dentro. n., interno m.

insidious, in-sid'-i-os, a., insidioso

insight, in'-sait, n.,discernimento m.;conoscenza f.

insignificant, in-sigh-nif'-i-kant, a., insignificante

insincere, in-sin-sir', a., poco sincero, falso

insinuate, in-sin'-iu-eit, v., insinuare

insipid, in-sip'-id, a., insipido

insist (on), in-sist', v., insistere

insolence, in'-so-lens, n., insolenza f.

insolent, in'-so-lent, a., insolente

insolvent, in-sol'-vent, a., insolvibile

inspect, in-spekt', v., ispezionare

inspection, in-spek'-shon, n., ispezione f.

inspector, in-spek'-ta, n., ispettore m.

inspiration, in-spi-rei'-shon, n., inspirazione f.

inspire, in-spair', v., inspirare

install, in-stool', v., installare

installation, in-stoo-lei'-shon, n., installazione f.

instalment, in-stool'-ment, n., rata f.; **to pay —s**, v., pagare a rate

instance, in'-stans, n., esempio m., caso m.

instant, in'-stant, n., istante m.; (date) corrente m.

instantaneous*, in-stan-tei'-ni-os, a., istantaneo

instantly, in'-stant-li, adv., all'istante

instead of, in-sted' ov, adv., invece di

instep, in'-step, n., collo del piede m.

instigate, in'-sti-gheit, v., istigare

instil, in-stil', v., istillare

instinct, in'-stingkt, n., istinto m.

institute, in'-sti-tiuut, n., istituto m.

instruct, in'-strōkt, v., istruire; (order) ordinare

instruction, in-strōk'-shon, n., istruzione f.

instrument, in'-stru-ment, n., strumento m.

insubordination, in-su-boor-di-nei'-shon, n., insubordinazione f.

insufferable, in-sōf'-er-a-bl, a., insopportabile

insufficient*, in-suf-ish'-ent, a., insufficiente

insulation, in-siu-lei'-shon, n., isolamento m.

insult, in-sōlt', v., insultare

insult, in'-sōlt, n., insulto m.

insurance, in-shūr'-ans, n., assicurazione f.

insure, in-shūr', v., assicurare

insurrection, in-sĕr-rek'-shon, n., insurrezione f.

intellect, in'-tel-ekt, n., intelletto m.

intelligence, in-tel'-i-chens, n., intelligenza f.

intelligent, in-tel'-i-chent, a., intelligente

intemperate, in-tem'-per-et, a., intemperante

intend, in-tend', v., aver l'intenzione, volere
intense°, in-tens', a., intenso
intent, in-tent', n., intento m. a., intento
intention, in-ten'-shon, n., intenzione f.
intentional°, in-ten'-shon-al, a., intenzionale, fatto
inter, in-tĕr', v., sotterrare [apposta
intercept, in-ter-sept', v., intercettare
interchange, in-ter-cheinch', v., scambiare
intercourse, in'-ter-kors, n., rapporto m.
interdict, in-ter-dikt', v., interdire
interest, in'-ter-est, n., interesse m.
interesting, in'-ter-est-ing, a., interessante
interfere, in-ter-fir', v., intromettersi
interference, in-ter-fi'-rens, n., intromissione f.;
(radio) interferenza f.
interior, in-ii'-ri-or, a., interiore, interno. n., in-
interlace, in-ter-leis', v., intrecciare [terno m.
interloper, in-ter-lou'-pa, n., intruso m.
interlude, in'-ter-liuud, n., intermezzo m.
intermediate, in-ter-mii'-di-et, a., intermediario
interment, in-tĕr'-ment, n., sepoltura f.
intermingle, in-ter-ming'-gol, v., frammischiare
intermission, in-ter-mish'-on, n., interruzione f.
intermittent°, in-ter-mit'-ent, a., intermittente
intermix, in-ter-miks', v., mischiare
intern, in-tĕrn', v., internare, confinare
internal°, in-tĕr'-nal, a., interno
international, in-tĕr-nash'-on-al, a., internazionale
interpret, in-tĕr'-pret, v., interpretare
interpreter, in-tĕr'-pre-ta, n., interprete m.
interrogate, in-ter'-o-gheit, v., interrogare
interrupt, in-ter-öpt', v., interrompere
interval, in'-ter-val, n., intervallo m.
intervene, in-ter-viin', v., intervenire
intervention, in-ter-ven'-shon, n., intervenzione f.
interview, in'-ter-viuu, n., intervista f. v., inter-
intestate, in-tes'-tet, a., intestato [vistare
intestine, in-tes'-tin, n., intestino m.
intimacy, in'-ti-ma-si, n., intimità f.
intimate°, in'-ti-met, a., intimo
intimate°, in'-ti-meit, v., (point out) far conoscere
intimation, in-ti-mei'-shon, n., avviso m.

intimidate, in-tim′-i-deit, v., intimidire
into, in′-tu, prep., entro, in, dentro
intolerable, in-tol′-er-a-bl, a., intollerabile
intoxicate, in-tok′-si-keit, v., ubbriacare
intrepid°, in-trep′-id, a., intrepido
intricate°, in′-tri-ket, a., intricato
intrigue, in′-trigh, n., intrigo m.   v., intrigare
intriguing, in-trii′-ghing, a., intrigante
intrinsic, in-trin′-sik, a., intrinseco   [sentare
introduce, in-tro-diuus′, v., introdurre ; (people) pre-
introductory, in-tro-dŏk′-to-ri, a., introduttivo
intrude, in-truud′, v., disturbare ; introdurre
intruder, in-truu′-da, n., intruso m.
intuition, in-tiu-ish′-on, n., intuito m.
inundation, in-on-dei′-shon, n., innondazione f.
inure, in-iur′, v., abituare
invade, in-veid′, v., invadere
invader, in-veid′-a, n., invasore m.
invalid, in′-va-liid, n., invalido m. ; infermo m. ;
    — -chair, poltrona d'infermo f.
invalid, in-val′-id, a., invalido
invaluable, in-val′-iu-a-bl, a., inestimabile
invariable, in-ve′-ri-a-bl, a., invariabile
invasion, in-vei′-shon, n., invasione f.
inveigle, in-vii′-gol, v., sedurre ; adescare
invent, in-vent′, v., inventare ; —ion, n., inven-
    zione f. ; —or, inventore m.
inventory, in-vent′-ri, n., inventario m.
invert, in-vĕrt′, v., invertire
invest, in-vest′, v., (capital) investire
investigate, in-ves′-ti-gheit, v., investigare
investment, in-vest′-ment, n., investimento m.
investor, in-ves′-ta, n., investitore m.
inveterate°, in-vet′-er-et, a., inveterato
invigorate, in-vi′-gor-eit, v., dar vigore
invincible, in-vin′-si-bl, a., invincibile
invisible, in-vis′-i-bl, a., invisibile
invitation, in-vi-tei′-shon, n., invito m.
invite, in-vait′, v., invitare
invoice, in′-vois, n., fattura f.
invoke, in-vouk′, v., invocare
involuntary, in-vol′-ŏn-ta-ri, a., involontario

involve, in-volv′, v., involgere
inward, in′-uerd, a., interno ; intimo
iodine, ai′-o-din, n., iodio m.
I. O. U., ai oo iu, n., pagherò m.
ire, air, n., ira f.
iris, ai′-ris, n., (flower) ireos m. ; (eye) iride m.
irksome*, ĕrk′-som, a., tedioso
iron, ai′-ern, v., stirare. n., ferro m. ; flat-—, ferro da stiro m.
ironical*, ai-ron′-i-kal, a., ironico
ironmonger, ai′-ern-mong-gher, n., chincagliere m.
ironware, ai′-ern-uer, n., ferramenta f.
irony, ai′-ron-i, n., ironia f.   [bile
irreconcilable, i-rek-on-sai′-la-bl, a., irreconcilia-
irregular*, i-re′-ghiu-lar, a., irregolare
irrelevant, i-rel′-i-vant, a., fuor di luogo
irreproachable, i-ri-prouch′-a-bl, a., irreprensibile
irresistible, i-ri-sist′-i-bl, a., irresistibile
irrespective, i-re-spek′-tiv, a., indipendente
irresponsible, i-ri-spon′-si-bl, a., irresponsabile
irretrievable, i-ri-trii′-va-bl, a., irrecuperabile ; irrimediabile
irreverent*, i-rev′-er-ent, a., irriverente
irrigate, i′-ri-gheit, v., irrigare
irritable, i′-ri-ta-bl, a., irritabile
irritate, i′-ri-teit, v., irritare
irruption, i-rŏp′-shon, n., irruzione f.
isinglass, ai′-sing-glaas, n., colla di pesce f.
island, ai′-land, n., isola f. ; —er, isolano m.
isle, ail, n., isola f.
islet, ai′-let, n., isoletta f.
isolate, ai′-sol-eit, v., isolare
isolation, ai-so-lei′-shon, n., isolamento m.
issue, i′-shiuu, v., emanare ; pubblicare ; (shares)e-mettere. n., risultato m. ; (offspring) progenie f. ; (books) pubblicazione f. ; (shares) emissione f.
isthmus, is′-mos, n., istmo m.   [quella
it, it, pron., il, la, lo ; egli, ella ; esso, essa ; quello,
italic, i-tal′-ik, n., (type) caratteri corsivi m. pl.
itch, ich, v., prudere. n., prurito m.
item, ai′-tem, n., articolo m. ; (accounts) partita f.
itinerant, ai-tin′-er-ant, a., ambulante

its, its, pron., il suo, la sua ; suoi, sue

itself, it-self', pron., esso stesso, essa stessa ;
  by —, da sè stesso

ivory, ai'-ver-i, n., avorio m.

ivy, ai'-vi, n., edera f.

jabber, chab'-a, v., cicalare

jack, chak, n., (mech.) martinetto m., cricco m.

jackal, chak'-ool, n., sciacallo m.

jacket, chak'-et, n., giacchetta f.

jade, cheid, n., (stone) giado m.

jaded, chei'-did, a., spossato

jag, chagh, n., tacca f. v., indentare

jail, cheil, n., carcere m. v., incarcerare

jailor, chei'-la, n., carceriere m.

jam, cham, n., (conserve) marmellata f. ; (traffic) ingombro m. v., incastrare ; (block) bloccare

jangle, chang'-gol, n., suono discordante m.
  v., far rumore discordante

January, chan'-iu-a-ri, n., gennaio m.

jar, chaar, n., vaso m.; (shock) scossa f. v., (annoy) urtare

jaundice, choon'-dis, n., itterizia f.

jaw, choo, n., mandibola f. v., (vulg.) cianciare

jay, chei, n., ghiandaia f.

jealous*, chel'-os, a., geloso

jealousy, chel'-o-si, n., gelosia f.

jeer, chir, v., beffarsi. n., burla f., beffa f.

jelly, chel'-i, n., gelatina f.; — -fish, medusa f.

jeopardize, chep-er-dais', v., arrischiare

jeopardy, chep'-er-di, n., pericolo m.

jerk, chërk, v., scuotere. n., scossa f.

jersey, chër'-si, n., giacca di lana f.

jest, chest, v., scherzare. n., facezia f., scherzo m.

jester, ches'-ta, n., burlone m.; (court) buffone m.

jet, chet, n.,(mineral) ambra nera f.; (liquid)getto m.;
  (nozzle) lancia f. v., lanciare ; (fountain) zampillare

jettison, chet'-i-son, v., gettar a mare

jetty, chet'-i, n., gettata f.

Jew, chuu, n., ebreo m. ; —ess, ebrea f.

jewel, chuu'-el, n., gioia f., gioiello m.

jeweller, chuu'-el-a, n., gioielliere m.

jewellery, chuu'-el-ri, n., gioie f. pl., gioielli m. pl.

jig, chigh, n., giga f. v., ballare la giga

jilt, chilt, v., lasciar in asso ; (tease) civettare

jingle, ching'-gol, v., tintinnare

job, chob, n., lavoro m.

jobber, chob'-a, n., (stock) sensale in Borsa m.

jockey, chok'-i, n., fantino m.

jocular*, chok'-iu-lar, a., faceto

join, choin, v., unire, unirsi ; (a club, etc.) asso-
    ciarsi ; — in, partecipare a

joiner, choi'-na, n., falegname m.

joint, choint, n., (meat) taglio m. ; (carpentry) gi-
    unta f. ; (anatomy) articolazione f. ; —stock
    Co., società in accomandita per azioni f.

jointly, choint'-li, adv., congiuntamente

joke, chook, n., burla f., scherzo m. v., scherzare

joker, choo'-ka, n., burlone m.

jolly, chol'-i, a., lieto, gaio

jolt, choult, n., sussulto m. v., sussultare

jostle, chos'-l, v., spingere

journal, cher'-nal, n., giornale m.

journalism, cher'-na-lism, n., giornalismo m.

journalist, cher'-na-list, n., giornalista m. & f.

journey, cher'-ni, n., viaggio m. v., viaggiare

jovial*, chou'-vi-al, a., gioviale

joy, choi, n., gioia f.

joyful*, choi'-ful, a., gioioso, allegro

jubilant, chuu'-bi-lant, a., giubilante

jubilee, chuu'-bi-li, n., giubileo m.   [dicare

judge, choch, n., giudice m. ; conoscitore m. v., giu-

judgment, choch'-ment, n., giudizio m. ; sentenza f.

judicial*, chu-dish'-al, a., giudiziale

judicious*, chu-dish'-os, a., giudizioso

jug, chogh, n., brocca f.

juggle, chogh'-l, v., far il giocoliere

juggler, chogh'-la, n., giocoliere m.

juice, chuus, n., sugo m.

juicy, chuu'-si, a., succoso

July, chu-lai', n., luglio m.   [m.

jumble, chom'-bl, v., imbrogliare. n., guazzabuglio

jumbled, chom'-beld, a., confuso

jump, chomp, n., salto m. v., saltare

jumper, chŏm'-p*a*, n., saltatore m. ; (blouse) farsetto m.

junction, chŏngk'-shon, n., giuntura f. ; (railway) stazione di smistamento f. ; (road) crocevia m.

juncture, chŏngk'-ch*u*r, n., (period) congiuntura f.

June, chuun, n., giugno m.

jungle, chŏng'-gol, n., giungla f.

junior, chuu'-ni-*or*, a., più giovane, iuniore ; — **partner**, n., socio meno anziano m.

juniper, chuu'-ni-p*a*, n., ginepro m.

jurisdiction, chu-ris-dik'-shon, n., giurisdizione f.

juror, chu'-r*or*, n., giurato m.

jury, chu'-ri, n., (law) giurì m. [proprio

just, chŏst, a., (fair) giusto. adv., (now) appunto.

justice, chŏst'-is, n., giustizia f.

justification, chŏs-ti-fi-kei'-shon, n., giustificazione

justify, chŏst'-i-fai, v., giustificare [f.

justly, chŏst'-li, adv., giustamente

jut (out), chŏt, v., sporgere fuori

jute, chuut, n., iuta f.

juvenile, chuu'-vi-nail, a., giovanile

kangaroo, kan-g*a*-ruu', n., canguro m.

keel, kiil, n., chiglia f.

keen, kiin, a., ansioso ; (blade) acuto ; —**ness**, n., ardore m. ; (mind) penetrazione f.

keep, kiip, n., mantenimento m. v., (retain) tenere ; (support) mantenere ; (preserve) conservare ; — **back**, trattenere ; — **off**, tener lontano ; — **to**, mantenere

keeper, kiip'-*a*, n., guardiano m.

keepsake, kiip'-seik, n., ricordo m.

keg, kegh, n., barile m.

kennel, ken'-l, n., canile m.

kerbstone, kĕrb'-stoun, n., orlo di marciapiedi m.

kernel, kĕr'-nl, n., (nut) gheriglio m.

kettle, ket'-l, n., caldaia f. ; — **drum**, timballo m.

key, kii, n., chiave f. ; — **board**, tastiera f. ; — **hole**, buco di serratura m.

kick, kik, n., calcio m. v., calciare

kid, kid, n., capretto m. ; (fig.) bambino m

kidnap, kid'-nap, v., rapire

kidney, kid′-ni, n., rene m. ; (animal) rognone m.

kill, kil, v., uccidere

kiln, kiln, n., forno m. ; fornace f.

kin, kin, n., affine m. & f. ; —**dred**, a., affine ; —**sfolk**, n., parenti m. pl. ; —**sman**, parente m., affine m. ; —**swoman**, parente f., affine f.

kind, kaind, n., specie f., genere m., sorta f. a., °buono, amabile ; —**ness**, n., bontà f.; (favour) gentilezza f.

kindle, kin′-dl, v., accendere

king, king, n., re m.

kingdom, king′-dom, n., regno m.

kipper, kip′-a, n., arringa affumicata f.

kiss, kis, n., bacio m. v., baciare

kit, kit, n., equipaggiamento m.

kitchen, kit′-shin, n., cucina f.

kite, kait, n., cervo volante m. ; (bird) nibbio m.

kitten, kit′-n, n., gattino m. ; gattina f.

knack, nak, n., talento m. ; abilità f.

knapsack, nap′-sak, n., zaino m.

knave, neiv, n., briccone m. ; (cards) fante m.

knead, niid, v., impastare

knee, nii, n., ginocchio m.; —**breeches**, calzoncini m. pl. ; —**cap**, rotella del ginocchio f.

kneel, niil, v., inginocchiarsi

knell, nel, n., rintocco funebre m.   [m. pl.

knickers, nik′-ers, n., (ladies) calzoncini da donna

knife, naif, n., coltello m.

knight, nait, n., cavaliere m.; —**hood**, ordine di

knit, nit, v., far la maglia   [cavaliere m.

knitting, nit′-ing, n., lavoro a maglia m.

knob, nob, n., bottone m. ; (stick) pomo m. ; (of a door) maniglia f.

knock, nok, v., picchiare ; (strike) urtare ; (hit) colpire ; —**against,** urtare contro ; —**down,** gettare a terra

knocker, nok′-a, n., (door) martello m.

knoll, noul, n., monticello m.

knot, not, n., nodo m. v., annodare

knotty, not′-i, a., nodoso

know, nou, v., conoscere ; sapere

knowledge, noul′-ich, n., conoscenza f.: sapere m

knuckle, nŏk′-l, n., nocca f.; giuntura f.

label, lei'-bl, n., etichetta f. v., fissare etichette
laboratory, lab'-o-*ra-to-ri*, n., laboratorio m.
laborious°, la-bo'-ri-os, a., laborioso
labour, lei'-ba, n., lavoro m.; fatica f. v., lavorare; affaticarsi; coltivare
labourer, lei'-ber-*a*, n., lavoratore m., bracciante m.
laburnum, la-ber'-nom, n., alburno m.
lace, leis, n., merletto m.; (shoe) laccio m.; (galloon) gallone m. v., allacciare
lacerate, las'-er-eit, v., lacerare
lack, lak, n., (shortage) mancanza f. v., **mancare**
lackey, lak'-i, n., lacchè m.
lacquer, lak'-*a*, n., lacca f.
lad, lad, n., ragazzo m., garzone **m.**
ladder, lad'-*a*, n., scala f. [carico f.
lading, lei'-ding, n., carico m.; bill of —, polizza di
ladle, leid'-l, n., cucchiaione m. v., scodellare
lady, lei'-di, n., dama f., signora f.; — -**bird**, bestia di Dio f., coccinella f.
lag, lagh, v., trascinarsi; — **behind**, restar in dietro
lagoon, la-guun', n., laguna f.
lair, ler, n., covo m.
lake, leik, n., lago m.
lamb, lam, n., agnello m. v., partorire gli agnelli
lame, leim, a.,° storpio, zoppo. v., storpiare
lameness, leim'-nes, n., storpiatura f.
lament, la-ment', v., lamentarsi. n., lamento m.
lamp, lamp, n., lampada f.; (street) lampione m.
lance, laans, n., lancia f. v., lanciare; (med.) tagliare colla lancetta
lancer, laans'-*a*, n., (mil.) lanciere m.
land, land, n., terra f.; (property) terreno m. v., sbarcare; —**ing**, n., sbarcatoio m.; (stairs) pianerottolo m.; —**ing-port**, (for aeroplanes) terreno d'atterraggio m.
landlady, land'-lei-di, n., padrona di casa f.
landlord, land'-loord, n., (land-owner) padrone del terreno m.; (inn) oste m.; (house-owner) padrone di casa m.
landmark, land'-maark, n., pietra terminale **f.**; (naut.) punto di riferimento m.
landscape, land'-skeip, n., paesaggio m.

landslide, land'-slaid, n., frana f.

lane, lein, n., sentiero m. ; (town) vicolo m.

language, lang'-guich, n., lingua f.; linguaggio **m.**

languid*, lang'-guid, a., languido

languish, lang'-guish, v., languire

lanky, lang'-ki, a., mingherlino

lantern, lan'-*tern*, n., lanterna f. [care

lap, lap, n., grembo m.;(sport) giro **m. v.,** (drink) lec-

lapel, lap'-l, n., falda f.

lapse, laps, n., mancanza f. ; (time) lasso di tempo m. v., trascorrere

larceny, laar'-si-ni, n., furto **m.**

lard, laard, n., strutto m.

larder, laar'-da, n., dispensa f.

large*, laarch, a., grande ; grosso ; considerevole

lark, laark, n., allodola f. ; (pop.) scappata f.

lash, lash, n., (whip) sferza f.; (stroke) sferzata f.;
(eye) ciglio m. v., sferzare ; (tie) legare

lassitude, las'-i-tiuud, n., stanchezza f.

last, laast, v., durare. n., (shoe) forma f. a.,* ultimo

lasting*, laast'-ing, a., (durable) durevole

latch, lach, n., saliscendi m. v., dare il chiavistello

latchkey, lach'-kii, n., chiave di casa f.

late, leit, a., tardi ; (belated) in ritardo ; **(for-**
merly) già ; (deceased) defunto

lately, leit'-li, adv., ultimamente

latent, lei'-tent, a., latente

lathe, leiD, n., tornio m.

lather, laD'-a, n., spuma f. v., insapon**are**

latitude, lat'-i-tiuud, n., latitudine f.

latter, lat'-*a*, a., questi, questo

lattice, lat'-is, n., graticcio m.

laudable, loo'-da-bl, a., lodevole

laudanum, loo'-da-nom, n., laudano m.

laugh, laaf, n., riso m. v., ridere ; — **at,** ridersi
di ; —**able,** a., comico, ridicolo ; —**ing-**
stock, n., ludibrio m. ; —**ter,** riso m.

launch, loonch, n., lancia f. ; (naut.) varo **m.**
v., varare ; (enterprise) lanciare

laundress, loon'-dres, n., lavandaia f.

laundry, loon'-dri, n., (works) lavanderia f.

laureate, loo'-ri-eit, n., (poet) laureato **m.**

laurel, loo*r'*-l, n., lauro m.

lavatory, lav'-*a*-to-ri, n., gabinetto m.; (washing) lavabo m.

lavender, lav'-en-d*a*, n., lavanda f.

lavish, lav'-ish, a.,° ricco, largo, prodigo. v., largire

law, loo, n., legge f.; —**ful**, a., legale; —**less**, illegale; (person) senza legge

lawn, loon, n., prato verde m.

lawsuit, loo'-siuut, n., processo m., causa f.

lawyer, loo'-i*a*, n., avvocato m.

lax°, laks, a., fiacco, floscio; rilassato

laxative, lak'-s*a*-tiv, n., lassativo m.

lay, lei, v., mettere, porre; (hen) far le uova

layer, lei'-*a*, n., (stratum, coating) strato m.

layman, lei'-m*a*n, n., laico m.

laziness, lei'-*s*i-nes, n., pigrizia f.

lazy, lei'-*s*i, a., pigro   [bare

lead, led, n.,piombo m.; (sounding) sonda f. v., piom-

lead, liid, v., condurre; guidare; (in a game of cards) toccare; —**ing**, a., primo; principale; —**ing article**, n., articolo di fondo m.

leader, lii'-d*a*, n., conduttore m.; (political) condottiero m.; —**ship**, guida f.; comando m.

leaf, liif, n., foglia f.

leaflet, liif'-let, n., (handbill) foglietto m.

leafy, lii'-fi, a., frondoso

league, liigh, n., lega f.

leak, liik, v., perdere; trapelare; (fluid) colare; (boats) far acqua.   n., fuga f.; perdita f.; (boats, etc.) via d'acqua f.

lean, liin, a.,magro; —**against**, v.,appoggiarsi contro; —**on**, appoggiarsi su; —**out**, sporgersi fuori

leap, liip, v. balzare.   n., sbalzo m.

leap-year, liip'-iir, n., anno bisestile m.

learn, lĕrn, v., imparare; (news, experience) apprendere; —**ed**, a., erudito; —**er**, n., allievo m.; apprendista m. & f.; —**ing**, sapere m.; istruzione f.

lease, liis, n., contratto d'affitto m.   v., affittare; dar in affitto

leash, liish, v., tenere al guinzaglio. n., guinzaglio m.

least, liist, a., il più piccolo, il minimo; **at —**, adv., almeno, per lo meno

leather, leD′-*a*, n., cuoio m.; pelle f., pellame **m.**

leave, liiv. n., (permission, furlough) licenza **f.**
v., partire; (bequeath, desert) lasciare; **— be-**
hind, lasciare dietro di sè; **— off,** cessare;
—out, tralasciare; **— to,** (hand over) lasciare a

lecture, lek′-ch*u*r, n., conferenza f.; (admonition) ammonizione f. v., fare una conferenza

lecturer, lek′-ch*u*r-*a*, n., conferenziere m.

ledge,lech.n.,(window) davanzale m.; (rock) orlo **m**

ledger, lech′-*a*, n., libro mastro m.

leech, liich, n., sanguisuga f.

leek, liik, n., porro m.

leer, li*r*, v., guatare di soppiatto   [mancino

left, left, adv., a sinistra. a., sinistro; **— -handed,**

leg, legh, n., gamba f.; (meat) coscia f.

legacy, leg′-*a*-si, n., legato m.

legal, lii′-gal, a., legale; **—ize,** v., legalizzare

legation, li-ghei′-sh*on*, n., legazione f.

legend, lech′-end, n., leggenda f.

legging, legh′-ing, n., uosa f.

legible, lech′-i-bl, a., leggibile

legion, lii′-ch*on*, n., legione f.

legislate, lech′-is-leit, v., legislare

legislation, lech-is-lei′-sh*on*, n., legislazione **f.**

legitimacy, lech-it′-i-ma-si, n., legittimità **f.**

legitimate, lech-it′-i-met, v., legittimare

legitimately, lech-i′-ti-met-li, adv., (justly) legit-
timamente

leisure, lesh′-*er*, n., tempo libero m.; agio m.

leisurely, lesh′-*er*-li, adv., con comodo, a bell'agio

lemon, lem′-*on*, n., limone m.

lemonade, lem-on-eid′, n., limonata f.

lend, lend, v., prestare

length, leng′-gZ, n., lunghezza f.; (time) durata f.;
—en, v., allungare; prolungare; **—ways,** adv.,
in lunghezza; **—y,** a., alquanto lungo; prolisso

leniency, lii′-ni-ens-i, n., mitezza **f.**

lenient*, lii′-ni-ent, a., mite

lens, lens, n., (glass) lente f.

Lent, lent, n., Quaresima f.

lentil, len′-til, n., lenticchia f.

leopard, lep′-a*r*d, n., leopardo **m**

leper, lep'-*a*, n., lebbroso m.

leprosy, lep'-*ro*-si, n., lebbra f.

leprous, lep'-ros, a., lebbroso

less, les, adv., meno. a., minore

lessee, les-ii', n., locatario m.; (land) affittuario m

lessen, les'-n, v., diminuire; (pain) attenuare

lesson, les'-n, n., lezione f.

let, let, v., lasciare; (house, etc.) affittare

letter, let'-*a*, n., lettera f.; — -**box,** buca da lettere f.; — **of credit,** lettera di credito f.

lettuce, let'-os, n., lattuga f.

levee, lev'-i, n., ricevimento regale m.

level, lev'-l, a., a livello. v., livellare. n., livello m.; — -**crossing,** passaggio a livello m.

lever, lii'-va, n., leva f.; (of a watch) ancora f.

levity, lev'-i-ti, n., leggerezza f.

levy, lev'-i, v., (taxes) levare. n., imposta f.; (troops) leva f.

lewd*, liuud, a., impudico; dissoluto

lewdness, liuud'-nes, n., impudicizia f.

liability, lai-*a*-bil'-i-ti, n., responsabilità f.; (legal) rischio m.; (commercial) debito m.

liable, lai'-*a*-bl, a., responsabile; (law) soggetto; — **to,** (inclined) soggetto a

liar, lai'-*a*, n., bugiardo m.

libel, lai'-bl, n., libello m.

libellous, lai'-bel-os, a., diffamatorio

liberal, lib'-er-*a*l, a., liberale

liberate, lib'-er-eit, v., liberare

liberty, lib'-er-ti, n., libertà f.

librarian, lai-bre'-ri-*a*n, n., bibliotecario m.

library, lai'-bre-ri, n., biblioteca f.

licence, lai'-sens, n., licenza f.

license, lai'-sens, v., autorizzare

licentious*, lai-sen'-shos, a., licenzioso

lichen, lai'-ken, n., lichene m.

lick, lik, v., leccare

lid, lid. n., coperchio m.; **eye-** —, palpebra f.

lie, lai, n., (untruth) bugia f. v., (tell lies) dire bugie

lie, lai, n., (position) giacitura f. v., giacere; — **about,** giacere qua e là; — **down,** mettersi a giacere

lieutenant, lef-ten'-*ant,* n., tenente m.
life, laif, n., vita f. ; **—-belt,** salvagente m. ;
 —-boat, battello di salvataggio m. ; **—-insur-
 ance,** assicurazione sulla vita f. ; **—less,** a., inanimato ; (dead) senza vita ; **—like,** vivente ;
 —long, a vita ; di tutta la vita ; **—-size,** n.,
 grandezza naturale f. ; **—time,** tutta la vita ;
 in **our —time,** nei nostri tempi
lift, lift, n., ascensore m. ; (goods) **elevatore** m.
 v., elevare, alzare ; (raise) sollevare
light, lait, n., luce f. a.,* chiaro ; (weight) leggero.
 v., accendere ; (illuminate) illuminare
lighten, lai'-tn, v., rischiarare ; (weight) alleggerire
lighter, lai'ta, n., (flint) accenditore m.; (boat) chi-
lighthouse, lait'-haus, n., faro m.   [atta f.
lighting, lai'-ting, n., illuminazione f.
lightness, lait'-nes, n., (weight) leggerezza f.
lightning, lait'-ning, n., fulmine m. ; **—-conduc-
 tor,** parafulmine m.
like, laik, v., piacere. a., simile ; ugale ; **—lihood,**
 n., probabilità f.; **—ly,** adv., probabile ; **—ness,**
 n., rassomiglianza f. ; **—wise,** adv., similmente
liking, lai'-king, n., gusto m.; inclinazione f.
lilac, lai'-lak, n., lilla f.   [to m.
lily, lil'-i, n., giglio m.; **— of the valley,** mughet-
limb, lim, n., (anatomy) membro m.
lime, laim, n., calce f. ; (bird-lime) vischio m. ;
 (fruit) cedro m. ; (tree) tiglio m. ; **—-juice,**
 acqua di cedro f. ; **—-light,** (stage) luce di riflettore f. ; (fig.) rilievo m.
limit, lim'-it, n., limite m. v., limitare ; **—ed,** a.,
 limitato ; **Ltd. Co.,** n., società anonima f.
limp, limp, v., zoppicare. a., (soft) molle, soffice
limpet, lim'-pet, n., patella f.
line, lain, n., linea f.; (fishing) lenza f.; (rope) corda f. v., (garment) foderare
lineage, lin'-i-ich, n., lignaggio m.
linen, lin'-en, n., lino m. ; (laundry) biancheria f.
liner, lain'-*a,* n., transatlantico m.
linger, ling'-*ga,* v., indugiare ; **—ing,** a.,* languente
linguist, ling'-guist, n., linguista m. & f.
lining, lain'-ing, n., (of clothes) fodera f.

link, lingk, v., unire ; allacciare. n., anello m. ; (fig.) vincolo m.

links, lingks, n. pl., (cuff) bottoni da polsini m. pl.

linnet, lin'-et, n., fanello m.

linoleum, lin-oul'-i-am, n., linoleo m.

linseed, lin'-siid, n., semi di lino m. pl.

lint, lint, n., filaccia f.

lion, lai'-on, n., leone m. ; —ess, leonessa f.

lip, lip, n., labbro m. :— -stick, rosso per le labbra m.

liquefy, lik'-ui-fai, v., liquefare, liquefarsi

liqueur, li-kor', n., liquore m.

liquid, lik'-uid, n., liquido m. a., liquido

liquidate, lik'-ui-deit, v., liquidare ; (debts) saldare

liquidation, lik-ui-dei'-shon, n., liquidazione f.

liquor, lik'-or, n., (alcoholic drink) liquore m. ; (cookery) sugo m.

liquorice, lik'-o-ris, n., liquorizia f.

lisp, lisp, v., biascicare

list, list, n., lista f. ; (naut.) sbandamento m. v., (naut.) sbandare

listen, lis'-n, v., ascoltare

listener, lis'-na, n., ascoltatore m. ; uditore m.

literal, lit'-er-al, a., letterale

literary, lit'-er-a-ri, a., letterario

literature, lit'-er-a-chur, n., letteratura f.

lithograph, liZ'-o-graf, n., litografia f. v., litografare

litigation, lit-i-ghei'-shon, n., litigio m.

litigate, lit'-i-gheit, v., litigare

litter, lit'-a, n., (stretcher) lettiga f. ; (untidiness) confusione f. ; (dirt) porcheria f. ; (straw) strame m. ; (animals) parto m. v., metter in disordine

little, lit'-l. a., (size) piccolo ; (time, quantity) poco, poca, pochi, poche. adv., poco

live, liv, v., vivere ; (reside) risiedere

live, laiv, (see **alive**)

lively, laiv'-li, a., vivace, gaio

liver, liv'-a, n., fegato m.

livery, liv'-er-i, n., livrea f. ; — -stable, stalla di cavalli da nolo f.

livid, liv'-id, a., livido   [vivente

living, liv'-ing, n., vita f. ; (eccl.) benefizio m. a., vivo

lizard, lis'-erd, n., lucertola f.

load, loud, v., caricare. n., **carico** m.

loaf, louf, v.,(about) bighellonare. n.,(bread)**pane m.,** pagnotta f. ; — -**sugar**, zucchero in zolle m.

loafer, lou'-fa, n., bighellone m.

loam, loum, n., **terra grassa** f.

loamy, loum'-i, a., di terra grassa

loan, loun, v., prestare. n., prestito m. ; **on —,** adv., su prestito, a prestito

loathe, louD, v., detestare

loathing, louD'-ing, n., avversione f.

loathsome, louD'-som, a., detestabile

lobby, lob'-i, n., anticamera f.;(theatre) vestibolo m.

lobe, loub, n., (ear) lobo m.

lobster, lob'-sta, n., aragosta f.

local, lou'-kl, a., locale ; —**ity,** n., località f.

locate, lou'-keit, v., localizzare

lock, lok, n., serratura f.; (canal, etc.) chiusa f.; (hair) ciocca f. v., serrare ; — **in,** rinchiudere ; — **out,** chiudere fuori. n., (industrial) serrata f.; — **up,** v., chiudere ; (imprison) imprigionare

locket, lok'-et, n., medaglione m.

lock-jaw, lok'-choo, n., tetano m.

locksmith, lok'-smiZ, n., magnano m.

locomotive, lou'-ko-mou-tiv, n., locomotiva f.

locum-tenens, lou'-kom-tii'-nens, n., sostituto m.

locust, lou'-kust, n., locusta f.

lodge, loch, n., padiglione m. ; (masonic) loggia f. v., alloggiare

lodger, loch'-a, n., inquilino m.

lodging, loch'-ing, n., alloggio m.

loft, loft, n., soffitta f. ; —**y,** a., alto, elevato

log, logh, n.,(wood) ceppo m. ; — -**book,** registro di bordo m.

logic, loch'-ik, n., logica f. ; —**al*,** a., logico

loin, loin, n., lombo m. ; (meat) lombata f.

loiter, loi'-ta, v., girovagare

loiterer, loi'-ter-a, n., fannullone m.

loll, lol, v., reclinare ; (tongue) penzolare

loneliness, loun'-li-nes, n., solitudine f.

lone(ly), loun('-li), a., solitario, isolato

long, long, a., lungo ; — **for,** v., anelare

longing, long'-ing, n., bramosia f.

longitude, lon'-chi-tiuud, n., longitudine f.

look, luk, n., sguardo m. v., guardare ; (appear) sembrare ; — after, attendere ; — at, guardare ; —er on, n., spettatore m. ; — for, v., cercare ; —ing-glass, n., specchio m.; — out, v., guardare fuori. n., (naut.) vedetta f. interj., attenzione ; to be on the — out, v., stare sull'aspettativa

loom, lum, n., telaio m. v., apparire in distanza

loop, luup, n., laccio m., nodo m. ; —hole, scappatoia f. ; (fort) feritoia f. ; — the loop, v., far le capriole

loose, luus, a., sciolto ; (morals) dissoluto

loosen, luus'-n, v., sciogliere ; allentare

loot, luut, v., depredare. n., bottino m.

lop, lop, v., (prune) potare. a., (ears) pendente

loquacious, lo-kuei'-shos, a., loquace

Lord (the), loord, n., Signore m.

Lord's Prayer, loords pre'-er, n., Paternostro m.

lord, loord, n., (peer) lord m.

lorry, lor'-i, n., (motor) autocarro m. [dere

lose, luus, v., perdere ; (watch) ritardare ; (train) per-

loser, luu'-sa, n., perdente m. & f.

loss, los, n., perdita f.

Lost Property Office, lost prop'-er-ti of'-is, n., ufficio oggetti smarriti m.

lot, lot, n., (auction) lotto m. ; (fate) sorte f. ; — of, quantità di f. a., molto, molta, molti, molte

lotion, lou'-shon, n., lozione f.

lottery, lot'-er-i, n., lotteria f.

loud*, laud, a., alto ; (colours) vistoso ; — -speaker, n., (radio) alto parlante m.

lounge, launch, n., salone d'entrata m. v., andar in

lounger, laun-cha, n., fannullone m. [giro

louse, laus, n., pidocchio m.

lout, laut, n., tanghero m.

love, lŏv, n., amore m. v., amare

loveliness, lŏv'-li-nes, n., grazia f., bellezza f.

lovely, lŏv'-li, a., bello, grazioso

lover, lŏv'-a, n., innamorato m.; (illicit) amante m.; (of animals, etc.) amatore m.

low, lou, a.,* basso. v., (cattle) muggire

lower, lou'-*a*, v., abbassare
lowland, lou'-land, n., pianura f.
loyal, loi'-*al*, a., leale ; **—ty**, n., lealtà f.
lozenge, los'-ench, n., pastiglia f.
lubricate, liuu'-bri-keit, v., lubrificare
lucid*, liuu'-sid, a., lucido
luck, lŏk, n., sorte f. ; fortuna f.   [tuna
lucky, lŏk'-i, a., fortunato ; (charm) che porta for-
ludicrous, liuu'-di-kros, a., ridicolo, comico
luggage, lŏgh'-ech, n., bagaglio m. ; **—office**,
    ufficio bagagli m.
lukewarm, liuuk'-uoorm, a., tiepido
lull, lŏl, v., placare ; (child) ninnare.
    n., (pause) pausa f., bonaccia f.
lullaby, lŏl'-*a*-bai, n., ninna-nanna f.
lumbago, lom-bei'-gou, n., lombaggine f.
lumber, lŏm'-*ba*, n., cose vecchie f.pl. ; (timber) le-
    gno da costruzione m.
luminous*, liuu'-mi-*nos*, a., luminoso
lump, lŏmp. n., pezzo m. ; (throat) nodo m. ;
    (sugar) zolla f. ; **—y**, a., grumoso
lunacy, luu'-*na*-si, n., demenza f.
lunar, luu'-nar, a., lunare
lunatic, luu'-*na*-tik, n., demente m & f. ;
    — asylum, manicomio m.
lunch(eon), lŏnch ('-n), n., colazione f.
lung, lŏng-gh, n., polmone m.
lurch, lĕrch, v., (ship) rullare ; (person) traballare ;
    to leave in the —, lasciar in asso
lure, liur, v., adescare, allettare. n., adescamento.
lurid, liu'-rid, a., lurido   [m.
lurk, lĕrk, v., essere in agguato ; celarsi
luscious, lŏ'-shos, a., succoso
lust, lŏst, n., lussuria f. ; (greed) concupiscenza f.
    v., bramare ; **—ful**, a., libidinoso
lustre, lost'-*a*, n., splendore m. ; (pendant) lampa-
lute, liuut, n., liuto m.   [dario m.
luxurious*, lŏk-siu'-ri-os, a., suntuoso
luxury l ŏk-sher-i, n., lusso m.
lying-in, lai'-ing-in, n., parto m.
lymph, limf, n., linfa f.
lynch, linch, v., linciare

macaroni, mak-*a*-ron'-ni, n., maccheroni m. pl.

macaroon, mak-*a*-ruun', n., amaretto m.

mace, meis, n., mazza f.

machine, m*a*-shiin', n., macchina f. ; —**ry**, meccanismo m. ; —-**gun**, mitragliatrice f.

machinist, m*a*-shin'-ist, n., macchinista m.

mackerel, mak'-*e*-rel, n., sgombro m.

mackintosh, mak'-in-tosh, n., impermeabile m.

mad, mad, a., pazzo

madam, mad'-m, n., signora f.

madman, mad'-man, n., pazzo m.

madness, mad'-nes, n., pazzia f.

magazine, ma-g*a*-siin', n., magazzino m. ; (periodical) rivista f.

maggot, magh'-ot, n., verme m.

magic, mach'-ik, n., magia f. a., magico

magistrate, mach'-is-treit, n., magistrato m. [f.

magnanimity, magh-n*a*-nim'-i-ti, n., magnanimità

magnanimous*, magh-nan'-i-mos, a., magnanimo

magnesia, magh-nii'-sh*a*, n., magnesia f.

magnesium, magh-nii'-si-*a*m, n., magnesio m.

magnet, magh'-net, n., magnate m. ; —**ic**, a., magnetico ; —**ism**, n., magnetismo m. ; —**ize**, v., magnetizzare

magneto, magh-nii'-to, n., magnete m.

magnificent*, magh-nif'-i-sent, a., magnifico

magnify, magh'-ni-f*a*i, v., ingrandire ; —**ing glass**, n., lente d'ingrandimento f.

magnitude, magh'-ni-tiuud, n., (size) grandezza f.

magpie, magh'-pai, n., gazza f.

mahogany, m*a*-hogh'-*a*-ni, n., mogano m.

Mahomedan, (see **Mohammedan**)

maid, meid, n., (young girl) giovanetta f. ; (servant) domestica f. : old —, zitellona f.

maiden, meid'-n, n., ragazza f., vergine f.

mail, meil, n., posta f. ; (armour) maglia di ferro f. v., spedire per posta ; —-**bag**, n., sacco della posta m. ; —-**boat**, battello postale m.

maim, meim, v., mutilare

main, mein, a., principale ; essenziale. n., (water, gas) tubo principale m. ; —**land**, terra firma f.

maintain, mein-tein', v., mantenere

maintenance, mein'-*te*-nans, n., mantenimento m.

maize, meis, n., granoturco m., maiz m.

majestic, m*a*-ches'-tik, a., maestoso

majesty, ma'-ches-ti, n., maestà f.

major, meich'-*or*, n., (mil.) maggiore m.; (age) maggiorenne m. & f.; a., maggiore

majority, m*a*-chor'-i-ti, n., maggioranza f.; (of age) maggiorità f.

make, meik, n., (abbricazione f. v., fare; (manufacture) fabbricare; — **believe**, far credere

maker, mei'-k*a*, n., fabbricante m.

makeshift, meik'-shift, n., espediente m.

make-up, meik'-öp, n., (face) truccatura f., belletto m. v., decidere; truccare, imbellettare

making, mei'-king, n., creazione f.; composizione f.

malady, mal'-*a*-di, n., malattia f.

malaria, m*a*-le'-ri-*a*, n., malaria f.

male, meil, a., maschio. n., maschio m.

malediction, mal-i-dik'-shon, n., maledizione f.

malevolent, mal-ev'-*o*-lent, a., malevolo

malice, mal'-is, n., malizia f.

malicious*, m*a*-lish'-os, a., malizioso

malign, m*a*-lain', v., malignare, calunniare

malignant*, m*a*-ligh'-nant, a., maligno

malinger, m*a*-lingh'-*a*, v., fingersi malato

mallet, mal'-*et*, n., maglio m.

malt, moolt, n., malto m.

maltreat, mal-trīt', v., maltrattare

mammal, mam'-mel, n., mammifero m.

man, man, n., uomo m. v., equipaggiare; —**hood**, n., virilità f.; —**kind**, razza umana f.; —**ly**, a., virile; — **servant**, n., domestico m.; —**slaughter**, omicidio m.

manacle, man'-*a*-kl, v., mettere le manette. n., manette f. pl.

manage, man'-ich, v., (business) condurre; (accomplish) venire a capo di; —**ment**, n., amministrazione f., direzione f.

manager, man'-ich-*a*, n., direttore m.

mandate, man'-deit, n., mandato m.

mandoline, man'-dol-in, n., mandolino m.

mane, mein, n., criniera f.

manger, mein'-cha, n., mangiatoia f.   [mangano

mangle, mang'-gol, n., mangano m.   v., passare al

mania, mei'-ni-a, n., mania f.

maniac, mei'-ni-ak, n., maniaco m.

manicure, man'-i-kiuur, n., manicure m. & f.

manifest, man'-i-fest, a., manifesto.   n., manifesto m.   v., manifestare

manifold, man'-i-fould, a., molteplice

manipulate, man-ip'-iu-leit, v., manipolare

manner, man'-er, n., maniera f.;   modo m.;   sorte f., qualità f.

manners, man'-ers, n.pl., maniere f.pl.; modi m.pl.

manoeuvre, ma-nuu'-ver, n., manovra f.   v., manovrare

manor, man'-or, n., maniero m.   [novrare

mansion, man'-shon, n., casa signorile f.

mantel-piece, man'-tl-piis, n., mensola di camino f.

mantle, man'-tl, n., mantello m.;   (gas) reticella d'incandescenza f.

manual, man'-iu-al, n., (handbook) manuale m.;   — labour, lavoro manuale m.

manufactory, man-iu-fak'-to-ri, n., manifattura f.

manufacture, man-iu-fak'-chur, n., manifattura f.   v., manifatturare;   —r, n., fabbricante m.

manure, ma-niur', n., concime m.   v., concimare

manuscript, man'-iu-skript, n., manoscritto m.

many, men'-i, a., molti, molte;   — a, più di un

map, map, n., carta f., mappa f.; (town) pianta f.   v., tracciare il piano di

maple, mei'-pl, n., acero m.

mar, maar, v., guastare;   turbare

marble, maar'-bl, n., marmo m.;   (toy) pallina f.

March, maarch, n., marzo m.

march, maarch, v., marciare.   n., marcia f.

marchioness, maar'-shon-es, n., marchesa f.

mare, mer, n., giumenta f.;   **night—,** incubo m.

margarine, maar'-ga-rin, n., margarina f.

margin, maar'-chin, n., margine m.

marginal, maar-chi'-nal, a., marginale

marigold, mar'-i-gould, n., calendola f.

marine, ma-riin', n., fanteria marina f.   a., marino

mariner, mar'-i-ner, n., marinaio m.

maritime, mar'-i-tiim, a., marittimo

mark, maark, n., marca f., marchio m., segno m.
v., marcare, segnare ; —ing-ink, n., inchiostro
da marcare m.; trade—, marca di fabbrica f.

market, maar'-ket, n., mercato m. v., trovare un
mercato

marmalade, maar'-ma-leid, n., marmellata f.

marmot, maar'-mot, n., marmotta f.

maroon, ma-ruun', a., marrone. v., abbandonare

marquee, maar-kii', n., (tent) tendone m.

marquess, maar'-kues, n., marchese m.

marriage, mar'-ich, n., matrimonio m., sposalizio m.; (feast) nozze f. pl.

marrow, mar'-ou, n., midollo m.; (vegetable) zuc-
marry, mar'-i, v., sposare   [chino m.

marsh, maarsh, n., maremma f.

marshal, maar'-shal, n., maresciallo m.

marten, maar'-tn, n., martora f.

martial, maar'-shal, a., marziale; court—, n.,
tribunale di guerra m.; —law, legge marziale f.

martyr, maar'-ter, n., martire m.& f. v., martirizzare

martyrdom, maar'-ter-dom, n., martirio m.

marvel, maar'-vl, v., meravigliarsi. n., meraviglia f.

marvellous*, maar'-vel-os, a., meraviglioso

masculine, mas'-kiu-lin, a., maschile

mash, mash, v., schiacciare ; far un purè

mask, mask, v., mascherare ; n., maschera f.

mason, mei'-son, n., muratore m.; framassone m.

masonic, mei-son'-ik, a., massonico

masonry, mei'-son-ri, n., (stone) muratura f.

masquerade, mas-ker-eid', v., travestirsi. n., mascherata f.; travestimento m.

mass, mas, n., massa f.; (eccl.) messa f. v., ammassare

massacre, mas'-a-ker, n., massacro m. v., massa-
crare

massage, mas-saach', n., massaggio m. v., far un
massive*, mas'-iv, a., massiccio   [massaggio

mast, maast, n., albero m.

master, maas'-ta, v., dominare ; vincere ; sormontare. n., padrone m.; (teacher) maestro m.;
—ful, a., imperioso ; —ly, adv., abilmente ;
—piece, n., capolavoro m.

masticate, mas'-ti-keit, v., masticare

mastiff, mas'-tif, n., mastino m.

mat, mat, n., stuoia f.

match, mach, n., fiammifero m.; cerino m., zolfanello m.; (contest) partita f. v., (colours, etc.) assortire, appaiare

matchless, mach'-les, a., senza pari

mate, meit, v., appaiare; (chess) dar matto. n., (work) compagno m.; (naut.) secondo di bordo m.

material, ma-ti'-ri-al, n., materiale m.

materialize, ma-ti'-ri-al-ais, v., prendere corpo

maternal*, ma-tĕr'-nal, a., materno

mathematics, maZ-i-mat'-iks, n., matematica f.

matrimony, mat'-ri-mo-ni, n., matrimonio m.

matrix, mei'-triks, n., matrice f.

matron, mei'-tron, n., (hospital) capo infermiera f.

matter, mat'-a, n., materia f.; questione f.; cosa f.; soggetto m.; (pus) materia f.

matting, mat'-ing, n., stuoia f.

mattress, mat'-res, n., materasso m.

mature, ma-tiur', a., maturo; (bills) scadente. v., maturare; venire a scadenza

maturity, ma-tiur'-i-ti, n., maturità f.; (bill) scadenza f.

maul, mool, v., (by beasts) lacerare cogli artigli

mauve, mouv, a., malva

maxim, mak'-sim, n., massima f.

maximum, mak'-si-mom, n., massimo m.

may, mei, v., essere permesso; essere possibile

May, mei, n., maggio m.

mayor, mei'-or, n., sindaco m., podestà m.

maze, meis, n., labirinto m.

me, mii, pron., mi, me; to —, a me

meadow, med'-ou, n., prato m.

meagre, mii'-ga, a., magro, meschino

meal, miil, n., farina f.; (repast) pasto m.

mean, miin, v., voler dire; (signify) significare. a., meschino; (action) basso; (poor) misero

meaning, miin'-ing, n., significato m.; senso m.

meaningless, miin'-ing-les, a., senza senso

means, miins, n.pl., mezzi m.pl.

meanwhile, miin'-huail, adv., frattanto

measles, mii'-sls, n. pl., rosolia f.

measure, mesh'-er, v., misurare. n., misura f.; (stick, tape) metro m.; —**ment**, misura f.

meat, miit, n., carne f.

mechanic, mi-kan'-ik, n., meccanico m.; —**al**, a., meccanico; —**s**, n., meccanica f.

mechanism, mek'-a-nism, n., meccanismo m.

medal, med'-l, n., medaglia f.

meddle, med'-l, v., immischiarsi

mediæval, med-i-i'-vl, a., medioevale

mediate, mii'-di-eit, v., intercedere

medical, med'-i-kl, a., medicinale; **medico**

medicine, med'-i-sin, n., medicina f.

mediocre, mii'-di-ou-kr, a., mediocre

meditate, med'-i-teit, v., meditare

medium, mii'-di-om, n., mezzo m.; (person) medio m. a., medio

meek*, milk, a., mansueto

meerschaum, miir'-shom, n., schiuma di mare f.

meet, miit, v., incontrare; (chance) incontrarsi; (obligations) far onore a. n., (hunt) radunata f.

meeting, miit'-ing, n., incontro m.; riunione f.; (public) comizio m.

melancholy, mel'-an-kol-i, n., melanconia f. a., melanconico

mellow, mel'-ou, a., molle, maturo; (tone) dolce

melodious*, mi-lou'-di-os, a., melodioso

melody, mel'-o-di, n., melodia f.

melon, mel'-on, n., melone m.

melt, melt, v., fondere

member, mem'-ba, n., membro m.; (club) socio m.; (parliament) deputato m.; —**ship**, qualità di socio f.; quota di associazione f.

memento, mi-men'-tou, n., memento m.

memoirs, mem'-uaars, n. pl., memorie f. pl.

memorandum, mem-o-ran'-dom, n., memorandum m.; —**book**, agenda f.

memorial, mi-mou'-ri-al, n., ricordo m.

memory, mem'-o-ri, n., memoria f.

menace, men'-as, n., minaccia f. v., minacciare

menagerie, mi-nach'-er-i, n., serraglio m.

mend, mend, v., riparare; (sew) rammendare

mendacious, men-dei'-sh*o*s. a., mendace

menial, mee'-ni-*al*, n., servo m. a., servile

mental, men'-t*l*, a., mentale

mention, men'-sh*o*n, v., menzionare

menu, men'-iu, n., lista dei piatti f.

mercantile, m*ĕr*-kan-tail, a., mercantile

merchandise, m*ĕr*'-ch*a*n-dai*s*, n., mercanzia f.

merchant, m*ĕr*'-ch*a*nt, n., mercante m., negoziante m.; — -fleet, flotta mercantile f.

merciful*, m*ĕr*'-si-f*u*l, a., misericordioso

mercury, m*ĕr*'-kiu-ri, n., mercurio m.

mercy, m*ĕr*'-si, n., misericordia f.

mere, mir, a.,• puro ; semplice. n., laghetto m.

merge, m*ĕr*ch, v., fondere ; assorbire

meridian, mi-ri'-di-*a*n, n., meridiano m.

merit, mer'-it, v., meritare. n., merito m. ; on one's —s, meritato ; per proprio merito

meritorious*, mer-i-to'-ri-*o*s, a., meritorio

mermaid, m*ĕr*'-meid, n., sirena f.

merriment, mer'-i-m*e*nt, n., gaiezza f., allegria f.

merry, mer'-i, a., gaio, gioioso

mesh, mesh, n., maglia f.

mesmerize, me*s*'-m*ĕr*-ai*s*, v., magnetizzare

mess, mes, v., sporcare. n., (dirt) porcheria f.; (bungle) guazzabuglio m.; (naut., mil.) mensa f.

message, mes'-ich, n., messaggio m.

messenger, mes'-en-ch*a*, n., messaggero m.

metal, met'-l, n., metallo m. ; —lic, a., metallico

meteor, mii'-ti-*o*r, n., meteora f.

meter, mii'-t*a*, n., contatore m.

method, me*Z*'-*o*d, n., metodo m.   [brucio m.

methylated (spirit), mii'-*Z*i-lei-tid, n., spirito da

metropolis, mi-trop'-*o*-lis, n., metropoli f.

mica, mai'-k*a*, n., mica f.

Michaelmas, mik'-*e*l-m*a*s, n., festa di San Michele f.

microscope, mai'-kros-koup, n., microscopio m.

midday, mid'-dei, n., mezzogiorno m.

middle, mid'-l, n., mezzo m., centro m. a., di mezzo ; — -age, n., medio evo m.; — -class (people), classe media f. ; —man, intermediario m.

midge, mich, n., moscherino m.

midget, mich'-*e*t, n., (dwarf) nano m.

midnight, mid'-nait. n., mezzanotte f.

midshipman, mid'-ship-man, n., guardia marina m.

midst, midst. prep., mezzo

midwife, mid'-uaif, n., levatrice f.

mien, miin, n., ciera f., aspetto m.

might, mait, n., potere m.: —y, a., potente

mignonette, min-ion-et', n., reseda f.

migrate, mai'-greit, v., emigrare

mild*, maild, a., mite; (not strong) leggero

mildew, mil'-diuu, n., muffa f.

mile, mail, n., miglio m.;—stone, pietra migliare f.

military, mil'-i-ta-ri, n., militare m. a., militare

milk, milk, n., latte m.

milky, milk'-i, a., di latte; —way, n., via lattea f.

mill, mil, n., mulino m.; (textile) stabilimento tessile m.; (paper) fabbrica di carta f.

miller, mil'-a, n., mugnaio m.

milliner, mil'-i-na, n., modista f.

millinery, mil'-i-ner-i, n., mode f.pl. modisteria f.

million, mil'-ion, n., milione m.; —aire, milionario [m.

mimic, mim'-ik, v., imitare

mince, mins, v., tritare

mince-meat, mins-miit, n., carne trita f.

mind, maind, n., mente f.; opinione f. v., fare attenzione; (look after) attendere; (object) importare; —ful*, a., attento; memore

mine, main, poss.pron., di me, mio, il mio; mia, la mia; miei, i miei; mie, le mie

mine, main, n., (pit) miniera f.; (explosive) mina f.

miner, main'-a, n., minatore m.

mineral, min'-er-al, n., minerale m.

mingle, ming'-gol, v., mischiare

miniature, min'-ia-tiur, n., miniatura f.

minimize, min'-i-mais, v., ridurre al minimo

minister, min'-is-ta, n., (cabinet) ministro m.; (parson) pastore m. v., provvedere; amministrare

ministry, min'-is-tri, n., ministero m.

mink, mink, n., visone m.

minor, mai'-na, n., minore m. & f., minorenne m. & f. a., piccolo

minority, mi-nor'-i-ti, n., (number) minoranza f.

minstrel, min'-strel, n., menestrello m.

mint, mint, n., (coin) zecca f. ; (plant) menta f.
v., batter moneta
minuet, min-iu-et', n., minuetto m.
minus, mai'-nos, adv., meno. prep., senza
minute, min'-it, n., minuto m.   [nuzioso
minute*, mai-niuut', a., minuscolo ; (precise) mi-
miracle, mi'-ra-kl, n., miracolo m.
miraculous*, mi-rak'-iu-los, a., miracoloso
mirage, mi-raash', n., miraggio m.
mire, mair, n., melma f.
mirror, mir'-or, n., specchio m. v., riflettere
mirth, mĕrZ, n., allegria f., gaiezza f.
misadventure, mis-ad-ven'-chur, n., sfortuna f.
misapprehension, mis-ap-ri-hen'-shon, n., malinteso m.
misappropriate, mis-a-prou'-pri-eit, v., appro-
priare indebitamente
misbehave, mis-bi-heiv', v., condursi male
miscarriage, mis-kar'-ich, n., insuccesso m. ;
(birth) aborto m. ; (justice) giudizio ingiusto m.
miscarry, mis-kar'-i, v., fallire ; (med.) abortire
miscellaneous*, mis-el-ei'-ni-os, a., miscellaneo
mischief, mis'-chif, n., malizia f.; (harm) male m.
mischievous*, mis'-chii-vos, a., malizioso
misconduct, mis-kon'-dŏkt, n., mala condotta f.;
(law) adulterio m.
misconstruction, mis-kon-strŏk'-shon, n., falsa
interpretazione f.
miscount, mis-kaunt', v., calcolare male
miscreant, mis'-kri-ant, n., miscredente m.
misdeed, mis'-diid, n., misfatto m.
misdemeanour, mis-di-mii'-na, n., (law) trasgressione alla legge f.
misdirect, mis-di-rekt', v., dirigere male
miser, mai'-sa, n., avaro m. ; —ly, a., avaro
miserable, mis'-er-a-bl, a., miserabile
misery, miis'-er-y, n., miseria f.
misfit, mis-fit', n., vestiario inadatto m.
misfortune, mis-foor'-chon, n., sfortuna f.
misgiving, mis-ghiiv'-ing, n., timore m.
misgovern, mis-gŏv'-ern, v., governare male
misguide, mis-gaid', v., fuorviare, traviare

mishap, mis-hap', n., accidente m. ; contrattempo

misinform, mis-in-foorm', v., informare male [m.

misjudge, mis-chŏch', v., giudicare male

mislay, mis-lei', v., smarrire

mislead, mis-liid', v., sviare ; (fraud) ingannare

mismanage, mis-man'-ich, v., condurre male

misplace, mis-pleis', v., porre male

misprint, mis-print', n., sbaglio di stampa m.

mispronounce, mis-prou-nauns', v., pronunciare male

misrepresent, mis-rep-ri-sent', v., snaturare ; falsare

miss, mis, v., (train, etc.) perdere ; (feel lack of) sentire la mancanza : (shots) sbagliare il bersaglio

Miss, mis, n., signorina f.

missile, mis'-il, n., proiettile m.

missing, mis'-ing, a., mancante, assente, perduto, n., (casualties) assente m.

mission, mish'-on, n., missione f.

missionary, mish'-on-a-ri, n., missionario m.

misstatement, mis-steit'-ment, n., dichiarazione erronea f.

mist, mist, n., bruma f. ; —y, brumoso

mistake, mis-teik', n., errore m. v., sbagliare

mistaken, mis-tei'-kn, a., erroneo

Mister (Mr.), mis'-ta, n., signore m.

mistletoe, mis'-el-tou, n., vischio m.

mistress, mis'-tres, n., (house) padrona f.:(school) maestra f.; (kept) amante f.; (Mrs.) signora f.

mistrust, mis-trŏst', v., diffidare di. n., diffidenza f.

misunderstand, mis-ŏn-der-stand', v., comprendere male ; —ing, n., malinteso m.

misuse, mis-iuus', v., usare male ; abusare di

mitigate, mit'-i-gheit, v., mitigare

mitre, mai'-ta, n., mitra f.

mix, miks, v., mescolare ; —ed, a., misto

mixture, miks'-chur, n., mistura f.

moan, moun, v., gemere. n., gemito m.

moat, mout, n., fosso m.

mob, mob, v., sclamare attorno. n., plebaglia f.

mobile, mou'-bil, a., mobile

mobilize, mob'-i-lais, v., mobilizzare

mock, mok, v., beffarsi ; —at, ridersi di

I—17

mockery, mok′-er-i, n., beffeggiamento m.

mockingly, mok′-ing-li, adv., beffardamente

mode, moud, n., moda f.; (manner) maniera f.

model, mod′-l, n., modello m. v., modellare

moderate, mod′-er-eit, v., moderare. a.,° moderato

moderation, mod-er-ei′-shon, n., moderazione f.

modern, mod′-ern, a., moderno

modest*, mod′-ist, a., modesto

modify, mod′-i-fai, v., modificare   [m.

Mohammedan, mou-ham′-e-dan, n., maomettano

moist, moist, a., umido; —en, v., umettare; inumidire; —ure, n., umidità f.

mole, moul, n., talpa f.; (mark) neo m.; (naut.) molo m.; —hill, tana di talpa f.

molest, mo-lest′, v., molestare

molten, moul′-tn, a., fuso

moment, mou′-ment, n., momento m.   [solenne

momentous, mou-men′-tos, a., molto importante;

momentum, mou-men′-tom, n., impulso m.

monarch, mon′-ark, n., monarca m.; —y, monar-

monastery, mon′-as-tri, n., monastero m.   [chia f.

Monday, mon′-di, n., lunedì m.

monetary, mon′-e-ta-ri, a., monetario

money, mon′-i, n., denaro m.; —box, cassetta dei denari f.; —changer, cambiavalute m.; —lender, usuraio m.; —order, vaglia postale m.

mongrel, mong′-grel, n., (dog) bastardo m.

monk, mongk, n., monaco m.   [f.

monkey, mong′-ki, n., scimmia f.; —nut, arachide

monocle, mon′-ok-l, n., monocolo m.

monogram, mon′-ou-gram, n., monogramma m.

monoplane, mon′-ou-plein, n., monoplano m.

monopolize, mo-nop′-o-lais, v., monopolizzare

monopoly, mo-nop′-o-li, n., monopolio m.

monotonous*, mon-ot′-o-nos, a., monotono

monster, mon′-sta, n., mostro m.

monstrous*, mon′-stros, a., mostruoso

month, monZ, n., mese m.; —ly, a., mensile

monument, mon′-iu-ment, n., monumento m.

mood, muud, n., umore m.; (gram.) modo m.

moody, muud′-i, a., di cattivo umore

moon, muun, n., luna f.; —light, chiaro di luna m.

Moor, muer, n., moro m.; **—ish,** a., **moresco**

moor, muer, n., (heath) brughiera f.

moor, muer, v., (ship) amarrare

mop, mop, n., (ship's) radazza f. **v., pulire**

mope, moup, v., essere scoraggiato

moral, mor'-al, n., morale f.

morass, mo-ras', n., maremma f.

moratorium, mour-a-tou'-ri-om, n., **moratoria f.**

morbid*, moor'-bid, a., morboso

more, mor, adv., più, più di ; **once —, ancora una** volta ; **—over,** di più, per di più

morning, moor'-ning, n., mattino m.; **mattinata f.**

morocco, mo-rok'-ou, n., (leather) marocchino m.

morose, mo-rous', a., mesto

morphia, moor'-fi-a, n., morfina f.

morrow, mor'-ou, n., domani m.

morsel, moor'-sl, n., tozzo m., boccone m.

mortal, moor'-tl, n., mortale m. a., mortale ; **fatale**

mortality, moor-tal'-i-ti, n., mortalità f.

mortar, moor'-ta, n., calcina f.; (gun) mortaio m.

mortgage, moor'-gheich, n., ipoteca f. [m.

mortgagee, moor-ghe-chii',n.,creditore ipotecario

mortification, moor-ti-fi-kei'-shon, n., mortificazione f.; (medical) cancrena f.

mortuary, moor'-tiu-a-ri, n., camera **mortuaria f.**

mosaic, mou'-sa-ik, n., mosaico m.

mosque, mosk, n., moschea f.

mosquito, mos-kii'-tou, n., **zanzara f.**

moss, mos, n., musco m. [il più **spesso**

most, moust, a., il più ; la maggior parte ; **—ly,** adv.,

moth, moZ, n., tignuola f.

mother, möD'-a, n., madre f.; **—hood,** maternità f.; **—-in-law,** suocera f.; **— of pearl,** madreperla f.; **—ly,** a., materno

motion, mou'-shon, n., mozione f.; (machine) **movimento m.** ; **—less,** a., immobile

motive, mou'-tiv, n., motivo m.

motor, mou'-ta, n., motore m.; **— bus,** autobus m. ; **— car,** automobile f.; **— cycle,** motocicletta f. ; **—ing,** automobilismo m. ; **—ist,** automobilista m. & f.

mottled, mot'-ld, a., screziato ; **marezzato**

motto, mot'-ou, n., motto m.

mould, mould, n., (matrix) forma f., stampo m.; (mildew) muffa f.; (earth) terriccio m. v., model-**moulder,** moul'-da, n., modellatore m. [lare

mouldy, moul'-di, a., ammuffito

moult, moult, v., mudare

mound, maund, n., monticello di terra m.

mount, maunt, n., (horse) cavallo da sella m.; (picture) quadro m v., salire, montare; (jewels) montare; —**ed,** a., (horseback) a cavallo

mountain, maun'-tin, n., montagna f.;—**eer,** montanaro m.; —**ous,** a., montagnoso; — **range,** n., catena di monti f.

mourn, moorn, v., lamentare; piangere; —**er,** n., persona in lutto f.; —**ful***, a., triste, lagrimoso; —**ing,** n., lutto m.; (apparel) abito da lutto m.

mouse, maus, n., topo m.; —**trap,** trappola da topi f.

moustache, mus-tash', n., mustacchi m. pl.

mouth, mauZ, n., bocca f.; (river) imboccatura f.; —**ful,** boccata f.; —**piece,** (pipe. etc.) bocchino m.; (musical instrument) imboccatura f.

movable, muu'-va-bl, a., mobile

move, muuv, v., muovere; (removal) cambiare di casa n., (games. action) mossa f.

movement, muuv'-ment, n., movimento m.

mow, mou, v., falciare; —**er,** n., falciatrice f.

much, moch, adv., molto; **how** — ? quanto?

mud, mod, n., fango m.; —**dy,** a., fangoso

muddle, mod'-l, n., pasticcio m.; disordine m.

mudguard, mod'-gaard, n., parafango m.

muffle, mof'-l, v., imbaccucare; (sound) attutire

muffler, mof'-la, n., sciarpa f.

mug, mogh, n., vaso m.; (earthenware) ciotola f.

mulatto, miu-lat' ou, n., mulatto m.

mulberry, mol'-be-ri, n., mora f.; —**tree,** gelso m.

mule, miuul, n., mulo m. [m.

multifarious, mol-ti-fe'-ri-os, a., multiforme

multiplication, mol-ti-pli-kei'-shon, n., (arithmethic) multiplicazione f.

multiply, mol'-ti plai, v., moltiplicare

multitude, mol'-ti-tiuud, n., moltitudine f.

mumble, mŏm'-bl, v., mormorare [f.

mummery, mŏm'-er-i, n., mascherata f.; buffoneria

mummy, mŏm'-i, n., mummia f.

mumps, mŏmps, n. pl., orecchioni m. pl.

munch, mŏnch, v., masticare rumorosamente

municipal, miu-nis'-i-pal, a., municipale

munificent, miu-nif'-i-sent, a., munifico

munition, miu-nish'-on, n., munizione f.

murder, mer'-da, n., assassino m. v., assassinare ;
—er, n., assassino m. ; —ess, assassina f. ;
—ous, a., omicida

murky, mer'-ki, a., fosco, tenebroso

murmur, mer'-ma, n., mormorio m. v., mormorare

muscle, mŏs'-l, n., muscolo m.

muse, miuus, v., meditare. n., musa f.

museum, miu-sii'-om, n., museo m.

mushroom, mŏsh'-rum, n., fungo m.

music, miuu'-sik, n., musica f. ; —al, a., musicale

musician, miu-sish'-an, n., musico m., musicista
[m. & f.

musk, mŏsk, n., muschio m.

musket, mŏs'-ket, n., moschetto m.

muslin, mŏs'-lin, n., mussolina f.

mussel, mŏs'-l, n., muscolo m., pidocchio di mare m.

must, mŏst, v., dovere ; abbisognare. n., (wine) mosto

mustard, mŏs'-tard, n., mostarda f. [m.

muster, mŏs'-ta, v., riunire, passare in rassegna.
n., mostra f.

musty, mŏs'-ti, a., ammuffito ; di muffa

mute, miuut, a., muto. n., muto m.

mutilate, miuu'-ti-leit, v., mutilare

mutineer, miuu-ti-nir', n., ammutinato m.

mutinous, miuu'-ti-nos, a., sedizioso, ammutinato

mutiny, miuu'-ti-ni, n., ammutinamento m.

mutter, mŏt'-a, v., mormorare

mutton, mŏt'-on, n., montone m., castrato m.

mutual, miuu'-tiu-al, a., mutuo

muzzle, mŏs'-l, n., (for dogs, etc.) museruola f. ;
(snout) muso m. : (gun) bocca f.

my, mai, a., mio, mia, miei, mie ; il mio, la mia,
[i miei, le mie

myrrh, mer, n., mirra f.

myrtle, mer'-tl, n., mirto m.

myself, mai-self', pron., io stesso, io stessa

mysterious*, mis-ti'-ri-os, a., misterioso

mystery, mis'-ter-i, n., mistero m.

mystify, mis'-ti-fai, v., mistificare

myth, miZ, n., mito m.; —**ology**, mitologia f.

nag, nagh, v., rampognare. n., (horse) ronzino m.

nail, neil, n., chiodo m.; (human, etc.) unghia f.
  v., inchiodare; —**brush**, n., spazzola per le
  unghie f.; —**file**, lima per le unghie f.

naive*, ne-iv', a., ingenuo

naked, nei'-kid, a., nudo

name, neim, n., nome m.; **Christian** —, nome
  di battesimo m.; **sur**—, cognome m.

nameless, neim'-les, a., senza nome; anonimo

namely, neim'-li, adv., cioè

namesake, neim'-seik, n., omonimo m.

nap, nap, n., sonnellino m.; (cloth) pelo m.

nape, neip, n., nuca f.

naphtha, nap'-Za, n., nafta f.

napkin, nap'-kin, n., tovagliolo m.

narcissus, nar-sis'-os, n., narciso m.

narcotic, nar-kot'-ik, n., narcotico m.

narrate, nar-eit', v., narrare

narrative, nar'-a-tiv, n., narrazione f.

narrow, nar'-ou, a., stretto; —**minded**, di
  mente ottusa; —**ness**, n., strettezza f.

nasal, nei'-sal, a., nasale

nasturtium, nas-těr'-shom, n., nasturzio m.

nasty, naas'-ti, a., sudicio; (individual) brutto

nation, nei'-shon, n., nazione f.

national, nash'-on-al, a., nazionale

nationality, nash-on-al'-i-ti, n., nazionalità f.

native, nei'-tiv, a., nativo m.; (aborigines) indigeno m.

natural, nat'-iu-ral, a., naturale

naturalization, nat-iu-ra-li-Sei'-shon, n., natura-
nature, nei'-chur, n., natura f.   [lizzazione f.

naught, noot, n., nulla m.; niente m.; zero m.

naughty, noo'-ti, a., cattivo

nauseous*, noo'-shi-os, a., nauseabondo

nautical, noo'-ti-kl, a., nautico

naval, nei'-val, —**officer**, n., ufficiale di marina m.;
  —**engagement**, combattimento navale m.

navel, nei'-vl, n., ombelico m.

navigate, nav'-i-gheit, v., (ship) navigare

navigation, nav-i-ghei'-shon, n., navigazione f.

navigator, nav-i-ghei'-ta, n., navigatore m.

navvy, nav'-i, n., manovale m.

navy, nei'-vi, n., marina f. ; flotta f.

nay, nei, adv., anzi

near, nir, a., vicino, prossimo. v., avvicinarsi ;
   —ly, adv., quasi ; —sighted, a., miope

neat°, niit, a., (spruce) accurato ; (dainty) grazioso ;
   (tidy) ordinato ; —ness, n., accuratezza f. ;
   (elegance) pulizia f.

necessarily, nes'-es-a-ri-li, adv., necessariamente

necessary, nes'-es-a-ri, a., necessario

necessitate, ni-ses'-i-teit, v., necessitare

necessity, ni-ses'-i-ti, n., necessità f.

neck, nek, n., collo m. ; —lace, collana f.

need, niid, v., abbisognare. n., bisogno m. ; mancanza f. ; —less, a., inutile ; —y, bisognoso

needful, niid'-ful, a.,° necessario. n., necessario m.

needle, nii'-dl, n., ago m. ; —woman, cucitrice f.

negation, ni-ghei'-shon, n., negazione f.

negative, neg-a-tiv, n., negativa f. a.,° negativo

neglect, ni-ghlekt', v., negligere

negligence, negh'-lich-ens, n., negligenza f.

negligent, negh'-lich-ent, a., negligente

negotiate, ni-gou'-shi-eit, v., negoziare

negotiation, ni-gou-shi-ei'-shon, n., negoziazione f.

negress, nii'-gres, n., negra f.

negro, nii'-grou, n., negro m.

neigh, nei, v., nitrire

neighbour, nei'-ber, n., vicino m. ; —hood, vicinanza f. ; —ly, a., da buon vicino

neither, nai'-Da, conj., nè ; ... nor, ... nè

nephew, nev'-iu, n., nipote m.

nerve, nĕrv, n., nervo m. ; (pluck) coraggio m.

nervous°, nĕr'-vos, a., nervoso ; (timid) timido

nest, nest, n., nido m. v., nidificare

nestle, nes'-l, v., alloggiare ; (birds) annidare

net, net, n., rete f. v., cogliere colla rete. a., netto ;
   nett weight, n., peso netto m.

nettle, net'-l, n., ortica f.

neuralgia, niu-ral′-chi-a, n., nevralgia f.

neuritis, niu-rai′-tis, n., neurite f.

neuter, niuu′-ta, a., (gram.) neutro

neutral, niuu′-tral, a., neutrale. n., neutrale m.

never, nev′-a, adv., mai; —**more**, non ... mai; —**theless**, nonostante, tuttavia

new*, niuu, a., nuovo; —**year**, n., anno nuovo m.

news, niuus, n. pl., notizie f. pl.; nuove f. pl.; —**agent**, giornalaio m.; —**paper**, giornale m.

next, nekst, a., vicino; seguente; prossimo; (besides) a lato. adv., in seguito

nib, nib, n., pennino m.

nibble, nib′-l, v., rodere; (fish) abboccare

nice*, nais, a., gentile; (pretty) bello, grazioso

nick, nik, n., tacca f.

nickel, nik′-l, n., nickel m. a., (plated) nickelato

nickname, nik′-neim, n., soprannome m.

nicotine, ni′-kø-tiin, n., nicotina f.

niece, niis, n., nipote f. [mente

niggard, ni′-gherd, n., avaro m.; —**ly**, adv., avara-

night, nait, n., notte f.; —**dress**, camicia da notte f.; —**fall**, cadere della notte m.; —**ingale**, usignolo m.; —**ly**, adv., di notte; ogni notte; —**mare**, n., incubo m.

nimble, nim′-bl, a., lesto; agile; vivo

nine, nain, a., nove

nineteen, nain′-tiin, a., diciannove

nineteenth, nain′-tiinZ, a., diciannovesimo

ninetieth, nain′-ti-iiZ, a., novantesimo

ninety, nain′-ti, a., novanta

ninth, nainZ, a., nono; (date) nove

nip, nip, v., pizzicare; — **off**, staccare

nipple, nip′-l, n., capezzolo m.

nitrate, nai′-treit, n., nitrato m.

nitrogen, nai′-tro-chen, n., azoto m.

no, nou, adv., no

nobility, no-bil′-i-ti, n., nobiltà f.

noble, nou′-bl, a., nobile; —**man**, n., nobile m.

nobody, nou′-bod-i, pron., nessuno. n., nessuno m.

nod, nod, v., far cenno di testa. n., cenno di testa m.

noise, nois, n., rumore m.

noiseless*, nois′-les, a., senza rumore; tranquillo

noisily, noi'-*si*-li, adv., rumorosamente

noisy, noi'-*si*, a., rumoroso

nominal, nom'-i-nal, a., nominale

nominate, nom'-i-neit, v., nominare

nominee, nom-i-nii', n., persona designata f.

non-commissioned officer, non-ko-mish'-*ond* of'-is-*a*, n., sott'ufficiale m.

none, nŏn, pron., nessuno

nonplussed, non'-plŏst, a., interdetto

nonsense, non'-sens, n., assurdità f.

non-skid, non'-skid, a., non sdrucciolevole

non-stop, non'-stop, a., continuo ; (train, etc.) di-nook, nuk, n., canto m.   [retto

noon, nuun, n., mezzogiorno m.

noose, nuus, n., nodo scorsoio m.

nor, noor, conj., ... nè ; non più

normal, noor'-mal, a., normale

north, noorZ, n., nord m.

northerly, noor'-*Der*-li, a., nordico ; del nord

nose, nous, n., naso m.

nostril, nos'-tril, n., narice f. ; (horse) froge f. pl.

not, not, adv., non ; punto

notable, nou'-*ta*-bl, a., notevole

notary, nou'-ta-ri, n., notaio m.

notch, noch, v., intaccare. n., tacca f.

note, nout, v., notare. n., nota f. ; banconota f.; (letter) biglietto m. ; — -**book,** libro di note m.; — -**paper,** carta da scrivere f.

noted, nou'-tid, a., famoso, celebre   [nota

noteworthy, nout'-*uĕr*-Di, a., notevole, degno di

nothing, nŏ'-Zing, adv., niente ; for —, per niente ; invano

notice, nou'-tis, v., notare ; osservare. n., avviso m.; attenzione f.; (to quit) avviso m., preavviso m.

noticeable, nou'-tis-*a*-bl, a., notevole, percettibile

notify, nou'-ti-fai, v., comunicare

notion, nou'-shon, n., nozione f.

notoriety, nou-to-rai'-i-ti, n., notorietà f.

notorious*, no-tou'-ri-os, a., insigne ; notorio

notwithstanding, not-uiD-stan'-ding, conj., non-dimeno, nonostante. prep., malgrado

nought, noot, adv., niente, nulla. n., zero m., nulla f.

noun, naun, n., (gram.) sostantivo m.

nourish, nŏr'-ish, v., alimentare, nutrire ; **—ing,** a., nutritivo ; **—ment,** n., alimento m., nutrimento m.

novel, nov'-l, n., romanzo m.; a., nuovo

novelist, nov'-l-ist, n., romanziere m.

novelty, nov'-l-ti, n., novità f.

November, no-vem'-ba, n., novembre **m.**

novice, nov'-is, n., novizio m.

now, nau, adv., ora, adesso ; **— and then,** di tempo in tempo ; **just —,** or ora

nowadays, nau'-a-deis, adv., oggigiorno, oggidì

nowhere, nou'-huer, adv., in nessun luogo

noxious*, nok'-shos, a., nocivo

nozzle, nos'-l, n., (of hose) lancia f.

nucleus, niuu'-kli-os, n., nucleo m.

nude, niud, a., nudo

nudge, nŏch, v., toccare col **gomito**

nugget, nŏ'-ghit, n., pepita f.

nuisance, niuu'-sens, n., fastidio m.; flagello m.

null, nŏl, a., nullo ; **—ify,** v., annullare

numb, nŏm, a., intirizzito ; torpido ; **—ness,** n., intirizzimento m.; intorpidimento f.

number, nŏm'-ba, v., numerare ; (count) contare. n., (figure) numero m.; (many) gran numero m.

numberless, nŏm'-ber-les, a., innumerevole

numerous*, niuu'-mer-os, a., numeroso

nun, nŏn, n., monaca f.; **—nery,** convento di monuptial,** nŏp'-shal, a., nuziale [nache m.

nuptials, nŏp'-shals, n. pl., nozze f.pl.

nurse, nĕrs, n., infermiera f.; (male) infermiere m.; (maid) bambinaia f. v., curare ; (suckle) nutrire

nursery, nĕrs'-ri, n., camera dei bambini f.; (horticulture) vivaio m. ; **— -rhyme,** racconto di bambini m.

nut, nŏt, n., noce f.; (of screw) testa di vite f.

nut-cracker, nŏt'-krak-a, n., schiaccianoci **m.**

nutmeg, nŏt'-megh, n., noce moscata f.

nutriment, niuu'-tri-ment, n., nutrimento **m.**

nutritious, niuu-trish'-os, a., nutritivo

nutshell, nŏt'-shel, n., scorza di noce f.; **in a —,** (fig.) **in breve**

oak, ouk, n., quercia f.
oakum, ou'-kom, n., stoppa f.
oar, or, n., remo m.; —sman, rematore m.
oasis, ou-ei'-sis, n., oasi f.
oat, out, n., avena f.; —meal, tritello d'avena m.
oath, ouZ, n., giuramento m.; (curse) impreca-
    zione f., bestemmia f.; take one's —, v.,
    prestare giuramento
obdurate*, ob'-diu-ret, a., ostinato
obedience, o-bii'-di-ens, n., ubbedienza f.
obedient, o-bii'-di-ent, a., ubbediente
obese, o-biis', a., obeso
obesity, o-bes'-i-ti. n., obesità f.
obey, o-bei', v., obbedire
obituary, o-bit'-ju-a-ri, n., (notice) necrologia f.
object, ob-chekt', v., obiettare; (oppose) opporsi
object, ob'-chekt, n., oggetto m.; (aim) scopo m.
objection, ob-chek'-shon, n., obiezione f.
objectionable, ob-chek-shon-a-bl, a., biasimevole
objective, ob-chek'-tiv, n., obbiettivo m.
obligation, ob-li-ghei'-shon, n., obbligazione f.
obligatory, ob'-li-ga-to-ri, a., obbligatorio
oblige, ob-laich', v., obbligare ; (favour) far il favore
obliging, ob-laich'-ing. a., compiacente, gentile
obliterate, ob-lit'-er-eit, v., obliterare
oblivion, ob-liv'-i-on, n., oblio m.
oblivious*, ob-liv'-i-os. a., dimentico, assente
oblong, ob'-long a., oblungo
obnoxious*, ob-nok'-shos, a., nocivo ; ripugnante
obscene*, ob-siin', a., osceno
obscure, ob-skiu', a.,* oscuro. v., oscurare
observance, ob-sér'-vans,n.,(comply) osservanza f.
observant, ob-sér'-vant, a., osservante
observation, ob-sér-vei-shon, n., osservazione f.
observatory, ob-sér'-va-to-ri, n., osservatorio m.
observe, ob-sérv', v., osservare
obsolete, ob'-so-liit, a., obsoleto
obstacle, ob'-sta-kl, n., ostacolo m.   [daggine f.
obstinacy, ob'-sti-na-si, n., ostinazione f. ; testar-
obstinate*, ob'-sti-net, a., ostinato
obstreperous*, ob-strep'-er-os, a., turbolento
obstruct, ob-strökt', v., ostruire, ingombrare

obstruction, ob-strŏk'-shon, n., ostruzione f. ; in-
obtain, ob-tein', v., ottenere   [gombro m.
obtrude, ob-truud', v., imporsi
obtrusive, ob-truu'-siv, a., importuno
obtuse°, ob-tiuus', a., ottuso
obviate, ob'-vi-eit, v., ovviare
obvious°, ob'-vi-os, a., evidente, chiaro
occasion, o-kei'-shon, n., occasione f. ; (cause) motivo m.   v., motivare ; —al, a., occasionale,
casuale ; —ally, adv., di tempo in tempo
occult°, o-kŏlt', a., occulto
occupation, o-kiu-pei'-shon, n., occupazione f.
occupier, o'-kiu-pai-a, n., occupante m. & f. ;
(tenant) inquilino m.
occupy, o'-kiu-pai, v., (possess) occupare ; (oneself) occuparsi ; (use) necessitare
occur, o-kŏr', v., occorrere ; — **to one**, accadere
occurrence, o-kŏr'-ens, n., occorrenza f.
ocean, ou'-shon, n., oceano m.
ochre, ou'-kr, n., ocra f.
o'clock, o-klok', n., ... ora f. ; ... ore f.pl.
octagonal, ok-tagh'-on-al, a., ottagonale
octave, ok'-teiv, n., ottavo m. ; (music) ottava f.
October, ok-tou'-ba, n., ottobre m.
oculist, ok'-iu-list, n., oculista m.
odd, od, a., (number) impari ; (single) spaiato
oddly, od'-li, adv., stranamente
odds, ods, n.pl., probabilità f. ; — **and ends**, un pò
odious°, ou'-di-os, a., odioso   [di tutto
odium, ou'-di-om, n., (hatred) odio m.
odour, ou'-da, n., odore m.
of, ov, prep., di, da
off, oof, prep., lungi ; lontano da ; da ; fuori ;
— **and on**, ad intervalli
offal, of'-l, n., frattaglie f.pl.
offence, o-fens', n., offesa f.
offend, o-fend', v., offendere
offensive, o-fen'-siv, a.,° offensivo. n., (mil.) offen-
offer, of'-a, v., offrire. n., offerta f.   [siva f.
offering, of'-er-ing, n., offerta f.
office, of'-is, n., ufficio m. ; funzione f.
officer, of'-is-a, n., ufficiale m.

official, *o*-fish′-l. n., ufficiale m. **a.,** **ufficiale**

officious*, *o*-fish′-*os*. a., ufficioso

offspring, of′-spring. n., discendente m. & f.

oft, often, oft. of′-n. adv., sovente

ogle, ou′-gol, v., occhieggiare

oil, oil. n., olio m. v., lubrificare

oil-cloth, oil′-klooZ. n., tela cerata f.

ointment, oint′-ment, n., unguento m.

old, ould, a., vecchio ; —**fashioned,** all'antica

olive, ol′-iv, n., oliva f. a., (colour) olivastro

omelet, om′-let, n., frittata f. ometletta f.

omen, ou′-men, n., presagio m.

ominous, ou′-mi-*nos*, a., di presagio

omission, o-mish′-on, n., (leave out) omissione f.; (neglect) dimenticanza f.

omit, o-mit′, v., omettere

omnibus, om′-ni-*bus*, n., (motor) autobus m.

omnipotent, om-nip′-*o*-*tent*, a., onnipotente

on, on. prep., (upon) su, sopra ; (date) a ; (foot, horse) a. adv., (onward) avanti

once, uŏns, adv., una volta ; (formerly) un tempo ; all at —, improvvisamente ; **at** —, subito

one, uŏn, (number) un, uno, una. **a.,** un, uno, una ; any—, qualunque ; no —, nessuno, nessuna ; some —, qualcuno, qualcuna

onerous*, on′-*er*-*os*. a., oneroso

oneself, uŏn-self′, pron., sè stesso, sè stessa

onion, ŏn′-i-on, n., cipolla f.

only, ounn′-li, adv., solamente. a., solo, unico

onslaught, on′-sloot, n., attacco m., assalto m.

onward, on′-*uerd*. adv., in avanti

onyx, on′-iks, n., onice m.

ooze, uus, v., trapelare, stillare. n., melma f.

opal, ou′-pal, n., opale m.

opaque, o-peik′, a., opaco

open, ou′-pn, v., aprire. a., *aperto

opener, oup′-na, n., (tool) ferro da aprir scatole m.

opening, oup′-ning. n., opportunità f. ; apertura f.

opera, op′-*er*-*a*, n., opera f. ; —**glass,** binoccolo da teatro m. ; —**hat,** gibus m. ; —**house,** teatro d'opera m.

operate, op′-*er*-eit, v., operare

operation, op-er-ei'-shon, n., operazione f.

operator, op'-er-ei-ta, n., operatore m. ; **(telephone)** signorina del telefono f.

ophthalmia, of-Zal'-mi-a, n., oftalmia f.

opiate, ou'-pi-et, n., sonnifero m. ; narcotico **m.**

opinion, o-pin'-ion, n., opinione f.

opium, ou'-pi-om, n., oppio m.

opossum, ou-pos'-om, n., opossum m.   [m. & f.

opponent, o-pou'-nent, n., competitore m. ; rivale

opportune*, o'-por-tiuun, a., opportuno

opportunity, o-por-tiuu'-ni-ti, n., opportunità f.

oppose, o-pous', v., opporre

opposite, op'-o-sit, n., opposto m., contrario **m.** adv., dirimpetto

opposition, o-pou-si'-shon, n., opposizione f. ; resistenza f.

oppress, o-pres', v., opprimere ; —**ion**, n., oppressione f.; —**ive***, a., oppressivo

optician, op-tish'-an, n., ottico m.

option, op'-shon, n., opzione f.; —**al***, a., facoltativo

opulence, op'-iu-lens, n., opulenza f.

opulent, op'-iu-lent, a., opulento

or, or, conj., o, oppure ; — **else**, o bene, altrimenti

oral, o'-ral, a., orale

orange, or'-inch, n., arancia f. a., (colour) arancio

orator, or'-a-ta, n., oratore m.

oratory, or'-a-to-ri, n., (speaking) oratoria f.

orb, oorb, n., orbe m.; (sphere) sfera f.

orchard, oor'-cherd, n., frutteto m.

orchestra, oor'-kes-tra, n., orchestra f.

orchid, oor'-kid, n., orchidea f.

ordain, oor-dein', v., prescrivere ; (clergy) ordinare

ordeal, oor'-diil, n., prova f.

order, oor'-da, n., ordine m. v., ordinare

orderly, oor'-der-li, a., ordinato, metodico. n., (mil.) ordinanza f.

ordinary, oor'-di-na-ri, a., ordinario

ordinance, oord'-nans, n., artiglieria f.

ore, or, n., minerale m.

organ, oor'-gan, n., organo m. ; —**ic**, a., organico

organisation, oor-gan-i-sei'-shon, n., organizza-

organize, oor'-gan-ais, v., organizzare   [zione f

orgy, oor'-ohi, n., orgia f.

orient, o'-ri-ent, n., oriente m.

oriental, o-ri-en'-tal, a., orientale

origin, or'-i-chin, n., origine f.

original, o-rich'-in-al, a., originale

originate, o-rich'-in-eit, v., creare, dar forma, dar vita ; aver origine

ornament, oor'-na-ment, n., ornamento m.

ornamental, oor-na-men'-tal, a., ornamentale

orphan, oor'-fan, n., orfano m.

orphanage, oor'-fan-ich, n., orfanotrofio m.

orthodox, oor'-Zo-doks, a., ortodosso

orthography, oor-Zogh'-ra-fi, n., ortografia f.

oscillate, os'-il-eit, v., oscillare

ostentatious*, os-ten-tei'-shos, a., vanitoso, fastoso

ostler, os'-la, n., stalliere m.

ostrich, os'-trich, n., struzzo m.

other, ŏD'-a, a., altro, altra, altri, altre ; the — one, l'altro, l'altra ; —wise, adv., differentemente ; (else) altrimenti

otter, ot'-a, n., lontra f.

ought, oot, v., dovere ; bisognare

ounce, auns, n., oncia f.

our, aur, a., nostro, nostra, nostri, nostre

ours, aurs, pron., il nostro, la nostra, i nostri, le nostre

ourselves, aur-selvs', pron., noi stessi

out, aut, adv., fuori, di fuori. a., (extinguished) estinto ; —and-out, adv., completamente, del tutto, pienamente ; —bid, v., fare una offerta maggiore ; —break, n., scoppio m. ; —burst, esplosione f. ; —cast, reietto m. ; —cry, clamore m. ; —do, v., superare, sorpassare ; —fit, n., (equipment) equipaggiamento m. ; —fitter, fornitore di vestiti fatti m. ; (ships) armatore m. ; —goings, spese f. pl. ; —grow, v., ingrandire troppo per ; —ing, n., sortita f., escursione f. ; —last, v., durare più a lungo di ; —law, n., persona fuori della legge f. ; —lay, sborsi m.pl. ; —let, uscita f. ; (market) sbocco m. ; —line, abbozzo m. ; rilievo m. ; contorno m. ; —live, v., sopravvivere a ; —look, n., prospettiva f. ; aspetto m. ; —lying, a., remoto ; limitrofo ;

— number, v., superare in numero; —of
-bounds, a. fuor dei limiti; —-of-fashion,
antiquato; —-of-sight, fuori di vista; — -of
-step, fuori di passo; — -of-tune, stonato;
— -of-work, disoccupato; — -patient, n.,
ammalato esterno m.; —-post, avamposto m.;
—put, rendimento m.; —rage, oltraggio m.,
offesa f.; —rageous°, a., oltraggioso; —right,
adv., addirittura; —run, v., oltrepassare; infestare; —side, n., il di fuori m. a., esterno.
adv., (outdoors) di fuori, all'esterno; —size,
n., misura extra f.; —skirts, periferia f.;
—standing. a., prominente; (debts) non pa-
gato; —ward, adv., al di fuori. a., esteriore;
—ward-bound, (shipping) a destinazione
dell'estero; —wit, v., mostrarsi più astuto
oval, ou′-val, n., ovale m. & f. a., ovale
oven, ŏ′-vn, n., forno m.
over, ou′-va, prep., sopra; al di sopra di; al di là di.
adv., per di sopra. a., (past) finito; —alls, n.,
vestito di lavoro m.; (one-piece) tuta f.; —bear-
ing, a., arrogante; —board, adv., fuori bordo;
—cast, a., coperto; —charge, n., (price) prezzo
eccessivo m. v., far pagare troppo; —coat, n.,
soprabito m.; —come, v., superare; (over-
power) sopraffare; —do, far troppo; eccedere;
(cooking) cuocer troppo; —dose, n., dose troppo
forte f.; —draw, v., eccedere il proprio credito;
—due, a., (late) in ritardo; (debt) scaduto, in
sofferenza; —flow, v., traboccare; —grow,
crescere troppo; (botanical) coprire; —hang,
curvarsi sopra; —haul, ispezionare; —head,
adv., sopra la testa; —hear, v., udire casual-
mente; —land, a., per terra; —lap, v., sovrap-
porsi; —load, caricare troppo; —look,
(forgive) passar sopra; (forget) negligere;
(view) guardar sopra; —power, dominare;
vincere; —rate, esagerare; stimar troppo;
—rule, (set aside) rigettare; —run, coprire;
infestare; —seas, adv., oltre mare; —see, v.
sorvegliare, sopraintendere; —seer, n., sorve
gliante m. & f.; —sight, svista f.; —sleep-

v., dormire troppo ; —step, eccedere ; —take, raggiungere ; —throw, rovesciare ; —time, n., (work) lavoro straordinario m. ; —ture, proposta f. ; (mus.) preludio m. ; —turn, v., rovesciare ; rovesciarsi ; —weight, n., eccedenza di peso f. ; —whelm, v., colmare ; (conquer) sopraffare ; —work, lavorare troppo

owe, ou, v., dovere

owing, ou'-ing, a., (money) dovuto ; — to, prep., a causa di

owl, aul, n., gufo m. [causa di

own, Oun, v., possedere ; ammettere

owner, ou'-na, n., proprietario m.

ox, oks, n., bue m.

oxygen, oks'-i-chen, n., ossigeno m.

oyster, ois'-ta, n., ostrica f. ; —bed, ostricaio m.

pace, peis, v., camminare su e glù ; (sport) dare il passo. n., passo m. ; (speed) marcia f.

pacific, pas'-i-fik, a., pacifico

pacify, pas'-i-fai, v., pacificare

pack, pak, v., imballare ; impaccare. n., (bundle) pacco m. ; (gang) banda f. ; (hounds) muta f. ; (cards) pacco m. ; —age, collo m. ; —et, pacchetto m. ; —ing, imballaggio m. ; impacco m. ; (mech.) guarnizione f.

pact, pakt, n., patto m.

pad, pad, v., imbottire. n., imbottitura f. ; (stamp) tampone m. ; (paper) blocco di carta da scrivere m. ; —ding, imbottitura f. ; superfluità f.

paddle, pad'-l, v., remare colla pagaia ; (feet) guazzare. n., pagaia f. ; —box, tamburo di ruota m. ; —ste;mer, vapore a ruote m. ; —wheel, ruota f.

paddock, pad'-ok, n., (meadow) pascolo m. ; (at races) recinto dei cavalli m.

padlock, pad'-lok, n., lucchetto m. v., chiudere a lucchetto

pagan, pei'-gan, n., pagano m. [lucchetto

page, peich, n., pagina f. ; —boy, paggio m. ; (hotel, etc.) ragazzo d'albergo m.

pageant, pach'-ent, n., corteo m. ; parata f.

pail, peil, n., secchio m.

pain, pein, n., dolore m. ; —ful*, a., doloroso ; —less, senza dolore

paint, peint, v., dipingere ; (make up) imbellettare.
n., pittura f., colore m. ; —**er,** pittore m. ;
—**ing,** pittura f., quadro m., dipinto m.

pair, per, n., paio m.

palace, pal'-is, n., palazzo m.

palatable, pal'-a-ta-bl, a., gustoso

palate, pal'-et, n., palato m. [pallidezza f.

pale, peil, a., pallido. v., impallidire ; —**ness,** n.,

palette, pal'-et, n., tavolozza f.

pallid, pal'-id, a., pallido

palm, paam, n., palma f. ; —**ist,** chiromante m. &
f. ; —**istry,** chiromanzia f. ; — **Sunday,** domenica delle Palme f.

palpitation, pal-pi-tei'-shon, n., palpitazione f.

paltry, pool'-tri, a., meschino

pamper, pam'-pa, v., guastare

pamphlet, pam'-flet, n., opuscolo m.

pan, pan, n., padella f. ; —**sauce—,** casseruola f.

pancake, pan'-keik, n., frittella f.

pander, pan'-da, v., (to toady) compiacere

pane, pein, n., vetro m. ; (large) invetriata f.

panel, pan'-l, n., pannello m. ; (list) ruolo m.

pang, pang, n., dolore m. ; (mental) angoscia f.

panic, pan'-ik, n., panico m.

pansy, pan'-si, n., viola del pensiero f.

pant, pant, v., palpitare ; anelare

panther, pan'-Za, n., pantera f.

pantomime, pan'-to-maim, n., pantomima f. ;
(Xmas) farsa di Natale f.

pantry, pan'-tri, n., (food) dispensa f.

pants, pants, n.pl., mutande f.pl.

pap, pap, n., (food) pappa f. ; (fruit) polpa f.

papal, pei'-pal, a., papale

paper, pei'-pa, n., carta f. v., tappezzare di carta

par, paar, n., pari f. a., alla pari

parable, par'-a-bl, n., parabola f.

parachute, par'-a-shut, n., paracadute m.

parade, pa-reid', n., parata f. ; (troops) rivista f.

paradise, par'-a-dais, n., paradiso m.

paraffin, par'-a-fin, n., paraffina f.

parallel, par'-a-lel, a., parallelo

paralyse, par'-a-lais, v., paralizzare

paralysis, pa-ral'-i-sis, n., paralisi f.
parapet, par'-a-pet, n., parapetto m.
parasite, par'-a-sait, n., parassita m.
parcel, paar'-sl, n., pacco m.
parched, paart-sht, a., disseccato
parchment, paart'-shment, n., pergamena f.
pardon, paar'-dn, v., perdonare ; (grant) **graziare.**
n., perdono m. ; grazia f.
parents, per'-ents, n. pl., genitori m. pl.
parish, par'-ish, n., parrocchia f.
park, paark, n., parco m. ; —**ing**, (motors) posteggio m.; —**ing-place**, posteggio per automobili m.
parley, paar'-li, v., parlamentare
parliament, paar'-li-ment, n., parlamento m.
parlour, paar'-la, n., parlatorio m. ; salottino m.
parrot, par'-ot, n., pappagallo m.
parry, par'-i, v., parare
parse, paars, v., analizzare   [nioso
parsimonious*, paar-si-mou'-ni-os, a., parsimo-
parsley, paar'-sli, n., prezzemolo m.
parsnip, paar'-snip, n., pastinaca f.
parson, paar'-sn, n., parroco m.;—**age**, parrocchia f.
part, paart, v.(divide)dividere in parti ; (separate)se-
parare ; (the hair) dividere. n., parte f.
partake, paar-teik', — **in**, v., participare a ; — **of**,
aver parte di
partial, paar'-shal, a., parziale ; — **to**, favorevole a ; —**ity**, n., parzialità f.
participate, paar-tis'-i-peit, v., participare
participle, paar'-ti-si-pl, n., participio m.
particle, paar'-ti-kl, n., particella f.
particular*, par-tik'-iu-lar, a., particolare ; (fastidious) esigente ; (exact) minuzioso
particulars, par-tik'-iu-lars, n.pl., particolari m.pl.;
(details) dettagli m.pl. ; (data) dati m.pl.
parting, paar'-ting,n.,separazione f.;(hair) divisione
partition, paar-tish'-on, n., divisione f.   [f.
partly, paart'-li, adv., parzialmente, in parte
partner, paart'-na, n., (business) socio m. ;
(cards) compagno m. ; (dance) ballerino m.,
ballerina f. ; —**ship**, associazione f.
partridge, paar'-trich, n., pernice f.

party, paar'-ti, n., partito m.; (social) riunione f., festa f.

pass, paas, v., passare; (examination) superare

passage, pas'-ich, n., passaggio m., corridoio m.; (travel) traversata f.

passbook, paas'-buk, n., libretto di banca m.

passenger, pas'-in-cha, n., passeggiero m.

passer-by, pas'-r-bai, n., passante m. & f.

passion, pash'-on, n., passione f.; (anger) collera f.; **—ate***, a., appassionato; vivo, impetuoso

passover, paas'-ou-va, n., Pasqua degli Ebrei f.

passport, paas'-port, n., passaporto m.

past, paast. n., passato m. a., passato. prep., oltre, al di là di

paste, peist, n., colla f.; (cakes, etc.) pasta f.; (gem) gioiello artificiale m. v., incollare

pastime, paas'-taim, n., passatempo m.

pastor, paas'-ta, n., curato m.

pastries, peis'-triš, n.pl., pasticceria f. [ceria f.

pastry, peis'-tri, n., pasticceria f.; **—cook's**, pasticpasticceria f.

pasture, paas'-chur, n., pastura f.

pat, pat, v., battere dolcemente. n., colpetto m.

patch, pach, n., pezza f. v., rappezzare

patent, pei'-tent, n., brevetto m. v., brevettare; **—-leather**, n., pelle verniciata f.

paternal*, pa-tĕr'-nal, a., paterno

path, paaZ, n., sentiero m.

pathetic, pa-Zet'-ik, a., patetico

patience, pei'-shens, n., pazienza f. [malato m.

patient, pei'-shent, a., paziente. n., paziente m.& f.,

patriot, pei'-tri-ot, n., patriotta m. & f.

patriotic, pei-tri-ot'-ik, a., patriottico

patrol, pa-troul', n., pattuglia f. v., pattugliare

patronize, pat'-ron-ais, v., patrocinare; frequentare; farla da protettore

pattern, pat'-ern, n., modello m.; (sample) campione

patty, pat'-i, n., pasticcino m. [m.

paunch, poonch, n., pancia f.

pauper, poo'-pa, n., indigente m. & f.

pause, pooš, n., pausa f. v., fare pausa

pave, peiv, v., lastricare; **—-ment**, n., lastricato m., selciato m.; (street) marciapiede m.

pavilion, pa-vil'-ion, n., padiglione m.

paw, poo, n., zampa f. v., raspare

pawn, poon, v., impegnare. n., (pledge) **pegno m.;** (chess) pedina f.; —**broker's**, casa di pegno f.

pay, pei, v., pagare ; —**able**, a., pagabile

payer, pei'-a, n., pagatore m.

payment, pei'-ment, n., pagamento m.

pea, pii, n., pisello m.

peace, piis, n., pace f.; —**ful°**, a., pacifico

peach, piich, n., pesca f.

peacock, pii'-kok, n., pavone m.

peak, piik, n., picco m.

peal, piil, n., (bells) scampanio m. ; (thunder) rimbombo m. v., suonare

peanut, pii'-nŏt, n., arachide f.

pear, pér, n., pera f, ; — **-tree**, pero m.

pearl, pĕrl, n., perla f.

peasant, pes'-ant, n., contadino m., rustico m.

peasantry, pes'-ant-ri, n., gente dei campi f.

peat, piit, n., torba f.

pebble, peb'-l, n., ciottolo m.

peck, pek, v., beccare. n., beccata f.

peculiar°, pi-kiuu'-li-a, a., singolare, strano

peculiarity, pi-kiuu-li-ar'-i-ti, n., singolarità f.

pecuniary, pi-kiuu'-ni-a-ri, a., pecunario

pedal, ped'-l, n., pedale m. v., pedalare

pedantic, pi-dan'-tik, a., pedante, pedantesco

pedestal, ped'-es-tl, n., piedestallo m.

pedestrian, pi-des'-tri-an, n., pedone m.

pedigree, ped'-i-grii, n., linea di progenitura f., razza f. a., di razza pura

pedlar, ped'-la, n., merciaio ambulante m.

peel, piil, n., buccia f. v., sbucciare ; perdere la pelle

peep, piip, v., (look) guardar furtivamente

peer, pir, n., pari m. ; —**less**, a., senza pari

peerage, pir'-ich, n., dignità di pari f.

peevish, pii'-vish, a., di cattivo umore

peg, pegh, n., (tent) cavicchio m.; (hats) attaccapanni m.; (violin) bischero m. ; (washing) caviglia f.

pellet, pel'-et, n., pallottola f.; (shot) pallino m.

pelt, pelt, v., assalire a colpi di. n., pelle f.; (fur) pelliccia f.

pen, pen, n., penna f.; (sheep) ovile m.; — **-holder,** portapenne m.; — **-knife,** temperino m.
penal, pii'-nl, a., penale ; — **servitude,** n., reclu-
penalty, pen'-al-ti, n., pena f., punizione f. [sione f.
penance, pen'-ans, n., penitenza f.
pencil, pen'-sl, n., matita f., lapis m.
pendant, pen'-dant, n., pendente m.
pending, pen'-ding, a., pendente. prep., **durante**
pendulum, pen'-diu-lom, n., pendolo m.
penetrate, pen'-i-treit, v., penetrare
penguin, pen'-gu-in, n., pinguino m.
peninsula, pen-in'in-siu-la, n., penisola f.
penis, pii'-nis, n., pene m.
penitent, pen'-i-tent, a., penitente
penniless, pen'-i-les, a., senza un soldo
pension, pen'-shon, n., pensione f.
pensioner, pen'-shon-a, n., pensionato m.
pensive*, pen'-siv, a., pensieroso
penurious, pi-niu'-ri-os, a., indigente
people, pii'-pl, n., popolo m.; (community) **gente** f.
    v., popolare
pepper, pep'-a, n., pepe m.; — **-mint,** menta f.
per, per, prep., per ; — **cent,** per cento ;
    — **centage,** n., percentuale f.
perambulator, per-am'-biu-lei-ta, n., carrozzella
    da bambini f.
perceive, per-siiv', v., percepire
perception, per-sep'-shon, n., percezione f.
perch, perch, n., posatoio m. ; (fish) perca f.
perchance, per-chaans', adv., per caso
perdition, per-dish'-on, n., perdizione f.
peremptory, per-emp'-to-ri, a., perentorio
perfect, per-fikt, a.,* perfetto. v., perfezionare
perfection, per-fek'-shon, n., perfezione f.
perfidious*, per-fid'-i-os, a., perfido
perfidy, per'-fi-di, n., perfidia f.
perforate, per'-for-eit, v., perforare
perform, per-foorm', v., eseguire ; (fulfil) com-
    piere ; (stage) rappresentare ; — **ance,** n.,
    (stage) rappresentazione f.
perfume, per'-fiuum, n., profumo m. v., profumare
perhaps, per-haps', adv., forse

peril, per'-il, n., pericolo m. ; **—ous°,** a., pericoloso
period, pi'-ri-od, n., periodo m. ; **—ical,** a., periodico. n., periodico m.
periscope, per'-is-koup, n., periscopio m.
perish, per'-ish, v., perire
perishable, per'-i-sha-bl, a., caduco, deperibile
perjury, per'-chiu-ri, n., spergiuro m.
permanent, per'-ma-nent, a., permanente
permeate, per'-mi-eit, v., permeare
permission, per-mish'-on, n., permesso m.
permit, per-mit', v., permettere
permit, per'-mit, n., permesso m., benestare **m.**
pernicious°, per-nish'-os, a., pernicioso
perpendicular, per-pen-dik'-iu-la, a., perpendico-
perpetrate, per'-pi-treit, v., perpetrare [lare
perpetual°, per-pet'-iu-al, a., perpetuo
perplex, per-pleks', v., imbarazzare
perquisites, per'-kui-sits, n. pl., utili m. pl.
persecute, per'-si-kiuut, v., perseguitare
persecution, per-si-kiuu'-shon, n., persecuzione f.
perseverance, per-si-vi'-rens, n., perseveranza f.
persevere, per-si-vir', v., perseverare
persist, per-sist', v., persistere
person, per'-son, n., persona f.; **—al,** a., personale ;
—ality, n., personalità f.; **—ate,** v., prendere
il posto di ; **—ify,** personificare
perspective, per-spek'-tiv, n., prospettiva f.
perspicacity, per-spi-kas'-i-ti, n., perspicacia f.
perspiration, per-spi-rei'-shon, n., traspirazione f.
perspire, per-spair', v., traspirare
persuade, per-sueid', v., persuadere
persuasion, per-suei'-shon, n., persuasione f.
pert°, pert, a., svegliato, sfacciato
pertain, per-tein', v., appartenere ; concernere
pertinent, per'-ti-nent, a., pertinente
perturb, per-terb', v., perturbare
perverse°, per-vers', a., perverso
pervert, per-vert', v., pervertire [tare
pest, pest, n., peste f.; **—er,** v., annoiare, tormen-
pet, pet, v., vezzeggiare. n., favorito m., beniamino
petal, pet'-l, n., petalo m. [m.
petition, pi-tish'-on, n., petizione f., **richiesta f.**

petitioner, pi-tish'-on-*a*, n., postulante m. & f.
petrify, pet'-ri-fai, v., pietrificare
petrol, pet'-rol, n., benzina f.
petroleum, pi-trou'-li-*om*, n., petrolio m.
petticoat, pet'-i-kout, n., gonnella f., **sottana** f.
petty, pet'-i, a., piccolo, meschino
pew, piuu, n., banco di chiesa m.
pewter, piuu'-t*a*, n., peltro m.
phantom, fan'-tom, n., fantasma m.
phase, feis, n., fase f.
pheasant, fes'-ant, n., fagiano m.
phenomenon, fi-nom'-i-non, n., fenomeno m.
phial, fai'-al, n., fiala f.
philosopher, fi-los'-o-f*a*, n., filosofo m.
phlegm, flem, n., flemma f.
phonograph, fou'-no-graf, n., fonografo m.
phosphate, fos'-feit, n., fosfato m.
phosphorous, fos'-fo-ros, n., fosforo m.
photograph, fou'-to-graf, n., fotografia f.
photographer, fou-togh'-raf-*a*, n., fotografo m.
phrase, freis, n., frase f.
physic, fis'-ik, n., medicina f.; **—al°,** a., fisico
physician, fi-sish'-an, n., medico m.
piano, pi-a'-no, n., pianoforte m. ; (grand) pianoforte a coda m.
pick, pik, n., piccone m.   v., scegliere ; (gather) cogliere ;   (bones) rosicchiare ;   (teeth) curare ;
  — up, pigliare su
pickle, pik'-l, v., conservare in aceto
pickles, pik'-ls, n. pl., conserve in aceto f. pl.
pick-pocket, pik'-pok-*et*, n., borsaiuolo m.
picnic, pik'-nik, n., merenda in campagna f.
picture, pik'-ch*ur*, n., dipinto m.; quadro m.; illustrazione f.
pie, pai, n., pasticcio m., torta f.
piece, piis, n., pezzo m.; **—meal,** adv., a fram-
  menti ; **—work;** n., lavoro a cottimo m.
pied, paid, a., pezzato ; screziato
pier, pir, n., (seaside) gittata f.
pierce, pirs, v., forare, perforare ; (fig.) trafiggere
piercing, pir'-sing, a., penetrante, trafiggente
piety, pai'-i-ti, n., pietà f.

pig, pigh, n., porco m. ; — -**sty**, porcile m.

pigeon, pich′-in, n., piccione m.

pigeon-hole, pich′-in-houl, n., (division) casella f.

pig-iron, pigh′-ai-ern, n., massa di ferro f.

pike, paik, n., (fish) luccio m.

pilchard, pil′-cherd, n., sardella f.

pile, pail, n., (beam) palo m., **palafitta** f.; (heap) pila f. v., ammucchiare

pilfer, pil′-fa, v., rubacchiare   [naggio m.

pilgrim, pil′-grim, n., pellegrino m.; —**age**, pellegri-

pill, pil, n., pillola f.

pillage, pil′-ich, n., saccheggio m.

pillar, pil′-a, n., pilastro m.

pillory, pil′-o-ri, n., berlina f.

pillow, pil′-ou, n., guanciale m.

pilot, pai′-lot, n., pilota m. v., pilotare

pimpernel, pim′-per-nel, n., pimpinella f.

pimple, pim′-pl, n., foruncoletto m.

pin, pin, n., spillo m. ; (bolt, etc.), **caviglia** f. v., fissare con spilli

pinafore, pin′-a-for, n., grembialino m.

pincers, pin′-sers, n. pl., pinze f. pl.; tanaglie f. pl.

pinch, pinch, n., pizzicotto m. ; v., pizzicare ; (press) far male

pine, pain, n., pino m. v., consumarsi ; —**for**, languire

pine-apple, pain′-a-pel, n., ananasso m.

pinion, pin′-ion, v., legare le braccia. n., (mech.) pi-gnone m.

pink, pingk, n., rosa f.; (flower) garofano m. a., rosa

pinnacle, pin′-a-kl, n., pinnacolo m.

pint, paint, n., pinta f.

pioneer, pai-o-nir′, n., pioniere m.

pious*, pai′-os, a., pio

pip, pip, n., seme m. ; granello m.

pipe, paip, n., tubo m. ; (tobacco) pipa f.

pirate, pai′-ret, n., pirata m. v., pubblicare in frode

pistol, pis′-tl, n., pistola f.

piston, pis′-ton, n., pistone m.

pit, pit, n., fosso m.; (theatre) platea f.

pitch, pich, n., (tar) pece f.; (mus.) tono m. v., (throw) lanciare ; (naut.) beccheggiare

pitcher, pich′-a, n., brocca f.

pitchfork, pich'-foork, n., forcone m.

piteous, pi'-ti-os, a., pietoso

pitfall, pit'-fool, n., trabocchetto m.

pith, piZ, n., midollo m. ; quintessenza f.

pitiable, pit'-i-a-bl, a., lamentevole ; pietoso

pitiful, pit'-i-ful, a., compassionevole

pitiless, pit'-i-les, a., senza pietà   [cato !

pity, pit'-i, n., compassione f. ; **what a —** ! che pec-

pivot, piv'-ot, n., perno m.   v., girare sul perno

placard, plak'-aard, n., cartello m. v., affiggere un
    cartello

placate, pla'-keit, v., placare

place, pleis, n., piazza f. ; (locality) luogo m., sito m. ;
    (home) posto m. v., mettere ; (lay) porre

placid, plas'-id, a., placido

plagiarism, plei-chi-a-rism, n., plagio m.

plague, pleigh, n., peste f. v., appestare

plaice, pleis, n., sogliola f.

plain, plein, n., piano m., pianura f. a., (simple) sem-
    plice ; (looks) ordinario ; (clear) chiaro

plaint, pleint, n., lamento m. ; (legal) querela f.

plaintiff, plein'-tif, n., querelante m. & f.

plaintive, plein'-tiv, a., lamentevole

plait, pleit, n., treccia f. v., intrecciare

plan, plann, n., progetto m. ; (draft) pian-
    ta f. v., progettare ; (contrive) divisare

plane, plein, v., piallare. n., pialla f. ; **— -tree**,

planet, plan'-et, n., pianeta m.   [platano m.

plank, plangk, n., tavola f., asse m.

plant, plaant, v., piantare. n., pianta f.; (mech.) mac-
    chinario m.

plantation, plan-tei'-shon, n., piantagione f.

plaster, plaas'-ta, v., ingessare. n., gesso m. ;
    (building) intonaco m., malta f. ; (med.) impia-
    stro m. ; **court—**, taffetà m. ; **—of Paris**,
    gesso di Parigi m.

plate, pleit, v., galvanizzare ; (gild) dorare ; (sil-
    ver) argentare. n., (food) piatto m. ; (metal) plac-
    ca f. ; (family) argenteria f. ; **—-glass**, lastra
    di vetro f.

platform, plat'-foorm, n., piattaforma f.

platinum, plat'-i-nom, n., platino m.

play, plei, v., giuocare ; (music) suonare. n., giuoco m.; (theatre) rappresentazione f.; **—er**, giuocatore m.; suonatore m.; attore m.; **—ful,** a., scherzoso, giocoso ; **—ground**, n., campo di giuoco m.; **—ing-cards**, carte da giuoco f. pl.

plea, plii, n., lite f.; pretesto m.; difesa f.; supplica f.

plead, pliid, v., supplicare ; difensa ; (law) difendere

pleasant, ples'-ant, a., gradevole, piacevole

please, pliis, v., piacere a ; **—d**, a., contento

pleasing, pliis'-ing, a., piacente ; gradevole

pleasure, plesh'-er, n., piacere m.

pledge, plech, n., pegno m.; (oath) **garanzia f.,** parola f. v., (pawn) impegnare

plenipotentiary, plen-i-po-ten'-shi-a-ri, n., **plenipotenziario m.**

plenty, plen'-ti, a., molto, abbondanza

pleurisy, pliuu'-ri-si, n., pleurite f.

pliable, plai'-a-bl, a., flessibile

pliers, plai'-as, n.pl., tenaglie f.pl.

plight, plait, n., stato m.; imbarazzo m.

plod, plod, v., (work) lavorare faticosamente ; **— along**, camminare lentamente

plodder, plod'-a, n., sgobbone m.

plot, plot, n., complotto m.; (story) intreccio m.; (land)lotto m. v.,complottare ;**—ter**, n., cospira-tore m.

plough, plau, v., arare. n., aratro m.

ploughman, plau'-man, n., aratore m.

plover, plov'-a, n., piviere m.

pluck, plok, v., (flowers) cogliere ; (feathers) spennare. n., (fig.) fegato m.

plug, plogh, n., turare; tamponare. n., turacciolo m.; tampone m.; (electric) contatto m.

plum, plom, n., susina f.; **—tree**, susino m.

plumage, plu'-mich, n., piumaggio m.

plumb, plom, n., piombo m. v., (sound) **sondare**

plumber, plom'-a, n., stagnino m.

plump, plomp, a., grassotto ; (animal) grasso

plunder, plon'-da, n.,saccheggio m. v., saccheggiare

plunderer, plon'-der-a, n., saccheggiatore m.

plunge, plonch, v., tuffarsi ; (dagger) **immergere**

plural, pluu'-ral, n., plurale m.

plus, plos, adv., più

plush, plŏsh, n., felpa f.

ply, plai, v., (trade) esercitare. n., (ply-wood) legno compensato m. ; (ply-wool) lana a molti fili f. ; — **between**, v., far servizio fra

pneumatic, niu-mat'-ik, a., pneumatico

pneumonia, niu-mon'-ni-a, n., polmonite f.

poach, pooch, v., (stealing) cacciare di frodo ; —**ed eggs**, n. pl., uova affogate f. pl.

poacher, pooch'-a, n., bracconiere m.

pocket, pok'-it, v., intascare. n., tasca f.

pod, pod, n., guscio m. ; (peas, etc.) baccello **m**.

poem, pou'-em, n., poema m.

poet, pou'-et, n., poeta m. ; —**ry**, poesia f.

point, point, v., indicare ; mostrare ; (sharpen) appuntire. n., (tip) punta f. ; (punctuation, position) punto m. ; —**er**, indicatore m. ; (dog) cane da ferma m.

poise, pois, n., (deportment) portamento **m**.

poison, poi'-sn, n., veleno m. v., avvelenare

poisonous, pois'-nos, a., velenoso

poke, pouk, n., urto m. v., urtare ; (fire) attizzare

poker, pou'-ka, n., attizzatolo m. ; (cards) poker m.

pole, poul, n., palo m. ; pertica f. ; (artic) polo m.

police, po-liis', n., polizia f. ; —**man**, poliziotto m. ; — -**station**, posto di polizia m.

policy, pol'-i-si, n., politica f. ; (insurance) polizza f.

polish, pol'-ish, v., lucidare, verniciare, incerare. n., (gloss) lucido m. ; **furniture** —, (wax) cera da mobili f. ; **shoe** —, cera da scarpe f.

polite, po-lait', a., cortese ; —**ness**, n., cortesia f.

political, po-lit'-i-kl, a., politico ; — -**economy**, n., economia politica f.

politician, pol-i-tish'-an, n., uomo politico **m**.

politics, pol'-i-tiks, n. pl., politica f.

poll, poul, n., (election) votazione f. v., **votare**

pollute, po-liuut', v., contaminare

pomade, pou-meid', n., pomata f.

pomegranate, pŏm'-gra-neit, n., melagrano **m**.

pomp, pomp, n., pompa f. ; —**ous**,* a., pomposo

pond, pond, **n.**, laghetto m.

ponder, pon'-da, v., ponderare

ponderous*, pon'-der-os, a., ponderoso, pesante

pontiff, pon′-tif, n., pontefice m.

pony, pou′-ni, n., cavallino m.

poodle, puu′-dl, n., cane barbone m.

pool, puul, n., (pond) stagno m., bacino m.; (puddle, blood) pozza f.; (cards) messa f. v., mettere assieme [sieme

poop, puup, n., poppa f.

poor, pur, a., povero. n., povero m.

poorness, pur′-nes, n., poverta f.

pop, pop, v., scoppiettare. n., scoppiettio m.

Pope, poup, n., papa m.

poplar, pop′-la, n., pioppo m.

poplin, pop′-lin, n., poplina f.

poppy, pop′-i, n., papavero m.

populace, pop′-iu-las, n., plebe f.

popular, pop′-iu-la, a., popolare

populate, pop′-iu-leit, v., popolare

population, po-piu-lei′-shon, n., popolazione f.

populous, pop′-iu-los, a., popoloso

porcelain, pors′-lin, n., porcellana f.

porch, porch, n., portico m.

porcupine, por′-kiu-pain, n., porcospino m.

pore, por, n., poro m.; — over, v., sprofondarsi in

pork, pork, n., porco m.; — -butcher, pizzica-gnolo m. [gnolo m.

porous, po′-ros, a., poroso

porpoise, poor′-pos, n., marsuino m.

porridge, por′-ich, n., pappa d'avena f.

port, port, n., (wine) Oporto m.; (harbour) porto m.; (naut.) babordo m.; —-hole, sabordo m., fine-strino m. [strino m.

portable, por′-ta-bl, a., portabile

portend, por-tend′, v., presagire

porter, por′-ta, n., (door) portinaio m.; (luggage) facchino m.; —-age, porto m., trasporto m.

portfolio, port-fou′-li-ou, n., cartella f.; (ministerial) portafoglio m.

portion, por′-shon, n., porzione f.; (share) parte f.

portly, port′-li, a., (stout) imponente

portmanteau, port-man′-tou, n., valigia f.

portrait, por′-tret, n., ritratto m.

portray, por-trei′, v., ritrattare; (describe) descrivere

pose, pous, n., posa f. v., posare; —as, farsi passare per

position, po-sish′-on, n., posizione f.

positive, pos′-i-tiv, a., positivo; (certain) convinto

possess, po-ses', v., possedere ; **—ion**, n., posses-
possessor, po-ses'-er, n., possessore m. [sione f.
possibility, pos-i-bil'-i-ti, n., possibilità f.
possible, pos'-i-bl, a., possibile
possibly, pos'-i-bli, adv., possibilmente
post, poust, v., impostare. n., posta f.; (wood,
iron) pilastro m.; (job) posto m.; —**age**, porto m.,
affrancatura f.; — **-card**, cartolina postale f.;
— **-date**, v., postdatare ; — **-free**, a., franco
di porto ; —**man**, n., portalettere m.;—**master**,
direttore di ufficio postale m.; — **-mortem**, au-
topsia f.; — **-office**, ufficio postale m.;—**pone**,
v., posporre ; —**script**, n., poscritto m.
poster, pous'-ta, n., affisso m.
posterior, post-i'-ri-a, a. & n., di dietro m.
posterity, pos-ter'-i-ti, n., posterità f.
posture, pos'-tiur, n., postura f.
pot, pot, n., vaso m. ; (cooking) pentola f.;
(tea) teiera f. v., mettere in vaso
potash, pot'-ash, n., potassa f.
potato, po-tei'-to, n., patata f.
potent, pou'-tent, a., potente
potion, pou'-shon, n., pozione f.
pottery, pot'-er-i, n., ceramica f.
pouch, pauch, n., borsa f.
poulterer, poul'-ter-a, n., pollaiuolo m.
poultice, poul'-tis, n., impiastro m.
poultry, poul'-tri, n., pollame m.
pounce, pauns, v., (on, upon) piombare addosso
pound, paund, n., sterlina f.; (weight) libbra f.
v., (pulverise) pestare
pour, por, v., versare ; (rain) piovere a dirotto ;
— out, (serve) versare
pout, paut, v., far smorfie. n., smorfia f.
poverty, pov'-er-ti, n., povertà f.
powder, pau'-da, v.,polverizzare ; (face)dar la cipria.
n., polvere f.; cipria f.; — puff, fiocco da cipria m.
power, pau'-a, n., potere m. ; (mech.) forza f.;
—**ful**², a., poderoso ; —**less**, a., impotente
practicable, prak'-ti-ka-bl, a., fattibile
practical², prak'-ti-kl, a., pratico [m.
practice, prak'-tis, n., pratica f.; (custom)costume

practise, prak'-tis, v., far pratica; (med.) esercitare
practitioner, prak-tish'-on-a, n., (med.) medico m.
praise, preis, v., lodare. n., lode f.
praiseworthy, preis'-uĕr-Di, a., lodevole
prance, praans, v., impennarsi; (fig.) pavoneggiarsi
prank, prangk, n., scappata f.; burla f., beffa f.
prattle, prat'-l, v., chiacchierare. n., chiacchiera f.
prawn, proon, n., gamberetto m.
pray, prei, v., pregare
prayer, pre'-ĕr, n., preghiera f.; — -book, libro di
    preghiere m.; Lord's Prayer, Paternostro m.
preach, priich, v., predicare; —er, n., predicatore m.
precarious*, pri-ke'-ri-os, a., precario
precaution, pri-koo'-shon, n., precauzione f.
precede, pre-siid', v., precedere
precedence, pre'-si-dens, n., precedenza f.
precedent, pre'-si-dent, n., precedente m.
precept, prii'-sept, n., precetto m.
preceptor, pri-sep'-ta, n., precettore m.
precinct(s), prii'-singkt(s), n., limite m.; distretto m.
precious*, presh'-os, a., prezioso
precipice, pres'-i-pis, n., precipizio m.
precipitate, pri-sip'-i-teit, v., precipitare
precise*, pri-sais', a., preciso
precision, pri-sish'-on, n., precisione f.
preclude, pri-kluud', v., escludere, precludere
precocious*, pri-kou'-shos, a., precoce
predatory, pred'-a-to-ri, a., rapace
predecessor, pri-di-ses'-a, n., predecessore m.
predicament, pri-dik'-a-ment, n., posizione difficile f.
predicate, pred'-i-ket, n., (gram.) predicato m.
predict, pri-dikt', v., predire
prediction, pri-dik'-shon, n., predizione f.
predominant, pri-dom'-i-nant, a., predominante
pre-eminent, prii-em'-i-nent, a., preminente
preface, pref'-is, n., prefazione f.
prefect, prii'-fekt, n., prefetto m.
prefer, pri-fĕr', v., preferire
preferable, pref'-ĕr-a-bl, a., preferibile
preference, pref'-ĕr-ens, n., preferenza f.
prefix, prii-fiks', n., prefisso m. v., prefiggere
pregnancy, pregh'-nan-si, n., gravidanza f.

pregnant, pregh'-nant, a., gravida

prejudice, prech'-u-dis, v., pregiudicare. n., pregiudizio m.; **without —**, senza pregiudizio

prejudiced, prech'-u-dist, a., prevenuto

prejudicial*, prech-u-dish'-al, a., nocivo

prelate, prel'-et, n., prelato m. [liminare m.

preliminary, pri-lim'-i-na-ri, a.,preliminare. n.,pre-

prelude, pre'-liuud, n., preludio m.

premature*, prem'-a-tiur, a., prematuro

premeditate, pri-med'-i-teit, v., premeditare

premier, prii'-mi-a, n., presidente del consiglio m. a., principale

premises, prem'-i-sis, n.pl., locali m.pl.

premium, prii'-mi-om, n., premio m.

preparation, prep-a-rei'-shon, n., preparazione f.

prepare, pri-per', v., preparare

prepay, prii-pei', v., pagare in anticipo

prepossessing, pri-po-ses'-ing, a., avvenente

preposterous*, pri-pos'-ter-os, a., assurdo

prerogative, pri-rogh'-a-tiv, n., prerogativa f.

presage, pres'-ich, n., presagio m.

prescribe, pri-skraib', v., prescrivere

prescription, priis-skrip'-shon, n., (med.) ricetta f.

presence, pres'-ens, n., presenza f.; **— of mind**, presenza di spirito f.

present, pri-sent', v., presentare; (give) donare

present, pres'-ent, n., dono m., regalo m. a., presente; **—ation**, n., presentazione f.; (gift) presente m.; **—ly**, adv., ora, subito [m.

presentiment, pri-sen'-ti-ment, n., presentimento

preservation, pri-ser-vei'-shon, n., (state, condition) conservazione f.

preserve, pri-serv', v.,(defend) proteggere; (in good state' conservare; (fruit. etc.) mettere in conserva

preserves, pri-servs', n.pl., riserve f.pl.; conserve

preside, pri-said', v., presiedere [f. pl.

president, pres'-i-dent, n., presidente m.

press, pres. n..(mech.) pressa f.; (editorial) stampa f.; (throng) ressa f. v., pressare; (clothes) stirare; (fruit) spremere; **—ing**, a., (urgent) pressante

pressman, pres'-man, n., giornalista m.

pressure, presh'-er, n., pressione f.

presume, pri-siuum'. v., presumere
presumption, pri-sŏmp'-shon, n., presunzione f.
pretence, pri-tens', n., pretesa f.
pretend, pri-tend', v., pretendere
pretentious* , pri-ten'-shos, a., pretenzioso
pretext, pri-text', n., pretesto m.
pretty, pri'-ti, a., grazioso, carino
prevail, pri-veil', v., prevalere ; (upon) persuadere
prevalent, prev'-a-lent, a., prevalente   [ricare
prevaricate, pri-var'-i-keit. v., tergiversare ; preva-
prevent, pri-vent', v. prevenire ; impedire ; —ion,
    n., prevenzione f. ; —ive*, a., preventivo
previous, prii'-vi-os, a., anteriore, precedente
prevision, pri-vi'-shon, n., previsione f.
prey, prei, n., preda f. v., predare
price, prais, n., prezzo m. ; —less, a., inestimabile
prick, prik, n., puntura f. v., pungere
prickle, prik'-l, n., punta f. ; (thorn) spina f.
prickly, prik'-li, a., pungente ; (thorny) spinoso
pride, praid, n., orgoglio m. v., inorgoglirsi
priest, priist, n., prete m.
prig, prigh, n., borioso m.
prim, prim, a., ricercato   [pale
primary, prai'-ma-ri, a., primario ; (main) princi-
primate, prai'-met, n., (eccl.) primate m.
prime, praim, n., (of life, period) fiore m. a., (qua-
    lity) migliore. v., (prepare) preparare ; —mini-
    ster, n., primo ministro m.
primer, praim'-a, n., libro elementare m.
primitive, prim'-i-tiv, a., primitivo
primrose, prim'-rous, n., primula f.
prince, prins, n., principe m.
princely, prins'-li, a., principesco
princess, prin'-ses, n., principessa f.
principal, prin'-si-pl, n., (chief) capo m. ; (own-
    er) padrone m. ; (school) rettore m.; (funds) ca-
    pitale m. a., principale
principle, prin-si-pl, n., principio m. ; on —, per
    principio
print, print, n., stampa f.; (photo) stampa f., copia f.
    v., stampare ; —er, n., stampatore m. ; —ing,
    stampa f. ; —ing-works, stamperia f.

prior, prai'-or, n., priore m. a., anteriore. adv., an-
priority, prai-or'-i-ti, n., priorità f. [teriormente
priory, prai'-or-i, n., priorato m.
prism, prism, n., prisma m. : —**atic**, a., prismatico
prison, pri'-sn, n., prigione f.; —**er**, prigioniero m.
privacy, prai'-va-si, n., intimità f.
private°, prai'-vet, a., privato ; particolare
privation, prai-vei'-shon, n., privazione f. [giare
privilege, priv'-i-lich, n., privilegio m. v., privile-
privy, priv'-i, a., privato ; —**council**, n., consiglio
    della Corona m.
prize, prais, n., premio m. ; (ship) cattura f.
    v., valutare
pro, prou, prep., per, in favore di ; — **& con**, pro e
probable, prob'-a-bl, a., probabile [contro
probate, prou'-bet, n., registrazione di testamento f.
probation, pro-bei'-shon, n., legge del perdono f.;
    —**er**, beneficiario della legge del perdono m.;
    (eccl.) novizio m.
probe, proub, v., sondare. n., sonda f.
probity, prob'-i-ti, n., probità f.
problem, prob'-lem, n., problema m.
procedure, pro-sii'-diur, n., procedimento m.
proceed, pro-siid', v., procedere ; —**s**, n. pl., ri-
    cavo m., prodotto m. ; —**ings**, procedura f.,
    (legal) atti processuali m. pl.
process, prou'-ses, n., processo m.
procession, pro-sesh'-on, n., processione f.
proclaim, pro-kleim', v., proclamare [f.
proclamation, prok-la-mei'-shon, n., proclamazione
proclivity, pro-kliv'-i-ti, n., proclività f.
procrastination, pro-kras-ti-nei'-shon, n., pro-
    crastinazione f.
proctor, prok'-ta, n., (university) censore nelle
    università inglesi m.
procurable, pro-kiu'-ra-bl, a., procurabile [zano
procure, pro-kiur', v., procurare ; (pimp) far il mez-
prod, prod, n., puntata f. v., dare una puntata
prodigal, prod'-i-gal, n., prodigo m. a.,° prodigo
prodigious°, pro-dich'-os, a., prodigioso
prodigy, prod'-ich-i, n., prodigio m. [colo m.
produce, prou-diuus, v., produrre. n., prodotto agri-

producer, pro-diuus'-*a*, n., produttore m.
product, pro'-dŏkt, n., prodotto m.
production, pro-dŏk'-shon, n., produzione f.
profane, pro-fein', a.,* profano. v., profanare
profess, pro-fes', v., professare
profession, pro-fesh'-on, n., professione f.
professional, pro-fesh'-on-*al*, a., professionale
professor, pro-fes'-*a*, n., professore m. [f.
proficiency, pro-fish'-en-si, n., progresso m.; capacità
proficient, pro-fish'-ent, a., competente ; valente
profile, prou'-fail, n., profilo m.
profit, prof'-it, n., beneficio m. v., approfittare
profitable, prof-it'-*a*-bl, a., profittevole
profiteer, pro-fi-tiir', n., profittatore m.
profligate, pro'-fli-gheit, a., dissoluto
profound*, pro-faund', a., profondo
profuse*, pro-fiuus', a., profuso
prognosticate, progh-nos'-ti-keit, v., pronosticare
programme, prou'-gram, n., programma m.
progress, prou'-gres, n., progresso m.
progress, pro-gres', v., progredire ; avanzare
prohibit, prou-hib'-it, v., proibire
prohibition, prou-hib-ish'-on, n., proibizione f.
project, pro'-chekt, n., progetto m.
project, pro-chekt', v., progettare
projectile, pro-chek'-til, n., proiettile m.
projection, pro-chek'-shon, n., proiezione f.
proletarian, prou-li-te'-ri-*an*, n., proletario m.
prologue, prou'-logh, n., prologo m.
prolong, prou-long', v., prolungare
promenade, prom-i-naad', n., passeggiata f., passeggio m. v., passeggiare
prominent, prom'-i-nent, a., prominente
promiscuous*, pro-mis'-kiu-os, a., promiscuo
promise, pro'-mis, n., promessa f. v., promettere
promissory note, prom'-is-o-ri nout, n., pagherò m.
promote, pro-mout', v., promuovere
promoter, pro-mou'-ta, n., promotore m., iniziatore m. ; company —, lanciatore d'affari m.
promotion, pro-mou'-shon, n., promozione f.
prompt, prompt, a.,* pronto. v., (stage) suggerire; (induce) istigare ; —er, n., suggeritore m.

prone, proun, a., inclinato ; (lying) prono

prong, prong, n., punta f., dente m.

pronoun, prou'-naun, n., pronome m.

pronounce, pro-nauns', v., pronunciare   [f.

pronunciation, pro-nŏn-si-ei'-shon, n., pronunzia

proof, pruuf, n., prova f.; bozza f.

prop, prop, n., sostegno m. ; puntello m. v., sostenere ; puntellare

propagate, prop'-a-gheit, v., propagare

propel, pro-pel', v., propulsare ; —ler, n., elica f.

proper*, prop'-a, a., appropriato ; (decent) corretto

property, prop'-er-ti, n., proprietà f.

prophecy, prof'-i-si, n., profezia f.

prophesy, prof'-i-sai, v., profetizzare

prophet, prof'-et, n., profeta m.

propitious*, pro-pish'-os, a., propizio

proportion, pro-por'-shon, n., proporzione f.

proposal, pro-pou'-sal, n., proposta f.

propose, pro-pous', v., proporre

proprietor, pro-prai'-e-ta, n., proprietario m.

proprietress, pro-prai'-e-tres, n., proprietaria f.

propriety, pro-prai'-e-ti, n., proprietà f.

proscribe, pro-skraib', v., proscrivere

prose, prous, n., prosa f.

prosecute, pros'-i-kiut, v., (law) processare

prosecution, pros-i-kiu'-shon, n., processo m.

prosecutor, pros'-i-kiu-ta, n., querelante m. ; attore m. ; public —, pubblico ministero m.

prospect, pros'-pekt, n., prospetto m.

prospective, pros-pek'-tiv, a., probabile

prospectus, pros-pek'-tos, n., prospetto m.

prosper, pros'-pa, v., prosperare

prosperity, pros-per'-i-ti, n., prosperità f.

prosperous*, pros'-per-os, a., prospero, fiorente

prostitute, pros'-ti-tiuut, n., prostituta f. v., prostituire

prostrate, pros-treit', v., (oneself) prostrarsi, prosternarsi. a., (sorrow) prostrato

prostration, pros-trei'-shon, n., prostrazione f.

protect, pro-tekt', v., proteggere ; —ion, n., pro-

protest, pro'-test, n., protesta f.   [tezione f.

protest, pro-test', v., protestare

protract, pro-trakt', v., protrarre
protrude, pro-truud', v., protrudere
proud*, praud, a., orgoglioso
provable, pruu'-va-bl, a., provabile
prove, pruuv, v., provare
proverb, prov'-erb, n., proverbio m.
provide, pro-vaid', v., fornire, provvedere
provided, pro-vai'-did, conj., a condizione che
providence, prov'-i-dens, n., provvidenza f.
provident, prov'-i-dent, a., previdente
provider, pro-vai'-da, n., provveditore m.
province, prov'-ins, n., provincia f.; (sphere) competenza f.
provision, pro-vish'-on, n., provvisione f.
provisional, pro-vish'-on-al, a., provvisorio
provisions, pro-vish'-ons, n.pl., viveri m. pl.
provocation, prov-o-kei'-shon, n., provocazione f.
provoke, pro-vouk', v., provocare
provost, prov'-ost, n., prevosto m. [funzionario inglese]
prow, prau, n., prua f.
prowess, prau'-is, n., prodezza f.
prowl, praul, v., girovagare per preda
proximity, prok-sim'-i-ti, n., prossimità f.
proxy, prok'-si, n., procuratore m.; by —, per procura
prude, pruud, n., schizzinosa f.;—nce, prudenza f.;
—nt, a.,prudente ;—ry, n.,rigorismo m.; ritrosia f.
prudish, pruu'-dish, a., schizzinoso, ritroso
prune, pruun, n., prugna f. v., potare
prussic acid, prū-sik as'-id, n., acido prussico m.
pry, prai, v., scrutare, spiare
psalm, saam, n., salmo m.
pseudonym, siuu'-do-nim, n., pseudonimo m.
psychology, sai-kol'-o-chi, n., psicologia f.
public, pŏb'-lik, a.* & n., pubblico m.
publican, pŏb'-li-kan, n., oste m.
publication, pŏb-li-kei'-shon, n., pubblicazione f.
public-house, pŏb'-lik-haus, n., taverna f.
publish, pŏb'-lish, v., fare pubblico; (books) pubblicare ;—er, n., editore m.
pucker, pŏk'-a, v., arrugare; (fold) fare pieghe.
n., ruga f.

pudding, pud'-ing. n., budino m. ; **black —**, san-
puddle, pŏd'-l n., pozza f.   [guinaccio m.

puerile, piu'-*er*-ail, a., puerile

puff, pŏf. n., (breath) soffio m. ; (wind) buffo **m.**
     v., soffiare ; (swell) gonfiarsi ; **powder- —**, n.,
     fiocco da cipria m.

puffy, pŏf'-i, a., gonfiato

pug, pŏgh, n., (dog) cagnuolo m. ; **—nacious, a.,**
     pugnace ; **—nosed**, dal naso schiacciato

pugilist, piu'-chi-list, n., pugilista m.

pull, pul, n., tirata f. ; (tension) sforzo m.   v., tirare ;
     — down, tirare giù ; (demolish) abbattere ;
     — out, estrarre, strappare ; **— up**, issare

pullet, pul'-et, n., pollastra f.

pulley, pul'-i, n., puleggia f.

pulp, pŏlp, v., convertire in polpa. n., polpa f. ;
     wood- —, polpa di legno f.

pulpit, pul'-pit, n., pulpito m.

pulse, pŏls, n., polso m.

pulverize, pŏl'-ver-ais, v., polverizzare

pumice-stone, pŏm'-is-stoun, n., pietra pomice **..**

pump, pŏmp, n., pompa f.   v., pompare

pun, pŏn, n., gioco di parole m.

punch, pŏnch, v., battere ; (pierce) punzonare.
     n., pugno m.; (tool) punzone m.; (drink) ponce m.;
     (of Punch and Judy show) pulcinella m.

punctilious[e], pŏngk-til'-i-os, a., puntiglioso

punctual, pŏngk'-tiu-*al*, a., puntuale

punctuate, pŏngk'-tiu-eit, v., punteggiare   [ra f.

punctuation, pŏngk'-tiu-ei'-shon, n., punteggiatu-

puncture, pŏngk'-ch*ur*, n., (prick) puntura f. ;
     (tyre) bucatura f.

pungency, pŏn'-chen-si, n.,pungenza f.; asprezza f.

pungent, pŏn'-chent, a., pungente

punish, pŏn'-ish, v., punire ; **—able, a.,** punibile ;
     —ment, n., punizione f. ; castigo m.

punitive, piuu'-ni-tiv, a., punitivo

punt, pŏnt, n., barca a fondo piatto f.   v., puntare

puny, piuu'-ni, a., meschino

pupil, piuu'-pil, n., allievo m.; (eye) pupilla f.

puppet, pŏp'-et, n., marionetta f., burattino m.

puppy, pŏp'-i, n., cucciolo m.; (fig.) millantatore **m.**

purchase, pĕr'-chis, n., compera f. v., comprare
purchaser, pĕr-chis'-a, n., compratore m.
pure*, piur, a., puro; (chaste) casto
purgative, pĕr'-ga-tiv, n., purgante m.
purgatory, pĕr'-ga-to-ri, n., purgatorio m.
purge, pĕrch, v., purgare
purify, piu'-ri-fai, v., purificare
purity, piu'-ri-ti, n., purità f.
purlieu, pĕr'-liuu, n., vicinanze f. pl.
purloin, pĕr-loin', v., sottrarre
purple, pĕr'-pl, n., porpora f. a., purpureo
purport, pĕr-port', n., fine m. v., voler dire
purpose, pĕr'-pos, n., proposito m., intenzione f.
purposely, pĕr'-pos-li, adv., di proposito
purr, pĕr, v., far le fusa
purse, pĕrs, n., borsa f., borsellino m.
purser, pĕr'-sa, n., commissario di bordo m.
pursuant, pĕr-siuu'-ant, a., conforme
pursue, pĕr-siuu', v., inseguire; (aim) perseguire
pursuit, pĕr-siuut', n.,inseguimento m.; aspirazione f.
purveyor, pĕr-vei'-a, n., fornitore m.   [f.
pus, pos, n., pus m.
push, push, v., premere, spingere. n., spinta f.
pushing, push'-ing, a., (enterprising) intraprendente
puss, pus, n., miccio m.
put, put, v., porre, mettere; — off, rimettere, diffe-
    rire; — on, mettere su, indossare
putrefy, piuu'-tri-fai, v., putrefare
putrid, piuu'-trid, a., putrido
putty, pŏt'-i, n., stucco ad olio m.
puzzle, pŏs'-l, v., confondere, essere perplesso.
    n., indovinello m.; cross word —, parole incrocia-
pyjamas, pi-chaa'-mas, n.pl., pigiama m. [te f.pl.
pylon, pai'-lon, n., pilone m.
pyramid, pir'-a-mid, n., piramide f.
python, pai'-Zon, n., pitone m.

quack, kuak, v., gridare. n., ciarlatano m.; —ery,
    ciarlatanismo m.; —ing, grido delle anitre m.
quadrille, kua-dril', n., quadriglia f.
quadruped, kuod'-ru-ped, n., quadrupede m.
quadruple, kuod'-ru-pl, a., quadruplo

quagmire, kuagh'-mair, n., pantano m.

quail, kueil, n., quaglia f. v., tremare di paura

quaint°, kueint, a., bizzarro ; —ness, n., bizzarria f.

quake, kueik, v., tremare ; earth—, n., terremoto m.

quaker, kuei'-ka, n., quacchero m.

qualification, kuol-i-fi-kei'-shon, n., **qualifica f.**

qualify, kuol'-i-fai, v., qualificare

quality, kuol'-i-ti, n., qualità f.

quandary, kuon'-da-ri, n., perplessità f.

quantity, kuon'-ti-ti, n., quantità f.

quarantine, kuor'-an-tiin, n., quarantena f.

quarrel, kuor'-el, n., alterco m. v., altercare

quarrelsome, kuor'-el-som, a., litigioso

quarry, kuor'-i, n., cava f. ; (prey) preda f.

quart, kuoort, n., quarto m. ; (music) quarta f.

quarter, kuoor'-ta, v., squartare ; alloggiare. n., quarto m.; (period) trimestre m.; —ly, a. & adv., trimestralmente

quarter-master, kuoor'-ta-maas'-ta, n., furiere m.; (naut.) quartiermastro m.

quartet, kuoor-tet', n., quartetto m.

quartz, kuoorts, n., quarzo m.

quash, kuosh, v., reprimere ; (a verdict) cassare

quaver, kuei'-va, v., tremare. n., (music) trillo m.

quay, kii, n., molo m.

queen, kuiin, n., regina f. ; (at cards) dama f.

queer°, kuir, a., strano

quell, kuel, v., domare ; (allay) calmare

quench, kuench, v., estinguere

querulous, kuer'-u-los, a., dolente

query, kui'-ri, (see question)

quest, kuest, n., ricerca f.

question, kues'-tion, n., domanda f., interrogazione f. v., interrogare ; (doubt) dubitare ; —able, a., discutibile ; — mark, n., punto interrogativo m.

queue, kiu, n., coda f. v., far la coda

quibble, kui'-bl, v., (evade) cavillare. n., cavillo m.

quick, kuik, a.,° pronto ; veloce, celere ; vivace. interj. & adv., presto ; —en, v., accelerare ; animare ; —lime, n., calce viva f. ; —ness, rapidità f. ; (smart) vivacità f. ; —sands, sabbie mobili f.pl. ; —silver, mercurio m.

quiet, kuai'-*et,* a.,* quieto. n., quiete f. v., acquie-
quill, kuil, n., penna d'oca f [tare
quilt, kuilt, n., piumino m.
quince, kuins, n., mela cotogna f.
quinine, kui-niïn', n., chinino m.
quire, kuair, n., (paper) quinterno m.
quit, kuit, v., lasciare ; —s, a., pari
quite, kuait, adv., completamente ; affatto
quiver, kuiv'-*a,* n., (sheath) faretra f. v., fremere
quoit, koit. n., piastrella f.
quota, kuou'-ta, n., quota f.
quotation, kuou-tei'-shon, n., (citation) citazione f. ; (price) stima f., prezzo m.
quote, kuout, v., quotare

rabbi, rab'-ai, n., rabbino m.
rabbit, rab'-it, n., coniglio m.
rabble, rab'-l, n., plebaglia f. ; (riffraff) canaglia f.
rabid°, rab'-id, a., rabbioso ; fanatico
rabies, rei'-bi-iis, n., rabbia f.
race, reis, v., correre. n., (breed) razza f. ; (contest) gara f. ; (motor) corsa f. ; — course,
campo di corse m. ; —horse, cavallo da corsa m. ; —s, (horse) corse f. pl.
rack, rak, n., rastrelliera f. ; (luggage) rete per bagagli f.; (torture) ruota f. v., (brain) tormentarsi
racket, rak'-*et,* n., (bat) racchetta f.
radiant, rei'-di-*ant,* a., raggiante, radioso
radiate, rei'-di-eit, v., irradiare
radiator, rei'-di-e-ta, n., radiatore m.
radio, rei'-di-o, n., radio f.
radish, rad'-ish, n., ravano m.
radium, rei'-di-om, n., radio m.
radius, rei'-di-os, n., raggio m.
raffle, raf'-l, n., riffa f. v., mettere in lotteria
raft, raaft, n., zattera f.
rafter, raaf'-ta, n., travicello m.
rag, ragh, n., cencio m. ; —ged, a., cencioso
rage, reich, n., rabbia f. v., infuriarsi
raid, reid. n., incursione f. ; (air) attacco m. ;
(police) irruzione della polizia f. v., fare incursione
rail, reil, n., rotaia f. ; (stairs) ringhiera f.

rail, reil, v., chiudere con ringhiera

raillery, rei'-ler-i, n., motteggio m.

railway, reil'-uei, n., ferrovia f.

rain, rein, v., piovere. n., pioggia f. ; **—bow**, arcobaleno m. ; **—coat**, impermeabile m.; **—fall**, caduta di pioggia f. ; **—y**, a., piovoso

raise, reis, v., alzare ; (increase) aumentare ; (cultivate) coltivare ; (breed) allevare ; (hoist) sollevare

raisin, rei'-sn, n., uva passa f.

rake, reik, n., rastrello m. ; (person) dissoluto m. v., rastrellare ; (fire) scuotere

rally, ral'-i, v., (collect, reunite) riunire, raccogliere

ram, ram, n., montone m. ; (battering) ariete m. ; (naut.) sperone m. v., sfondare ; (naut.) speronare

ramble, ram'-bl, v., andare a zonzo ; (mind) divagare. n., escursione a piedi f.

rampant, ram'-pant, a., ritto ; (heraldic) rampante

rampart, ram'-paart, n., bastione m.

rancid, ran'-sid, a., rancido

rancour, rang'-ka, n., rancore m.

random, ran'-dom, at —, adv., a casaccio

range, reinch, v., ordinare. n., (kitchen) fornello m.; (extent) distesa f. ; (projectile) portata f. ; **rifle —**, campo di tiro m. ; **mountain —**, catena di montagne f.

ranger, reinch'-a, n., (forest) guardaboschi m.

rank, rangk, v., classificare ; prendere il rango. a., (taste, smell) rancido. n., (grade) grado m., rango m.; (row) fila f.; **—and file**, ranghi m.pl.

rankle, rang'-kl, v., (fig.) inasprirsi

ransack, ran'-sak, v., saccheggiare

ransom, ran'-som, n., riscatto m. v., riscattare

rap, rap, v., (hit) picchiare ; (knock) bussare. n., colpo

rapacious, ra-pei'-shos, a., rapace   [m.

rape, reip, v., rapire. n., ratto m.

rapid[a], rap'-id, a., rapido ; **—ity**, n., rapidità f.

rapids, rap'-ids, n. pl., rapide f. pl.

rapier, rei'-pi-a, n., spadone m.

rapture, rap'-chur, n., rapimento **m.**

rare[a], rer, a., raro ; (air) rarefatta

rarity, re'-ri-ti, n., rarità f.

rascal, raas'-kl, n., furfante m.

rash, rash, n., (skin) eruzione f. a.,° avventato

rasher, rash'-*a*, n., fetta f.

rashness, rash'-nes, n., avventatezza f.

rasp, raasp, n., raspa f. v., raspare

raspberry, raas'-ber-i, n., lampone m.

rat, rat, n., sorcio m.; — -**trap**, trappola da sorci f.

rate, reit, n., (exchange) tasso m.; (proportion) proporzione f.; (tax) tasso d'imposta m.; (speed) velocità f. v., (value) valutare, stimare

rather, raaD'-*a*, adv., piuttosto ; (somewhat) alquanto ; (prefer) preferibilmente

ratify, ra'-ti-fai, v., ratificare

ratio, rei'-shi-ou, n., rapporto m. ; proporzione f.

ration, rei'-shon, n., razione f. v., razionare

rational, rash'-on-*al*, a., razionale

rattle, rat'-l,v.,strepitare. n.,(noise) scuotimento m.; (toy) raganella f.; (death) rantolo m.

rattlesnake, rat'-l-sneik, n., serpente a sonagli m.

ravage, rav'-ich, v., devastare. n., devastazione f.

rave, reiv, v., delirare ; — **about**, (fig.) far pazzie

raven, reiv'-n, n., corvo m. [per

ravenous, rav'-en-os, a., vorace

ravine, ra-viin', n., burrone m.

raving, reiv'-ing, a., delirante

ravish, rav'-ish, v., rapire ; —**ing**, a., incantevole

raw, roo, a., crudo ; (rough) greggio ; (wound) in [carne viva

ray, rei, n., raggio m.

raze, reis, v., radere ; (trees) abbattere

razor, rei'-*sa*, n., rasoio m. ; — **blade**, lama da rasoio f. ; — -**strop**, cuoio da rasoio m. ; **safety** —, rasoio di sicurezza m.

reach, riich, v., arrivare ; estendersi

react, rii-akt', v., reagire

reaction, rii-ak'-shon, n., reazione f.

read, riid, v., leggere ; —**er**, n., lettore m. ; (proof) correttore m.; (book) libro di lettura m.; —**ing**, lettura f. ; lezione f.

readily, red'-i-li, adv., prontamente ; volentieri

ready, red'-i, a., pronto ; — -**made**, fatto. n., (clothes) abiti confezionati m. pl.

real, riil, a., reale ; (genuine) vero ; — **estate**, n., beni immobili m. pl.

realize, rii'-*a*-lais, v., rendersi conto di ; (sell) realizzare

really, riil'-i, adv., realmente [lizzare

realm, relm, n., regno m., reame m.

ream, riim, n., (paper) risma f.

reap, riip, v., mietere, raccogliere ; —**er**, n., (labourer) mietitore m.;—**ing-machine**, mietitrice f.

rear, rir, v., (children) allevare ; (prance) impennarsi. n., (background) retrovie f. pl. ; **in the —**, (mil.) di dietro, in coda

rear-admiral, rir-ad'-mi-ral, n., contr'ammiraglio

reason, rii'-*s*n, v., ragionare. n., ragione f. [m.

reasonable, rii'-*s*n-*a*-bl, a., ragionevole

reassure, rii-*a*-shur', v., rassicurare

rebate, rii-beit', n., ribasso m.

rebel, reb'-l, n., ribelle m. & f.

rebel, ri-bel', v., ribellarsi ; —**lion**, n., ribellione f.

rebound, ri-baund', v., rimbalzo m. v., rimbalzare

rebuff, ri-böf', v., rabbuffare. n., rabbuffo m.

rebuke, ri-biuuk', n., rimprovero m. v., rimproverare

recall, ri-kool', v., richiamare ; (mind) rammentarsi

recapitulate, ri-*ka*-pit'-iu-leit, v., ricapitolare

recede, ri-siid', v., ritirarsi

receipt, ri-siit', v., quittanzare. n., ricevuta f.; (reception) ricevimento m.

receipts, ri-siits', n. pl., (business) incassi m. pl.

receive, ri-siiv', v., ricevere

receiver, ri-sii'-va, n., ricevitore m. ; (bankruptcy) procuratore fallimentare m.; (stolen goods) ricettatore m.

recent, rii'-sent, a. & adv., recente

recently, rii'-sent-li, adv., recentemente

receptacle, ri-sep'-ta-kl, n., ricettacolo m.

reception, ri-sep'-shon, n., accoglienza f., ricevuta f.; ricevimento m.

recess, ri-ses', n., recesso m.; (parl.) vacanze f. pl.

recipe, res'-i-pi, n., ricetta f.

reciprocate, ri-sip'-ro-keit, v., reciprocare

recital, ri-sai'-tl, n., recitazione f.

recite, ri-sait', v., recitare

reckless, rek'-les, a., imprudente

reckon, rek'-n, v., contare, calcolare

reclaim, ri-kleim′, v., reclamare ; (land) bonificare

recline, ri-klain′, v., reclinare

recluse, ri-kluus′, n., recluso m. [m.

recognition, rek-ogh-nish′-on, n., riconoscimento

recognize, rek′-ogh-nais, v., riconoscere

recoil, ri-koil′, v., rinculare. n., (gun) rinculo m.

recollect, rek-o-lekt′, v., ricordarsi

recollection, rek-o-lek′-shon, n., ricordo m.

recommence, rii-ko-mens′, v., ricominciare

recommend, rek-o-mend′, v., raccomandare ; —ation, n., raccomandazione f.

recompense, rek′-om-pens, v., ricompensare. n., ricompensa f.

reconcile, rek′-on-sail, v., riconciliare

reconnoitre, rek-on-oit′-a, v., fare una ricognizione

reconsider, rii-kon-sid′-a, v., riconsiderare

record, ri-koord′, v., ricordare ; registrare

record, rek′-oord, n., record m. ; (gramophone) disco m. ; (law) archivio m.

recoup, rii-kuup′, v., rifarsi di

recourse, ri-kors′, n., ricorso m.

recover, ri-kŏv′-a, v., ricuperare

re-cover, ri-kŏv′-a, v., ricoprire

recovery, ri-kŏv′-er-i, n., ricupero m.

recreation, rek-ri-ei′-shon, n., ricreazione f. ; —-ground, campo di giuochi m.

recruit, ri-kruut′, n., recluta f. v., reclutare

rectangular, rek-tang′-ghiu-lar, a., rettangolare

rectify, rek′-ti-fai, v., rettificare

rector, rek′-ta, n., rettore m. ; parroco m.

rectory, rek′-to-ri, n., casa parrocchiale f.

recumbent, ri-kŏm′-bent, a., coricato

recuperate, ri-kiu′-per-eit, v., ricuperare

recur, ri-kĕr′, v., ricorrere

red, red, a., rosso. n., rosso m. :—**breast,** pettirosso m. ; —**den**, v., arrossire ; —**dish**, a., rossiccio ; —-**hot**, rovente ; —**ness**, n., rossezza f.

redeem, ri-diim′, v., (pledge) disimpegnare ; (bonds) redimere ; (soul) redimere ; (promise) mantenere

redemption, ri-demp′-shon, n., redenzione f.

redouble, ri-dŏb′-l, v., raddoppiare

redress, ri-dres′, n., riparazione f. v., riparare

reduce, ri-diuus', v., ridurre

reduction, ri-dŏk'-shon, n., riduzione f.

reed, riid, n., canna f.   [terzaruoli

reef, riif, n., scoglio m.: (sail) terzaruolo m. v., dar i

reek, riik, n., fumo m.: tanfo m. v., sentire di tanfo

reel, riil, n., (roll) rocchetto m.; (film) rotolo m. v., (sway) barcollare

refer, ri-fёr', v., riferirsi; (apply) dirigersi; (consult) consultare

referee, ref-er-ii', n., arbitro m.

reference, ref'-er-ens, n., referenza f.; **with — to**, in riferimento a

refine, ri-fain', v., raffinare; **—d***, a., distinto

refinement, ri-fain'-ment, n., raffinamento m.

re-fit, ri-fit', v., modernizzare; riparare

reflect, ri-flekt', v., riflettere; **—ion**, n., riflessione f.; (reproach) biasimo m.

reflector, ri-flek'-tor, n., riflettore m.

reform, rii-foorm', v., riformare; (moral) correggersi. n., riforma f.; correzione f.

reformation, rii-foor-mei'-shon, n., riforma f.

refrain, ri-frein', v., astenersi. n., ritornello m.

refresh, ri-fresh', v., rinfrescare

refreshment, ri-fresh'-ment, n., rinfresco m.

refrigerator, ri-frich'-er-ei-tor, n., frigorifero m.

refuge, ref'-iuuch, n., (place) rifugio m.

refugee, ref-iuu-chii', n., profugo m.

refund, ri-fŏnd', v., rimborsare, rifondare

refusal, ri-fiuu-sl, n., rifiuto m.

refuse, ri-fiuus', v., rifiutare

refuse, ref'-iuus, n., rifiuti m. pl.

regain, ri-ghein', v., riguadagnare

regal*, rii'-gal, a., regale

regale, ri-gheil', v., regalare

regard, ri-gaard', v., riguardare; considerare. n., sguardo m.; (esteem) riguardo m.; **—less**, a., senza riguardi; **kind —s**, complimenti m.pl.; **with — to**, in relazione a

regatta, ri-gat'-ta, n., regata f.

regenerate, ri-chen'-er-eit, v., rigenerare

regent, ri'-chent, n., reggente m.

regiment, reʤ'-i-ment, n., reggimento m.

region, rii'-ch*o*n, n., regione f.

register, rech'-is-t*a*, n., registro m. v., registrare

registrar, rech'-is-traar, n., ufficiale di stato civile m.; (courts) cancelliere m.

registration, rech-is-trei'-sh*o*n, n., registrazione f.

registry, rech'-is-tri, n., ufficio di registrazione m.; servants' —, agenzia di servizio f.

regret, ri-gret', v., rammaricarsi. n., rammarico m.

regrettable, ri-gret'-*a*-bl, a., lamentevole

regular*, re'-ghiu-l*a*, a., regolare

regulate, regh'-iu-leit, v., regolare

regulation, re-ghiu-lei'-sh*o*n, n., regolamento m.

rehearsal, ri-hĕr'-sal, n., (stage) prova f.

rehearse, ri-hŏrs', v., far le prove

reign, rein, v., regnare. n., regno m.

reimburse, rii-im-bĕrs', v., rimborsare

rein, rein, n., redine f.

reindeer, rein'-dir, n., renna f.

reinforce, rii-in-fors', v., rinforzare

reinstate, rii-in-steit', v., reintegrare

re-insure, re-in-shur', v., riassicurare

reject, ri-chekt', v., rigettare

rejoice, ri-chois', v., rallegrarsi

rejoicing, ri-chois'-ing, n., allegria f.

rejuvenate, ri-chu'-ven-eit, v., ringiovanire

relapse, ri-laps', n., ricaduta f. v., ricadere

relate, ri-leit', v., raccontare

related, ri-lei'-tid, a., parente

relation, ri-lei'-sh*o*n, n., (reference) rapporto m.; (kinship) parente m. & f.; —ship, parentela f.

relax, ri-laks', v., riposarsi; (abate) rilasciare; —ation, n., (rest) riposo m.: —ing, a., rilassante

relay, ri-lei', v., (radio) ritrasmettere

release, ri-liis', n., liberazione f. v., liberare

relent, ri-lent', v., intenerirsi

relentless*, ri-lent'-les, a., implacabile

relevant, rel'-i-v*a*nt, a., applicabile

reliable, ri-lai'-*a*-bl, a., degno di fiducia; sicuro

reliance, ri-lai'-*a*ns, n., fiducia f.

relic, rel'-ik, n., reliquia f.

relief, ri-liif', n., sollievo m.; (raised) rilievo m.; (mil.) cambio m.; (siege) liberazione f.

relieve, ri-liiv', v., alleviare : soccorrere
religion, ri-lich'-on, n., religione f.
religious*, ri-lich'-os, a., religioso
relinquish, ri-ling'-kuish, v., rinunziare
relish, rel'-ish, n., sapore m. v., assaporare
reluctance, ri-lŏk'-tans, n., riluttanza f.
reluctant*, ri-lŏk'-tant, a., riluttante, ritroso
rely, ri-lai', v., fidarsi, contar su [m.
remain, ri-mein', v., rimanere ; —der, n., rimanente
remand, ri-maand', v., (law) rinviare
remark, ri-maark', v., rimarcare. n., appunto m.
remarkable, ri-maark'-a-bl, a., rimarchevole
remedy, rem'-i-di, n., rimedio m. v., rimediare
remember, ri-mem'-ba, v., ricordarsi
remembrance, ri-mem'-brans, n., ricordo m.
remind, ri-maind', v., ricordare
remit, ri-mit', v.,(money) rimettere ; (fine, etc.) condonare ; —tance, n., (money) rimessa f.
remnant, rem'-nant, n., avanzo m. : scampolo m.
remonstrate, ri-mon'-streit, v., rimostrare
remorse, ri-moors', n., rimorso m.
remote*, ri-mout', a., remoto
removal, ri-muu'-val, n., (furniture) trasloco m.
remove, ri-muuv', v., (furniture) traslocare ;
(shift) rimuovere ; (dismissal) dimettere
remunerate, ri-miuu'-ner-eit, v., rimunerare
remunerative, ri-miuu'-ner-a-tiv, a.,rimunerativo
rend, rend, v., lacerare
render, ren'-da, v., rendere ; —ing, n., (music,
etc.) interpretazione f.
renegade, ren'-i-gheid, n., rinnegato m.
renew, ri-niuu', v., rinnovare
renewal, ri-niuu'-al, n., rinnovo m.
renounce, ri-nauns', v., rinunciare
renovate, ren'-o-veit, v., rinnovare
renown, ri-naun', n., rinomanza f.; (repute) fama f.
rent, rent, v., affittare. n., (hire) affitto m.;
(tear) squarcio m., strappo m.
renunciation, ri-nŏn-si-ei'-shon, n., rinunzia f
reorganize, ri-oor'-gan-ais, v., riorganizzare
repair, ri-per', n., riparo m. v., riparare
reparation, rep-a-rei'-shon, n., riparazione f.

repartee, rep-*ar*-tii', n., pronta risposta f.

repeal, ri-piil', v., abrogare. n., abrogazione f.

repeat, ri-piit', v., ripetere

repel, ri-pel', v., respingere

repellent, ri-pel'-ent. a., repulsivo

repent, ri-pent', v., pentirsi

repetition, ri-pi-tish'-on. n., ripetizione f.

replace, ri-pleis', v., sostituire ; (put back) ricollocare

replenish, ri-plen'-ish, v., riempire

reply, ri-plai', n., risposta f. v., rispondere

report, ri-port', v., far rapporto. n., rapporto m.; (shot) rimbombo m.

reporter, ri-por'-ta, n., corrispondente m. & f.

repose, ri-pous', v., riposare. n., riposo m.

repository, ri-pos'-i-to-ri, n., deposito m.

represent, rep-ri-sent', v., rappresentare ;—**ation**, n., rappresentazione f.;—**ative**, rappresentante m.

reprieve, ri-priiv', n., commutazione f. v., commutare ; rimettere

reprimand, rep-ri-maand', n., riprensione f. v., riprendere

reprint, ri-print', n., ristampa f. v., ristampare

reprisal, ri-prais'-al, n., rappresaglia f.

reproach, ri-prouch', n., rimprovero m. v., rimproverare

reprobate, rep'-ro-bet, n., reprobo m. [proverare

reproduce, rii-pro-diuus', v., riprodurre

reproduction, ri-pro-dŏk'-shon, n., riproduzione f.

reproof, ri-pruuf', n., riprensione f.

reprove, ri-pruuv', v., riprendere

reptile, rep'-tail, n., rettile m.

republic, ri-pŏb'-lik, n., repubblica f.

repudiate, ri-piuu'-di-eit, v., ripudiare

repugnant, ri-pŏgh'-nant, a., ripugnante

repulse, ri-pŏls', v., (enemy) respingere

repulsive*, ri-pŏl'-siv, a., repulsivo

reputation, rep-iu-tei'-shon, n., riputazione f.

repute, ri-piuut', n., riputazione f.

request, ri-kuest', n., richiesta f. v., richiedere

require, ri-kuair', v., (need) abbisognare ; (demand) richiedere ; —**ment**, n., bisogno m. ; richiesta f. ; esigenza f.

requisite, rek'-ui-sit, n., requisito m. a., richiesto

rescue, res'-kiuu, v., soccorrere. n., soccorso m.
research, ri-sěrch', n., ricerca f.
resemble, ri-sem-bl, v., rassomigliare
resent, ri-sent', v., risentirsi di :—ful*, a., risentito ; facile al risentimento :—ment, n., risentimento m.
reserve, ri-sěrv', n., riserva f. v., riservare
reservoir, res'-ěr-vo-ar, n., serbatoio m.
reside, ri-said', v., risiedere
residence, res'-i-dens, n., residenza f.
resident, res'-i-dent, a. & n., residente m. & f.
resign, ri-sain', v., dare le dimissioni ; (claim) cedere ; — oneself, rassegnarsi
resin, res'-in, n., resina f.
resist, ri-sist', v., resistere ; —ance, n., resistenza f.
resolute*, res'-o-liuut, a., risoluto
resolution, res-o-liuu'-shon, n., risoluzione f.
resolve, ri-solv', v., risolvere
resort, ri-soort', n., (health) stazione di cura f. ; — to, v., ricorrere a
resound, ri-sound', v., risuonare
resource, ri-sors', n., risorsa f.
resources, ri-sor'-sis, n.pl., mezzi m.pl., risorse f.pl.
respect, ri-spekt', v., rispettare. n., rispetto m. ; —ability, n., rispettabilità f.;—able, a., rispettabile : —ful*, rispettoso ;—ing, prep., riferenti
respite, res'-pait, n., respiro m.; dilazione f.   [tesi
respond, ri-spond', v., (reply) rispondere
respondent, ri-spon'-dent, n., (law) imputato m., querelato m.
response, ri-spons', n., risposta f.   [tà f.
responsibility, ri-spon-si-bi'-li-ti, n., responsabili-
responsible, ri-spon'-si-bl, a., responsabile
rest, rest, n., (repose) riposo m. ; (remainder) resto m. v., (repose) riposarsi ; —ful, a., calmo ; —ive*, restio ; —less*, irrequieto
restaurant, res'-to-rant, n., ristorante m.;—car, vagone ristorante m.
restore, ri-stor', v., (give back) restituire ; (repair) restaurare
restrain, ri-strein', v., (to check) raffrenare
restraint, ri-streint', n., costrizione f.; arresto m.
restrict, ri-strikt', v., restringere

restriction, ri-strik'-shon, n., restrizione f.
result, ri-sŏlt', n., risultato m. v., risultare
resume, ri-siuum', v., riassumere
resumption, ri-sŏmp'-shon, n., ripresa f.
resurrection, res-ĕr-rek'-shŏn, n., resurrezione f.
retail, ri-teil', v., vendere al minuto
retail, rii'-teil, n., dettaglio m. ; —er, venditore al
retain, ri-tein', v., ritenere   [minuto m.
retaliate, ri-tal'-i-eit, v., usare rappresaglie
retard, ri-taard', v., ritardare
reticent, ret'-i-sent, a., reticente
retinue, ret'-i-niuu, n., seguito m.
retire, ri-tair', v., ritirarsi ; —ment, n., ritiro m.;
    (enemy) ritirata f.
retort, ri-toort', n., ritorsione f. v., ritorcere
retract, ri-trakt', v., ritrattare
retreat, ri-triit', v., ritirare. n., ritirata f.
retrench, ri-trench', v., economizzare
retrieve, ri-triiv', v., ricuperare, riparare
return, ri-tĕrn', v., (come back) rivenire ; (go
    back) ritornare ; (give back) restituire. n., ri-
    torno m.; restituzione f.; —ticket, biglietto
    di andata e ritorno m.
returns, ri-tĕrns', n.pl., (turnover) guadagno m.
reveal, ri-viil', v., rivelare
revel, rev'-l, v., gozzovigliare. n., gozzoviglia f.
revenge, ri-vench', v., rivendicarsi. n., vendetta f.
revenue, rev'-i-niuu, n., rendita f.; (state) fisco m.
reverse, ri-vĕrs', v., fare marcia indietro ; (en-
    gine) dare marcia indietro. n.,(back) rovescio m.;
    (defeat) rovescio m.; (contrary) contrario m.
revert, ri-vĕrt', v., ritornare
review, ri-viuu', v., (consider) esaminare ; (in-
    spect) passare in rivista ; (edit) far la recensione.
    n., recensione f.; (army) rivista f.; (stage) rivista
revile, ri-vail', v., vilipendere   [f.
revise, ri-vais', v., rivedere
revision, ri-vish'-on, n., revisione f.
revive, ri-vaiv', v., rianimare ; (matter) ravvivare
revoke, ri-vouk', v., revocare ; (cards) rifiutare
revolt, ri-volt', v., rivoltarsi. n., rivolta f.
revolution, ri-vo-liuu'-shon, n., rivoluzione f.

revolve, ri-volv', v., girare; rivolgere

revolver, ri-vol'-va, n., rivoltella f.

reward, ri-uoord', v., ricompensare. n., ricompensa f.

rheumatism, ruu'-ma-tism, n., reumatismo m.

rhinoceros, rai-nos'-i-ros, n., rinoceronte m.

rhubarb, ruu'-baarb, n., rabarbaro m.

rhyme, raim, n., rima f. v., rimare

rib, rib, n., costola f.

ribbon, rib'-on, n., nastro m.

rice, rais, n., riso m.

rich*, rich, a., ricco; (food) grasso

richness, rich'-nes, n., ricchezza f.

rick, rik, n., fienile m.

rickets, rik'-ets, n., rachitismo m.

rickety, rik'-et-i, a., (shaky) vacillante

rid, rid, v., sbarazzare; liberare; **to get — of**, sbarazzarsi di

riddle, rid'-l, n., (puzzle) enigma m. v., (perforate) crivellare

ride, raid, v., andare a cavallo; (cycle) andare in bicicletta. n., cavalcata f.

rider, rai'-da, n., cavalcatore m.; ciclista m. & f.

ridge, rich, n., (mountain) groppa f.

ridicule, rid'-i-kiuul, v., porre in ridicolo

ridiculous*, ri-dik'-iu-los, a., ridicolo

rifle, rai'-fl, n., fucile m. v., (rob) svaligiare

rift, rift, n., (crack) fessura f.; (cleft) spacco m.

rig, righ, n., (ship) attrezzatura f. v., attrezzare

right, rait, n., diritto m.; (side) destra f. a., diritto; giusto; destro. v., raddrizzare; **all —**, benissimo; **on the —**, a destra

rigid, rich'-id, a., rigido

rigorous*, righ'-or-os, a., rigoroso

rigour, righ'-a, n., rigore m.

rim, rim, n., orlo m.; (hat) falda f.; (wheel) cerchio m.

rind, raind, n., (fruit) scorza f.; (cheese) crosta f.; (bacon, etc.) cotenna f.

ring, ringh, n., circolo m.; (metal) anello m.; (napkin) porta tovagliolo m.; (of bell) suonata f. v., suonare

ringleader, ringh'-lii-da, n., caporione m.

rinse, rins, v., sciacquare

riot, rai'-*ot*, n., tumulto m.

rip, rip, v., squarciare ; (cloth) strappare

ripe, raip, a., maturo ; **—n**, v., maturare

ripple, rip'-l, n., crespa f. ; (sound) mormorio m.

rise, rais, v., alzarsi ; (river) gonfiarsi ; (prices) crescere ; (revolt) rivoltarsi. n., elevazione f. ; (sun) levata f. ; (salary) aumento m.

risk, risk, n., rischio m. v., arrischiare

rite, rait, n., rito m.

rival, rai'-vl, n., rivale m. & f. ; (competitor) concorrente m.

river, riv'-*a*, n., fiume m.

rivet, riv'-*et*, n., (metal) bullone m.

road, roud, n., strada f.

roam, roum, v., girare [gire

roar, r*o*r, n., ruggito m. ; (gun) rombo m. v., ruggire

roast, roust, n., arrosto m. v., arrostire

rob, rob, v., rubare ; **—ber**, n., ladro m.

robbery, rob'-*er*-i, n., furto m.

robe, roub, n., veste f. ; (lawyers) toga f.

robin, rob'-in, n., pettirosso m.

robust°, ro-b*o*st', a., robusto

rock, rok, n., scoglio m., roccia f. v., rullare ; (cradle) ninnare ; (quake) oscillare ; **—y**, a., roccioso

rocket, rok'-*et*, n., razzo m.

rod, rod, n., canna f. ; (birch) verga f.

roe, rou, n., (deer) capriolo m. ; (of fish) uova f.pl.

rogue, rough, n., briccone m. ; **—ry**, bricconeria f.

roll, roul, n., rullio m. ; (bread) panino m. v., rullare ; **—up**, arrotolare ; **—call**, n., appello m.

roller, roul'-*a*, n., rullo m. ; (street) compressore m. ; **—skates**, pl., pattini a ruote m. pl.

romance, rou-mans', n., romanzo m.

romp, romp, v., giuocare rumorosamente

roof, ruuf, n., tetto m. ; (mouth) palato m.

rook, ruk, n., cornacchia f.

room, ruum, n., stanza f. ; (space) spazio m.

roomy, ruum'-i, a., spazioso

roost, ruust, v., appollaiarsi. n., posatoio m.

root, ruut, n., radice f. v., prendere radice

rope, roup, n., corda f., fune f.

rosary, rou'-*sa*-ri, n., rosario m.

rose, rou*s*, n., rosa f. ; (nozzle) getto a rosa m.

rosemary, rous'-ma-ri, n., rosmarino m.

rosy, rou'-si, a., roseo

rot, rot, n., putredine f.　v., imputridire

rotate, rou-teit', v., ruotare

rotten, rot'-n, a., putrido ; fradicio

rouge, ruush, n., (face) belletto m.

rough*, rŏf, a., ruvido ; (rude) rozzo ; (sea) grosso ; (bumpy) cattivo ; —ness, n., rozzezza f.

round, raund, a., rotondo.　v., arrotondare. n., (sport) assalto m.; —about, (merry-go-round)

roundness, raund'-nes, n., rotondità f.　[giostra f.

rouse, raus, v., svegliare ; (anger) eccitare

rout, rout, v., (mil.) mettere in rotta.　n., rotta f.

route, ruut, n., via f., rotta f.

routine, ru-tiin', n., pratica f.

rove, rouv, v., vagare

row, rou, n., fila f.; (boating) remata f.　v., remare

row, rau, n., lite f. ; (noise) schiamazzo m.

royal*, roi'-al, a., reale ; —ty, n., (royal family) reali m.pl.; (author's) diritti d'autore m. pl.

rub, rŏb, v., fregare ; — off, pulir strofinando ; — out, (erase) cancellare

rubber, rŏb'-a, n., gomma f.

rubbish, rŏb'-ish, n., rifiuti m.pl.; (trash) robaccia

ruby, ruu'-bi, n., rubino m.　a., rubino　[f.

rudder, rŏd'-a, n., timone m.

ruddy, rŏd'-i, a., rosso

rude*, ruud, a., rozzo, ruvido

rudiment, ruu'-di-ment, n., rudimento m.

rue, ruu, v., deplorare ; —ful*, a., triste

ruffian, rŏf'-i-an, n., farabutto m.

ruffle, rŏf'-l, v., arruffare

rug, rŏgh, n., (travelling) coperta da viaggio f. ; (hearth) tappeto da caminetto m.

rugged*, rŏ'-ghid, a., scabro, ineguale

ruin*, ruu'-in, v., rovinare.　n., rovina f.

rule, ruul, v., tirar linee ; (govern) governare. n., (regulation) regola f.

ruler, ruul'-a, n., governante m.; (drawing) riga f.

rum, rŏm, n., rum m.

rumbling, rŏm'-bling, n., (thunder, guns, traffic) rombo m. ; (stomach) brontolio m.

rummage, rŏm'-ich, v., frugare

rumour, ruu'-ma, n., rumore m.

run, rŏn, v., correre. n., corsa f.; — **away,** v., fuggire, scappare. n., (horse) cavallo in fuga m.

rupture, rŏp'-chur, n., rottura f.; (med.) ernia f.

rural*, ru'-ral, a., rurale

rush, rŏsh, n., (water) torrente m.; (panic) corsa precipitosa f.; (reed) giunco m.; — **at,** v., precipitarsi

rust, rŏst, n., ruggine f. v., arrugginire; —**y,** a., arrugginito

rustic, rŏs'-tik, a. & n., rustico m.

rustle, rŏs'-l, v., frusciare. n., fruscio m.

rut, rŏt, n., carreggiata f.

rye, rai, n., segale f.

sable, sei'-bl, n., (fur) zibellino m. a., nero

sabre, sei'-br, n., sciabola f.

sack, sak, n., sacco m. v., (mil.) saccheggiare

sacrament, sa'-kra-ment, n., sacramento m.

sacred*, sei'-krid, a., sacro

sacrifice, sak'-ri-fais, n., sacrificio m. v., sacrificare

sacrilege, sak'-ri-lich, n., sacrilegio m.

sad*, sad, a., triste; —**ness,** n., tristezza f.

saddle, sad'-l, n., sella f. v., insellare

saddler, sad'-la, n., sellaio m.

safe, seif, a.* salvo; sicuro. n., cassaforte f.; (ice) ghiacciaia f.; (strong room) camera di sicurezza f.; —**guard,** salvaguardia f. v., salvaguardare; —**ty,** n., sicurezza f.; —**ty-razor,** rasoio di sicurezza m.

sag, sahg, v., afflosciarsi

sagacious*, sa-ghei'-shos, a., sagace

sage, seich, n., saggio m.; (herb) salvia f.

sail, seil, n., vela f. v., veleggiare; (leave) salpare

sailing, sei'-ling, n., veleggiare m.

sailor, sei'-la, n., marinaio m.

saint, seint, n., santo m.

sake, seik, n., for ... sake, per amore ...

salad, sal'-ad, n., insalata f.

salary, sal'-a-ri, n., salario m.

sale, seil, n., vendita f.; (bargains) liquidazione f.; (auction) asta f.; —**able,** a., vendibile

salesman, seils'-man, n., venditore m.

salient, sei'-li-ent, n., saliente m. a., saliente

saliva, sa-lai'-va, n., saliva f.

sallow, sal'-ou, a., gialliccio

salmon, sam'-on, n., salmone m.

saloon, sa-luun', n., salone m.; dining —, sala da pranzo f.

salt, soolt, n., sale m. a., salato : — cellar, n., saliera f

salute, sa-liuut', n., (mil.) saluto m. v., salutare

salvage, sal'-vich, n., salvataggio m. v., ricuperare

salvation, sal-vei'-shon, n., salvazione f.; (theol.) salvezza f.: — army, esercito della salute m.

salver, sal'-va, n., vassoio m.

same (the), seim, a., lo stesso, la stessa, gli stessi, le stesse ; (immaterial) medesimo

sample, saam'-pl, v., assaggiare ; provare. n., campione m.

sanctify, sangk'-ti-fai, v., santificare [pione m.

sanction, sangk'-shon, n., sanzione f. v., sanzionare

sanctity, sangk'-ti-ti, n., santità f.

sanctuary, sangk'-tiu-a-ri, n., santuario m.

sand, sand, n., sabbia f.; —y, a., sabbioso

sandal, san'-dl, n., sandalo m.

sandpaper, sand'-pei-pa, n., carta vetrata f.

sandwich, sand'-uich, n., panino imbottito m.

sane*, sein, a., sano

sanguine*, sang'-ghuin, a., sanguigno ; (fig.) fiducioso

sanitary, san'-i-ter-i, a., sanitario ; — towels, n. pl., salviette igieniche f. pl.

sanity, san'-i-ti, n., sanità f.; igiene f.

sap, sap, n., (juice) succo m. v., minare

sapper, sap'-a, n., zappatore m.

sapphire, saf'-air, n., zaffiro m.

sarcasm, saar'-kasm, n., sarcasmo m.

sarcastic, saar-kast'-ik, a., sarcastico

sardine, saar-diin', n., sardina f.

sash, sash, n., corda f.; (belt) fascia f.

satchel, satsh'-l, n., (school) cartella f.

satiate, sei-shi-eit, v., saziare

satin, sat'-in, n., raso m. a., di raso

satire, sat'-air, n., satira f.

satisfaction, sat-is-fak'-shon, n., soddisfazione f.

satisfactory, sat-is-fak'-to-ri, a., soddisfacente

satisfy, sat'-is-fai, v., soddisfare

saturate, sat'-iu-reit, v., saturare

Saturday, sat'-er-di, n., sabato m.

satyr, sat'-er, n., satiro m.

sauce, soos, n., salsa f. ; — -pan, casseruola f.

saucer, soo'-sa, n., piattino m.

saunter, soon'-ta, v., girovagare

sausage, so'-sich, n., salsiccia f.

savage, sav'-ich, n., selvaggio m. a.,• selvaggio

save, seiv, v., salvare ; (economise) risparmiare ; (keep) conservare ; (theol.) salvare

saving, sei'-ving, a., frugale. n., risparmio m.

savings, sei'-vings, n. pl., risparmi m. pl.

Saviour, sei'-via, n., (Jesus) Salvatore m.

savoury, sei'-ver-i, n., manicaretto m. a., saporito

saw, soo, n., sega f. v., segare

say, sei, v., dire ; —ing, n., detto m.

scabbard, skab'-erd, n., fodero m.

scaffold, skaf'-old, n., (execution) patibolo m.

scaffolding, skaf'-old-ing, n., impalcatura f.

scald, skoold, v., scottare

scale(s), skeil(s), n. pl., bilancia f.; (fish) squama f.; (measure) scala metrica f. ; (music) scale f. pl. v., squamare ; (climb) scalare

scallop, skall'-op, n., (shell-fish) petonchio m.

scalp, skalp, n., cuoio capelluto m.; cranio m.

scamp, skamp, n., furfante m.

scamper, skam'-pa, v., battersela

scan, skan, v., scrutare ; (verse) scandire   [loso

scandal, skan-dl, n., scandalo m.; —ous•, a., scanda-

scanty, skan'-ti, a., scarso

scapegoat, skeip'-gout, n., capro espiatorio m.

scar, skaar, n., cicatrice f. v., cicatrizzare

scarce, skers, a., scarso, raro

scarcely, skers-li, adv., raramente ; appena

scarcity, sker'-si-ti, n., scarsità f.

scare, skeir, v., impaurire ; — away, spaventare

scarecrow, skeir'-krou, n., spauracchio m.

scarf, skaarf, n., sciarpa f.

scarlet, skaar'-let, a., scarlatto ; — fever, n., scar-

scathing, skei'-Ding, a., sferzante   [lattina f.

scatter, skat'-a, v., spargere

scavenger, skav'-en-cha, n., spazzino m.

scene, siin, n., scena f. [m.
scenery, siî'-ner-i, n., panorama f.; (stage) scenario
scent, sent, n., profumo m.; (trail) pista f. v., pro-
sceptical*, skep'-ti-kal, a., scettico [fumare
sceptre, sep'-tr, n., scettro m.
schedule, shed'-iuul, n., lista f.
scheme, skiim, n., piano m., progetto m. v., pro-
schism, sism, n., scisma m. [gettare
scholar, skol'-a, n., erudito m.; (pupil) scolaro m.;
    —**ship,** (prize) borsa di studio f.
school, skuul, n., scuola f.; —**master,** maestro m.;
    —**mistress,** maestra f.
schooner, skuun'-a, n., goletta f.
sciatica, sai-at'-i-ka, n., sciatica f.
science, sai'-ens, n., scienza f.
scientific, sai-en-tif'-ik, a., scientifico
scissors, sis'-ers, n. pl., forbici f. pl.
scoff, skof, v., beffeggiare; — **at,** farsi beffe di
scold, skould, v., sgridare. n., sgridata f.
scoop, skuup, n., (shovel) pala f.; —**out,** scavare
scope, skoup, n., campo d'azione m.; (aim) scopo m
scorch, skoorch, v., abbruciacchiare
score, skor, n., (cut) intaglio m.; (games) punti m.pl.
    v., (cut) intaccare; (win) guadagnare; (keeping
    count) marcare i punti
scorn, skoorn, n., scorno m. v., scornare
scornful*, skoorn'-ful, a., sdegnoso
scoundrel, skaun'-drel, n., briccone m.; (fig.) scel-
scour, skaur, v., fregare [lerato m.
scourge, skërch, n., sferza f.; flagello m.
scout, skaut, v., esplorare. n., esploratore m.
    boy-—, ragazzo esploratore m.
scowl, skaul, v., guardar torvo
scraggy, skra'-ghi, a., ruvido, rozzo
scramble, skram'-bl, n., (struggle) parapiglia f.
    v., (climb) arrampicarsi; — **for,** urtarsi
scrap, skrap, n., bricciolo m.; brano m.; (cloth) pez-
    zo m. v., (dispose of) eliminare
scrape, skreip, v., raschiare; —**r,** n., raschiatoio m.
scratch, skrach, n., graffio m.; (sport) linea di par-
    tenza f. v., graffiare; (rub itch) grattare; (glass)
    scalfire; (sport) ritirare; — **out,** cancellare

scream, skriim, v., gridare. n., grido m.

screen, skriin, v., proteggere. n., (cinema) schermo m. ; (room) paravento m. ; (fire) parafuoco m. ; **wind-—**, cristallo paravento m.

screw, skruu, n., vite f. v., avvitare

screwdriver, skruu-drai'-va, n., cacciavite m.

scribble, skrib'-l, n., scarabocchio m. v., [scribac-

Scripture, skrip'-chur, n., Sacra Scrittura f. [chiare

scroll, skroul, n., rotolo m.; (sculptural) voluta f.

scrub, skrŏb, v., fregare. n., (bush) bosco ceduo m.

scruple, skruu'-pl, n., scrupolo m.

scrupulous*, skruu'-piu-los, a., scrupoloso

scrutinize, skruu'-ti-nais, v., scrutare

scuffle, skŏf'-l, n., rissa f. v., rissare

scull, skŏl, n., (rowing) remo corto m. v., remare

scullery, skŏl'-er-i, n., spazzacucina f.

sculptor, skŏlp'-ta, n., scultore m.

sculpture, skŏlp'-chur, n., scultura f.

scum, skŏm, v., schiumare. n., schiuma f.

scurf, skĕrf, n., (head) forfora f.;**—y**, a., con forfora

scurvy, skĕr'-vi, n., scorbuto m. a., (fig.) vile

scuttle, skŏt'-l, n., secchio m. v., (naut.) affondare

scythe, saiD, n., falce f.

sea, sii, n., mare m.; **—man**, marinaio m. ; **—-sick**, a., con mal di mare f. ; **—-side**, n., riva del mare f. ; **—-weed**, alga f. ; **—-worthy**, a., atto a tener il mare

seal, siil, n., sigillo m.; (animal) foca f. v., sigillare ; **—ing-wax**, n., ceralacca f.

seal-skin, siil'-skin, n., pelle di foca f.

seam, siim, v., orlare. n., cucitura f.; (mine) vena f., filone m. ; **—stress**, cucitrice f.

sear, sir, v., (burn) bruciare ; (brand) marcare con ferro rovente

search, sĕrch, n., ricerca f., esame m. v., cercare, frugare

searchlight, sĕrch'-lait, n., proiettore m.

season, sii'-sn, n., stagione f. v., (food) condire ; (timber) stagionare ; **—able**, a., di stagione ; **—ing**, n., condimento m.; **—-ticket**, tessera f.

seat, siit, n., sedile m.; (bench) banco m.; (trousers) fondo m. ; (estate) proprietà f.

secluded, si-kluu'-did, a., appartato
seclusion, si-kluu'-shon, n., ritiro m.
second, sek'-ond, n., secondo m. a.,* (numeral) secondo. v., (support) appoggiare ; **—ary**, a.,
secondario ; **— hand**, d'occasione
secondly, sek'-ond-li, adv., in secondo luogo
secrecy, sii'-kri-si, n., segretezza f.
secret, sii'-krit, a.* & n., segreto m.
secretary, sek'-ri-ta-ri, n., segretario m.
secrete, si-kriit', v., nascondere ; (glands) **secernere**
secretion, si-krii'-shon, n., secrezione f.
sect, sekt, n., setta f.
section, sek'-shon, n., sezione f.
secular,* sek'-iu-lar, a., secolare
secure, si-kiu'-r, a.,* sicuro. v., assicurare
security, si-kiu'-ri-ti, n., sicurezza f. ; **garanzia f.**
sedate, si-deit', a., sedato
sedative, sed'-a-tiv, n., sedativo m.
sedentary, sed'-en-ta-ri, a., sedentario
sediment, sed'-i-ment, n., sedimento **m.**
sedition, si-dish'-on, n., sedizione f.
seditious,* si-dish'-os, a., sedizioso
seduce, si-diuus', v., sedurre
see, sii, v., vedere ; (visit) visitare ; **— through**,
(glass, a person, etc.) vedere attraverso ; **— to**,
seed, siid, n., seme m. [occuparsi di
seek, siik, v., cercare
seem, siim, v., sembrare ; **—ly**, a., **conveniente**
seethe, siiD, v., bollire ; ribollire
seize, siis, v., prendere ; **sequestrare**
seizure, sii'-sher, n., attacco m.
seldom, sel'-dom, adv., raramente
select, si-lekt', v., scegliere. a., **scelto**
selection, si-lek'-shon, n., selezione f., scelta f.
self, self, **one—**, pron., stesso, stessa ; **—con-**
scious, a., conscio di sè stesso ; **—ish**, egoista :
—ishness, n., egoismo m. ; **—starter**,
(motor) messa in moto automatica f.
sell, sel, v., vendere ; **—er**, n., venditore m.
semblance, sem'-blans, n., sembianza f.
semi, sem'-i, **—circle**, n., semicircolo **m.** :
—colon, punto e virgola m.

seminary, sem'-i-na-ri, n., seminario m.

semolina, sem-o-lii'-na, n., semolina f.

senate, sen'-et, n., senato m.

send, send, v., mandare ; spedire ; — **away**, mandar via ; — **back**, rinviare ; —**er**,n.,speditore m.; — **for**, v., mandare a cercare ; — **in advance**, mandare in anticipo ; — **off**, spedire

senile, sii'-nail, a., senile

senior, sii'-ni-a, n., seniore m. a., seniore ;—**ity**, n., priorità f. ; anzianità f. ; —**partner**, socio princi-

sensation, sen-sei'-shon, n., sensazione f. [pale m.

sense, sens, n., senso m.; —**less***, a., **senza sensi** ; (stupid) insensato

sensible, sen'-si-bl, a., sensato

sensitive, sen'-si-tiv, a., sensibile

sensual*, sen'-shu-al, a., sensuale

sentence, sen'-tens, n., frase f.; (law) sentenza f.

sentiment, sen'-ti-ment, n., sentimento m.; (conviction) opinione f.; —**al**, a., sentimentale

sentinel, sen'-ti-nl, n., sentinella f.

sentry, sen'-tri, n., sentinella f.; — **-box**, garetta f.

separate, sep'-a-reit, v., separare. a.,* separato

separation, sep-a-rei'-shon, n., separazione f.

September, sep-tem'-ba, n., settembre m.

septic, sep'-tik, a., settico

sequel, sii'-kuel, n., risultato m.

sequence, sii'-kuens, n., seguito m.

serenade, ser-i-neid', n., serenata f.

serene*, si-riin', a., sereno

serge, serch, n., saia f.

sergeant, saar'-chent, n., sergente m.

serial, sii'-ri-al, a., in serie. n.,(story) romanzo d'ap-series, sii'-ri-iis, n., serie f.   [pendice m.

serious*, sii'-ri-os, a., serio

sermon, ser'-mn, n., predica f.

serpent, ser'-pent, n., serpente m.   [stica f.

servant, ser'-vant, n., servitore m.; (maid) dome-

serve, serv, v., servire ; (tennis) lanciare la palla ; (legal) presentare formalmente

service, ser'-vis, n., servizio m.; (Divine) ufficio divino m. ; —**able**, a., servizievole, utile

servile, ser'-vail, a., servile

servitude, sĕr'-vi-tiud, n., servitù f.; (imprisonment) reclusione f.

session, sesh'-on, n., sessione f.

set, set, v., (type ; to music) comporre ; (fowls) covare ; (trap) tendere ; (clock) regolare ; (example) dare ; (task) imporre ; (blade) affilare ; (plants) piantare ; (fracture)ridurre ; (bones) mettere a posto ; (solidify) rapprendere ; (jewels) montare ; (sun) tramontare. n., collezione f.; serie f.; gruppo m.; (china, etc.) servizio m.; — **dog at**, v., eccitare un cane contro ; — **on fire**, mettere a fuoco

settee, set'-ii, n., canapè m.

settle, set'-l, v., (accounts) liquidare ; (decide) decidere ; (bequeath) assegnare ; (domicile) stabilirsi

settlement, set'-l-ment, n., (completion) decisione f., fine f.; (accounts) liquidazione f.; (colony) colonia f.; (foundations) sedimento m.; (agreement) aggiustamento m.; (bequest) dote f.

seven, sev'-n, a., sette

seventeen, sev'-n-tiin, a., diciasette

seventh, sev'-nZ, a., settimo

seventy, sev'-n-ti, a., settanta

sever, sev'-a, v., separare ; (cut) tagliare **netto**

several, sev'-er-al, a., diversi

severe°, si-vir', a., intenso ; (stern) severo

severity, si-ver'-i-ti, n., severità f.

sew, sou, v., cucire ; (med.) suturare ; —**ing**, n., cucitura f.; —**ing-cotton**, cotone da cucire m.; —**ing-machine**, macchina da cucire f.

sewage, siuu'-ich, n., acqua di fognatura f.

sewer, siuu'-a, n., fogna f.

sex, seks, n., sesso m.; —**ual**, a., sessuale [m. **sexton**, seks'-ton, n., sagrestano m.; (digger) becchino

shabby, shab'-i, a., logoro ; (action) meschino

shackle, shak'-l, n., manetta f. v., incatenare

shade, sheid, n., ombra f.; (colour) tinta f.; (lamp) paralume m.; (eyes) visiera f. v., proteggere ; (art) ombreggiare

shadow, shad'-ou, n., ombra f. v., (follow) stare alle calcagna di

shady, shei'-di, a., ombroso ; (fig.) di dubbia onestà

shaft, shaaft, n., (arrow) freccia f.; (mech.) albero di trasmissione m. ; (mine) pozzo m.

shafts, shaafts, n. pl., (vehicle) stanghe f. pl.

shaggy, shagh'-i, a., irsuto

shake, sheik, v., scuotere ; (tremble) tremare ; (loose) vacillare ; (quake) tremare

shaky, shei'-ki, a., malfermo ; tremolante

shallow, shal'-ou, a., poco profondo

sham, sham, n., finta f. v., fingere

shame, sheim, n., vergogna f.; (modesty) pudore m. v., svergognare ; **—ful**, a., vergognoso

shameless, sheim'-les, a., sfacciato

shampoo, sham-puu', n., shampooing m.

shamrock, sham'-rok, n., trifoglio m.

shape, sheip, n., forma f. v., formare

share, sher, v., dividere ; partecipare. n., parte f.; (stock) azione f. ; **—holder**, azionista m. & f.

shark, shaark, n., pescecane m.

sharp, shaarp, a., *affilato ; (mind) acuto. n., (music) diesis m. ; **—en**, v., affilare ; (point) fare la punta ; **—ness**, n., affilatezza f.; (fig.) acutezza f.

sharper, shaar'-pa, n., (crook) scroccone m.

shatter, shat'-a, v., fracassare ; (nerves) infrangere

shave, sheiv, v., radere ; radersi

shaving, shei'-ving, n., **—brush**, n., pennello da barba m. ; **—cream**, pasta di sapone f.

shavings, shei'-vings, n. pl., trucioli m. pl.

shawl, shool, n., scialle m. [f.

she, shii, pron., ella, essa, lei. n., (female) femmina

sheaf, shiif, n., (corn) covone m.; (papers) fascio m.

shear, shir, v., tosare

shears, shirs, n. pl., cesoie f. pl.

sheath, shiiZ, n., astuccio m., guaina f.

shed, shed, n., tettoia f. v., (tears, blood) versare ; (hair, leaves and feathers) perdere

sheen, shiin, n., lustro m.

sheep, shiip, n., pecora f.

sheer, shir, a., puro, semplice ; (steep) verticale

sheet, shiit, n., (bed) lenzuolo m.: (paper, metal) foglio m. ; **—lightning**, bagliori m. pl.

shelf, shelf, n., scaffale m.

shell, shel, n., (hard) conchiglia f.; (soft) baccello m.; (nut, etc.) guscio m.; (artillery) granata f.
v., sgusciare; sbaccellare; bombardare

shell-fish, shel´-fish, n., crostaceo m.

shelter, shel´-ta, n., ricovero m. v., ricoverarsi; proteggere

shepherd, shep´-erd, n., pastore m.   [teggere

sheriff, sher´-if, n., sceriffo m.

sherry, sher´-i, n., vino di Xeres m.

shield, shiild, n., scudo m. v., difendere

shift, shift, n., (workers) turno m. v., spostare

shilling, shil´-ing, n., scellino m.

shin, shin, n., stinco m.

shine, shain, v., risplendere; luccicare; brillare.
n., splendore m., brillo m.

shingle, shing´-gol, n., (stones) ciottoli m. pl.

ship, ship, n., nave f., battello m. v., imbarcare;
spedire; **—broker,** n., sensale marittimo m.;
—ment, imbarco m.; **—owner,** armatore m.;
—ping, (traffic) navigazione f.;   **—wreck,**
[naufragio m.

shire, shair, n., contea f.

shirk, sherk, v., schivare; **—er,** n., scansafatiche m.

shirt, shert, n., camicia f.; **—ing,** tessuto da camicie

shiver, shiv´-a, v., tremare. n., brivido m.   [m.

shoal, shool, n., (crowd) folla f.; (fish) frotta di
pesci f.; (shallows) basso fondo m.

shock, shok, n., scossa f.; (fright) emozione f.
v., (disgust) offendere; **—absorber,** n., smorzatore di scosse m.; **—ing*,** a., offensivo; orribile

shoddy, shod´-i, n., tessuto di lana vecchia m.
a., (goods) di poco valore; (material) logorato

shoe, shuu, n., scarpa f.; (horse) ferro di cavallo m.
v., (horse) ferrare; **—black,** n., (man) lustrascarpe m.; **—horn,** corno da scarpe m.; **—maker,**
calzolaio m.; **—polish,** cera da scarpe f.

shoot, shuut, v., sparare, tirare; (murder) uccidere
d'un colpo; (execute) fucilare; (grow) germinare. n., caccia f.; (growth) germoglio m.;
—ing, tiro m.; **—ing-star,** stella cadente f.

shop, shop, n., bottega f., negozio m. v., fare acquisti; **—keeper,** n., negoziante m., bottegaio m.; **—ping,** acquisti m. pl.; **—walker,**
sorvegliante di negozio m.

shore, shor, n., (sea) lido m.; (beach) spiaggia f.; (river *or* lake) riva f.; (coast) costa f.; (ashore) terra f.; (support) puntello m. v., puntellare

shorn, shorn, a., tosato; (fig.) spogliato

short, shoort, a., corto; (small) basso; (need) privo; **—age**, n., deficienza f.; **—en**, v., raccorciare; abbreviare; **—hand**, n., stenografia f.; **—ly**, adv., in breve; **—ness**, n., cortezza f.; **—sighted**, a., miope

shot, shot, n., tiro m.; (marksman) tiratore m.; (pellet) pallini m.pl.

shoulder, shoul′-da, n., spalla f. v., mettere in spalla; (fig.) portare; **—strap**, n., cinghia da spalla f.

shout, shaut, n., grido m. v., gridare

shove, shŏv, n., spinta f.; urto m. v., spingere

shovel, shŏv′-l, n., pala f. v., spalare

show, shou, v., mostrare. n., mostra f.; (play) spettacolo m.; (exhibition) esposizione f.; **—room**, sala di esposizione f.; **—y**, a., (gaudy) vistoso

shower, shau′-a, n., acquazzone m.; **—bath**, doccia f.; **—y**, a., piovoso

shred, shred, n., (tatter) brano m. v., mettere a brani

shrew, shruu, n., megera f.

shrewd°, shruud, a., sagace; fino

shriek, shriik, n., strillo m. v., strillare

shrill, shril, a., strillante   [tolo m.

shrimp, shrimp, n., gamberettino m.; (fig.) omiciat-

shrine, shrain, n., reliquario m.; santuario m.

shrink, shringk, v., raccorciarsi

shrivel, shriv′-l, **—up**, v., raggrinzarsi

shroud, shraud, n., sudario m.   [grasso m.

Shrove Tuesday, shrouv tiuus′-di, n., martedì

shrub, shrŏb, n., arbusto m.; **—bery**, arbusti m.pl.

shrug, shrŏgh, v., (shoulders) alzare le spalle

shudder, shŏd′-a, n., fremito m. v., fremere

shuffle, shŏf′-l, v., (gait) trascinare il passo; (cards)   [mescolare

shun, shŏn, v., scansare

shunt, shŏnt, v., (trucks, etc.) manovrare

shut, shŏt, v., chiudere; **—ter**, n., imposte f. pl.; (camera) otturatore m.

shuttle, shŏt′-l, n., (sewing) spola f.

shy, shai, a.,° timido. v., adombrarsi

shyness, shai'-nes, n., timidezza f.

sick, sik, a., ammalato; **—en,** v., ammalarsi; **—ly,** adv., malaticcio; **—ness,** n., malattia f.

sickle, sik'-l, n., falcetto m.

side, said, v., prendere le parti di. n., lato m.; (hill) versante m.; (river) riva f.; (party) parte f.; **—board,** credenza f.; **—car,** carrozzella f.; **—slip,** scivolata di fianco f.; **—ways,** adv., di fianco, di lato; **on the one —,** da un lato; **on the other —,** dall'altro lato

siding, sai'-ding, n., binario laterale m.

siege, siich, n., assedio m.

sieve, siiv, n., staccio m. v., stacciare

sift, sift, v., vagliare

sigh, sai, n., sospiro m. v., sospirare

sight, sait, v., avvistare. n., (eye) vista f.; (spectacle) spettacolo m.; (gun) mira f.; **by —,** di vista

sights, saits, n. pl., punti interessanti m. pl.

sign, sain, n., segno m.; (board) insegna f. v., firmare; **—post,** n., palo indicatore m.

signal, sigh'-nal, n., segnale m. v., segnalare

signature, sigh'-na-chur, n., firma f.

significant*, sigh-nif'-i-kant, a., significante

signification, sigh-ni-fi-kei'-shon, n., significato m.

signify, sigh'-ni-fai, v., significare

silence, sai'-lens, n., (quiet) silenzio m. interj., silenzio! v., imporre silenzio

silencer, sai'-len-sa, n., (motor) silenziatore m.

silent*, sai'-lent, a., silenzioso

silk, silk, n., seta f.; **—cloth,** stoffa di seta f.; **—en,** a., di seta; **—thread,** n., filo di seta m.; **—worm,** baco da seta m.; **—y,** a., serico

sill, sil, n., davanzale m.

silly, sil'-i, a., sciocco

silver, sil'-va, n., argento m. a., argenteo. v., inargentare; **—smith,** n., argentiere m.

similar*, sim'-i-la, a., simile

similarity, sim-i-lar'-i-ti, n., somiglianza f.

simile, sim'-i-li, n., simile m.

simmer, sim'-a, v., bollire lentamente

simple, sim'-pl, a., semplice

simplicity, sim-plis'-i-ti, n., semplicità f.

simplify, sim'-pli-fai, v., semplificare

simultaneous*, si-mol-tei'-ni-os, a., simultaneo

sin, sin, n., peccato m. v., peccare ; **—ful***, a., peccaminoso ; **—less,** senza peccato ; **—ner,** n., peccatore m.

since, sins, prep., dappoichè. adv., dacchè ; d'allora. conj., poichè

sincere*, sin-sir', a., sincero

sinew, sin'-iuu, n., tendine m.

sing, sing, v., cantare ; **—er,** n., cantante m. & f.

singe, sinch, v., bruciare ; (scorch) abbruciacchiare

single, sing'-gol, a., solo ; (unmarried) celibe. n., (ticket) biglietto d'andata m. ; **—file,** fila indiana f. ; **—handed,** a., da solo

singly, sing'-ghli, adv., uno ad uno

singular, sing'-ghiu-la, a.* & n., singolare m.

sinister, sin'-is-ta, a., sinistro

sink, singk, v., affondare ; (shaft) scavare. n., (kitchen) lavatoio m.

sip, sip, n., sorso m. v., sorseggiare

siphon, sai'-fn, n., sifone m.

siren, sai'-ren, n., sirena f.

sirloin, sër'-loin, n., lombata f.

sister, sis'-ta, n., sorella f. ; (nun) suora f. ; **—in-law,** cognata f.

sit, sit, v., sedere ; (hens) covare ; **—down,** sedersi ; **—ting,** n., (session, etc.) seduta f. ; (incubation) covata f. ; **—ting-room,** salotto m.

site, sait, n., sito m. ; (building) posto m.

situated, sit'-iu-ei-tid, a., situato

situation, sit-iu-ei'-shon, n., situazione f.

six, siks, a., sei

sixteen, siks'-tiin, a., sedici

sixteenth, siks'-tiinZ, a., sedicesimo

sixth, siksZ, a., sesto

sixtieth, siks'-ti-iZ, a., sessantesimo

sixty, siks'-ti, a., sessanta

size, sais, n., dimensione f. ; (measure) misura f.; (width) larghezza f. ; (glue) colla f. v., incollare

skate, skeit, v., pattinare. n., pattino m. ; (fish) razza

skater, skei'-ta, n., pattinatore m. **[f.**

skein, skein, n., matassa f.

skeleton, skel'-*e*-ton, n., scheletro m.

sketch, skech, n., schizzo m. v., schizzare

skewer, skiuu'-*a*, n., spiedo m. v., infilare colle

skid, skid, v., slittare. n., slittata f. [spiedo

skiff, skif, n., schifo m.

skilful°, skil'-f*u*l, a., abile, destro

skill, skil, n., abilità f.

skim, skim, v., schiumare ; (cream) scremare

skin, skin, n., pelle f.; (hide) cuoio m.; (peel) buccia f. v., scuoiare ; (peel) sbucciare

skip, skip, v., saltare ; (omit) passar sopra

skipper, skip'-*a*, n., capitano m.

skirmish, skër'-mish, n., scaramuccia f.

skirt, skërt, n., sottana f.; (edge) orlo m.

skittle, skit'-l, n., birillo m.

skull, skŏl, n., cranio m.; (skeleton) teschio m.

skunk, skonk, n., skunk m.

sky, skai, n., cielo m.; —**light**, abbaino m.

sky-scraper, skai'-skrei-*pa*, n., grattacielo m.

slab, slab, n., lastra di pietra f.

slack, slak, n., (coal) polvere di carbone f.
a., (loose) allentato ; (business) fiacco

slacken, slak'-n, v., allentare ; (pace) rallentare

slam, slam, v., sbattere. n., cappotto m.

slander, slaan'-da, n., diffamazione f.; —**er**, calunniatore m.

slang, slang, n., gergo m.

slant, slaant, n., declivio m. v., inclinare

slanting, slaant'-ing, a., obliquo

slap, slap, n., manata f. v., dare una manata

slash, slash, n., (wound) sfregio m. ; (clothes,
etc.) taglio m. v., sfregiare ; tagliuzzare

slate, sleit, n., ardesia f.; (school) lavagna f. v., coprire d'ardesie ; —**pencil**, n.,lapis di lavagna m.

slaughter, sloo'-ta, n., macello m. v., macellare ;
—**er**, n., macellaio m. ; —**-house**, macello m.

slave, sleiv, n., schiavo m. v., lavorare come uno
schiavo ; —**ry**, n., schiavitù f.

slay, slei, v., trucidare ; ammazzare

sledge, slech, n., (vehicle) slitta f.; —**-hammer**,
mazza ferrata f.

sleek°, sliik, a., liscio ; (manners) dolciastro

sleep, sliip, n., sonno m. v., dormire ; **—ing-car,** n., vagone letto m. ; **—less,** a., insonne ; **—lessness,** n., insonnia f. ; **—y,** a., sonnolento

sleet, sliit, n., nevischio m.

sleeve, sliiv, n., manica f.

sleigh, slei, n., slitta f.

sleight, slait, **—of hand,** n., giuoco di prestigio m.

slender, slen'-*da*, a., snello, sottile ; (means) pochi

slice, slais, n., fetta f. v., affettare   [mezzi

slide, slaid, v., sdrucciolare. n., (ice) slittata f. ; (microscopic) vetrino m.

slight, slait, n., (offend) spregio m. a.,* leggero ; (slender) sottile. v., spregiare

slim, slim, a., snello, smilzo. v., dimagrire

slime, slaim, n., (mud) limo m.

slimy, slai'-mi, a., limaccioso ; (fig.) untuoso

sling, sling, n., fionda f. ; (med.) sciarpa f. v., (throw) scagliare

slink, slingk, v., svignarsela

slip, slip, n., scivolare ; **—pery,** a., sdrucciolevole

slipper, slip'-*a*, n., pantofola f.

slit, slit, n., taglio m. v., fendere, spaccare

sloe, slou, n., prugnola f.

slop, slop, n., (waste) acqua sporca f.; **—-pail,** secchio da lavatura m.

slope, sloup, n., china f. v., essere in pendio

slot, slot, n., fessura f.

sloth, slouZ, n., indolenza f.

slouch, slauch, v., camminare pesantemente

slouch-hat, slauch'-hat, n., cappello a cencio m.

slough, slau, n., pantano m.

slovenly, slóv'-n-li, a., trascurato

slow*, slou, a., lento ; to be —, v., (watch) ritardare ; **—-train,** n., treno omnibus m.

slug, slógh, n., lumaca f.; (ingot) pane di piombo m.

sluggish*, sló'-ghish, a., lento

sluice, sluus, n., chiusa f. ; **— gate,** paratoia f.

slum, slóm, n., quartiere basso m.

slumber,slóm'-ba,v.,sonnecchiare. n.,sonnellino m.

slump, slómp, n., caduta f.

slur, slér, v., imbrattare. n., macchia f.

slush, slósh, n., fanghiglia f.

slut, slŏt, n., sgualdrina f.

sly*, slai, a., sornione, scaltro

smack, smak, n., (hit) schiaffo m.; (boat) barca da pesca f. v., dar scapaccioni ; (lips) schioccar la lingua

small, smool, a., piccolo ; —**ness**, n., piccolezza f.

small-pox, smool'-poks, n., vaiuolo m.

smart, smaart, a.,* vivace ; (clever) intelligente ; (spruce) elegante. v., (pain) far dolore

smash, smash, n., (collision) scontro m.; (commercial) crac m. v., frantumare

smattering, smat'-er-ing, n., conoscenza superficiale

smear, smir, v., imbrattare. n., imbrattatura f. [f.

smell, smel, n., odore m. v., odorare ; —**ing-salts**, n. pl., sali da fiuto m. pl.

smelt, smelt, v., fondere. n., (fish) perlano m.

smile, smail, n., sorriso m. v., sorridere

smite, smait, v., percuotere

smith, smiZ, n., fabbro m. ; —**y**, fucina f.

smoke, smouk, n., fumo m. v., fumare ; —**less**, a., senza fumo ; —**r**, n., fumatore m.

smoky, smouk'-i, a., fumoso

smooth, smuuD, a.,* liscio. v., lisciare ; calmare

smother, smŏD'-a, v., soffocare

smoulder, smoul'-da, v., ardere lentamente

smudge, smŏch, n., sgorbio m. v., sgorbiare

smug, smŏgh, a., soddisfatto di sè

smuggle, smŏgh'-l, v., contrabbandare

smuggler, smŏgh'-la, n., contrabbandiere **m.**

smut, smŏt, n., punto nero m.

snack, snak, n., spuntino m.

snail, sneil, n., lumacone m.

snake, sneik, n., serpe f., biscia **f.**

snap, snap, n., (noise) schiocco m.; (bite) colpo di dente m. ; (catch) fermaglio m. v., (break) schiantare ; (fingers) schioccare ; —**at**, cercar di mordere

snapshot, snap'-shot, n., istantanea f.

snare, sner, n., trappola f. v., intrappolare

snarl, snaarl, v., ringhiare

snatch, snach, —**at**, v., cercar d'afferrare ; — **from**, strappare da

sneak, sniik, n., (school) sornione m. v., strisciare ; —**away**, andarsene furtivamente

sneer, snīr, n., ghigno m. v., sogghignare
sneeze, sniis. n., starnuto m. v., starnutire
sniff, snif, v., annusare
snip, snip. — off, v., ritagliare
snipe, snaip, n., beccaccino m.
sniper, snaip'-a, n., scelto tiratore m.
snob, snob, n., posatore m., pretensioso m.
snobish, snob'-ish, a., pretensioso
snore, snōr, v., russare
snort, snoort, n., sbuffata f. v., sbuffare
snout, snaut, n., muso m.; (pig) grugno m.
snow, snou, n., neve f. v., nevicare; —drop,
    n., bucaneve m.; —storm, tempesta di neve f.
snub, snob, n., rabbuffo m. v., rabbuffare
snub-nose, snob'-nous, n., naso camuso m.
snuff, snof, n., tabacco da presa m.
snug, snogh, a., compatto; comodo
so, sou, adv.,così, in tal modo; tanto; (therefore) per-   [ciò
soak, souk, v., inzuppare
soap, soup, n., sapone m.
soar, sōr, v., elevarsi
sob, sob, n., singhiozzo m. v., singhiozzare
sober°, sou'-ba, a., sobrio; grave
sociable, sou'-sha-bl, a., socievole
social, sou'-shal, a., sociale; —ism, n., socialismo m.
society, so-sai'-i-ti, n., società f.
sock, sok, n., calzettino m.; (sole) suola interna f.
socket, sok'-it, n., incastro m.; incavo m.; (eyes) oc-
    chiaia f.; (teeth) alveolo m.
sod, sod, n., zolla erbosa f.
soda, sou'-da, n., soda f.; —water, acqua gas-   [sosa f.
soft°, soft, a., molle; —en, v., ammollare
softness, soft'-nes, n., mollezza f.
soil, soil, n., suolo m. v., imbrattare
sojourn, sŏch'-ern, n., soggiorno m. v., soggiornare
solace, sol'-as, n., consolazione f. v., consolare
solder, sol'-da, n., saldatura f. v., saldare
soldier, soul'-cha, n., soldato m.
sole, soul, n., risuolare. n., (shoe) suola f.; (foot)
    pianta del piede f.; (fish) sogliola f. a., solo, unico
solemn°, sol'-em, a., solenne; (serious) grave
solicit, so-lis'-it, v., sollecitare

solicitor, so-lis'-i-ta, n., avvocato m.

solicitude, sol-is'-i-tiuud, n., sollecitudine f.

solid*, sol'-id, a., solido

solidify, sol-id'-i-fai, v., solidificare

solitary, sol'-i-ta-ri, a., solitario ; (single) solingo

solitude, sol'-i-tiuud, n., solitudine f.

soluble, sol'-iu-bl, a., solubile

solution, sol-iuu'-shon, n., soluzione f.

solve, solv, v., solvere ; (puzzle) risolvere

solvency, sol'-ven-si, n., solvibilità f.

solvent, sol'-vent, a., solvibile ; (chemistry) solvente

sombre, sombr, a., cupo, tetro

some, sŏm, a. & pron., qualche, alcune, alcuni ; del, dello, della, delle, degli ; un po'di ; —body, n., qualcuno m. ; —how, adv., comunque ; —thing, n., qualcosa f. ; —times, adv., qualche volte ; —what, alquanto ; —where, in qualche luogo

somersault, som'-er-soult, n., salto mortale m.

somnambulist, som-nam'-biu-list, n., sonnambulo m.

son, sŏn, n., figlio m. ; —in-law, genero m.

song, song, n., canto m., canzone f.

soon, suun, adv., presto ; as — as, non appena

soot, sut, n., fuliggine f.

soothe, suud, v., blandire ; (pain) calmare

sorcerer, sor'-ser-a, n., stregone m.

sorcery, sor'-ser-i, n., stregoneria f.

sordid*, soor'-did, a., sordido

sore, sor, n., piaga f. a., che fa male

sorrel, sor'-el, n., acetosa f.

sorrow, sor'-ou, n., affanno m.; afflizione f. v., afflig-   [gersi

sorrowful*, sor'-ou-ful, a., triste

sorry, sor'-i, a., dispiacente ; I am —, mi dispiace

sort, soort, n., sorte f. v., assortire

soul, soul, n., anima f.

sound, saund, n., rumore m.; suono m. v., suonare. a.,* (health) sano ; (thorough) retto ;(sleep) profondo ; —film, n., pellicola sonora f.

soundings, saund'-ings, n.pl., (naut.) sondaggio m.

soup, suup, n., minestra f.; —tureen, zuppiera f.

sour*, saur, a., agro, acido, aspro

source, sors, n., sorgente f.

south, sauZ, n., sud m.

southerly, sŏD'-er-li, a., meridionale

souvenir, su'-ven-iir, n., ricordo m.

sovereign, sov'-er-in, n., (ruler) sovrano m.; (£) lira sterlina f. a., sovrano

sow, sou, v., seminare ; —**er**, n., seminatore m.

sow, sau, n., troia f.

space, speis, n., spazio m.; (time) intervallo m.

spacious*, spei'-shos, a., spazioso

spade, speid, n., vanga f.; (cards) picca f.

span, span, n., palmo m.; (architecture) arcata f.; (fig.) durata f. v., varcare

spangle, spang'-gol, n., lustrino m. v., costellare

spaniel, span'-iel, n., cane spagnuolo m.

spanner, span'-a, n., (tool) chiave inglese f.

spar, spaar, v., allenarsi alla box

spare, sper, v., perdonare ; (life) risparmiare ; (afford) dare ; (part with) disporre. a., frugale ; magro ; sovrabbondante ; —**part**, n., parte di ricambio f.

sparing*, spe'-ring, a., (thrifty) economo

spark, spaark, n., scintilla f. v., mandare scintille

sparking-plug, spaark'-ing-plŏgh, n., candela f.

sparkle, spaar'-kl, v., scintillare ; (wine) spumare

sparrow, spar'-ou, n., passero m.

spasm, spaṣm, n., spasimo m.

spasmodic, spaṣ-mo'-dik, a., spasmodico

spats, spats, n. pl., ghette f. pl.

spatter, spat'-a, v., inzaccherare

spawn, spoon, n., fregola f. v., essere in fregola

speak, spiik, v., parlare ; —**er**, n., oratore m.

spear, spir, n., lancia f. v., trafiggere colla lancia

special*, spesh'-al, a., speciale ;—**ity**, n., specialità f.

specie*, spii'-shii, n., numerario m.; —**s**, specie f.

specification, spes-i-fi-kei'-shon, n., specificazione f.

specify, spes'-i-fai, v., specificare

specimen, spes'-i-men, n., esemplare m.

specious*, spii'-shos, a., specioso

speck, spek, n., macchia f., punto m.

spectacle, spek'-ta-kl, n., spettacolo m.;—**s**, occhiali

spectator, spek-tei'-ta, n., spettatore m. [m. pl.

spectre, spek'-tr, n., spettro m.

speculate, spek'-iu-leit, v., speculare

speech, spiich, n., linguaggio m. ; parola f. ; (discourse) discorso m. ; **—less,** a., (fig.) interdetto
speed, spiid, n., velocità f. v., affrettarsi
speedy, spii'-di, a., pronto ; celere
spell, spel, v., compitare. n., (charm) incanto m.
spend, spend, v., spendere ; **—thrift,** n., scialacquatore [m.
sphere, sfir, n., sfera f.
spice, spais, n., spezie f.pl. v., condire con spezie
spicy, spai'-si, a., aromatico ; (fig.) piccante
spider, spai'-da, n., ragno m.; **—'s web,** telaragna f.
spike, spaik, n., spuntone m. v., inchiodare
spill, spil, v., spandere
spin, spin, v., far girare ; (web, etc.) filare ; **—ning,** n., filatura f.
spinach, spin'-ich, n., spinaci m. pl.
spinal, spai'-nl, a., dorsale
spindle, spin'-dl, n., fuso m.
spine, spain, n., spina f.
spinster, spin'-sta, n., zitella f.
spiral, spai'-rl, n., spirale f. a., spirale
spire, spair, n., (church) guglia f.
spirit, spir'-it, n., spirito m. ; (alcohol) alcool m. ; (vitality) energia f.; (drinks) bibite alcooliche f.pl.; **—ed*,** a., focoso ; **—ual*,** spirituale ; **—ualist,** n., spiritualista m. & f.
spit, spit, v., sputare. n., sputo m.; (roasting) spiedo m.
spite, spait, n., dispetto m. v., causare dispetto ; **—ful*,** a., dispettoso ; **in — of,** conj., nonostante
spittle, spit'-l, n., sputo m.
spittoon, spit-uun', n., sputacchiera f.
splash, splash, n., spruzzo m. v., spruzzare
splendid*, splen'-did, a., splendido
splendour, splen'-dor, n., splendore m.
splint, splint, n., (surgical) stecca f.
splinter, splin'-ta, n., scheggia f. v., scheggiarsi
split, split, n., fessura f. v., fendere
spoil, spoil, v., guastare
spoils, spoils, n.pl., spoglie f.pl.
spoke, spouk, n., raggio m.
spokesman, spouks'-man, n., porta parola m.
sponge, spónch, n., spugna f.   [drino m.
sponsor, spon'-sor, n., garante m. & f.; (baptism) pa-

spontaneous*, spon-tei'-ni-os, a., spontaneo

spool, spuul, n., rocchetto m.

spoon, spuun, n., cucchiaio m. ; (tea, etc.) cucchiaino m. ; **—ful**, cucchiaiata f.

sport, sport, n., sport m., giuoco m. ; **—ive***, a., sportivo ; **—sman**, n., uomo sportivo m. ; (hunter) cacciatore m.

spot, spot, n., punto m. ; (dirt) chiazza f. ; (place) luogo m. v., chiazzare ; **—ted**, a., punteggiato ; chispotless***, spot'-les, a., immacolato   [azzato

spout, spaut, n., (gutter) grondaia f. ; (pot or jug) becco m. v., zampillare

sprain, sprein, n., distorsione f. v., **storcere**

sprat, sprat, n., spratto m.

sprawl, sprool, v., sdraiarsi

spray, sprei, v., (water, etc.) spruzzare. n., spruzzo m. ; (branch) rametto m. ; **—er**, spruzzatore m.

spread, spred, v., estendersi ; (butter, etc.) spalmare ; (news) diffondere

sprig, sprigh, n., ramoscello m.

sprightly, sprait'-li, a., gaio, brioso

spring, springh, n., primavera f. ; (leap) salto m. ; (water) sorgente f. ; (metal) molla f. v., **saltare**

springy, spring'-ghi, a., elastico

sprinkle, spring'-kl, v., aspergere

sprout, spraut, n., germoglio m. v., **germogliare**

spur, spör, n., sperone m. v., speronare

spurious*, spiu-ri-os, a., spurio

spurn, spörn, v., disprezzare

spy, spai, n., spia f., spione m. v., **spiare**

squabble, skuob'-l, n., alterco m. v., altercare

squad, skuod, n., (mil.) squadra f. ; **—ron**, (mil. air) squadrone m. ; (naval) squadra f.

squalid*, skuol'-id, a., squallido   [schiamazzare

squall, skuool, n., (wind) raffica f. v., (scream)

squalor, skuol'-or, n., squallore m.

squander, skuon'-da, v., dissipare

square, skuer, a.,* quadrato. n., quadrato m. ; (public) piazza f.

squash, skuosh, v., schiacciare. n., (fig.) calca f.

squat, skuot, v., accoccolarsi. **a.**, (figure) tozzo

squeak, skuiik, v., squittire

squeeze, skuiiß, n., stretta f. v., spremere ; stringere

squint, skuint, n., strabismo m. v., guardare strabico

squirrel, skuir'-l, n., scoiattolo m.

squirt, skuȅrt, v., schizzettare. n., inaffiatore m.

stab, stab, n., pugnalata f. v., pugnalare

stability, sta-bil'-i-ti, n., stabilità f.

stable, stei'-bl, n., scuderia f. a., stabile

stack, stak, n., (wood) catasta f. ; (hay) mucchio di fieno m. ; (chimney) ciminiera f. v., ammucchiare

staff, staaf, n., bastone m. ; (flag) asta f. ; (employees) personale m. ; (mil.) stato maggiore m.

stag, stagh, n., cervo m.

stage, steich, n., (theatre) scena f., palco scenico m. ; (step) fase f. v., mettere in scena

stagger, stagh'-a, v., vacillare ; (astonish) sbalordire

stagnate, stagh'-neit, v., stagnare

staid*, steid, a., posato, serio

stain, stein, v., tingere ; (soil) macchiare. n., macchia f. ; —less, a., (metal) inossidabile

stair, ster, n., scalino m. ; —case, scala f.

stake, steik, n., palo m. ; (wager) posta f. v., plantare piuoli ; (wager, etc.) scommettere

stale, steil, a., (bread) stantio ; (liquor) sciocco

stalk, stoolk, n., gambo m. v., cacciare alla posta

stall, stool, n., banchetto m. ; (theatre) poltrona f.

stalwart, stool'-uȅrt, a., robusto

stamina, stam'-i-na, n., resistenza f. [ziente m.

stammer, stam'-a, v., balbuziare ; —er, n., balbu-

stamp, stamp, n., (postage) francobollo m. ; (rubber, etc.) timbro m. ; (seal) sigillo m. v., (letters) bollare ; (imprint) timbrare ; (foot) pestare i piedi

stampede, stam-piid', n., fuga precipitosa f.

stand, stand, n., tribuna f. ; resistenza f. ; (receptacle) attaccapanni m. ; (exhibition) posto m v., stare ; stare in piedi ; (endure) soffrire ; —ing, n., posizione f. ; —ing-room, posto in piedi m. ; — up ! (command) in piedi !

standard, stan-dard, n., (flag) insegna f. ; (cavalry) stendardo m. ; (fig.) modello m. a., normale ; (weights, etc.) tipo

standstill, stand'-stil, n., ristagno m.

staple, stei'-pl, a., principale. n.,(loop) cavalletta f.

star, staar, n., stella f. ; —**ry**, a., stellato

starboard, staar'-bŏrd, n., tribordo m.

starch, staarch, n., amido m. v., inamidare

stare, stēr, n., sguardo fisso m. v., guardare fisso

starling, staar'-ling, n., stornello m.

start, staart, n., (commencement) inizio m.; (departure) partenza f. ; (shock) colpo m. v., (commence) cominciare : (mech.) porre in moto ; (depart) partire

startle, staar'-tl, v., trasalire ; (frighten) spaventare

starvation, staar-vei'-shon, n., inedia f.

starve, staarv, v., morire d'inedia

state, steit, v., dichiarare. n., stato m. ; (condition) condizione f. ; (pomp) pompa f. ; —**ly**, a., maestoso ; —**ment**, n., dichiarazione f.; (account) rendiconto m. ; —**sman**, statista m.

station, stei'-shon, n., (railway) stazione f.; (police, fire) posto m.; (position) posizione f. v., appostare

stationary, stei'-shon-a-ri, a., stazionario

stationer, stei'-shon-a, n., cartolaio m.

stationery, stei'-shon-er-i, n., cancelleria f.

statistics, sta'-tis-tiks, n. pl., statistica f.

statue, stat'-iu, n., statua f.

statute, stat'-iuut, n., statuto m.

staunch, stŏŏnch, a., fedele. v., stagnare

stave, steiv, n., doga f. ; — **in**, v., sfondare

stay, stei, n., soggiorno m. v., (remain) rimanere

stead, sted, n., luogo m. ; **in— of**, adv., invece di

steadfast, sted'-faast, a., saldo, fermo

steady, sted'-i, a., serio ; costante ; stabile ; solido

steak, steik, n., bistecca f.

steal, stiil, v., rubare

stealth, stelZ, n., segretezza f.; **by —**, furtivamente

steam, stiim, n., vapore m.; —**er**, piroscafo m.

steel, stiil, n., acciaio m.

steep, stiip, a., erto. v., (soak) imbevere

steeple, stii'-pl, n., campanile m.

steer, stir, v., guidare. n., (ox) torello m.

steerage, stir'-ich, n., classe emigranti f.

stem, stem, v., respingere. n., stelo m.; (naut.) prua f.;

stench, stench, n., tanfo m. [(pipe) canna f.

step, step, n., passo m. ; (stair) gradino m. v., fare un passo ; **—father**, n., padrigno m. ; **—mother**, madrigna f.

sterile, ster'-il, a., sterile

sterilize, ster'-i-lais, v., sterilizzare

sterling, stĕr'-ling, a., puro. n., sterlina f.

stern, stĕrn, n., (ship) poppa f. a.,* austero

stevedore, stii'-ve-dor, n., stivatore m.

stew, stiuu, n., stufato m. v., mettere in stufato

steward, stiuu'-erd, n., cameriere di bordo m. ; (estate) intendente m.

stick, stik, n., bacchetta f. ; (walking, etc.) bastone m. v., attaccare ; (to paste) incollare

sticky, stik'-i, a., appiccicaticcio

stiff, stif, a., duro ; rigido ; **—en**, v., indurire

stifle, stai'-fl, v., soffocare

stigmatize, stigh'-ma-tais, v., stigmatizzare

stile, stail, n., barriera f.

still, stil, n., (distil) lambicco m. a., quieto ; calmo. adv., tuttora. conj., nondimeno. v., calmare

stimulate, stim'-iu-leit, v., stimolare

sting, sting, v., pungere. n., puntura f.; (barb) pungiglione m.

stingy, stin'-chi, a., spilorcio [giglione m.

stink, stingk, v., puzzare. n., puzzo m.

stint, stint, v., restringere ; limitare

stipend, stai'-pend, n., stipendio m.

stipulate, stip'-iu-leit, v., stipulare

stipulation, stip-iu-lei'-shon, n., stipulazione f.

stir, stĕr, v., rimestare ; (to move) commuovere

stirrup, stĕr'-op, n., staffa f.

stitch, stich, v., cucire. n., punto m.; (knitting) maglia f. ; (pain) fitta f.

stock, stok, n., (trunk) tronco m.; (gun) cassa f.; (flower) violacciocca f.; (store) merci in magazzino f.pl.; (broth) carne da brodo f.; (live) bestiame m. v., (keep) avere in magazzino ; **— book**, n., libro di magazzino m.; **— broker**, agente di borsa m. ; **—exchange**, borsa f. ; **— size**, misura corrente f. ; **—taking**, inventario m.

stocking, stok'-ing, n., calza f. [gogna f.

stocks, stoks, n. pl., valori pubblici m.pl. ; (pillory)

stoke, stouk, v., attizzare ; **—r**, n., fuochista m.
stolid, stol'-id, a., stolido
stomach, stŏm'-ak, n., stomaco m.
stone, stoun, n., pietra f. ; (pebble) ciottolo m. ; (of fruit) nocciolo m. v., lapidare ; (fruit) cavare il nocciolo
stool, stuul, n., sgabello m. ; (med.) evacuazione f.
stoop, stuup, v., abbassarsi
stop, stop, n., fermata f. ; (interruption) pausa f. ; (punctuation) punto m. v., fermare ; (stay) rimanere ; (payment) sospendere ; (teeth) impiombare ; (cease) interrompere ; (to remain standing) fermarsi ; **— up**, ostruire
stopper, stop'-a, n., tappo m.
storage, stor'-ich, n., magazzinaggio m. [m.
store, stor, v., immagazzinare. n., (shop) magazzino
stork, stoork, n., cicogna f.
storm, stoorm, n., temporale m. v., attaccare
stormy, stoor'-mi, a., tempestoso
story, sto'-ri, n., novella f. ; (narrative) storia f. ; (untruth) storiella f. ; **— -book**, libro di racconti m.
stout*, staut, a., corpulento ; (strong) forte
stove, stouv, n., stufa f. ; (range) fornello m.
stow, stou, v., (naut.) stivare
stowaway, stou'-a-uei, n., passeggero abusivo m.
straggle, stragh'-l, v., (lag) ritardare
straight, streit, a., dritto. adv., diritto ; **—en, v.**, raddrizzare ; **— forward***, a., simplice ; retto
strain, strein, n., (effort) sforzo m. ; (music) aria f. ; (tension) tensione f. v., sforzarsi ; (tendon) storcere ; (liquid) filtrare
strainer, strein'-a, n., filtro m. ; (tea) passa tè m.
straits, streits, n. pl., (channel) stretto m.
strand, strand, n., riva f. ; (rope) filo di corda m. v., incagliare
strange*, streinch, a., straniero ; (peculiar) strano
stranger, strein'-cha, n., straniero m.
strangle, strang'-gol, v., strangolare
strap, strap, n., correggia f. v., legare con cinghie
straw, stroo, n., paglia f. ; **—berry**, fragola f.
stray, strei, v., smarrirsi
streak, striik, n., striscia f. ; **—y**, a., striato

stream, striim, n., corrente f.

street, striit, n., via f.

strength, strengZ, n., forza f. ; **—en**, v., fortificare

strenuous*, stren'-iu-os, a., strenuo

stress, stres, n., accento tonico m. ; pressione f. ; importanza f. v., accentuare

stretch, strech, n., distesa f. v., stirare

stretcher, strech'-a, n., barella f.

strew, struu, v., spargere

strict*, strikt, a., severo ; esatto [passi lunghi

stride, straid, n., passo lungo m. v., camminare a

strife, straif, n., disputa f. ; contesa f.

strike, straik, n., sciopero m. v., (work) scioperare ; (thrash) battere ; (hit) colpire ; (match) accendere ; **— out**, (delete) eliminare

striker, straik'-a, n., (of work) scioperante m.

string, string, n., cordicella f. ; (violin) corda f.

stringency, strin'-chen-si, n., rigore m.; brevità f.

strip, strip, n., striscetta f. v., svestirsi

stripe, straip, n., striscia f. ; (mil.) **gallone m.** ; (lash) sferzata f. v., rigare

strive, straiv, v., sforzarsi, lottare

stroke, strouk, n., (blow) colpo m. ; (med.) attacco m. ; (pen) tratto m. ; (piston) corsa f.

stroll, stroul, n., giro m. v., far un giro

strong*, strong, a., forte ; (firm) solido

strop, strop, n., cuoio da rasoio m. v., affilare

structure, strok'-chur, n., struttura f.

struggle, strögh'-l, n., lotta f. v., lottare

strut, strot, v., pavoneggiarsi

stubborn*, stöb'-ern, a., testardo

stud, stöd, n.,(nail) borchia f.; (collar) bottoncino m.; (breeding) luogo da monta m. v.,guarnire di borchie

student, stiuu'-dent, n., studente m. & f.

studio, stiuu'-di-ou, n., studio m.

studious*, stiuu'-di-os, a., studioso [diare

study, stöd'-i, n., studio m.; (room) libreria f. v., stu-

stuff, stöf, v.,(pad) imbottire ; (preserve) impagliare ; (seasoning) infarcire ; (gorge) impinzarsi. n., materia f. ; **—ing**, (cookery) ripieno m.

stuffy, stöf'-i, a., (air) afoso

stumble, stöm'-bl, v., inciampare

stump, stŏmp, n., (limb) moncone m.; (tree, etc.) ceppo m.; (cigar, etc.) mozzicone m.; (cricket) bastone m.

stun, stŏn, v., stordire; —**ning**, a., (fig.) abbagliante

stunted, stŏnt′-id, a., (growth) mal cresciuto

stupefy, stiuu′-pi-fai, v., stupefare

stupendous°, stiu-pen′-dŏs, a., stupendo

stupid°, stiuu′-pid, a., stupido; —**ity**, n., stupidità f.

stupor, stiuu′-pr, n., stupore m.

sturdy, stĕr′-di, a., vigoroso; robusto

sturgeon, stĕr′-chon, n., storione m.

stutter, stŏt′-a, v., balbuziare

sty, stai, n., porcile m.; (eye) orzaiuolo m.

style, stail, n., stile m.; modo m.; maniera f.

stylish, stail′-ish, a., distinto

subdue, sob-diuu′, v., soggiogare; (soften) mitigare; —**d**, a., sommesso

subject, sob-chekt′, v., assoggettare

subject, sŏb′-chekt, n., soggetto m.; (a national) suddito m.; — **to**, a., soggetto a

subjection, sob-chek′-shon, n., soggezione f.

subjunctive, sob-chŏnk′-tiv, n., soggiuntivo m.

sublime, sob-laim′, a., sublime

submarine, sob-ma-riin′, n., sottomarino m.

submerge, sob-mĕrch′, v., sommergere

submission, sob-mish′-on, n., sommissione f.

submit, sob-mit′, v., sottomettere

subordinate, sob-or′-di-neit, a., subordinato

subpœna, sob-pii′-na, n., citazione di testimonio f.

subscribe, sob-skraib′, v., sottoscrivere; (journals) abbonarsi; —**r**, n., sottoscrittore m.; abbonato m.

subscription, sob-skrip′-shon, n., sottoscrizione f.; abbonamento m.

subsequent°, sŏb′-sii-kuent, a., susseguente

subservient, sob-sĕr′-vi-ent, a., subordinato

subside, sob-said′, v., avvallarsi; (abate) abbassarsi

subsidiary, sob-sid′-ia-ri, a., sussidiario

subsidy, sŏb′-si-di, n., sussidio m.

subsist, sob-sist′, v., sussistere

substance, sŏb′-stans, n., sostanza f.

substantial, sob-stan′-shal, a., sostanziale; solido

substantiate, sŏb-stan'-shi-eit, v., provare

substantive, sŏb-stan-tiv, n., sostantivo m.

substitute, sŏb'-sti-tiuut, n., (proxy) rappresentante m.; (thing) sostituto m. v., sostituire

subterranean, sob-ter-re'-ni-an, a., sotterraneo

subtle, sŏt'-l, a., fino; sottile

subtract, sŏb'-trakt, v., sottrarre

suburb, sŏb'-ĕrb, n., sobborgo m., suburbio m.

subway, sŏb'-uei, n., passaggio sotterraneo m.

succeed, sok-siid', v., succedere; (inherit) ereditare; (achieve) riuscire

success, sŏk'-ses, n., successo m.; —**ful**, a., pieno di successo; —**ion**, n., successione f.

successor, sok-ses'-or, n., successore m.

succour, sŏk'-er, n., soccorso m. v., soccorrere

succumb, sok-ŏm', v., soccombere

such, sŏch, pron. & a., tale, simile; — **a**, un tal

suck, sŏk, v., succhiare; —**le**, allattare

suction, sŏk'-shon, n., aspirazione f.; gorgo m.

sudden*, sŏd'-n, a., subitaneo

sue, siuu, v., citare in giudizio

suet, siuu'-et, n., grasso di bue m.

suffer, sŏf'-a, v., soffrire; —**ing**, n., sofferenza f.; on —**ance**, per tolleranza

suffice, so-fais', v., bastare

sufficient*, so-fish'-ent, a., sufficiente

suffocate, sŏf'-o-keit, v., soffocare

suffrage, sŏf'-rech, n., suffragio m. [zucchero f.pl.

sugar, shu'-ga, n., zucchero m.; — **tongs**, molle da

suggest, so-chest', v., suggerire; —**ion**, n., suggerimento m.; —**ive**, a., suggestivo

suicide, siuu'-i-said, n., suicidio m.

suit, siuut, v., convenire; (dress, etc.) star bene. n., abito completo m.; (law) processo m.; —**able**, a., conveniente; —**or**, n.,(wooer) pretendente m.

suite, su-iit', n., (retinue) seguito m.; (rooms) appartamento m.; (furniture) fornitura completa f.

sulk, sŏlk, v., essere di cattivo umore; —**y**, a., imsullen*, sŏl'-n, a., tetro [bronciato

sulphur, sŏl'-fr, n., zolfo m.

sultry, sŏl'-tri, a., soffocante, afoso

sum, sŏm, n., somma f.; — **up**, v., ricapitolare

summary, sŏm'-a-ri, n., sommario m. a., sommario
summer, sŏm'-a, n., estate f.
summit, sŏm'-it, n., sommità f., cima f.
summon, sŏm'-n, v., citare ; (call) convocare
summons, sŏm'-ns, n., (legal) citazione f.
sumptuous*, sŏmp'-tiu-os, a., sontuoso
sun, sŏn, n., sole m.; —**beam**, raggio di sole m.;
— -**dial**, orologio solare m.; —**flower**, girasole m.; —**ny**, a., di sole, soleggiato ; —**rise**,
n., aurora f.; —**set**, tramonto m.; —**shine**,
[luce di] sole f.; —**stroke**, colpo di sole m.
Sunday, sŏn'-di, n., domenica f.
sundries, sŏn'-dris, n. pl., diversi m. pl.
sundry, sŏn'-dri, a., vario
sunken, sŏng'-kn, a., (features) incavato
super, siuu'-pa, n., (theatrical) comparsa m. & f.;
—**abundant**, a., sovrabbondante ; —**annu-**
ation, n., pensione f.; —**cilious***, a., arrogante ; —**ficial***, superficiale ; —**fine**, sopraf-
fino ; —**intend**, v., sorvegliare ; —**intendent**,
n., sovraintendente m.; —**natural**, a., soprannaturale ; —**sede**, v., surrogare ; —**vise**, sorvegliare ; —**vision**, n., sorveglianza f.
superb*, siu-pĕrb', a., superbo
superfluous*, siuu-pĕr'-flu-os, a., superfluo
superior, siuu-pi'-ri-a, a. & n., superiore m.
superlative, siuu-pĕr'-la-tiv, n., superlativo m.
superstition, siuu-per-stish'-on, n., superstizione f.
superstitious*, siuu-per-stish'-os, a., superstizioso
supper, sŏp'-a, n., cena f.
supplant, so-plaant', v., soppiantare
supple, sŏp'-l, a., flessibile
supplement, sŏp'-li-ment, n., supplemento m.
supplier, so-plai'-a, n., fornitore m.
supply, so-plai', v., (with) fornire ; (deliver) consegnare. n., fornitura f.; (stock) provvista f.
support, so-port', v., sostegno m. v., sostenere
suppose, so-pous', v., supporre
supposition, so-pou-sish'-on, n., supposizione f.
suppress, so-pres', v., sopprimere ; (conceal) nascondere
supremacy, siu-prem'-a-si, n., supremazia f.

supreme*, siu-priim', a., supremo

surcharge, sĕr-chaarch', v., sopraccaricare. n., (postage) sopratassa f.

sure*, shur, a., sicuro, certo

surety, shur'-ti, n., cauzione f.; (person) garante m.

surf, sĕrf, n., risacca f.

surface, sĕr'-fis, n., superficie f.

surge, sĕrch, v., urtare. n., marosi m. pl.

surgeon, sĕr'-chon, n., chirurgo m.

surgery, sĕr'-cher-i, n., chirurgia f.

surgical, sĕr'-chi-kl, a., chirurgico

surly, sĕr'-li, a., burbero ; irascibile

surmise, ser-mais', n., supposizione f. v., supporre

surmount, ser-maunt', v., sormontare

surname, sĕr'-neim, n., cognome m.

surpass, ser-paas', v., sorpassare ; superare

surplus, sĕr'-plos, n., soprappiù m. ; eccedente m.

surprise, ser-prais', n., sorpresa f. v., sorprendere

surrender, se-ren'-da, n., (mil.) resa f. v., capitolare ; (cede) cedere

surround, se-raund', v., circondare

surroundings, se-raund'-ings, n.pl., dintorni m.pl.

survey, sĕr'-vei, n., (land) misura f. v., misurare ; (to glance) ispezionare

surveyor, ser-vei'-or, n., geometra m.; ispettore m.

survival, ser-vai'-vl, n., sopravvivenza f.

survive, ser-vaiv', v., sopravvivere

survivor, ser-vai'-vr, n., sopravvivente m.

susceptible, so-sep'-ti-bl, a., suscettibile

suspect, sos-pekt', v., sospettare. n., sospetto m.

suspend, sos-pend', v., sospendere

suspenders, sos-pen'-ders, n.pl., giarettiere f.pl.

suspense, sos-pens', n., incertezza f.

suspension, sos-pen'-shon, n., sospensione f.

suspicion, sos-pish'-on, n., sospetto m.

suspicious*, so-spish'-os, a., sospettoso

sustain, sos-tein', v., sostenere ; (maintain) sostentare ; (suffer) sopportare ; (loss) subire

sustenance, sŏs'-ti-nans, n., mantenimento m.

swagger, suagh'-a, n., millanteria f. v., vantarsi

swallow, suol'-ou, v., inghiottire. n., inghiottita f.; (bird) rondine f.

swamp, suomp, n., palude f. v., (boat) sommergere

swan, suon, n., cigno m.

swarm, suoOrm, n., sciame m. v., sciamare

sway, suei, n., (power) potere m.; (influence) influenza f. v., influenzare; (to rock) oscillare; (to reel) vacillare

swear, suer, v., giurare; (curse) bestemmiare

sweat, suet, n., sudore m. v., sudare

sweep, suiip, v., spazzare. n., (chimney) spazzacamino m.; —er, spazzino m.

sweet, suitt, n., dolce m. a.,° dolce; —bread, n., animella f.; —en, v., inzuccherare; —heart, n., carino m.; —ness, dolcezza f.; (smell) fragranza f.; —pea, pisello odorato m.

swell, suel, v., gonfiarsi. n., (sea) onda di fondo f.

swelling, suel′-ing, n., gonfiezza f.

swerve, suerv, v., deviare; (skid) slittare

swift*, suift, a., presto, veloce

swim, suim, n., nuotata f. v., nuotare

swindle, suin′-dl, n., scroccone m. v., scroccare

swindler, suin′-dla, n., scroccone m.

swine, suain, n., maiale m.

swing, suingh, n., oscillazione f.; (child′s) altalena f. v., dondolare, oscillare; brandire

switch, suich, n., (riding) frustino m.; (electrical) interruttore m. v., (train) scambiare; — off, (electric) togliere; — on, dare

swivel, sui′-vl, n., perno m.

swoon, suun, v., svenire

swoop, suup, — down, v., piombare dall′alto

sword, sord, n., spada f.

sworn, suorn, a., giurato

syllable, sil′-a-bl, n., sillaba f.

syllabus, sil′-a-bos, n., compendio m.

symbol, sim′-bol, n., simbolo m.

symmetry, sim′-et-ri, n., simmetria f.

sympathetic, sim-pa-Zet′-ik, a., pieno di simpatia

sympathize, sim-pa-Zais′, v., simpatizzare

sympathy, sim′-pa-Zi, n., simpatia f.

symptom, simp′-tom, n., sintomo m.

synchronize, sin′-kron-ais, v., concordare

syndicate, sin′-di-keit, n., sindacato m.

synonymous*, si-non'-i-mos, a., sinonimo
syphilis, si-fil'-is, n., sifilide f.
syphon, sai'-fon, n., sifone m.
syringe, sir'-inch, n., siringa f. v., siringare
syrup, sir'-op, n., sciroppo m.
system, sis'-tem, n., sistema m.

tabernacle, tab'-er-na-kl, n., tabernacolo m.
table, tei'-bl, n., tavola f.; (list) tabella f.; — -**cloth**,
 tovaglia f.;   — -**cover**, tappeto da tavola m.;
 — -**land**, altipiano m.;   — -**spoon**, cucchiaio
 da tavola m.
tablet, tab'-let, n., tavoletta f.; pastiglia f.
tack, tak, n., (nail) bulletta f. v., imbullettare;
 (sew) imbastire; (sailing) bordeggiare
tackle, tak'-l, n., (fishing) arnesi da pesca m. pl.;
 (naut.) sartiame m. v., (to attack, to set to
 work) dar di piglio
tact, takt, n., tatto m.;   — **ful***, a., accorto;
 — **ics**, n., tattica f.;   — **less**, a., senza tatto
tadpole, tad'-poul, n., girino m.
tag, tagh, n., cartellino m. v., appendere
tail, teil, n., coda f.
tailor, tei'-lr, n., sarto m.
taint, teint, v., infettare; insozzare
take, teik, v., prendere; accompagnare; portare;
 — **away**, portar via; — **off**, togliere
takings, tei'-kings, n. pl., incasso m.
tale, teil, n., racconto m.; (fairy) favola f.
talent, tal'-ent, n., talento m.
talk, took, v., parlare. n., conversazione f.
talkative, took'-a-tiv, a., loquace
tall, tool, a., alto; grande
tallow, tal'-ou, n., sego m.
tally, tal'-i, v., (agree) concordare
talon, tal'-on, n., artiglio m.
tame, teim, a., mansueto,   v., domare; — **ness**,
 n., mansuetudine f.; — **r**, domatore m.
tamper, tam'-pa, v., — **with**, porre le mani su
tan, tan, n., concia f. v., conciare; (sunburn) abbronzare;   — **ner**, n., conciatore di pelli m.;
 — **nery**, conciatura di pelli f.

tangerine, tan'-che-riin, n., mandarino m.

tangible, tan'-chi-bl, a., tangibile

tangle, tang'-gol, n., imbroglio m. v., imbrogliare

tank, tangk, n., cisterna f.; (mil.) carro d'assalto m.

tankard, tang'-kerd, n., boccale m.

tantalize, tan'-ta-lais, v., tormentare

tantamount, tan'-ta-mount, a., equivalente

tap, tap, v., bussare ; (barrel) forare. n., rubinetto m.

tape, teip, n., passamano m.; — measure, misura a nastro f.; — worm, tenia f.; red —, burocrazia f.

taper, tei'-pa, v., terminare in punta. n., cerino m.

tapestry, tap'-es-tri, n., arazzo m.

tar, taar, n., catrame m. v., incatramare

tardiness, taar'-di-nes, n., tardezza f.

tardy, taar'-di, a., (slow) lento

tare, ter, n., (weight) tara f.; (weed) loglio m.

target, taar'-ghet, n., bersaglio m.

tariff, tar'-if, n., tariffa f.

tarnish, taar'-nish, v., perdere il lustro

tarpaulin, taar-poo'-lin, n., tela incatramata f.

tart, taart, n., torta f. a.,* agro

task, taask, n., tema m. ; compito m.

tassel, tas'-l, n., nappina f.

taste, teist, n., gusto m. v., gustare ; — ful, a., di buon gusto ; — less, insipido, senza gusto

tasty, teis'-ti, a., saporito

tatter, tat'-a, n., straccio m. ; — ed, a., straccioso

tattle, tat'-l, v., ciarlare. n., ciarla f.

tattoo, ta-tuu', n., (mil.) ritirata f. v., (the skin) ta-
taunt, toont, n., beffa f. v., beffare [tuare

tavern, tav'-ern, n., taverna f.

tawdry, too'-dri, a., barocco

tax, taks, n., tassa f. v., tassare

taxi, taks'-i, n., auto m., taxi m.

tea, tii, n., tè m. ; — pot, teiera f.

teach, tiich, v., insegnare ; — er, n., maestro m.

teaching, tiich'-ing, n., istruzione f.

team, tiim, n., tiro m. ; (sport) squadra f.

tear, ter, n., strappo m. v., lacerare

tear, tir, n., lagrima f.

tease, tiis, v., stuzzicare

teat, tiit, n., tetta f.; (dummy) tettina f.

technical*, tek'-ni-kl, a., tecnico
tedious*, tii'-di-os, a., tedioso
tedium, tii'-di-om, n., tedio m.
teem, tiim, v., — **with**, formicolare
teething, tii'-Ding, n., dentizione f.
teetotaller, tii'-too-tla, n., astemio m.
telegram, tel'-i-gram, n., telegramma m.
telegraph, tel'-i-graf, v., telegrafare
telephone, tel'-i-foun, n., telefono m. v., telefonare
telescope, tel'-i-skoup, n., telescopio m.
tell, tel, v., dire ; (relate) raccontare   [pera f.
temper, tem'-pa, n., umore m., indole f.; (steel) tem-
temperance, tem'-per-ans, n., temperanza f.
temperate, tem'-per-et, a., (moderate) moderato ,
   (habits) sobrio
temperature, tem'-pra-chur, n., temperatura f.
tempest, tem'-pest, n., tempesta f.
temple, tem'-pl, n., tempio m. ; (head) tempia f.
temporary, tem'-po-ra-ri, a., temporaneo
tempt, tempt, v., tentare ; **—ation**, n., tentazione f.
ten, ten, a., dieci
tenable, ten'-a-bl, a., sostenibile
tenacious*, ti-nei'-shos, a., tenace
tenacity, ti-nas'-i-ti, n., tenacità f.
tenancy, ten'-an-si, n., locazione f.
tenant, ten'-ant, n., locatario m.; (land) fittavolo m.
tend, tend, v., aver tendenza ; (nurse) curare
tendency, ten'-en-si, n., tendenza f.
tender, ten'-da, v., fare un'offerta. n., (offer) offerta f.; (public) offerta d'appalto f. a.,* tenero ;
   (sensitive) sensibile ; **— -hearted**, di cuore
   tenero ; **—ness**, n., (affection) tenerezza f.
tenement, ten'-i-ment, n., alloggio m.
tennis, ten'-is, n., tennis m.
tenor, ten'-or, n., tenore m.
tense, tens, a.,* teso. n., (gram.) tempo m.
tension, ten'-shon, n., tensione f.
tent, tent, n., tenda f.
tentative, ten'-ta-tiv, a., di prova
tenth, tenZ, a.,decimo. n., (fraction) un decimo m.
tenure, ten'-iur, n., possesso m.
tepid, tep'-id, a., tiepido

term, tĕrm, n., espressione f.; (time) durata f.; (quarter) trimestre m.

terminate, tĕr'-mi-neit, v., terminare

terminus, tĕr'-mi-nos, n., stazione capolinea f.

terms, tĕrms, n. pl., condizioni f. pl.

terrace, ter'-is, n., terrazza f.

terrible, ter'-i-bl, a., terribile

terrific, ter-if'-ik, a., terrifico

terrify, ter'-i-fai, v., terrorizzare

territory, ter'-i-to-ri, n., territorio m.

terror, ter'-or, n., terrore m.; **—ize**, v., terrorizzare

terse*, tĕrs, a., terso

test, test, n., prova f.; (exam.) prova d'esame f. v., provare; esaminare; **—ify**, testimoniare; **—imonial**, n., certificato m.; (presentation) dono di riconoscimento m.; **—imony**, testimonianza f.

Testament, tes'-ta-ment, n., Testamento m.

testicle, tes'-ti-kl, n., testicolo m.

tether, teD'-a, n., pastoia f. v., impastoiare

text, tekst, n., testo m.; **— -book**, libro di testo m.

textile, teks'-tail, a., tessile

texture, teks'-chur, n., tessuto m.; (weave) tessitura

than, Dan, conj., che; di   [f.

thank, Zangk, v., ringraziare; **— you!** interj., grazie! **—ful***, a., grato; **—less**, ingrato; **—s**, n. pl., grazie f. pl.; **—s to**, prep., in grazia a; **—sgiving**, n., resa di grazie f.; (festival) giorno di grazie m.

that, Dat, pron., quello, quella; ciò; chi; quegli; colui. conj., che; affinchè

thatch, Zach, n., paglia f. v., coprire di paglia

thaw, Zoo, n., sgelo m. v., sgelare

the, Di, art., il, lo, la; pl., i, gli, le; the ... the ..., quanto ... tanto ...; example: the later the better, quanto più tardi tanto meglio

theatre, Zii'-a-ta, n., teatro m.

thee, Dii, pron., te; ti; **to —**, a te

theft, Zeft, n., furto m.   [le loro

their, Der, a., loro; **—s**, pron., il loro, la loro, i loro,

them, Dem, pron., li, le, loro, essi, esse; **—selves**, sè stessi; loro medesimi; **to —**, a loro

theme, Ziim, n., tema m.

then, Den, adv. allora; poi; quindi. conj. dunque

thence, Dens, adv. d'allora; di là; **—forth,** d'allora in poi

theology, Zi-ol'-*o*-chi, n., teologia f.

theoretical,* Zi-*o*-ret'-i-kal, a., teorico

theory, Zii'-*o*-ri, n., teoria f.

there, Der, adv. li, là, colà, ivi, vi, ci; **—after,** dopo ciò; **—by,** perciò; **—fore,** pertanto; **—upon,** indi

thermal, Zer'-ml, a., termale

thermometer, Zer-mom'-i-ter, n., termometro m.

these, Diis, pron., questi, queste

thesis, Zi'-sis, n., tesi f.

they, Dei. pron., essi, esse, loro

thick,* Zik, a., spesso, denso; (big) grosso; **—en,** v., condensarsi; addensare;**—ness,** n., spessore m.

thicket, Zik'-*et*, n., boschetto m.   [densità f.

thief, Ziif, n., ladro m.

thieve, Ziiv, v., rubare

thigh, Zai, n., coscia f.

thimble, Zim'-bl, n., ditale m.

thin, Zin, a.,* sottile; (lean) magro; (sparse) rado. v., assottigliare; (trees, etc.) diradare; **—ness,** n., sottigliezza f.; magrezza f.

thine, Dain, pron., il tuo, la tua; i tuoi, le tue

thing, Zing, n., cosa f.

think, Zingk, v., pensare; (believe) credere; **— over,** pensare su

third, Zerd, a., terzo. n., (fraction) un terzo m.

thirdly, Zerd'-li, adv., in terzo luogo

thirst, Zerst, n., sete f.; **—y,** a., assetato

thirteen, Zer'-tiin, a., tredici

thirteenth, Zer'-tiinZ, a., tredicesimo

thirtieth, Zer'-ti-iiZ, a., trentesimo

thirty, Zer'-ti, a., trenta

this, Dis, pron. & a., questo, questa

thistle, Zis'-l, n., cardo m.

thong, Zong, n., correggia f.

thorn, Zoorn, n., spino m.; **—y,** a., spinoso

thorough,* Zŏr'-o, a., intero; completo, perfetto; **—bred,** n., puro sangue m.; **—fare,** via f.; (main street) via principale f.; **no —fare,** via sbarrata f.

those, Dou**s**, a. & pron., quei, quegli ; quelli, quelle,

thou, Dau, pron., tu   [coloro

though, Dou, conj., benchè, quantunque

thought, Zoot, n., pensiero m. ; **—ful***, a., pensieroso ; (considerate) riguardoso ; **—less***, (inconsiderate) sbadato, sconsiderato

thousand, Zau'-**s**and, a., mille, mila ; **—th**, millesimo

thrash, Zrash, v., battere ; **—ing**, n., percosse f.; **—ing-machine,** trebbiatrice f.

thread, Zred, n., filo m. v., infilare

threadbare, Zred'-ber, a., logoro

threat, Zret, n., minaccia f.; **—en,** v., minacciare **; —ening***, a., minacciante

three, Zrii, a., tre ; **—fold,** triplo

thresh, Zresh, v., battere

threshold, Zresh'-hould, n., soglia f.

thrice, Zrais, adv., tre volte

thrift, Zrift, n., economia f.; **—less,** a., prodigo

thrifty, Zrift'-ti, a., economo

thrill, Zril, v., far fremere. n., fremito m.

thrilling, Zril'-ing, a., che fa fremere

thrive, Zraiv, v., prosperare

throat, Zrout, n., gola f.

throb, Zrob, v., pulsare ; (heart) palpitare

throes, Zrou**s**, n. pl., dolore m. ; (fig.) angoscia f.

throne, Zroun, n., trono m.

throng, Zrong, n., calca f. v., accalcare

throttle, Zrot'-l, v., (mech.) togliere pressione ; (kill) strangolare. n., (anatomy) trachea f. ; (mech.) valvola di strozzamento f.

through, Zruu, prep., attraverso ; per ; **—out,** adv., (wholly) interamente ; (everywhere) dappertutto ; **—train,** n., treno diretto m.

throw, Zrou, v., gettare. n., gettata f.

thrush, Zrôsh, n., tordo m.

thrust, Zrôst, n., colpo m. v., dare una puntata

thud, Zôd, n., tonfo m.

thumb, Zôm, n., pollice m.   [gno

thump, Zômp, n., (blow) pugno m. v., dar un pu-

thunder, Zôn'-da, n., tuono m. v., tuonare ; **—bolt,** n., fulmine m.; **—storm,** temporale m.

Thursday, Zêrs'-di, n., giovedì m.

thus, Dŏs, adv., così, perciò [riare

thwart, Zuoŏrt, v., frustrare ; (someone) contra-

thy, Dai, pron., tuo, tua, tuoi, tue

thyme, taim, n., timo m.

tick, tik, n., (cattle) zecca f. v., (clock) fare tic tac ; (check) marcare ; —**ing**, n., battito m.

ticket, tik'-*et*, n., biglietto m. ; (label) etichetta f. ; **season**-—, tessera f.

tickle, tik'-l, v., solleticare [broso

ticklish, tik'-lish, a., soggetto a solletico ; (fig.) sca-

tidal, tai'-dl, a., di marea

tide, taid, n., (high) alta marea f. ; (low) bassa ma-

tidings, tai'-ding**s**, n.pl., notizie f. pl. [rea f.

tidy, tai'-di, a., in ordine ; (neat) lindo. v., mettere in ordine

tie, tai, n., (bow) cravatta a farfalla f.; (necktie) cra-vatta f. v., legare ; (bow, etc.) annodare

tier, tir, n., piano m. ; (theatre) ordine m.

tiff, tif, n., (altercation) picca f.

tiger, tai'-*ga*, n., tigre m.

tight°, tait, a., (close) fisso ; (garments, etc.) stretto

tighten, tait'-*en*, v., stringere ; (a screw) serrare

tights, taits, n. pl., maglia f.

tile, tail, n., (roof) tegola f. ; (floor and wall) pia-strella f. v., coprire di tegole

till, til, n., cassetto del denaro m. v., (land) lavo-rare. conj. & prep., fino a che ; — **now**, finora

tiller, til'-*a*, n., coltivatore m. ; (naut.) barra del ti-

tilt, tilt, v., inclinare, pendere [mone f.

timber, tim'-*ba*, n., legname m.

time, taim, v., misurare il tempo. n., (hour) ora f.; (period) tempo m. ; (occasion) volta f. ; (mu-sic) tempo m. ; (step) passo m. ; —**ly**, a. & adv., opportuno ; —-**keeper**, n., cronometrista f. ; controllore m. ; —-**table**, orario m.

timid°, tim'-id, a., timido

tin, tin, n., stagno m. ; (sheet) latta f. v., stagnare ; (can) mettere in iscatola ; — **box**, n., scatola di latta f. ; —-**foil**, stagnola f. ; —-**plate**, lami-na di stagno f.

tincture, tingh'-chur, n., tintura f.

tinge, tinch, n., tinta f. v., tingere

tingle, ting'-gol, v., formicolare ; (sound) tintinnare

tinkle, tingk'-l, v., tintinnare. n., tintinnio m.

tinsel, tin'-sl, n., orpello m.

tint, tint, n., tinta f. v., tingere

tiny, tai'-ni, a., minuscolo

tip, tip, n., punta f.: (hint) suggerimento m.: (gratuity) mancia f. v., (cart, etc.) capovolgere ; (waiters, etc.) dare la mancia ; **on— -toe,** adv., sulla punta dei piedi

tire, tair, n., (rim) cerchione di ferro m. v., stancare : —d, a., stanco ; — **of,** v., stancarsi di ; —**some,** a., faticoso ; (boring) noioso

tissue, tish'-iu, n., tessuto m. ; — **-paper,** carta velina f.

tithe, taiD, n., decima f.

title, tai'-tl, n., titolo m.: — **-deed,** titolo di proprietà m. ; — **-page,** frontespizio m.

titter, tit'-a, n., risata soffocata f. v., ridere sotto baffi

to, tu, prep. & adv., (until) fino ; (towards) verso : (to a place or person) da ; (intention) per : (writing to someone) a ; (going to a country) in ; (going to a town) a ; (secretary, etc., **to**) di

toad, toud, n., rospo m.

toast, toust, n., (bread) crostino m. v., tostare

toast, toust,n.,(health) brindisi m. v.,fare un brindisi

tobacco, to-bak'-ou, n., tabacco m. ; —**nist,** tabaccaio m. ; — **-pouch,** borsa da tabacco f.

toboggan, to-bogh'-an, n., slitta f. v., slittare

to-day, tu-dei', adv., oggi

toe, tou, n., dito del piede m.

toffee, tof'-i, n., caramella al burro f.

together, to-gheD'-a, adv., insieme, assieme

toil, toil, n., fatica f. v., affaticare

toiler, toi'-la, n., lavoratore m.

toilet, toi'-let, n., toeletta f.

token, tou'-kn, n., segno m., marca f.

tolerable, tol'-er-a-bl, a., tollerabile

tolerance, tol'-er-ans, n., tolleranza f.

tolerant, tol'-er-ant, a., tollerante

tolerate, tol'-er-eit, v., tollerare

toll, toul, n., (tax) pedaggio m. ; (bell) rintocco m. v., suonare a rintocco

tomato, to-maa'-tou, n., pomodoro m.   [f.
tomb, tuum, n., tomba f.;—**stone,** lapide funeraria
tomboy, tom'-boi, n., biricchina f.
tomcat, tom'-kat, n., gatto m.
tomfoolery, tom-fuul'-er-i, n., balordaggine f.
to-morrow, tu-mor'-ou, adv., domani
tomtit, tom'-tit, n., cingallegra f.
ton, tön, n., tonnellata f. ; —**nage,** tonnellaggio m.
tone, toun, n., tono m.
tongs, tonghs, n.pl., molle f.pl.
tongue, töng, n., lingua f.; —**tied,** a., ammutolito
tonic, ton'-ik, n., tonico m.
to-night, tu-nait', adv., stanotte
tonsil, ton'-sil, n., tonsilla f.;—**itis,** tonsillite f.
too, tuu, adv., troppo ; (also) anche ;— **much,** troppo
tool, tuul, n., arnese m., ferro m.
tooth, tuuz, n., dente m.;—**ache,** mal di denti m.;
  — **-brush,** spazzolino da denti m. ; —**paste,**
  dentifricio m.; — **-pick,** stuzzicadenti m.
top, top, n., cima f. ; (toy) trottola f. ; (scholar) il
  primo m. a., primo ; **on —,** in cima ; di sopra ;
  — **-boot,** n., stivalone f.; — **-hat,** cilindro m.
topic, top'-ik, n., argomento m.
topple (over), top'-l, v., (headlong fall) capitom-
  bolare ; (car, etc.) rovesciarsi
topsy-turvy, top'-si-tér'-vi, adv., sottosopra
torch, toorch, n., torcia f.
torment, toor'-ment, n., tormento m. v., tormentare
tornado, toor-nei'-dou, n., uragano m.
torpedo, toor-pii'-dou, n., siluro m. ; — **-boat,**
  torpediniera f.
torpid*, toor'-pid, a., torpido ; intorpidito
torpor, toor'-pa, n., torpore m.
torrent, tor'-ent, n., torrente m.
torrid, tor'-id, a., torrido   [ruga f.
tortoise, toor'-tos, n., tartaruga f.;—**shell,** tarta-
torture, toor'-chur, n., tortura f. v., torturare
toss, tos, n., (bull) cornata f.   v., gettare in aria ;
  (coin) giuocare a testa e corona ; — **about,** agitarsi ; (naut.) sballottare
total, tou'-tl, n., totale m. v., sommare. a.,*totale
totalisator, tou-tl-i-se'-ta, n., totalizzatore m.

totter, tŏt'-*a*, v., barcollare ; —**ing***, a., barcollante

touch, tŏch, v., toccare. n., (contact) tocco m. ; (feeling) tatto m. ; (mus.) toccata f. ; —**ing**, a., (emotion) commovente ; —**y**, (fig.) suscettibile

tough*, tŏf, a., tiglioso ; duro

tour, tür, n., viaggio m. ; (excursion) giro m. v., girare ; —**ist**, n., turista m. & f. ; —**nament**, torneo m.

tout, taut, v., (seats, etc.) adescare. n., bagarino m.

tow, tou, v., (haul) rimorchiare. n., (flax) stoppa f. ; —**age**, rimorchio m. ; —**ing-path**, banchina di rimorchio f. ; —**rope**, corda di rimorchio f.

towards, tou'-*erds*, prep., verso

towel, tau'-*el*, n., tovaglia f.

tower, tau'-*a*, n., torre f.

town, taun, n., città f. ; —**-hall**, municipio m.

toy, toi, n., giuocattolo m. v., giuocare

trace, treis, n., traccia f. v., tracciare ; (track) rintracciare ; (copy) calcare

tracing, treis'-ing, n., calco m. ; —**paper**, carta da calco f.

track, trak, n., traccia f. ; (race) pista f. ; (railway) strada f. v., seguire la traccia

tract, trakt, n., tratto m. ; (religious) opuscolo m.

traction, trak'-shon, n., trazione f. ; —**engine**, locomotiva di trazione f.

trade, treid, v., commerciare. n., commercio m. ; (craft) mestiere m. ; —**mark**, marca di fabbrica f. ; —**r**, commerciante m. ; —**sman**, negoziante m. ; —**union**, corporazione di mestiere f.

tradition, tra-dish'-on, n., tradizione f.

traditional*, tra-dish'-on-al, a., tradizionale

traduce, tra-diŭus', v., calunniare

traffic, traf'-ik, n., traffico m.

tragedian, tra-chii'-di-*an*, n., tragico **m**.

tragedy, trach'-i-di, n., tragedia f.

tragic, trach'-ik, a., tragico

trail, treil, n., pista f. ; via f. v., seguire la pista ; (drag) strascicare

trailer, treil'-*a*, n., (van) rimorchio m.

train, trein, v., addestrare ; (educate) istruire. n., (railway) treno m. ; (dress) strascico m. ; —**er**, allenatore m. ; —**ing**, addestramento **m**.

traitor, trei'-ta, n., traditore m.

tram, tram, n., tranvia m. [dare

tramp, tramp, n., vagabondo m. v.,(walk) vagabon-

trample, tram'-pl, v., calpestare

trance, traans, n., (joy)estasi f.; (hypnotic) sonno m.

tranquil, trang'-kuil, a., tranquillo [zione f.

transact, tran-sakt', v., trattare ; —ion, n., transa-

transcribe, tran-skraib', v., trascrivere

transfer, trans-fër', v., trasferire. n., trasferimen-
to m.; —-ticket, biglietto cumulativo m.

transform, trans-foorm', v., trasformare

transgress, trans-gres', v., trasgredire

tranship, tran-ship', v., trasbordare

transit, tran'-sit, n., transito m.

translate, trans-leit', v., tradurre

translation, trans-lei'-shon, n., traduzione f.

translator, trans-lei'-ta, n., traduttore m.

transmit, trans-mit', v., trasmettere

transparent, trans-pë'-rent, a., trasparente

transpire, trans-pair', v., traspirare

transport, trans'-port, n., trasporto m.

transport, trans-port', v., trasportare

transpose, trans-pous', v., trasporre

transverse, trans-vërs', a., trasversale

trap, trap, n., trappola f. v., intrappolare

trap-door, trap'-dor, n., trabocchetto m.

trappings, trap'-ings, n.pl., finimenti m.pl. [f.pl.

trash, trash, n., robaccia f.; (nonsense) sciocchezze

trashy, trash'-i, a., di rifiuto

travel, trav'-l, v., viaggiare ; —ler, n., viaggiatore m.

traverse, trav'-ers, v., traversare. a., traverso

trawler, trool'-a, n., battello per pesca a strascico m.

tray, trei, n., vassoio m. ; **ash- —**, porta cenere m.

treacherous, trech'-er-os, a., traditore

treachery, trech'-er-i, n., tradimento m.; perfidia f.

treacle, trii'-kl, n., sciroppo m.

tread, tred, n., passo m.; (stair) scalino m. v., camminare ; — upon, calpestare

treason, trii'-sn, n., tradimento m.

treasure, tresh'-er, n., tesoro m. v., valutare

treasurer, tresh'-er-a, n., tesoriere m.

treasury, tresh'-er-i, n., tesoro m.

treat, triit, n., (outing) gita f.; (enjoyment) pia-
    cere m. v., trattare; (fig.) offrire

treatise, trii'-tis, n., trattato m.

treatment, triit'-ment, n., trattamento m.

treaty, trii'-ti, n., trattato m.

treble, treb'-l, n., (mus.) suono più alto m. a., tri-
    plice. v., triplicare

tree, trii, n., albero m.; **family —**, albero genea-
    [logico m.

trellis, trel'-is, n., graticcio m.

tremble, trem'-bl, v., tremare

tremendous*, tri-men'-dos, a., tremendo

tremulous*, trem'-iu-los, a., tremulo

trench, trench, n., trincea f. v., trincerare

trend, trend, n., tendenza f.

trespass, tres'-pas, v., violare

trespasser, tres'-pas-a, n., trasgressore m.

trestle, tres'-l, n., trespolo m.

trial, trai'-al, n., prova f.; (law) processo m.

triangle, trai'-ang-gol, n., triangolo m.

triangular, trai-ang'-ghiu-la, a., triangolare

tribe, traib, n., tribù f.

tribunal, trai-biuu'-nal, n., tribunale m.

tribune, tri'-biuun, n., tribuna f.

tributary, trib'-iu-ta-ri, n., (stream) tributario m,

tribute, trib'-iuut, n., tributo m.

trick, trik, n., (fraud) artifizio m., tiro m.;
    (joke) burla f.; (dexterity) giuoco m.; (cards
    score) plico m. v., ingannare; **—ery**, n., bir-
    bonata f.; **—ster**, furfante m.

trickle, trik'-l, v., stillare; (flow) scorrere

trifle, trai'-fl, n., bagatella f. v. burlarsi di

trifling, trai'-fling, a., insignificante

trigger, trigh'-a, n., (gun) grilletto m.

trill, tril, n., trillo m. v., trillare

trim, trim, v., (dress) guarnire; (hair) acconciare

trimming, trim'-ing, n., (garments) guarnizione f.

trinity, tri'-ni-ti, n., trinità f.

trinket, tring'-ket, n., ciondolo m.

trio, tri'-ou, n., trio m.
    [pare

trip, trip, n., (journey) gita f. v., (stumble) inciam-

tripe, traip, n., trippa f.

triple, trip'-l, a., triplo

I—20

triplets, trip'-lets, n. pl., trigemini m. pl.

tripod, trai'-pod, n., tripode m.

tripper, trip'-*a*, n., escursionista m. & f.

triumph, trai'-omf, n., trionfo m.

trivial°, triv'-i-*a*l, a., triviale [smissione f.

trolley, trol'-i, n., carrello m. : (electric) asta di tra-

trombone, trom'-boun, n., trombone m.

troop, truup, v., attrupparsi. n., truppa f.

trooper, truu'-p*a*, n., (mil.) cavalleggero m.

troopship, truup'-ship, n., trasporto di truppe m.

trophy, trou'-fi, n., trofeo m.

tropical, trop'-i-kl, a., tropicale

tropics, trop'-iks, n. pl., tropici m. pl.

trot, trot, v., trottare. n., trotto m.

trotter, trot'-*a*, n., trottatore m. ; (pig) piede di porco m.

trouble, trŏb'-l, n., (cares) noia f., pena f.; (inconvenience) seccatura f.; (disturbance) disturbo m.; (difficulty) imbarazzo m.   v., darsi la pena ; annoiare ; disturbare ; —**some,** a., noioso

trough, trôf, n., (cattle, etc.) abbeveratoio m.

trounce, trauns, v., battere ; punire

trousers, trau-*s*ers, n. pl., pantaloni m. pl.

trout, trout, n., trota f.

trowel, trau'-*e*l, n., cazzuola f.

truant, truu'-*a*nt, play —, v., marinare la scuola

truce, truus, n., tregua f.

truck, trŏk, n., carretto m.; (railway) vagone merci

truckle, trŏk'-l, v., (yield) umiliarsi [m.

truculent°, trŏk'-iu-lent, a., truculento

trudge, trŏch, v., marciare penosamente

true, truu, a., vero ; (faithful) leale

truffle, trŏf'-l, n., tartufo m.

truism, truu-i*s*m, n., evidenza lampante f.

trump, trŏmp, n., trionfo m.   v., prendere con un trionfo

trumpery, trŏm'-per-i, a., di nessun valore

trumpet, trŏm'-pet, n., tromba f.

truncheon, trŏn'-shon, n., randello m.

trunk, trŏngk, n., (tree, body) tronco m. ; (elephant) proboscide f. ; (travelling) baule m. ; —**call,** telefonata interurbana f.

truss, trŏs, n., (bundle, etc.) fardello m. ; (surgical) cinto erniario m. v., (poultry) legare

trust, trŏst, n., fiducia f. ; (combine) cartello m. v., fidarsi

trustee, trŏs'-tii, n., curatore m.; (legal) esecutore testamentario m.

trustworthy, trŏst'-uĕr-Di, a., fidato

truth, truuZ, n., verità f.

truthful*, truuZ'-ful, a., veritiero

try, trai, v., provare ; (taste) assaggiare ; (law) processare

trying, trai'-ing, a., penoso

tub, tŏb, n., tinozza f.

tube, tiuub, n., tubo m.

tuck, tŏk, n., piega f. v., ripiegare ; — in, (rug, etc.) rimboccare ; — up, (dress) rincalzare

Tuesday, tiuus'-di, n., martedì m.

tuft, tŏft, n., ciuffo m.

tug, tŏgh, n., tirata f. v., tirare ; (tow) rimorchiare ; — of war, n., tiro alla fune m.

tug-boat, tŏgh'-bout, n., rimorchiatore m.

tuition, tiu-ish'-on, n., istruzione f.

tulip, tiuu'-lip, n., tulipano m.

tumble, tŏm'-bl, v., (person) inciampare ; (things) cadere

tumbler, tŏm'-bla, n., bicchierone m.

tumour, tiuu'-mor, n., tumore m.

tumult, tiuu'-molt, n., tumulto m.

tune, tiuun, n., aria f. v., accordare

tuneful, tiuun'-ful, a., armonioso

tunic, tiuu'-nik, n., (mil.) giubba f.

tuning-fork, tiuu'-ning foork, n., diapason m.

tunnel, tŏn'-l, n., galleria f. v., traforare

tunny, tŏn'-i, n., tonno m.

turbine, tĕr'-bain, n., turbina f.

turbot, tĕr'-bot, n., rombo m.

turbulent*, tĕr'-biu-lent, a., turbolento

tureen, tiu-riin', n., zuppiera f.

turf, tĕrf, n., zolla erbosa f. ; (peat) torba f.

turkey, tĕr'-ki, n., tacchino m.

Turkish, tĕr'-kish, a., turco

turmoil, tĕr'-moil, n., tumulto m.

turn, tĕrn, v., girare. n., (service) servizio m.; (order of succession) turno m.; — **about,** v., fare dietrofront ; — **aside,** stornare ; — **back,** volgere in dietro ; — -**coat,** n., (fig.) banderuola f.; —**ing,** (corner) voltata f.; —**ing-point,** punto decisivo m. ; — **into,** v., cambiarsi in ; — **off,** chiudere ; — **on,** aprire ; — **out,** espellere ; (extinguish) spegnere ; — **over,** voltare ; voltarsi. n., (commerce) giro d'affari m. ; — **to,** v., ricor-   [rere

turner, tĕr'-na, n., (artisan) tornitore m.

turnip, tĕr'-nip, n., rapa f.

turnstile, tĕrn'-stail, n., arganello m.

turpentine, tĕr'-pen-tain, n., trementina f.

turret, tŏr'-et, n., torretta f.

turtle, tĕr'-tl, n., tartaruga f. ; — -**dove,** tortorella f. ; **turn** —, v., capovolgere

tusk, tŏsk, n., zanna f.

tussle, tŏs'-l, n., schiamazzo m. v., lottare

tutor, tiuu'-ta, n., precettore m.

twang, tuang, n., accento nasale m.; (sound) suono m. ; (taste) sapore speciale m.

tweezers, tuii'-sas, n., pl., pinzette f. pl.

twelfth, tuelfZ, a., dodicesimo. n., (fraction) un dodicesimo m.

twelve, tuelv, a., dodici

twentieth, tuen'-ti-iZ, a., ventesimo. n., (fraction) un ventesimo m.

twenty, tuen'-ti, a., venti

twice, tuais, adv., due volte

twig, tuigh, n., ramoscello m.

twilight, tuai'-lait, n., crepuscolo **m.**

twill, tuil, n., stoffa diagonale f.

twin, tuin, n., gemello m. a., gemello

twine, tuain, n., spago m. v., torcere, intrecciare

twinge, tuinch, n., fitta f. v., tormentare

twinkle, tuing'-kl, v., sfavillare

twirl, tuĕrl, v., girare vorticosamente ; (twist) torcere

twist, tuist, v., torcere

twit, tuit, v., (tease) biasimare

twitch, tuich, n., ticchio nervoso m. v., contrarsi

twitter, tuit'-a, v., garrire. n., gorgheggio m.

two, tuu, a., due ; —**fold,** doppio

type, taip, n., tipo m.; sorte f.; (printing) **carat**
tere m.   v., scrivere a macchina
typewriter, taip'-rai-ta, n., macchina da scrivere f.
typhoid, tai'-foid, n., febbre tifoidea f.
typical*, tip'-i-kal, a., tipico
typist, tai'-pist, n., dattilografo m.
typography, tai-po'-gra-fi, n., tipografia f.
tyrannical*, ti-ran'-i-kl, a., tirannico
tyrannize, tir'-an-ais, v., tiranneggiare
tyrant, tai'-rant, n., tiranno m.
tyre, tair, n., (rim) cerchione di ferro m.; (pneumatic) copertone m.

ubiquitous, iuu-bik'-ui-tos, a., onnipresente
udder, ŏd'-a, n., mammella f.
ugliness, ŏgh'-li-nes, n., bruttezza f.
ugly, ŏgh'-li, a., brutto
ulcer, ŏl'-sa, n., ulcera f.
ulcerate, ŏl'-ser-eit, v., ulcerare
ulterior, ŏl-ti'-ri-or, a., ulteriore
ultimate*, ŏl'-ti-met, a., ultimo
ultimatum, ŏl-ti-me'-tom, n., ultimatum m.
ultimo, ŏl'-ti-mou, adv., ultimo scorso
ultra, ŏl'-tra, a., ultra
umbrella, ŏm-brel'-a, n., ombrello m., ombrella f.;
— -stand, porta ombrelli m.
umpire, ŏm'-pair, n., arbitro m.
unabashed, ŏn-a-basht', a., senza vergogna
unabated, ŏn-a-bei'-tid, a., non affievolito
unable, ŏn-ei'-bl, a., incapace; to be —, v.,
non potere
unacceptable, ŏn-ak-sep'-ta-bl, a., inaccettabile
unaccountable, ŏn-a-kaun'-ta-bl, a., inesplicabile
unacquainted, ŏn-a-kuen'-tid, a., ignorante; (person) sconosciuto
unaffected, ŏn-a-fek'-tid, a., naturale; impassibile
unaided, ŏn-ei'-did, a., da solo
unalterable, ŏn-ool'-tĕr-a-bl, a., inalterabile
unaltered, ŏn-ool'-tĕrd, a., inalterato
unanimity, iuu-nan-i'-mi-ti, n., unanimità f.
unanimous*, iuu-nan'-i-mos, a., unanime
unanswerable, ŏn-aan'-ser-a-bl, a., incontestabile

unapproachable, ŏn-*a*-prouch'-*a*-bl, a., inaccessi-
unarmed, ŏn-aarmd', a., inerme   [bile
unassailable, ŏn-*a*-sei'-*la*-bl, a., inattaccabile
unattainable, ŏn-*a*-tei'-*na*-bl, a., inaccessibile
unattended, ŏn-*a*-ten'-did, a., solo
unavoidable, ŏn-*a*-voi'-da-bl, a., inevitabile
unaware, ŏn-*a*-uer', a., ignaro
unawares, ŏn-*a*-uers', adv., all'improvviso
unbearable, ŏn-ber'-*a*-bl, a., insopportabile
unbecoming*, ŏn-bi-kŏm'-ing, a., sconveniente
unbeliever, ŏn-bi-liiv'-*a*, n., incredulo m.
unbend, ŏn-bend', v., (yield) essere inflessibile
unbending, ŏn-ben'-ding, a., inflessibile
unbiassed, ŏn-bai'-*a*st, a., imparziale
unbleached, ŏn-bliicht', a., naturale ; crudo
unblemished, ŏn-blem'-isht, a., senza taccia
unbounded, ŏn-baun'-did, a., illimitato
unbreakable, ŏn-breik'-*a*-bl, a., irrompibile
unburden, ŏn-bĕr'-n, v., scaricare
unbutton, ŏn-bŏt'-n, v., sbottonare
uncalled for, ŏn-koold'-for, a., non richiesto
uncanny, ŏn-kan'-i, a., strano
uncared, ŏn-kerd'. — for, a., negletto
unceasing*, ŏn-siis'-ing, a., incessante
uncertain*, ŏn-sĕr'-tin, a., incerto
unchangeable, ŏn-chein'-*cha*-bl, a., immutabile
uncivil, ŏn-siv'-l, a., scortese
unclaimed, ŏn-kleimd', a., non reclamato
uncle, ong'-kl, n., zio m.
unclean*, ŏn-kliin'. a., sporco ; impuro
uncomfortable, ŏn-kŏm'-for-ta-bl, a., incomodo
uncommon*, ŏn-kom'-on, a., non comune
unconcern, ŏn-kon-sĕrn', n., indifferenza f.
unconditional*, ŏn-kon-dish'-*o*-nl, a., incondizio-
    nale
uncongenial, ŏn-kon-chii'-ni-*a*l, a., antipatico
unconscious*, ŏn-kon'-shos, a., incosciente
uncontrollable, ŏn-kon-trou'-la-bl, a., irrefre-
    nabile
unconventional, ŏn-kon-ven'-shon-l, a., libero da
    convenzioni
uncork, ŏn-koork', v., stappare

uncouth, ŏn-kuuZ', a., grossolano ; (**awkward**) goffo
uncover, ŏn-kŏv'-a, v., scoprire
uncultivated, ŏn-kol'-ti-vei-tid, a., incolto
undated, ŏn-dei' tid, a., senza data
undaunted*, ŏn-dŏon'-tid, a., intrepido
undeceive, ŏn-di-siiv', v., disingannare
undecided, ŏn-di-sai'-did, a., indeciso
undefiled, ŏn-di-faild', a., intemerato
undelivered, ŏn-di-liv'-erd, a., non consegnato
undeniable, ŏn-di-nai'-a-bl, a., innegabile
under, ŏn'-da, adv. & prep., sotto, al di sotto di ;
— **age**, a., minorenne ; —**clothing**, n., biancheria f.; —**done**, a., poco cotto ; —**estimate**,
v., sotto stimare ; —**fed**, a., mal nutrito ; —**go**,
v., subire ; (**suffer**) soffrire ; —**graduate**, n.,
studente universitario m.; —**ground**, a., sotterraneo. n., (**railway**) ferrovia sotterranea f.;
—**hand**, a., sottomano ; —**line**, v., sottolineare ;
—**mine**, minare ; —**neath**, prep., disotto ;
— **proof**, a., sotto gradazione ; —**rate**, v., sotto
stimare ; —**sell**, tagliare i prezzi ; —**signed**, n.,
sottoscritto m.; —**sized**, a., di misura piccola ;
—**stand**, v., comprendere ; —**standing**, n.,
comprensione f. ; (**accord**) accordo m. ; **on the**
—**standing**, conj., a condizione di ; —**state**,
v., attenuare ; —**study**, n., sostituto m. ;
—**take**, v., intraprendere ; —**taker**, n., (**funeral**) impresario di pompe funebre m. ;—**taking**,
impresa f.; —**tone**, voce bassa f.; —**wear**, biancheria f. ; —**world**, malavita f. ; —**writer**,
assicuratore m.
undeserved*, ŏn-di-s̆erv'd', a., immeritato
undesirable, ŏn-di-sai'-ra-bl, a., sgradito
undignified, ŏn-digh'-ni-faid, a., senza dignità
undiminished, ŏn-di-mi'-nisht, a., non scemato
undismayed, ŏn-dis-meid', a., imperturbato
undisturbed, ŏn-dis-t̆erbd', a., indisturbato
undo, ŏn-duu', v., disfare
undoing, ŏn-duu'-ing, n., (**downfall**) caduta f.
undoubted*, ŏn-dau'-tid, a., indubbio
undress, ŏn-dres', v., svestirsi
undue, ŏn-diuu', a., (**improper**) ingiusto

undulating, ŏn'-diu-lei-ting, a., ondeggiante
unduly, ŏn-diuu'-li, adv., (overdone) indebitamente
unearned, ŏn-ĕrnd', a., non guadagnato ; immeritato
unearth, ŏn-ĕrZ', v., dissotterrare ; (fig.) scoprire
unearthly, ŏn-ĕrZ'-li, a., soprannaturale
uneasy, ŏn-ii'-si, a., inquieto
uneducated, ŏn-ed'-iu-kei-tid, a., senza istruzione
unemployed, ŏn-em-ploid', a., disoccupato
unemployment, ŏn-em-plo'-i-ment, n., disoccupazione f.
unequal, ŏn-ii'-kual, a., disuguale
unequalled, ŏn-ii'-kuald, a., senza eguale
unerring*, ŏn-ĕr'-ing, a., infallibile
uneven, ŏn-ii'-vn, a., ineguale ; (road) scabroso
unexpected*, ŏn-eks-pek'-tid, a., inaspettato
unfailing, ŏn-fei'-ling, a., infallibile
unfair*, ŏn-fer', a., ingiusto
unfaithful*, ŏn-feiZ'-ful, a., infedele
unfaltering, ŏn-fool'-ter-ing, a., non esitante
unfasten, ŏn-faas'-n, v., slegare ; disfare
unfathomable, ŏn-faD'-om-a-bl, a., insondabile
unfavourable, ŏn-fei'-vor-a-bl, a., sfavorevole
unfeeling, ŏn-fii'-ling, a., insensibile
unfit, ŏn-fit', a., improprio ; inetto
unflagging, ŏn-fla'-ghing, a., indefesso
unflinching*, ŏn-flinch'-ing, a., fermo ; risoluto
unfold, ŏn-fould', v., spiegare ; (reveal) rivelare
unforeseen, ŏn-for-siin', a., imprevedito
unfortunate*, ŏn-foor'-tiu-net, a., sfortunato
unfounded, ŏn-faun-did, a., infondato
unfriendly, ŏn-frend'-li, a., poco amichevole ; ostile
unfulfilled, ŏn-ful-fild', a., incompiuto
unfurl, ŏn-fĕrl', v., spiegare
unfurnished, ŏn-fĕr'-nisht, a., non ammobiliato
ungainly, ŏn-ghein'-li, a., senza grazia ; pesante
ungrateful*, ŏn-greit'-ful, a., ingrato
unguarded, ŏn-gaar'-did, a., incustodito ; (fig.) incauto   [cauto
unhappy, ŏn-hap'-i, a., infelice
unharness, ŏn-haar'-nes, v., levare gli arnesi
unhealthy, ŏn-helZ'-i, a., insalubre
unheard, ŏn-hĕrd', a., sconosciuto ; — of, inaudito

unheeded, ŏn-hii´-did, a., negletto

unhinge, ŏn-hinch´, v., sgangherare

unhinged, ŏn-hinchd´, a., (mind) disordinato

unhurt, ŏn-hĕrt´, a., sano e salvo

uniform, iuu´-ni-foorm, n., uniforme m. a., uniforme ; **—ity,** n., uniformità f.

unimaginable, ŏn-i-mach´-in-a-bl, a., inconcepibile

unimpaired, ŏn-im-perd´, a., intatto

unimpeachable, ŏn-im-piich´-a-bl, a., irreprensibile

unimportant, ŏn-im-po´-tant, a., insignificante

uninhabitable, ŏn-in-hab´-i-ta-bl, a., inabitabile

unintelligible, ŏn-in-tel´-ich-i-bl, a., incomprensibile

unintentional*, ŏn-in-ten´-shon-al, a., involontario

uninviting, ŏn-in-vai´-ting, a., non attraente

union, iuu´-ni-on, n., unione f.

unique, iu-niik´, a., unico

unit, iuu´-nit, n., unità f.

unite, iu-nait´, v., unire

unity, iuu´-ni-ti, n., unità f.

universal*, iuu-ni-vĕrs´-l, a., universale

universe, iuu´-ni-vĕrs, n., universo m.

university, iuu-ni-vĕrs´-i-ti, n., università f.

unjust*, ŏn-chŏst´, a., ingiusto

unkind*, ŏn-kaind´, a., poco gentile

unknown, ŏn-noun´, a., sconosciuto

unlawful*, ŏn-loo´-ful, a., illegale ; illecito

unless, ŏn-les´, conj., a meno che

unlike, ŏn-laik´, a., poco somigliante

unlikely, ŏn-laik´-li, a., improbabile

unlimited, ŏn-lim´-i-tid, a., illimitato

unload, ŏn-loud´, v., scaricare

unlock, ŏn-lo-k´, v., aprire

unlooked for, ŏn-lukt´ for, a., inatteso

unlucky, ŏn-lŏk´-i, a., sfortunato

unmannerly, ŏn-man´-er-li, a., sgarbato

unmarried, ŏn-mar´-id, a., (man) celibe ; **(woman)** nubile

unmerciful*, ŏn-mĕr´-si-ful, a., spietato

unmistakable, ŏn-mis-tei´-ka-bl, a., evidente

unmoved, ŏn-muuvd´, a., (unemotional) impassibile

unnatural, ŏn-nat′-iu-rl, a., non naturale ; **snaturato**

unnecessary, ŏn-nes′-ses-a-ri, a., non necessario

unnerve, ŏn-nĕrv′, v., snervare

unnoticed, ŏn-nou′-tist, a., inosservato

unobtainable, ŏn-ob-tei′-na-bl, a., inottenibile

unoccupied, ŏn-ok′-iu-paid, a., disoccupato ; libero

unopposed, ŏn-o-pousd′, a., senza opposizione

unpack, ŏn-pak′, v., disfare

unpardonable, ŏn-paar′-don-a-bl, a., imperdonabile

unpleasant*, ŏn-ples′-ant, a., spiacevole

unpopular, ŏn-pop′-iu-lr, a., impopolare

unprecedented, ŏn-pres′-i-den-tid, a., senza precedente

unprepared, ŏn-pri-perd′, a., impreparato

unproductive, ŏn-pro-dŏk′-tiv, a., improduttivo

unprofitable, ŏn-prof′-i-ta-bl, a., senza profitto

unpromising, ŏn-prom′-is-ing, a., non promettente

unpropitious*, ŏn-pro-pish′-os, a., impropizio

unprotected, ŏn-pro-tek′-tid, a., improtetto

unprovided, ŏn-pro-vai′-did, a., sprovvisto

unpunctual, ŏn-pŏngh′-tiu-al, a., poco puntuale

unquestionable, ŏn-kues′-tion-a-bl, a., incontestabile

unravel, ŏn-rav′-l, v., sbrogliare

unread, ŏn-red′, a., non letto

unreadable, ŏn-rii′-da-bl, a., illeggibile

unreasonable, ŏn-rii′-son-a-bl, a., irragionevole

unrelated, ŏn-ri-lei′-tid, a., senza legame

unrelenting, ŏn-ri-len′-ting, a., implacabile

unreliable, ŏn-ri-lai′-a-bl, a., di cui non si può fidarsi

unremitting, ŏn-ri-mit′-ing, a., incessante

unreserved, ŏn-ri-sĕrvd′, a., non riservato

unrest, ŏn-rest′, n., agitazione f.

unrestrained, ŏn-ri-streind′, a., sfrenato

unrestricted, ŏn-ri-strik′-tid, a., illimitato

unripe, ŏn-raip′, a., verde, acerbo

unroll, ŏn-roul′, v., svolgere

unruly, ŏn-ruu′-li, a., turbolento

unsafe, ŏn-seif′, a., poco sicuro

unsaleable, ŏn-seil′-a-bl, a., invendibile

unsatisfactory, ŏn-sat-is-fak'-to-ri, a., non soddisfacente

unscrew, ŏn-skruu', v., svitare

unscrupulous, ŏn-skruu'-piu-los, a., senza scrupoli

unseasonable, ŏn-sii'-ßn-a-bl, a., fuori di stagione

unseemly, ŏn-siim'-li, a., disdicevole

unseen, ŏn-siin', a., inosservato

unselfish, ŏn-sel'-fish, a., altruista

unsettled, ŏn-set'-ld, a., insicuro ; (weather. mind) instabile

unshaken, ŏn-shei'-kn, a., risoluto

unshrinkable, ŏn-shringk'-a-bl, a., irrestringibile

unshrinking, ŏn-shringk'-ing, a., intrepido

unsightly, ŏn-sait'-li, a., spiacente

unskilful*, ŏn-skil'-ful, a., inabile

unskilled, ŏn-skild', a., inesperto

unsociable, ŏn-sou'-sha-bl, a., non socievole

unsold, ŏn-sould', a., invenduto

unsolicited, ŏn-so-lis'-i-tid, a., non richiesto

unsolved, ŏn-solvd', a., insoluto

unstinted, ŏn-stin'-tid, a., illimitato

unsuccessful*, ŏn-sŏk-ses'-ful, a., senza successo ; vano

unsuitable, ŏn-siuu'-ta-bl, a., inadatto

unsuited, ŏn-siuu'-tid, a., inatto

unsurpassed, ŏn-sor-paast', a., non sorpassato

untack, ŏn-tak', v., scucire

untamed, ŏn-teimd', a., indomito

untarnished, ŏn-taar'-nisht, a., senza macchia

untenable, ŏn-ten'-a-bl, a., intenibile

untenanted, ŏn-ten'-an-tid, a., disoccupato

unthankful*, ŏn-Zangk'-ful, a., ingrato

unthinking, ŏn-Zingk'-ing, a., stordito

untidy, ŏn-tai'-di, a., disordinato ; sporco

untie, ŏn-tai', v., snodare

until, ŏn-til', prep., finchè, sino a che

untimely, ŏn-taim'-li, a., intempestivo

untiring, ŏn-tai'-ring, a., instancabile

untold, ŏn-tould', a., inespresso ; (vast) inaudito

untouched, ŏn-tŏcht', a., intatto ; placido

untranslatable, ŏn-trans-lei'-ta-bl, a., intraducibile

untried, ŏn-traid', a., intentato ; non giudicato
untrodden, ŏn-trŏd'-n, a., non battuto
untrue, ŏn-truu', a., falso ; infedele
untrustworthy, ŏn-trŏst'-uerD-ĭ, a., indegno di fiducia
untruth, ŏn-truuZ', n., falsità f.
untwist, ŏn-tuist', v., storcere
unusual*, ŏn-iuu'-shu-al, a., insolito
unvaried, ŏn-vē'-rĭd, a., invariato
unvarying, ŏn-vē'-ri-ing, a., invariabile
unveil, ŏn-veil', v., svelare ; scoprire
unwarrantable, ŏn-uor'-an-ta-bl, a., ingiustificabile
unwavering, ŏn-uei'-ver-ing, a., fermo
unwelcome, ŏn-uel'-kom, a., mal accolto ; sgradito
unwell, ŏn-uel', a., indisposto
unwholesome, ŏn-hŏul'-som, a., malsano ; viziato
unwieldy, ŏn-uiil'-di, a., pesante
unwilling, ŏn-uil'-ing, a., di mala voglia
unwind, ŏn-uaind', v., disfare ; svolgere
unwise*, ŏn-uais', a., malaccorto
unwittingly, ŏn-uit'-ing-li, a., senza pensarci
unworthy, ŏn-uŏrD'-i, a., indegno
unwrap, ŏn-rap', v., disfare
unwritten, ŏn-rit'-n, a., non scritto
unyielding, ŏn-iiil'-ding, a., inflessibile
up, ŏp, adv. & prep., su, insù, sopra, in alto ; — **and down**, su e giù ; — **here**, (position) quassù ; — **there**, lassù ; — **to**, fino a
upbraid, ŏp-breid', v., rimproverare
upheaval, ŏp-hii'-vl, n., sollevamento m.
uphill, ŏp-hil', a., in salita ; (toilsome) penoso
uphold, ŏp-hŏuld', v., sostenere
upholsterer, ŏp-hŏul'-ster-a, n., tappezziere **m.**
upkeep, ŏp'-kiip, n., mantenimento m.
upland, ŏp'-land, n., altipiano m.
uplift, ŏp-lift', v., alzare, elevare
upon, ŏp-on', prep., sopra
upper, ŏp'-a, a., superiore ; —**hand**, n., superiorità f. ; —**most**, a., il più alto ; —**part**, n., parte superiore f.
upright, ŏp'-rait, a., dritto ; (honest) probo

uprising, ŏp-rai'-sing, n., sollevazione f.

uproar, ŏp'-ror, n., strepito m. ; clamore **m.**

uproot, ŏp-ruut', v., sradicare

upset, ŏp-set', v., capovolgere ; (feelings) sconvolgere

upside, ŏp'-said, — **down**, sottosopra

upstairs, ŏp'-sters, adv., di sopra

upstart, ŏp-staart, n., villano rifatto m.

upwards, ŏp'-uerds, adv., su, insù, in alto, **all'insù**

urban, ĕr'-bn, a., urbano

urchin, ĕr'-chin, n., biricchino **m.**

urge, ĕrch, v., urgere

urgency, ĕr'-chen-si, n., urgenza **f.**

urgent*, ĕr'-chent, a., urgente

urine, iu'-rin, n., urina f.

urn, ĕrn, n., urna f.

us, ŏs, pron., ci, ce, noi

use, iuus, v., usare ; servirsi di ; — **up, consumare**

use, iuus, n., uso m. ; utilità f.; —d **to, a., (accus-**
tomed) usato a

useful*, iuus'-ful, a., utile

useless*, iuus'-les, a., inutile

usher, ŏsh'-a, n., usciere m. ; — **in, v., introdurre**

usual*, iuu-shu-al, a., usuale

usurp, iu-sĕrp', v., usurpare

usurper, iu-sĕr'-pa, n., usurpatore **m.**

usury, iuu'-shu-ri, n., usura f.

utensil, iu-ten'-sil, n., utensile **m.**

utility, iuu-til'-i-ti, n., utilità f.

utilize, iuu'-til-ais, v., utilizzare

utmost, ŏt'-a, v., & adv., sommo ; estremo ;
tutto il possibile

utter, ŏt'-a, v., (coin) spacciare ; (sound) emettere. a., completo

utterance, ŏt'-er-ans, n., emissione f.

uttermost, ŏt'-er-moust, a., estremo

vacancy, vei'-kan-si, n., vacanza f.; (gap) vacuo m.

vacant, vei'-kant, a., vacante ; (mind) distratto

vacate, va-keit', v., sgombrare ; (a post) lasciare

vacation, va-kei'-shon, n., vacanza f.

vaccinate, vak'-si-neit, v., vaccinare

vacillate, vas'-i-leit, v., vacillare

vacuum, vak'-iu-om, n., vacuo m.; **—-cleaner,** aspiratore di polvere m.

vagabond, vagh'-*a*-bond, n., vagabondo m.

vagary, va-ghe'-ri, n., capriccio m.

vagina, va-chii'-na, n., vagina f.

vagrancy, va'-gran-si, n., vagabondaggio m.

vague°, veigh, a., vago

vain°, vein, a., vanitoso; **in —,** invano

vainglory, vein-ghlo'-ri, n., vanagloria f.

vale, veil, n., valle f.

valet, val'-et, n., valletto m.

valiant°, val'-i-*a*nt, a., valoroso

valid°, val'-id, a., valido

valley, val'-i, n., valle f.

valorous°, val'-*o*-ros, a., valoroso

valour, val'-*r*, n., valore m.

valuable, val'-iu-*a*-bl, a., di valore; prezioso

valuation, val-iu-ei'-shon, n., valutazione f.

value, val'-iu, n., valore m. v., valutare

valuer, val'-iu-*a*, n., stimatore m.

valve, valv, n., valvola f.

vamp, vamp, n., tomaio m.; (woman) donna irresistibile f. v., rimontare; improvvisare

vampire, vam'-pair, n., vampiro m.

van, van, n., furgone m.; (railway) bagagliaio m.; (foremost) avanguardia f.

vane, vein, n., banderuola f.; (windmill) ala f.

vanilla, va-nil'-*a*, n., vainiglia f.

vanish, van'-ish, v., svanire

vanity, van'-i-ti, n., vanità f.

vanquish, vang-kuish, v., vincere

vapour, vei'-pa, n., vapore m.

variable, ve'-ri-*a*-bl, a., variabile

variance, ve'-ri-*a*ns, n., disaccordo m.

variation, ve-ri-ei'-shon, n., variazione f.

varicose vein, ve'-ri-kous vein, n., varice f.

varied, ve'-rid, a., vario, svariato

variegated, ve'-ri-i-ghei-tid, a., variegato

variety, va-rai'-i-ti, n., varietà f.

various°, ve'-ri-os, a., vario; diverso

varnish, vaar'-nish, n., vernice m. v., verniciare

vary, ve'-ri, v., variare

vase, vaa*s*, n., vaso m.

vaseline, vaa*s*'-e-liin, n., vaselina f.

vast*, vaast, a., vasto

vat, vat, n., tino m.

vault, voolt, n., (crypt, burial) volta f.; (wine) **can-**
tina f. v., saltare

veal, viil, n., vitello m.

veer, vi*r*, v., girare ; (naut.) vivare

vegetables, vech'-i-ta-bl*s*, n.pl., legumi m. pl.

vegetarian, vech-i-tei'-ri-an, n., vegetariano m.

vegetation, vech-i-tei'-shon, n., vegetazione f.

vehement*, vii'-hi-ment, a., veemente

vehicle, vii'-i-kl, n., veicolo m.

veil, veil, n., velo m. v., velare ; (cloak) celare

vein, vein, n., vena f.; (mood) disposizione f.

vellum, vel'-m, n., pergamena fina f.

velocity, vi-los'-i-ti, n., velocità f.

velvet, vel'-vet, n., velluto m.

velveteen, vel-vi-tiin', n., velluto di cotone m.

vendor, ven'-da, n., venditore m.

veneer, vi-ni*r*', n., impiallacciatura f. v., impial-
lacciare

venerable, ven'-er-ei-bl, a., venerabile

veneration, ven-er-ei'-shon, n., venerazione f.

venereal, vi-ni'-ri-al, a., venereo

vengeance, ven'-chans, n., vendetta f.; **with**
a —, furiosamente

venial, vii'-ni-al, a., veniale

venison, ven'-i-*s*n, n., selvaggina f.

venom, ven'-m, n., veleno m.

venomous, ven'-o-mos, a., velenoso

vent, vent, n., sfogo m.; (cask) buco m.; **give**
— to, v., dare libero corso, sfogare

ventilate, ven'-ti-leit, v., ventilare

ventilator, ven'-ti-lei-ta, n., ventilatore m.

ventriloquist, ven-tril'-o-kuist, n., ventriloquio m.

venture, ven'-chur, n., impresa avventurosa f.
v., osare ; rischiare

venturesome, ven'-chur-som, a., ardito ; avventuroso

veracity, vi-ras'-i-ti, n., veracità f.

veranda, vi-ran'-da, n., veranda f.

verb, vĕrb, n., verbo m.

verbal*, vĕr'-bl, a., verbale

verbatim, vĕr-bei'-tim, adv., letteralmente

verbose, vĕr-bous', a., verboso

verdant, vĕr'-dant, a., verdeggiante

verdict, vĕr'-dikt, n., (judgment) verdetto m.

verdigris, vĕr'-di-gris, n., verderame m.

verge, vĕrch, v., lambire. — n., (brink) orlo m.

verger, vĕr'-cha, n., sagrestano m.

verify, ver'-i-fai, v., verificare

vermilion, vĕr-mil'-ion, n., vermiglione m.

vermin, vĕr'-min, n., insetti e animali nocivi m. pl.

vernacular, vĕr-nak'-iu-lar, n., vernacolo m.

versatile, vĕr'-sa-tail, a., versatile

verse, vĕrs, n., verso m.; (bible) versetto m.

versed, vĕrst, a., versato

version, vĕr'-shon, n., versione f.

versus, vĕr'-sos, prep., contro

vertical*, vĕr'-tik-l, a., verticale

vertigo, vĕr'-ti-gou, n., vertigine f.

very, ver'-i, adv., molto; proprio; (that is the very idea=quella è proprio l'idea)

vessel, ves'-l, n., vaso m.; (naut.) nave f.

vest, vest, n., maglia f.

vested, ves'-tid, a., (interest; rights) acquisito

vestige, ves'-tich, n., vestigio m.

vestment, vest'-ment, n., vestimento m.

vestry, ves'-tri, n., sagrestia f.

veteran, vet'-e-ran, n., veterano m.

veterinary, vet'-e-ri-na-ri, a., veterinario; --**surgeon**, n., veterinario m.

veto, vii'-tou, n., veto m. v., porre il veto

vex, veks, v., vessare

vexation, vek-sei'-shon, n., vessazione f.

vexatious*, vek-sei'-shos, a., noioso, molesto; (law) vessatorio

via, vai'-a, prep., via, per

viaduct, vai'-a-dŏkt, n., viadotto m.

viaticum, vai-at'-i-kom, n., (eccl.) viatico m.

vibrate, vai'-breit, v., vibrare

vibration, vai-brei'-shon, n., vibrazione f.

vicar, vik'-a, n., vicario m.

vicarage, vik'-er-ich, n., casa del vicario f.
vice, vais, n., vizio m. ; (mech.) morsa f.
vice, vais, (prefix) vice-
viceroy, vais'-roi, n., vicerè m.
vicinity, vi-sin'-i-ti, n., vicinanza f.
vicious°, vish'-os, a., vizioso ; (dog) maligno
viciousness, vish'-os-nes, n., viziosità f. ; malignità f.
victim, vik'-t'm, n., vittima f.
victimize, vik'-tim-ais, v., rendere vittima
victor, vik'-ta, n., vincitore m.
victorious°, vik-tor'-i-os, a., vittorioso
victory, vik'-to-ri, n., vittoria f.
victual, vit'-l, v., vettovagliare
victuals, vit'-ls, n.pl., vettovaglie f.pl., viveri m.pl.
vie, vai, v., gareggiare
view, viuu, n., vista f.; opinione f. v., ispezionare
vigil, vich'-il, n., veglia f.
vigilance, vich'-il-ans, n., vigilanza f.
vigilant°, vich'-il-ant, a., vigilante
vigorous°, vigh'-or-os, a., vigoroso
vigour, vigh'-r, n., vigore m.
vile, vail, a., vile, abbietto
vilify, vil'-i-fai, v., avvilire
village, vil'-ich, n., villaggio m.
villager, vil'-ich-a, n., villico m.
villain, vil'-in, n., scellerato m.; (fig.) furfante m.
villainous°, vil'-a-nos, a., basso, infame
villainy, vil'-a-ni, n., infamia f.
vindicate, vin'-di-keit, v., difendere
vindication, vin-di-kei'-shon, n., rivendicazione f.
vindictive°, vin-dik'-tiv, a., vendicativo
vindictiveness, vin-dik'-tiv-nes, n., rancore m.
vine, vain, n., vite f.; sermento m.
vinegar, vin'-i-ga, n., aceto m.
vineyard, vin'-iaard, n., vigna f.
vintage, vin'-tich, n., vendemmia f.; (year) annata f.
violate, vai'-o-leit, v., (dishonour) oltraggiare; (law) violare
violence, vai'-o-lens, n., violenza f.
violent°, vai'-o-lent, a., violento

violet, vai'-o-let, n., violetta f.

violin, vai'-o-lin, n., violino m.

violinist, vai'-o-lin-ist, n., violinista m. & f.

viper, vai'-pa, n., vipera f.

virgin, věr'-chin, n., vergine f.

virginian, věr-chii'-ni-an, a., di Virginia

virile, vir'-ail, a., virile

virtual*, věr'-tiu-al, a., virtuale

virtue, věr'-tiuu, n., virtù f.; castità f.

virtuous*, věr'-tiu-os, a., virtuoso

virulent*, vir'-u-lent, a., virulento

viscount, vai'-kaunt, n., visconte m.

viscountess, vai'-kaunt-es, n., viscontessa f.

vise, vii'-sei, n., visto m. v., vistare

visibility, vis-i-bil'-i-ti, n., visibilità f.

visible, vis'-i-bl, a., visibile

vision, vish'-on, n., visione f.

visit, vis'-it, n., visita f. v., visitare; —ing-card, n., biglietto di visita m.

visitor, vis'-i-ta, n., visitatore m.

vital*, vai'-tl, a., vitale

vitality, vai-tal'-i-ti, n., vitalità f.

vitals, vai'-tls, n., pl., organi vitali m. pl.

vitiate, vish'-i-eit, v., viziare

vitriol, vit'-ri-ol, n., vitriolo m.

vivacious*, vi-vei'-shos, a., vivace

vivacity, vi-vas'-i-ti, n., vivacità f.

vivid*, viv'-id, a., vivido

vivify, viv'-i-fai, v., vivificare

vixen, vik'-sen, n., volpe f.; (fig.) megera f.

viz=namely, neim'-li, adv., cioè

vocabulary, vou-kab'-iu-la-ri, n., vocabolario m.; (command of words) ricchezza di lingua f.

vocal, vou'-kl, a., vocale; — chords, n. pl., corde vocali f. pl.

vocation, vo-kei'-shon, n., vocazione f.

vociferous*, vo-sif'-er-os, a., vociferante

vogue, vough, n., voga f., moda f.

voice, vois, n., voce f.

void, void, a., vuoto; nullo. n., vuoto m.

volatile, vol'-a-tail, a., volatile

volcano, vol-kei'-nou, n., vulcano m.

volley, vol'-i, n., (mil.) scarica f., salva f.
volt, volt, n., (electric) volt m.
voluble, vol'-iu-bl, a., (tongue) loquace
volume, vol'-ium, n., volume m.
voluminous[2], vol-iuu'-mi-nos, a., voluminoso
voluntary, vol'-on-ta-ri, a., volontario
volunteer, vol-on-tir', n., volontario m.
voluptuous[2], vo-lŏp'-tiu-os, a., voluttuoso
vomit, vom'-it, v., vomitare
voracious[2], vo-rei'-shos, a., vorace
vortex, voor'-teks, n., vortice m.
vote, vout, n., voto m. v., votare
voter, vou'-ta, n., votante m. & f.
vouch, vauch, v., attestare; — for, garantire per
voucher, vauch'-a, n., documento giustificativo m.
vow, vau, n., voto m. v., fare voto; giurare
vowel, vau'-il, n., vocale f.
voyage, voi'-ich, n., viaggio m. v., viaggiare
vulcanite, vŏl'-ke-nait, n., gomma vulcanizzata f.
vulgar[2], vŏl'-gar, a., volgare
vulnerable, vŏl'-nĕr-a-bl, a., vulnerabile
vulture, vŏl'-chur, n., avvoltoio m.

wabble, uob'-l, v., vacillare
wad, uod, n., (cartridge) boraccia f.; (surgical) tampone m. v., tamponare
wadding, uod'-ing, n., bambagia f.; (padding) ovatta f.
waddle, uod'-l, v., dondolarsi
wade, ueid, v., guadare; guazzare
wafer, uei'-fa, n., cialda f.; (eccl.) ostia f.
wag, uagh, v., scodinzolare. n., burlone m.
wage, ueich, n., paga f.; — war, v., guerreggiare
wager, uei'-cha, n., scommessa f. v., scommettere
wages, uei'-chis, n. pl., salario m.
waggle, uagh'-l, v., scodinzolare, dimenare
waggon, uagh'-n, n., carro m.; (railway) vagone m.
waif, ueif, n., (child) fanciullo abbandonato m.
wail, ueil, n., lamento m. v., lamentare
waist, ueist, n., vita f.
waistcoat, ueist'-kot, n., panciotto m.

wait, ueit, v., aspettare ; (at table) servire ; —**for,** aspettare ; —**ing,** n., attesa f.; (service) servizio m.; —**ing-room,** sala di aspetto f. ; —**upon,** v., servire

waiter, uei′-tɑ, n., cameriere m.

waitress, uei′-tres, n., cameriera f.

waive, ueiv, v., rinunciare a

wake, ueik, v., (to awake) svegliarsi ; (to call or be called) svegliare. n., (ship's) scia f.

walk, uook, v., camminare. n., passeggiata f.; —**er,** camminatore m. ; —**ing-tour,** escursione a piedi f.

wall, uool, n., muro m. ; (room, etc.) parete f.; —**-paper,** carta da muri f.

wallet, uol′-it, n., portafoglio m.

wallflower, uool′-flau-ɑ, n., violaciocca f.

wallow, uol′-ou, v., ravvoltolarsi

walnut, uool′-nŏt, n., noce f.

walrus, uool′-ros, n., tricheco m.

waltz, uoolts, n., valzer m. v., ballare il valzer

wander, uoon′-dɑ, v., errare ; (mentally) delirare

wane, uein, v., scemare

want, uoont, n., (lack) mancanza f.; (distress) bisogno m. v., volere ; abbisognare

wanton, uon′-ton, a., (lustful) lascivo ; (malicious) scellerato. n., persona libertina f.

war, uoor, n., guerra f. v., guerreggiare ; —**like,** a., guerriero ; —**loan,** n., prestito di guerra m.; —**-office,** ministero della guerra m.

warble, uoor′-bl, v., gorgheggiare

warbler, uoor′-blɑ, n., uccello cantore m.

ward, uoord, n., (minor) pupillo m., pupilla f.; (hospital) sala f.; —**en,** (guard) guardiano m.; (college) rettore m.; —**er,** custode m.; — **off,** v., deviare ; —**ress,** n., guardiana f.; —**robe,** (clothes) guardaroba f.; — **-room,** (naval) quadrato degli ufficiali m.

ware, uer, n., merce f. ; —**house,** magazzino m.

warily, ue′-ri-li, adv., cautamente

warm, uourm, a.,* caldo. v., riscaldare

warmth, uoormZ, n., calore m.

warn, uoorn, v., avvertire

warning, uoorn'-ing. n., avvertimento m.

warp, uoorp, v., (wood) torcersi: (mind) pervertire

warrant, uor'-ant. n., (security) garanzia f.; (authority) procura f.; (for arrest) mandato d'arresto m.; (voucher) mandato m.

warranty, uor'-an-ti, n., garanzia f.

warrior, uor'-i-a, n., guerriero m.

warship, uoor'-ship, n., nave da guerra f.

wart, uoort, n., porro m.

wary, ue'-ri, a., accorto, cauto

wash, uoosh, v., lavare; lavarsi; —-basin, n., bacinella f.; —ing, (laundry) biancheria f.; —-stand, lavabo m.

washer, uoosh'-a, n., (mech.) anello m.

washerwoman, uoosh'-a-uu-man, n., lavandaia f.

wasp, uoosp, n., vespa f.

waste, ueist, n., sperpero m.; (refuse) rifiuti m.pl.; (land) terra incolta f. v., sperperare; —away, deperire; —-paper, n., carta straccia f.; —-paper basket, cesto della carta straccia m.

wasteful, ueist'-ful, a., sperperato

watch, uoch, n., orologio m.; (wrist) orologio da polso m.; (look-out) guardia f.; —ful, a., attento; —man, n., guardia notturna m.; — over, v., (guard) sorvegliare; —word, n., parola d'ordine f.

watchmaker, uoch'-mei-ka, n., orologiaio m.

water, uoo'-ta, v., irrigare; (cattle, etc.) abbeverare. n., acqua f.; hot — bottle, scaldapiedi m.; —-closet, (W.C.) gabinetto m.; —-colour, acquarello m.; —-cress, crescione m.; —-fall, cascata f.; —-jug, brocca f.; —-level, livello dell'acqua m.; —-line, linea d'immersione f.; —-lily, ninfea f.; —logged, a., pieno d'acqua; —mark, n., (paper) filigrana f.; —-proof, a. & n., impermeabile m.; —-tank, cisterna f.; —tight, a., stagno; —y, acquoso

watering, uoo'-ter-ing, n., innaffiamento m.; —-can, innaffiatoio m.; —-place, stazione balneare f.

wave, ueiv, n., onda f. v., agitare ; (hand) salutare colla mano ; (hair) ondulare

waver, uei'-va, v., vacillare

wavering, uei'-ver-ing, a., vacillante

wavy, uei'-vi, a., ondulato

wax, uaks, n., cera f. v., incerare ; (grow) divenire

wax-works, uaks'-uėrks, n. pl., museo di figure di cera m.

way, uei, n., via f. ; (manner) modo m. ; **— in,** entrata f. ; **—lay,** v., tendere un agguato a ; **— out,** n., uscita f. ; **—through,** passaggio m.

wayward, uei'-uerd, a., capriccioso ; perverso

we, uii, pron., noi

weak*, uiik, a., debole ; **—en,** v., indebolire ; **—ening,** a., che indebolisce. n., indebolimento m.

weakling, uiik'-ling, n., persona debole f.

weakness, uiik'-nes, n., debolezza f.

weal, uiil, n., benessere m. ; (wale) segno m.

wealth, uelZ, n., ricchezza f.

wealthy, uelZ'-i, a., ricco

wean, uiin, v., spoppare ; (fig.) alienare

weapon, uep'-n, n., arma f.

wear, uer, n., (wear and tear) logorio m. ; (clothes) uso m. v., portare ; (last) durare ; **— out,** consumare ; (fatigue) spossare

weariness, ui'-ri-nes, n., spossatezza f. ; (fig.) noia f.

weary, ui'-ri, a., affaticato. v., affaticare

weasel, ui'-sl, n., donnola f.

weather, ueD'-a, n., tempo m. v., reggere a ; **— -beaten,** a., logoro dai tempo ; **—bound,** impedito dal tempo ; **—forecast,** n., bollettino meteorologico m. ; **—report,** informazione meteorologica f.

weave, uiiv, v., tessere

weaver, uii'-va, n., tessitore m.

web, ueb, n., tessuto m. ; (spider) telaragna f.

webbing, ueb'-ing, n., cinghia di sedia f.

web-footed, ueb-fut'-id, a., palmipede

wed, ued, v., sposare, sposarsi

wedding, ued'-ing, n., sposalizio m. ; (ceremony) nozze f. pl. ; **—ring,** anello nuziale m.

wedge, ueoh, n., cuneo m. v., incuneare

wedlock, ued'-lok, n., matrimonio m.

Wednesday, uens'-di, n., mercoledì m.

weed, uiid, n., erbaccia f. v., sarchiare

week, uiik, n., settimana f. ; **—-day,** giorno di lavoro m. ; **—-end,** fine di settimana f.

weekly, uiik'-li, a., settimanale

weep, uiip, v., piangere

weevil, uii'-vl, n., gorgoglione m.

weigh, uei, v., pesare ; considerare ; **—-ing-machine,** n., bascula f., bilancia f.

weight, ueit, n., peso m.

weighty, uei'-ti, a., pesante ; (serious) grave

weir, uir, n., sbarramento m.

weird, uird, a., strano ; bizzarro

welcome, uel'-kom, v., dare il benvenuto. a. & n., benvenuto m.

weld, ueld, v., saldare

welfare, uel'-fer, n., benessere m.

well, uel, n., pozzo m. adv., bene ; **—-being,** n., benessere m. : **—done,** a., (food) ben cotto

well-bred, uel'-bred, a., ben educato

well-wisher, uel'-uish-a, n., chi fa auguri

welt, uelt, n., (shoe, etc.) orlatura f.

wend, uend, v., incamminarsi

west, uest, n., ovest m.

westerly, uest'-er-li, a., occidentale

wet, uet, n., umidità f. v., inumidire

wet-nurse, uet'-nĕrs, n., balia f.

whack, huak, n., botta f. v., bastonare

whale, hueil, n., balena f.

whale-bone, hueil'-boun, n., osso di balena m.

whaler, hueil'-a, n., (ship) nave baleniera f.

wharf, huoorf, n., molo m.

what, huot, pron., che, ciò, ciò che, quello che ; **—ever,** adv., qualunque ; tutto quel che

wheat, huiit, n., frumento m.

wheedle, huii'-dl, v., estrarre con lusinghe

wheel, huiil, v., condurre. n., ruota f. ; **—-bar-row,** carruola f. ; **—-wright,** carraio m.

wheezy, huii'-si, a., asmatico

whelk, huelk, n., buccino m.

when, huen, adv., quando

whence, huens, adv., da dove, donde

whenever, huen'-ev-a, conj., ogni qualvolta

where, huer, adv., dove, ove; **—about,** dove, ove; **—as,** conj., laddove; **—at,** adv., al che; **—by,** a mezzo di che; **—fore,** cosicchè, così; **—in,** in che, in cui; **—on,** su di che, su cui; **—to,** a cui, a che

wherever, huer-ev'-a, adv., ovunque

whet, huet, v., affilare; (appetite) stimolare

whether, hueD'-a, conj., se, sia

which, huich, pron., quale, quali, che, cui

whichever, huich-ev'-a, pron., qualunque

while, huail, n., tempo m. conj., mentre. v., passare; **to be worth —,** valer la pena

whim, huim, n., ghiribizzo m.

whimper, huim'-pa, v., gemere. n., gemito m.

whine, huain, v., guaire

whip, huip, n., frusta f., sferza f. v. sferzare

whirl, huĕrl, v., turbinare. n., turbine m.

whirlpool, huĕrl'-pul, n., vortice m.

whirlwind, huĕrl'-uind, n., mulinello m.

whisk, huisk, n., (switch) cacciamosche m.; (beater) battitore m. v., sbattere; **— off,** spazzare via

whiskers, huis'-kers, n.pl., bassette f.pl.; (animal) baffi m.pl.

whisky, huis'-ki, n., whisky m.

whisper, huis'-pa, v., sussurrare. n., sussurro m.

whist, huist, interj., zitto ! n., (cards) whist m.

whistle, huis'-l n., fischietto m.; (sound) fischio m. v., fischiare

whit, huit, n., iota m.

white, huait, a.&n., bianco m.; **—of egg,** chiara f.

whiteness, huait'-nes, n., bianchezza f.

whitewash, huait'-uoosh, n., calce f. v., imbiancare

whither, huiD'-a, adv., dove

whiting, huai'-ting, n., merlano m.

Whitsun, huit'-sŏn, n., Pentecoste f.

whiz, huis, v., sibilare

who, huu, pron., chi, che

whoever, huu-ev'-a, pron., chiunque

whole, houl, n., intero m.   a., tutto
wholesale, houl'-seil, a., all'ingrosso
wholesome*, houl'-som, a., sano ; salubre
wholly, houl'-i, adv., interamente
whom, huum, pron., chi, che, cui
whoop, huup, n., urlo m.   v., urlare
whooping-cough, huu'-ping-koof, n., tosse canina f.
whore, hoor, n., puttana f.   v., prostituirsi
whose, huus, pron., cui ; di cui ; di chi
whosoever, huu-so-ev'-a, pron., chiunque
why, uai, adv., perchè
wick, uik, n., stoppino m.
wicked*, uik'-id, a., malvagio ; (morally) perverso
wickedness, uik'-id-nes, n., malvagità f.
wicker, uik'-a, — -**basket,** n., paniere di vimini m.
wicket, uik'-it, n., (cricket) stanghette f. pl.
wide*, uaid, a., largo ; (dresses, etc.) ampio ;
  — **awake,** ben sveglio :—-**spread,** esteso ; divul-   [gato
widen, uaid'-n, v., allargare
widow, uid'-ou, n., vedova f.
widower, uid'-ou-a, n., vedovo m.
width, uidZ, n., larghezza f. ; ampiezza f.
wield, uiild, v., maneggiare
wife, uaif, n., moglie f.
wig, uigh, n., parrucca f.
wild*, uaild, a., selvaggio ; (fig.) furioso
wilderness, uil'-der-nes, n., deserto m.
wile, uail, n., furberia f. ; astuzia f.
wilful*, uil'-ful, a., volontario ; (act) premeditato
will, uil, n., volontà f. ; (legal) testamento m., ul-   time volontà f. pl.   v., volere ; (bequeath) legare
willing*, uil'-ing, a., volonteroso ; compiacente
willingness, uil'-ing-nes, n., buona volontà f.
will-o'-the-wisp, uil-o-Di-uisp', n., fuoco fatuo m.
willow, uil'-ou, n., salice m. ; **weeping —,** salice   piangente m.
wily, uai'-li, a., astuto
win, uin, v., guadagnare ; (victorious) vincere ;
  —**ner,** n., vincitore m. ; —**ning,** a., (man-   ners) cattivante ;   —**ning-post,** n., tra-   guardo m. ;   —**nings,** pl., guadagni m. pl.

wince, uins, v., trasalire

winch, uinch, n., mancina f. ; (reel) manovella f.

wind, uaind, v., serpeggiare ; girare ; **—ing**, a., (road, etc.) serpeggiante ; (stairs) a chiocciola ; **— up**, v., caricare ; (business) liquidare

wind, uind, n., vento m. ; flatulenza f. ; **—fall**, (luck) fortuna inesperata f. ; **—mill**, mulino a vento m. ; **—pipe**, trachea f. ; **—ward**, adv., sotto vento ; **—y**, a., ventoso

windlass, uind′-las, n., argano m.

window, uin′-dou, n., finestra f.

wine, uain, n., vino m. ; **— -glass**, bicchiere da vino m.

wing, uingh, n., ala f. ; (of car) parafango m.

wink, uingk, v., far l'occhiolino ; (blink) sbattere gli occhi

winter, uin′-ta, n., inverno m. v., svernare

wipe, uaip, v., pulire

wire, uair, n., filo di metallo m. v., legare con filo di metallo

wireless, uair′-les, n., telegrafia senza fili f. ; radio f. ; (message) radiogramma m. v., radio-telegrafare

wisdom, uis′-dom, n., sapienza f.

wise*, uais, a., saggio

wish, uish, n., desiderio m. v., desiderare

wishful, uish′-ful, a., desideroso

wisp, uisp, n., ciuffo m.

wistaria, uis-te′-ri-a, n., glicine f. pl.

wistful*, uist′-tul, a., pensoso

wit, uich, n., spirito m. ; **—s**, pl., sensi m. pl. ; **—ticism**, arguzia f. ; **—ty**, a., spiritoso

witch, uich, n., strega f.

witchcraft, uich′-kraaft, n., sortilegio m.

with, uiD, prep., con ; presso ; di ; da ; **—draw**, v., ritirare ; **—hold**, trattenere ; **—in**, adv., dentro ; entro ; **—out**, prep., senza. adv., (outside) fuori ; **—stand**, v., resistere

wither, uiD′-a, v., appassire

withering, uiD′-er-ing, a., (look) fulminante

witness, uit′-nes, n., testimonio m. v., (testify) testimoniare

wizard, uis'-*erd*, n., stregone m.

wobble, uob'-l, v., dondolarsi ; (sway) vacillare

woe, uou, n., guaio m., calamità f. ; — **to him,** guai a lui

woeful*, uou'-*ful*, a., misero

wolf, uulf, n., lupo m. ; **she- —,** lupa f.

woman, uu'-*man*, n., donna f. ; —**hood,** stato di donna m.

womanly, uu'-*man*-li, a., femminile

womb, uum, n., matrice f., utero m. ; (fig.) grembo m.

wonder, uŏn'-*da*, n., meraviglia f. ; miracolo m. v., meravigliarsi ; (ask oneself) domandarsi

wonderful*, uŏn'-*der*-*ful*, a., meraviglioso

woo, uu, v., corteggiare ; —**er,** n., pretendente m.

wood, uud, n., legno m. ; (forest) bosco m. ; —**bine,** caprifoglio m. ; —**cock,** beccaccia f. ; —**en,** a., di legno ; —**pecker,** n., picchio m. ; —**y,** a., legnoso ; (trees) boscoso

wool, uul, n., lana f. ; —**len,** a., di lana

woolly, uul'-i, a., lanoso

word, uĕrd, v., compilare : redigere. n., parola f. ; (news) nuova f. ; —**ing,** redazione f. ; (style) stile m. ; — **of honour,** parola d'onore f.

work, uĕrk, v., lavorare. n., lavoro m., opera f. ; (occupation) occupazione f.

worker, uĕr'-*ka*, n., operaio m., lavoratore m.

workhouse, uĕrk'-*haus*, n., asilo dei poveri m.

working, uĕr'-*king*, n., effetto m. ; risultato m. ; (business) condotta f. ; (machine) funzionamento m. ; (mine) sfruttamento m. ; — **ex-penses,** pl., spese di produzione f. pl.

workman, uĕrk'-*man*, n., operaio m.

workmanship, uĕrk'-*man*-ship, n., lavoro m. ; opera f.

works, uĕrks, n. pl., fabbrica f. ; (mech.) movimento

workshop, uĕrk'-*shop*, n., officina f. [m.

world, uĕrld, n., mondo m. ; terra f.

worldly, uĕrld'-li, a., mondano ; di mondo

worm, uĕrm, n., verme m. ; (wood) tarlo m.

worm-eaten, uĕrm-ii'-*tn*, a., tarlato

worry, uŏr'-i, n., tormento m. ; ansietà f. ; (bother) noia f. v., tormentarsi

worse, uĕ*rs*, a., peggiore. adv., peggio

worship, uĕr'-ship, n., adorazione f.; (divine) culto m. v., adorare ; compiere le pratiche religiose

worst, uĕrst, a. & n., il peggiore m.; la peggiore f. adv., il peggio ; **to get the — of it**, aver la peggio

worsted, uĕr'-stid, n., (yarn) lana filata f.

worth, uĕr*Z*, valore m.; merito m. a., che vale ; **—ily**, adv., degnamente ; **—less**, a., senza valore ; (person) indegno ; **to be — while**, valere la pena

worthy, uĕr'-*D*i, a., degno

would-be, uud*'*-bii, a., sedicente, preteso

wound, uund, n., ferita f. v., ferire

wrangle, rang*'*-gol, v., litigarsi. n., litigio m.

wrap, rap, n., sortita f.; **— up**, v., avvolgere ; (oneself) imbacuccarsi

wrapper, rap'-*a*, n., (postal) fascia f.; (book) copertina f.

wrath, roo*Z*, n., collera f., ira f.

wrathful, roo*Z'*-ful, a., adirato

wreath, rii*Z*, n., corona f.

wreathe, rii*D*, v., intrecciare ; (fig.) incoronare

wreck, rek, n., naufragio m.; (fig.) rovina f. v., naufragare ; far naufragare ; (destroy) distruggere ; (fig.) rovinare ; **—age**, n., resto di naufragio m.; (debris) rimasugli m. pl.

wrecked, rekt, a., naufragato ; (fig.) rovinato

wren, ren, n., reattino m.

wrench, rench, n., strappo violento m.; (sprain) torsione f.; (tool) chiave inglese f. v., (twist) torcere ; (tear away) strappare

wrestle, res'-l, v., lottare

wrestler, res'-la, n., lottatore m.

wretch, rech, n., miserabile m. & f.; diavolo m.

wretched, rech'-id, a., triste

wretchedness, rech'-id-nes, n., miseria f.

wriggle, righ'-l, v., contorcersi ; (eels, etc.) guizzare

wring, ring, v., (clothes) spremere ; (hands : neck) torcere

wrinkle, ring'-kl, n., ruga f. v., aggrinzare

wrist, rist, n., polso m.

writ, rit, n., mandato m.; ordine m.

write, rait, v., scrivere
writer, rai'-ta, n., scrivente m. ; (author) **scrittore** m.
writhe, raiD, v., contorcersi
writing, rai'-ting, n., scrittura f. ; **hand—**, calligrafia f.; **in —**, adv., per iscritto ; **—-pad**, blocco di carta da scrivere m. ; **—-paper**, (note paper) carta da scrivere f. ; **—-table**, scrittoio m.
written, rit'-n, a., scritto
wrong, rong, n., torto m. v., far torto a a.,*falso, sbagliato ; (moral) cattivo, ingiusto
wroth, rooZ, a., arrabbiato
wrought-iron, root'-ai-ern, n., ferro battuto m.
wry, rai, a., sbieco ; **— face**, n., smorfia f.
wryneck, rai'-nek, n., torcicollo m.

Xmas (=Christmas), kris'-mas, n., Natale m.
Xmas-eve, kris'-mas-iiv, n., vigilia di Natale f.
X-ray, eks'-rei, n., raggio X m. ; (X-ray photography) radiografia f. v., radiografare
xylophone, sai'-lo-foun, n., silofono m.

yacht, iot, n., yacht m.
yachting, iot'-ing, n., sport della vela m.
yard, iaard, n., cortile m. ; (measure) iarda f. ; **ship-—**, cantiere m. ; **timber-—**, deposito di legname m.
yarn, iaarn, n., filo m. ; (tale) storiella f.
yawn, ioon, v., sbadigliare. n., sbadiglio m.
year, iir, n., anno m.
yearling, iir'-ling, n., animale d'ün anno m.
yearly, iir'-li, a., annuo. adv., annualmente
yearn, iërn, v., bramare ; sospirare
yearning, iërn'-ing, n., brama f.
yearningly, iërn'-ing-li, adv., bramosamente
yeast, iiist, n., lievito m.
yell, iel, v., strillare. n., strillo m., urlo m.
yellow, iel'-ou, a., giallo. n., giallo m.
yelp, ielp, v., guaire. n., guaito m.
yeomanry, iou'-man-ri, n., (mil.) milizia a cavallo f.

yes, ies. adv., sì

yesterday, ies'-*ter*-di, adv., ieri

yet, iet. adv., ancora, tuttavia. conj., eppure

yew, iuu, n., tasso m.

yield, iiild, n., prodotto m., ricavo m. v., produrre ; (give way) cedere

yoke, iouk, n., giogo m. v., aggiogare

yokel, iou'-kl, n., rustico m.

yolk, iouk, n., rosso d'uovo m.

yonder, ion'-*da*, adv., colà, laggiù. a., quello

you, iuu, pron., tu ; voi ; lei ; ella ; loro

young, iŏng, a., giovane ; the —, n.pl., giovani m.pl.· (of animals) piccoli m.pl.

younger, iŏng'-*gha*, a., più giovane

youngster, iŏng-sta, n., giovinotto m.

your, iur, pron., tuo [or suo] ; di lei ; vostro ; loro

yours, iur*s*, pron.· il tuo ; il suo ; il vostro ; il loro

youth, iuuZ, n., gioventù f. ; (lad) giovane m.

youthful*, iuuZ'-*ful*, a., giovane

youthfulness, iuuZ'-*ful*-nes, n., giovinezza f.

Yule-tide, iuul'-taid, n., tempo di Natale m.

zeal, *s*iil, n., zelo m.

zealous*, *s*el'-*os*, a., zelante

zebra, *s*ii'-bra, n., zebra f.

zenith, *s*en'-iZ, n., zenit m.

zephyr, *s*ef'-*r*, n., zeffiro m.

zero, *s*i'-rou, n., zero m.

zest, *s*est, n., gusto m., piccante m.

zinc, *s*ingk, n., zinco m. v., zincare

zip-fastener, *s*ip-faas'-na, n., chiusura lampo f

zone, *s*oun, n., zona f.

zoological, *s*ou-o-looh'-i-kl, a., zoologico

zoology, *s*ou-ol'-och-i, n., zoologia f.

hugo

Pocket Dictionaries

French–English/English–French
German–English/English–German
Spanish–English/English–Spanish
Italian–English/English–Italian
Dutch–English/English–Dutch
Russian–English/English–Russian

all with Imitated Pronunciation

English Pocket Dictionary
(without pronunciation)

Tourist Phrasebooks

France, Germany, Spain, Italy, Greece,
Holland, Portugal and Scandinavia.

*Essential words and phrases for most
holiday travel situations.*

"Three Months" books

French, German, Spanish, Italian, Portuguese, Greek, Dutch, Norwegian, Danish, Swedish, Russian, Latin and English for foreign students.

Complete, concise courses which are essentially practical.

Audio Cassette Courses

French, German, Spanish, Italian, Dutch, Greek, Portuguese and Swedish.

The most up-to-date way of learning a language quickly and easily.
For details of these and other language-learning aids, write to:

Hugo's Language Books Ltd
104 Judd Street, London WC1H 9NF